The Columbia Dictionary
of Quotations from Shakespeare

The Columbia Dictionary
of Quotations from Shakespeare

Mary and Reginald Foakes

COLUMBIA UNIVERSITY PRESS   NEW YORK

Columbia University Press
New York   Chichester, West Sussex
Copyright © 1998 Columbia University Press

Library of Congress Cataloging-in-Publication Data

Shakespeare, William, 1564-1616.
   The Columbia dictionary of quotations from Shakespeare / [selected by]
Mary and Reginald Foakes.
      p.   cm.
   Includes indexes.
   ISBN 0–231–10434–0
   1. Shakespeare, William, 1564–1616—Quotations—Dictionaries.
   2. Quotations, English—Dictionaries.   I. Foakes, Mary.
   II. Foakes, R. A.   III. Title.
   PR2892.F48   1998
   822.3'3—DC21   97–44894
                                                            CIP

Casebound editions of Columbia University Press books are printed on
permanent and durable acid-free paper.

Printed in the United States of America

c 10 9 8 7 6 5 4 3 2 1

Contents

Introduction

In the English-speaking world William Shakespeare and his works have an extraordinary status. He has long been accepted as a figure of enormous cultural authority. This is evidenced both in the education provided by schools and colleges, where his works are widely studied, and in the theaters, summer festivals and libraries dedicated to preserving his achievements. This cultural authority has paradoxically ensured that Shakespeare has been democratized as a representative consciousness, whose works embody in memorable language much of the wisdom of our civilization. Passages from his plays and poems are frequently cited in all sorts of contexts to support legal or political arguments, validate advertisements, justify prejudices, and generally sanction a whole range of beliefs and opinions. In this process, his words have floated free of their moorings in the context of his plays, have become detached from the characters for whom the lines were written, and are treated as if they represent Shakespeare's own convictions.

So in support of their nominees or arguments politicians may quote speeches from *Othello* or *Richard III* without realizing that the words may be appropriate in ways they have not imagined, since they were written to be spoken by Iago and Richard, characters noted for their manipulation of others and their consummate hypocrisy. Such mindless use of quotations is encouraged by dictionaries that do not identify the speaker of particular lines, or indicate what sort of character he or she represents. However much we may feel Shakespeare put a lot of himself into figures like Hamlet, we cannot be sure that any character speaks for him as embodying his beliefs. He was steeped in the Bible and in folk-wisdom as represented, for instance, by proverbs, and he lived in an age when people noted down clever sayings or "sentences" (Latin "*sententiae*") in their commonplace books. His plays certainly contain many such sayings, and some memorable formulations of accepted wisdom that have passed into the language. However, many other quotations need to be understood in context if their full implications are to be appreciated. This new selection identifies characters for each citation, and provides annotations designed to help the reader to understand the dramatic context and meaning of passages that offer any kind of difficulty. For an example, consider the line "Respect and reason wait on wrinkled age," from *The Rape of Lucrece*, which might seem to need no explanation as stating a general truth. It makes a lot of difference, however, if we know that these words are spoken by Tarquin as he premeditates raping Lucrece, and tries to justify his deed by arguing that it is proper for the young to follow their heart's desire and reject reason. The line should give us food for thought; it is not simply expressing received wisdom.

So much of Shakespeare's language is quotable that every collection of quotations from his works differs from earlier ones, and there is no sense in which any collection can be "complete." What makes a quotation? In going through Shakespeare's works for the present collection, our first thought was that in general quotations should be brief, not more than six lines or so, and memorable. In fact we found we could not make this a rule, and we include a few longer passages as well as two sonnets. We had in mind several other criteria in choosing passages. Some were selected for their current aptness, as in this entry from *Antony and Cleopatra* under "Business":

To business that we love we rise betime,
And go to't with delight.

Antony is preparing for battle, but the lines may seem appealing or ironic as they might relate to commuters rushing towards another day in the office; the word "business" has taken on wider meanings since Shakespeare's day. Others were selected for their descriptive beauty, for their pithy expression of an opinion or wise saying, or for their wit and forcefulness of style, or their sheer quality as poetry. Shakespeare was brilliant at rewording proverbial sayings and recycling phrases from the Bible in such a way that his formulations have often passed into common use. The more notable allusions to the Bible are recorded in commentary notes on the passages, and there is a section devoted to proverbs which do not fit easily under another topic heading.

The quotations are arranged under topics, which are in alphabetical order. Topic headings are necessarily arbitrary, and it is often the case that a single passage of a few lines could be linked to several topics. For example, the line cited above, "Respect and reason wait on wrinkled age," could be placed under "Respect" or "Reason," but in fact appears under "Old Age." Some quotations are printed under two different topics, but to do this with every one that could be located under two or more possible headings would swell the collection enormously. So as a further aid to the reader this collection has an exceptionally full index to significant words in quotations, an index that offers a more thorough guide to the collection than the list of topics which is also provided. A further index ties each quotation by topic heading to the work from which it is cited, identifying in the case of Shakespeare's plays the character who speaks the words. It is thus possible, by looking up the play in this index, to trace what passages are cited from it, and also what passages attributed to any particular character are quoted. The list of topics, index of words, and index of plays and characters together provide a full reference guide to what is contained in the quotations.

The text of the quotations has been modernized. Line references, for convenience, are to the *Riverside Shakespeare* (Boston: Houghton Mifflin), and may be slightly different in other editions. Shakespeare's plays and poems were written between about 1588 and 1613, when the English language was being greatly enriched by an influx of new coinages. Shakespeare had a huge vocabulary, and seems to have introduced a great many words that have remained current; but there have been many changes since his day, both in the meanings of some words, and in grammatical usage. The annotations to quotations in this collection provide explanations of changes in meaning or style. Thus the indexes and annotations are intended to give the reader all possible help in finding and in appreciating the passages quoted. Their relevance for our own time is best left to the individual reader.

I am grateful to Curt Whitaker for assistance in checking and proof-reading.

The basic selection of quotations in this volume was made by my dear wife, Mary (F. Mary White), who, sadly, did not live to see its completion; the book is lovingly dedicated to her memory.

Reginald Foakes

List of Topics

The Columbia Dictionary
of Quotations from Shakespeare

Quotations

Absence

1   Shall I abide
In this dull world, which in thy
absence is
No better than a sty?

Cleopatra in *Antony and Cleopatra*,
4.15.60–2

On the death of Antony.

2   I shall be loved when I am lacked.

Coriolanus in *Coriolanus*, 4.1.15

Referring to his banishment from Rome.

3   There is not one among them but I
dote on his very absence.

Portia in *The Merchant of Venice*,
1.2.109–10

Dismayed by all her suitors, she wishes they
would go away.

4   How like a winter hath my absence
been
From thee, the pleasure of the fleeting year!
What freezings have I felt, what
dark days seen,

What old December's bareness
everywhere!

Sonnet 97, 1–4

For the speaker, the absence of his lover has
turned summer into winter.

Achievement

1   All's well that ends well; still the
fine's the crown.
Whate'er the course, the end is the
renown.

Helena in *All's Well That Ends Well*,
4.4.35–6

The play's proverbial title is repeated at
5.4.35; "the end crowns all" ("fine" = end,
from the Latin) is also proverbial.

Acting
(see also Plays, Theater)

1   When good will is showed, though
it come too short,
The actor may plead pardon.

Cleopatra in *Antony and Cleopatra*,
2.5.8–9

2 You have put me now to such a
part which never
I shall discharge to the life.

Coriolanus in *Coriolanus*, 3.2.105–6

Speaking of the requirement that he stand in
the gown of humility and ask the public for
votes.

3 Like a dull actor now
I have forgot my part, and I am out,
Even to a full disgrace.

Coriolanus in *Coriolanus*, 5.3.40–2

Coriolanus, about to make war on Rome, is
ashamed to be at a loss for words ("out")
when confronted by his family, come to plead
with him.

4 How strange or odd some'er I bear
myself,
As I perchance hereafter shall think
meet
To put an antic disposition on.

Hamlet in *Hamlet*, 1.5.170–2

Announcing to Horatio and Marcellus his idea
of pretending to be mad whenever it suits him
("shall think meet").

5 He that plays the king shall be welcome.

Hamlet in *Hamlet*, 2.2.319

Welcoming the actors who come to play at
court.

6 The best actors in the world,
either for tragedy, comedy, history,
pastoral, pastoral-comical, histori-
cal-pastoral, tragical-historical,
tragical-comical-historical-pastoral,
scene individable, or poem
unlimited.

Polonius in *Hamlet*, 2.2.396–400

Listing every kind of play, and then some.

7 Will you see the players well
bestowed? Do you hear, let them
be well used, for they are the
abstracts and brief chronicles of the
time. After your death you were
better have a bad epitaph than their
ill report while you live.

Hamlet in *Hamlet*, 2.2.522–6

Speaking to Polonius about the actors who
have just arrived in Elsinore; "bestowed" =
lodged.

8 What's Hecuba to him, or he to
Hecuba,
That he should weep for her? What
would he do
Had he the motive and the cue for
passion
That I have?

Hamlet in *Hamlet*, 2.2.559–62

Meditating on the player who weeps as he
narrates the death of Hecuba, Queen of Troy,
and on his own failure to act.

9 Speak the speech, I pray you, as I
pronounced it to you, trippingly
on the tongue; but if you mouth it
as many of your players do, I had
as lief the town-crier spoke my
lines.

Hamlet in *Hamlet*, 3.2.1–4

To the actors, who are to perform a play with
a speech by Hamlet inserted; "as lief" = just as
willingly.

10 Be not too tame neither, but let
your own discretion be your tutor.
Suit the action to the word, the
word to the action, with this special
observance, that you o'erstep not
the modesty of nature.

Hamlet in *Hamlet*, 3.2.16–19

Instructing the actors; "modesty" =
moderation.

11 The purpose of playing, whose end,
both at the first and now, was and
is, to hold as 'twere the mirror up
to nature: to show virtue her feature, scorn her own image, and the
very age and body of the time his
form and pressure.

Hamlet in *Hamlet*, 3.2.20–4

Hamlet's advice to the actors has its origins in
classical rhetoric; they are to show plainly the
appearance (feature) of virtue and of vice, and
reflect the present state of affairs; "pressure" =
impression, as if in wax.

12 O Jesu, he doth it as like one of
these harlotry players as ever I see!

Hostess in *Henry IV, Part 1*, 2.4.395–6

On Falstaff's extempore portrayal of King
Henry IV; "harlotry" = rascal.

13 　　　　But pardon, gentles all,
The flat unraisèd spirits that hath
dared
On this unworthy scaffold to bring
forth
So great an object.

Chorus in *Henry V*, Prologue, 8–11

Apologizing to the audience ("gentles" = gentlemen and gentlewomen) for the inadequacy
of the actors on their stage ("scaffold").

14 　　　　Still be kind,
And eke out our performance with
your mind.

Chorus in *Henry V*, 3.Prologue, 34–5

Appealing to the audience.

15 Good gentlemen, look fresh and
merrily.
Let not our looks put on our purposes,
But bear it as our Roman actors do,

With untired spirits and formal
constancy.

Brutus in *Julius Caesar*, 2.1.224–7

As the conspirators set off towards the Capitol.

16 　　　　How many ages hence
Shall this our lofty scene be acted
over
In states unborn and accents yet
unknown!

Cassius in *Julius Caesar*, 3.1.111–13

Referring to the assassination of Caesar.

17 I hold the world but as the world,
Gratiano,
A stage, where every man must play
a part,
And mine a sad one.

Antonio in *The Merchant of Venice*,
1.1.77–9

18 *Bottom.* What is Pyramus? A lover
or a tyrant?
Quince. A lover that kills himself,
most gallant, for love.
Bottom. That will ask some tears in
the true performing of it. If I do
it, let the audience look to their
eyes.

***A Midsummer Night's Dream*, 1.2.22–6**

Peter Quince is casting Bottom for the play of
Pyramus and Thisbe.

19 My chief humor is for a tyrant.
I could play Ercles rarely, or a part
to tear a cat in, to make all split.

**Bottom in *A Midsummer Night's
Dream*, 1.2.28–30**

"Humor" = inclination; "Ercles" is Bottom's
corruption of Hercules; to "tear a cat" on the
stage is to rant and bluster.

20 *Snug.* Have you the lion's part written? Pray you, if it be, give it me; for I am slow of study. *Quince.* You may do it extempore, for it is nothing but roaring.
A Midsummer Night's Dream, 1.2.66–9

21 I will aggravate my voice so that I will roar you as gently as any sucking dove. I will roar you and 'twere any nightingale.
Bottom in *A Midsummer Night's Dream,* 1.2.81–4

Bottom offers the gentlest of lions' roars so as not to frighten ladies; he means to say "moderate."

22 There we may rehearse most obscenely and courageously.
Bottom in *A Midsummer Night's Dream,* 1.2.107–8

"Obscenely" is Bottom's mistake for "seemly" (fitly), or some such word.

23 You speak all your part at once, cues and all.
Quince in *A Midsummer Night's Dream,* 3.1.99–100

On Flute, who is rehearsing for the part of Thisbe in the play they are to stage for the wedding of Theseus and Hippolyta.

24 We do not come, as minding to content you,
Our true intent is. All for your delight
We are not here.
Quince in *A Midsummer Night's Dream,* 5.1.113–15

He wrecks the sense of his prologue by confusing the punctuation.

25 *Theseus.* The best in this kind are but shadows; and the worst are no worse, if imagination amend them.
Hippolyta. It must be your imagination then, and not theirs.
Theseus. If we imagine no worse of them than they of themselves, they may pass for excellent men.
A Midsummer Night's Dream, 5.1.211–16

Watching "Pyramus and Thisbe" as staged by Bottom, Quince and their crew.

26 I can counterfeit the deep tragedian,
Speak, and look back, and pry on every side,
Tremble and start at wagging of a straw,
Intending deep suspicion. Ghastly looks
Are at my service like enforcèd smiles,
And both are ready in their offices
At any time to grace my stratagems.
Buckingham in *Richard III,* 3.5.5–11

"Intending" = pretending; Buckingham is putting his ability to act a part at the service of Richard.

27 They thought it good you hear a play,
And frame your mind to mirth and merriment,
Which bars a thousand harms and lengthens life.
Messenger in *The Taming of the Shrew,* Induction, 2.134–6

Inviting the tinker Sly to watch the play.

28 Our revels now are ended. These our actors,

As I foretold you, were all spirits,
and
Are melted into air, into thin air.
Prospero in *The Tempest*, 4.1.148–50

Dismissing the masquers who have entertained Ferdinand and Miranda.

29 *Olivia.* Whence came you, sir?
Viola. I can say little more than I
have studied, and that question's
out of my part.
Twelfth Night, 1.5.177–9

Olivia thinks Viola is a man, Cesario; Viola is indeed playing a part, that of Orsino's messenger of love.

30   I see the play so lies
That I must bear a part.
Perdita in *The Winter's Tale*, 4.4.655

Spoken as she is asked to disguise herself as a man.

31   We may leisurely
Each one demand and answer to his
part
Performed in this wide gap of time
since first
We were dissevered.
Leontes in *The Winter's Tale*, 5.3.152–5

Winding up the play; only the audience knows the whole story.

Action

1   In such business
Action is eloquence, and the eyes of
th' ignorant
More learned than the ears.
Volumnia in *Coriolanus*, 3.2.75–7

Coriolanus's mother advises him to look humble in front of the Roman people in order to win votes.

2 She stripped it from her arm. I see
her yet:
Her pretty action did outsell her
gift,
And yet enriched it too.
Jachimo in *Cymbeline*, 2.4.101–3

A charming description of an imaginary act; Jachimo is lying about how he came by Imogen's bracelet.

3 Duller shouldst thou be than the fat
weed
That roots itself in ease on Lethe
wharf,
Wouldst thou not stir in this.
Ghost in *Hamlet*, 1.5.32–4

Urging Hamlet to revenge his murder; "Lethe" = the underworld river of forgetfulness.

4 I am not yet of Percy's mind, the
Hotspur of the north, he that kills
me some six or seven dozen of
Scots at a breakfast, washes his
hands, and says to his wife,
"Fie upon this quiet life! I want
work."
Prince Hal in *Henry IV, Part 1*, 2.4.101–5

Mocking Hotspur's devotion to fighting.

5 The undeserver may sleep when the
man of action is called on.
Falstaff in *Henry IV, Part 2*, 2.4.376–7

Falstaff, late as usual, is summoned to help fight rebels.

6 A very little little let us do
And all is done.
Constable in *Henry V*, 4.2.33–4

Convinced the French will have an easy victory.

7 Strike now, or else the iron cools.

Richard of Gloucester in *Henry VI, Part 3*, 5.1.49

Proverbial; the idea is that iron is malleable and can be worked by the smith while it is hot.

8 He's sudden if a thing comes in his head.

King Edward in *Henry VI, Part 3*, 5.5.86

On Richard, soon to be Richard III; "sudden" = quick to act, impetuous.

9   We must not stint
Our necessary actions in the fear
To cope malicious censurers.

Cardinal Wolsey in *Henry VIII*, 1.2.76–8

Defending the imposition of a savage tax; "to cope" = of encountering.

10 If we shall stand still
In fear our motion will be mocked
    or carped at,
We should take root here where we
    sit, or sit
State-statues only.

Cardinal Wolsey in *Henry VIII*, 1.2.85–8

On hearing of complaints made about his use of power; "motion" = proposals, actions.

11 'Tis a kind of good deed to say well,
And yet words are no deeds.

King Henry in *Henry VIII*, 3.2.153–4

On discovering the gap between Wolsey's words and his actions.

12 If it were done when 'tis done, then
    'twere well
It were done quickly. If the assassi-
    nation
Could trammel up the conse-
    quence, and catch
With his surcease success—that but
    this blow

Might be the be-all and the end-
    all!—here,
But here, upon this bank and shoal
of time,
We'd jump the life to come.

Macbeth in *Macbeth*, 1.7.1–7

"If it were done when 'tis done" = if the deed were at an end, completely finished, at the moment it is done; Macbeth thinks that if he could avoid ("trammel up" = catch in a net) the consequences of murder with the death ("surcease") of Duncan, he would take a chance on the life to come (on earth, and in heaven or hell).

13 O, what men dare do! What men
may do! What men daily do, not
knowing what they do!

Claudio in *Much Ado About Nothing*, 4.1.19–20

His words reflect ironically on himself, as he is about to reject Hero as they are due to be married.

14 Pleasure and action make the hours
seem short.

Iago in *Othello*, 2.3.379

Iago has just contrived to get Cassio, his superior officer, dismissed by Othello.

15 A stirring dwarf we do allowance
    give
Before a sleeping giant.

Agamemnon in *Troilus and Cressida*, 2.3.137–8

Achilles is the "sleeping giant," who refuses to fight; "allowance" = praise, honor.

16   This action I now go on
Is for my better grace.

Hermione, *The Winter's Tale*, 2.1.121–2

She is being sent to prison by her husband, Leontes, an "action" that will elicit her fortitude and patience.

Adoration

1   She speaks!
O, speak again, bright angel, for
  thou art
As glorious to this night, being o'er
  my head,
As is a wingèd messenger of heaven.

Romeo in *Romeo and Juliet*, 2.2.25–8

On Juliet at her window.

Adultery

1   What was thy cause? Adultery?
Thou shalt not die. Die for adul-
  tery? No,
The wren goes to't, and the small
  gilded fly
Does lecher in my sight.
Let copulation thrive.

King Lear in *King Lear*, 4.6.109–14

Addressing Gloucester, who fathered the bastard Edmund.

2   There have been,
Or I am much deceived, cuckolds
  ere now,
And many a man there is, even at
  this present,
Now, while I speak this, holds his
  wife by th'arm,
That little thinks she has been
  sluiced in's absence,
And his pond fished by his next
  neighbor, by
Sir Smile, his neighbor.

Leontes in *The Winter's Tale*, 1.2.190–6

Beginning to believe the worst of his own wife.

3   Should all despair
That have revolted wives, the tenth
  of mankind
Would hang themselves.

**Leontes in *The Winter's Tale*,
1.2.198–200**

Suspecting his own wife of adultery.

Adversity

1   O how full of briers is this working-
  day world!

Rosalind in *As You Like It*, 1.3.11–12

Sighing for love, she finds the everyday world thorny.

2   Sweet are the uses of adversity,
Which like the toad, ugly and venomous,
Wears yet a precious jewel in his
  head.

**Duke Senior in *As You Like It*,
2.1.12–14**

A common belief about toads; it was proverbial that adversity makes men wise.

3   A wretched soul, bruised with
  adversity,
We bid be quiet when we hear it
  cry;
But were we burdened with like
  weight of pain,
As much, or more, we should ourselves complain.

**Adriana in *The Comedy of Errors*,
2.1.34–7**

4   Adversity's sweet milk, philosophy,
To comfort thee, though thou art
  banished.

**Friar Lawrence in *Romeo and Juliet*,
3.3.55–6**

Seeking to comfort the banished Romeo.

5   O, give me thy hand,
One writ with me in sour misfortune's book!

Romeo in *Romeo and Juliet*, 5.3.81–2

Addressing Paris, whom he has just fought
and killed.

6   Let's shake our heads and
say,
As 'twere a knell unto our master's
fortunes,
We have seen better days.

Flavius in *Timon of Athens*, 4.2.25–7

To Timon's servants as they depart from his
house.

Advice

1   Love all, trust a few,
Do wrong to none.

**Countess of Rossillion in *All's Well
That Ends Well*, 1.1.64–5**

A mother's advice to her young son Bertram,
as he is summoned by the King to Paris.

2   Be checked for silence,
But never taxed for speech.

**Countess of Rossillion in *All's Well
That Ends Well*, 1.1.67–8**

Advice to her son on how to behave at court:
don't mind being rebuked for saying nothing,
but never be charged with saying too much.

3 For I must tell you friendly in your
ear,
Sell when you can, you are not for
all markets.

Rosalind in *As You Like It*, 3.5.59–60

To Phebe, who rejects Silvius's love.

4 Do not, as some ungracious pastors
do,
Show me the steep and thorny way
to heaven,
Whilst like a puffed and reckless
libertine
Himself the primrose path of dalliance treads,
And recks not his own rede.

Ophelia in *Hamlet*, 1.3.47–51

To her brother, Laertes, who has been urging
her not to listen to Hamlet's advances; "ungracious" = lacking grace; "puffed" = bloated;
"recks" = heeds; "rede" = advice.

5 Give every man thy ear, but few thy
voice,
Take each man's censure, but
reserve thy judgment.

Polonius in *Hamlet*, 1.3.68–9

Advice to his son; "censure" = opinion.

6 Neither a borrower nor a lender be,
For loan oft loses both itself and
friend,
And borrowing dulls the edge of
husbandry.

Polonius in *Hamlet*, 1.3.75–7

Advice to his son, going to live abroad; "husbandry" = thrift.

7 This above all: to thine own self be
true,
And it must follow, as the night the
day,
Thou canst not then be false to any
man.

Polonius in *Hamlet*, 1.3.78–80

The last of a list of precepts addressed to his
son, who is going to live abroad.

8 You shall be as a father to my
youth,

My voice shall sound as you do
prompt mine ear,
And I will stoop and humble my
intents
To your well-practiced wise directions.

Prince Hal in *Henry IV, Part 2,*
5.2.118–121

Accepting the guidance of the Chief Justice.

9 Heat not a furnace for your foe so
hot
That it do singe yourself.

Norfolk in *Henry VIII,* 1.1.140–1

To Buckingham, who has proclaimed his
enmity to Wolsey.

10 Let go thy hold when a great wheel
runs down a hill lest it break thy
neck with following; but the great
one that goes upward, let him draw
thee after.

Fool in *King Lear,* 2.4.71–4

Giving Kent politic advice, to abandon Lear;
he goes on to say "I would have none but
knaves follow it."

11 It is a good divine that follows his
own instructions; I can easier teach
twenty what were good to be done,
than to be one of the twenty to follow mine own teaching.

Portia in *The Merchant of Venice,*
1.2.14–17

Echoing the proverb, "practice what you
preach."

12   Pause awhile,
And let my counsel sway you in this
case.

Friar Francis in *Much Ado About
Nothing,* 4.1.200–1

Trying to help the distraught Leonato.

13 I pray thee, cease thy counsel,
Which falls into mine ears as profit-
less
As water in a sieve.

Leonato in *Much Ado About Nothing,*
5.1.3–5

Refusing his brother's attempt to comfort him.

14 And what's he then that says I play
the villain,
When this advice is free I give, and
honest,
Probal to thinking, and indeed the
course
To win the Moor again?

Iago in *Othello,* 2.3.336–9

Addressing the audience after advising
Cassio to apply to Desdemona; "probal" =
reasonable.

15 Wise men ne'er sit and wail their
woes,
But presently prevent the ways to
wail.

Bishop of Carlisle in *Richard II,*
3.2.178–9

Giving the downcast Richard some good
advice.

16 O Lord, I could have stayed here all
the night
To hear good counsel. O, what
learning is!

Nurse in *Romeo and Juliet,* 3.3.159–60

On hearing Friar Lawrence counseling
Romeo, who has tried to kill himself.

17   Thou dost advise me
Even so as I mine own course have
set down.

Leontes in *The Winter's Tale,* 1.2.339–40

On hearing Camillo's advice to treat
Hermione well.

Affectation

1 *Holofernes.* He is too picked, too spruce, too affected, too odd as it were, too peregrinate as I may call it.
   Nathaniel. A most singular and choice epithet.
   Love's Labor's Lost, 5.1.12–15

   Speaking of Armado; "picked" = fastidious; "peregrinate" = outlandish.

Affliction (see also Grief, Misery, Suffering)

1 You do draw my spirits from me
   With new lamenting ancient over-sights.
   Northumberland in *Henry IV, Part 2*, 2.3.46–7

   Hearing old mistakes lamented saps his courage.

2 *Cassius.* I did not think you could have been so angry.
   Brutus. O Cassius, I am sick of many griefs.
   Julius Caesar, 4.3.143–4

   Cassius does not know that Portia, Brutus's wife, has taken her own life.

3 O madam, my old heart is cracked, it's cracked!
   Gloucester in *King Lear*, 2.1.90

   Supposing his son Edgar has sought to kill him.

4 You see me here, you gods, a poor old man,
   As full of grief as age, wretched in both.
   King Lear in *King Lear*, 2.4.272–3

   The old king is cast out by his daughters, Goneril and Regan.

5 The worst is not
   So long as we can say, "This is the worst."
   Edgar in *King Lear*, 4.1.27–8

6 Henceforth I'll bear
   Affliction till it do cry out itself
   "Enough, enough," and die.
   Gloucester in *King Lear*, 4.6.75–7

   Believing he has miraculously survived falling off a cliff.

7 O, full of scorpions is my mind, dear wife!
   Macbeth in *Macbeth*, 3.2.36

8 My heart is turned to stone; I strike it, and it hurts my hand.
   Othello in *Othello*, 4.1.182–3

9 Had it pleased Heaven
   To try me with affliction, had they rained
   All kind of sores and shames on my bare head,
   Steeped me in poverty to the very lips,
   Given to captivity me and my utmost hopes,
   I should have found in some place of my soul
   A drop of patience.
   Othello in *Othello*, 4.2.47–53

   No affliction could match that of Desdemona's supposed adultery.

10   O ill-starred wench,
Pale as thy smock! When we shall
meet at compt,
This look of thine will hurl my soul
from heaven,
And fiends will snatch at it. Cold,
cold, my girl,
Even like thy chastity.
Othello in *Othello*, 5.2.272–6

Looking at Desdemona's lifeless body;
"compt" = the Day of Judgment.

11 Comfort's in heaven, and we are on
the earth,
Where nothing lives but crosses,
cares and grief.
York in *Richard II*, 2.2.78–9

He is left alone to cope with rebellion;
"crosses" = vexations.

12 Affliction is enamored of thy parts,
And thou art wedded to calamity.
**Friar Lawrence in *Romeo and Juliet*,
3.3.2–3**

Telling the newly-married Romeo that he is
banished.

13 *Camillo.* Prosperity's the very bond
of love,
Whose fresh complexion and
whose heart together
Affliction alters.
Perdita.   One of these is true:
I think affliction may subdue the
cheek,
But not take in the mind.
The Winter's Tale, 4.4.573–7

Camillo is trying to help Perdita escape from
the anger of Polixenes.

14 It easeth some, though none it ever
cured,

To think their dolor others have
endured.
The Rape of Lucrece, 1581–2

Afterlife (see also Heaven)

1 But this eternal blazon must not be
To ears of flesh and blood.
Ghost in *Hamlet*, 1.5.21–2

Refusing to describe to Hamlet his afterlife;
"eternal blazon" = revelation of eternal things.

2   Who would fardels bear
To grunt and sweat under a weary
life
But that the dread of something
after death,
The undiscovered country, from
whose bourn
No traveler returns, puzzles the will,
And makes us rather bear those ills
we have,
Than fly to others that we know not
of?
Hamlet in *Hamlet*, 3.1.75–81

The "fardels" or burdens of this life are made
tolerable by fear of worse after death.

3 Would I were with him, wheresoe'er he is, either in heaven or in
hell!
Bardolph in *Henry V*, 2.3.7–8

On hearing that Falstaff is dead.

4 Nay sure, he's not in hell; he's in
Arthur's bosom, if ever man went
to Arthur's bosom. 'A made a finer
end, and went away an it had been
any christom child.
Mistress Quickly in *Henry V*, 2.3.9–12

On Falstaff: she confuses King Arthur with
Abraham (a beggar is carried by angels to
"Abraham's bosom" in Luke 16:22); by "chris-
tom child" she means new christened baby.

5   So part we sadly in this troublous
    world
    To meet with joy in sweet
    Jerusalem.
    Queen Margaret in *Henry VI, Part 3*,
    5.5.7–8

    Parting from her allies who are about to be
    executed; "sweet Jerusalem" is heaven, the
    holy city of the new Jerusalem promised in
    Revelation 21:2 and 10.

6   Beating and hanging are terrors to
    me. For the life to come, I sleep out
    the thought of it.
    Autolycus, *The Winter's Tale*, 4.3.29–30

Age (see also Middle Age, Old Age)

1   Unregarded age in corners thrown.
    Adam in *As You Like It*, 2.3.42

    On being dismissed at the age of "almost
    fourscore" from the household where he has
    served all his life.

2   He that doth the ravens feed,
    Yea, providently caters for the spar-
    row,
    Be comfort to my age!
    Adam in *As You Like It*, 2.3.43–5

    Calling on God's help.

3   Therefore my age is as a lusty win-
    ter,
    Frosty, but kindly.
    Adam in *As You Like It*, 2.3.52–3

4   The sixth age shifts
    Into the lean and slippered pan-
    taloon,

With spectacles on nose, and pouch
    on side,
His youthful hose, well saved, a
    world too wide
For his shrunk shank, and his big
    manly voice,
Turning again toward childish tre-
    ble, pipes
And whistles in his sound.
    Jaques in *As You Like It*, 2.7.157–63

    The sixth of the "seven ages" of man;
    "pantaloon" = old fool, from a character type
    in Italian comedy.

5   Last scene of all,
    That ends this strange eventful his-
    tory,
    Is second childishness, and mere
    oblivion,
    Sans teeth, sans eyes, sans taste,
    sans everything.
    Jaques in *As You Like It*, 2.7.163–6

    The seventh of the "seven ages" of man.

6   The satirical rogue says here that
    old men have grey beards, that their
    faces are wrinkled, their eyes purg-
    ing thick amber and plum-tree
    gum, and that they have a plentiful
    lack of wit, together with most
    weak hams.
    Hamlet in *Hamlet*, 2.2.196–200

    Mocking the aging Polonius by pretending to
    quote from a book he is reading.

7   What doth gravity out of his bed at
    midnight?
    Falstaff in *Henry IV, Part 1*, 2.4.294

    On an old nobleman arriving with a message
    for Hal.

8   That he is old, the more the pity,
    his white hairs do witness it.

Falstaff in *Henry IV, Part 1*, 2.4.467–8

Inviting sympathy because of old age.

9   If sack and sugar be a fault, God
    help the wicked! If to be old and
    merry be a sin, then many an old
    host that I know is damned.

Falstaff in *Henry IV, Part 1*, 2.4.470–2

Defending himself against Prince Henry's
denunciation.

10 Your lordship, though not clean
    past your youth, have yet some
    smack of age in you, some relish of
    the saltness of time in you.

Falstaff in *Henry IV, Part 2*, 1.2.96–9

Insulting the Chief Justice; "saltness" = sharp
or bitter taste.

11 You that are old consider not the
    capacities of us that are young.

Falstaff in *Henry IV, Part 2*, 1.2.173–4

In fact Falstaff is as old as the Chief Justice he
is teasing.

12 Have you not a moist eye, a dry
    hand, a yellow cheek, a white beard,
    a decreasing leg, an increasing
    belly? Is not your voice broken,
    your wind short, your chin double,
    your wit single, and every part
    about you blasted with antiquity?
    And will you yet call yourself
    young?

Chief Justice in *Henry IV, Part 2*,
1.2.180–5

Rebuking old Falstaff for calling himself
young.

13 A man can no more separate age
    and covetousness than 'a can part
    young limbs and lechery.

Falstaff in *Henry IV, Part 2*, 1.2.228–30

14 *Shallow.* Doth she hold her own
    well?
    Falstaff. Old, old, Master Shallow.
    Shallow. Nay, she must be old, she
    cannot choose but be old, certain
    she's old.

Henry IV, Part 2, 3.2.205–8

Recalling what happened fifty-five years
previously.

15 Lord, Lord, how subject we old
    men are to this vice of lying!

Falstaff in *Henry IV, Part 2*, 3.2.303–4

Falstaff speaking truth for once.

16 The old folk, time's doting chroni-
    cles.

Clarence in *Henry IV, Part 2*, 4.4.126

"Doting" implies they are extravagantly fond
of recalling the past.

17 I know thee not, old man. Fall to
    thy prayers.
    How ill white hairs becomes a fool
    and jester!

Prince Hal, now King Henry V, in
Henry IV, Part 2, 5.5.47–8

His famous rejection of his old companion,
Falstaff.

18 A good soft pillow for that good
    white head
    Were better than a churlish turf of
    France.

King Henry in *Henry V*, 4.1.14–15

Addressing the old soldier Erpingham.

19 My comfort is that old age, that ill
    layer-up of beauty, can do no more
    spoil upon my face.

King Henry in *Henry V*, 5.2.229–31

Apologizing for his plainness.

20 You see how full of changes his age
    is.
    Goneril in *King Lear* , 1.1.288
    Speaking of her father, King Lear.

21   Idle old man,
    That still would manage those
    authorities
    That he hath given away!
    Goneril in *King Lear*, 1.3.16–18
    She is speaking about her father, King Lear.

22 Old fools are babes again, and must
    be used
    With checks as flatteries.
    Goneril in *King Lear*, 1.3.19–20
    Speaking about her father, King Lear, and
    varying the proverb "an old man is twice a
    child"; "checks" or rebukes are the flattery
    they require.

23 As you are old and reverend,
    should be wise.
    Goneril in *King Lear*, 1.4.240
    To her father, implying he is anything but
    wise.

24 Thou shouldst not have been old
    till thou hadst been wise.
    Fool in *King Lear*, 1.5.44–5
    Addressing King Lear.

25   O sir, you are old;
    Nature in you stands on the very
    verge
    Of his confine.
    Regan in *King Lear*, 2.4.146–8
    "Confine" = limit, bounds.

26 Do you but mark how this becomes
    the house!
    "Dear daughter, I confess that I am
    old;
    Age is unnecessary. On my knees I
    beg
    That you'll vouchsafe me raiment,
    bed, and food."
    King Lear in *King Lear*, 2.4.153–6
    Scorning the idea of begging his daughter's
    forgiveness; "becomes the house" = befits the
    decorum of the royal house.

27 I am a very foolish fond old man,
    Fourscore and upward, not an hour
    more nor less;
    And to deal plainly,
    I fear I am not in my perfect mind.
    King Lear in *King Lear*, 4.7.59–62
    "Fond" = silly, in my dotage.

Air

1 Hover through the fog and filthy
    air.
    The Witches (Weird Sisters) in *Macbeth*, 1.1.12

2 *Adrian.* The air breathes upon us
    here most sweetly.
    Sebastian. As if it had lungs, and
    rotten ones.
    Antonio. Or as 'twere perfumed by
    a fen.
    ***The Tempest*, 2.1.47–9**
    Shipwrecked courtiers, whose characters are
    reflected in their attitudes to the island on
    which they find themselves.

Ambition

1   Ambition
(The soldier's virtue) rather makes
   choice of loss
Than gain which darkens him.

Ventidius in *Antony and Cleopatra*,
3.1.22–4

Having won a victory, he decides not to do
more, so as not to outshine the emperor,
Antony.

2   Ill-weaved ambition, how much art
   thou shrunk!
When that this body did contain a
   spirit,
A kingdom for it was too small a
   bound,
But now two paces of the vilest
   earth
Is room enough.

Prince Hal in *Henry IV, Part 1*,
5.4.88–92

On the death of Hotspur.

3   These days are dangerous;
Virtue is choked with foul ambition,
And charity chased hence by ran-
   cor's hand.

Gloucester in *Henry VI, Part 2*,
3.1.142–4

On plots against the king.

4   No man's pie is freed
From his ambitious finger.

Buckingham in *Henry VIII*, 1.1.52–3

On Cardinal Wolsey.

5   Cromwell, I charge thee, fling away
   ambition,
By that sin fell the angels; how can
   man then,
The image of his maker, hope to
   win by it?

Cardinal Wolsey in *Henry VIII*,
3.2.440–2

Lucifer's sin is usually called pride, but he was
ambitious too: "I will exalt my throne above
the stars of God" (Isaiah 14:13).

6   Love and meekness,
   lord,
Become a churchman better than
   ambition.

Archbishop Cranmer in *Henry VIII*,
5.2.97–8

Rebuking the Bishop of Winchester.

7   'Tis a common proof
That lowliness is young ambition's
   ladder.

Brutus in *Julius Caesar*, 2.1.21–2

8   Ambition's debt is paid.

Brutus in *Julius Caesar*, 3.1.83

Meaning the ambition of the assassinated
Caesar.

9   But Brutus says he was ambitious,
And Brutus is an honorable man.

Mark Antony in *Julius Caesar*, 3.2.86–7

Speaking to the people after the death of
Caesar.

10   When that the poor have cried,
   Caesar hath wept;
Ambition should be made of
   sterner stuff.

Mark Antony in *Julius Caesar*, 3.2.91–2

11   Thou wouldst be great;
      Art not without ambition, but
        without
      The illness should attend it. What
        thou wouldst highly
      That wouldst thou holily; wouldst
        not play false,
      And yet wouldst wrongly win.

Lady Macbeth in *Macbeth*, 1.5.18–22

"Illness" = wickedness; describing the moral
confusion in Macbeth as they think about
murdering Duncan.

12   I have no spur
      To prick the sides of my intent, but
        only
      Vaulting ambition, which o'erleaps
        itself,
      And falls on th' other.

Macbeth in *Macbeth*, 1.7.25–8

The image is of a rider vaulting into the saddle
and falling on the other side of the horse;
Macbeth is contemplating the murder of
Duncan.

13   Thriftless ambition, that will raven
        up
      Thine own life's means!

Ross in *Macbeth*, 2.4.28–9

Supposing Duncan's sons have killed their
father, and hence their means of subsistence;
"raven up" = devour greedily.

14   The aim of all is but to nurse the
        life
      With honor, wealth and ease in
        waning age.

***The Rape of Lucrece*, 141–2**

Anarchy (see also Chaos, Disorder)

1   If that the heavens do not their visi-
        ble spirits
      Send quickly down to tame these
        vile offenses,
      It will come:
      Humanity must perforce prey on
        itself,
      Like monsters of the deep.

Albany in *King Lear*, 4.2.46–9

Albany is horrified by what King Lear's daughters, Goneril and Regan, have done to their
father, thrust out into a wild storm; but his
words carry a more general meaning, impli-
cating everyone.

2   Force should be right, or, rather,
        right and wrong—
      Between whose endless jar justice
        resides—
      Should lose their names, and so
        should justice too.
      Then everything includes itself in
        power,
      Power into will, will into appetite;
      And appetite, an universal wolf,
      So doubly seconded with will and
        power,
      Must make perforce an universal
        prey,
      And last eat up himself.

Ulysses in *Troilus and Cressida*, 1.3.116–24

Ulysses' vision of anarchy if social ranks and
hierarchy are abolished.

Androgyny

1   They shall yet belie thy happy years
      That say thou art a man. Diana's
        lip
      Is not more smooth and rubious;
        thy small pipe
      Is as the maiden's organ, shrill and
        sound,
      And all is semblative a woman's
        part.

Orsino in *Twelfth Night*, 1.4.30–4

Almost penetrating Viola's disguise as his
page Cesario; "rubious" = red; "pipe" = voice;
"is semblative" = resembles. (Viola was originally played by a boy).

2 A woman's face with Nature's own
   hand painted
   Hast thou, the master-mistress of
   my passion;
   A woman's gentle heart, but not
   acquainted
   With shifting change as is false
   women's fashion.

Sonnet 20, 1–4

Addressing his male "friend."

Angels

1 Angels are bright still, though the
   brightest fell.
   Though all things foul would wear
   the brows of grace,
   Yet grace must still look so.

Malcolm in *Macbeth*, 4.3.22–4

Referring to Lucifer; see Isaiah 14:12.

2 For every man that Bolingbroke
   hath pressed
   To lift shrewd steel against our
   golden crown,
   God for his Richard hath in heavenly pay
   A glorious angel. Then if angels
   fight,
   Weak men must fall; for heaven still
   guards the right.

King Richard in *Richard II*, 3.2.58–62

Trying to comfort himself.

Anger

1 Anger's my meat; I sup upon
   myself,
   And so shall starve with feeding.

Volumnia in *Coriolanus*, 4.2.50–1

Refusing an invitation to supper after Coriolanus's banishment.

2 Must I give way and room to your
   rash choler?
   Shall I be frighted when a madman
   stares?

Brutus in *Julius Caesar*, 4.3.39–40

Responding to the angry Cassius.

3 Sir, sir, impatience hath his privilege.

Pembroke of *King John*, 4.3.32

Meaning that strong emotion permits a freedom from the restraints of good manners.

4 Come not between the dragon and
   his wrath.

King Lear in *King Lear*, 1.1.122

King Lear himself is the "dragon," the absolute
monarch, speaking to Kent.

5 O, when she is angry she is keen
   and shrewd;
   She was a vixen when she went to
   school,
   And though she be but little, she is
   fierce.

Helena in *A Midsummer Night's
Dream*, 3.2.323–5

On Hermia; "keen and shrewd" = caustic and
malicious.

6 Now you strike like the blind man;
'twas the boy that stole your meat,
and you'll beat the post.
Benedick in *Much Ado About Nothing,*
2.1.198–200

Claudio lashes out wildly on thinking he has
been betrayed.

7 O God, that I were a man! I would
eat his heart in the market-place.
Beatrice in *Much Ado About Nothing,*
4.1.306–7

Angry with Claudio for abandoning Hero.

8 Like an unseasonable stormy day,
Which makes the silver rivers
drown their shores,
As if the world were all dissolved to
tears,
So high above his limits swells the
rage
Of Bolingbroke.
Sir Stephen Scroop in *Richard II,*
3.2.106–10

Bringing news that the whole country has
gone over to Henry Bolingbroke.

9 To be in anger is impiety;
But who is man that is not angry?
Alcibiades in *Timon of Athens,* 3.5.56–7

Seeking mercy for a friend who has killed, he
claims, in self-defense.

Animals (see also Creatures, Dogs, Horses)

1 A lioness, with udders all drawn
dry,
Lay couching, head on ground,
with cat-like watch

When that the sleeping man should
stir; for 'tis
The royal disposition of that beast
To prey on nothing that doth seem
as dead.
Oliver in *As You Like It,* 4.3.114–18

Describing the danger from which Orlando
rescued him.

2 Pray you no more of this, 'tis like
the howling of Irish wolves against
the moon.
Rosalind in *As You Like It,* 5.2.109–10

Dogs or wolves barking at the moon offered a
proverbial image of ineffectual outcry. She is
calling on the lovers to stop complaining.

3 The cat will mew, and dog will have
his day.
Hamlet in *Hamlet,* 5.1.292

Meaning that one cannot stop a creature from
acting according to its nature. Hamlet may
refer to Laertes (as the cat), and himself (as the
dog whose turn will come). The saying about
the dog was proverbial.

4 Wanton as youthful goats, wild as
young bulls.
Vernon in *Henry IV, Part 1,* 4.1.103

Prince Hal and his companions, ready for
war against the rebels; "wanton" = merry,
frolicsome.

5 The fox barks not when he would
steal the lamb.
Suffolk in *Henry VI, Part 2,* 3.1.55

6 But when the fox hath once got in
his nose,
He'll soon find means to make the
body follow.
Richard of Gloucester in *Henry VI,
Part 3,* 4.7.25–6

7 And when the lion fawns upon the lamb,
   The lamb will never cease to follow him.
   King Henry in *Henry VI, Part 3*, 4.8.49–50

   Henry wrongly imagines that the people will support him because of his mild rule.

8 A harmless necessary cat.
   Shylock in *The Merchant of Venice*, 4.1.55

   Commenting on what some people for no reason dislike.

9 *King Richard.* Lions make leopards tame.
   Mowbray. Yea, but not change his spots.
   ***Richard II*,** 1.1.174–5

   Richard sees himself as a lion, king of beasts.

10 The lion dying thrusteth forth his paw
   And wounds the earth, if nothing else, with rage
   To be o'erpowered.
   Queen in *Richard II*, 5.1.29–31

   Urging the woebegone Richard to behave like the lion, the king of beasts.

11 Villain, thou know'st nor law of God nor man;
   No beast so fierce but knows some touch of pity.
   Lady Anne in *Richard III*, 1.2.70–1

   To Richard, displaying the corpse of Henry VI, slain by him; "nor law" = neither law.

12 *Exit pursued by a bear.*
   Stage direction in *The Winter's Tale*, 3.3.58

A famous stage direction, thought to be Shakespeare's own, for the exit of Antigonus; probably an actor dressed in a bear-skin was used.

Answers

1 Your answer, sir, is enigmatical.
   Benedick in *Much Ado about Nothing*, 5.4.27

   He is puzzled by Leonato's reference to the trick played on him to make him fall in love with Beatrice.

Anticipation

1 All things that are
   Are with more spirit chasèd than enjoyed.
   Gratiano in *The Merchant of Venice*, 2.6.12–13

   Referring to Lorenzo's plan to elope with Jessica.

2 A day in April never came so sweet,
   To show how costly summer was at hand,
   As this fore-spurrer comes before his lord.
   Messenger in *The Merchant of Venice*, 2.9.93–5

   On the messenger who announces the coming of Bassanio; "costly" = rich, splendid.

3 Gallop apace, you fiery-footed steeds,
   Towards Phoebus' lodging.
   Juliet in *Romeo and Juliet*, 3.2.1–2

   Trying to hurry on the horses of the sun (Phoebus) towards nightfall, when she expects Romeo to come.

4 I am giddy; expectation whirls me
   round.
   Th'imaginary relish is so sweet
   That it enchants my sense.

   Troilus in *Troilus and Cressida*,
   3.2.18–20

   Anticipating his first chance to make love to
   Cressida.

Anti-Semitism

1 You call me misbeliever, cut-throat
   dog,
   And spit upon my Jewish gaberdine,
   And all for use of that which is
   mine own.

   Shylock in *The Merchant of Venice*,
   1.3.111–13

   "Gaberdine" = loose cape or cloak.

2 He hath disgraced me, and hin-
   dered me half a million, laughed at
   my losses, mocked at my gains,
   scorned my nation, thwarted my
   bargains, cooled my friends, heated
   mine enemies; and what's his reason? I am a Jew.

   Shylock in *The Merchant of Venice*,
   3.1.54–8

   On the Christian merchant, Antonio.

Anxiety

1 Undone, and forfeited to cares for
   ever!

   Bertram in *All's Well That Ends Well*,
   2.3.266

   On being forced to marry Helena.

2 So shaken as we are, so wan with
   care,
   Find we a time for frighted peace to
   pant.

   King Henry in *Henry IV, Part 1*, 1.1.1–2

   Hoping for a breathing-space and the end of
   civil war.

3 Care is no cure, but rather corro-
   sive.
   For things that are not to be reme-
   died.

   Joan la Pucelle in *Henry VI, Part 1*,
   3.3.3–4

   Speaking to the French leaders, after the English have taken Rouen.

4 Between the acting of a dreadful
   thing
   And the first motion, all the interim
   is
   Like a phantasma or a hideous
   dream.
   The genius and the mortal instruments
   Are then in council, and the state of
   man,
   Like to a little kingdom, suffers
   then
   The nature of an insurrection.

   Brutus in *Julius Caesar*, 2.1.63–9

   A marvelous expression of a tormented mind
   living as it were a hallucination ("phantasma"), while the soul ("genius") on the one
   hand, and the mental and physical functions
   of the body on the other, are at odds.

5 You have some sick offense within
   your mind,
   Which by the right and virtue of
   my place
   I ought to know of.

   Portia in *Julius Caesar*, 2.1.268–70

Demanding, as Brutus's wife, to know what troubles him.

6   Better be with the dead,
Whom we, to gain our peace, have sent to peace,
Than on the torture of the mind to lie
In restless ecstasy.

Macbeth in *Macbeth*, 3.2.19–22

To Lady Macbeth; those they have murdered have gone to "peace" or heaven, but their deeds have not brought peace of mind to Macbeth, only "ecstasy," or a frenzied anxiety.

7   Then comes my fit again. I had else been perfect,
Whole as the marble, founded as the rock,
As broad and general as the casing air.
But now I am cabined, cribbed, confined, bound in
To saucy doubts and fears.

Macbeth in *Macbeth*, 3.4.20–4

On learning that his murderers failed to kill Fleance; "broad and general" = free and unconfined; "casing" = surrounding.

8   You have too much respect upon the world.
They lose it that do buy it with much care.

Gratiano in *The Merchant of Venice*, 1.1.74–5

Telling Antonio he has too anxious a regard ("respect") for his business affairs ("upon the world").

9   Although I joy in thee,
I have no joy of this contract tonight.

It is too rash, too unadvised, too sudden,
Too like the lightning which doth cease to be
Ere one can say it lightens.

Juliet in *Romeo and Juliet*, 2.2.116–20

To Romeo; she already has a premonition that their love may not last.

10   O, the thorns we stand upon!

Florizel in *The Winter's Tale*, 4.4.585

To Perdita; a proverbial expression for anxiety about the problems they face.

11   Not mine own fears, nor the prophetic soul
Of the wide world, dreaming on things to come,
Can yet the lease of my true love control,
Supposed as forfeit to a confined doom.

Sonnet 107, 1–4

Anxiety about the future in these lines may have been sparked by the uncertainties of the last years of the reign of Queen Elizabeth I; the "lease" or allotted term may be of the speaker's life and love, or of the loved one's life and love, or both; "forfeit to a confined doom" is usually taken to mean "subject to a fixed term."

Aphorisms and Epigrams

1   He that wants money, means, and content is without three good friends.

Corin in *As You Like It*, 3.2.24–6

"Means" = opportunity.

2   He's mad that trusts in the tameness of a wolf, a horse's health, a boy's love, or a whore's oath.

Fool in *King Lear*, 3.6.18–19

3   Wisdom and goodness to the vile
    seem vile.
    Albany in *King Lear*, 4.2.38

4   Things without all remedy
    Should be without regard: what's
    done is done.
    Lady Macbeth in *Macbeth*, 3.2.11–12

    "Be without regard" = not be brooded on.
    She speaks as though it is easy to forget the
    past, but see 7 below.

5   Things bad begun make strong
    themselves by ill.
    Macbeth in *Macbeth*, 3.2.55

6   Receive what cheer you may;
    The night is long that never finds
    the day.
    Malcolm in *Macbeth*, 4.3.239–40

7   What's done cannot be undone.
    Lady Macbeth in *Macbeth*, 5.1.68

    Her involvement in murders returns to haunt
    her; compare 4 above.

8   Shall quips and sentences and
    these paper bullets of the brain awe
    a man from the career of his
    humor? No, the world must be
    peopled.
    **Benedick in *Much Ado About Nothing*,
    2.3.240–2**

    Refusing to be intimidated by mocking words
    ("sentences" = maxims) from pursuing his
    inclination, and loving Beatrice.

9   Everyone can master a grief but he
    that has it.
    **Benedick in *Much Ado About Nothing*,
    3.2.28–9**

Pretending he has a toothache in order to
avoid confessing he is in love; "grief" = pain
or anguish.

10 She never yet was foolish that was
    fair,
    For even her folly helped her to an
    heir.
    Iago in *Othello*, 2.1.136–7

    No matter how silly, a beautiful woman may
    win a rich husband and have a child; "heir"
    may carry both senses.

11 Poor and content is rich, and rich
    enough,
    But riches fineless is as poor as win-
    ter
    To him that ever fears he shall be
    poor.
    Iago in *Othello*, 3.3.172–4

    "Fineless" = unlimited.

Apologies (see also Excuses)

1   I would I could
    Quit all offenses with as clear
    excuse
    As well as I am doubtless I can
    purge
    Myself of many I am charged
    withal.
    **Prince Hal in *Henry IV, Part 1*,
    3.2.18–21**

    Apologizing to his father, King Henry; "quit" =
    be clear of.

2   I should not urge thy duty past thy
    might.
    I know young bloods look for a
    time of rest.
    Brutus in *Julius Caesar*, 4.3.261–2

    To his servant Lucius.

3 Pardon this fault, and by my soul I
swear
I never more will break an oath
with thee.

Bassanio in *The Merchant of Venice*,
5.1.247–8

The "fault" lay in giving Portia's ring away.

4 I have been long a sleeper; but I
trust
My absence doth neglect no great
design
Which by my presence might have
been concluded.

King Richard in *Richard III*, 3.4.23–5

Apologizing for his late arrival at a council
meeting; "great design" = important proposal
or business.

5 My business was great, and in such
a case as mine a man may strain
courtesy.

Romeo in *Romeo and Juliet*, 2.4.49–51

Apologizing for dodging away from Mercutio;
his "business" was to make love to Juliet.

Apparitions (see also Ghosts)

1 What, has this thing appeared again
tonight?

Horatio in *Hamlet*, 1.1.21

Addressed to the sentinels at the king's castle,
regarding the ghost of the dead King Hamlet
of Denmark.

2 What art thou that usurp'st this
time of night,
Together with that fair and warlike
form
In which the majesty of buried
Denmark
Did sometimes march? By heaven I
charge thee speak!

Horatio in *Hamlet*, 1.1.46–9

Addressing the ghost of Hamlet's father, the
dead King of Denmark; Horatio questions the
ghost's right to assume that likeness, and its
right to invade the night, by the use of the
term "usurp'st."

3 In the most high and palmy state of
Rome,
A little ere the mightiest Julius fell,
The graves stood tenantless and the
sheeted dead
Did squeak and gibber in the
Roman streets.

Horatio in *Hamlet*, 1.1.113–16

The apparition of the dead King Hamlet suggests some impending calamity, like portents
before the assassination of Julius Caesar.

4 How ill this taper burns! Ha! Who
comes here?
I think it is the weakness of mine
eyes
That shapes this monstrous apparition.

Brutus in *Julius Caesar*, 4.3.275–7

On the entry of the ghost of Caesar.

5 Art thou some god, some angel, or
some devil,
That mak'st my blood cold, and my
hair to stare?

Brutus in *Julius Caesar*, 4.3.279–80

Seeing the ghost of Caesar.

6 Is this a dagger which I see before
me,
The handle toward my hand?
Come, let me clutch thee:
I have thee not, and yet I see thee
still.

Macbeth in *Macbeth*, 2.1.33–5

The imaginary dagger that symbolizes his anxiety about killing Duncan.

7 Art thou not, fatal vision, sensible
To feeling as to sight? Or art thou
but
A dagger of the mind, a false cre-
ation
Proceeding from the heat-
oppressèd brain?

Macbeth in *Macbeth*, 2.1.36–9

The vision is "fatal" as prompting him to murder; "heat-oppressed" = fevered.

8 Can such things be
And overcome us like a summer's
cloud,
Without our special wonder?

Macbeth in *Macbeth*, 3.4.109–11

On seeing the ghost of the murdered Banquo.

Appearance

1 *Gertrude.* Why seems it so particu-
lar with thee?
Hamlet. Seems, madam? Nay, it is,
I know not "seems."

Hamlet, 1.2.75–6

Gertrude has attempted to console Hamlet for
his father's death by urging that death is common, i.e., universal, not "particular."

2 There's no art
To find the mind's construction in
the face:
He was a gentleman on whom I
built
An absolute trust.

Duncan in *Macbeth*, 1.4.11–14

Referring to the traitor Cawdor.

3 Mislike me not for my complexion,
The shadowed livery of the burnished sun,
To whom I am a neighbor and near
bred.

**Prince of Morocco in *The Merchant of
Venice*, 2.1.1–3**

Asking Portia to be color-blind as he is black.

4 Lord worshipped might he be, what
a beard hast thou got!

**Old Gobbo in *The Merchant of Venice*,
2.2.93–4**

The blind old man mistakes his son's long hair
for a beard.

5 O wise and upright judge!
How much more elder art thou
than thy looks!

**Shylock in *The Merchant of Venice*,
4.1.150–1**

On Portia, who has led him to think he can
have his pound of flesh.

6 *Claudio.* The old ornament of his
cheek hath already stuffed tennis-
balls.
Leonato. Indeed, he looks younger
than he did, by the loss of a beard.

Much Ado About Nothing, 3.2.46–9

Benedick appears clean-shaven for the sake of
Beatrice, who said she could not stand a
bearded man.

7 Give not this rotten orange to your
friend;
She's but the sign and semblance of
her honor.

**Claudio in *Much Ado About Nothing*,
4.1.32–3**

Rejecting Hero as unchaste at the wedding
ceremony; "sign and semblance" = outward
appearance.

8 Men should be what they seem,
Or those that be not, would they
might seem none.

Iago in *Othello*, 3.3.126

Ironic in relation to his own hypocrisy.

9   Opinion's but a fool that makes us scan
     The outward habit for the inward man.
     Simonides in *Pericles*, 2.2.56–7

     Or judge people by appearances.

10   I think there's never a man in Christendom
     Can lesser hide his love or hate than he,
     For by his face straight shall you know his heart.
     Hastings in *Richard III*, 3.4.51–3

     Showing his mistaken trust in Richard.

11   I will believe thou hast a mind that suits
     With this thy fair and outward character.
     Viola in *Twelfth Night*, 1.2.50–1

     To the captain of the ship that brought her to Illyria.

12   He's as tall a man as any's in Illyria.
     Sir Toby Belch in *Twelfth Night*, 1.3.20

     Defending his friendship with Sir Andrew Aguecheek.

13   *Mamillius.* What color are your eyebrows?
     First Lady. Blue, my lord.
     Mamillius. Nay, that's a mock. I have seen a lady's nose
     That has been blue, but not her eyebrows.
     ***The Winter's Tale*, 2.1.13–15**

     Hermione's little son talks with court ladies.

Appetite

1   The sweetest honey
     Is loathsome in his own deliciousness,
     And in the taste confounds the appetite.
     Friar Lawrence in *Romeo and Juliet*, 2.6.11–13

     Varying the proverb, "too much honey cloys the stomach," and hinting at the idea of love turning into hate.

Argument (see also Reason)

1   You shall have time to wrangle in when you have nothing else to do.
     Enobarbus in *Antony and Cleopatra*, 2.2.105–6

     Intervening to stop Antony and Octavius arguing about who is to blame for their differences.

2   He is too disputable for my company. I think of as many matters as he, but I give heaven thanks, and make no boast of them.
     Jaques in *As You Like It*, 2.5.35–7

     "Disputable" = fond of argument.

3   Your reasons at dinner have been sharp and sententious, pleasant without scurrility, witty without affection, audacious without impudency, learned without opinion, and strange without heresy.
     Nathaniel in *Love's Labor's Lost*, 5.1.2–6

     The curate praises the conversation of the pedant; "affection" = affectation; "without opinion" = without being opinionated.

4   He draweth out the thread of his
     verbosity finer than the staple of his
     argument.

Holofernes in *Love's Labor's Lost*,
5.1.16–17

Describing Armado's extravagant language;
"staple" = fiber.

5   You have both said well,
     And on the cause and question now
        in hand
     Have glozed, but superficially—not
        much
     Unlike young men whom Aristotle
        thought
     Unfit to hear moral philosophy.

Hector in *Troilus and Cressida*,
2.2.163–7

Referring to Paris and Troilus in the debate
about whether to keep Helen; "glozed" =
commented. Aristotle lived long after the Trojan War took place.

6   The reasons you allege do more
        conduce
     To the hot passion of distempered
        blood
     Than to make up a free determina-
        tion
     'Twixt right and wrong; for plea-
        sure and revenge
     Have ears more deaf than adders to
        the voice
     Of any true decision.

Hector in *Troilus and Cressida*,
2.2.168–73

Criticizing Troilus and Paris for being besotted
on Helen; "free" = unbiased.

Arithmetic

1   *Moth.* How many is one, thrice
     told?

Armado. I am ill at reckoning; it
fitteth the spirit of a tapster.

Love's Labor's Lost, 1.2.39–41

"Tapster" = barman.

Arrogance

1   But most it is presumption in us
        when
     The help of heaven we count the act
        of men.

Helena in *All's Well That Ends Well*,
2.1.151–2

She is urging the King of France, who has
refused her offer to treat his illness, to think of
her as heaven's agent.

2   Possessed he is with greatness,
     And speaks not to himself but with
        a pride
     That quarrels at self-breath.

Ulysses in *Troilus and Cressida*,
2.3.170–2

Commenting on Achilles; "quarrels at self-
breath" = finds fault with what he says about
himself (as not measuring up to his greatness).

Asceticism

1   A man whose blood
     Is very snow-broth; one who never
        feels
     The wanton stings and motions of
        the sense,
     But doth rebate and blunt his nat-
        ural edge
     With profits of the mind, study,
        and fast.

Lucio in *Measure for Measure*, 1.4.57–61

Describing Angelo as an ascetic who never
feels sexual passion ("wanton stings and
motions of the sense").

Aspiration

1 Why, then, I do but dream on sovereignty
Like one that stands upon a promontory
And spies a far-off shore where he would tread,
Wishing his foot were equal with his eye.

Richard of Gloucester in *Henry VI, Part 3*, 3.2.134–7

Already dreaming of becoming King Richard III.

Assassination

1 Let's kill him boldly, but not wrathfully;
Let's carve him as a dish fit for the gods,
Not hew him as a carcass fit for hounds.

Brutus in *Julius Caesar*, 2.1.172–4

On the idea of killing Caesar.

2 Let our hearts, as subtle masters do,
Stir up their servants to an act of rage
And after seem to chide 'em. This shall make
Our purpose necessary, and not envious;
Which so appearing to the common eyes,
We shall be called purgers, not murderers.

Brutus in *Julius Caesar*, 2.1.175–80

"Servants" = bodily agents; "envious" = malicious; he is trying to make the murder of Caesar look like a sacrifice.

Assault

1 These hands do lack nobility that they strike
A meaner than myself.

Cleopatra in *Antony and Cleopatra*, 2.5.82–3

On losing dignity in striking the messenger who brings bad news.

Astrology

1 We make guilty of our disasters the sun, the moon, and stars, as if we were villains on necessity, fools by heavenly compulsion.

Edmund in *King Lear*, 1.2.120–2

Edmund's contempt for astrology passes into a rejection of religion and morality; "on" = by.

2 My father compounded with my mother under the Dragon's tail, and my nativity was under Ursa Major, so that it follows, I am rough and lecherous. Fut, I should have been that I am, had the maidenliest star in the firmament twinkled on my bastardizing.

Edmund in *King Lear*, 1.2.128–33

The constellations Draco ("Dragon's tail") and Ursa Major, or Great Bear, were supposed to have a malignant influence. Edmund's belief contrasts with that of Kent in the same play; see the next entry

3   It is the stars,
The stars above us, govern our conditions.

Kent in *King Lear*, 4.3.32–3

He cannot explain the difference between King Lear's two wicked elder daughters and his youngest, the gentle Cordelia; "conditions" = natures, dispositions.

4   I find my zenith doth depend upon
     A most auspicious star, whose
        influence
     If now I court not, but omit, my
        fortunes
     Will ever after droop.

Prospero in *The Tempest*, 1.2.181–4

"Zenith" = height of fortune.

Authority

1   I must be patient; there is no fetter-
     ing of authority.

Parolles in *All's Well That Ends Well*,
2.3.236–7

Referring to Lord Lafew, who has seen
through his affectations, and treats him with
contempt.

2   Hear you this Triton of the min-
        nows? Mark you
     His absolute "shall"?

Coriolanus in *Coriolanus*, 3.1.89–90

Showing his contempt for Sicinius, a tribune
of the people; Triton was a minor sea-god in
ancient Greece.

3   He'll shake
     Your Rome about your ears.

Cominius in *Coriolanus*, 4.6.98–9

Said of Coriolanus, when news comes that he
has joined with the Volscians against Rome.

4   I think he'll be to Rome
     As is the osprey to the fish, who
        takes it
     By sovereignty of nature.

Aufidius in *Coriolanus*, 4.7.33–5

Speaking of Coriolanus; fish were said to sur-
render themselves to the osprey.

5   O, sir, your presence is too bold
        and peremptory,

And majesty might never yet
   endure
The moody frontier of a servant
   brow.

King Henry in *Henry IV, Part 1*,
1.3.17–19

"Moody frontier" = angry frown; King Henry
is dismissing the rebellious Earl of Worcester.

6   *Kent.* You have that in your coun-
     tenance which I would fain call
     master.
     Lear. What's that?
     Kent. Authority.

King Lear, 1.4.27–30

7   *Lear.* Thou hast seen a farmer's
        dog bark at a beggar?
     Gloucester. Ay, sir.
     Lear. And the creature run from
        the cur? There thou mightst
        behold the great image of author-
        ity: a dog's obeyed in office.

King Lear, 4.6.154–9

8   Thus can the demigod, Authority
     Make us pay down for our offense,
        by weight,
     The words of heaven: on whom it
        will, it will;
     On whom it will not, so; yet still 'tis
        just.

Claudio in *Measure for Measure*,
1.2.120–3

On being committed to prison for getting
Juliet with child; the "words of heaven" are
from Romans 9:15–18, where God's pleasure
is to have mercy or otherwise as He pleases.

9   But man, proud man,
     Dressed in a little brief authority,
     Most ignorant of what he's most
        assured,

His glassy essence, like an angry ape
Plays such fantastic tricks before
   high heaven
As makes the angels weep.

Isabella in Measure for Measure,
2.2.117–22

Pleading with Angelo for her brother's life, she reminds him of the pride that goes with authority, and how ignorant men are of their souls, the "essence" that like a glass or mirror is reflected from God.

10   Authority, though it err like others,
   Hath yet a kind of medicine in
      itself,
   That skins the vice o' the top.

Isabella in Measure for Measure,
2.2.134–6

Reminding Angelo that men may use authority to cover ("skin") their vices without remedying them.

11   Though authority be a stubborn
   bear, yet he is oft led by the nose
   with gold. Show the inside of your
   purse to the outside of his hand,
   and no more ado.

Clown in The Winter's Tale, 4.4.801–4

Advising his father to bribe Autolycus, whom he takes to be a great courtier.

Autumn, see Seasons

Avarice

1   How quickly nature falls into revolt
   When gold becomes her object!

King Henry in Henry IV, Part 2,
4.5.65–6

"Nature" = human nature, or natural affection; mistakenly thinking Prince Hal is greedy for power.

2   Poorly rich so wanteth in his store
   That, cloyed with much, he pineth
      still for more.

The Rape of Lucrece, 97–8

On the rich person who yet feels poor.

Banishment, see Exile

Bastardy

1   I grow, I prosper:
   Now, gods, stand up for bastards!

Edmund in King Lear, 1.2.21–2

2   I am a bastard too. I love bastards.
   I am bastard begot, bastard
   instructed, bastard in mind,
   bastard in valor, in every thing
   illegitimate.

Thersites in Troilus and Cressida,
5.7.16–18

Encountering the bastard Margarelon on the field of battle.

Beauty

1   For her own person,
   It beggared all description: she did
      lie
   In her pavilion—cloth of gold, of
      tissue—
   O'er-picturing that Venus where we
      see
   The fancy outwork nature.

Enobarbus in Antony and Cleopatra,
2.2.197–201

Cleopatra as she first appeared to Antony, out-doing Venus, the goddess of love.

2 Alas, what danger will it be to us,
   Maids as we are, to travel forth so
      far!
   Beauty provoketh thieves sooner
      than gold.

Rosalind in *As You Like It*, 1.3.108–10

Commenting on Celia's suggestion that they
escape to the forest of Arden.

3 'Tis not your inky brows, your
      black silk hair,
   Your bugle eyeballs, nor your cheek
      of cream
   That can entame my spirits to your
      worship.

Rosalind in *As You Like It*, 3.5.46–8

Disguised as Ganymede, she rejects Phebe's
love; bugles were shiny black glass beads.

4 You are a thousand times a prop-
      erer man
   Than she a woman. 'Tis such fools
      as you
   That makes the world full of ill-
      favored children.

Rosalind in *As You Like It*, 3.5.51–3

Disguised as a man, she advises Silvius, who
loves Phebe, who is in love with Rosalind;
"properer" = more handsome.

5 How bravely thou becom'st thy
      bed! fresh lily,
   And whiter than the sheets!

Jachimo in *Cymbeline*, 2.2.15–16

Looking at Imogen asleep.

6   On her left breast
   A mole cinque-spotted, like the
      crimson drops
   I'the bottom of a cowslip.

Jachimo in *Cymbeline*, 2.2.37–9

Looking at Imogen asleep; "cinque-spotted" =
having five spots, an accurate description of
the cowslip flower.

7 See what a grace was seated on this
      brow:
   Hyperion's curls, the front of Jove
      himself,
   An eye like Mars, to threaten and
      command.

Hamlet in *Hamlet*, 3.4.55–7

To Gertrude, seeing his father in a picture as
like Hyperion, the ancient Greek sun-god, for
beauty; having a forehead (front) like Jupiter;
and an eye like the god of war.

8 'Tis beauty that doth oft make
      women proud.

York in *Henry VI, Part 3*, 1.4.128

9 The fairest hand I ever touched: O
      beauty,
   Till now I never knew thee.

King Henry in *Henry VIII*, 1.4.75–6

On meeting Anne Boleyn.

10 Beauty and honor in her are so
       mingled
    That they have caught the king.

**Lord Chamberlain in *Henry VIII*,
2.3.76–7**

On Anne Boleyn, soon to be queen.

11 Thou hast the sweetest face I ever
       looked on.
    Sir, as I have a soul, she is an angel.

**Second Gentleman in *Henry VIII*,
4.1.43–4**

On seeing Anne Boleyn, now crowned as
queen.

12   My beauty, though but mean,
    Needs not the painted flourish of
       your praise.
    Beauty is bought by judgment of
       the eye.

Princess in *Love's Labor's Lost*, 2.1.13–15

Rejecting Boyet's flattery of her.

13 Beauty doth varnish age as if new
    born,
    And gives the crutch the cradle's
    infancy.
    O, 'tis the sun that maketh all
    things shine!

Berowne in *Love's Labor's Lost,*
4.3.240–2

In love with Rosaline, Berowne claims for her
a beauty that could restore youth to the aged.

14   Look on beauty,
    And you shall see 'tis purchased by
    the weight,
    Which therein works a miracle in
    nature,
    Making them lightest that wear
    most of it.

Bassanio in *The Merchant of Venice,*
3.2.88–91

Referring to cosmetics as making the wearer
"light" or lascivious.

15   O happy fair!
    Your eyes are lodestars, and your
    tongue's sweet air
    More tuneable than lark to shep-
    herd's ear
    When wheat is green, when
    hawthorn buds appear.

Helena in *A Midsummer Night's
Dream,* 1.1.182–5

To Hermia, whose eyes, she says, draw those
of Demetrius just as navigators fix their eyes
on a guiding star.

16   He hath achieved a maid
    That paragons description and wild
    fame;
    One that excels the quirks of bla-
    zoning pens.

Cassio in *Othello,* 2.1.61–3

The maid is Desdemona, who surpasses
("paragons") description, and goes beyond the
witty conceptions ("quirks") of those who

would proclaim her beauty; "blazon" is a term
from heraldry, meaning originally a shield or
badge.

17   O thou weed!
    Who art so lovely fair and smell'st
    so sweet
    That the sense aches at thee, would
    thou hadst ne'er been born!

Othello in *Othello,* 4.2.67–9

Thinking of Desdemona as false to him.

18   Yet I'll not shed her
    blood,
    Nor scar that whiter skin of hers
    than snow,
    And smooth as monumental
    alabaster.

Othello in *Othello,* 5.2.3–5

Seeing Desdemona as like an effigy in
alabaster on a tomb.

19 See where she comes, apparelled
    like the spring,
    Graces her subjects, and her
    thoughts the king
    Of every virtue gives renown to
    men.

Pericles in *Pericles,* 1.1.12–14

Admiring the approach of the daughter of
Antiochus.

20 *Simonides.* And she is fair too, is
    she not?
    Pericles. As a fair day in summer,
    wondrous fair.

Pericles, 2.5.35–6

They are speaking of Thaisa, the daughter of
Simonides.

21 O, she doth teach the torches to
    burn bright!

Romeo in *Romeo and Juliet,* 1.5.44

On first seeing Juliet.

22 Beauty too rich for use, for earth too dear!

Romeo in *Romeo and Juliet*, 1.5.47

On Juliet; "dear" = precious.

23   But he's something stained
With grief, that's beauty's canker,
   thou mightst call him
A goodly person.

Prospero in *The Tempest*, 1.2.415–17

Describing Ferdinand; the cankerworm feeds on buds.

24 Most radiant, exquisite, and unmatchable beauty.

Viola in *Twelfth Night*, 1.5.170–1

Addressing Olivia in Orsino's flowery style.

25 *Olivia.* Is't not well done?
Viola. Excellently done, if God did all.
Olivia. 'Tis in grain, sir, 'twill endure wind and weather.
Viola. 'Tis beauty truly blent, whose red and white
Nature's own sweet and cunning hand laid on.

***Twelfth Night*, 1.5.235–40**

Viola admires the blending of colors in Olivia's beauty, which is fast-dyed or natural ("in grain"), not contrived with cosmetics.

26 Who is Silvia? What is she,
That all our swains commend her?
Holy, fair, and wise is she.
The heaven such grace did lend her
That she might admirèd be.

Song in *The Two Gentlemen of Verona*, 4.2.39–43

Sung under Sylvia's window at the instigation of Thurio, who, like Proteus, is courting her.

27 Is she kind as she is fair?
For beauty lives with kindness.

Song in *The Two Gentlemen of Verona*, 4.2.44–5

28   Black brows they say
Become some women best, so that
   there be not
Too much hair there, but in a semi-circle,
Or a half-moon made with a pen.

Mamillius in *The Winter's Tale*, 2.1.8–11

A precocious boy talking to the ladies who attend his mother, Hermione.

29 Beauty itself doth of itself persuade
The eyes of men without an orator.

***The Rape of Lucrece*, 29–30**

Collatine has been boasting of the beauty of his wife, Lucrece.

30 From fairest creatures we desire
   increase,
That thereby beauty's rose might
   never die.

***Sonnet 1*, 1–2**

Urging his friend to perpetuate his beauty by "increase," i.e., by having a child.

31 Shall I compare thee to a summer's day?
Thou art more lovely and more
   temperate:
Rough winds do shake the darling
   buds of May,
And summer's lease hath all too
   short a date.

***Sonnet 18*, 1–4**

Addressed to his friend; "temperate" = moderate or even-tempered.

32 O how much more doth beauty
    beauteous seem
    By that sweet ornament which
    truth doth give!

Sonnet **54,** 1–2

The word "truth" means both fidelity ("troth")
and integrity.

33 My mistress' eyes are nothing like
    the sun;
    Coral is far more red than her lips'
    red;
    If snow be white, why then her
    breasts are dun;
    If hairs be wires, black wires grow
    on her head . . .
    And yet, by heaven, I think my
    love as rare
    As any she belied with false com-
    pare.

Sonnet 130, 1–4, 13–14

Begging

1 I see, sir, you are liberal in offers.
   You taught me first to beg, and now
     methinks
   You teach me how a beggar should
     be answered.

Portia in *The Merchant of Venice*,
4.1.438–40

In disguise, she demands that Bassanio give
her the ring she gave him, and which he
swore should never leave his finger.

2 *Pericles.* He asks of you that never
     used to beg.
   First Fisherman. No, friend, cannot
   you beg? Here's them in our

country of Greece gets more with
begging than we can do with
working.

Pericles, 2.1.62–5

Pericles, cast up on shore by a storm, is begging the fishermen to help him.

Belief

1 Before my God, I might not this
     believe
   Without the sensible and true
     avouch
   Of mine own eyes.

Horatio in *Hamlet*, 1.1.56–8

He is skeptical about the ghost until he sees it;
"sensible" = perceived by, or relating to, the
senses.

Bells

1 Go, bid thy mistress, when my
     drink is ready,
   She strike upon the bell.

Macbeth in *Macbeth*, 2.1.31–2

To a servant.

2 I go, and it is done; the bell invites
     me.
   Hear it not, Duncan, for it is a
     knell
   That summons thee to heaven, or
     to hell.

Macbeth in *Macbeth*, 2.1.62–4

On his way to murder Duncan.

Betrayal

1   Where you are liberal of your loves
    and counsels,
  Be sure you be not loose; for those
    you make friends
  And give your hearts to, when they
    once perceive
  The least rub in your fortunes, fall
    away
  Like water from ye, never found
    again
  But where they mean to sink ye.

Buckingham in *Henry VIII*, 2.1.126–31

"Loose" = unrestrained; "rub" = check (from the game of bowls).

2   Yet I well remember
  The favors of these men. Were they
    not mine?
  Did they not sometimes cry "All
    hail!" to me?
  So Judas did to Christ; but He, in
    twelve,
  Found truth in all but one; I, in
    twelve thousand, none.

King Richard in *Richard II*, 4.1.167–71

Appearing, in effect, as Henry's prisoner; "favors" = looks as well as support. Judas Iscariot betrayed Christ; see Matthew 26:25.

Birds

1   When he had occasion to be
    seen
  He was but as the cuckoo is in June,
  Heard, not regarded.

King Henry in *Henry IV, Part 1*,
3.2.74–6

To the Prince, about Richard II.

2   Being fed by us you used us so
  As that ungentle gull, the cuckoo's
    bird,
  Useth the sparrow.

Worcester in *Henry IV, Part 1*, 5.1.59–61

The cuckoo lays its eggs in nests of other birds, such as the sparrow, which feeds the cuckoo's young at the expense of its own chicks.

3   O Westmorland, thou art a sum-
    mer bird,
  Which ever in the haunch of winter
    sings
  The lifting up of day.

King Henry in *Henry IV, Part 2*,
4.4.91–3

"Haunch" = backside, latter part.

4   Like to a pair of loving turtle-doves
  That could not live asunder day or
    night.

Burgundy in *Henry VI, Part 1*, 2.2.30–1

Referring to the Dauphin and Joan of Arc.

5   So doth the swan her downy
    cygnets save,
  Keeping them prisoner underneath
    her wings.

Suffolk in *Henry VI, Part 1*, 5.3.56–7

Showing his affection for Margaret of France, taken prisoner by the English, and placed in his care.

6   This guest of summer,
  The temple-haunting martlet, does
    approve,
  By his loved mansionry, that the
    heaven's breath
  Smells wooingly here.

Banquo in *Macbeth*, 1.6.3–6

"Martlet" = house-martin, that migrates in winter, and builds nests under the eaves of houses.

7   No jutty, frieze,
Buttress, nor coign of vantage, but this bird
Hath made his pendant bed and procreant cradle;
Where they most breed and haunt, I have observed
The air is delicate.

Banquo in *Macbeth*, 1.6.6–10

Referring to the house-martin; "coign of vantage" = favorable corner.

8   It was the owl that shrieked, the fatal bellman,
Which gives the stern'st good night.

Lady Macbeth in *Macbeth*, 2.2.3–4

A duty of the "bellman" or town-crier was to announce deaths, and the owl was thought a bird of ill-omen.

9   A falcon, towering in her pride of place,
Was by a mousing owl hawked at and killed.

Old Man in *Macbeth*, 2.4.12–13

"Towering in her pride of place" = having risen to the point where it was ready to swoop down on its prey.

10   The crow doth sing as sweetly as the lark
When neither is attended.

Portia in *The Merchant of Venice*, 5.1.102–3

"When neither is attended" = when no one is listening.

11   I think
The nightingale, if she should sing by day
When every goose is cackling, would be thought
No better a musician than the wren.

Portia in *The Merchant of Venice*, 5.1.103–6

12   The ousel cock so black of hue,
With orange-tawny bill,
The throstle with his note so true,
The wren with little quill.

Bottom in *A Midsummer Night's Dream*, 3.1.125–8

Singing to cheer himself up; the "ousel cock" is the blackbird; the wren has only a small pipe ("little quill") or thin song.

13   The finch, the sparrow, and the lark,
The plainsong cuckoo grey,
Whose note full many a man doth mark
And dares not answer nay—

Bottom in *A Midsummer Night's Dream*, 3.1.130–3

The cuckoo invades the nests of other birds, and is associated with cuckoldry; Bottom sings because he is afraid.

14   The eagle suffers little birds to sing,
And is not careful what they mean thereby,
Knowing that with the shadow of his wings
He can at pleasure stint their melody.

Tamora in *Titus Andronicus*, 4.4.83–6

Tamora is trying to cheer up the Emperor Saturninus with this image of royal power.

Birth and Death

1 A terrible childbed hast thou had,
my dear;
No light, no fire: th'unfriendly elements
Forgot thee utterly.

Pericles in *Pericles*, 3.1.56–8

He supposes Thaisa is dead, after giving birth
to his daughter in a storm at sea.

2 Thou met'st with things dying, I
with things new-born.

**Shepherd in *The Winter's Tale*,
3.3.113–14**

His son has seen Antigonus die, while the
Shepherd has found the baby, Perdita, left on
the shore.

Birthdays

1 It is my birthday,
I had thought t' have held it poor;
but since my lord
Is Antony again, I will be
Cleopatra.

**Cleopatra in *Antony and Cleopatra*,
3.13.184–6**

After her reconciliation with Antony.

Blessings

1 God's benison go with you, and
with those
That would make good of bad, and
friends of foes!

Old Man in *Macbeth*, 2.4.40–1

"Benison" = blessing.

2 Heaven give thee joy!
What cannot be eschewed must be
embraced.

**Page in *The Merry Wives of Windsor*,
5.5.236–7**

Discovering that Fenton has married his
daughter.

3 Heaven give you many, many
merry days!

**Mistress Page in *The Merry Wives of
Windsor*, 5.5.240**

To Fenton on his marriage to Anne Page.

4 God keep your worship! I wish
your worship well; God restore you
to health! I humbly give you leave
to depart; and if a merry meeting
may be wished, God prohibit it!

**Dogberry in *Much Ado About
Nothing*, 5.1.323–6**

Dogberry presumably means to ask leave to
depart, and for God to permit a merry meeting.

5 Honor, riches, marriage-blessing,
Long continuance, and increasing,
Hourly joys be still upon you!

Juno in *The Tempest*, 4.1.106–8

The goddess of marriage sings a blessing on
Ferdinand and Miranda.

6 Earth's increase, foison plenty,
Barns and garners never empty,
Vines with clustering bunches
growing,
Plants with goodly burden bowing;
Spring come to you at the farthest
In the very end of harvest.

Ceres in *The Tempest*, 4.1.110–15

Ceres, goddess of fertility, offers her blessing
to Ferdinand and Miranda.

Body

1   I will through and through
Cleanse the foul body of th'
infected world,
If they will patiently receive my
medicine.

Jaques in *As You Like It*, 2.7.60–1

Claiming a godlike ability to purge people of
their sins.

2   Bear your body more seeming,
Audrey.

Touchstone in *As You Like It*, 5.4.68–9

"Seeming" = seemly, decorously.

3   When he was naked he was, for all
the world, like a forked radish, with
a head fantastically carved upon it
with a knife.

Falstaff in *Henry IV, Part 2*, 3.2.310–12

Falstaff describing Shallow as a young man.

4   What is the body when the head is
off?

King Edward in *Henry VI, Part 3*, 5.1.41

Speaking to Warwick, he threatens to kill King
Henry, who is his prisoner.

Books (see also Education, Learning, Study)

1   Whereas, before, our forefathers
had no other books but the score
and the tally, thou hast caused
printing to be used, and, contrary
to the king, his crown and dignity,
thou hast built a paper-mill.

Jack Cade in *Henry VI, Part 2*, 4.7.34–7

A peasant's idea of a treasonable offense; the
score and tally were matching notched sticks
used by creditor and debtor to keep primitive
accounts.

2   All delights are vain, but that
most vain
Which, with pain purchased, doth
inherit pain,
As painfully to pore upon a book
To seek the light of truth.

Berowne in *Love's Labor's Lost*, 1.1.72–5

Berowne has in mind the "light" of love as
found in a beautiful woman's eyes.

3   My library
Was dukedom large enough.

Prospero in *The Tempest*, 1.2.109–10

Claiming he never cared for power as Duke of
Milan.

4   Knowing I loved my books, he furnished me
From mine own library with volumes that
I prize above my dukedom.

Prospero in *The Tempest*, 1.2.166–8

On the loyal Gonzalo, who provided him
with books in his exile.

5   Come and take choice of all my
library,
And so beguile thy sorrow.

Titus in *Titus Andronicus*, 4.1.34–5

To Lavinia, who has no hands to cope with
books.

Boys (see also Parents and Children, Youth)

1 Then the whining schoolboy, with his satchel
And shining morning face, creeping like snail
Unwillingly to school.

Jaques in *As You Like It*, 2.7.145–7

The second of the "seven ages" of man.

2   The boy disdains me,
He leaves me, scorns me. Briefly die their joys
That place them on the truth of girls and boys.

Lucius in *Cymbeline*, 5.5.105–7

His page Fidele (really Imogen in disguise) abandons Lucius on spying Jachimo wearing a ring stolen from her; "truth" = loyalty or trust.

3   O, 'tis a parlous boy,
Bold, quick, ingenious, forward, capable.
He is all the mother's, from the top to toe.

King Richard in *Richard III*, 3.1.154–6

Describing Prince Edward; "parlous" = dangerously clever.

4 When that I was and a little tiny boy,
With hey, ho, the wind and the rain,
A foolish thing was but a toy,
For the rain it raineth every day.

Feste in *Twelfth Night*, 5.1.389–92

A sobering thought at the end of the comedy, as the play may seem a "foolish thing," or trifle ("toy").

5 Two lads that thought there was no more behind

But such a day tomorrow as today,
And to be boy eternal.

Polixenes in *The Winter's Tale*, 1.2.63–5

Recalling his boyhood with Leontes.

Brevity

1 Brevity is the soul of wit.

Polonius in *Hamlet*, 2.2.90

2 *Brackenbury.* What, so brief?
Second Murderer. 'Tis better, sir, than to be tedious.

Richard III, 1.4.88–9

The murderer who has come for Clarence treats the Lieutenant of the Tower with scant respect.

Building

1   When we mean to build,
We first survey the plot, then draw the model,
And when we see the figure of the house,
Then must we rate the cost of the erection,
Which if we find outweighs ability,
What do we then but draw anew the model
In fewer offices, or at least desist
To build at all?

Lord Bardolph in *Henry IV, Part 2*, 1.3.41–8

On confining plans within the scope of available resources; "offices" = rooms.

2 The singing masons building roofs of gold.

Archbishop of Canterbury in *Henry V*, 1.2.198

The best-known line in his vision of bees as exemplifying an ordered society.

3   Having waste ground enough,
Shall we desire to raze the sanctuary,
And pitch our evils there?

Angelo in *Measure for Measure*, 2.2.169–71

The general idea is of destroying what is good in order to build (as in pitching a tent) something nasty; but "evils" is thought by some to mean privies or toilets. Angelo is brooding on his urge to violate the chastity of Isabella.

Burial (see also Epitaphs, Graves, Mourning)

1   *Rosencrantz.* What have you done, my lord, with the dead body?
Hamlet. Compounded it with dust, whereto 'tis kin.

Hamlet, 4.2.5–6

The body of Polonius, killed by Hamlet; "dust thou art, and unto dust shalt thou return," Genesis 3:19.

2   I cannot choose but weep to think they would lay him in the cold ground.

Ophelia in *Hamlet*, 4.5.69–70

Thinking of her father Polonius, killed by Hamlet.

3   Lay her i' th' earth,
And from her fair and unpolluted flesh
May violets spring.

Laertes in *Hamlet*, 5.1.238–40

On the burial of Ophelia.

4   According to his virtue let us use him,
With all respect and rites of burial.

Octavius in *Julius Caesar*, 5.5.76–7

On the death of Brutus.

Business (see also Money)

1   To business that we love we rise betime,
And go to't with delight.

Antony in *Antony and Cleopatra*, 4.4.20–21

Arming for a final battle; "betime" = early. The word "business" now suggests routines of the workplace so that these lines out of context take on quite a new meaning.

2   In the way of bargain, mark ye me, I'll cavil on the ninth part of a hair.

Hotspur in *Henry IV, Part 1*, 3.1.137–8

Talking with other rebels about the division of the spoils they hope to win.

3   Our hands are full of business, let's away,
Advantage feeds him fat while men delay.

King Henry in *Henry IV, Part 1*, 3.2.179–80

"Feeds him fat" = grows lazy, loses its edge.

4   A good wit will make use of anything. I will turn diseases to commodity.

Falstaff in *Henry IV, Part 2*, 1.2.247–8

Planning to claim he has been lamed in battle, not by gout brought on by drinking; "commodity" = profit.

5   Our bad neighbor makes us early
    stirrers,
    Which is both healthful and good
    husbandry.
    King Henry in *Henry V*, 4.1.6–7

    "Husbandry" = management or thrift.

6   I thank my fortune for it,
    My ventures are not in one bottom
    trusted,
    Nor to one place.
    Antonio in *The Merchant of Venice*,
    1.1.41–3

    He is glad that his merchandise is not
    exported in a single ship ("bottom").

7   I will buy with you, sell with you,
    talk with you, walk with you, and so
    following; but I will not eat with
    you, drink with you, nor pray with
    you.
    Shylock in *The Merchant of Venice*,
    1.3.35–8

    Speaking to the Christian Bassanio.

8   When rich villains have need of
    poor ones, poor ones may make
    what price they will.
    Borachio in *Much Ado About Nothing*,
    3.3.113–4

    Reporting he has been well paid by Don John
    to prevent the marriage of Claudio and Hero.

9   Let us, like merchants, show our
    foulest wares,
    And think perchance they'll sell; if
    not,
    The luster of the better yet to show
    Shall show the better.
    Ulysses in *Troilus and Cressida*,
    1.3.358–61

Plotting with Nestor to ensure that Ajax, not
Achilles, meets Hector's challenge.

10   You do as chapmen do,
    Dispraise the thing that they desire
    to buy.
    Paris in *Troilus and Cressida*, 4.1.76–7

    He is responding to the bitter criticism of
    Helen by Diomedes; "chapmen" = merchants.
    Compare Proverbs 20:14.

11 Let me have no lying. It becomes
    none but tradesmen.
    Autolycus in *The Winter's Tale*,
    4.4.722–3

    Addressing the old Shepherd and his son; the
    comment is ironic since Autolycus is himself a
    talented liar.

Caesar

1   I rather tell thee what is to be feared
    Than what I fear; for always I am
    Caesar.
    Caesar in *Julius Caesar*, 1.2.211–12

    Caesar thinks of himself as an embodiment of
    power, and his name has passed into dictio-
    naries as such (compare the German
    "Kaiser").

2   Know, Caesar doth not wrong, nor
    without cause
    Will he be satisfied.
    Caesar in *Julius Caesar*, 3.1.47–8

    To Metellus, whose brother has been exiled.

3   As Caesar loved me, I weep for him;
    as he was fortunate, I rejoice at it; as
    he was valiant, I honor him; but as
    he was ambitious, I slew him.
    There is tears for his love; joy for

his fortune; honor for his valor; and death for his ambition.

Brutus in *Julius Caesar*, 3.2.24–9

Defending the killing of Caesar.

4   Here was a Caesar! When comes such another?

Mark Antony in *Julius Caesar*, 3.2.252

The name "Caesar" already begins to take on the meaning of "ruler" or "monarch."

5   O Julius Caesar, thou art mighty yet!
Thy spirit walks abroad and turns our swords
In our own proper entrails.

Brutus in *Julius Caesar*, 5.3.94–6

Brutus has just learned of the death of his friend Cassius; "own proper" = very own.

Capriciousness

1   If you find him sad,
Say I am dancing; if in mirth, report
That I am sudden sick.

Cleopatra in *Antony and Cleopatra*, 1.3.3–5

Teasing Antony by being contrary.

2   The unruly waywardness that infirm and choleric years bring with them.

Goneril in *King Lear*, 1.1.298–9

On the behavior of her father, the old King Lear.

Castles

1   This castle hath a pleasant seat; the air

Nimbly and sweetly recommends itself
Unto our gentle senses.

Duncan in *Macbeth*, 1.6.1–3

"Seat" = situation; "gentle senses" = sense made gentle by the air or breeze.

2   There stands the castle, by yon tuft of trees.

Percy in *Richard II*, 2.3.53

Berkeley castle, defended by Richard.

Cause

1   I know no personal cause to spurn at him,
But for the general: he would be crowned.
How that might change his nature, there's the question.

Brutus in *Julius Caesar*, 2.1.11–13

Thinking about the conspiracy against Caesar.

2   The cause is in my will: I will not come.
That is enough to satisfy the Senate.

Caesar in *Julius Caesar*, 2.2.71–2

Refusing to offer excuses for not going to the Capitol.

3   You all did love him once, not without cause;
What cause withholds you then to mourn for him?

Mark Antony in *Julius Caesar*, 3.2.102–3

Speaking to the people about Caesar.

4   Is there any cause in nature that make these hard hearts?

King Lear in *King Lear*, 3.6.77–8

5   It is the cause, it is the cause, my
    soul.
    Let me not name it to you, you
       chaste stars!
    It is the cause.

Othello in *Othello*, 5.2.1–3

Othello has no "cause," meaning both reason
and legal cause, to murder Desdemona other
than her imagined unchastity.

Celibacy

1   Shall I never see a bachelor of
    threescore again?

Benedick in *Much Ado About Nothing*,
1.1.199–200

Dismayed that his friend Claudio intends to
marry.

2   He that hath a beard is more than a
    youth, and he that hath no beard is
    less than a man; and he that is more
    than a youth is not for me, and he
    that is less than a man, I am not for
    him.

Beatrice in *Much Ado About Nothing*,
2.1.36–9

Rejecting the idea of marrying.

3   Good Lord, for alliance! Thus goes
    every one to the world but I, and I
    am sunburnt; I may sit in a corner
    and cry "Heigh-ho for a husband"!

Beatrice in *Much Ado About Nothing*,
2.1.318–20

To Claudio, who claims the privilege through
marriage of "alliance" in calling Beatrice
cousin; she feels left out, or "sunburnt" = dry
and withered.

Censorship

1   Art made tongue-tied by authority.

Sonnet 66, 9

Censorship was one of the many evils in his
society listed by the narrator in this sonnet;
"art" = letters (literature) and learning rather
than fine art.

Ceremony

1   What infinite heart's ease
    Must kings neglect, that private
       men enjoy!
    And what have kings, that privates
       have not too,
    Save ceremony, save general cere-
       mony?

King Henry in *Henry V*, 4.1.236–9

On the burdens of responsibility; "ceremony"
suggests deference as well as the pomp and
display of majesty.

2   And what art thou, thou idol cere-
       mony?
    What kind of god art thou, that suf-
       fer'st more
    Of mortal griefs than do thy wor-
       shippers?
    What are thy rents? What are thy
       comings-in?

King Henry in *Henry V*, 4.1.240–3

Dismissing the pomp of majesty as worthless.

3   To my judgment your highness is
    not entertained with that ceremoni-
    ous affection as you were wont.

Knight in *King Lear*, 1.4.58–9

On the treatment of King Lear by his daughter
Goneril.

4   To feed were best at home;
      From thence, the sauce to meat is
      ceremony;
      Meeting were bare without it.

Lady Macbeth in *Macbeth*, 3.4.34–6

"From thence" = away from home.

5   Ceremony was but devised at first
      To set a gloss on faint deeds, hollow
      welcomes,
      Recanting goodness, sorry e'er 'tis
      shown;
      But where there is true friendship,
      there needs none.

Timon in *Timon of Athens*, 1.2.15–18

Timon claims true friendship needs no ceremony; "recanting goodness" = generosity
withdrawn even as it is offered.

Challenges

1   You are a villain. I jest not. I will
      make it good how you dare, with
      what you dare, and when you dare.

Benedick in *Much Ado About Nothing*,
5.1.145–7

Challenging Claudio to fight.

2   *Sir Andrew Aguecheek*. Here's the
      challenge, read it. I warrant
      there's vinegar and pepper in't.
      Fabian. Is't so saucy?

Twelfth Night, 3.4.143–5

Sir Andrew is challenging Cesario (Viola in
disguise) to fight. "Saucy" = both spicy and
impertinent.

3   I will meditate the while upon some
      horrid message for a challenge.

Sir Toby Belch in *Twelfth Night*,
3.4.199–200

In place of Sir Andrew's silly written challenge
to Cesario.

Chance (see also Fortune)

1   This is the night
      That either makes me, or fordoes
      me quite.

Iago in *Othello*, 5.1.128–9

"Fordoes me quite" = destroys me utterly.

2   In the reproof of chance
      Lies the true proof of men.

Nestor in *Troilus and Cressida*, 1.3.33–4

The true test of men, says Nestor, lies in the
way they cope with chance.

3   We profess
      Ourselves to be the slaves of
      chance, and flies
      Of every wind that blows.

Florizel in *The Winter's Tale*, 4.4.539–41

Having no idea where to take Perdita.

Change (see also Mutability)

1   When clouds are seen, wise men
      put on their cloaks;
      When great leaves fall, then winter
      is at hand;
      When the sun sets, who doth not
      look for night?

Third Citizen in *Richard III*, 2.3.32–4

Fearing the worst on learning of the death of
Edward IV.

Chaos (see also Anarchy, Confusion)

1   Men, wives, and children stare, cry
    out, and run,
    As it were doomsday.

Trebonius in *Julius Caesar*, 3.1.97–8

After the death of Caesar.

2   Though castles topple on their
    warders' heads,
    Though palaces and pyramids do
    slope
    Their heads to their foundations;
    though the treasure
    Of nature's germens tumble all
    together,
    Even till destruction sicken—
    answer me
    To what I ask you.

Macbeth in *Macbeth*, 4.1.56–61

A warder is a guardian; "nature's germens" =
the seeds or rudiments from which it was
thought all living organisms developed.

3   Nay, had I power, I should
    Pour the sweet milk of concord
    into hell,
    Uproar the universal peace, con-
    found
    All unity on earth.

Malcolm in *Macbeth*, 4.3.97–100

"Uproar" = throw into confusion. Malcolm is
making out that he would be a worse king
than Macbeth.

Character

1   Along with them
    They brought one Pinch, a hungry
    lean-faced villain,
    A mere anatomy, a mountebank,
    A threadbare juggler and a fortune-
    teller,
    A needy, hollow-eyed, sharp look-
    ing wretch,
    A living dead man.

**Antipholus of Ephesus in *The Comedy
of Errors*, 5.1.237–42**

Doctor Pinch, a schoolmaster and charlatan
("mountebank"), called in by Adriana to help
restore Antipholus when she supposed her
husband was mad; "anatomy" = skeleton.

2   You would play upon me, you
    would seem to know my stops, you
    would pluck out the heart of my
    mystery, you would sound me from
    my lowest note to the top of my
    compass; and there is much music,
    excellent voice, in this little organ.

Hamlet in *Hamlet*, 3.2.364–8

Hamlet shows Guildenstern he is more difficult to comprehend and play on than a
recorder.

3   Before I knew thee, Hal, I knew
    nothing, and now am I, if a man
    should speak truly, little better than
    one of the wicked.

Falstaff in *Henry IV, Part 1*, 1.2.92–5

Blaming his faults on Prince Hal.

4   The Moor—howbeit that I endure
    him not—
    Is of a constant, loving, noble
    nature,
    And I dare think he'll prove to Des-
    demona
    A most dear husband.

Iago in *Othello*, 2.1.288–91

Speaking to the audience about Othello.

5   He plays o' the viol-de-gamboys,
    and speaks three or four languages

word for word without book, and
hath all the good gifts of nature.
Sir Toby Belch in *Twelfth Night,*
1.3.25–8

Over-praising Sir Andrew Aguecheek; the viola da gamba, or bass viol, was held between the legs, and the image has sexual overtones; "without book" = by heart.

Charity

1 He hath a tear for pity, and a hand
Open as day for melting charity.
King Henry in *Henry IV, Part 2,*
4.4.31–2

Praising Prince Hal.

2 For charity itself fulfills the law,
And who can sever love from charity?
Berowne in *Love's Labor's Lost,*
4.3.361–2

Referring to the words of Saint Paul, Romans 13:8, "he that loveth another hath fulfilled the law"; "charity," from the Latin "caritas" = caring or compassion, love in the largest sense. Hence the last verse of I Corinthians 13, "And now abideth faith, hope and charity, these three; but the greatest of these is charity."

3 'Twere good you do so much for
charity.
Portia in *The Merchant of Venice,*
4.1.261

Asking Shylock to allow a surgeon to be present when he takes his pound of flesh.

Charm

1 Fie, wrangling queen!
Whom everything becomes—to
chide, to laugh,
To weep.

Antony in *Antony and Cleopatra,*
1.1.48–50

Cleopatra's "infinite variety" (see 3 below).

2 I saw her once
Hop forty paces through the public
street;
And having lost her breath, she
spoke, and panted,
That she did make defect perfection.
Enobarbus in *Antony and Cleopatra,*
2.2.228–231

Cleopatra's charm in her less than queenly behavior.

3 Age cannot wither her, nor custom
stale
Her infinite variety.
Enobarbus in *Antony and Cleopatra,*
2.2.234–5

On Cleopatra's undying charm.

Chastity (see also Virginity)

1 Chaste as the icicle
That's curdied by the frost from
purest snow
And hangs on Dian's temple.
Coriolanus in *Coriolanus,* 5.3.65–7

On Valeria, friend of his wife, Virgilia; "curdied" = congealed; Diana was goddess of the moon and of chastity.

2 The heavens hold firm
The walls of thy dear honor; keep
unshaked
That temple, thy fair mind, that
thou mayst stand
T'enjoy thy banished lord, and this
great land
Second Lord in *Cymbeline,* 2.1.62–5

Speaking of Imogen and her banished husband, Posthumus.

3   Me of my lawful pleasure she
    restrained,
    And prayed me oft forbearance; did
    it with
    A pudency so rosy the sweet view
    on't
    Might well have warmed old Sat-
    urn; that I thought her
    As chaste as unsunned snow.

    Posthumus in *Cymbeline*, 2.5.9–13

    Speaking of Imogen, when he believes,
    falsely, that she has been unfaithful;
    "pudency" = modesty. Saturn was one of the
    ancient gods, father of Jupiter.

4   Weigh what loss your honor may
    sustain
    If with too credent ear you list his
    songs,
    Or lose your heart, or your chaste
    treasure open
    To his unmastered importunity.

    Laertes in *Hamlet*, 1.3.29–32

    Speaking to Ophelia of Hamlet's professions
    of love to her; "credent" = credulous; "chaste
    treasure" = virginity.

5   The chariest maid is prodigal
    enough
    If she unmask her beauty to the
    moon.

    Laertes in *Hamlet*, 1.3.36–7

    Warning Ophelia not to listen to Hamlet's
    protestations of love; "chariest" = most mod-
    est.

6   In the morn and liquid dew of
    youth
    Contagious blastments are most
    imminent.

    Laertes in *Hamlet*, 1.3.41–2

    Warning his sister Ophelia against Hamlet's
    advances; "contagious blastments" = disease-
    bringing blights.

7   A virgin from her tender infancy,
    Chaste and immaculate in very
    thought.

    **Joan la Pucelle in *Henry VI, Part 1*,
    5.4.50–1**

    Joan of Arc defending herself.

Cheerfulness

1   A light heart lives long.

    Katherine in *Love's Labor's Lost*, 5.2.18

    "Light" = merry, but could also mean
    unchaste.

Chiding

1   Better a little chiding than a great
    deal of heart-break.

    **Mistress Page in *The Merry Wives of
    Windsor*, 5.3.9–10**

    She expects to be rebuked by her husband for
    encouraging their daughter Anne to marry a
    man he despises.

Children (see also Boys, Girls, Parents and Children)

1   Barnes are blessings.

    **Lavatch in *All's Well That Ends Well*,
    1.3.25–6**

    "Barnes" means bairns, or children.

2   He makes a July's day short as
    December,
    And with his varying childness
    cures in me
    Thoughts that would thick my
    blood.

Polixenes in *The Winter's Tale*,
1.2.169–71

On the pleasure his son gives him.

Chivalry

1   When first this order was ordained,
    my lords,
    Knights of the Garter were of noble
    birth,
    Valiant and virtuous, full of
    haughty courage.

    Talbot in *Henry VI, Part 1*, 4.1.33–5

    On the founding of the Order of the Garter,
    founded about 1344 by Edward III, who is
    said to have picked up the garter of a lady he
    was dancing with. It is a blue ribbon buckled
    with gold, worn on the left leg, and bears the
    inscription "*Honi soit qui mal y pense*," or
    curst be he who thinks evil of this.

Choice

1   To be, or not to be, that is the ques-
    tion:
    Whether 'tis nobler in the mind to
    suffer
    The slings and arrows of outra-
    geous fortune,
    Or to take arms against a sea of
    troubles,
    And by opposing, end them.

    Hamlet in *Hamlet*, 3.1.55–9

    His most famous soliloquy, much debated; the
    choice in context is between suffering in
    silence or taking action by fighting; but the
    first line is often associated with a death-wish.

2   "Who chooseth me shall get as
    much as he deserves."

    **Prince of Morocco in *The Merchant of
    Venice*, 2.7.23**

    Reading the message on the silver casket.

3   Here do I choose, and thrive I as I
    may!

    **Prince of Morocco in *The Merchant of
    Venice*, 2.7.60**

    Choosing the golden casket in the hope of
    winning Portia.

4   O, these deliberate fools, when they
    do choose,
    They have the wisdom by their wit
    to lose.

    **Portia in *The Merchant of Venice*,
    2.9.80–1**

    "Deliberate" = calculating; referring to the
    Prince of Aragon's mistaken choice of the sil-
    ver casket.

5   Let me choose,
    For as I am, I live upon the rack.

    **Bassanio in *The Merchant of Venice*,
    3.2.24–5**

    Facing the three caskets.

6   Here choose I. Joy be the conse-
    quence!

    **Bassanio in *The Merchant of Venice*,
    3.2.107**

    Choosing the leaden casket to win Portia.

7   "You that choose not by the view,
    Chance as fair, and choose as true:
    Since this fortune falls to you,
    Be content, and seek no new."

    **Bassanio in *The Merchant of Venice*,
    3.2.131–4**

    The message he finds in the leaden casket
    telling him he has won Portia.

8   There's small choice in rotten
    apples.

    **Hortensio in *The Taming of the
    Shrew*, 1.1.134–5**

    Shakespeare may have coined this proverb.

Cities

1 Sweep on, you fat and greasy citizens,
'Tis just the fashion.

First Lord in *As You Like It*, 2.1.55–6

Quoting Jaques, moralizing over the fate of a
wounded stag, ignored by its fellows.

2 A city on whom plenty held full
hand,
For riches strewed herself even in
her streets;
Whose towers bore heads so high
they kissed the clouds,
And strangers ne'er beheld but
wondered at.

Cleon in *Pericles*, 1.4.22–5

On the former prosperity of Tarsus, now
afflicted by famine.

3 This world's a city full of straying
streets,
And death the market-place where
each one meets.

Third Queen in *The Two Noble Kinsmen*, 1.5.15–16

Civil War

1 Civil dissension is a viperous worm
That gnaws the bowels of the commonwealth.

King Henry in *Henry VI, Part 1*, 3.1.72–3

2 'Tis much when scepters are in children's hands,
But more when envy breeds unkind
division:
There comes the ruin, there begins
confusion.

Exeter in *Henry VI, Part 1*, 4.1.192–4

While Henry was young the country was
ruled by his uncle, Duke of Gloucester, the
Lord Protector.

3 *First Plebeian*. Tear him to pieces,
he's a conspirator!
Cinna. I am Cinna the poet! I am
Cinna the poet!
Fourth Plebeian. Tear him for his
bad verses, tear him for his bad
verses.

Julius Caesar, 3.3.28–31

The angry plebeians are indiscriminate in their
violence.

4 O, if you raise this house against
this house
It will the woefullest division prove
That ever fell upon this cursèd
earth.

Bishop of Carlisle in *Richard II*, 4.1.145–7

Prophesying civil war in England.

Cleverness

1 I know a trick worth two of that.

First Carrier in *Henry IV, Part 1*, 2.1.36–7

Varying a proverb; meaning "I'm too clever to
be taken in by your trick."

Clothing (see also Fashion)

1 There can be no kernel in this light
nut; the soul of this man is in his
clothes.

Lafew in *All's Well That Ends Well*, 2.5.43–4

Referring to the extravagant dress of Parolles,
the braggart soldier.

2 Good Hamlet, cast thy nighted
   color off.

Gertrude in *Hamlet*, 1.2.68

Referring to Hamlet's black mourning dress
for his father's death.

3 Costly thy habit as thy purse can
   buy,
   But not expressed in fancy, rich,
   not gaudy,
   For the apparel oft proclaims the
   man.

Polonius in *Hamlet*, 1.3.70–2

Advice to his son, going to live abroad;
"fancy" = ornamentation.

4   Youth no less becomes
   The light and careless livery that it
   wears
   Than settled age his sables and his
   weeds,
   Importing health and graveness.

Claudius in *Hamlet*, 4.7.78–81

"Sables" = dark robes trimmed with sable fur;
"weeds" = appropriate clothes.

5 There's not a shirt and a half in all
   my company, and the half shirt is
   two napkins tacked together and
   thrown over the shoulders like a
   herald's coat without sleeves.

Falstaff in *Henry IV, Part 1*, 4.2.42–5

Describing the men he has conscripted to
fight the rebels.

6 The naked truth of it is, I have no
   shirt; I go woolward for penance.

**Armado in *Love's Labor's Lost*,
5.2.710–11**

He wears no linen beneath his outer woolen
clothes.

7   Now does he feel his title

Hang loose about him like a giant's
robe
Upon a dwarfish thief.

Angus in *Macbeth*, 5.2.20–2

As if Macbeth has become too small for his
office as King of Scotland.

8 Rammed me in with foul shirts and
   smocks, socks, foul stockings,
   greasy napkins, that, Master Brook,
   there was the rankest compound of
   villainous smell that ever offended
   nostril.

**Falstaff in *The Merry Wives of Wind-
sor*, 3.5.89–93**

On his experience of being hidden in a basket
of foul linen.

9 Ne'er ask me what raiment I'll
   wear, for I have no more doublets
   than backs, no more stockings than
   legs, nor no more shoes than feet—
   nay, sometime more feet than
   shoes, or such shoes as my toes look
   through the overleather.

**Sly in *The Taming of the Shrew*,
Induction, 2.8–12**

The drunkard, Sly, protests he has hardly any
clothes.

10 Our purses shall be proud, our garments poor,
   For 'tis the mind that makes the
   body rich,
   And as the sun breaks through the
   darkest clouds,
   So honor peereth in the meanest
   habit.

**Petruchio in *The Taming of the Shrew*,
4.3.171–4**

Proposing to take his wife, Katherine, to her
father's house in poor clothes; "peereth in" =
shows through.

11 *Trinculo.* O worthy Stephano!
Look what a wardrobe here is for
thee!
Caliban. Let it alone, thou fool, it is
but trash.

The Tempest, 4.1.222–4

Stephano and Trinculo are readily distracted
by gaudy clothes from their plot to kill Prospero.

12 These clothes are good enough to
drink in, and so be these boots too.

Sir Toby Belch in *Twelfth Night*,
1.3.11–12

13 Sure this robe of mine
Does change my disposition.

Perdita, *The Winter's Tale*, 4.4.133

She is dressed up as the goddess Flora.

14 He hath ribbons of all the colors
i'the rainbow.

Servant in *The Winter's Tale*, 4.4.204–5

On Autolycus's stock of goods for sale.

15 Lawn as white as driven snow,
Cyprus black as e'er was crow,
Gloves as sweet as damask roses,
Masks for faces and for noses.

Autolycus in *The Winter's Tale*,
4.4.218–21

Singing his catalogue of wares, linen ("lawn"),
crepe (imported from Cyprus), and masks used
by women to protect their faces.

Comfort

1 How mightily sometimes we make
us comforts of our losses!

**First Lord in *All's Well That Ends
Well*,** 4.3.65–6

2 I will reward thee,
Once for thy sprightly comfort, and
tenfold
For thy good valor.

Antony in *Antony and Cleopatra*,
4.7.14–16

To Eros or Scarus, on learning they have won
a battle against Caesar.

3 I must comfort the weaker vessel, as
doublet and hose ought to show
itself courageous to petticoat.

Rosalind in *As You Like It*, 2.4.5–7

In disguise as a boy; "the weaker vessel" is
woman, a biblical phrase (Paul's first epistle to
Peter 3:7).

4 I beg cold comfort, and you are so
strait
And so ingrateful, you deny me
that.

King John in *King John*, 5.7.42–3

"Cold comfort" = empty consolation; "strait" =
severe.

5 Things at the worst will cease, or
else climb upward
To what they were before.

Ross in *Macbeth*, 4.2.24–5

Trying to comfort Lady Macduff in speaking of
the condition of Scotland under the tyranny of
Macbeth.

6 He receives comfort like cold por-
ridge.

Sebastian in *The Tempest*, 2.1.10

On Alonso, who is sad supposing his son Ferdinand to be drowned.

Company, see Society

Comparisons

1   Now I perceive that she hath made
    compare
    Between our statures; she hath
    urged her height,
    And with her personage, her tall
    personage,
    Her height, forsooth, she hath pre-
    vailed with him.
    **Hermia in *A Midsummer Night's
    Dream*, 3.2.290–3**

    Jealous of the taller Helena to whom her
    former lover, Lysander, has switched his
    affections.

2   So doth the greater glory dim the
    less:
    A substitute shines brightly as a
    king
    Until a king be by.
    **Portia in *The Merchant of Venice*,
    5.1.93–5**

    On the way moonlight makes the light of a
    candle seem faint.

Condescension

1   An honest soul, i'faith, sir, by my
    troth he is, as ever broke bread. But
    God is to be worshipped; all men
    are not alike.
    **Dogberry in *Much Ado About
    Nothing*, 3.5.38–40**

    Dogberry, as Constable of the Watch, patron-
    izes his assistant, Verges.

2   Your worship speaks like a most
    thankful and reverend youth, and I
    praise God for you.
    **Dogberry in *Much Ado About
    Nothing*, 5.1.315–16**

    To old Leonato; Dogberry is comically mud-
    dled as ever.

Confidence

1   I am armed,
    And dangers are to me indifferent.
    Cassius in *Julius Caesar*, 1.3.114–15

    "Indifferent" = immaterial.

2   Nothing that can be can come
    between me and the full prospect of
    my hopes.
    Malvolio in *Twelfth Night*, 3.4.81–2

    Convinced that Olivia loves him.

Confusion (see also Chaos, Disorder)

1   My soul aches
    To know, when two authorities are
    up,
    Neither supreme, how soon confu-
    sion
    May enter 'twixt the gap of both
    and take
    The one by the other.
    Coriolanus in *Coriolanus*, 3.1.108–12

    The two authorities set up ("up") in the play
    are the consuls and the tribunes of the people.

2   Fair is foul, and foul is fair;
    Hover through the fog and filthy
    air.
    **The Witches (Weird Sisters) in *Mac-
    beth*, 1.1.11–12**

3   So from that spring whence com-
    fort seemed to come,
    Discomfort swells.
    Sergeant in *Macbeth*, 1.2.27–8

    Reporting news that is at once good and bad.

4   My thought, whose murder yet is
     but fantastical,
     Shakes so my single state of man,
     That function is smothered in sur-
     mise,
     And nothing is but what is not.
     Macbeth in *Macbeth*, 1.3.139–42

What he imagines overwhelms his ability to
act ("function"), and nothing exists for him
but the thought of murder; "fantastical" =
imaginary.

5   Confusion now hath made his mas-
     terpiece!
     Most sacrilegious murder hath
     broke ope
     The Lord's anointed temple, and
     stole thence
     The life o' the building.
     Macduff in *Macbeth*, 2.3.66–9

Echoing biblical ideas of the king as the
"Lord's anointed" (anointed with holy oil; II
Samuel 1:16), and of the body as "the temple
of God" (I Corinthians 3:16).

6   But cruel are the times when we are
     traitors
     And do not know ourselves, when
     we hold rumor
     From what we fear, yet know not
     what we fear,
     But float upon a wild and violent
     sea
     Each way and move.
     Ross in *Macbeth*, 4.2.18–22

"When we hold rumor/From what we fear" =
when we are led by fear to believe rumors;
"Each way and move" = this way and that,
making no headway.

7   All is uneven,
     And everything is left at six and
     seven.
     York in *Richard II*, 2.2.121–2

The phrase "six and seven," or more commonly in later usage "sixes and sevens" (= in
confusion) is derived from games with dice,
with the idea that all is at risk of being lost.

Conquest

1   Sir, you have wrestled well, and
     overthrown
     More than your enemies.
     Rosalind in *As You Like It*, 1.2.254–5

Orlando has defeated Charles the wrestler and
"overthrown" Rosalind, who has fallen in love
with him.

2   He saw me, and yielded, that I may
     justly say, with the hook-nosed fel-
     low of Rome, "I came, saw, and
     overcame."
     Falstaff in *Henry IV, Part 2*, 4.3.40–2

Ironically comparing himself with Julius Caesar, who is said to have announced a victory
with the words "*Veni, vidi, vici*," I came, I
saw, I conquered.

Conscience (see also Guilt)

1   Taint not thy mind, nor let thy soul
     contrive
     Against thy mother aught. Leave
     her to heaven,
     And to those thorns that in her
     bosom lodge
     To prick and sting her.
     Ghost in *Hamlet*, 1.5.85–8

His father's ghost warning Hamlet.

2   Thus conscience does make cow-
     ards of us all,

And thus the native hue of resolution
Is sicklied o'er with the pale cast of thought.

Hamlet in *Hamlet*, 3.1.82–4

"Conscience" = consciousness, and also moral judgment.

3   Thus hulling in
The wild sea of my conscience, I did steer
Toward this remedy, whereupon we are
Now present here together.

King Henry in *Henry VIII*, 2.4.200–3

"Hulling" = drifting about; offering reasons for divorcing Katherine.

4   The worm of conscience still begnaw thy soul!

Queen Margaret in *Richard III*, 1.3.221

Addressing Richard; "still" = continually.

5   *First Murderer.* Where's thy conscience now?
. . .
Second Murderer. I'll not meddle with it. It makes a man a coward. . . . It fills a man full of obstacles. It made me once restore a purse of gold that by chance I found. It beggars any man that keeps it. It is turned out of towns and cities for a dangerous thing, and every man that means to live well endeavors to trust to himself and live without it.

Richard III, 1.4.127, 134–5, 139–44

Debating what they have been hired to do, i.e., murder Clarence.

6   O coward conscience, how dost thou afflict me!

King Richard in *Richard III*, 5.3.179

Starting out of a nightmare.

7   My conscience hath a thousand several tongues,
And every tongue brings in a several tale,
And every tale condemns me for a villain.

King Richard in *Richard III*, 5.3.193–5

For the first time Richard is afflicted with a sense of guilt.

8   Conscience is but a word that cowards use,
Devised at first to keep the strong in awe.

King Richard in *Richard III*, 5.3.309–10

Dismissing the conscience that had so troubled him in his dreams before the battle with Richmond.

9   I'll haunt thee like a wicked conscience still.

Troilus in *Troilus and Cressida*, 5.10.28

Speaking of Achilles, who has slain the unarmed Hector.

10   Love is too young to know what conscience is,
Yet who knows not conscience is born of love?

***Sonnet 151*, 1–2**

Cupid is suggested by "young," but also innocence; "conscience" may mean both knowledge, specifically carnal knowledge, and moral awareness, or sense of guilt.

Consideration

1   What you have said
      I will consider; what you have to
      say
      I will with patience hear, and find a
      time
      Both meet to hear and answer such
      high things.
      Brutus in *Julius Caesar*, 1.2.167–70

      "Meet" = fitting.

Conspiracy

1   I'll read you matter deep and dan-
      gerous,
      As full of peril and adventurous
      spirit
      As to o'erwalk a current roaring
      loud
      On the unsteadfast footing of a
      spear.
      Worcester in *Henry IV, Part 1*, 1.3.190–3

      Proposing rebellion against the king.

2   Be factious for redress of all these
      griefs,
      And I will set this foot of mine as
      far
      As who goes farthest.
      Casca in *Julius Caesar*, 1.3.118–20

      Speaking to Cassius; "factious" = actively par-
      tisan; "griefs" = grievances.

3   The complexion of the element
      In favor's like the work we have in
      hand,
      Most bloody-fiery, and most terri-
      ble.

Cassius in *Julius Caesar*, 1.3.128–30

On the terrible storms that occur the night
before Caesar is assassinated.

4   Since the quarrel
      Will bear no color for the thing he
      is,
      Fashion it thus: that what he is,
      augmented,
      Would run to these and these
      extremities.
      Brutus in *Julius Caesar*, 2.1.28–31

      Finding specious reasons to join the conspir-
      acy, and admitting it cannot be justified ("Will
      bear no color") by what Caesar has done.

5   O conspiracy,
      Sham'st thou to show thy dan-
      g'rous brow by night,
      When evils are most free? O then,
      by day
      Where wilt thou find a cavern dark
      enough
      To mask thy monstrous visage?
      Brutus in *Julius Caesar*, 2.1.77–81

      On the arrival at his house of the conspirators,
      hiding their faces in their cloaks.

6   Security gives way to conspiracy.
      Artemidorus in *Julius Caesar*, 2.3.7–8

      The soothsayer's message, but Caesar is too
      busy to look at it.

7   I see your brows are full of discon-
      tent,
      Your hearts of sorrow, and your
      eyes of tears.
      **Abbot of Westminster in *Richard II*,
      4.1.331–2**

      Speaking to the deposed King Richard's sup-
      porters.

8   O, heinous, strong, and bold con-
       spiracy!
King Henry IV in Richard II, 5.3.59

On learning of a plot to murder him;
"heinous" = abominable.

9   For conspiracy,
     I know not how it tastes, though it
       be dished
     For me to try how.
Hermione in The Winter's Tale,
3.2.71–3

Defending herself in court against accusations
that she conspired with Camillo.

Constancy

1   I am constant as the northern
       star,
     Of whose true-fixed and resting
       quality
     There is no fellow in the firma-
       ment.
Caesar in Julius Caesar, 3.1.60–2

The pole star thought of as constant and
immovable.

2   So in the world: 'tis furnished well
       with men,
     And men are flesh and blood, and
       apprehensive;
     Yet in the number I do know but
       one
     That unassailable holds on his rank,
     Unshaked of motion; and that I am
       he.
Caesar in Julius Caesar, 3.1.66–70

Boasting of his steadiness in holding his posi-
tion unshaken by movement around him, or
by "motions" = petitions; "apprehensive" =
capable of perception.

3   When this ring
     Parts from this finger, then parts
     life from hence.
Bassanio in The Merchant of Venice,
3.2.183–4

On the ring Portia has just given him; of
course he does part with it when she demands
it as her reward for defending his friend Antonio.

4   The sun was not so true unto the
       day
     As he to me.
**Hermia in A Midsummer Night's
Dream, 3.2.50–1**

Lamenting the disappearance of Lysander.

5   Nay, had she been true,
     If heaven would make me such
       another world
     Of one entire and perfect chrysolite,
     I'd not have sold her for it.
Othello in Othello, 5.2.143–6

Speaking of the now dead Desdemona;
"chrysolite" = topaz.

6   Our kindred, though they be long
     ere they be wooed, they are con-
     stant being won; they are burrs, I
     can tell you, they'll stick where they
     are thrown.
Pandarus in Troilus and Cressida,
3.2.109–12

Praising his niece, Cressida.

7   I am as true as truth's simplicity,
     And simpler than the infancy of
       truth.
Troilus in Troilus and Cressida,
3.2.169–70

Swearing eternal constancy in love to Cressida.

8   If I be false, or swerve a hair from truth,
When time is old and hath forgot itself,
When waterdrops have worn the stones of Troy,
And blind oblivion swallowed cities up,
And mighty states characterless are grated
To dusty nothing, yet let memory
From false to false among false maids in love
Upbraid my falsehood.

Cressida in _Troilus and Cressida_, 3.2.184–91

An oath she notoriously breaks when she is in the Greek camp; "characterless are grated" = reduced to ruins without written records.

9   If ever thou shalt love,
In the sweet pangs of it remember me;
For such as I am, all true lovers are,
Unstaid and skittish in all motions else
Save in the constant image of the creature
That is beloved.

Orsino in _Twelfth Night_, 2.4.15–20

His constancy is indeed to the "image" of Olivia, who refuses to see him; "motions" = urges, feelings.

10   I cannot
Be mine own, nor anything to any, if
I be not thine. To this I am most constant,
Though destiny says no.

Florizel in _The Winter's Tale_, 4.4.43–6

He is saying he will be no use to himself or anyone unless he can marry Perdita.

11   In all external grace you have some part,
But you like none, none you, for constant heart.

Sonnet 53, 13–14

12   Love's not Time's fool, though rosy lips and cheeks
Within his bending sickle's compass come;
Love alters not with his brief hours and weeks,
But bears it out even to the edge of doom.
If this be error, and upon me proved,
I never writ, nor no man ever loved.

Sonnet 116, 9–14

Time is imaged as a reaper rapidly despoiling human youth and beauty, but love is out of his range ("compass"), and endures till the brink of death (or perhaps doomsday).

13   If my dear love were but the child of state,
It might for Fortune's bastard be unfathered,
As subject to Time's love or to Time's hate,
Weeds among weeds, or flowers with flowers gathered.
No, it was builded far from accident;
It suffers not in smiling pomp, nor falls
Under the blow of thrallèd discontent,
Whereto th'inviting time our fashion calls;
It fears not policy, that heretic,
Which works on leases of short-numbered hours,

But all alone stands hugely politic,
That it nor grows with heat, nor
   drowns with showers.
To this I witness call the Fools of
   Time,
Which die for goodness, who have
   lived for crime.

Sonnet 124

The stability of the speaker's love is set against
the unstable world of "state" or politics, where
accident, changes of fashion with passing
time, discontent, and machination are all concerned with immediate change or advantage
("short-numbered hours"). "Fools of Time"
presumably waste their lives in pursuit of gain,
and claim "goodness" only when at death's
door; but see the quotation from *Sonnet* 116
(12 above).

Constraint

1 Nor stony tower, nor walls of
      beaten brass,
   Nor airless dungeon, nor strong
      links of iron,
   Can be retentive to the strength of
      spirit.

   Cassius in *Julius Caesar*, 1.3.93–5

   Trying to persuade Casca that they will have
   no freedom under Caesar.

2 I am trusted with a muzzle and
      enfranchised with a clog; therefore I
      have decreed not to sing in my
      cage.

   **Don John in *Much Ado About
   Nothing*, 1.3.32–4**

   Although treated generously by his brother
   Don Pedro, after fighting as his enemy, Don
   John grudgingly compares himself to a muz-
   zled or hobbled animal, or a caged bird.

Contempt (see also Scorn)

1 How much methinks, I could
      despise this man,
   But that I am bound in charity
      against it.

   **Cardinal Wolsey in *Henry VIII*,
   3.2.297–8**

   Speaking of the Earl of Surrey.

2 This is a slight unmeritable man,
   Meet to be sent on errands.

   **Mark Antony in *Julius Caesar*,
   4.1.12–13**

   To Octavius, showing his contempt for the
   third member of the triumvirate, Lepidus.

3 He must be taught, and trained and
      bid go forth;
   A barren-spirited fellow; one that
      feeds
   On objects, arts and imitations,
   Which, out of use and staled by
      other men,
   Begin his fashion.

   **Mark Antony in *Julius Caesar*,
   4.1.35–9**

   On Lepidus, whose attention is taken by
   curiosities, tricks, and copying fashions that
   are already obsolete.

4 O, what a deal of scorn looks beau-
      tiful
   In the contempt and anger of his
      lip!

   Olivia in *Twelfth Night*, 3.1.145–6

   After an interview with Cesario, really Viola in
   disguise.

Contentment (see also Happiness)

1 I earn that I eat, get that I wear, owe no man hate, envy no man's happiness, glad of other men's good, content with my harm.

Corin in *As You Like It*, 3.2.73–6

The shepherd's contentment with a pastoral life.

Conversation

1 More of your conversation would infect my brain.

Menenius in *Coriolanus*, 2.1.94

Speaking to the tribunes of the people.

2 Who can converse with a dumb show?

Portia in *The Merchant of Venice*, 1.2.73

Referring to her English suitor, who speaks no Italian.

Cooking (see also Food)

1 But his neat cookery! He cut our roots in characters,
And sauced our broths, as Juno had been sick
And he her dieter.

Guiderius in *Cymbeline*, 4.2.49–51

Speaking of Imogen, in disguise as a youth, making a meal fit for the gods; "characters" = letters.

2 'Tis an ill cook that cannot lick his own fingers.

Second Servingman in *Romeo and Juliet*, 4.2.6–7

Corruption

1 They say this town is full of cozenage:
As nimble jugglers that deceive the eye,
Dark-working sorcerers that change the mind,
Soul-killing witches that deform the body,
Disguisèd cheaters, prating mountebanks,
And many such-like liberties of sin.

Antipholus of Syracuse in *The Comedy of Errors*, 1.2.97–102

On the reputation of Ephesus, where Antipholus has just arrived; "mountebanks" were quack doctors or charlatans.

2 Something is rotten in the state of Denmark.

Marcellus in *Hamlet*, 1.4.90

Hamlet's general conclusion about the appearance of his father's ghost.

3 Lay not that flattering unction to your soul
That not your trespass but my madness speaks;
It will but skin and film the ulcerous place,
Whilst rank corruption, mining all within,
Infects unseen.

Hamlet in *Hamlet*, 3.4.145–9

Speaking to his mother, who thinks he is mad; "flattering unction" = soothing ointment of flattery.

4   Love thyself last, cherish those
      hearts that hate thee;
      Corruption wins not more than
      honesty.

Cardinal Wolsey in *Henry VIII*,
3.2.443–4

After his own downfall he advises Cromwell.

5   You yourself
      Are much condemned to have an
      itching palm,
      To sell and mart your offices for
      gold
      To undeservers.

Brutus in *Julius Caesar*, 4.3.9–12

Accusing his friend Cassius; "mart" = traffic
in.

6   Shall we now
      Contaminate our fingers with base
      bribes,
      And sell the mighty space of our
      large honors
      For so much trash as may be
      graspèd thus?
      I had rather be a dog and bay the
      moon
      Than such a Roman.

Brutus in *Julius Caesar*, 4.3.23–8

Reprimanding Cassius.

7   Who lives that's not depravèd or
      depraves?
      Who dies that bears not one spurn
      to their graves
      Of their friend's gift?

Apemantus in *Timon of Athens*,
1.2.140–1

A cynic's view of humanity; "spurn" = contemptuous rejection (literally, a kick).

Councils

1   Let us presently go sit in council,
      How covert matters may be best
      disclosed
      And open perils surest answerèd.

Mark Antony in *Julius Caesar*, 4.1.45–7

To Octavius, as they take power in Rome.

2   Now sit we close about this taper
      here,
      And call in question our necessities.

Brutus in *Julius Caesar*, 4.3.164–5

To Cassius, Titinius and Messala; "call in
question" = take stock of.

3   Words before blows; is it so, coun-
      trymen?

Brutus in *Julius Caesar*, 5.1.27

On meeting Octavius before the battle of
Philippi.

Countries

1   Hath Britain all the sun that shines?
      day? night?
      Are they not but in Britain?

Imogen in *Cymbeline*, 3.4.136–7

Alluding to the proverb, "The sun shines on
all alike."

2   I'the world's volume
      Our Britain seems as of it, but not
      in't;
      In a great pool a swan's nest.

Imogen in *Cymbeline*, 3.4.139

She thinks of going into exile abroad.

3   *Hamlet.* Why was he sent into Eng-
    land?
    Grave-digger. Why, because 'a was
    mad. 'A shall recover his wits
    there; or if 'a do not, 'tis no great
    matter there.
    Hamlet. Why?
    Grave-digger. 'Twill not be seen in
    him there. There the men are as
    mad as he.
    Hamlet, 5.1.149–55

    The Grave-digger does not recognize Hamlet,
    who he supposes to be in England; "'a" = he.

4   But it was alway yet the trick of our
    English nation, if they have a good
    thing, to make it too common.
    Falstaff in *Henry IV, Part 2,* 1.2.214–16

    "Alway yet" = ever till now.

5   This royal throne of kings, this
    sceptered isle,
    This earth of majesty, this seat of
    Mars,
    This other Eden, demi-paradise.
    John of Gaunt in *Richard II,* 2.1.40–2

    His grand vision of England, as both warlike
    ("seat of Mars") and a garden of innocence
    ("Eden").

6   This happy breed of men, this little
    world,
    This precious stone set in the silver
    sea,
    Which serves it in the office of a
    wall,
    Or as a moat defensive to a house,
    Against the envy of less happier
    lands,
    This blessèd plot, this earth, this
    realm, this England.
    John of Gaunt in *Richard II,* 2.1.45–50

    The dying Gaunt's vision of England.

7   That England, that was wont to
    conquer others,
    Hath made a shameful conquest of
    itself.
    John of Gaunt in *Richard II,* 2.1.65–6

    Criticizing Richard's corrupt mode of
    governing.

8   *Viola.* What country, friends, is
    this?
    Sea Captain. This is Illyria, lady.
    Viola. And what should I do in
    Illyria? My brother he is in Ely-
    sium.
    Twelfth Night, 1.2.1–4

    Viola thinks her brother is dead and in
    heaven; "Elysium" parallels "Illyria," an area
    in the Balkans adjacent to the Adriatic sea.

Country Life and Countryside

1   They say he is already in the forest
    of Arden, and a many merry men
    with him; and there they live like
    the old Robin Hood of England.
    Charles in *As You Like It,* 1.1.114–16

    On the exiled Duke Senior; the Ardennes in
    Shakespeare's source becomes Arden, then a
    forest near Stratford-on-Avon.

2   This our life, exempt from public
    haunt,
    Finds tongues in trees, books in the
    running brooks,
    Sermons in stones, and good in
    everything.
    Duke Senior in *As You Like It,* 2.1.15–17

    Finding consolation in the forest.

3   Under the greenwood tree
     Who loves to lie with me,
     And turn his merry note
     Unto the sweet bird's throat,
     Come hither, come hither, come
     hither!
          Here shall he see
          No enemy
     But winter and rough weather.

Amiens in *As You Like It*, 2.5.1–8

This picture of ideal pastoral life nevertheless
includes winter; "turn" means adapt or attune.

4   Who doth ambition shun,
     And loves to live i' the sun,
     Seeking the food he eats,
     And pleased with what he gets,
     Come hither, come hither, come
     hither!

Amiens in *As You Like It*, 2.5.38–42

Second stanza of a song praising the pastoral
life.

5   If it do come to pass
     That any man turn ass,
     Leaving his wealth and ease
     A stubborn will to please,
     Ducdame, ducdame, ducdame!
     Here shall he see
     Gross fools as he,
     And if he will come to me.

Jaques in *As You Like It*, 2.5.50–7

His ridicule of the pastoral life so idealized by
the Duke and Amiens.

6   To get your living by the copulation
     of cattle.

Touchstone in *As You Like It*, 3.2.79–80

Speaking to Corin the shepherd; Touchstone
remains unimpressed by life in the country.

7   In respect that it is solitary, I like it
     very well; but in respect that it is
     private, it is a very vile life. In
     respect it is in the fields, it pleaseth
     me well; but in respect it is not in
     the court, it is tedious.

Touchstone in *As You Like It*, 3.2.15–19

On life in the forest of Arden as contrasted
with life at court.

8   West of this place, down in the
     neighbor bottom,
     The rank of osiers by the murmur-
     ing stream
     Left on your right hand brings you
     to the place.

Celia in *As You Like It*, 4.3.78–80

Directions to Oliver to the house Celia and
Rosalind live in; "left" = passed by.

9   O, this life
     Is nobler than attending for a
     check;
     Richer than doing nothing for a
     bauble;
     Prouder than rustling in unpaid-for
     silk.

Belarius in *Cymbeline*, 3.3.21–4

Contrasting a simple country life with life at
the king's court; "attending for a check" =
doing service only for a rebuke.

10   What should we speak of
     When we are old as you? When we
     shall hear
     The rain and wind beat dark
     December, how,
     In this our pinching cave, shall we
     discourse
     The freezing hours away?

Arviragus in *Cymbeline*, 3.3.35–9

On growing up in remotest Wales.

11   Of all these bounds, even from this
line to this,
With shadowy forests and with
champains riched,
With plenteous rivers and wide-
skirted meads,
We make thee lady.

King Lear in *King Lear*, 1.1.63–6

Giving his daughter Goneril a third of the
kingdom; "champains" = open country;
"meads" = meadows.

Courage (see also Valor)

1   Husband, I come!
Now to that name my courage
prove my title!

**Cleopatra in *Antony and Cleopatra*,
5.2.287–8**

She welcomes death like a bride going to her
husband.

2   There's neither honesty, manhood,
nor good fellowship in thee, nor
thou cam'st not of the blood royal,
if thou darest not stand for ten
shillings.

Falstaff in *Henry IV, Part 1*, 1.2.139–41

"Stand" = stand and fight. The gold ten
shilling coin was called a "royal."

3   The smallest worm will turn being
trodden on,
And doves will peck in safeguard of
their brood.

Clifford in *Henry VI, Part 3*, 2.2.17–18

The first line is proverbial.

4   Why, courage then! what cannot be
avoided

'Twere childish weakness to lament
or fear.

**Queen Margaret in *Henry VI, Part 3*,
5.4.37–8**

Encouraging her army in their fight against
King Edward.

5   When the cross blue lightning
seemed to open
The breast of heaven, I did present
myself
Even in the aim and very flash of it.

Cassius in *Julius Caesar*, 1.3.50–2

Boasting to Casca that he is not afraid of ominous storms.

6   *Macbeth.* If we should fail?
Lady Macbeth.   We fail?
But screw your courage to the stick-
ing place,
And we'll not fail.

***Macbeth*, 1.7.59–61**

Plotting the murder of Duncan. The image
may relate to screwing the pegs of a musical
instrument to the point where the strings are
taut.

7   He hath borne himself beyond the
promise of his age, doing, in the
figure of a lamb, the feats of a lion.

**Messenger in *Much Ado About Noth-
ing*, 1.1.13–15**

On the feats of young Claudio in battle.

Court

1   I have trod a measure, I have flattered a lady, I have been politic
with my friend, smooth with mine
enemy.

Touchstone in *As You Like It*, 5.4.44–6

Part of Touchstone's claim to be a courtier.

Courtesy

1 I am the king of courtesy . . . a Corinthian, a lad of mettle, a good boy.

Prince Hal in *Henry IV, Part 1*, 2.4.10–11, 12

Terms of approval given to him by the bartenders of a tavern; Corinthians were noted as spendthrifts and profligates.

2 I am the very pink of courtesy.

Mercutio in *Romeo and Juliet*, 2.4.57

"Pink" = embodiment or perfection.

Courtship (see also Adoration, Devotion, Love)

1 *Orlando.* Fair youth, I would I could make thee believe I love. *Rosalind.* Me believe it? You may sooner make her that you love believe it, which I warrant she is apter to do than to confess she does.

As You Like It, 3.2.387–9

Orlando is trying to make her believe that he loves her.

2 Come, woo me, woo me; for now I am in a holiday humor, and like enough to consent.

Rosalind in *As You Like It*, 4.1.68–9

Pretending to be able to cure Orlando of his love-sickness.

3 *Rosalind.* I will be your Rosalind in a more coming-on disposition; and ask me what you will, I will grant it.

Orlando. Then love me, Rosalind. *Rosalind.* Yes, faith, will I, Fridays and Saturdays and all.

As You Like It, 4.1.112–17

Orlando is practicing how to woo Rosalind, who is disguised as a youth.

4 Sing, siren, for thyself, and I will dote; Spread o'er the silver waves thy golden hairs, And as a bed I'll take them, and there lie.

Antipholus of Syracuse in *The Comedy of Errors*, 3.2.47–9

To Luciana, who has been pleading with him on her sister's behalf; "take" = make use of.

5 It is thyself, mine own self's better part: Mine eye's clear eye, my dear heart's dearer heart, My food, my fortune, and my sweet hope's aim, My sole earth's heaven, and my heaven's claim.

Antipholus of Syracuse in *The Comedy of Errors*, 3.2.61–4

Lovesick for Luciana.

6 *Adriana.* With what persuasion did he tempt thy love? *Luciana.* With words that in an honest suit might move. First he did praise my beauty, then my speech.

The Comedy of Errors, 4.2.13–15

They both suppose Adriana's husband has been making love to Luciana; they have mistaken his twin brother for him.

7 Will you vouchsafe to teach a soldier terms
Such as will enter at a lady's ear
And plead his love-suit to her gentle heart?

King Henry in *Henry V*, 5.2.99–101

Having defeated the French Henry tries to make love to Katherine, daughter of the French king.

8 An angel is like you, Kate, and you are like an angel.

King Henry in *Henry V*, 5.2.109–10

Wooing Katherine of France.

9 I know no ways to mince it in love, but directly to say, "I love you"; then if you urge me farther than to say, "Do you in faith?," I wear out my suit.

King Henry in *Henry V*, 5.2.126–9

"Wear out my suit" = use up all my words of love; Henry presents himself as a plain man to Katherine.

10 If thou canst love a fellow of this temper, Kate, whose face is not worth sunburning, that never looks in his glass for love of anything he sees there, let thine eyes be thy cook.

King Henry in *Henry V*, 5.2.146–9

Henry presents himself as a plain soldier in making love to Katherine; her eye will have to dress him up to find beauty, as a cook embellishes food.

11 A good leg will fall, a straight back will stoop, a black beard will turn white, a fair face will wither, a full

eye will wax hollow; but a good heart, Kate, is the sun and the moon—or rather the sun and not the moon, for it shines bright and never changes, but keeps his course truly.

King Henry in *Henry V*, 5.2.159–64

Wooing the French Princess Katherine.

12 What other pleasure can the world afford?
I'll make my heaven in a lady's lap,
And deck my body in gay ornaments,
And witch sweet ladies with my words and looks.

Richard of Gloucester in *Henry VI*, Part 3, 3.2.147–50

A lesser pleasure for the deformed Richard than aiming to get the crown.

13 He capers, he dances, he has eyes of youth; he writes verses, he speaks holiday, he smells April and May.

Host in *The Merry Wives of Windsor*, 3.2.67–9

Recommending Fenton as a suitor for Anne Page.

14 We cannot fight for love, as men may do;
We should be wooed, and were not made to woo.

Helena in *A Midsummer Night's Dream*, 2.1.241–2

Following Demetrius who is trying to shake her off.

15 Thou and I are too wise to woo peaceably.

Benedick in *Much Ado About Nothing*, 5.2.72

To Beatrice; neither of them wants to admit to passion.

Romeo in *Romeo and Juliet*, 1.1.212–14

Speaking of Rosaline, who rejects his advances.

16 She thanked me,
And bade me, if I had a friend that
    loved her,
I should but teach him how to tell
    my story,
And that would woo her.

Othello in *Othello*, 1.3.163–6

Desdemona's indirect way of making known her love for Othello.

17 Look how my ring encompasseth
    thy finger;
Even so thy breast encloseth my
    poor heart.
Wear both of them, for both of
    them are thine.

King Richard in *Richard III*, 1.2.203–5

Lady Anne succumbs to his wily courtship by accepting the ring he gives her.

18 Was ever woman in this humor
    wooed?
Was ever woman in this humor
    won?

King Richard in *Richard III*, 1.2.227–8

Having successfully wooed the Lady Anne in presence of her father-in-law's corpse.

19 She will not stay the siege of loving
    terms,
Nor bide the encounter of assailing
    eyes,
Nor ope her lap to saint-seducing
    gold.

20 Say that she rail, why then I'll tell
    her plain
She sings as sweetly as a nightin-
    gale.
Say that she frown, I'll say she looks
    as clear
As morning roses newly washed
    with dew.
Say she be mute, and will not speak
    a word,
Then I'll commend her volubility,
And say she uttereth piercing elo-
    quence.

Petruchio in *The Taming of the Shrew*, 2.1.170–6

Petruchio's plan for wooing Katherine.

21 She is a woman, therefore may be
    wooed;
She is a woman, therefore may be
    won.

Demetrius in *Titus Andronicus*, 2.1.82–3

Proposing to woo Lavinia, Titus's daughter.

22 But though I loved you well, I
    wooed you not;
And yet, good faith, I wished myself
    a man,
Or that we women had men's privi-
    lege
Of speaking first.

Cressida in *Troilus and Cressida*, 3.2.126–9

Confessing she has long desired Troilus.

23 Make me a willow cabin at your
     gate,
   And call upon my soul within the
     house;
   Write loyal cantons of contemnèd
     love,
   And sing them loud even in the
     dead of night;
   Halloo your name to the reverber-
     ate hills,
   And make the babbling gossip of
     the air
   Cry out "Olivia!" O, you should
     not rest
   Between the elements of air and
     earth
   But you should pity me.
   Viola in *Twelfth Night*, 1.5.268–76

   Her sentimental description of a devoted
   lover; the willow was a symbol of unrequited
   love; "my soul" = Olivia; "cantons" = songs.

24 That man that hath a tongue I say is
     no man
   If with his tongue he cannot win a
     woman.
   **Valentine in *The Two Gentlemen of
   Verona*, 3.1.104–5**

   Making it seem easy in advising the Duke,
   who in fact knows that Valentine is aiming to
   elope with his daughter Sylvia.

Cowardice

1 We'll have a swashing and a martial
     outside,
   As many other mannish cowards
     have
   That do outface it with their sem-
     blances.
   Rosalind in *As You Like It*, 1.3.118–22

   Proposing a swashbuckling disguise as a fighting man.

2 I could brain him with his lady's
     fan.
   Hotspur in *Henry IV, Part 1*, 2.3.23

   Exasperated by the writer of a letter criticizing
   a plot, which Hotspur is involved in, against
   the king.

3 A plague of all cowards, I say, and a
     vengeance too!
   Falstaff in *Henry IV, Part 1*, 2.4.114–15

   Blustering after running away himself from
   Hal and Poins; "of" = on.

4   Wouldst thou have that
   Which thou esteem'st the orna-
     ment of life,
   And live a coward in thine own
     esteem,
   Letting "I dare not" wait upon "I
     would,"
   Like the poor cat i' th' adage?
   Lady Macbeth in *Macbeth*, 1.7.41–5

   Goading her husband, and alluding to the
   proverb, "the cat would eat fish but she will
   not wet her feet."

5 That which in mean men we entitle
     patience
   Is pale cold cowardice in noble
     breasts.
   **Duchess of Gloucester in *Richard II*,
   1.2.33–4**

   Accusing John of Gaunt of cowardice for taking no action about the murder of his brother.

6 A milksop, one that never in his life
   Felt so much cold as over shoes in
     snow.
   King Richard in *Richard III*, 5.3.325–6

   Trying to raise the spirits of his troops by abusing Richmond.

7 A coward, a most devout coward,
religious in it.

Fabian in *Twelfth Night*, 3.4.389–90

Persuading Sir Andrew that Cesario is a coward.

8 If you had but looked big and spit
at him, he'd have run.

Clown in *The Winter's Tale*, 4.3.105–6

To Autolycus, who claims to have been assaulted by a rogue.

Creatures (see also Animals, Birds, Dogs, Horses, Insects, Snakes)

1 *Lepidus.* What manner o' thing is
your crocodile?
Antony. It is shaped, sir, like itself,
and it is as broad as it hath
breadth.

Antony and Cleopatra, 2.7.41–3

Antony mocks the drunken Lepidus, with whom he and Octavius share power.

2 'Tis a strange serpent.

Lepidus in *Antony and Cleopatra*,
2.7.48

The crocodile.

3 You spotted snakes with double
tongue,
Thorny hedgehogs, be not seen.
Newts and blindworms, do no
wrong,
Come not near our Fairy Queen.

First Fairy in *A Midsummer Night's
Dream*, 2.2.9–12

Singing a charm to keep creatures thought to be poisonous away from the sleeping Titania;

"blindworms" are harmless snakes but sometimes confused with adders.

4 Weaving spiders, come not here;
Hence, you longlegged spinners,
hence!
Beetles black approach not near;
Worm nor snail, do no offense.

First Fairy in *A Midsummer Night's
Dream*, 2.2.20–3

A charm to protect the sleeping Titania from tiny creatures common in England, and all harmless, though once thought to be venomous.

5 Come on, poor babe,
Some powerful spirit instruct the
kites and ravens
To be thy nurses. Wolves and
bears, they say,
Casting their savageness aside, have
done
Like offices of pity.

Antigonus in *The Winter's Tale*,
2.3.185–9

He obeys Leontes' command to deposit his baby daughter Perdita in a remote place.

Crime (see also Law, Murder, Punishment, Theft)

1 If little faults, proceeding on distemper,
Shall not be winked at, how shall
we stretch our eye
When capital crimes, chewed, swallowed, and digested,
Appear before us?

King Henry in *Henry V*, 2.2.54–7

Forgiving the fault of a man who abused him as caused by drunkenness ("proceeding on distemper").

2   I am in blood
Stepped in so far, that should I
wade nor more
Returning were as tedious as go
o'er.

Macbeth in *Macbeth*, 3.4.135–7

The psychology of a serial killer?

Criticism

1 In such a time as this it is not meet
That every nice offense should bear
his comment.

Cassius in *Julius Caesar*, 4.3.7–8

To Brutus; "nice" = trivial; "bear his comment" = be subject to criticism.

2   Cassius is aweary of the world;
Hated by one he loves; braved by
his brother;
Checked like a bondman; all his
faults observed,
Set in a notebook, learned and
conned by rote
To cast into my teeth.

Cassius in *Julius Caesar*, 4.3.95–9

Quarreling with Brutus: "braved" = defied;
"Checked" = rebuked; "conned by rote" =
learned by heart.

3 So turns she every man the wrong
side out,
And never gives to truth and virtue
that
Which simpleness and merit purchaseth.

**Hero in *Much Ado About Nothing*,
3.1.68–70**

Making sure that Beatrice hears this criticism
of her as too judgmental, and as denying
integrity ("simpleness") and merit what they
deserve ("purchaseth").

4 O gentle lady, do not put me to't,
For I am nothing if not critical.

Iago in *Othello*, 2.1.118–19

Desdemona has invited him to praise her.

Cruelty (see also Ruthlessness)

1 O tiger's heart wrapped in a
woman's hide!

York in *Henry VI, Part 3*, 1.4.137

To Queen Margaret, who is gloating over the
murder of his son.

2 All pity choked with custom of fell
deeds.

Mark Antony in *Julius Caesar*, 3.1.269

In the wake of Caesar's death, cruel ("fell")
deeds will become so familiar ("choked with
custom") that no-one will feel pity.

3   Come, you spirits
That tend on mortal thoughts,
unsex me here,
And fill me from the crown to the
toe, top-full
Of direst cruelty!

Lady Macbeth in *Macbeth*, 1.5.40–3

Summoning evil spirits that attend on murderous ("mortal") thoughts.

4 Did you say all? O hell-kite! All?
What, all my pretty chickens and
their dam
At one fell swoop?

Macduff in *Macbeth*, 4.3.217–19

On learning that his wife and children have
been murdered by Macbeth.

5   Thou art come to answer
A stony adversary, an inhuman
wretch,
Uncapable of pity, void and empty
From any dram of mercy.

Duke in *The Merchant of Venice*,
4.1.3–6

To Antonio, about Shylock; "answer" =
defend yourself; "dram" = minute amount.

6   The pound of flesh which I demand
of him
Is dearly bought as mine, and I will
have it.

Shylock in *The Merchant of Venice*,
4.1.99–100

Insisting on having a pound of Antonio's flesh.

7   For thy desires
Are wolvish, bloody, starved, and
ravenous.

Gratiano in *The Merchant of Venice*,
4.1.137–8

On Shylock demanding his pound of flesh.

Curses

1   What, shall we curse the planets of
mishap
That plotted thus our glory's over-
throw?

Exeter in *Henry VI, Part 1*, 1.1.23–4

Attributing the early death of Henry V to the
influence of the planets.

2   Let this pernicious hour
Stand aye accursèd in the calendar!

Macbeth in *Macbeth*, 4.1.133–4

He has just seen the apparitions that show the
descendants of Banquo ruling in Scotland, not
his own; "aye" = forever.

3   Infected be the air whereon they
ride,
And damned all those that trust
them!

Macbeth in *Macbeth*, 4.1.138–9

Cursing the Witches.

4   The devil damn thee black, thou
cream-faced loon!

Macbeth in *Macbeth*, 5.3.11

The stupid servant ("loon") is white with fear.

5   Curses, not loud but deep, mouth-
honor, breath
Which the poor heart would fain
deny, and dare not.

Macbeth in *Macbeth*, 5.3.27–8

"Mouth-honor" = merely superficial respect,
which is all Macbeth's achievement of the
crown of Scotland has brought him.

6   The devil take one party and his
dam the other!

**Falstaff in *The Merry Wives of Wind-
sor*,** 4.5.106–7

On being tricked by Mrs. Ford and Mistress
Page; "dam" = dame or woman.

7   The day will come when thou shalt
wish for me
To help thee curse this poisonous
bunch-backed toad.

Queen Margaret in *Richard III*,
1.3.244–5

Foreshadowing the misery Richard (the
"toad") will inflict on Edward's Queen, Elizabeth.

8   A plague o' both your houses!

Mercutio in *Romeo and Juliet*, 3.1.99

As he is dying in their quarrel, Mercutio
curses both Capulets and Montagues.

9 The common curse of mankind,
   folly and ignorance, be thine in
   great revenue!

Thersites in _Troilus and Cressida_,
2.3.27–9

Cursing Patroclus.

Custom

1   Custom calls me to't.
   What custom wills, in all things
      should we do't,
   The dust on antique time would lie
      unswept,
   And mountainous error be too
      highly heaped
   For truth to o'erpeer.

Coriolanus in _Coriolanus_, 2.3.117–121

Coriolanus hates following the custom that
requires him to solicit votes from the citizens
of Rome for election as consul; if we obey
custom, he says ("should we do't"), nothing
would ever change.

2 But to my mind, though I am
      native here
   And to the manner born, it is a cus-
      tom
   More honored in the breach than
      the observance.

Hamlet in _Hamlet_, 1.4.14–16

Commenting on the music accompanying the
king's carousing and revelry by night; "manner" = custom; "more honored in the breach
than the observance" = which it is more honorable to break than to observe.

3 Use almost can change the stamp of
      nature.

Hamlet in _Hamlet_, 3.4.168

Proverbial; "stamp of nature" = innate charac-
teristics.

4 O Kate, nice customs curtsy to
   great kings. Dear Kate, you and I
   cannot be confined within the weak
   list of a country's fashion. We are
   the makers of manners, Kate.

King Henry in _Henry V_, 5.2.268–71

"Nice" = punctilious or particular; "weak list"
= feeble bounds or barriers.

5 How use doth breed a habit in a
      man!

**Valentine in _The Two Gentlemen of
Verona_, 5.4.1**

"Use" = continual usage or practice.

Damnation

1 For Banquo's issue have I filed my
      mind;
   For them the gracious Duncan have
      I murdered;
   Put rancors in the vessel of my
      peace
   Only for them; and mine eternal
      jewel
   Given to the common enemy of
      man,
   To make them kings, the seeds of
      Banquo kings!

Macbeth in _Macbeth_, 3.1.64–9

He has defiled ("filed") his mind, filled the
cup of his peace with enmity, and given his
soul ("eternal jewel") to the devil; "seeds" =
descendants.

Dancing

1 If you will patiently dance in our
      round,
   And see our moonlight revels, go
      with us.

Titania in *A Midsummer Night's Dream*, 2.1.140–1

Titania inviting Oberon to join in the fairy dance or "round."

2   He capers nimbly in a lady's chamber
    To the lascivious pleasing of a lute.

King Richard in *Richard III*, 1.1.12–13

The warrior has become the courtier in peacetime.

3   You and I are past our dancing days.

Capulet in *Romeo and Juliet*, 1.5.31

Old Capulet talks with his cousin while watching the dance.

4   When you do dance, I wish you
    A wave o'the sea, that you might ever do
    Nothing but that, move still, still so,
    And own no other function.

Florizel in *The Winter's Tale*, 4.4.140–3

Describing Perdita, with whom he is in love.

Danger

1   Out of this nettle, danger, we pluck this flower, safety.

Hotspur in *Henry IV, Part 1*, 2.3.9–10

On a lord who has refused out of fear to join his rebellion.

2   I must go and meet with danger there,
    Or it will seek me in another place,
    And find me worse provided.

Northumberland in *Henry IV, Part 2*, 2.3.48–50

He is wondering whether to join with other rebels to fight King Henry; "provided" = prepared.

3   Gloucester, 'tis true that we are in great danger;
    The greater therefore should our courage be.

King Henry in *Henry V*, 4.1.1–2

Preparing to fight the French army.

4   *Williams.* I pray you, what thinks he of our estate?
    King Henry. Even as men wrecked upon a sand, that look to be washed off the next tide.

Henry V, 4.1.96–8

"Estate" = state of affairs, condition; the disguised king can say what he really thinks.

5   *Soothsayer.* Beware the Ides of March.
    Caesar. He is a dreamer. Let us leave him. Pass.

Julius Caesar, 1.2.23–4

Caesar was assassinated on the Ides (15th) of March.

6   It is the bright day that brings forth the adder,
    And that craves wary walking.

Brutus in *Julius Caesar*, 2.1.14–15

"Craves" = requires.

7   Think him as a serpent's egg,
    Which, hatched, would as his kind grow mischievous,
    And kill him in the shell.

Brutus in *Julius Caesar*, 2.1.32–4

The snake (Caesar) will behave according to its nature ("as his kind").

8   Danger knows full well
        That Caesar is more dangerous
            than he.
        We are two lions littered in one day,
        And I the elder and more terrible,
        And Caesar shall go forth.

Caesar in *Julius Caesar*, 2.2.44–8

He feels he has to live up to his name.

9   We are at the stake
        And bayed about with many ene-
            mies;
        And some that smile have in their
            hearts, I fear,
        Millions of mischiefs.

Octavius in *Julius Caesar*, 4.1.48–51

To Antony; the image is from bear-baiting;
bears were tied to a stake and mastiff dogs set
on them.

10   I am amazed, methinks, and lose
            my way
        Among the thorns and dangers of
            this world.

**The Bastard Falconbridge in *King
John*, 4.3.140–1**

On finding the young prince Arthur murdered;
"amazed" = astonished, but also carries the
sense "lost as in a maze."

11   The bow is bent and drawn; make
            from the shaft.

King Lear in *King Lear*, 1.1.143

Threatening Kent; "make" = get away.

12   There's daggers in men's smiles.

Donalbain in *Macbeth*, 2.3.140

Feeling unsafe after the murder of his father,
Duncan.

13   We have scorched the snake, not
            killed it:

She'll close and be herself.

Macbeth in *Macbeth*, 3.2.13–14

Macbeth fails to find the security he thought
the death of Duncan would bring him;
"scorched" = slashed, scored; "close" = heal
up.

14   Why strew'st thou sugar on that
            bottled spider
        Whose deadly web ensnareth thee
            about?

**Queen Margaret in *Richard III*,
1.3.241–2**

Speaking to Edward's Queen, Elizabeth, who
does not join her in her denunciation of
Richard.

15   Thus have I shunned the fire for
            fear of burning,
        And drenched me in the sea, where
            I am drowned.

**Proteus in *The Two Gentlemen of
Verona*, 1.3.78–9**

Having concealed his love for Julia, his reason
for staying at home in Verona, Proteus now
finds he is sent off by his father to further his
education in Milan.

Darkness (see also Night)

1   O sun,
        Burn the great sphere thou mov'st
            in! darkling stand
        The varying shore o' the world!

**Cleopatra in *Antony and Cleopatra*,
4.15.9–11**

Calling for universal darkness to mark the
death of Antony.

2   There's husbandry in heaven,
        Their candles are all out.

Banquo in *Macbeth*, 2.1.4–5

"Husbandry" = thrift, meaning the stars are
not visible.

3   This thing of darkness I
Acknowledge mine.

Prospero in *The Tempest*, 5.1.275–6

Owning that he is responsible for Caliban;
"darkness" suggests both ignorance and evil
(as commonly in the Bible).

Dawn (see also Sunrise)

1   But look, the morn in russet mantle
    clad
  Walks o'er the dew of yon high
    eastward hill.

Horatio in *Hamlet*, 1.1.166–7

2   But soft, methinks I scent the
    morning air,
  Brief let me be.

Ghost in *Hamlet*, 1.5.58–9

3   The glow-worm shows the matin to
    be near,
  And 'gins to pale his ineffectual fire.

Ghost in *Hamlet*, 1.5.89–90

Signaling the end of his interview with Hamlet
as day approaches.

4   Yonder shines Aurora's harbinger.

**Puck in *A Midsummer Night's Dream*,
3.2.380**

The morning star, or Venus, precursor of
dawn; Venus is also goddess of love, and here
heralds the reconciliation of the lovers in the
play.

5   The grey-eyed morn smiles on the
    frowning night,
  Checkering the eastern clouds with
    streaks of light.

**Friar Lawrence in *Romeo and Juliet*,
2.3.1–2**

6   It was the lark, the herald of the
    morn,
  No nightingale. Look, love, what
    envious streaks
  Do lace the severing clouds in yon-
    der east.

Romeo in *Romeo and Juliet*, 3.5.6–8

To Juliet; their wedding night has ended all
too soon.

7   Night's candles are burnt out, and
    jocund day
  Stands tiptoe on the misty moun-
    tain tops.
  I must be gone and live, or stay and
    die.

Romeo in *Romeo and Juliet*, 3.5.9–11

The exiled Romeo parts from Juliet after their
wedding night.

8   O Cressida! But that the busy day,
  Waked by the lark, hath roused the
    ribald crows,
  And dreaming night will hide our
    joys no longer,
  I would not from thee.

**Troilus in *Troilus and Cressida*,
4.2.8–11**

The morning after their first night together.

Death (see also Death-Wish, Dying, Mortality)

1   There's a great spirit gone!

**Antony in *Antony and Cleopatra*,
1.2.122**

Antony has just learned of the death of his
wife, Fulvia.

2   I will be
A bridegroom in my death, and run
    into't
As to a lover's bed.

Antony in *Antony and Cleopatra,*
4.14.99–101

Only in dying does he think of Cleopatra in
terms of marriage.

3   Where art thou, death?
Come hither, come! Come, come,
    and take a queen
Worth many babes and beggars!

Cleopatra in *Antony and Cleopatra,*
5.2.46–8

Preferring death to being a captive.

4   His biting is immortal; those that
do die of it do seldom or never
recover.

Clown in *Antony and Cleopatra,*
5.2.246–8

Referring to the asp or snake he brings to
Cleopatra.

5   Now boast thee, death, in thy pos-
    session lies
A lass unparalleled! Downy win-
    dows, close,
And golden Phoebus never be
    beheld
Of eyes again so royal!

Charmian in *Antony and Cleopatra,*
5.2.315–18

Closing Cleopatra's eyes after her death.

6   She looks like sleep,
As she would catch another Antony
In her strong toil of grace.

Octavius Caesar in *Antony and*
Cleopatra, 5.2.346–8

Looking at the dead Cleopatra; a "toil" is a net
or snare.

7   To die, to sleep—
To sleep, perchance to dream—ay,
    there's the rub,
For in that sleep of death what
    dreams may come,
When we have shuffled off this
    mortal coil,
Must give us pause.

Hamlet in *Hamlet,* 3.1.63–7

Sleep was proverbially the image of death;
"rub" = snag (a term from the game of bowls);
"coil" = turmoil.

8   He is dead and gone, lady,
    He is dead and gone;
At his head a grass-green turf,
    At his heels a stone.

Ophelia in *Hamlet,* 4.5.29–32

Singing in her madness, after her father's
death.

9   Had I but time—as this fell
    sergeant, Death,
Is strict in his arrest—O, I could tell
    you—
But let it be.

Hamlet in *Hamlet,* 5.2.336–8

As he lies dying, to Horatio; "fell" = fierce;
"sergeant" = officer of the law-courts.

10   O proud death,
What feast is toward in thine eter-
    nal cell,
That thou so many princes at a shot
So bloodily hast struck?

Fortinbras in *Hamlet,* 5.2.364–7

Arriving after the deaths of Hamlet, Laertes,
Claudius and Gertrude; "toward" = in prepa-
ration; "eternal cell" = the grave.

11 Doomsday is near, die all, die merrily.

Hotspur in *Henry IV, Part 1*, 4.1.134

A rallying call to his fellow rebels as they face a battle against the king's forces.

12 *Prince Hal.* Why, thou owest God a death.
Falstaff. 'Tis not due yet, I would be loath to pay him before his day.

Henry IV, Part 1, 5.1.126–8

Hal's phrase is proverbial, and true for everyone.

13 Death, as the Psalmist saith, is certain to all, all shall die.

Shallow in *Henry IV, Part 2*, 3.2.37–8

Psalms 89:48.

14 A man can die but once, we owe God a death.

Feeble in *Henry IV, Part 2*, 3.2.234–5

Proverbial (see also 12 above); Feeble shows his courage.

15 This sleep is sound indeed, this is a sleep
That from this golden rigol hath divorced
So many English kings.

Prince Hal in *Henry IV, Part 2*, 4.5.35–7

Sitting by his father's bedside, he thinks his father is dead; "rigol" = circle (compare "regal").

16 Here was a royal fellowship of death.

King Henry in *Henry V*, 4.8.101

On hearing of the 126 French princes and nobles killed in the battle of Agincourt.

17 Cowards die many times before their deaths;
The valiant never taste of death but once.

Caesar in *Julius Caesar*, 2.2.32–3

18 It seems to me most strange that men should fear,
Seeing that death, a necessary end,
Will come when it will come.

Caesar in *Julius Caesar*, 2.2.35–7

The idea that nothing is more certain than death, and nothing more uncertain than the time it will come, is proverbial.

19 That we shall die we know, 'tis but the time
And drawing days out that men stand upon.

Brutus in *Julius Caesar*, 3.1.99–100

"Drawing days out" = prolonging their lives.

20   She's gone for ever.
I know when one is dead, and when one lives;
She's dead as earth.

King Lear in *King Lear*, 5.3.260–2

Looking at his dead or dying daughter Cordelia.

21 And my poor fool is hanged! No, no, no life!
Why should a dog, a horse, a rat have life,
And thou no breath at all? Thou'lt come no more,
Never, never, never, never, never.

King Lear in *King Lear*, 5.3.306–9

"Poor fool" affectionately refers to his daughter Cordelia, whose body he is looking at (but may recall the Fool, who has not been seen since Act 3).

22   The sleeping and the dead
Are but as pictures; 'tis the eye of
   childhood
That fears a painted devil.

Lady Macbeth in *Macbeth*, 2.2.50–2

To Macbeth, who cannot face looking on the
scene of the murder he has carried out.

23   Shake off this downy sleep, death's
   counterfeit,
And look on death itself!

Macduff in *Macbeth*, 2.3.76–7

On the death of Duncan; varying the proverb,
"sleep is the image of death."

24   Banquo, thy soul's flight,
If it find heaven, must find it out
   tonight.

Macbeth in *Macbeth*, 3.1.140–1

Having arranged the murder of Banquo.

25   Duncan is in his grave;
After life's fitful fever he sleeps well.

Macbeth in *Macbeth*, 3.2.22–3

The murder of Duncan has not cured Macbeth's "fitful fever."

26   Be absolute for death. Either death
   or life
Shall thereby be the sweeter. Reason thus with life:
If I do lose thee I do lose a thing
That none but fools would keep.

Duke in *Measure for Measure*, 3.1.5–8

Preparing Claudio to face the death penalty.

27   The sense of death is most in apprehension,
And the poor beetle that we tread
   upon
In corporal sufferance finds a pang
   as great

As when a giant dies.

**Isabella in *Measure for Measure*,
3.1.77–80**

Trying to reconcile Claudio, her brother, to
the idea that he must die; "apprehension" =
anticipation.

28   If I must die,
I will encounter darkness as a bride,
And hug it in mine arms.

**Claudio in *Measure for Measure*,
3.1.83–5**

Claudio has been sentenced to death for getting Juliet with child.

29   Death is a fearful thing.

**Claudio in *Measure for Measure*,
3.1.115**

He is in prison, and sentenced to death.

30   The weariest and most loathèd
   worldly life
That age, ache, penury, and
   imprisonment
Can lay on nature is a paradise
To what we fear of death.

**Claudio in *Measure for Measure*,
3.1.128–31**

He is in prison, and sentenced to death; "To"
= compared to.

31   A man that apprehends death no
more dreadfully but as a drunken
sleep, careless, reckless, and fearless
of what's past, present, or to come;
insensible of mortality, and desperately mortal.

**Provost in *Measure for Measure*,
4.2.142–5**

On Barnardine, long since sentenced to die,
and who has no fear of death, and no hope of
escaping it ("desperately mortal").

32 Death may usurp on nature many
hours,
And yet the fire of life kindle again
The o'erpressed spirits.
Cerimon in *Pericles*, 3.2.82–4

He restores to life the shipwrecked and almost
dead Thaisa.

33 Cry woe, destruction, ruin, and
decay:
The worst is death, and death will
have his day.
King Richard in *Richard II*, 3.2.102–3

Despairing at ever more bad news.

34 Nothing can we call our own but
death,
And that small model of the barren
earth
Which serves as paste and cover to
our bones.
King Richard in *Richard II*, 3.2.152–4

The "model" is the body, made of earth (Genesis 3:19).

35   Within the hollow crown
That rounds the mortal temples of
a king
Keeps Death his court, and there
the antic sits,
Scoffing his state and grinning at
his pomp,
Allowing him a breath, a little
scene,
To monarchize, be feared, and kill
with looks.
King Richard in *Richard II*, 3.2.160–5

Death was often personified as a grinning
skeleton, as in the common images of the
Dance of Death; "antic" = grotesque clown.

36 'Tis a vile thing to die, my gracious
lord,
When men are unprepared, and
look not for it.
Catesby in *Richard III*, 3.2.62–3

Speaking to Hastings, who is unaware that
Richard will shortly have him executed.

37 Death lies on her like an untimely
frost
Upon the sweetest flower of all the
field.
Capulet in *Romeo and Juliet*, 4.5.28–9

Old Capulet thinks Juliet is dead.

38 Death, that hath sucked the honey
of thy breath,
Hath had no power yet upon thy
beauty.
Thou art not conquered. Beauty's
ensign yet
Is crimson in thy lips and in thy
cheeks,
And death's pale flag is not
advanced there.
Romeo in *Romeo and Juliet*, 5.3.92–6

He has opened the tomb where Juliet lies,
thought to be dead, but really unconscious
and still alive.

39 Grim death, how foul and loath-
some is thine image.
**Lord in *The Taming of the Shrew*,
Induction, 1.35**

The "image" is that of a drunken man.

40 Come away, come away, death,
   And in sad cypress let me be laid.
Fly away, fly away, breath,
   I am slain by a fair cruel maid.
Feste in *Twelfth Night*, 2.4.51–4

A song for Orsino; a reminder of mortality, as
cypress was an emblem of mourning; the
image is of the lover slain by the power of a
maid's beauty, suggesting also Cupid's arrow.

Death-Wish

1 Unarm, Eros, the long day's task is
done,
And we must sleep.

Antony in *Antony and Cleopatra*,
4.14.35–6

To his servant, Eros, preparing for death.

2 Finish, good lady, the bright day is
done,
And we are for the dark.

Iras in *Antony and Cleopatra*, 5.2.193–4

Encouraging Cleopatra to take her own life.

3 Give me my robe, put on my
crown, I have
Immortal longings in me.

Cleopatra in *Antony and Cleopatra*,
5.2.280–1

To Iras; Cleopatra is preparing her death
scene.

4 Look,
I draw the sword myself; take it and
hit
The innocent mansion of my love,
my heart.
Fear not, 'tis empty of all things but
grief.

Imogen in *Cymbeline*, 3.4.66–9

She draws Pisanio's sword on learning he has
been ordered by her husband Posthumus to
kill her.

5 'Tis a consummation
Devoutly to be wished.

Hamlet in *Hamlet*, 3.1.62–3

"Consummation" = final completion of this
life.

6 Live a thousand years,
I shall not find myself so apt to die.
No place will please me so, no
mean of death,
As here by Caesar, and by you cut
off,
The choice and master spirits of
this age.

Mark Antony in *Julius Caesar*,
3.1.159–63

To Brutus and the conspirators who assassinated Caesar.

7 Death, death! O amiable, lovely
Death!
Thou odoriferous stench, sound
rottenness!
Arise forth from the couch of last-
ing night,
Thou hate and terror to prosperity,
And I will kiss thy detestable bones.

Constance in *King John*, 3.4.25–9

Behind these lines lies the image of Death as
often depicted in drawings of the "Dance of
Death," a skeleton seizing victims at random.
Her son, Arthur, is imprisoned, and she fears
for his life.

8 Hath no man's dagger here a point
for me?

Leonato in *Much Ado About Nothing*,
4.1.109

Reacting to the public defamation of his
daughter Hero.

9 O that I were a mockery king of
snow,
Standing before the sun of Bolingbroke,
To melt myself away in water
drops!

King Richard in *Richard II*, 4.1.260–2

Humiliated in front of the whole court.

10   O, here
Will I set up my everlasting rest,
And shake the yoke of inauspicious
    stars
From this world-wearied flesh.

Romeo in *Romeo and Juliet*, 5.3.109–12

He supposes Juliet is dead, and resolves (sets
up his rest) to seek everlasting repose and die
himself.

11   Sir, spare your
    threats;
The bug that you would fright me
    with, I seek.
To me life can be no commodity.

Hermione in *The Winter's Tale*,
3.2.92–4

She is threatened with death by Leontes;
"bug" = bugbear, terror; "commodity" = benefit.

12   Tired with all these, for restful
    death I cry.

***Sonnet* 66, 1**

"All these" are the wrongs and corruption the
narrator finds widespread in society.

Deceit/Deception (see also Duplicity, Hypocrisy)

1   Apparel vice like virtue's harbinger;
    Bear a fair presence, though your
      heart be tainted;
    Teach sin the carriage of a holy
      saint;
    Be secret-false.

Luciana in *The Comedy of Errors*,
3.2.12–15

Her advice is wasted on the twin brother of
her sister's husband.

2   O,
Dissembling courtesy! How fine
    this tyrant
Can tickle where she wounds!

Imogen in *Cymbeline*, 1.1.83–5

On her step-mother, the Queen, as pretending
to care for her.

3   What says she, fair one? That the
    tongues of men are full of deceits?

King Henry in *Henry V*, 5.2.117–8

Discovering that Katherine understands his
English flattery.

4   To beguile the time,
Look like the time, bear welcome in
    your eye,
Your hand, your tongue; look like
    the innocent flower,
But be the serpent under't.

Lady Macbeth in *Macbeth*, 1.5.63–6

"To beguile the time, Look like the time" = to
deceive people, behave as they do ("time" =
society at large); the idea of the snake in the
grass is proverbial.

5   Away, and mock the time with
    fairest show;
False face must hide what the false
    heart doth know.

Macbeth in *Macbeth*, 1.7.81–2

Recalling the proverb, "false face, foul heart."

6   So may the outward shows be least
    themselves—
The world is still deceived with
    ornament.

Bassanio in *The Merchant of Venice*,
3.2.73–4

Thinking about his choice of caskets; outward
appearance may conceal inner reality.

7 There is no vice so simple but assumes
Some mark of virtue on his outward parts.

Bassanio in *The Merchant of Venice*, 3.2.81–2

"Simple" = plain or unadulterated.

8 Thus ornament is but the guilèd shore
To a most dangerous sea; the beauteous scarf
Veiling an Indian beauty; in a word,
The seeming truth which cunning times put on
To entrap the wisest.

Bassanio in *The Merchant of Venice*, 3.2.97–101

Rejecting the silver and gold caskets; "guiled" = treacherous.

9 O, what authority and show of truth
Can cunning sin cover itself withal!

Claudio in *Much Ado About Nothing*, 4.1.35–6

To Leonato, who, he thinks, is deceiving him; "authority" = assurance.

10 When my outward action doth demonstrate
The native act and figure of my heart
In compliment extern, 'tis not long after
But I will wear my heart upon my sleeve
For daws to peck at: I am not what I am.

Iago in *Othello*, 1.1.61–5

Boasting of concealing his true feelings; "compliment extern" = external show or behavior to others; "daws" = jackdaws, i.e., fools.

11 Look to her, Moor, if thou hast eyes to see;
She has deceived her father, and may thee.

Brabantio in *Othello*, 1.3.292–3

Brabantio's last words to Othello about his daughter, Desdemona.

12 The Moor is of a free and open nature,
That thinks men honest that but seem to be so,
And will as tenderly be led by the nose
As asses are.

Iago in *Othello*, 1.3.399–402

Speaking of Othello as artless ("free and open") and easily ("tenderly") deceived.

13 'Tis here, but yet confused. Knavery's plain face is never seen till used.

Iago in *Othello*, 2.1.311–12

Scheming against Othello.

14 I know our country disposition well;
In Venice they do let God see the pranks
They dare not show their husbands; their best conscience
Is not to leave't undone, but keep't unknown.

Iago in *Othello*, 3.3.201–4

Cynically suggesting Venetian women are all covert adulterers.

15 Who makes the fairest show means most deceit.

Cleon in *Pericles*, 1.4.75

Misinterpreting the arrival of the fleet of Pericles that is bringing aid to Tarsus; proverbial.

16 Ah, that deceit should steal such
gentle shape,
And with a virtuous visor hide deep
vice!
Duchess of York in *Richard III*,
2.2.27–8

On Richard, who wears a mask ("visor") of
virtue.

17 We know each other's faces; for our
hearts,
He knows no more of mine than I
of yours,
Or I of his, my lord, than you of
mine.
Buckingham in *Richard III*, 3.4.10–12

Deceiving the Bishop of Ely; Buckingham is
conspiring with Richard.

18 Here's a good world the while!
Who is so gross
That cannot see this palpable
device?
Yet who's so bold but says he sees it
not.
Scrivener in *Richard III*, 3.6.10–12

On an indictment written after the execution
of Hastings.

19 Be not easily won to our requests;
Play the maid's part: still answer
nay, and take it.
Buckingham in *Richard III*, 3.7.50–1

Advising Richard on how to behave when he
is offered the crown; it was proverbial that
maids said no when they meant yes.

20 For God doth know, and you may
partly see,

How far I am from the desire of
this.
King Richard in *Richard III*, 3.7.235–6

Pretending he does not want power and the
throne.

21 If ye should lead her in a fool's paradise, as they say, it were a very
gross kind of behavior.
Nurse in *Romeo and Juliet*, 2.4.165–7

Speaking to Romeo about Juliet; "a fool's
paradise" = a state of delusory happiness;
proverbial.

22 O serpent heart, hid with a
flow'ring face!
Juliet in *Romeo and Juliet*, 3.2.73

On learning that Romeo has killed Tybalt;
varying the idea of the proverbial "snake in
the grass."

23 Was ever book containing such vile
matter
So fairly bound? O that deceit
should dwell
In such a gorgeous palace!
Juliet in *Romeo and Juliet*, 3.2.83–5

Thinking Romeo has deceived her.

24 So shall I live, supposing thou art
true,
Like a deceivèd husband, so love's
face
May still seem love to me, though
altered new,
Thy looks with me, thy heart in
other place.
***Sonnet 93*, 1–4**

Fearing his lover is deceiving him, he will be
content with the appearance of love ("love's
face").

Decline (see also Downfall)

1 O Hamlet, what a falling off was
   there!
   Ghost in *Hamlet*, 1.5.45–7

   On the part of his widow, Gertrude, who has
   married his brother Claudius.

2 So now prosperity begins to mellow
   And drop into the rotten mouth of
   death.
   Queen Margaret in *Richard III*, 4.4.1–2

   Happy to see Richard's fortunes declining and
   her enemies being destroyed.

3 'Tis certain, greatness, once fallen
   out with fortune,
   Must fall out with men too. What
   the declined is,
   He shall as soon read in the eyes of
   others
   As feel in his own fall.
   **Achilles in *Troilus and Cressida*,
   3.3.75–8**

   On finding he is ignored by the other Greek
   generals.

Defeat

1 Our enemies have beat us to the pit.
   It is more worthy to leap in our-
   selves
   Than tarry till they push us.
   Brutus in *Julius Caesar*, 5.5.23–5

   Accepting defeat; the "pit" could be a trap for
   wild animals.

Dejection

1 How weary, stale, flat, and unprofitable

Seem to me all the uses of this
world!
Fie on't, ah fie! 'tis an unweeded
garden
That grows to seed, things rank and
gross in nature
Possess it merely.
Hamlet in *Hamlet*, 1.2.133–7

Expressing his world-weariness after his
mother's remarriage.

2 I have of late—but wherefore I
   know not—lost all my mirth, for-
   gone all custom of exercise.
   Hamlet in *Hamlet*, 2.2.295–7

   To Rosencrantz and Guildenstern, on his
   melancholy.

3 I, of ladies most deject and
   wretched,
   That sucked the honey of his music
   vows,
   Now see that noble and most sovereign reason
   Like sweet bells jangled out of tune
   and harsh.
   Ophelia in *Hamlet*, 3.1.155–8

   On Hamlet's supposed madness.

4 I have not that alacrity of spirit
   Nor cheer of mind that I was wont
   to have.
   King Richard in *Richard III*, 5.3.73–4

   A premonition of his defeat to come.

Delay

1   I do not know
   Why yet I live to say, "This thing's
   to do,"
   Since I have cause, and will, and
   strength, and means
   To do't.

Hamlet in *Hamlet*, 4.4.43–6

On his failure to carry out his revenge on Claudius.

2   That we would do
We should do when we would, for this "would" changes,
And hath abatements and delays as many
As there are tongues, are hands, are accidents.

Claudius in *Hamlet*, 4.7.118–21

"Abatements" = loss of momentum; what people do or say, and mere chance, may cause us to delay doing what we should.

3   Defer no time; delays have dangerous ends.

Reignier in *Henry VI, Part 1*, 3.2.33

Urging immediate assault by the French on Rouen, held by the English.

Demons

1   As I stood here below, methought his eyes
Were two full moons; he had a thousand noses,
Horns whelked and waved like the enridgèd sea.
It was some fiend.

Edgar in *King Lear*, 4.6.69–72

Deceiving his father into thinking he has been led by a fiend; "whelked" = twisted.

Deserving (see also Merit)

1   We wound our modesty, and make foul the clearness of our deservings, when of ourselves we publish them.

Steward in *All's Well That Ends Well*, 1.3.5–7

"Make foul" = obscure or sully; "publish" = boast of.

2   Use every man after your own desert, and who should scape whipping? Use them after your own honor and dignity—the less they deserve, the more merit is in your bounty.

Hamlet in *Hamlet*, 2.2.529–32

Speaking to Polonius about the actors who have come to court.

3   Well you deserve. They well deserve to have
That know the strong'st and surest way to get.

King Richard in *Richard II*, 3.3.200–1

To Bolingbroke, who has seized power.

4   Plead what I will be, not what I have been;
Not my deserts, but what I will deserve.

King Richard in *Richard III*, 4.4.414–15

Begging Queen Elizabeth to plead on his behalf with her daughter for her hand in marriage.

Desire (see also Lust)

1   Yet have I fierce affections, and think
What Venus did with Mars.

Mardian in *Antony and Cleopatra*, 1.5.17–18

A eunuch speaks of his desires.

2 He will to his Egyptian dish again.
Enobarbus in _Antony and Cleopatra_,
2.6.126

Forseeing that Antony, though married and in
Rome, will not stay away from Cleopatra.

3 Your heart's desires be with you!
Celia in _As You Like It_, 1.2.199

To Orlando as he is about to fight with
Charles, the wrestler.

4 _Phebe._ Thou hast my love; is not
that neighborly?
Silvius. I would have you.
Phebe. Why, that were
covetousness.
As You Like It, 3.5.90–1

"Thou shalt not covet . . . any thing that is thy
neighbor's" is God's commandment, Exodus
20:17.

5 Can one desire too much of a good
thing?
Rosalind in _As You Like It_, 4.1.123–4

An ambiguous question; proverbially "The
more common a good thing is the better," and
also "Too much of one thing is good for nothing."

6 I hope it is no dishonest desire to
desire to be a woman of the world.
Audrey in _As You Like It_, 5.3.3–5

"A woman of the world" = married woman;
"dishonest" = dishonorable.

7 Is it not strange that desire should
so many years outlive performance?
Poins in _Henry IV, Part 2_, 2.4.260–1

Commenting on old Falstaff with Doll
Tearsheet sitting on his lap.

8 O, the difference of man and man!
To thee a woman's services are due.

Goneril in _King Lear_, 4.2.26–7

Making love to Edmund, so different from her
husband, Albany.

9 Stars, hide your fires;
Let not light see my black and deep
desires!
The eye wink at the hand; yet let
that be
Which the eye fears, when it is
done, to see.
Macbeth in _Macbeth_, 1.4.50–3

Contemplating murder; "wink at" = overlook,
or connive at what the hand does.

10 Nought's had, all's spent,
Where our desire is got without
content.
Lady Macbeth in _Macbeth_, 3.2.4–5

"Content" = contentment.

11 It oft falls out,
To have what we would have, we
speak not what we mean.
Isabella in _Measure for Measure_,
2.4.117–18

To Angelo; she has overpitched her pleading
for the life of her brother.

12 "Who chooseth me shall gain what
many men desire."
Why, that's the lady, all the world
desires her.
**Prince of Morocco in _The Merchant of
Venice_, 2.7.37–8**

Reading the message on the golden casket.

13 "Who chooseth me shall gain what
many men desire."
What many men desire! That
many may be meant

By the fool multitude that choose
by show.

Prince of Aragon in *The Merchant of Venice*, 2.9.24–6

He starts by examining the golden casket.

14 I know a lady in Venice would have
walked barefoot to Palestine for a
touch of his nether lip.

Emilia in *Othello*, 4.3.38–9

15 That she was never yet that ever
knew
Love got so sweet as when desire
did sue.
Therefore this maxim out of love I
teach:
Achievement is command;
ungained, beseech.

**Cressida in *Troilus and Cressida*,
1.2.290–3**

Realizing that once she has yielded to a man
she will be subject to his whims ("command"), but if she holds off he will remain a
suitor.

16 O, when mine eyes did see Olivia
first,
Methought she purged the air of
pestilence;
That instant was I turned into a
hart,
And my desires, like fell and cruel
hounds,
E'er since pursue me.

Orsino in *Twelfth Night*, 1.1.18–22

The image of Actaeon, transformed into a stag
by Diana, lies behind these lines.

17 The trustless wings of false desire.

The Rape of Lucrece, 2

"Trustless" = not to be trusted.

18 What win I if I gain the thing I
seek?
A dream, a breath, a froth of fleeting joy.
Who buys a minute's worth to wail
a week?
Or sells eternity to gain a toy?

The Rape of Lucrece, 211–4

Tarquin struggles with his conscience about
the rape; "toy" = a trivial thing.

19 Desire my pilot is, beauty my prize,
Then who fears sinking where such
treasure lies?

Tarquin in *The Rape of Lucrece*, 279–80

Inventing reasons to pursue the rape of the
chaste Lucrece.

20 The sweets we wish for turn to
loathèd sours
Even in the moment that we call
them ours.

The Rape of Lucrece, 867–8

Lucrece reflects on the rape she has suffered.

21 "In night," quoth she, "desire sees
best of all."

Venus and Adonis, 720

Venus is trying to seduce Adonis.

Despair

1 I am so lated in this world, that I
Have lost my way for ever.

**Antony in *Antony and Cleopatra*,
3.11.3–4**

Despairing after losing the Battle of Actium;
"lated" means belated, or benighted as if
obscured in darkness.

2   The happiest youth, viewing his
    progress through,
    What perils past, what crosses to
    ensue,
    Would shut the book, and sit him
    down and die.

King Henry in _Henry IV, Part 2_,
3.1.54–6

If the happiest youth could foresee his life's
passage ("progress through"), and what afflictions ("crosses") he would have to face, he
might be content to die rather than live.

3   I 'gin to be aweary of the sun,
    And wish th' estate o' the world
    were now undone.

Macbeth in _Macbeth_, 5.5.48–9

At the end of his tether; " 'gin" = begin; "th'
estate o' the world" = the condition or fixed
order of the universe.

4   I will despair, and be at enmity
    With cozening hope.

Queen in _Richard II_, 2.2.68–9

On learning that Henry Bolingbroke makes
war against Richard; "cozening" = deceiving.

5   Of comfort no man speak.
    Let's talk of graves, of worms and
    epitaphs,
    Make dust our paper, and with
    rainy eyes
    Write sorrow on the bosom of the
    earth.
    Let's choose executors and talk of
    wills.

King Richard in _Richard II_, 3.2.144–8

In despair as he realizes all is lost.

6   What comfort have we now?
    By heaven, I'll hate him everlast-
    ingly

That bids me be of comfort any
    more.

King Richard in _Richard II_, 3.2.206–8

Rejecting comfort in favor of despair.

7   I shall despair. There is no creature
    loves me,
    And if I die no soul will pity me.
    And wherefore should they, since
    that I myself
    Find in myself no pity to myself?

King Richard in _Richard III_, 5.3.200–3

Realizing that he has cut himself off from
everyone.

8   Come weep with me, past hope,
    past cure, past help!

Juliet in _Romeo and Juliet_, 4.1.45

Unable to see a way out of being forced to
marry Paris, she turns to Friar Lawrence.

Desperation

1   A horse! A horse! My kingdom for
    a horse!

King Richard in _Richard III_, 5.4.7

His famous line in the heat of battle; the kingdom he so ruthlessly sought has become
worthless.

Determination (see also Resolution)

1   Unhand me, gentlemen.
    By heaven, I'll make a ghost of him
    that lets me!

Hamlet in _Hamlet_, 1.4.84–5

To his companions who try to stop Hamlet
following his father's ghost; "lets" = hinders.

2 I'll have my bond, speak not against
my bond,
I have sworn an oath that I will
have my bond.
Shylock in *The Merchant of Venice*,
3.3.4–5

The bond demands a pound of Antonio's
flesh.

3   By my soul I swear
There is no power in the tongue of
man
To alter me.
Shylock in *The Merchant of Venice*,
4.1.240–2

Standing on his legal right to cut flesh from
Antonio.

4 He's fortified against any denial.
Malvolio in *Twelfth Night*, 1.5.145

On Cesario (Viola in disguise), who is determined to speak with Olivia.

The Devil (see also Hell)

1 He must needs go that the devil
drives.
Lavatch in *All's Well That Ends Well*,
1.3.29–30

Proverbial.

2   The spirit that I have seen
May be the devil, and the devil hath
power
T'assume a pleasing shape.
Hamlet in *Hamlet*, 2.2.598–600

Reflecting on his father's ghost.

3 Now I perceive the devil understands Welsh.
Hotspur in *Henry IV, Part 1*, 3.1.229

Alluding to Glendower's claim to supernatural
powers.

4 Give the devil his due.
Orleans in *Henry V*, 3.7.116–17

Orleans and the Constable of France swap
proverbs; even the devil may deserve some
credit.

5 The prince of darkness is a gentleman.
Edgar in *King Lear*, 3.4.143

Referring to Ephesians 6:12, "we wrestle not
against flesh and blood, but against principali-
ties, against powers, against the rulers of the
darkness of this world"; the Geneva Bible,
used by Shakespeare, has "princes" for
"rulers."

6 Devils soonest tempt, resembling
spirits of light.
Berowne in *Love's Labor's Lost*, 4.3.253

Referring to the black-eyed Rosaline.

7 What, can the devil speak true?
Banquo in *Macbeth*, 1.3.107

On one of the Witches' prophecies being fulfilled; varying the proverb, "the devil sometimes speaks the truth."

8 The devil can cite scripture for his
purpose.
Antonio in *The Merchant of Venice*,
1.3.98

Proverbial, alluding to Matthew 4:6, where
the devil tempts Jesus.

9 Naked in bed, Iago, and not mean
harm?
It is hypocrisy against the devil.
They that mean virtuously and yet
do so,
The devil their virtue tempts, and
they tempt heaven.

Othello in *Othello*, 4.1.5–8

Imagining Cassio in bed with Desdemona; as
good covering up evil is hypocrisy against
God, so evil actions that claim to be virtuous
constitute hypocrisy against the devil.

10 Now the devil that told me I did
well
Says that this deed is chronicled in
hell.

Sir Pierce of Exton in *Richard II*,
5.5.115–16

He has just killed Richard in prison.

11 What, man, defy the devil. Consider, he's an enemy to mankind.

Sir Toby Belch in *Twelfth Night*,
3.4.97–8

Treating Malvolio as if he is mad.

Deviousness

1 Your bait of falsehood takes this
carp of truth,
And this do we of wisdom and of
reach,
With windlasses and with assays of
bias,
By indirections find directions out.

Polonius in *Hamlet*, 2.1.60–3

Sending Reynaldo to spy on his son Laertes,
and spread a few lies about him; "windlasses"
= roundabout methods; "assays of bias" =
indirect attempts, "bias" referring to the curv-
ing line in which a bowl runs.

2 I am well acquainted with your
manner of wrenching the true
cause the false way.

Chief Justice in *Henry IV, Part 2*,
2.1.109–11

On Falstaff's deviousness.

3 God knows, my son,
By what by-paths and indirect
crooked ways
I met this crown.

King Henry in *Henry IV, Part 2*,
4.5.183–5

On the devious means by which he came to
power.

Devotion (see also Infatuation, Love)

1 He has my heart yet, and shall have
my prayers
While I shall have my life.

Queen Katherine in *Henry VIII*,
3.1.180–1

Speaking about Henry, who has just divorced
her.

2 All the faith, the virtue of my heart,
The object and the pleasure of mine
eye,
Is only Helena.

**Demetrius in *A Midsummer Night's
Dream*, 4.1.169–71**

Though he had been in love with Hermia until
Puck made him see differently.

3 To her, my lord,
Was I betrothed ere I saw Hermia;
But like a sickness did I loathe this
food.

But, as in health come to my nat-
ural taste,
Now I do wish it, love it, long for it,
And will for evermore be true to it.

Demetrius in *A Midsummer Night's
Dream*, 4.1.171–6

Protesting his eternal loyalty to Helena.

4   My heart's subdued
Even to the very quality of my lord.
I saw Othello's visage in his mind,
And to his honors and his valiant
     parts
Did I my soul and fortunes conse-
crate.

Desdemona in *Othello*, 1.3.250–4

Rejecting her father's assumption that she
could not love a black man.

5   My love doth so approve
     him,
That even his stubbornness, his
     checks, his frowns—
Prithee unpin me—have grace and
favor in them.

Desdemona in *Othello*, 4.3.19–21

To Emilia, about Othello's harsh behavior.

6   All my fortunes at thy foot I'll lay,
     And follow thee my lord through-
     out the world.

Juliet in *Romeo and Juliet*, 2.2.147–8

Offering to marry Romeo.

7   Being your slave, what should I do
     but tend
     Upon the hours and times of your
     desire?
     I have no precious time at all to
     spend,

Nor services to do, till you require.

Sonnet 57, 1–4

The narrator's total devotion to his friend is
imaged as slavery; "tend" = attend.

Dignity

1   I am a wise fellow, and, which is
     more, an officer; and, which is
     more, a householder; and, which is
     more, as pretty a piece of flesh as
     any is in Messina; and one that
     knows the law, go to; and a rich fel-
     low enough, go to; and a fellow that
     hath had losses; and one that hath
     two gowns and everything hand-
     some about him.

Dogberry in *Much Ado About
Nothing*, 4.2.80–6

Priding himself on his modest wealth and
status.

Disappointment

1   Thus do the hopes we have in him
     touch ground
     And dash themselves to pieces.

Mowbray in *Henry IV, Part 2*, 4.1.17–18

On Northumberland's failure to support the
rebels.

2   Thus hath the candle singed the
     moth.

Portia in *The Merchant of Venice*,
2.9.79

On the Prince of Aragon's disappointment in
choosing the wrong casket.

Discontent

1   But whate'er I be,
Nor I, nor any man that but man is,
With nothing shall be pleased till he
be eased
With being nothing.

King Richard in *Richard II*, 5.5.38–41

Brooding in prison that he cannot be content
with having nothing until he is nothing, i.e.,
dead.

Disease, see Sickness

Disillusion

1   Heigh-ho, sing heigh-ho! unto the
green holly,
Most friendship is feigning, most
loving mere folly.

Amiens in *As You Like It*, 2.7.180–1

Sung by a follower of the banished rightful
Duke Senior.

Dismissal

1   Get you hence, sirrah! Saucy fellow, hence!

Brutus in *Julius Caesar*, 4.3.134

Dismissing a poet who seeks to reconcile him
with Cassius.

Disorder (see also Anarchy, Chaos, Confusion)

1   Love cools, friendship falls off,
brothers divide: in cities, mutinies;
in countries, discord; in palaces,
treason; and the bond cracked
'twixt son and father.

Gloucester in *King Lear*, 1.2.106–9

Thinking of King Lear's banishment of Kent,
and believing his own son Edgar seeks his life.

2   We have seen the best of our time.
Machinations, hollowness, treachery, and all ruinous disorders follow us disquietly to our graves.

Gloucester in *King Lear*, 1.2.112–14

3   Our sea-walled garden, the whole
land,
Is full of weeds, her fairest flowers
choked up,
Her fruit-trees all unpruned, her
hedges ruined,
Her knots disordered, and her
wholesome herbs
Swarming with caterpillars.

Gardener's Man in *Richard II*, 3.4.43–7

Recalling the image of King Richard's favorites
as "caterpillars of the commonwealth";
"knots" were patterned beds of flowers.

4   Have you no wit, manners nor
modesty, to gabble like tinkers at
this time of night?

Malvolio in *Twelfth Night*, 2.3.87–8

Olivia's steward rebukes Sir Toby Belch, Feste
and Sir Andrew Aguecheek for making merry
late at night in her house.

5   Is there no respect of place, persons, nor time in you?

Malvolio in *Twelfth Night*, 2.3.91–2

Reprimanding Sir Toby and his companions
for their rowdiness at night.

Dogs

1   As familiar with me as my dog.
    Prince Hal in *Henry IV, Part 2*,
    2.2.106–7

2   That island of England breeds very
    valiant creatures; their mastiffs are
    of unmatchable courage.
    Rambures in *Henry V*, 3.7.140–2

3   The little dogs and all,
    Trey, Blanch and Sweetheart, see,
    they bark at me.
    King Lear in *King Lear*, 3.6.62–3

    The mad old king's imaginary dogs might sug-
    gest his three daughters, Goneril, Regan
    (betrayal and fear; "blanch" = make pale with
    fear), and Cordelia, his favorite.

4   Ay, in the catalogue ye go for men,
    As hounds and greyhounds, mon-
    grels, spaniels, curs,
    Shoughs, water-rugs, and demi-
    wolves, are clept
    All by the name of dogs.
    Macbeth in *Macbeth*, 3.1.91–4

    Speaking to the murderers he has hired;
    "shoughs" are rough mongrels, and "water-
    rugs" dogs used for fowling; "clept" = called.

5   My love shall hear the music of my
    hounds.
    **Theseus in *A Midsummer Night's
    Dream*, 4.1.106**

    Speaking to Hippolyta.

6   My hounds are bred out of the
    Spartan kind,
    So flewed, so sanded; and their
    heads are hung

With ears that sweep away the
morning dew;
Crook-kneed, and dewlapped like
Thessalian bulls;
Slow in pursuit, but matched in
mouth like bells,
Each under each.
**Theseus in *A Midsummer Night's
Dream*, 4.1.119–24**

Praising sand-colored ("sanded") hunting
dogs; "flews" are the large hanging chaps of a
hound; Thessaly was in ancient Greece.

7   I think Crab, my dog, be the
    sourest-natured dog that lives: my
    mother weeping, my father wailing,
    my sister crying, our maid howling,
    our cat wringing her hands, and all
    our house in a great perplexity, yet
    did not this cruel-hearted cur shed
    one tear. He is a stone, a very peb-
    ble-stone, and has no more pity in
    him than a dog.
    **Launce in *The Two Gentlemen of
    Verona*, 2.3.5–11**

Doomsday

1   Doomsday is near; die all, die mer-
    rily.
    Hotspur in *Henry IV, Part 1*, 4.1.134

    Spoken as he prepares for battle.

2   *Kent.*   Is this the promised
    end?
    Edgar. Or image of that horror?
    Albany.   Fall and
    cease.
    ***King Lear*, 5.3.264–5**

    Imagining doomsday on seeing King Lear
    enter carrying his dying or dead daughter
    Cordelia.

3   What, will the line stretch out to
      the crack of doom?

Macbeth in *Macbeth*, 4.1.117

Referring to the line of Banquo's descendants;
"crack of doom" = the peal of thunder on
Judgment Day.

Doubt

1   Doubting things go ill often hurts
      more
      Than to be sure they do; for cer-
      tainties
      Either are past remedies, or, timely
      knowing,
      The remedy then born.

Imogen in *Cymbeline*, 1.6.95–8

To Jachimo, who has hinted that all is not well
with her; "Doubting" = suspecting; "timely
knowing" = knowing in time.

2   Our doubts are traitors,
      And makes us lose the good we oft
      might win,
      By fearing to attempt.

Lucio in *Measure for Measure*, 1.4.77–9

Urging Isabella to plead for her brother with
Angelo.

Downfall (see also Decline)

1   I have touched the highest point of
      all my greatness,
      And from that full meridian of my
      glory
      I haste now to my setting. I shall
      fall
      Like a bright exhalation in the
      evening,
      And no man see me more.

**Cardinal Wolsey in *Henry VIII*,
3.2.223–7**

Cardinal Wolsey contemplates his downfall.

2   O how wretched
      Is that poor man that hangs on
      princes' favors!
      There is betwixt that smile we
      would aspire to,
      More pangs and fears than wars or
      women have;
      And when he falls, he falls like
      Lucifer,
      Never to hope again.

**Cardinal Wolsey in *Henry VIII*,
3.2.366–72**

Comparing himself to Lucifer, the brightest
angel, who fell from heaven to hell (Isaiah
14:12).

3   Men so noble,
      However faulty, yet should find
      respect
      For what they have been. 'Tis a
      cruelty
      To load a falling man.

Cromwell in *Henry VIII*, 5.2.109–12

Speaking on behalf of Archbishop Cranmer.

4   Men shut their doors against a set-
      ting sun.

Apemantus in *Timon of Athens*, 1.2.145

Foreshadowing the fall of Timon.

Dreams (see also Sleep)

1   I dreamt there was an Emperor
      Antony.
      O, such another sleep, that I might
      see
      But such another man!

Cleopatra in *Antony and Cleopatra*,
5.2.76–8

After Antony's death.

2   *Cleopatra.* Think you there was or
   might be such a man
   As this I dreamt of?
   Dolabella.   Gentle madam, no.
   Antony and Cleopatra, 5.2.93–4

   Dolabella punctures Cleopatra's fantasy of
   Antony as superman.

3   I could be bounded in a nutshell
   and count myself a king of infinite
   space, were it not that I have bad
   dreams.
   Hamlet in *Hamlet*, 2.2.254–6

   To his college friends Rosencrantz and
   Guildenstern.

4   *Guildenstern.* The very substance of
   the ambitious is merely the
   shadow of a dream.
   Hamlet. A dream itself is but a
   shadow.
   Hamlet, 2.2.257–60

   Guildenstern thinks Hamlet's problem may be
   ambition.

5   That, he awaking when the other
   do,
   May all to Athens back again repair,
   And think no more of this night's
   accidents
   But as the fierce vexation of a
   dream.
   Oberon in *A Midsummer Night's
   Dream*, 4.1.66–9

   Planning to release the lovers and Bottom
   from the magic spell; "other" = others; "vexation" = affliction.

6   I have had a most rare vision. I
   have had a dream, past the wit of
   man to say what dream it was.
   Man is but an ass if he go about to
   expound this dream.
   Bottom in *A Midsummer Night's
   Dream*, 4.1.204–7

7   The eye of man hath not heard, the
   ear of man hath not seen, man's
   hand is not able to taste, his tongue
   to conceive, nor his heart to report
   what my dream was!
   Bottom in *A Midsummer Night's
   Dream*, 4.1.211–14

   Bottom confuses the senses, in a garbled recollection of I Corinthians 2:9–10, just as his
   dream is confused in recollection.

8   O, I have passed a miserable night,
   So full of fearful dreams, of ugly
   sights,
   That, as I am a Christian faithful
   man,
   I would not spend another such a
   night
   Though 'twere to buy a world of
   happy days,
   So full of dismal terror was the
   time.
   Clarence in *Richard III*, 1.4.2–7

   In prison, his dream foreshadows his death.

9   O Lord, methought what pain it
   was to drown,
   What dreadful noise of waters in
   my ears!
   What sights of ugly death within
   my eyes!
   Clarence in *Richard III*, 1.4.21–3

   Describing a fearful dream; anticipating his
   own death.

10 Methought I saw a thousand fearful wrecks,
A thousand men that fishes gnawed upon,
Wedges of gold, great anchors, heaps of pearl,
Inestimable stones, unvalued jewels,
All scattered in the bottom of the sea.

Clarence in *Richard III*, 1.4.24–8

Describing his dream of wealth scattered among dead bodies.

11 Methought a legion of foul fiends
Environed me, and howlèd in mine ears
Such hideous cries that with the very noise
I trembling waked, and for a season after
Could not believe but that I was in hell,
Such terrible impression made my dream.

Clarence in *Richard III*, 1.4.58–63

His fearful dream, anticipating his own death.

12 *Romeo.* I dreamt a dream tonight.
Mercutio. And so did I.
Romeo. Well, what was yours?
Mercutio. That dreamers often lie.
Romeo. In bed asleep, while they do dream things true.
Mercutio. O then I see Queen Mab hath been with you.
She is the fairies' midwife, and she comes
In shape no bigger than an agate stone
On the forefinger of an alderman,
Drawn with a team of little atomi
Over men's noses as they lie asleep.

Romeo and Juliet, 1.4.50–8

Mercutio's fairy-tale seems meant to divert Romeo from his preoccupation with Rosaline; agates were carved with tiny figures (like "atomi") and used as seal-rings by town officials ("aldermen").

13 *Romeo.* Peace, peace, Mercutio, peace!
Thou talk'st of nothing.
Mercutio. True, I talk of dreams,
Which are the children of an idle brain,
Begot of nothing but vain fantasy,
Which is as thin of substance as the air,
And more inconstant than the wind.

Romeo and Juliet, 1.4.95–100

Mercutio implies that Romeo's love for Rosaline is as much a vain fantasy as a dream.

14 If I may trust the flattering truth of sleep,
My dreams presage some joyful news at hand.

Romeo in *Romeo and Juliet*, 5.1.1–2

In exile, Romeo hopes for good news from Verona.

15 In dreaming,
The clouds methought would open, and show riches
Ready to drop upon me; that, when I waked,
I cried to dream again.

Caliban in *The Tempest*, 3.2.140–3

16 Dreams are toys.
Yet for this once, yea, superstitiously,
I will be squared by this.

Antigonus in *The Winter's Tale*,
3.3.39–41

Dreams are trifles ("toys"), yet Antigonus allows himself to be directed ("squared") in his course of action by his dream of Hermione.

17 Thus have I had thee as a dream doth flatter,
In sleep a king, but waking no such matter.

Sonnet 87, 13–14

From a sonnet that relates to a quarrel with his friend.

Drinking

1 Come, thou monarch of the vine.

Song in *Antony and Cleopatra*, 2.7.113

Song to Bacchus, god of wine.

2 In my youth I never did apply Hot and rebellious liquors in my blood.

Adam in *As You Like It*, 2.3.48–9

Adam's recipe for a healthy old age.

3 One that loves a cup of hot wine with not a drop of allaying Tiber in't.

Menenius in *Coriolanus*, 2.1.48–9

Portraying himself as a drinker, who prefers his wine undiluted; the Tiber is the river that flows through Rome.

4 One that converses more with the buttock of the night than with the forehead of the morning.

Menenius in *Coriolanus*, 2.1.51–3

Presenting himself as liking to carouse at night rather than rise early.

5 We'll teach you to drink deep ere you depart.

Hamlet in *Hamlet*, 1.2.175

To his friend, Horatio, visiting him in Denmark.

6 These mad mustachio purple-hued maltworms.

Gadshill in *Henry IV, Part 1*, 2.1.74–5

Beer-drinkers whose moustaches are stained with drink.

7 O monstrous! but one half-penny-worth of bread to this intolerable deal of sack!

Prince Hal in *Henry IV, Part 1*, 2.4.540–1

Reading the tavern bill found in Falstaff's pocket.

8 Doth it not show vilely in me to desire small beer?

Prince Hal in *Henry IV, Part 2*, 2.2.5–6

Implying that a prince should want strong drink, not weak ("small") beer.

9 A good sherris-sack hath a twofold operation in it. It ascends me into the brain, . . . makes it apprehensive, quick, forgetive, full of nimble, fiery, and delectable shapes.

Falstaff in *Henry IV, Part 2*, 4.3.96–7, 99–100

Praising the effects of drinking sherry ("sherris-sack," from "Xeres" in Spain and "seco" = dry), that stimulates the imagination to be creative ("forgetive," from the verb to forge).

10 The second property of your excellent sherris is the warming of the blood.

Falstaff in *Henry IV, Part 2*, 4.3.102–3

Drinking wine or sherry was thought to heat the blood.

11 It illumineth the face, which as a beacon gives warning to all the rest of this little kingdom, man, to arm . . . this valor comes of sherris.

Falstaff in *Henry IV, Part 2*, 4.3.107–9, 112–13

On drinking wine or sherry as promoting courage.

12 If I had a thousand sons, the first humane principle I would teach them should be, to forswear thin potations and to addict themselves to sack.

Falstaff in *Henry IV, Part 2*, 4.3.122–5

"Sack" = sherry; see 9 above.

13 That which hath made them drunk hath made me bold;
What hath quenched them hath given me fire.

Lady Macbeth in *Macbeth*, 2.2.1–2

Referring to the wine she has given Duncan's attendants.

14 *Macduff.* What three things does drink especially provoke?
Porter. Marry, sir, nose-painting, sleep, and urine. Lechery, sir, it provokes, and unprovokes: it provokes the desire, but it takes away the performance.

***Macbeth*, 2.3.26–30**

"Marry" = by the Virgin Mary (an oath); "nose-painting" = red noses.

15 When he is best, he is a little worse than a man, and when he is worst, he is little better than a beast.

Portia in *The Merchant of Venice*, 1.2.88–9

Describing her German suitor, who is often drunk.

16 I'll ne'er be drunk, whilst I live, again, but in honest, civil, godly company.

Slender in *The Merry Wives of Windsor*, 1.1.181–2

17 Come, gentlemen, I hope we shall drink down all unkindness.

Page in *The Merry Wives of Windsor*, 1.1.196–7

18 You love sack, and so do I; would you desire better sympathy?

Mistress Page in *The Merry Wives of Windsor*, 2.1.8–10

Mistress Page is reading Falstaff's letter, which shows his peculiar way of making love to her.

19 *Falstaff.* Go, brew me a pottle of sack, finely.
Bardolph. With eggs, sir?
Falstaff. Simple of itself; I'll no pullet-sperm in my brewage.

***The Merry Wives of Windsor*, 3.5.28–32**

Falstaff asks for two quarts of sherry to be heated.

20 I have very poor and unhappy brains for drinking. I could well wish courtesy would invent some other custom of entertainment.

Cassio in *Othello*, 2.3.33–6

21 O thou invisible spirit of wine, if thou hast no name to be known by, let us call thee devil!

Cassio in *Othello*, 2.3.281–3

His drunkenness has cost him his office.

22 O God, that men should put an enemy into their mouths to steal away their brains!

Cassio in Othello, 2.3.289–91

On losing his office because of drunkenness.

23 Good wine is a good familiar creature, if it be well used.

Iago in Othello, 2.3.309–10

Iago seems to praise wine as friendly, but a "familiar" was also the name for demons thought to attend on witches in the shape of creatures.

24 Prithee do not turn me about, my stomach is not constant.

Stephano in The Tempest, 2.2.114–15

The butler is drunk, having found a cask of wine driven ashore on the island where they have been shipwrecked.

25 *Sebastian.* He is drunk now. Where had he wine?
Alonso. And Trinculo is reeling ripe. Where should they Find this grand liquor that hath gilded 'em?

The Tempest, 5.1.278–80

On the arrival of the drunken butler Stephano and his companion Trinculo; "gilded" = flushed, made them red-faced.

26 Here's that which is too weak to be a sinner, Honest water, which ne'er left man i' the mire.

Apemantus in Timon of Athens, 1.2.58–9

As opposed to the wine that flows in Timon's house.

27 *Maria.* He's drunk nightly in your company.
Sir Toby Belch. With drinking healths to my niece. I'll drink to her as long as there is a passage in my throat, and drink in Illyria.

Twelfth Night, 1.3.36–40

Referring to Sir Andrew Aguecheek.

28 O, he's drunk, Sir Toby, an hour agone; his eyes were set at eight i' the morning.

Feste in Twelfth Night, 5.1.198–9

Referring to the surgeon who should attend to the injured Sir Toby.

Duplicity (see also Deceit/Deception, Hypocrisy)

1 Why, I can smile, and murder whiles I smile, And cry "Content!" to that which grieves my heart, And wet my cheeks with artificial tears, And frame my face to all occasions.

Richard of Gloucester in Henry VI, Part 3, 3.2.182–5

Boasting to the audience in soliloquy.

2 I can add colors to the chameleon, Change shapes with Proteus for advantages, And set the murderous Machiavel to school.

Richard of Gloucester in Henry VI, Part 3, 3.2.191–3

Proteus, the old man of the sea, could change himself into any shape. Machiavelli was identified with ruthless political cunning.

3   And that I love the tree from
    whence thou sprang'st,
    Witness the loving kiss I give the
    fruit.
    He kisses the infant prince
    [*Aside*] To say the truth, so Judas
    kissed his master,
    And cried "All hail!" whenas he
    meant all harm.
    **Richard of Gloucester in *Henry VI,
    Part 3*, 5.7.31–4**

    Richard of Gloucester, later Richard III,
    already has in mind getting rid of the prince
    he has just kissed, son of Edward IV. It was
    the kiss Judas Iscariot gave to Christ that
    betrayed him to the chief priests (Mark
    14:44–6).

4   An evil soul producing holy witness
    Is like a villain with a smiling cheek,
    A goodly apple rotten at the heart.
    **Antonio in *The Merchant of Venice*,
    1.3.99–101**

    Referring to Shylock.

5   O, what a goodly outside falsehood
    hath!
    **Antonio in *The Merchant of Venice*,
    1.3.102**

    Referring to Shylock, from whom he wants to
    borrow money.

6   Cannot a plain man live and think
    no harm,
    But that his simple truth must be
    abused
    With silken, sly, insinuating Jacks?
    King Richard in *Richard III*, 1.3.51–3

    Falsely protesting his honest simplicity;
    "Jacks" is a scornful term for people of lower
    rank or low breeding.

7   I do the wrong, and first begin to
    brawl.

The secret mischiefs that I set
abroach
I lay unto the grievous charge of
others.
King Richard in *Richard III*, 1.3.323–5

Laying the responsibility for his own wicked
schemes on others; "set abroach" = initiate,
set going.

Duty

1   He was disposed to mirth, but on
    the sudden
    A Roman thought hath struck him.
    **Cleopatra in *Antony and Cleopatra*,
    1.2.82–3**

    In Alexandria, Antony occasionally remem-
    bers his duties as a ruler and his wife in Rome.

2   Every subject's duty is the King's,
    but every subject's soul is his own.
    King Henry in *Henry V*, 4.1.176–7

    The king, disguised, speaks with common sol-
    diers.

3   I owe him little duty and less love.
    Somerset in *Henry VI, Part 1*, 4.4.34

    Referring to Richard, Duke of York; they are
    supposed to be supporting one another in
    fighting the French.

4   What wouldst thou do, old
    man?
    Think'st thou that duty shall have
    dread to speak
    When power to flattery bows?
    Kent in *King Lear*, 1.1.146–8

    Reminding the king of his age ("fourscore and
    upward" as we learn later).

5   I do perceive here a divided duty.

Desdemona in *Othello*, 1.3.181

To her father, Brabantio, and her husband,
Othello.

6   Duty never yet did want his meed.

Silvia in *The Two Gentlemen of
Verona*, 1.4.112

To Proteus, who is offering his service to her;
"want his meed" = lack his reward.

Dying (see also Death, Mortality)

1   I am dying, Egypt, dying.

Antony in *Antony and Cleopatra*,
4.15.18, 41

Antony's only reference to Cleopatra's title as
Queen of Egypt.

2   I am fire and air; my other elements
I give to baser life.

Cleopatra in *Antony and Cleopatra*,
5.2.289–90

Earth and water were the heavier of the four
elements of which it was thought life was
composed.

3   If thou and nature can so gently
part,
The stroke of death is as a lover's
pinch,
Which hurts, and is desired.

Cleopatra in *Antony and Cleopatra*,
5.2.294–6

Addressing Iras, one of her attendants, who
dies just before Cleopatra herself.

4   The poor world is almost six thousand years old, and in all this time

there was not any man died in his
own person, videlicet, in a love-
cause.

Rosalind in *As You Like It*, 4.1.94–7

"Videlicet" = namely; calculating from the
Bible, it was thought that the world was created about 4000 B.C.

5   Men have died from time to time,
and worms have eaten them, but
not for love.

Rosalind in *As You Like It*, 4.1.106–8

6   'A parted even just between twelve
and one, even at the turning o' the
tide; for after I saw him fumble
with the sheets, and play with flowers, and smile upon his finger's end,
I knew there was but one way; for
his nose was as sharp as a pen, and
'a babbled of green fields.

Mistress Quickly in *Henry V*, 2.3.12–17

On the death of Falstaff; " 'A parted" = he
departed.

7   So 'a bade me lay more clothes on
his feet. I put my hand into the bed
and felt them, and they were as cold
as any stone; then I felt to his knees,
and so upward and upward, and all
was as cold as any stone.

Mistress Quickly in *Henry V*, 2.3.22–6

On the death of Falstaff.

8   The sands are numbered that
makes up my life,
Here must I stay, and here my life
must end.

York in *Henry VI, Part 3*, 1.4.25–6

He is defeated and alone on the field of battle.

9   Why, what is pomp, rule, reign, but
     earth and dust?
     And live we how we can, yet die we
     must.

Warwick in *Henry VI, Part 3*, 5.2.27–8

He is wounded and near death; "die we must"
is proverbial.

10 He gave his honors to the world
     again,
     His blessèd part to heaven, and
     slept in peace.

Griffith in *Henry VIII*, 4.2.29–30

Reporting the death of Cardinal Wolsey.

11 My heart hath one poor string to
     stay it by.

King John in *King John*, 5.7.55

12   But his flawed heart
     (Alack, too weak the conflict to
     support!)
     'Twixt two extremes of passion, joy
     and grief,
     Burst smilingly.

Edgar in *King Lear*, 5.3.197–200

On the death of his father, Gloucester;
"flawed" = cracked.

13   Nothing in his life
     Became him like the leaving it. He
     died
     As one that had been studied in his
     death,
     To throw away the dearest thing he
     owed
     As 'twere a careless trifle.

Malcolm in *Macbeth*, 1.4.7–11

On the execution of the traitor Cawdor.

14   I will play the swan,
     And die in music.

Emilia in *Othello*, 5.2.247–8

Proverbially the swan sang before it died
(hence the term "swan song").

15 *Romeo.* Courage, man, the hurt
     cannot be much.
     Mercutio. No, 'tis not so deep as a
     well, nor so wide as a church
     door, but 'tis enough, 'twill serve.
     Ask for me tomorrow, and you
     shall find me a grave man.

Romeo and Juliet, 3.1.95–8

Even as he is dying, stabbed by Tybalt, Mercutio jests with a pun on the word "grave."

16   My long sickness
     Of health and living now begins to
     mend,
     And nothing brings me all things.

Timon in *Timon of Athens*, 5.1.186–8

Foreseeing his death.

Earthquakes

1   Diseasèd nature oftentimes breaks
     forth
     In strange eruptions; oft the teem-
     ing earth
     Is with a kind of colic pinched and
     vexed
     By the imprisoning of unruly wind
     Within her womb, which, for
     enlargement striving,
     Shakes the old beldame earth, and
     topples down
     Steeples and moss-grown towers.

Hotspur in *Henry IV, Part 1*, 3.1.26–32

Rejecting Glendower's claim that extraordinary events in nature at his birth were signs
that he was to be remarkable; "beldame" =
grandmother.

Eating (see also Food)

1   On the Alps
It is reported thou didst eat strange flesh,
Which some did die to look on.

Octavius Caesar in *Antony and Cleopatra*, 1.4.66–8

Hardships endured by Antony as a soldier.

2   Unquiet meals make ill digestions.

The Abbess in *The Comedy of Errors*, 5.1.74

To Adriana, who has been criticizing her husband.

3   They surfeited with honey and began
To loathe the taste of sweetness, whereof a little
More than a little is by much too much.

King Henry in *Henry IV, Part 1*, 3.2.71–3

Describing how the people became tired of seeing Richard II.

4   He hath eaten me out of house and home, he hath put all my substance into that fat belly of his.

Mistress Quickly in *Henry IV, Part 2*, 2.1.74–5

On Falstaff's gargantuan appetite.

5   We will eat a last year's pippin of mine own grafting, with a dish of caraways, and so forth.

Shallow in *Henry IV, Part 2*, 5.3.2–3

Apples were often eaten with caraway seeds.

6   Read o'er this,
And after this, and then to breakfast with
What appetite you have.

King Henry in *Henry VIII*, 3.2.201–3

Henry hands Cardinal Wolsey documents proving his disloyalty to the King.

7   Now good digestion wait on appetite,
And health on both!

Macbeth in *Macbeth*, 3.4.37–8

Welcoming his guests to a banquet.

8   Who riseth from a feast
With that keen appetite that he sits down?

Gratiano in *The Merchant of Venice*, 2.6.8–9

9   Truly, a peck of provender, I could munch your good dry oats. Methinks I have a great desire to a bottle of hay. Good hay, sweet hay hath no fellow.

Bottom in *A Midsummer Night's Dream*, 4.1.31–4

Bottom when transformed into an ass; a "bottle" is a truss.

10   Eat no onions nor garlic, for we are to utter sweet breath.

Bottom in *A Midsummer Night's Dream*, 4.2.42–3

Advising the actors who are to perform "Pyramus and Thisbe."

11   Things sweet to taste prove in digestion sour.

John of Gaunt in *Richard II*, 1.3.236

Proverbial; compare Revelation 10:9–10.

12 Nothing but sit and sit, and eat and eat!

Petruchio in *The Taming of the Shrew*, 5.2.12

At Lucentio's banquet to celebrate his marriage.

13 I am a great eater of beef, and I believe that does harm to my wit.

Sir Andrew Aguecheek in *Twelfth Night*, 1.3.85–6

Eating beef was proverbially linked to being stupid or "beef-witted."

14 A plague o' these pickle herring!

Sir Toby Belch in *Twelfth Night*, 1.5.120–1

Excusing a drunken belch.

15 Though the chameleon love can feed on the air, I am one that am nourished by my victuals, and would fain have meat.

Speed in *The Two Gentlemen of Verona*, 2.1.172–4

The chameleon, once supposed to live on air, changes its color, just as the lover varies in mood.

Education (see also Books, Learning, Study)

1 Thou hast most traitorously corrupted the youth of the realm in erecting a grammar school.

Jack Cade in *Henry VI, Part 2*, 4.7.32–4

The peasants' accusations against Lord Saye.

2   Ignorance is the curse of God,

Knowledge the wing wherewith we fly to heaven.

Lord Saye in *Henry VI, Part 2*, 4.7.73–4

3 He must be taught, and trained, and bid go forth:
A barren-spirited fellow; one that feeds
On objects, arts, and imitations,
Which, out of use and staled by other men,
Begin his fashion.

Mark Antony in *Julius Caesar*, 4.1.35–9

On Lepidus, the third member of the triumvirate ruling Rome as one whose attention is taken by curiosities, tricks and copying fashions that are already obsolete.

4   Those that do teach young babes
Do it with gentle means and easy tasks.

Desdemona in *Othello*, 4.2.111–12

5 While I play the good husband at home, my son and his servant spend all at the university.

Vincentio in *The Taming of the Shrew*, 5.1.68–70

Mistakenly thinking his son Lucentio is a spendthrift; "good husband" = careful manager.

6 I prithee let me bring thee where crabs grow,
And I with my long nails will dig thee pig-nuts,
Show thee a jay's nest, and instruct thee how
To snare the nimble marmoset.

Caliban in *The Tempest*, 2.2.267–70

Offering to educate Stephano and Trinculo in what the island has to offer in the way of interest and food, crab-apples, tubers ("pig-nuts").

7   A devil, a born devil, on whose nature
Nurture can never stick; on whom my pains
Humanely taken, all, all quite lost.
Prospero in *The Tempest*, 4.1.188–90

Complaining that a European mode of moral education is wasted on the native of the island, Caliban.

Effeminacy

1   He was perfumèd like a milliner.
Hotspur in *Henry IV, Part 1*, 1.3.36

Describing an effeminate courtier who appeared thus inappropriately on a battle-field.

2   A woman impudent and mannish grown
Is not more loathed than an effeminate man
In time of action.
Patroclus in *Troilus and Cressida*, 3.3.217–19

Speaking of his own reluctance to fight; Thersites calls Patroclus Achilles's "masculine whore."

Eloquence (see also Speech, Speechmaking)

1   Very good orators, when they are out, they will spit.
Rosalind in *As You Like It*, 4.1.75–6

"Out" = lost for words.

2   More matter with less art.
Gertrude in *Hamlet*, 2.2.95

To Polonius, who claims to know the cause of Hamlet's madness but is being longwinded in coming to the point; "art" = rhetorical decoration.

3   When he speaks,
The air, a chartered libertine, is still.
Archbishop of Canterbury in *Henry V*, 1.1.47–8

On King Henry's eloquence in stilling the air, which has license to move freely (as a "chartered libertine").

4   You have witchcraft in your lips, Kate. There is more eloquence in a sugar touch of them than in the tongues of the French council.
King Henry in *Henry V*, 5.2.275–7

The French council negotiates for peace while Henry makes love.

5   The gentleman is learned, and a most rare speaker.
King Henry in *Henry VIII*, 1.2.111

On Buckingham, arrested as a traitor.

6   With all the gracious utterance thou hast
Speak to his gentle hearing kind commends.
King Richard in *Richard II*, 3.3.125–6

Flattering Henry Bolingbroke, who has control of the kingdom.

7   Doubt not, my lord, I'll play the orator
As if the golden fee for which I plead
Were for myself.
Buckingham in *Richard III*, 3.5.95–7

Promising to persuade the people to acclaim Richard as king.

8　All orators are dumb when beauty
　　pleadeth.

The Rape of Lucrece, 268

Tarquin is finding excuses to pursue the rape
of the chaste Lucrece; her beauty, he claims,
silences objections.

Empire

1　Let Rome in Tiber melt, and the
　　wide arch
　　Of the ranged empire fall! Here is
　　my space.

Antony in *Antony and Cleopatra*,
1.1.33–4

Putting love before empire; already signaling
what leads to Antony's downfall.

2　The greater cantle of the world is
　　lost
　　With very ignorance, we have
　　kissed away
　　Kingdoms and provinces.

Scarus in *Antony and Cleopatra*,
3.10.6–8

After Antony has lost the Battle of Actium
against Caesar; "cantle" = portion.

Encouragement

1　Wise men ne'er sit and wail their
　　loss,
　　But cheerly seek how to redress
　　their harms.

Queen Margaret in *Henry VI, Part 3*,
5.4.1–2

Encouraging her allies after the death of their
leader, Warwick.

2　But wherefore do you droop? Why
　　look you sad?

Be great in act as you have been in
thought.

The Bastard Falconbridge in *King
John*, 5.1.44–5

Comforting the king.

3　What, courage, man! What though
　　care killed a cat, thou hast mettle
　　enough in thee to kill care.

Claudio in *Much Ado About Nothing*,
5.1.132–4

To Benedick, who is unusually serious and
full of care; "care will kill a cat" is proverbial.

Endings

1　　All's well that ends well yet,
　　Though time seem so adverse and
　　means unfit.

Helena in *All's Well That Ends Well*,
5.1.25–6

2　Our wooing doth not end like an
　　old play.
　　Jack hath not Jill.

Berowne in *Love's Labor's Lost*,
5.2.874–5

The courtiers have to practice austerity for a
year before the ladies will have them.

3　O most lame and impotent conclu-
　　sion!

Desdemona in *Othello*, 2.1.161

On Iago's anticlimactic winding-up of his
praise of women.

4　More are men's ends marked than
　　their lives before.
　　The setting sun, and music at the
　　close,

As the last taste of sweets, is sweetest last,
Writ in remembrance more than
things long past.

John of Gaunt in *Richard II*, 2.1.11–14

Spoken as he anticipates his death; "marked"
= noticed.

Endurance

1   Thou didst drink
The stale of horses and the gilded
    puddle
That beasts would cough at.

**Octavius Caesar in *Antony and
Cleopatra*, 1.4.61–3**

Hardships that Antony suffered as a soldier;
"stale" is urine.

2   Bid that welcome
Which comes to punish us, and we
    punish it
Seeming to bear it lightly.

**Antony in *Antony and Cleopatra*,
4.14.136–8**

The dying Antony asks his guard to carry him
to Cleopatra.

3   *Gloucester.* No further, sir, a man
    may rot even here.
Edgar. What, in ill thoughts again?
    Men must endure
Their going hence, even as their
    coming hither;
Ripeness is all.

***King Lear*, 5.2.8–11**

"Ripeness is all" may mean the gods deter-
mine when we die, or that we must await the
time of ripeness when we are ready for death.

4   He's truly valiant that can wisely
    suffer

The worst that man can breathe,
    and make his wrongs
His outsides, to wear them like his
    raiment carelessly,
And ne'er prefer his injuries to his
    heart,
To bring it into danger.

**First Senator in *Timon of Athens*,
3.5.31–5**

The idea is of enduring wrongs as merely
external ("outsides"), like clothes ("raiment"),
not taking them to heart (and seeking
revenge).

5   Jog on, jog on, the footpath way,
And merrily hent the stile-a.
A merry heart goes all the day,
Your sad tires in a mile-a.

**Autolycus in *The Winter's Tale*,
4.3.123–6**

Having tricked the shepherd's son, Autolycus
goes off with a song; "hent" = take hold of.

Enemies

1   Why, Harry, do I tell thee of my
    foes,
Which art my nearest and dearest
    enemy?

**King Henry in *Henry IV, Part 1*,
3.2.122–3**

To Prince Hal, reproaching him for failing to
support his father.

2   If the enemy is an ass and a fool
and a prating coxcomb, is it meet,
think you, that we should also, look
you, be an ass and a fool and a prating coxcomb, in your own conscience now?

Fluellen in *Henry V*, 4.1.77–80

Fluellen's quaint way of cautioning the army
against being noisy.

3   You have many enemies that
     know not
     Why they are so, but like to village
     curs
     Bark when their fellows do.
     King Henry in *Henry VIII*, 2.4.159–61

     To Cardinal Wolsey.

4   Keep this man safe;
     Give him all kindness. I had rather
     have
     Such men my friends than enemies.
     Mark Antony in *Julius Caesar*, 5.4.27–9

     On the capture of Lucilius.

Envy

1   Men that make
     Envy and crooked malice nourish-
     ment
     Dare bite the best.
     Archbishop Cranmer in *King Henry
     VIII*, 5.2.78–80

     Defending himself against the malice of Gar-
     diner, Bishop of Winchester.

Epitaphs (see also Burial, Graves, Mourning)

1   O, withered is the garland of the
     war,
     The soldier's pole is fallen!
     Cleopatra in *Antony and Cleopatra*,
     4.15.64–5

     "Garland" suggests the wreath of victory, and
     "pole" the standard-bearer, and also a phallus,
     reminding us of the dead Antony's sexuality.

2   Now boast thee, death, in thy pos-
     session lies
     A lass unparalleled.
     Charmian in *Antony and Cleopatra*,
     5.2.315–16

     The "lass" is Cleopatra, Queen of Egypt.

3   She shall be buried by her Antony;
     No grave upon the earth shall clip
     in it
     A pair so famous.
     Octavius Caesar in *Antony and
     Cleopatra*, 5.2.358–60

     He is speaking about Cleopatra.

4   Alas, poor Yorick! I knew him,
     Horatio, a fellow of infinite jest, of
     most excellent fancy.
     Hamlet in *Hamlet*, 5.1.184–5

     The grave-digger has turned up the skull of
     Yorick, the king's jester; on stage Hamlet usu-
     ally holds the skull while he says this; "fancy"
     = imagination.

5   Now cracks a noble heart. Good
     night, sweet prince,
     And flights of angels sing thee to
     thy rest!
     Horatio in *Hamlet*, 5.2.359–60

     On Hamlet's death; "flights of angels sing" =
     may flights of angels sing.

6   Adieu, and take thy praise with thee
     to heaven!
     Prince Hal in *Henry IV, Part 1*, 5.4.99

     Bidding farewell to the dead Hotspur.

7   Thy ignominy sleep with thee in the
     grave,

But not remembered in thy epitaph!

Prince Hal in *Henry IV, Part 1*,
5.4.100–1

On the rebel Hotspur, killed by Hal.

8   O mighty Caesar! Dost thou lie so
low?
Are all thy conquests, glories, tri-
umphs, spoils,
Shrunk to this little measure? Fare
thee well.

Mark Antony in *Julius Caesar*,
3.1.148–50

Seeing the dead body of Caesar.

9   Thou art the ruins of the noblest
man
That ever livèd in the tide of times.

Mark Antony in *Julius Caesar*, 3.1.256–7

Mourning Caesar; "tide of times" = course of
history.

10   Friends, Romans, countrymen, lend
me your ears.
I come to bury Caesar, not to praise
him.
The evil that men do lives after
them;
The good is oft interrèd with their
bones—
So let it be with Caesar.

Mark Antony in *Julius Caesar*, 3.2.73–7

11   The last of all the Romans, fare thee
well.
It is impossible that ever Rome
Should breed thy fellow.

Brutus in *Julius Caesar*, 5.3.99–101

On the death of Cassius.

12   His life was gentle, and the elements
So mixed in him that Nature might
stand up
And say to all the world, "This was
a man!"

Mark Antony in *Julius Caesar*, 5.5.73–5

On Brutus; human beings were thought to be
composed of the four elements, fire, air, earth
and water.

13   The ripest fruit first falls, and so
doth he.
His time is spent; our pilgrimage
must be.

King Richard in *Richard II*, 2.1.153–4

Referring to the death of his uncle John of
Gaunt; "pilgrimage" = journey through life.

14   Sweet peace conduct his sweet soul
to the bosom
Of good old Abraham!

Bolingbroke in *Richard II*, 4.1.103–4

On news of the death of his enemy Mowbray;
"Abraham's bosom" = heaven, from Luke
16:22.

15   Timon hath made his everlasting
mansion
Upon the beachèd verge of the salt
flood,
Who once a day with his embossèd
froth
The turbulent surge shall cover;
thither come,
And let my grave-stone be your
oracle.

Timon in *Timon of Athens*, 5.1.215–19

"Embossed" = foaming; "oracle" = source of
wisdom.

16   Repose you here in rest,
Secure from worldly chances and
 mishaps.
Here lurks no treason, here no envy
 swells,
Here grow no damnèd drugs, here
 are no storms,
No noise, but silence and eternal
 sleep.

Titus in *Titus Andronicus*, 1.1.151–5

Burying his sons, slain in war.

17 His part is played, and though it
  were too short,
He did it well.

**Theseus in *The Two Noble Kinsmen*,
5.4.102–3**

On the death of young Arcite, thrown acci-
dentally from his horse.

Eternity

1   When you sued staying,
Then was the time for words; no
 going then;
Eternity was in our lips and eyes.

**Cleopatra in *Antony and Cleopatra*,
1.3.33–5**

"Sued staying" = begged to stay; Antony is setting off for Rome.

2 But this eternal blazon must not be
To ears of flesh and blood.

Ghost in *Hamlet*, 1.5.21–2

Refusing to describe his afterlife to Hamlet;
"eternal blazon" = revelation of eternal things.

3 But thy eternal summer shall not
 fade,

Nor lose possession of that fair
 thou owest,
Nor shall Death brag thou wander-
 est in his shade,
When in eternal lines to time thou
 growest.
So long as men can breathe or
 eyes can see,
So long lives this, and this gives
 life to thee.

***Sonnet 18*, 9–14**

On the poet's lines as conferring eternity on
the transient beauty of his friend.

4 Poor soul, the center of my sinful
  earth,
[Slave to] these rebel powers that
 thee array,
Why dost thou pine within and suffer dearth,
Painting thy outward walls so costly
 gay?
Why so large cost, having so short a
 lease,
Dost thou upon thy fading mansion
 spend?
Shall worms, inheritors of this
 excess,
Eat up thy charge? Is this thy
 body's end?
Then, soul, live thou upon thy servant's loss,
And let that pine to aggravate thy
 store;
Buy terms divine in selling hours of
 dross,
Within be fed, without be rich no
 more:
 So shalt thou feed on Death, that
  feeds on men,
 And Death once dead, there's no
  more dying then.

Sonnet 146

A powerful sonnet that sets enriching the soul
("aggravate thy store" = increase your wealth)

against enriching the body, and the brevity of the "short lease" of this world's existence against eternal life ("terms divine"). "Slave to" in the second line is a guess; the first edition repeats "My sinful earth."

Evening

1 How still the evening is,
As hushed on purpose to grace harmony!

Claudio in *Much Ado About Nothing*, 2.3.38–9

Evil (see also Wrongdoing)

1 A very tainted fellow, and full of
wickedness.

Countess of Rossillion in *All's Well That Ends Well*, 3.2.87

Describing Parolles.

2 What rein can hold licentious
wickedness
When down the hill he holds his
fierce career?

King Henry in *Henry V*, 3.3.22–3

Suggesting a victorious army, like a horse in full gallop ("career"), cannot be restrained from rape and pillage.

3 Now let it work! Mischief, thou art
afoot,
Take thou what course thou wilt.

Mark Antony in *Julius Caesar*, 3.2.260–1

He has achieved his aim, as the people rush off to burn and destroy.

4 Those wicked creatures yet do look
well-favored
When others are more wicked; not
being the worst
Stands in some rank of praise.

King Lear in *King Lear*, 2.4.255–7

The "wicked creatures" are his two elder daughters; he hopes Goneril will treat him better than Regan.

5 Oftentimes, to win us to our
harm,
The instruments of darkness tell us
truths,
Win us with honest trifles, to
betray 's
In deepest consequence.

Banquo in *Macbeth*, 1.3.123–6

The Weird Sisters are the "instruments of dark-ness," or agents of evil; "in deepest conse-quence" = in matters of greatest importance.

6 Come to my woman's breasts,
And take my milk for gall, you
murdering ministers,
Wherever in your sightless sub-
stances
You wait on nature's mischief!

Lady Macbeth in *Macbeth*, 1.5.47–50

Summoning spirits ("ministers") to make her ruthless; "sightless" = invisible.

7 Ere the bat hath flown
His cloistered flight, ere to black
Hecate's summons
The shard-borne beetle with his
drowsy hums
Hath rung night's yawning peal,
there shall be done
A deed of dreadful note.

Macbeth in *Macbeth*, 3.2.40–4

Bats and dung-beetles ("shard-borne") were associated with darkness, and here with Hecate, goddess of witchcraft.

8
    Come, seeling night,
Scarf up the tender eye of pitiful
day,
And with thy bloody and invisible
hand
Cancel and tear to pieces that great
bond
Which keeps me pale.

Macbeth in *Macbeth*, 3.2.46–50

Night that "seels" or covers up (like stitching
the eyelids of a hawk in order to tame it) is
"bloody" because it provides concealment for
murder; the "bond" is the obligation of love to
all, as in Matthew 5:43–4, "Do good to them
which hate you."

9 By the pricking of my thumbs,
  Something wicked this way comes.

Second Witch in *Macbeth*, 4.1.44–5

Announcing the arrival of Macbeth.

10 I have't. It is engendered. Hell and
  night
  Must bring this monstrous birth to
  the world's light.

Iago in *Othello*, 1.3.403–4

Exactly what evil Iago has in mind is not yet
clear.

11   O mischief, thou art swift
To enter in the thoughts of desperate men!

Romeo in *Romeo and Juliet*, 5.1.35–6

On hearing news of Juliet's death, he thinks of
suicide, regarded as wicked because of he
biblical injunction against taking life, as at
Matthew 5:21.

Exaggeration

1 Well said—that was laid on with a
  trowel.

Celia in *As You Like It*, 1.2.105–6

Meaning something stated with exaggerated
force.

Excellence

1 So excellent a king that was to this
  Hyperion to a satyr, so loving to my
  mother
  That he might not beteem the
  winds of heaven
  Visit her face too roughly.

Hamlet in *Hamlet*, 1.2.139–42

Remembering his father as a sun-god compared to Claudius, the satyr, half-goat, half-
man; "beteem" = permit.

Excuses (see also Apologies)

1   I would I could
Quit all offences with as clear
excuse
As well as I am doubtless I can
purge
Myself of many I am charged
withal.

**Prince Hal in *Henry IV, Part 1*,
3.2.18–21**

Apologizing to the king, his father; "quit" = be
clear of.

2 Thou knowest in the state of innocency Adam fell, and what should
  poor Jack Falstaff do in the days of
  villainy?

Falstaff in *Henry IV, Part 1*, 3.3.164–6

To Prince Hal, who has exposed Falstaff's lies
about what was stolen from his pocket.

3   Thou seest I have more flesh than another man, and therefore more frailty.

Falstaff in *Henry IV, Part 1*, 3.3.166–8

4   Look what is done cannot be now amended:
Men shall deal unadvisedly sometimes,
Which after-hours gives leisure to repent.

King Richard in *Richard III*, 4.4.291–3

Trying to excuse his murder of Queen Elizabeth's relatives; proverbial (what's done cannot be undone).

Execution

1   Thou art a traitor.
Off with his head!

King Richard in *Richard III*, 3.4.75–6

Accusing and sentencing Hastings at the same time.

Exercise

1   A turn or two I'll walk
To still my beating mind.

Prospero in *The Tempest*, 4.1.162–3

He becomes angry as he recalls the "foul conspiracy" by Stephano, Trinculo and Caliban, who plot to kill him.

2   He hopes it is no other
But for your health and your digestion sake,
An after-dinner's breath.

Patroclus in *Troilus and Cressida*, 2.3.110–12

The Greek leaders, calling on Achilles, meet with this rebuff.

Exile

1   Now, my co-mates and brothers in exile,
Hath not old custom made this life more sweet
Than that of painted pomp?

Duke Senior in *As You Like It*, 2.1.1–3

The banished Duke moralizing in the forest of Arden.

2   Despising,
For you, the city, thus I turn my back;
There is a world elsewhere.

Coriolanus in *Coriolanus*, 3.3.133–5

Coriolanus is banished by the people of Rome.

3   This must my comfort be:
That sun that warms you here shall shine on me.

Bolingbroke in *Richard II*, 1.3.144–5

On being banished by King Richard.

4   Then thus I turn me from my country's light,
To dwell in solemn shades of endless night.

Mowbray in *Richard II*, 1.3.176–7

Seeing his exile as a kind of death.

5   Now no way can I stray;
Save back to England, all the world's my way.

Mowbray in *Richard II*, 1.3.206–7

"Stray" = take a wrong turn.

6   Then England's ground, farewell.
Sweet soil, adieu,
My mother and my nurse that bears
me yet!
Where e'er I wander, boast of this I
can:
Though banished, yet a true-born
Englishman.

Bolingbroke in *Richard II*, 1.3.306–9

Spoken as he goes off to exile.

7   Eating the bitter bread of banishment.

Bolingbroke in *Richard II*, 3.1.21

Recalling his years in exile.

8   Ha, banishment? Be merciful, say
"death";
For exile hath more terror in his
look,
Much more than death. Do not say
"banishment"!

Romeo in *Romeo and Juliet*, 3.3.12–14

On hearing from Friar Lawrence that he is
banished from Verona, and hence from Juliet.

9   There is no world without Verona
walls
But purgatory, torture, hell itself.
Hence "banishèd" is banished from
the world.

Romeo in *Romeo and Juliet*, 3.3.17–19

His "world" being Juliet.

Exorcism

1   I charge thee, Satan, housed within
this man,
To yield possession to my holy
prayers.

Doctor Pinch in *The Comedy of Errors*, 4.4.54–5

Treating the supposedly mad Antipholus of
Ephesus.

Expectation

1   Oft expectation fails, and most oft
there
Where most it promises; and oft it
hits
Where hope is coldest, and despair
most fits.

Helena in *All's Well That Ends Well*, 2.1.142–4

"Hits" = is fulfilled.

Experience

1   The oldest hath borne most; we
that are young
Shall never see so much, nor live so
long.

Edgar in *King Lear*, 5.3.326–7

These are the final lines of the play, referring
to the sufferings of the "oldest," King Lear and
Gloucester. The lines are assigned to Edgar in
the Folio text (1623), and to Albany in the
Quarto (1608).

2   A man loves the meat in his youth
that he cannot endure in his age.

Benedick in *Much Ado About Nothing*, 2.3.238–40

Justifying his sudden love for Beatrice.

3   Men
Can counsel and speak comfort to
that grief

Which they themselves not feel;
  but, tasting it,
Their counsel turns to passion.

Leonato in *Much Ado About Nothing,*
5.1.20–3

Proverbial; it is easy to advise others who are
suffering, but hard for those in pain to accept
counsel.

4   Experience is by industry achieved,
     And perfected by the swift course of
       time.

Antonio in *The Two Gentlemen of*
Verona, 1.3.22–3

He is thinking of sending his son off to court
to complete his education.

5   His years but young, but his experi-
       ence old;
     His head unmellowed, but his judg-
       ment ripe.

Valentine in *Two Gentlemen of*
Verona, 2.4.69–70

Praising his friend Proteus.

Extravagance

1   *Chief Justice.* Your means are very
       slender, and your waste is great.
     Falstaff. I would it were otherwise.
       I would my means were greater,
       and my waist slenderer.

Henry IV, Part 2, 1.2.140–3

"Waste" = expense; Falstaff lives beyond his
means.

2   To gild refinèd gold, to paint the
       lily,
     To throw a perfume on the violet,

To smooth the ice, or add another
  hue
Unto the rainbow, or with taper-
  light
To seek the beauteous eye of
  heaven to garnish,
Is wasteful and ridiculous excess.

Salisbury in *King John,* 4.2.11–16

"The beauteous eye of heaven" is the sun.

3   No care, no stop; so senseless of
       expense
     That he will neither know how to
       maintain it
     Nor cease his flow of riot, takes no
       account
     How things go from him, nor
       resumes no care
     Of what is to continue.

Flavius in *Timon of Athens,* 2.2.1–5

On Timon's reckless spending on feasting his
friends.

Eyes

1   Eyes, that are the frail'st and softest
       things,
     Who shut their coward gates on
       atomies.

Phebe in *As You Like It,* 3.5.12–13

"Atomies" are atoms or motes.

2   I think she means to tangle my eyes
       too!

Rosalind in *As You Like It,* 3.5.44

Phebe begins to fall in love with Rosalind,
who is disguised as a boy.

3   The flame o' the taper
Bows toward her, and would
   under-peep her lids,
To see th'enclosèd lights, now
   canopied
Under these windows, white and
   azure laced
With blue of heaven's own tinct.

Jachimo in *Cymbeline*, 2.2.19–23

Looking at the eyes of the sleeping Imogen.

4   I see before me, man; nor here,
   nor here,
Nor what ensues, but have a fog in
   them
That I cannot look through.

Imogen in *Cymbeline*, 3.2.78–80

On Pisanio advising her to think about what
she is doing.

5   Our very eyes
Are sometimes, like our judgments,
   blind.

Imogen in *Cymbeline*, 4.2.301–2

Not knowing whether she is dreaming or
awake.

6   With his head over his shoulder
   turned,
He seemed to find his way without
   his eyes,
For out o' doors he went without
   their help,
And to the last bended their light
   on me.

Ophelia in *Hamlet*, 2.1.94–7

Hamlet has appeared like a ghost or madman
to Ophelia.

7   The eye sees not itself
But by reflection.

Brutus in *Julius Caesar*, 1.2.52–3

8   *Old Man.*   You cannot see your
   way.
Gloucester. I have no way, and
   therefore want no eyes;
I stumbled when I saw.

King Lear, 4.1.17–19

Gloucester has been blinded by Regan and
Cornwall, and turned out of doors; he "stumbled" in misjudging his son Edgar.

9   *Macbeth.*   This is a sorry
   sight.
Lady Macbeth. A foolish thought,
   to say "A sorry sight."

Macbeth, 2.2.18–19

Referring to the blood on Macbeth's hands
after he has killed Duncan.

10   Show his eyes and grieve his heart.

Witches (Weird Sisters) in *Macbeth*,
4.1.110

What Macbeth sees is the line of Banquo's
descendants as kings.

11   *Claudio.* In mine eye she is the
   sweetest lady that ever I looked
   on.
Benedick. I can see yet without
   spectacles, and I see no such matter.

Much Ado About Nothing, 1.1.187–90

Claudio has fallen in love with Hero.

12   I have a good eye, uncle; I can see a
   church by daylight.

Beatrice in *Much Ado About Nothing*,
2.1.82–3

On her clear-sighted view of marriage.

13   He that is strucken blind cannot
   forget

The precious treasure of his eyesight lost.

Romeo in *Romeo and Juliet*, 1.1.232–3

14 The fringèd curtains of thine eye
    advance,
    And say what thou seest yond.

Prospero in *The Tempest*, 1.2.409–10

"Advance" = lift up, implying Miranda has
been demurely looking down; she now sees
young Ferdinand.

15   At the first sight
    They have changed eyes.

Prospero in *The Tempest*, 1.2.441–2

Watching Ferdinand and Miranda fall in love
at first sight.

16 What a pair of spectacles is here!

Pandarus in *Troilus and Cressida*,
4.4.14

Looking at Troilus and Cressida embracing,
and quibbling on "spectacles" = eyeglasses.

Faces

1 He'll make a proper man. The best
   thing in him
   Is his complexion.

Phebe in *As You Like It*, 3.5.115–16

On Rosalind disguised as a youth.

2 *Hamlet.* What, looked he frowningly?
   Horatio. A countenance more in
   sorrow than in anger.

Hamlet, 1.2.231–2

Describing the expression of the ghost of old
Hamlet.

3 Do thou amend thy face, and I'll
   amend my life.

Falstaff in *Henry IV, Part 1*, 3.3.24

Bardolph's face is inflamed with drinking.

4 I never see thy face but I think
   upon hell-fire.

Falstaff in *Henry IV, Part 1*, 3.3.31

To Bardolph, whose nose is red.

5 His face is all bubukles and whelks,
   and knobs, and flames of fire.

Fluellen in *Henry V*, 3.6.102–3

On Bardolph; "bubukles and whelks" = car-
buncles and pimples.

6 Your face, my thane, is as a book,
   where men
   May read strange matters.

Lady Macbeth in *Macbeth*, 1.5.62–3

Speaking to her husband; thanes were Scottish
noblemen.

7 He does smile his face into more
   lines than is in the new map with
   the augmentation of the Indies.

Maria in *Twelfth Night*, 3.2.78–80

On Malvolio, referring to the new Mercator
map showing the East Indies in full.

8   I do believe thee;
   I saw his heart in's face.

Polixenes in *The Winter's Tale*,
1.2.446–7

Leontes has shown in his expression his
hatred of Polixenes.

Fairies

1 Over hill, over dale,
   Thorough bush, thorough briar,
   Over park, over pale,
   Thorough flood, thorough fire;
   I do wander everywhere
   Swifter than the moon's sphere.

Fairy in *A Midsummer Night's Dream*,
2.1.2–7

"Thorough" = through (as in the modern "thoroughfare"); a pale is a fence, which would not stop fairies.

2 I must go seek some dewdrops
   here,
   And hang a pearl in every cowslip's
   ear.

Fairy in *A Midsummer Night's Dream*,
2.1.14–15

A charming image of fairies as responsible for scattering dew.

3 Either I mistake your shape and
   making quite,
   Or else you are that shrewd and
   knavish sprite
   Called Robin Goodfellow.

Fairy in *A Midsummer Night's Dream*,
2.1.32–4

Robin is better known as Puck, the mischievous ("shrewd") servant of Oberon, King of the Fairies.

4 *Fairy.* Those that "Hobgoblin" call
   you, and "Sweet Puck,"
   You do their work, and they shall
   have good luck.
   Are not you he?
   Puck.   Thou speakest aright;
   I am that merry wanderer of the
   night.

A Midsummer Night's Dream, 2.1.40–3

5 Peaseblossom, Cobweb, Moth, and
   Mustardseed!

Titania in *A Midsummer Night's*
Dream, 3.1.162

The charming names of Titania's diminutive fairy servants; "Moth" sounded like "mote" or speck.

6 And we fairies, that do run
   By the triple Hecate's team
   From the presence of the sun,
   Following darkness like a dream,
   Now are frolic. Not a mouse
   Shall disturb this hallowed house.

Puck in *A Midsummer Night's Dream*,
5.1.383–8

The goddess of the moon ruled under three names, Hecate in the underworld, Diana on earth, and Phoebe or Cynthia in the heavens; her chariot was supposed to be drawn across the sky by a team of dragons.

7 Hand in hand, with fairy grace,
   Will we sing, and bless this place.

Titania in *A Midsummer Night's*
Dream, 5.1.399–400

Blessing the bridal chamber of Theseus and Hippolyta.

8 Ye elves of hills, brooks, standing
   lakes, and groves,
   And ye that on the sands with
   printless foot
   Do chase the ebbing Neptune, and
   do fly him
   When he comes back. . . .

Prospero in *The Tempest*, 5.1.33–6

The beginning of the speech in which Prospero renounces his magic powers.

9 Where the bee sucks, there suck I,
   In a cowslip's bell I lie;
   There I couch when owls do cry.
   On the bat's back I do fly

After summer merrily.
Merrily, merrily shall I live now,
Under the blossom that hangs on
the bough.

Ariel in *The Tempest*, 5.1.88–94

Celebrating his freedom, Ariel dwindles into a
delicate fairy.

Falconry

1   My falcon now is sharp and passing
empty,
And till she stoop she must not be
full-gorged,
For then she never looks upon her
lure.

Petruchio in *The Taming of the Shrew*,
4.1.190–2

Like a falcon, Katherine has been starved in
order to tame her; the "lure," baited with
pieces of meat, was used by falconers to recall
the bird.

Fall, see Seasons

Fame (see also Reputation)

1   By being seldom seen, I could not
stir
But like a comet I was wondered at.

King Henry in *Henry IV, Part 1*,
3.2.46–7

Describing his own youthful renown to his
son.

2   Let fame, that all hunt after in their
lives,
Live registered upon our brazen
tombs,
And then grace us in the disgrace of
death;

When spite of cormorant devouring Time,
Th'endeavor of this present breath
may buy
That honor which shall bate his
scythe's keen edge,
And make us heirs of all eternity.

King of Navarre in *Love's Labor's Lost*,
1.1.1–7

The King of Navarre's lofty idea of gaining
eternal fame through the "breath" or breathing-space of three years of hermit-like study.

3   From the four corners of the earth
they come
To kiss this shrine, this mortal-
breathing saint.

Prince of Morocco in *The Merchant of
Venice*, 2.7.39–40

In adoration of Portia.

4   Death makes no conquest of this
conqueror,
For now he lives in fame though
not in life.

Prince Edward in *Richard III*, 3.1.87–8

Commenting on Julius Caesar.

5   Much attribute he hath, and much
the reason
Why we ascribe it to him; yet all his
virtues,
Not virtuously of his own part
beheld,
Do in our eyes begin to lose their
gloss,
Yea, like fair fruit in an unwhole-
some dish,
Are like to rot untasted.

Agamemnon in *Troilus and Cressida*,
2.3.116–21

Commenting on the scornful behavior of
Achilles; "attribute" = distinction, fame.

Familiarity

1 *Aeneas.* We know each other well.
Diomedes. We do, and long to
   know each other worse.
   Troilus and Cressida, 4.1.31–2

   A Trojan and a Greek meeting during a truce;
   they will know each other "worse" on the
   field of battle.

Farewells (see also Parting)

1 Fare thee well, dame. Whate'er
   becomes of me,
   This is a soldier's kiss.
   Antony in *Antony and Cleopatra*,
   4.4.29–30

   Renewing his role as a soldier, and bidding
   farewell to Cleopatra as if she were a housewife.

2 Hereafter, in a better world than
   this,
   I shall desire more love and knowledge of you.
   Le Beau in *As You Like It*, 1.2.284–5

   Addressing Orlando; "better world" may
   mean better conditions than under the Duke's
   tyranny, or the next world, heaven.

3 Adieu, adieu, adieu! Remember
   me.
   Ghost in *Hamlet*, 1.5.91

   His father's ghost gives a final command to
   Hamlet.

4 Come, my coach. Good night,
   ladies, good night, sweet ladies,
   good night, good night.
   Ophelia in *Hamlet*, 4.5.71–3

   In her madness Ophelia makes a grand exit;
   her words are quoted in a well-known passage in T.S. Eliot's *The Waste Land.*

5 Sweets to the sweet, farewell!
   Gertrude in *Hamlet*, 5.1.243

   Scattering flowers on the corpse of Ophelia.

6 Fare thee well, great heart!
   Prince Hal in *Henry IV, Part 1*, 5.4.87

   His farewell to the dead Hotspur.

7 What, old acquaintance! could not
   all this flesh
   Keep in a little life? Poor Jack,
   farewell!
   I could have better spared a better
   man.
   Prince Hal in *Henry IV, Part 1*,
   5.4.102–4

   He finds Falstaff pretending to be dead.

8 Well, fare thee well. I have known
   thee these twenty-nine years, come
   peascod-time, but an honester and
   truer-hearted man—well, fare thee
   well.
   Mistress Quickly in *Henry IV, Part 2*,
   2.4.382–4

   "Peascod-time" is in summer, when pea-pods
   are harvested.

9 Yet now farewell, and farewell life
   with thee!
   Queen Margaret in *Henry VI, Part 2*,
   3.2.356

   Bidding farewell to her banished lover, the
   Duke of Suffolk.

10 Farewell? A long farewell to all my
   greatness.
   This is the state of man; today he
   puts forth
   The tender leaves of hopes, tomorrow blossoms,

And bears his blushing honors thick upon him:
The third day comes a frost, a killing frost,
And when he thinks, good easy man, full surely
His greatness is a-ripening, nips his root,
And then he falls as I do.

Cardinal Wolsey in *Henry VIII*, 3.2.351–8

Wolsey's famous soliloquy, bidding farewell to his power.

11 Whether we shall meet again I know not.
Therefore our everlasting farewell take.

Brutus in *Julius Caesar*, 5.1.114–15

Saying farewell to Cassius.

12 Thus Kent, O princes, bids you all adieu;
He'll shape his old course in a country new.

Kent in *King Lear*, 1.1.186–7

13 Fair thoughts and happy hours attend on you!

Lorenzo in *The Merchant of Venice*, 3.4.41

Saying farewell to Portia as she sets off for Venice.

14   O, now for ever
Farewell the tranquil mind, farewell content,
Farewell the plumèd troops and the big wars
That makes ambition virtue! O, farewell!

Othello in *Othello*, 3.3.347–50

Jealousy in love destroys Othello as a soldier.

15 Once more, adieu. The rest let sorrow say.

King Richard in *Richard II*, 5.1.102

Bidding farewell to his Queen as they are separated.

16 Sleep dwell upon thine eyes, peace in thy breast.

Romeo in *Romeo and Juliet*, 2.2.186

To Juliet as she goes in from her window.

17 But that a joy past joy calls out on me,
It were a grief, so brief to part with thee.

Romeo in *Romeo and Juliet*, 3.3.173–4

On leaving Friar Lawrence to go to Juliet.

18   It is so very late that we
May call it early by and by. Good night.

Capulet in *Romeo and Juliet*, 3.4.34–5

Dismissing Paris, who has been waiting in hopes of seeing Juliet.

19   Eyes, look your last.
Arms, take your last embrace, and lips, O you
The doors of breath, seal with a righteous kiss
A dateless bargain to engrossing death.

Romeo in *Romeo and Juliet*, 5.3.112–15

Kissing Juliet before drinking the apothecary's poison; "engrossing" = 1. taking all; 2. preparing the contract or "bargain."

20 The gentleness of all the gods go with thee!

Antonio in *Twelfth Night*, 2.1.44

Bidding farewell to his friend Sebastian.

21 Farewell, thou art too dear for my
possessing,
And like enough thou know'st thy
estimate;
The charter of thy worth gives thee
releasing;
My bonds in thee are all determinate.

Sonnet 87, 1–4

On the superior wealth and status of the loved
one, who knows his worth ("estimate"), and
through the privilege ("charter") of his standing is released from the obligations ("bonds")
of love, which have expired; the imagery is
drawn from legal terms.

Farming

1 All her husbandry doth lie on
heaps,
Corrupting in its own fertility.
Burgundy in *Henry V*, 5.2.39–40

"Husbandry" = cultivation; French farms are
overgrown with noxious weeds because of
war.

2 The even mead, that erst brought
sweetly forth
The freckled cowslip, burnet, and
green clover,
Wanting the scythe, all uncor-
rected, rank,
Conceives by idleness, and nothing
teems
But hateful docks, rough thistles,
kecksies, burrs,
Losing both beauty and utility.
Burgundy in *Henry V*, 5.2.48–53

Describing France as overgrown with weeds
instead of flowers, as a result of war.

Fashion (see also Clothing)

1 Thou art not for the fashion of
these times,
When none will sweat but for promotion.
Orlando in *As You Like It*, 2.3.59–62

2 The glass of fashion and the mold
of form,
Th' observed of all observers.
Ophelia in *Hamlet*, 3.1.153–4

Seeing Hamlet as a mirror ("glass") by which
fashion is measured, and a pattern ("mold") of
the perfect courtier.

3 He was indeed the glass
Wherein the noble youth did dress
themselves.
Lady Percy in *Henry IV, Part 2*, 2.3.21–2

"Glass" = mirror; everyone imitated the fashion of Hotspur.

4 He was the mark and glass, copy
and book,
That fashioned others.
Lady Percy in *Henry IV, Part 2*, 2.3.31–2

On Hotspur as the ideal others sought to imitate; "mark" = target, aim; "glass" = mirror.

5 New customs,
Though they be never so ridiculous
(Nay, let 'em be unmanly) yet are
followed.
Lord Sands in *Henry VIII*, 1.3.2–4

On new fashions imported from France.

6 Thou art a lady;
If only to go warm were gorgeous,

Why, nature needs not what thou
gorgeous wear'st,
Which scarcely keeps thee warm.

King Lear in *King Lear*, 2.4.267–70

Speaking to his daughter Regan.

7   A man in all the world's new fashion planted,
That hath a mint of phrases in his
brain.
One who the music of his own vain
tongue
Doth ravish like enchanting harmony.

**King of Navarre in *Love's Labor's Lost*,
1.1.164–7**

Commenting on Armado and his extravagant
language.

8   I see that the fashion wears out
more apparel than the man.

**Conrade in *Much Ado About Nothing*,
3.3.139–40**

Changes in fashion often cause people to dis-
card clothing before it is worn out.

9   Report of fashions in proud Italy,
Whose manners still our tardy,
apish nation
Limps after in base imitation.

York in *Richard II*, 22.21–3

Accusing the English of being belatedly imita-
tive ("apish") of Italian fashions.

10   Old fashions please me best.

**Bianca in *The Taming of the Shrew*,
3.1.80**

11   One touch of nature makes the
whole world kin,
That all, with one consent, praise
new-born gauds,

Though they are made and molded
of things past,
And give to dust that is a little gilt
More laud than gilt o'erdusted;
The present eye praises the present
object.

**Ulysses in *Troilus and Cressida*,
3.3.175–80**

Appealing to the way human nature makes
everyone eager to follow new fashions; he is
trying to persuade Achilles to return to the
battlefield; "gauds" = trifles; "laud" = praise.

Fate (see also Necessity)

1   My fate cries out,
And makes each petty artery in this
body
As hardy as the Nemean lion's
nerve.

Hamlet in *Hamlet*, 1.4.81–3

Desperately trying, against his companions'
persuasion, to follow his father's ghost;
"Nemean lion" = slain by Hercules as one of
his twelve labors; "nerve" = sinew.

2   Our wills and fates do so contrary
run
That our devices still are overthrown.

Player King in *Hamlet*, 3.2.211–2

3   O God, that one might read the
book of fate,
And see the revolution of the times
Make mountains level, and the con-
tinent,
Weary of solid firmness, melt itself
Into the sea.

**King Henry in *Henry IV, Part 2*,
3.1.45–9**

Gloomily expecting one calamity after
another.

4   What fates impose, that men must
     needs abide;
     It boots not to resist both wind and
     tide.

King Edward in _Henry VI, Part 3_,
4.3.58–9

He has been taken prisoner by Warwick and
Somerset; "boots" = helps.

5   Men at some time are masters of
     their fates.

Cassius in _Julius Caesar_, 1.2.139

Urging Brutus to take action against Caesar.

6   What can be avoided
     Whose end is purposed by the
     mighty gods?

Caesar in _Julius Caesar_, 2.2.26–7

He refuses to be swayed by his wife's fears of
portents and predictions.

7   Who can control his fate?

Othello in _Othello_, 5.2.265

Accepting that he must die, though he has
made his own "fate" in murdering Desdemona.

Fatness

1   Falstaff sweats to death,
     And lards the lean earth as he walks
     along.

Prince Hal in _Henry IV, Part 1_,
2.2.108–9

"Lards" = covers in grease.

2   How now, my sweet creature of
     bombast, how long is't ago, Jack,
     since thou sawest thine own knee?

Prince Hal in _Henry IV, Part 1_,
2.4.326–8

To Falstaff; "bombast" = cotton padding.

3   A goodly portly man, i'faith, and a
     corpulent, of a cheerful look, a
     pleasing eye, and a most noble car-
     riage.

Falstaff in _Henry IV, Part 1_, 2.4.422–4

Under cover of playing King Henry IV, he
describes himself in flattering terms; "portly" =
stately; "carriage" = bearing.

4   That trunk of humors, that bolting-
     hutch of beastliness, that swollen
     parcel of dropsies, that huge bom-
     bard of sack, that stuffed cloak-bag
     of guts, that roasted Manningtree
     ox with the pudding in his belly.

Prince Hal in _Henry IV, Part 1_,
2.4.449–53

Describing Falstaff; "bolting-hutch" = flour
bin; "bombard" = leather wine vessel; "Man-
ningtree" = a town in Essex.

5   There's no room for faith, truth,
     nor honesty in this bosom of thine;
     it is all filled up with guts and
     midriff.

Prince Hal in _Henry IV, Part 1_,
3.3.153–5

Another comment on Falstaff.

Faults

1   A man who is the abstract of all
     faults
     That all men follow.

**Octavius Caesar in _Antony and
Cleopatra_, 1.4.9–10**

Commenting on Antony.

2   His taints and honors
Waged equal with him.

Maecenas in *Antony and Cleopatra*,
5.1.30–1

Another, more fair, assessment of Antony;
"taints" = faults.

3   A rarer spirit never
Did steer humanity; but you gods
     will give us
Some faults to make us men.

Agrippa in *Antony and Cleopatra*,
5.1.31–3

A kinder comment on Antony, after his death.

4   *Jaques.* The worst fault you have is
     to be in love.
Orlando. 'Tis a fault I will not
     change for your best virtue.

As You Like It, 3.2.282–4

5   Fie, 'tis a fault to heaven,
A fault against the dead, a fault to
     nature,
To reason most absurd, whose
     common theme
Is death of fathers, and who still
     hath cried,
From the first corse till he that died
     today,
"This must be so."

Claudius in *Hamlet*, 1.2.101–6

Trying to persuade Hamlet against persisting
in mourning for his father's death; "first corse"
= first corpse, Abel, murdered by his brother
Cain (Genesis 4).

6   The fault, dear Brutus, is not in our
     stars,
But in ourselves, that we are under-
     lings.

Cassius in *Julius Caesar*, 1.2.140–1

7   *Brutus.*   I do not like your
     faults.
Cassius. A friendly eye could never
     see such faults

Julius Caesar, 4.3.89–90

8   They say best men are molded out
     of faults,
And for the most, become much
     more the better
For being a little bad.

Mariana in *Measure for Measure*,
5.1.439–41

Speaking about Angelo, now her husband.

Fear

1   How now, Horatio? You tremble
     and look pale.
Is not this something more than
     fantasy?

Barnardo in *Hamlet*, 1.1.53–4

The skeptical Horatio has seen the ghost; "fantasy" = imagination.

2   What, frighted with false fire?

Hamlet in *Hamlet*, 3.2.266

He thinks Claudius has taken fright at the play
they have been watching; "false fire" is the
flash produced by a blank shot or cartridge.

3   He that but fears the thing he
     would not know
Hath by instinct knowledge from
     others' eyes
That what he feared is chanced.

Northumberland in *Henry IV, Part 2*,
1.1.85–7

He is anticipating the news that his son, Hotspur, is dead; "is chanced" = has happened.

4 Of all base passions, fear is the most accursed.

Joan la Pucelle in *Henry VI, Part 1*, 5.2.18

5 True nobility is exempt from fear: More can I bear than you can execute.

Suffolk in *Henry VI, Part 2*, 4.1.129–30

Spoken as he is about to be beheaded.

6 Suspicion always haunts the guilty mind; The thief doth fear each bush an officer.

Richard of Gloucester in *Henry VI, Part 3*, 5.6.11–12

To Henry VI, who rightly fears Richard intends to kill him.

7 Would he were fatter! But I fear him not. Yet if my name were liable to fear, I do not know the man I should avoid So soon as that spare Cassius.

Caesar in *Julius Caesar*, 1.2.198–201

Caesar's name has become a symbol of domination, and seems to exist separately from the man.

8 Caesar should be a beast without a heart If he should stay at home today for fear.

Caesar in *Julius Caesar*, 2.2.42–3

In spite of bad omens, he is determined to go to the Capitol.

9 Who dares not stir by day must walk by night.

The Bastard Falconbridge in *King John*, 1.1.172

Suggesting that his unknown father begot him obscurely; he claims to be the bastard son of King Richard I, Richard Lionheart.

10 I find the people strangely fantasied, Possessed with rumors, full of idle dreams, Not knowing what they fear, but full of fear.

The Bastard Falconbridge in *King John*, 4.2.144–6

Reporting that people are full of strange fancies and pre-occupied with fearful rumors.

11 *Albany.* Well, you may fear too far. *Goneril.* Safer than trust too far.

King Lear, 1.4.328

12 Present fears Are less than horrible imaginings.

Macbeth in *Macbeth*, 1.3.137–8

"Present" as contrasted with what may happen in the future.

13 When our actions do not, Our fears do make us traitors.

Lady Macduff in *Macbeth*, 4.2.3–4

She refers to her husband, who has fled to England.

14 I have almost forgot the taste of fears. The time has been, my senses would have cooled To hear a night-shriek, and my fell of hair Would at a dismal treatise rouse and stir

As life were in't. I have supped full
with horrors;
Direness, familiar to my slaughter-
ous thoughts,
Cannot once start me.

Macbeth in *Macbeth*, 5.5.9–15

Macbeth has destroyed his capacity to feel
emotion; "my fell" = my skin covered in hair,
or all my hair; "dismal treatise" = horror story.

15   I have a faint cold fear thrills
through my veins,
That almost freezes up the heat of
life.

Juliet in *Romeo and Juliet*, 4.3.15–16

She is afraid to drink the opiate Friar
Lawrence has given her.

16   Blind fear that seeing reason leads
finds safer footing than blind reason stumbling without fear. To
fear the worst oft cures the worst.

Cressida in *Troilus and Cressida*,
3.2.71–3

The last phrase is proverbial. She is expressing anxiety about accepting Troilus as her
lover.

Feasts

1   This is not yet an Alexandrian feast.

Pompey in *Antony and Cleopatra*,
2.7.96

A Roman feast proves less of an orgy than one
in Alexandria, Egypt.

2   Come,
Let's have one other gaudy night.

Antony in *Antony and Cleopatra*,
3.13.181–2

Calling, in defeat, for one more night of feasting (certain college feasts in Oxford and Cambridge are still called a "gaudy").

3   Small cheer and great welcome
makes a merry feast.

Balthazar in *The Comedy of Errors*,
3.1.26

Proverbial.

4   Let me see, what am I to buy for
our sheep-shearing feast? Three
pound of sugar, five pound of cur-
rants, rice—what will this sister of
mine do with rice? But my father
hath made her mistress of the feast,
and she lays it on.

Clown in *The Winter's Tale*, 4.3.36–40

"Lays it on" = does it thoroughly; the midsummer sheep-shearing feast celebrated country-
wide with festivity.

Fellowship (see also Society)

1   Watch tonight, pray tomorrow.
Gallants, lads, boys, hearts of gold,
all the titles of good fellowship
come to you!

Falstaff in *Henry IV, Part 1*, 2.4.277–9

Happy in the prospect of a night's festivity
("watch" = stay awake).

2   We few, we happy few, we band of
brothers.
For he today that sheds his blood
with me
Shall be my brother.

King Henry in *Henry V*, 4.3.60–2

Encouraging his soldiers before the battle of
Agincourt.

3   Misery acquaints a man with strange bedfellows.

Trinculo in *The Tempest*, 2.2.39–40

Creeping under Caliban's cloak to shelter from a storm.

4   Fellowship in woe doth woe assuage.

***The Rape of Lucrece*, 790**

Lucrece broods alone after being raped by Tarquin.

Festivals

1   Some say that ever 'gainst that season comes
Wherein our Savior's birth is celebrated,
This bird of dawning singeth all night long,
And then they say no spirit dare stir abroad,
The nights are wholesome, then no planets strike,
No fairy takes, nor witch hath power to charm,
So hallowed, and so gracious, is that time.

Marcellus in *Hamlet*, 1.1.158–64

The bird of dawning is the cock; planets were thought to exert malign influence, and fairies to bewitch people.

2   Tomorrow is Saint Valentine's Day,
All in the morning betime,
And I a maid at your window,
To be your Valentine.

Ophelia in *Hamlet*, 4.5.48–51

Singing in her madness after her father's death.

3   This day is called the Feast of Crispian.
He that outlives this day and comes safe home
Will stand a-tiptoe when this day is named
And rouse him at the name of Crispian.

King Henry in *Henry V*, 4.3.40–3

October 25th was the feast of St. Crispian, a legendary Roman martyr, and patron saint of shoemakers; "safe home" = to England.

4   He that shall see this day and live old age
Will yearly on the vigil feast his neighbors
And say, "Tomorrow is Saint Crispian."

King Henry in *Henry V*, 4.3.44–6

October 25th, the day the battle of Agincourt was fought.

5   No doubt they rose up early to observe
The rite of May.

Theseus in *A Midsummer Night's Dream*, 4.1.132–3

May Day festivities in England involved going to woods to gather flowers and bring them, as symbolic of new life, into towns and villages (the play is nominally set in Greece).

Fighting (see also Soldiers, War)

1   To the latter end of a fray and the beginning of a feast
Fits a dull fighter and a keen guest.

Falstaff in *Henry IV, Part 1*, 4.2.79–80

He prefers feasting to fighting; "fray" = battle.

2 Lay on, Macduff,
And damned be him that first cries,
"Hold, enough!"
Macbeth in *Macbeth*, 5.8.33–4

Macbeth's last words, as Macduff kills him in their fight.

3 You dare easier be friends with me than fight with mine enemy.
Beatrice in *Much Ado About Nothing*, 4.1.298–9

To Benedick, who hesitates at the idea of killing his friend Claudio.

4 Keep up your bright swords, for the dew will rust them.
Othello in *Othello*, 1.2.59

Preventing by his calm authority a fight between his supporters and those of Brabantio, who thinks Othello has stolen away his daughter Desdemona.

5 Were it my cue to fight, I should have known it
Without a prompter.
Othello in *Othello*, 1.2.83–4

Speaking as a soldier.

Fire

1 A little fire is quickly trodden out,
Which, being suffered, rivers cannot quench.
Clarence in *Henry VI, Part 3*, 4.8.7–8

"Being suffered" = being unchecked, allowed to grow.

2 Those that with haste will make a mighty fire
Begin it with weak straws.
Cassius in *Julius Caesar*, 1.3.107–8

Meaning that a huge conflagration can quickly be started with a few worthless straws (and so may a revolution be begun from nothing).

3 Tut, man, one fire burns out another's burning,
One pain is lessened by another's anguish.
Benvolio in *Romeo and Juliet*, 1.2.45–6

On Romeo's unrequited love for Rosaline; varying the proverb, "one fire drives out another."

4 Where two raging fires meet together,
They do consume the thing that feeds their fury.
Though little fire grows great with little wind,
Yet extreme gusts will blow out fire and all.
Petruchio in *The Taming of the Shrew*, 2.1.132–5

This is how he sees his relationship with Katherine, the shrew.

5 The fire i'the flint
Shows not till it be struck.
Poet in *Timon of Athens*, 1.1.22–3

Fish

1 *Third Fisherman.* I marvel how the fishes live in the sea.
First Fisherman. Why, as men do a-land: the great ones eat up the little ones.
Pericles, 2.1.26–9

2   A fish, he smells like a fish; a very
    ancient and fish-like smell.
    Trinculo in *The Tempest*, 2.2.25–6
    Finding a strange creature (Caliban) on Pros-
    pero's island.

Fishing

1   Give me mine angle, we'll to the
    river; there,
    My music playing far off, I will
    betray
    Tawny-finned fishes; my bended
    hook shall pierce
    Their slimy jaws; and as I draw
    them up,
    I'll think them every one an
    Antony,
    And say, "Ah, ha! y'are caught."
    Cleopatra in *Antony and Cleopatra*,
    2.5.10–15
    Imagining getting her hooks into Antony, as
    we now say; an "angle" is a fishing rod and
    line.

2   The pleasant'st angling is to see the
    fish
    Cut with her golden oars the silver
    stream,
    And greedily devour the treacher-
    ous bait.
    Ursula in *Much Ado About Nothing*,
    3.1.26–8
    "Oars" = fins.

3   Here's a fish hangs in the net like a
    poor man's right in the law; 'twill
    hardly come out.
    Second Fisherman in *Pericles*,
    2.1.116–18

Fitness

1   Now bid me run,
    And I will strive with things impos-
        sible,
    Yea, get the better of them.
    Ligarius in *Julius Caesar*, 2.1.324–6
    Though sick, Ligarius joins the conspirators
    against Caesar.

Flattery

1   Why should the poor be
    flattered?
    No, let the candied tongue lick
    absurd pomp,
    And crook the pregnant hinges of
    the knee
    Where thrift may follow fawning.
    Hamlet in *Hamlet*, 3.2 59–60
    Praising Horatio: "pregnant" = pliant, readily
    bending; "thrift" = profit.

2   Why, what a candy deal of courtesy
    This fawning greyhound then did
        proffer me!
    Hotspur in *Henry IV, Part 1*, 1.3.251–2
    Henry IV once needed the help of Hotspur to
    regain his rights; "candy deal" = sugary quan-
    tity.

3   There is flattery in friendship.
    Constable in *Henry V*, 3.7.114–15

4   When I tell him he hates flatterers,
    He says he does, being then most
        flattered.
    Decius in *Julius Caesar*, 2.1.207–8
    Speaking of Julius Caesar.

5   They told me I was everything. 'Tis
    a lie, I am not ague-proof.

    King Lear in *King Lear,* 4.6.104–5

    "They" are flattering courtiers; "ague-proof" =
    immune to fever.

6   He does me double wrong
    That wounds me with the flatteries
    of his tongue.

    King Richard in *Richard II,* 3.2.215–6

    "Double wrong" in deceiving and in raising
    false hopes.

7   He that loves to be flattered is wor-
    thy o'the flatterer.

    Apemantus in *Timon of Athens,*
    1.1.226–7

8   O that men's ears should be
    To counsel deaf, but not to flattery!

    Apemantus in *Timon of Athens,*
    1.2.249–50

    On Timon, who refuses to listen to his good
    advice.

9   Most smiling, smooth, detested
    parasites,
    Courteous destroyers, affable
    wolves, meek bears,
    You fools of fortune, trencher-
    friends, time's flies.

    Timon in *Timon of Athens,* 3.6.94–6

    Cursing his former friends; "fools of fortune" =
    playthings at the mercy of fortune; "flies"
    come in summer and disappear in winter.

Flowers

1   A violet in the youth of primy
    nature,

    Forward, not permanent, sweet, not
    lasting.

    Laertes in *Hamlet,* 1.3.7–8

    Describing Hamlet's love as expressed to
    Ophelia; "primy" = in its prime, in the spring.

2   There's rosemary, that's for
    remembrance; pray you, love,
    remember. And there is pansies,
    that's for thoughts.

    Ophelia in *Hamlet,* 4.5.175–7

    In her madness, handing out flowers; these
    meanings are traditional.

3   O that this blossom could be kept
    from cankers!

    Poins in *Henry IV, Part 2,* 2.2.94–5

    Referring to Falstaff's boy; "cankers" = corrup-
    tion, from canker-worms that eat into blos-
    soms.

4   I pluck this pale and maiden blos-
    som here.

    Vernon in *Henry VI, Part 1,* 2.4.47

    Plucking a white rose, the badge of the faction
    of York.

5   Yet marked I where the bolt of
    Cupid fell:
    It fell upon a little western flower,
    Before, milk-white; now purple
    with love's wound:
    And maidens call it "love-in-idle-
    ness."

    Oberon in *A Midsummer Night's
    Dream,* 2.1.165–8

    Describing how the arrow ("bolt") of Cupid
    falls on the pansy, and stains it the color of
    blood.

6   I know a bank where the wild
    thyme blows,
    Where oxlips and the nodding vio-
    let grows,
    Quite overcanopied with luscious
    woodbine,
    With sweet musk-roses, and with
    eglantine:
    There sleeps Titania sometime of
    the night,
    Lulled in these flowers with dances
    and delight.

    **Oberon in *A Midsummer Night's
    Dream*, 2.1.249–54**

    Describing the nighttime bower of the Queen
    of the Fairies; the flowers include scented wild
    roses and sweet-briar ("eglantine"), and all
    grow wild in the English countryside.

7   Who are the violets now
    That strew the green lap of the new-
    come spring?

    Duchess of York in *Richard II*, 5.2.46–7

    Asking her son Aumerle to tell her who is in
    favor with the new king, Henry IV.

8   Away before me to sweet beds of
    flowers.
    Love-thoughts lie rich when
    canopied with bowers.

    Orsino in *Twelfth Night*, 1.1.39–40

    Lovesick for Olivia, who has no interest in
    him.

9   There's rosemary and rue. These
    keep
    Seeming and savor all the winter
    long.
    Grace and remembrance be to you.

    Perdita in *The Winter's Tale*, 4.4.74–6

    Rosemary was an emblem of remembrance,
    and rue, or "herb grace," of repentance; she
    gives them to Polixenes and Camillo.

10 The year growing ancient,
    Not yet on summer's death, nor on
    the birth
    Of trembling winter, the fairest
    flowers o'the season
    Are our carnations and streaked
    gillyvors.

    Perdita in *The Winter's Tale*, 4.4.79–82

    "Gillyvors" are a kind of carnation or pink.

11   Here's flowers for you:
    Hot lavender, mints, savory, marjo-
    ram,
    The marigold, that goes to bed
    wi'the sun,
    And with him rises, weeping.

    Perdita in *The Winter's Tale*, 4.4.103–6

    Giving "hot" flowers to Polixenes and Camillo
    as appropriate to older men, perhaps as
    restorative in some way.

12   Daffodils,
    That come before the swallow
    dares, and take
    The winds of March with beauty.

    Perdita in *The Winter's Tale*, 4.4.118–20

    Perdita wishes for flowers to express her love
    for Florizel.

13   Pale primroses,
    That die unmarried ere they can
    behold
    Bright Phoebus in his strength.

    Perdita in *The Winter's Tale*, 4.4.122–4

    Spring flowers that do not live to see the sun
    ("Phoebus") at full strength in the summer.

14 The summer's flower is to the sum-
    mer sweet
    Though to itself it only live and die,
    But if that flower with base infec-
    tion meet,

The basest weed outbraves his dignity:
For sweetest things turn sourest
by their deeds;
Lilies that fester smell far worse
than weeds.

Sonnet 94, 9–14

The last line has become proverbial; "it only
live and die" = it lives and dies alone; "outbraves his dignity" = exceeds its worth
(though "his" points to the real subject, the
unfaithful lover).

Folly

1 The triple pillar of the world transformed
Into a strumpet's fool.

Philo in *Antony and Cleopatra*,
1.1.12–13

Antony, one of the three rulers of the Roman
Empire, unflatteringly described before we
meet him and Cleopatra.

2   I see still
A diminution in our captain's brain
Restores his heart.

Enobarbus in *Antony and Cleopatra*,
3.13.196–8

Pointing to Antony's folly thinking he can still
beat Octavius; "heart" = courage.

3 In everything the purpose must
weigh with the folly.

Prince Hal in *Henry IV, Part 2*,
2.2.175–6

Meaning that folly may be justified if the purpose is good.

4 I will keep where there is wit stirring, and leave the faction of fools.

Thersites in *Troilus and Cressida*,
2.1.118–19

Parting from Achilles and Ajax.

5 Alas, 'tis true, I have gone here and
there,
And made myself a motley to the
view,
Gored mine own thoughts, sold
cheap what is most dear,
Made old affections of offenses
new.

Sonnet 110, 1–4

The speaker has made a fool of himself (a
motley coat was the dress of the professional
fool), wounded ("gored") his own self-esteem,
and offended against old friendships by his
choice of new ones.

Food (see also Cooking, Eating)

1   Now I feed myself
With most delicious poison.

Cleopatra in *Antony and Cleopatra*,
1.5.26–7

Imagining the absent Antony.

2   Epicurean cooks
Sharpen with cloyless sauce his
appetite.

Pompey in *Antony and Cleopatra*,
2.1.24–5

Imagining Antony's luxurious idling in Egypt.

3 I found you as a morsel, cold upon
Dead Caesar's trencher.

Antony in *Antony and Cleopatra*,
3.13.116–17

Referring to Cleopatra's past affair with Julius
Caesar.

4 Truly, thou art damned, like an ill-roasted egg, all on one side.

Touchstone in *As You Like It*, 3.2.37–8

Part of a sophistical argument that Corin is damned for not being at court.

5 Sweetest nut hath sourest rind.

Touchstone in *As You Like It*, 3.2.155–7

Mocking Rosalind as sweet and sour.

6 Thrift, thrift, Horatio, the funeral baked meats
Did coldly furnish forth the marriage tables.

Hamlet in *Hamlet*, 1.2.180–1

In reply to Horatio's acknowledgment that Hamlet's mother's marriage took place very soon after her first husband's death; "coldly" = when cold.

7 What's a joint of mutton or two in a whole Lent?

Mistress Quickly in *Henry IV, Part 2*, 2.4.346–7

No meat was supposed to be eaten in the whole six weeks of Lent before Easter.

8 This making of Christians will raise the price of hogs. If we grow all to be pork-eaters, we shall not shortly have a rasher on the coals for money.

Launcelot Gobbo in *The Merchant of Venice*, 3.5.23–6

Referring to the conversion of Jessica, Shylock's daughter, to Christianity.

9 I will make an end of my dinner; there's pippins and cheese to come.

Evans in *The Merry Wives of Windsor*, 1.2.11–13

Apples and cheese round off the meal.

10 A surfeit of the sweetest things
The deepest loathing to the stomach brings.

Lysander in *A Midsummer Night's Dream*, 2.2.137–8

Finding he now hates his earlier love, Hermia.

11 Feed him with apricots and dewberries,
With purple grapes, green figs, and mulberries.

Titania in *A Midsummer Night's Dream*, 3.1.166–7

Infatuated with Bottom, she tells her fairies to indulge him.

12 Good Master Mustardseed, I know your patience well. That same cowardly, giant-like ox-beef hath devoured many a gentleman of your house. I promise you, your kindred hath made my eyes water ere now.

Bottom in *A Midsummer Night's Dream*, 3.1.191–5

Addressing one of Titania's fairies.

13 Come, thou shalt go home, and we'll have flesh for holidays, fish for fasting-days, and moreover puddings and flap-jacks, and thou shalt be welcome.

First Fisherman in *Pericles*, 2.1.80–3

The fisherman takes pity on the shipwrecked Pericles; "flap-jacks" = pancakes.

14 What say you to a piece of beef and mustard?

Grumio in *The Taming of the Shrew*, 4.3.23

Teasing Katherine, who is being denied anything to eat.

15 Though the chameleon love can feed on the air, I am one that am nourished by my victuals, and would fain have meat.

Speed in *Two Gentlemen of Verona*, 2.1.172–4

"Fain" = gladly.

Foolery

1   Being fooled, by foolery thrive;
There's place and means for every man alive.

Parolles in *All's Well That Ends Well*, 4.3.339

Shown up as a fool, he hopes to live by fooling others.

2 There was more foolery yet, if I could remember it.

Casca in *Julius Caesar*, 1.2.287

Reporting to Cassius what happened when Caesar addressed the people of Rome.

3 Foolery, sir, does walk about the orb like the sun, it shines everywhere.

Feste in *Twelfth Night*, 3.1.38–9

To Cesario (Viola in disguise), varying the proverb, "the sun shines on all alike"; "foolery" is Feste's profession, but also = foolish behavior.

4 More matter for a May morning.

Fabian in *Twelfth Night*, 3.4.142

That is, fit for May Day sports; Sir Andrew has arrived with his absurd challenge to Cesario.

Fools

1 A fool, a fool! I met a fool i' the forest,
A motley fool.

Jaques in *As You Like It*, 2.7.12–13

Delighted to encounter Touchstone, the professional fool.

2 Motley's the only wear.

Jaques in *As You Like It*, 2.7.34

"Motley" was the costume of a professional fool.

3   O that I were a fool!
I am ambitious for a motley coat.

Jaques in *As You Like It*, 2.7.42–3

"Motley," usually a parti-colored coat, was worn by the professional fool.

4 *Jaques.* I was seeking for a fool when I found you.
Orlando. He is drowned in the brook; look but in, and you shall see him.

As You Like It, 3.2.285–8

The lover Orlando wittily puts down the melancholy Jaques.

5 The fool doth think he is wise, but the wise man knows himself to be a fool.

Touchstone in *As You Like It*, 5.1.31–2

Echoing such biblical injunctions as that at I Corinthians 3:18, "If any man among you seemeth to be wise in this world, let him become a fool, that he may be wise."

6 Here comes a pair of very strange beasts, which in all tongues are called fools.

Jaques in *As You Like It*, 5.4.36–8

Referring to Touchstone and Audrey.

7 A fool's bolt is soon shot.

Orleans in *Henry V*, 3.7.122

Proverbial; a fool lets fly with his arrow ("bolt") too soon.

8 *Lear.* Dost thou call me fool, boy?
Fool. All thy other titles thou hast given away; that thou wast born with.

King Lear, 1.4.148–50

On King Lear, who has given away his kingdom to his daughters.

9 Shall we their fond pageant see?
Lord, what fools these mortals be!

Puck in *A Midsummer Night's Dream*, 3.2.114–5

Watching the quarrels of the lovers; "fond" = both foolish and affectionate.

10 Why, my cheese, my digestion, why hast thou not served thyself in to my table, so many meals?

Achilles in *Troilus and Cressida*, 2.3.41–2

Pleased to have Thersites attending on him as a scurrilous jester.

11 Better a witty fool than a foolish wit.

Feste in *Twelfth Night*, 1.5.36

Feste is a witty professional fool; "wit" = understanding or intelligence.

12 *Feste.* Beshrew me, the knight's in admirable fooling.
Sir Andrew Aguecheek. Ay, he does well enough if he be disposed, and so do I, too. He does it with a better grace, but I do it more natural.

Twelfth Night, 2.3.80–3

The "knight" is the witty Sir Toby Belch; Sir Andrew does it more naturally because he is a "natural," a born fool.

13 She will keep no fool, sir, till she be married, and fools are as like husbands as pilchards are to herrings— the husband's the bigger.

Feste in *Twelfth Night*, 3.1.33–5

Referring to Olivia; "pilchards," small fish, are common off European coasts.

14 I am indeed not her fool, but her corrupter of words.

Feste in *Twelfth Night*, 3.1.35–6

Referring to his function in relation to the Lady Olivia.

15 This fellow is wise enough to play the fool,
And to do that well craves a kind of wit.
He must observe their mood on whom he jests,
The quality of persons, and the time,
Not, like the haggard, check at every feather
That comes before his eye. This is a practice
As full of labor as a wise man's art.

Viola in *Twelfth Night*, 3.1.60–6

Recognizing that the Fool (Feste) may be wise; "quality" = rank or nature; a "haggard" was an untrained hawk.

Forbearance

1 Be angry when you will, it shall
have scope.
Do what you will, dishonor shall be
humor.

Brutus in *Julius Caesar*, 4.3.108–9

To Cassius, patching their quarrel by giving
his anger free rein ("scope"), and humoring
his questionable conduct.

2 Have you not love enough to bear
with me,
When that rash humor which my
mother gave me
Makes me forgetful?

Cassius in *Julius Caesar*, 4.3.119–21

To Brutus; "rash humor" = hasty temper.

3 Bear with me, good boy, I am much
forgetful.

Brutus in *Julius Caesar*, 4.3.255

To his servant Lucius.

Foreboding (see also Portents)

1 *Messenger.*   But yet, madam—
Cleopatra. I do not like "but yet."

***Antony and Cleopatra*, 2.5.49–50**

Heralding unwelcome news that Antony is
married.

2 *Francisco.* For this relief much
thanks. 'Tis bitter cold,
And I am sick at heart.

Barnardo. Have you had quiet
guard?
Francisco. Not a mouse stirring.

Hamlet, 1.1.8–10

Francisco's sense of foreboding ("I am sick at
heart") establishes right away the atmosphere
of the play.

3 In the gross and scope of mine
opinion,
This bodes some strange eruption
to our state.

Horatio in *Hamlet*, 1.1.68–9

This appearance of the ghost foretells some
political upheaval; "gross and scope" = general drift.

4 A mote it is to trouble the mind's
eye.

Horatio in *Hamlet*, 1.1.112

On the disturbing appearance of the ghost of
Hamlet's father.

5 My father's spirit in arms! All is
not well.
I doubt some foul play. Would the
night were come!
Till then sit still, my soul. Foul
deeds will rise,
Though all the earth o'erwhelm
them, to men's eyes.

Hamlet in *Hamlet*, 1.2.254–7

Left alone now he knows about the ghost,
Hamlet plans to watch for it that night; compare the proverb, "murder will out."

6 Thou wouldst not think how ill all's
here about my heart—but it is no
matter.

Hamlet in *Hamlet*, 5.2.212–13

Just before the fencing-match with Laertes.

7 *Portia.* Why, know'st thou any
harm's intended towards him?
Soothsayer. None that I know will
be, much that I fear may chance.
Julius Caesar, 2.4.31–2

The soothsayer fears for Caesar.

8   O that a man might know
The end of this day's business ere it
come!
Brutus in Julius Caesar, 5.1.122–3

Before the battle of Philippi.

9   The raven himself is hoarse
That croaks the fatal entrance of
Duncan
Under my battlements.
Lady Macbeth in Macbeth, 1.5.38–40

The croaking of the raven proverbially fore-
shadowed misfortune or death.

10 There is some ill a-brewing towards
my rest,
For I did dream of money-bags
tonight.
Shylock in The Merchant of Venice,
2.5.17–18

11   O, it comes o'er my memory
As doth the raven o'er the infected
house,
Boding to all!
Othello in Othello, 4.1.20–2

Recalling the handkerchief he thinks Desdemona gave Cassio; the raven proverbially
foreboded bad luck or death.

12   Methinks
Some unborn sorrow, ripe in fortune's womb,

Is coming towards me, and my
inward soul
With nothing trembles.
Queen in Richard II, 2.2.9–12

Anticipating the fall of Richard.

13 *Richard.*   Give me a calendar.
Who saw the sun today?
Ratcliffe.   Not I, my lord.
Richard. Then he disdains to shine,
for by the book
He should have braved the east an
hour ago.
A black day will it be to somebody.
Richard III, 5.3.276–80

Before the Battle of Bosworth; it turns out to
be a black day for Richard, who is killed by
Richmond.

Forgetfulness

1 O, my oblivion is a very Antony,
And I am all forgotten.
Cleopatra in Antony and Cleopatra,
1.3.90–1

Her forgetfulness (oblivion) is due to her preoccupation with Antony, so that she forgets
herself, and at the same time implies that he
forgets her in going to Rome.

2 Give me to drink mandragora. . . .
That I might sleep out this great
gap of time
My Antony is away.
Cleopatra in Antony and Cleopatra,
1.5.4, 5–6

An opiate Cleopatra desires to pass the time
while Antony is away.

3 Great thing of us forgot!
Albany in King Lear, 5.3.237

In the excitement of other events, he has forgotten to find out what has happened to Lear and Cordelia.

Forgiveness (see also Mercy)

1 Far from her nest the lapwing cries away;
My heart prays for him, though my tongue do curse.
Adriana in *The Comedy of Errors*, 4.2.27–8

On her husband, who, she thinks, is making love to her sister; the lapwing proverbially cries most when far from the nest.

2 The power that I have on you is to spare you;
The malice towards you, to forgive you. Live,
And deal with others better.
Posthumus in *Cymbeline*, 5.5.418–20

To Jachimo, after Jachimo's explanation of the way he deceived Posthumus.

3 What if this cursèd hand
Were thicker than itself with brother's blood,
Is there not rain enough in the sweet heavens
To wash it white as snow?
Claudius in *Hamlet*, 3.3.43–6

Claudius wishes he could be forgiven.

4 I as free forgive you
As I would be forgiven: I forgive all.
Buckingham in *Henry VIII*, 2.1.82–3

Speaking on his way to be executed.

5 Though with their high wrongs I am struck to the quick,
Yet with my nobler reason 'gainst my fury
Do I take part. The rarer action is
In virtue than in vengeance.
Prospero in *The Tempest*, 5.1.25–8

Abandoning thoughts of revenging himself on his enemies.

6 Do as the heavens have done, forget your evil;
With them, forgive yourself.
Cleomenes in *The Winter's Tale*, 5.1.5–6

Begging Leontes to forgive himself for causing, as he thinks, the death of his wife, Hermione.

Fortune (see also Chance)

1 I am a man whom Fortune hath cruelly scratched.
Parolles in *All's Well That Ends Well*, 5.2.26–7

Appealing for pity after being exposed as a liar and braggart.

2 Fortune knows
We scorn her most when most she offers blows.
Antony in *Antony and Cleopatra*, 3.11.73–4

3 Let us sit and mock the good huswife Fortune from her wheel, that her gifts may henceforth be bestowed equally.
Celia in *As You Like It*, 1.2.31–3

The goddess Fortune turns her wheel bringing both good and bad luck; Celia playfully refers to her as a housewife at a spinning wheel.

4 Fortune reigns in the gifts of the world, not in the lineaments of nature.

Rosalind in *As You Like It*, 1.2.41–2

Expressing the common idea that beauty and cleverness were thought of as given by nature, wealth and status by fortune.

5 Wear this for me: one out of suits with Fortune,
That could give more, but that her hand lacks means.

Rosalind in *As You Like It*, 1.2.246–7

Giving Orlando a chain; she is out of Fortune's favor because her father has been driven into exile.

6 Fortune brings in some boats that are not steered.

Pisanio in *Cymbeline*, 4.3.46

Putting his trust in chance.

7 A man that Fortune's buffets and rewards
Hast ta'en with equal thanks.

Hamlet in *Hamlet*, 3.2.67–8

Describing his friend Horatio.

8 Will Fortune never come with both hands full,
But write her fair words still in foulest terms?
She either gives a stomach and no food—
Such are the poor, in health; or else a feast
And takes away the stomach—such are the rich,
That have abundance and enjoy it not.

King Henry in *Henry IV, Part 2*, 4.4.105–8

Henry feels ill even as he receives good news.

9 Fortune is painted blind, with a muffler afore his eyes, to signify to you that Fortune is blind; and she is painted also with a wheel, to signify to you, which is the moral of it, that she is turning, and inconstant, and mutability, and variation; and her foot, look you, is fixed upon a spherical stone, which rolls and rolls and rolls.

Fluellen in *Henry V*, 3.6.30–6

Fluellen quaintly describes Fortune as the goddess was often represented, notably in emblem books.

10 Doth Fortune play the huswife with me now?

Pistol in *Henry V*, 5.1.80

"Huswife" = hussy; he complains that fortune is being fickle; proverbial.

11 Fortune is merry,
And in this mood will give us anything.

Mark Antony in *Julius Caesar*, 3.2.266–7

He has achieved his aim, to launch a civil war.

12 When Fortune means to men most good,
She looks upon them with a threatening eye.

Cardinal Pandulph in *King John*, 4.3.119–20

The French have been defeated, and the slippery Cardinal is encouraging the Dauphin to attack England.

13 A good man's fortune may grow out at heels.

Kent in *King Lear*, 2.2.157

"Out at heels" literally = threadbare, worn out; Kent is sitting in the stocks, so there's a bitter humor in his remark.

14 Fortune, good night; smile once
more, turn thy wheel.

Kent in *King Lear*, 2.2.173

Recalling the proverbs, "Fortune's wheel is ever turning," and "Fortune can both smile and frown."

15 He that has and a little tiny wit—
With heigh-ho, the wind and the rain—
Must make content with his fortunes fit,
Though the rain it raineth every day.

Fool in *King Lear*, 3.2.74–7

"Wit" = brain or intelligence; a spin-off from a song sung by Feste in *Twelfth Night*.

16 The wheel is come full circle.

Edmund in *King Lear*, 5.3.175

That is, fortune's wheel, ever turning.

17 So may I, blind fortune leading me,
Miss that which one unworthier
may attain,
And die with grieving.

Prince of Morocco in *The Merchant of Venice*, 2.1.36–8

Determined to take his chance in choosing among the caskets that will show whether he is to be Portia's husband; Fortune is proverbially blind.

18 Good fortune then!
To make me blest or cursed'st
among men.

Prince of Morocco in *The Merchant of Venice*, 2.1.45–6

He means he will be blessed if he chooses the right casket and wins Portia.

19 Well, if Fortune be a woman, she's
a good wench for this gear.

Launcelot Gobbo in *The Merchant of Venice*, 2.2.166–7

Fortune was depicted as a goddess; "gear" = business; Launcelot has the good fortune to be taken on as a servant by Bassanio.

20 Fortune now
To my heart's hope!

Prince of Aragon in *The Merchant of Venice*, 2.9.19–20

Hoping for good luck in choosing the right casket.

21 Herein Fortune shows herself more
kind
Than is her custom. It is still her
use
To let the wretched man outlive his
wealth,
To view with hollow eye and wrinkled brow
An age of poverty; from which lingering penance
Of such misery doth she cut me off.

Antonio in *The Merchant of Venice*, 4.1.267–72

Finding reasons to welcome the prospect of death.

22 If it be my luck, so; if not, happy
man be his dole.

Slender in *The Merry Wives of Windsor*, 3.4.64–5

On the possibility of marrying Anne Page; "dole" literally = lot; in effect he is saying, "good luck to him who wins her." The phrase is proverbial, and occurs also in *The Winter's Tale*, 1.2.163.

23   O Lady Fortune,
Stand you auspicious!

Perdita in *The Winter's Tale*, 4.4.51–2

Hoping nothing will prevent her marriage to
the prince, Florizel.

24 If I had a mind to be honest, I see
Fortune would not suffer me: she
drops booties in my mouth.

Autolycus in *The Winter's Tale*,
4.4.831–2

Thinking him a courtier, the Shepherds have
given him gold to conduct their business at
court.

Freedom

1   The fated sky
Gives us free scope, only doth backward pull
Our slow designs when we ourselves are dull.

Helena in *All's Well That Ends Well*,
1.1.217–9

Claiming, in effect, that she will have God on
her side in actively seeking a way to win
Bertram as a husband.

2   I must have liberty
Withal, as large a charter as the
wind,
To blow on whom I please.

Jaques in *As You Like It*, 2.7.47–8

He wants to be free to satirize everyone.

3 I had as lief not be as live to be
In awe of such a thing as I myself.

Cassius in *Julius Caesar*, 1.2.95–6

"As lief not be" = as soon not exist; he is
thinking of Caesar.

4 Liberty! Freedom! Tyranny is
dead!
Run hence, proclaim, cry it about
the streets!

Cinna in *Julius Caesar*, 3.1.78–9

After the assassination of Caesar.

5 Had you rather Caesar were living,
and die all slaves, than that Caesar
were dead, to live all free men?

Brutus in *Julius Caesar*, 3.2.22–24

Addressing the people after the death of
Caesar.

6 Liberty plucks justice by the nose.

Duke in *Measure for Measure*, 1.3.29

He means license, or too much freedom.

7 Thou shalt be as free
As mountain winds; but then
exactly do
All points of my command.

Prospero in *The Tempest*, 1.2.499–501

Promising Ariel his liberty, but demanding
obedience.

8 Freedom, high-day! high-day, freedom! freedom, high-day, freedom!

Caliban in *The Tempest*, 2.2.186–7

In fact Caliban is only exchanging one kind of
servitude, under Prospero, for another, under
Stephano and Trinculo.

9   Then to the elements
Be free, and fare thou well!

Prospero in *The Tempest*, 5.1.318–19

His final parting from his devoted spirit, Ariel.

Friendship

1   I cannot live out of her company.

Celia in *As You Like It*, 1.3.86

Referring to herself and her cousin Rosalind.

2   O! let me clip ye
In arms as sound as when I wooed, in heart
As merry as when our nuptial day was done
And tapers burnt to bedward!

Caius Martius, later Coriolanus, in *Coriolanus*, 1.6.29–32

Coriolanus seems happier embracing Cominius, his fellow commander, than his wife Virgilia.

3   Those friends thou hast, and their adoption tried,
Grapple them to thy soul with hoops of steel.

Polonius in *Hamlet*, 1.3.62–3

Advice to his son as he goes to live abroad; "their adoption tried" = their association with you tested.

4   In the beaten way of friendship, what make you at Elsinore?

Hamlet in *Hamlet*, 2.2.269–70

Questioning Rosencrantz and Guildenstern, his old school fellows, as to why they have come to Denmark; "beaten way" = well-trodden track, i.e., be honest with me.

5   Give me that man
That is not passion's slave, and I will wear him
In my heart's core, ay, in my heart of heart,
As I do thee.

Hamlet in *Hamlet*, 3.2.71–4

Praising the stoical Horatio.

6   I cannot flatter; I do defy
The tongues of soothers, but a braver place
In my heart's love hath no man than yourself.

Hotspur in *Henry IV, Part 1*, 4.1.6–8

To Douglas; they are joining forces with other nobles against King Henry; "soothers" = flatterers.

7   We were the first and dearest of your friends.

Worcester in *Henry IV, Part 1*, 5.1.33

Referring to the support Worcester and his allies gave to Bolingbroke before he became king.

8   Come, I'll be friends with thee, Jack. Thou art going to the wars, and whether I shall ever see thee again or no, there is nobody cares.

Doll Tearsheet in *Henry IV, Part 2*, 2.4.65–8

Bidding goodbye to Falstaff.

9   The man nearest my soul,
Who like a brother toiled in my affairs,
And laid his love and life under my foot.

King Henry in *Henry IV, Part 2*, 3.1.61–3

On Northumberland, once his friend, now his enemy.

10   At your return visit our house; let our old acquaintance be renewed.

Shallow in *Henry IV, Part 2*, 3.2.293–4

Inviting Falstaff to return.

11 A friend i'the court is better than a penny in purse.

Shallow in *Henry IV, Part 2*, 5.1.30–1

12 I have not from your eyes that gentleness
And show of love as I was wont to have.

Cassius in *Julius Caesar*, 1.2.33–4

To his friend Brutus, who is troubled in mind.

13 Good friends, go in, and taste some wine with me,
And we, like friends, will straightway go together.

Caesar in *Julius Caesar*, 2.2.126–7

14 What compact mean you to have with us?
Will you be pricked in number of our friends,
Or shall we on, and not depend on you?

Cassius in *Julius Caesar*, 3.1.215–17

To Mark Antony; "compact" = agreement; "pricked" = marked down.

15 Friends am I with you all, and love you all.

Mark Antony in *Julius Caesar*, 3.1.220

To Cassius and the conspirators who killed Caesar; Antony is being disingenuous.

16 He was my friend, faithful and just to me.

Mark Antony in *Julius Caesar*, 3.2.85

Praising the dead Caesar.

17 A friend should bear his friend's infirmities,

But Brutus makes mine greater than they are.

Cassius in *Julius Caesar*, 4.3.86–7

18 I think he only loves the world for him.

Solanio in *The Merchant of Venice*, 2.8.50

On Antonio's affection for Bassanio.

19   In companions
That do converse and waste the time together,
Whose souls do bear an equal yoke of love,
There must be needs a like proportion
Of lineaments, of manners, and of spirit.

Portia in *The Merchant of Venice*, 3.4.11–15

Arguing that Bassanio and his friend Antonio, who spend ("waste") so much time together, must be alike.

20 Life itself, my wife, and all the world,
Are not with me esteemed above thy life.
I would lose all, ay, sacrifice them all
Here to this devil, to deliver you.

Bassanio in *The Merchant of Venice*, 4.1.284–7

To his friend Antonio; the devil is Shylock, demanding his pound of flesh.

21 Is all the counsel that we two have shared,
The sisters' vows, the hours that we have spent

When we have chid the hasty-footed time
For parting us—O, is all forgot?
All schooldays' friendship, childhood innocence?

Helena in *A Midsummer Night's Dream*, 3.2.198–202

On finding her school-friend Hermia hostile to her.

22 My love is thine to teach; teach it but how,
And thou shalt see how apt it is to learn
Any hard lesson that may do thee good.

Don Pedro in *Much Ado About Nothing*, 1.1.291–3

Offering to help Claudio in any way to woo Hero.

23 Friendship is constant in all other things
Save in the office and affairs of love.

Claudio in *Much Ado About Nothing*, 2.1.175–6

Thinking he has been betrayed by his friend Don Pedro; "office" = business.

24 If I do vow a friendship, I'll perform it
To the last article.

Desdemona in *Othello*, 3.3.21–2

Going out of her way to help Cassio.

25 I count myself in nothing else so happy
As in a soul remembering my good friends.

Bolingbroke in *Richard II*, 2.3.46–7

He quarrels with them, however, once he becomes King Henry IV.

26 'Twixt such friends as we
Few words suffice.

Petruchio in *The Taming of the Shrew*, 1.2.65–6

To his good friend Hortensio.

27 Do as adversaries do in law,
Strive mightily, but eat and drink as friends.

Tranio in *The Taming of the Shrew*, 1.2.276–7

Speaking to the other suitors for Baptista's daughters.

28 What need we have any friends, if we should ne'er have need of 'em? They were the most needless creatures living, if we should ne'er have use for 'em.

Timon in *Timon of Athens*, 1.2.95–8

Believing his friends will help him if need be.

29 We are born to do benefits; and what better or properer can we call our own than the riches of our friends? O, what a precious comfort 'tis to have so many like brothers commanding one another's fortunes!

Timon in *Timon of Athens*, 1.2.101–5

Timon's naive and misplaced trust in his friends.

30 I weigh my friend's affection with mine own.

Timon in *Timon of Athens*, 1.2.216

Assuming his friends are like himself.

31 The amity that wisdom knits not,
folly may easily untie.
Ulysses in *Troilus and Cressida*,
2.3.101–2

Referring to the friendship of Ajax and
Achilles.

32 'Twere pity two such friends should
be long foes.
**Valentine in *The Two Gentlemen of
Verona*,** 5.4.118

Reconciled at last with his old friend Proteus

33 They have seemed to be together,
though absent; shook hands as over
a vast; and embraced as it were
from the ends of opposed winds.
Camillo in *The Winter's Tale*, 1.1.29–31

Describing the long friendship of Leontes of
Sicily and Polixenes of Bohemia.

Futility

1 The task he undertakes
Is numbering sands and drinking
oceans dry.
Green in *Richard II*, 2.2.145–6

Seeing it is impossible for the old Duke of
York to hold back the rebels led by Henry
Bolingbroke.

2 Nay, if our wits run the wild-goose
chase, I am done.
Mercutio in *Romeo and Juliet*, 2.4.71–2

To Romeo, giving up a futile argument.

Gardens and Gardening

1 Most subject is the fattest soil to
weeds.
King Henry in *Henry IV, Part 2*, 4.4.54

"Fattest" = richest, best; the "weeds" refer to
Prince Hal's base companions.

2 The strawberry grows underneath
the nettle,
And wholesome berries thrive and
ripen best
Neighbored by fruit of baser quality.
Bishop of Ely in *Henry V*, 1.1.60–2

Prince Hal was the strawberry growing under
the shade of base companions like Falstaff.

3 Now 'tis the spring, and weeds are
shallow-rooted;
Suffer them now, and they'll out-
grow the garden,
And choke the herbs for want of
husbandry.
Queen Margaret in *Henry VI, Part 2*,
3.1.31–3

She is speaking to the king about noblemen
who may challenge his power; "want of husbandry" = lack of proper cultivation.

4 Adam was a gardener.
Jack Cade in *Henry VI, Part 2*, 4.2.134

A peasant claiming all men are descended
from a working man, though Adam did not
have to work in the Garden of Eden.

5 Go bind thou up yon dangling apricots,
Which, like unruly children, make
their sire
Stoop with oppression of their
prodigal weight.
Gardener in *Richard II*, 3.4.29–31

Giving instructions to his assistant; "prodigal"
= excessive.

6   I will go root away
The noisome weeds which without
    profit suck
The soil's fertility from wholesome
    flowers.

Gardener in *Richard II*, 3.4.37–9

The gardener's care contrasts with King
Richard's failure to rid himself of parasites and
look after his kingdom.

7   Superfluous branches
We lop away, that bearing boughs
    may live.

Gardener in *Richard II*, 3.4.63–4

8   Thou, old Adam's likeness, set to
    dress this garden.

Queen in *Richard II*, 3.4.73

Speaking to the gardener as if he were the first
gardener, Adam.

9   Here did she fall a tear. Here in this
    place
I'll set a bank of rue, sour herb-of-
    grace.
Rue even for ruth here shortly shall
    be seen
In the remembrance of a weeping
    queen.

Gardener in *Richard II*, 3.4.104–7

Speaking of the distressed Queen; "fall" = let
fall; rue was a herb symbolic of repentance,
and signifying sorrow; "ruth" = pity.

10   How lush and lusty the grass looks!
    How green!

Gonzalo in *The Tempest*, 2.1.53–4

The good Gonzalo sees the island on which
he has been shipwrecked in the best light.

Generosity

1   For his bounty,
There was no winter in't; an
    autumn it was
That grew the more by reaping.

Cleopatra in *Antony and Cleopatra*, 5.2.86–8

Exaggerating Antony's generosity, after his
death.

2   Use every man after his desert, and
who should scape whipping? Use
them after your own honor and
dignity—the less they deserve, the
more merit is in your bounty.

Hamlet in *Hamlet*, 2.2.529–32

Asking Polonius to deal well with the actors.

3   A largess universal, like the sun,
His liberal eye doth give to every-
    one,
Thawing cold fear.

Chorus in *Henry V*, 4.Prologue, 43–5

On the influence of the King on his army;
"largess" = bounty.

4   The fashion of the world is to avoid
cost, and you encounter it.

Don Pedro in *Much Ado About Nothing*, 1.1.97–8

To Leonato, who offers hospitality to Don
Pedro and his companions.

5   There's none
Can truly say he gives if he receives.
If our betters play at that game, we
    must not dare
To imitate them; faults that are rich
    are fair.

Timon in *Timon of Athens*, 1.2.10–13

The "fault" is to expect something in return for
a gift.

6   No villainous bounty yet hath
      passed my heart;
    Unwisely, not ignobly, have I given.

Timon in *Timon of Athens*, 2.2.173–4

On being upbraided by his steward, Flavius.

7   At your request
    My father will grant precious things
    as trifles.

Florizel in *The Winter's Tale*, 5.1.221–2

To Perdita; "as" = as if they were.

Ghosts (see also Apparitions)

1   Such was the very armor he had on
    When he the ambitious Norway
      combated.

Horatio in *Hamlet*, 1.1.60–1

Speaking of the ghost which has just appeared
in the likeness of the dead King of Denmark;
"Norway" = King of Norway.

2   Thus twice before, and jump at this
      dead hour,
    With martial stalk hath he gone by
      our watch.

Marcellus in *Hamlet*, 1.1.65–6

Telling of earlier appearances of the ghost of
Hamlet's father, always exactly at midnight
("jump at this dead hour").

3   But soft, behold! lo where it comes
      again!
    I'll cross it though it blast me. Stay,
      illusion!

Horatio in *Hamlet*, 1.1.126–7

Seeing the ghost of Hamlet's father again;
"cross" = confront, and perhaps make the sign
of the cross; "blast" = wither or destroy.

4   We do it wrong, being so majesti-
      cal,
    To offer it the show of violence,
    For it is as the air, invulnerable,
    And our vain blows malicious
      mockery.

Marcellus in *Hamlet*, 1.1.143–6

On the apparition of the dead King Hamlet of
Denmark.

5   *Barnardo.* It was about to speak
      when the cock crew.
    Horatio. And then it started like a
      guilty thing
    Upon a fearful summons.

Hamlet, 1.1.147–9

Describing the ghost of Hamlet's father; "fearful" = terrifying.

6   The cock, that is the trumpet to the
      morn,
    Doth with his lofty and shrill-
      sounding throat
    Awake the god of day, and at his
      warning,
    Whether in sea or fire, in earth or
      air,
    Th' extravagant and erring spirit
      hies
    To his confine.

Horatio in *Hamlet*, 1.1.150–5

Wandering ("extravagant") spirits return to
where they came from in daylight.

7   Be thou a spirit of health, or goblin
      damned,
    Bring with thee airs from heaven,
      or blasts from hell,
    Be thy intents wicked or charitable,
    Thou com'st in such a questionable
      shape
    That I will speak to thee.

Hamlet in *Hamlet*, 1.4.40–4

Addressing the ghost as a spirit that appears in his father's shape; "questionable" = which invites questions.

8   What if it tempt you toward the flood, my lord,
    Or to the dreadful summit of the cliff
    That beetles o'er his base into the sea,
    And there assume some other horrible form
    Which might deprive your sovereignty of reason,
    And draw you into madness?
    Horatio in *Hamlet*, 1.4.69–74

    Trying to persuade Hamlet not to follow his father's ghost, uncertain whether the spirit is good or evil; "deprive your sovereignty of reason" = make you lose control of your mind.

9   I am thy father's spirit,
    Doomed for a certain term to walk the night,
    And for the day confined to fast in fires,
    Till the foul crimes done in my days of nature
    Are burnt and purged away.
    Ghost in *Hamlet*, 1.5.9–13

    The ghost, alone with Hamlet, describes his fate; it seems his days are spent in purgatory.

10   Art thou there, truepenny?
    You hear this fellow in the cellarage,
    Consent to swear.
    Hamlet in *Hamlet*, 1.5.151–2

    His father's honest ghost ("truepenny") speaks from under the stage ("the cellarage"), urging Hamlet's friends to swear secrecy.

11 Well said, old mole, canst work i'th' earth so fast?
    Hamlet in *Hamlet*, 1.5.162

    To the ghost, who seems to be moving about under the stage as it calls on Hamlet's friends to swear secrecy.

12 Rest, rest, perturbèd spirit!
    Hamlet in *Hamlet*, 1.5.182

    To his father's ghost, who has spoken from under the stage.

13 Thou canst not say I did it; never shake
    Thy gory locks at me.
    Macbeth in *Macbeth*, 3.4.49–50

    On seeing the ghost of the murdered Banquo.

14 Now it is the time of night
    That the graves, all gaping wide,
    Every one lets forth his sprite
    In the church-way paths to glide.
    Puck in *A Midsummer Night's Dream*, 5.1.379–82

    Ghosts were thought to wander abroad at midnight, returning to their graves at dawn.

15 I have heard, but not believed, the spirits o'the dead
    May walk again.
    Antigonus in *The Winter's Tale*, 3.3.16–17

    After dreaming that he saw Hermione, whom he believes to be dead.

Giddiness

1   He that is giddy thinks the world turns round.
    Widow in *The Taming of the Shrew*, 5.2.20

    Proverbial; meaning her husband, Hortensio, who finds his wife domineering, and not at all what he expected.

Gifts

1 What have I to give you back,
whose worth
May counterpoise this rich and precious gift?
Claudio in Much Ado About Nothing,
4.1.27–8

The "gift" is Leonato's daughter, Hero.

2   O you gods!
Why do you make us love your
goodly gifts,
And snatch them straight away?
Pericles in Pericles, 3.1.22–4

Thinking his wife Thaisa has died in giving
birth to their daughter.

3 Yet my good will is great, though
the gift small.
Thaisa in Pericles, 3.4.18

4 I am not in the giving vein today.
King Richard in Richard III, 4.2.116

Refusing to give Buckingham the reward he
promised.

5 Win her with gifts if she respect not
words.
Dumb jewels often in their silent
kind
More than quick words do move a
woman's mind.
**Valentine in The Two Gentlemen of
Verona, 3.1.89–91**

6 She prizes not such trifles as these
are.
The gifts she looks from me are
packed and locked

Up in my heart, which I have given
already,
But not delivered.
Florizel in The Winter's Tale, 4.4.357–60

Speaking to his disguised father, Polixenes,
about Perdita; his gifts are love and marriage.

Girls (see also Parents and Children, Youth)

1 Those girls of Italy, take heed of
them.
**King of France in All's Well That Ends
Well, 2.1.19**

2   Briefly die their joys
That place them on the truth of
girls and boys.
Lucius in Cymbeline, 5.5.106–5

Imogen, disguised as Fidele, a faithful page in
his service, loses interest in him in concern for
her husband, Posthumus, who is on stage as a
prisoner of the Romans.

3 An unlessoned girl, unschooled,
unpracticed;
Happy in this, she is not yet so old
But she may learn; happier in this,
She is not bred so dull but she can
learn.
**Portia in The Merchant of Venice,
3.2.159–62**

Describing herself to Bassanio, who is to be
her husband.

Glory

1 Glory is like a circle in the water,
Which never ceaseth to enlarge
itself,

Till by broad spreading it disperse to nought.

Joan la Pucelle (Joan of Arc) in *Henry VI, Part 1*, 1.2.133–5

The "glory" is that brought to England by Henry V, now dead.

God

1   He that of greatest works is finisher
Oft does them by the weakest minister.

Helena in *All's Well That Ends Well*, 2.1.136–7

Hoping that God will work through her as agent to cure the French king's disease.

2   *Gloucester.* I hope they will not come upon us now.
King Henry. We are in God's hands, brother, not in theirs.

Henry V, 3.6.168–9

Henry soothes Gloucester's anxiety that the French might attack.

3   O God, thy arm was here,
And not to us, but to thy arm alone Ascribe we all.

King Henry in *Henry V*, 4.8.106–8

Ascribing his victory to God's help.

4   God is our fortress.

Talbot in *Henry VI, Part 1*, 2.1.26

Claiming God's protection as he attacks the French at Orleans.

5   Now God be praised, that to believing souls

Gives light in darkness, comfort in despair!

King Henry in *Henry VI, Part 2*, 2.1.64–5

On the miracle of a blind man recovering his sight.

6   Let never day nor night unhallowed pass,
But still remember what the Lord hath done.

King Henry in *Henry VI, Part 2*, 2.1.83–4

To a blind man who recovered his sight; "unhallowed" = unblessed by prayers.

7   God shall be my hope,
My stay, my guide, and lantern to my feet.

King Henry in *Henry VI, Part 2*, 2.3.24–5

8   Heaven is above all yet; there sits a judge
That no king can corrupt.

Queen Katherine in *Henry VIII*, 3.1.100–1

Rejecting the corrupt advice of Wolsey and Campeius.

Gods and Goddesses

1   As flies to wanton boys are we to the gods,
They kill us for their sport.

Gloucester in *King Lear*, 4.1.36–7

A cynical or despairing view; "wanton" = playful.

2 That very time I saw (but thou
        couldst not)
Flying between the cold moon and
        the earth
Cupid all armed.

Oberon in *A Midsummer Night's Dream*, 2.1.155–7

Speaking to Puck; the cold moon symbolizes chastity (the goddess Diana).

3 Here she comes, curst and sad.
Cupid is a knavish lad
Thus to make poor females mad.

Puck in *A Midsummer Night's Dream*, 3.2.439–41

On Hermia, ill-tempered ("curst"), and thinking she is abandoned in the woods by night.

4   O you heavenly charmers,
What things you make of us! For
        what we lack
We laugh, for what we have are
        sorry, still
Are children in some kind.

Theseus in *The Two Noble Kinsmen*, 5.4.131–4

"For what we lack we laugh" = we happily anticipate getting what we desire.

5   The gods themselves,
Humbling their deities to love, have
        taken
The shapes of beasts upon them.
        Jupiter
Became a bull, and bellowed; the
        green Neptune
A ram, and bleated; and the fire-
        robed god,
Golden Apollo, a poor humble
        swain.

Florizel in *The Winter's Tale*, 4.4.25–30

What Florizel does not say to Perdita is that the aim of all these gods was to seduce a mortal girl; Apollo was god of the sun.

Gold (see also Money)

1 I see the jewel best enamelèd
Will lose his beauty; yet the gold
        bides still
That others touch, and often touch-
        ing will
Wear gold.

Adriana in *The Comedy of Errors*, 2.1.109–12

The sense is that jewels tarnish, while gold retains its luster.

2   'Tis gold
Which makes the true man killed
        and saves the thief;
Nay, sometimes hangs both thief
        and true man. What
Can it not do and undo?

Cloten in *Cymbeline*, 2.3.70–3

3 How quickly nature falls into revolt
When gold becomes her object!

King Henry in *Henry IV, Part 2*, 4.5.65–67

He thinks his son, Prince Hal, has stolen his golden crown.

4   Plate sin with gold
And the strong lance of justice
        hurtless breaks.

King Lear in *King Lear*, 4.6.165–6

The image is of plate armor, and suggests how wealth can buy out the law.

5   "All that glisters is not gold,
Often have you heard that told;
Many a man his life hath sold
But my outside to behold.
Gilded tombs do worms infold.
Had you been as wise as bold,
Young in limbs, in judgment old,
Your answer had not been
inscrolled.
Fare you well, your suit is cold."

**Prince of Morocco in *The Merchant of
Venice*, 2.7.65–73**

The message set down ("inscrolled") in the
golden casket, beginning with a well-known
proverb.

6   Gold? Yellow, glittering, precious
gold?
. . .
This yellow slave
Will knit and break religions, bless
th' accursed,
Make the hoar leprosy adored,
place thieves,
And give them title, knee and
approbation
With senators on the bench.

Timon in *Timon of Athens*, 4.3.26, 34–8

Digging for roots to eat, Timon finds buried
gold; "place" = place in office. The idea of a
leper as white (hoary) may be derived from I
Kings 5:27, "a leper white as snow."

Golden Age

1   They . . . fleet the time carelessly, as
they did in the golden world.

Charles in *As You Like It*, 1.1.118–19

The exiled Duke and his followers pass their
time free from care, recalling the mythical
golden age of man.

Goodness (see also Virtue)

1   They should be good men, their
affairs as righteous,
But all hoods make not monks.

**Queen Katherine in *Henry VIII*,
3.1.22–3**

Referring to the two Cardinals, Wolsey and
Campeius; it was proverbial that a monk's
hood did not guarantee holiness.

2   I never did repent for doing good,
Nor shall not now.

**Portia in *The Merchant of Venice*,
3.4.10–11**

On setting off to help Antonio.

3   How far that little candle throws his
beams!
So shines a good deed in a naughty
world.

**Portia in *The Merchant of Venice*,
5.1.90–1**

Seeing a light in her house as she arrives back
from Venice; "naughty" = wicked.

4   There's nothing ill can dwell in
such a temple.
If the ill spirit have so fair a house,
Good things will strive to dwell
with 't.

Miranda in *The Tempest*, 1.2.458–60

Her first impression of Ferdinand.

Gossip

1   What great ones do, the less will
prattle of.

Sea Captain in *Twelfth Night*, 1.2.33

"Less" = social inferiors.

Government

1 Let men say we be men of good
government, being governed, as the
sea is, by our noble and chaste mistress the moon, under whose countenance we steal.

Falstaff in *Henry IV, Part 1*, 1.2.27–9

Wittily claiming to be well-behaved ("of good
government"), under Diana, goddess of
chastity and the moon, while planning a robbery by night.

2 For government, though high, and
low, and lower,
Put into parts, doth keep in one
consent,
Congreeing in a full and natural
close,
Like music.

Exeter in *Henry V*, 1.2.180–3

Though divided among social groups, and
into various functions ("parts"), the aspects of
government agree together ("congreeing") in a
final harmony "close"; "parts" quibbles on the
parts in a musical score.

3 So work the honey-bees,
Creatures that by a rule in nature
teach
The act of order to a peopled kingdom.

**Archbishop of Canterbury in *Henry
V*, 1.2.187–9**

4 Woe to that land that's governed by
a child.

Third Citizen in *Richard III*, 2.3.11

Hearing news of the death of King Edward IV;
proverbial, from the Bible (Ecclesiastes 10:16).

5 I would with such perfection govern, sir,

T'excel the golden age.

Gonzalo in *The Tempest*, 2.1.168–9

The climax of his vision of a utopian society;
the mythical golden age of antiquity was an
age of innocence and plenty.

6 There is a mystery (with whom
relation
Durst never meddle) in the soul of
state,
Which hath an operation more
divine
Than breath or pen can give expressure to.

**Ulysses in *Troilus and Cressida*,
3.3.201–5**

He is mystifying the idea of government in
talking to Achilles; "relation" = report;
"expressure" = expression.

Grace

1 Grace me no grace, nor uncle me
no uncle;
I am no traitor's uncle, and that
word "grace"
In an ungracious mouth is but profane.

York in *Richard II*, 2.3.87–9

On being greeted as "gracious uncle" by
Henry Bolingbroke, who has invaded England.

2 O momentary grace of mortal men,
Which we more hunt for than the
grace of God!

Hastings in *Richard III*, 3.4.96–7

Sentenced to death, he realizes how uncertain
the favor ("grace") of Richard is.

Gratitude, see Thanks

Graves (see also Burial, Epitaphs, Mourning)

1   Ay, but to die, and go we know
not where;
To lie in cold obstruction and to
rot.
Claudio in *Measure for Measure*,
3.1.117–18

Expressing his fear of death.

2   Not a flower, not a flower sweet
On my black coffin let there be
strewn.
Not a friend, not a friend greet
My poor corpse, where my bones
shall be thrown.
A thousand thousand sighs to save,
Lay me, O, where
Sad true lover never find my grave,
To weep there.
Feste in *Twelfth Night*, 2.4.59–66

The image of sexual consummation as "dying"
here passes into a reminder of death indeed.

Greatness (see also Politics, Power)

1   The soul and body rive not more in
parting
Than greatness going off.
Charmian in *Antony and Cleopatra*,
4.13.5–6

On Antony's wild behavior in defeat.

2   Rightly to be great
Is not to stir without great argument,
But greatly to find quarrel in a
straw

When honor's at the stake.
Hamlet in *Hamlet*, 4.4.53–6

True greatness consists not in fighting for any
trivial cause, unless honor is involved, when it
is noble to act.

3   All the courses of my life do show
I am not in the roll of common
men.
Glendower in *Henry IV, Part 1*, 3.1.41–2

Boasting of his greatness.

4   Thus did I keep my person fresh
and new,
My presence, like a robe pontifical,
Ne'er seen but wondered at, and so
my state,
Seldom but sumptuous, showed
like a feast.
King Henry in *Henry IV, Part 1*,
3.2.55–8

Recalling his former renown when he was
able to appear more important than Richard II,
king at the time; "state" = greatness, pomp.

5   Greatness knows itself.
Hotspur in *Henry IV, Part 1*, 4.3.74

Implying that great men take power for
granted.

6   Th' abuse of greatness is when it
disjoins
Remorse from power.
Brutus in *Julius Caesar*, 2.1.18–19

Thinking of Caesar; "Remorse" = mercy.

7   Think not, thou noble Roman,
That ever Brutus will go bound to
Rome.
He bears too great a mind.
Brutus in *Julius Caesar*, 5.1.110–12

To Cassius, anticipating what may happen if
they lose the battle with Octavius.

8   Spirits are not finely touched
But to fine issues.

Duke in *Measure for Measure*, 1.1.35–6

Arguing that souls are given greatness (and put to the test, as gold by a touchstone) for noble purposes.

9   This did I fear, but thought he had no weapon;
For he was great of heart.

Cassio in *Othello*, 5.2.360–1

On Othello killing himself.

10 They that stand high have many blasts to shake them,
And if they fall, they dash themselves to pieces.

Queen Margaret in *Richard III*, 1.3.258–9

As she, the widow of Henry VI, has become an object of scorn in the court of Edward IV.

11 Some are born great, some achieve greatness, and some have greatness thrust upon 'em.

Malvolio in *Twelfth Night*, 2.5.145–6

Reading Maria's letter that feeds his self-importance.

12 The mightier man, the mightier is the thing
That makes him honored or begets him hate;
For greatest scandal waits on greatest state.

***The Rape of Lucrece*, 1004–6**

"Waits on greatest state" = attends on men of the highest rank.

Greed (see also Avarice)

1   My more-having would be as a sauce
To make me hunger more.

Malcolm in *Macbeth*, 4.3.81–2

Greetings (see also Welcome)

1   Health and fair time of day!

King Henry in *Henry V*, 5.2.3

Greeting the King of France and his nobility.

2   Give me your hands all over, one by one.

Brutus in *Julius Caesar*, 2.1.112

3   You are come in very happy time
To bear my greeting to the senators
And tell them that I will not come today.

Caesar in *Julius Caesar*, 2.2.60–2

To Decius, who has come to fetch him to the senate chamber.

4   Let each man render me his bloody hand.

Mark Antony in *Julius Caesar*, 3.1.184

Shaking hands with the murderers of Caesar, and seeming to make peace with them.

5   Ill met by moonlight, proud Titania!

Oberon in *A Midsummer Night's Dream*, 2.1.60

The first meeting between the King and Queen of the Fairies.

6 Good morrow, friends. Saint
Valentine is past;
Begin these woodbirds but to cou-
ple now?

**Theseus in *A Midsummer Night's
Dream*, 4.1.139–40**

Birds were proverbially supposed to choose
their mates on St. Valentine's Day, 14th February.

7 Joy, gentle friends, joy and fresh
days of love
Accompany your hearts!

**Theseus in *A Midsummer Night's
Dream*, 5.1.29–30**

Addressing the reconciled lovers.

8 What, my dear Lady Disdain! Are
you yet living?

**Benedick in *Much Ado About Nothing*,
1.1.118–19**

His first, mocking words to Beatrice.

9 Most potent, grave, and reverend
signiors,
My very noble and approved good
masters.

Othello in *Othello*, 1.3.76–7

Addressing the senate of Venice; "potent" =
powerful; "approved" = tested by experience.

10 Hail to thee, lady! and the grace of
heaven,
Before, behind thee, and on every
hand,
Enwheel thee round!

Cassio in *Othello*, 2.1.85–7

On Desdemona's arrival in Cyprus.

11 As a long-parted mother with her
child
Plays fondly with her tears and
smiles in meeting,
So weeping, smiling, greet I thee,
my earth.

King Richard in *Richard II*, 3.2.8–10

Returning from Ireland, he greets the soil of
England.

Grief (see also Affliction, Mourning, Sorrow)

1 Moderate lamentation is the right
of the dead, excessive grief the
enemy to the living.

**Lafew, *All's Well That Ends Well*,
1.1.55–6**

Referring to the Countess of Rossillion, whose
husband has died, and Helena, who has lost
her father.

2 A heavier task could not have been
imposed
Than I to speak my griefs unspeakable.

Egeon in *The Comedy of Errors*, 1.1.31–2

Beginning the story of how he was separated
from his wife and one of their twin sons.

3 O! grief hath changed me since you
saw me last,
And careful hours with time's
deformèd hand
Have written strange defeatures in
my face.

**Egeon in *The Comedy of Errors*,
5.1.298–300**

Meeting Antipholus and Dromio of Ephesus,
who do not recognize him; "defeatures" = dis-
figurement.

4 Great griefs, I see, medicine the less.

Belarius in *Cymbeline*, 4.2.243

Alluding to the proverb, a greater sorrow (for the supposed death of Imogen) drives out a lesser one (for the death of Cloten).

5 *Claudius.* How is it that the clouds still hang on you?
Hamlet. Not so, my lord, I am too much in the sun.

***Hamlet*, 1.2.66–7**

Claudius probes Hamlet's grief at his father's death, while Hamlet resists Claudius's attempts to treat him as a son in the quibble on "sun."

6 It is not, nor it cannot come to good.
But break, my heart, for I must hold my tongue.

Hamlet in *Hamlet*, 1.2.158–9

Expressing his grief and dismay at his mother's hasty marriage to his uncle after his father's death.

7 Mine eyes are full of tears, my heart of grief.

Gloucester in *Henry VI, Part 2*, 2.3.17

On the banishment of his wife.

8   My grief's so great
That no supporter but the huge firm earth
Can hold it up.

Constance in *King John*, 3.1.71–3

The widow of John's elder brother, she fears for the life of her young son Arthur.

9 Grief fills the room up of my absent child,
Lies in his bed, walks up and down with me,
Puts on his pretty looks, repeats his words,

Remembers me of all his gracious parts,
Stuffs out his vacant garments with his form;
Then have I reason to be fond of grief?

Constance in *King John*, 3.4.93–8

Lamenting for her son, Arthur, who is imprisoned; "remembers" = reminds.

10 Give sorrow words; the grief that does not speak
Whispers the o'er-fraught heart and bids it break.

Malcolm in *Macbeth*, 4.3.209–10

Addressing Macduff, who has just learned that his wife and children have been slaughtered; "whispers" = whispers to the overburdened heart.

11 *Malcolm.* Dispute it like a man.
Macduff.   I shall do so;
But I must also feel it as a man.
I cannot but remember such things were
That were most precious to me.

***Macbeth*, 4.3.220–3**

"Dispute it" = struggle against your grief.

12 Poor Desdemona! I am glad thy father's dead.
Thy match was mortal to him, and pure grief
Shore his old thread in twain.

Gratiano in *Othello*, 5.2.204–6

Cutting the thread of life alludes to the Fates who in ancient mythology spun the thread (Clotho) and cut it at death (Atropos); the phrase became proverbial; "shore" = sheared.

13 Shorten my days thou canst with sullen sorrow,

And pluck nights from me, but not
lend a morrow;
Thou canst help time to furrow me
with age,
But stop no wrinkle in his pilgrimage.

John of Gaunt in *Richard II*, 1.3.227–30

To King Richard, who has just banished his
son, Bolingbroke.

14   My grief lies all within,
And these external manners of
laments
Are merely shadows to the unseen
grief
That swells with silence in the tor-
tured soul.
There lies the substance.

King Richard in *Richard II*, 4.1.295–9

Lamenting his fall; "manners" = shows or
forms.

15 I am not prone to weeping, as our
sex
Commonly are, the want of which
vain dew
Perchance shall dry your pities; but
I have
That honorable grief lodged here
which burns
Worse than tears drown.

Hermione in *The Winter's Tale*,
2.1.108–12

On being accused of adultery and sent to
prison.

Guilt (see also Conscience)

1 O, my offense is rank, it smells to
heaven,
It hath the primal eldest curse
upon't,

A brother's murder.

Claudius in *Hamlet*, 3.3.36–8

Left alone, Claudius confesses to his crime,
alluding to Cain's slaughter of Abel (Genesis
4).

2 O limèd soul, that struggling to be
free
Art more engaged!

Claudius in *Hamlet*, 3.3.68–9

Attempting to pray for forgiveness, he
becomes more conscious of his guilt; "limed"
= caught in birdlime, a sticky substance
smeared on twigs to catch birds.

3 Thou turn'st my eyes into my very
soul,
And there I see such black and
grainèd spots
As will not leave their tinct.

Gertrude in *Hamlet*, 3.4.89–91

Hamlet has made her conscious of her guilt in
marrying Claudius; "grained" = ingrained,
fast-dyed.

4 To my sick soul, as sin's true nature
is,
Each toy seems prologue to some
great amiss.
So full of artless jealousy is guilt,
It spills itself in fearing to be spilt.

Gertrude in *Hamlet*, 4.5.17–20

"Toy" = trifle; "jealousy" = suspicion; "spills"
= reveals and destroys.

5 Will all great Neptune's ocean wash
this blood
Clean from my hand? No. This my
hand will rather
The multitudinous seas incarnadine,
Making the green one red.

Macbeth in *Macbeth*, 2.2.57–60

"Incarnadine" = turn red.

6 A little water clears us of this deed.
How easy is it then!

Lady Macbeth in *Macbeth*, 2.2.64–5

Referring to the blood on their hands after the
murder of Duncan.

7 Out, damned spot! Out, I say!

Lady Macbeth in *Macbeth*, 5.1.35

Sleepwalking, she imagines Duncan's blood is
still on her hands.

8 Here's the smell of the blood still:
all the perfumes ofArabia will not
sweeten this little hand.

Lady Macbeth in *Macbeth*, 5.1.50–1

Imagining in her sleepwalking that she can
smell Duncan's blood on her hands.

9 Foul whisp'rings are abroad.
Unnatural deeds
Do breed unnatural troubles.
Infected minds
To their deaf pillows will discharge
their secrets.
More needs she the divine than the
physician.

Doctor in *Macbeth*, 5.1.71–4

Unable to cure Lady Macbeth's disease of the
mind, the guilt confessed in her sleepwalking.

10 She, O, she is fallen
Into a pit of ink, that the wide sea
Hath drops too few to wash her
clean again
And salt too little which may season
give
To her foul tainted flesh!

**Leonato in *Much Ado About Nothing*,
4.1.139–43**

Believing his daughter to have been unchaste;
"season give" = make sound again (literally,
give relish to, like salt).

11 They whose guilt within their
bosoms lie
Imagine every eye beholds their
blame.

The Rape of Lucrece, 1342–3

Lucrece imagines everyone can see that she
has been raped.

Habit, see Custom

Hair

1 *Rosalind.* His very hair is of the dissembling color. . . .
Celia. An excellent color. Your
chestnut was ever the only color.

As You Like It, 3.4.10–12

Rosalind disparages Orlando (tawny or chestnut was said to be the color of Judas's hair), in
order to hear Celia praise him.

2 There's many a man has more hair
than wit.

**Antipholus of Syracuse in *The Com-
edy of Errors*, 2.2.82–3**

"Wit" = intelligence or sense.

3 I must to the barber's, monsieur,
for methinks I am marvellous hairy
about the face; and I am such a tender ass, if my hair do but tickle me,
I must scratch.

**Bottom in *A Midsummer Night's
Dream*, 4.1.23–6**

Bottom, who does not realize Puck has given
him an ass's head, addresses the fairy, Cobweb.

Happiness (see also Contentment, Joy)

1 O, how bitter a thing it is to look into happiness through another man's eyes!

Orlando in *As You Like It*, 5.2.43–5

The happiness is that of his brother Oliver, who is to marry Celia.

2 Believe me, I am passing light in spirit.

Archbishop of York in *Henry IV, Part 2*, 4.2.85

"Passing" = exceedingly.

3 O God! methinks it were a happy life
To be no better than a homely swain.

King Henry in *Henry VI, Part 3*, 2.5.21–2

Caught in a brutal civil war, the king wishes he were a shepherd.

4 Our content is our best having.

Old Lady in *Henry VIII*, 2.3.22–3

She would like to be rich all the same; "having" = possession.

5 Happy thou art not,
For what thou hast not, still thou striv'st to get,
And what thou hast, forget'st.

Duke in *Measure for Measure*, 3.1.21–3

Depicting life as an unrewarding struggle in order to prepare Claudio to face death.

6 If it were now to die,
'Twere now to be most happy; for I fear

My soul hath her content so absolute
That not another comfort like to this
Succeeds in unknown fate.

Othello in *Othello*, 2.1.189–93

This ironically does turn out to be Othello's happiest moment.

7 One feast, one house, one mutual happiness.

Valentine in *The Two Gentlemen of Verona*, 5.4.173

Marking the marriages promised at the end of the play.

Haste

1 To climb steep hills
Requires slow pace at first.

Norfolk in *Henry VIII*, 1.1.131–2

Advising the hasty Buckingham to act with caution.

2 Wisely and slow. They stumble that run fast.

Friar Lawrence in *Romeo and Juliet*, 2.3.94

Cautioning Romeo against marrying too hastily; varying the proverb "more haste, less speed."

Hate (see also Malice)

1 I care not for you,
And am so near the lack of charity
To accuse myself I hate you; which I had rather
You felt than make't my boast.

Imogen in *Cymbeline*, 2.3.108–11

To the stupid Cloten, whom she detests.

2 If I can cross him any way, I bless myself every way.

Don John in *Much Ado About Nothing*, 1.3.67–8

Referring to Claudio, whom he hates; "cross" = thwart, quibbling also on making the sign of the cross, so leading into "bless."

Health

1 *Ligarius.* What's to do?
Brutus. A piece of work that will make sick men whole.

Julius Caesar, 2.1.326–7

The "work" is the planned killing of Caesar.

Heaven

1 Where souls do couch on flowers, we'll hand in hand,
And with our sprightly port make the ghosts gaze.

Antony in *Antony and Cleopatra*, 4.14.51–2

Imagining a blissful afterlife united with Cleopatra.

2 The treasury of everlasting joy.

King Henry in *Henry VI, Part 2*, 2.1.18

Henry's formula for heaven.

3 There's not the smallest orb which thou behold'st
But in his motion like an angel sings,
Still quiring to the young-eyed cherubins;
Such harmony is in immortal souls,

But whilst this muddy vesture of decay
Doth grossly close it in, we cannot hear it.

Lorenzo in *The Merchant of Venice*, 5.1.60–5

It was thought that the soul liberated from the body ("vesture of decay") might hear the music made by the stars in their motions; cherubim were covered with eyes, according to Ezekiel 10:12.

Hedonism

1 I am sure care's an enemy to life.

Sir Toby Belch in *Twelfth Night*, 1.3.2–3

2 *Sir Toby Belch.* Does not our life consist of the four elements?
Sir Andrew Aguecheek. Faith, so they say, but I think it rather consists of eating and drinking.
Sir Toby Belch. Thou'rt a scholar; therefore let us eat and drink.

Twelfth Night, 2.3.9–14

All matter was thought to be composed of the four elements, earth, water, air, and fire.

Height

1 *Jaques.* What stature is she of?
Orlando. Just as high as my heart.

As You Like It, 3.2.268–9

A lover's answer to a pointless question.

2 He is not very tall—yet for his years he's tall.

Phebe in *As You Like It*, 3.5.118

Fondly describing Rosalind, who is disguised as a youth.

Hell (see also The Devil)

1 All hell shall stir for this.
Pistol in *Henry V*, 5.1.68

On being forced by Fluellen to eat a leek.

2 But this place is too cold for hell. I'll devil-porter it no further; I had thought to have let in some of all professions that go the primrose way to th' everlasting bonfire.
Porter in *Macbeth*, 2.3.16–19

The porter imagines Macbeth's castle as hell: the flowery path to hell is derived from Matthew 7:13, "broad is the way that leadeth to destruction."

3   Not in the legions
Of horrid hell can come a devil
    more damned
To top Macbeth.
Malcolm in *Macbeth*, 4.3.55–7

4 Hell is murky.
Lady Macbeth in *Macbeth*, 5.1.36

Speaking in her sleepwalking as if she is in hell.

5   You, mistress,
That have the office opposite to
    Saint Peter,
And keep the gate of hell!
Othello in *Othello*, 4.2.90–2

To Emilia, Desdemona's attendant, treating her as a bawd; the "harlot's house is the way to hell" in Proverbs 7:27.

6   Whip me, ye devils,
From the possession of this heavenly sight!
Blow me about in winds! Roast me in sulphur!

Wash me in steep-down gulfs of liquid fire!
Othello in *Othello*, 5.2.277–80

His vision, as he realizes the horror of his murder of Desdemona, of the torments of hell.

Helping

1 Well then, it now appears you need my help.
Shylock in *The Merchant of Venice*, 1.3.114

To Antonio, who has reviled him.

2 'Tis not enough to help the feeble up,
But to support him after.
Timon in *Timon of Athens*, 1.1.107–8

On Ventidius, imprisoned for debt.

Hindrance

1 Any bar, any cross, any impediment will be medicinable to me.
Don John in *Much Ado About Nothing*, 2.2.4–5

Hoping to prevent by any means the marriage of Claudio and Hero; any obstacle will do him good ("be medicinable").

History

1 'Tis no sinister nor awkward claim Picked from the wormholes of long-vanished days,
Nor from the dust of old oblivion raked.
Exeter in *Henry V*, 2.4.85–7

On Henry's claim to France; "sinister" = erroneous or underhand.

2 When went there by an age, since
   the great Flood,
   But it was famed with more than
   with one man?
   Cassius in *Julius Caesar*, 1.2.152–3

   Greek mythology and the Bible both describe
   a great flood; in the first Zeus spared Deu-
   calion, and in the second God spared Noah.

Holidays

1 If all the year were playing holidays,
   To sport would be as tedious as to
   work;
   But when they seldom come, they
   wished for come,
   And nothing pleaseth but rare accidents.
   Prince Hal in *Henry IV, Part 1*,
   1.2.204–7

   "Rare accidents" = unusual events.

2 A while to work, and after, holiday.
   Bolingbroke in *Richard II*, 3.1.44

   Seeing he needs only to defeat the Welsh to
   gain the kingdom.

Home

1 East, west, north, south, or like a
   school broke up,
   Each hurries toward his home and
   sporting-place.
   Hastings in *Henry IV, Part 2*, 4.2.104–5

   On an army dispersing for home.

Homelessness

1 Return to her? And fifty men dismissed?

   No, rather I abjure all roofs, and
   choose
   To wage against the enmity o' th'
   air,
   To be a comrade with the wolf and
   owl—
   Necessity's sharp pinch.
   King Lear in *King Lear*, 2.4.207–11

   Preferring to struggle against storms and winds
   ("the enmity o' th' air"), and live with wild
   beasts, than stay with his ungrateful daughters.

2 Poor naked wretches, wheresoe'er
   you are,
   That bide the pelting of this pitiless
   storm,
   How shall your houseless heads and
   unfed sides,
   Your looped and windowed
   raggedness, defend you
   From seasons such as these?
   King Lear in *King Lear*, 3.4.28–32

   "Bide" = endure; "looped and windowed
   raggedness" = ragged clothes full of holes and
   tatters.

3 Who can speak broader than he
   that has no house to put his head
   in? Such may rail against great
   buildings.
   **Varro's Second Servant in *Timon of
   Athens*,** 3.4.63–5

   "Broader" = more freely.

Honesty (see also Integrity, Truth)

1 Rich honesty dwells like a miser, sir,
   in a poor house, as your pearl in
   your foul oyster.

Touchstone in *As You Like It*, 5.4.59–61

Speaking of the sluttish Audrey.

2   To be honest, as this world goes, is to be one man picked out of ten thousand.

Hamlet in *Hamlet*, 2.2.178–9

Speaking to Polonius in real or pretended cynicism.

3   Where I could not be honest, I never yet was valiant.

Albany in *King Lear*, 5.1.23–4

He is unwilling to fight except in a good cause; "honest" = honorable.

4   An old man, sir, and his wits are not so blunt as, God help, I would desire they were; but, in faith, honest as the skin between his brows.

Dogberry in *Much Ado About Nothing*, 3.5.10–12

Commenting on his assistant, Verges, and, as often, in the word "blunt" (= sharp) saying the opposite of what he means; "honest as the skin between his brows" is proverbial.

5   I know thou'rt full of love and honesty, And weigh'st thy words before thou giv'st them breath.

Othello in *Othello*, 3.3.118–19

Iago has convinced everyone of his honesty.

6   This fellow's of exceeding honesty, And knows all qualities, with a learnèd spirit, Of human dealings.

Othello in *Othello*, 3.3.258–60

Trusting Iago as one who knows all types of characters ("qualities").

7   O wretched fool, That lov'st to make thine honesty a vice! O monstrous world! Take note, take note, O world, To be direct and honest is not safe.

Iago in *Othello*, 3.3.375–8

The "wretched fool" is Iago himself, hypocritically protesting his honesty to Othello.

8   What a fool Honesty is! and Trust, his sworn brother, a very simple gentleman!

Autolycus in *The Winter's Tale*, 4.4.595–6

Proverbial; he finds it easy to cheat the honest shepherds.

9   Though I am not naturally honest, I am so sometimes by chance.

Autolycus in *The Winter's Tale*, 4.4.712–13

The rogue finds it useful sometimes to tell the truth.

Honor

1   Honors thrive When rather from our acts we them derive Than our foregoers.

King of France in *All's Well That Ends Well*, 2.3.135–7

2   The honor of a maid is her name, and no legacy is so rich as honesty.

Mariana in *All's Well That Ends Well*, 3.5.12–13

3   By heaven, methinks it were an easy
    leap
    To pluck bright honor from the
    pale-faced moon,
    Or dive into the bottom of the
    deep,
    Where fathom-line could never
    touch the ground,
    And pluck up drownèd honor by
    the locks.

    Hotspur in *Henry IV, Part 1*, 1.3.201–5

    For Hotspur "honor" means fame or glory
    gained in battle; "locks" = hair.

4   Thou art the king of honor.

    Douglas in *Henry IV, Part 1*, 4.1.10

    To Hotspur, who has gained honor or fame on
    the battlefield.

5   Well, 'tis no matter, honor pricks
    me on. Yes, but how if honor prick
    me off when I come on? How
    then?

    Falstaff in *Henry IV, Part 1*, 5.1.129–31

    Quibbling on meanings of "honor" = moral
    obligation and fame; and "prick" = spur on
    and mark down as dead.

6   What is honor? A word. What is in
    that word honor? What is that
    honor? Air. A trim reckoning!
    Who hath it? He that died o'
    Wednesday.

    Falstaff in *Henry IV, Part 1*, 5.1.133–6

    Reducing fame and moral obligation to mere
    noise.

7   Honor's thought
    Reigns solely in the breast of every
    man.

    Chorus in *Henry V*, 2.Prologue, 3–4

8   The fewer men, the greater share of
    honor.

    King Henry in *Henry V*, 4.3.22

    In fighting against the French.

9   By Jove, I am not covetous for gold,
    . . .
    But if it be a sin to covet honor
    I am the most offending soul alive.

    King Henry in *Henry V*, 4.3.24, 28–9

    Before the battle of Agincourt.

10 I would not lose so great an honor
    As one man more methinks would
    share with me
    For the best hope I have.

    King Henry in *Henry V*, 4.3.31–3

    Rejecting Westmorland's wish for a larger
    army to fight the French.

11   In thy face I see
    The map of honor, truth, and loy-
    alty.

    King Henry in *Henry VI, Part 2*,
    3.1.202–3

    On his uncle, the Duke of Gloucester,
    arrested for treason.

12 If it be aught toward the general
    good,
    Set honor in one eye, and death
    i'th' other,
    And I will look on both indiffer-
    ently;
    For let the gods so speed me as I
    love
    The name of honor more than I
    fear death.

    Brutus in *Julius Caesar*, 1.2.85–9

    Proclaiming his integrity.

13 Well, honor is the subject of my
    story.

Cassius in *Julius Caesar*, 1.2.92

For Brutus honor concerns the general good,
but for Cassius it concerns his personal status.

14 Believe me for mine honor, and
    have respect to mine honor, that
    you may believe.

Brutus in *Julius Caesar*, 3.2.14–16

Speaking to the people.

15 Here, under leave of Brutus and the
    rest—
    For Brutus is an honorable man;
    So are they all, all honorable men—
    Come I to speak in Caesar's funeral.

Mark Antony in *Julius Caesar*, 3.2.81–4

Beginning to make the people question the
notion of "honor."

16 O, if thou wert the noblest of thy
    strain,
    Young man, thou couldst not die
    more honorable.

Brutus in *Julius Caesar*, 5.1.59–60

That is, if he were to die on the sword of Brutus.

17 Thou art a fellow of a good respect;
    Thy life hath had some smatch of
    honor in it.

Brutus in *Julius Caesar*, 5.5.45–6

Asking Strato to kill him; "respect" = reputation; "smatch" = touch, smack.

18 If you were born to honor, show it
    now;
    If put upon you, make the judgment good
    That thought you worthy of it.

Marina in *Pericles*, 4.6.92–4

Held in a brothel, she appeals to Lysimachus
not to attempt sex with her.

19 Mine honor is my life, both grow in
    one,
    Take honor from me, and my life is
    done.

Mowbray in *Richard II*, 1.1.182–3

"Honor" is a complex word; Mowbray seems
to mean by it both fame or reputation, and
moral probity.

20   Though mine enemy thou hast
      ever been,
      High sparks of honor in thee have I
      seen.

King Henry IV in *Richard II*, 5.6.28–9

Speaking to the Bishop of Carlisle, a supporter
of the dead Richard II; here "honor" = probity
or virtue.

21   Not a man, for being simply man,
      Hath any honor, but honor for
      those honors
      That are without him, as place,
      riches and favor—
      Prizes of accident as oft as merit.

**Achilles in *Troilus and Cressida*,
3.3.83–6**

Reducing "honor" to mere fame or dignity;
"without" = external to; "place" = office or
status.

22 Life every man holds dear, but the
    dear man
    Holds honor far more precious-
    dear than life.

Hector in *Troilus and Cressida*, 5.3.27–8

Refusing to be dissuaded from fighting by
pressure from his wife Andromache and Cassandra; "dear man" = man of worth, noble
man.

23 The painful warrior famous èd for
    fight,
    After a thousand victories once
    foiled
    Is from the book of honor rasèd
    quite,
    And all the rest forgot for which he
    toiled.

Sonnet 25, 9–12

Once defeated ("foiled"), the toil and pain
endured by a fighter in a thousand victories is
blotted out or erased.

Hope

1   It never yet did hurt
    To lay down likelihoods and forms
    of hope.

Hastings in Henry IV, Part 2, 1.3.34–5

To his fellow-conspirators, plotting rebellion.

2   To be worst,
    The lowest and most dejected thing
    of fortune,
    Stands still in esperance, lives not in
    fear.
    The lamentable change is from the
    best,
    The worst returns to laughter.

Edgar in King Lear, 4.1.2–6

"Esperance" = hope; alluding to the proverb,
"when things are at the worst they will mend."

3 The miserable have no other medicine
   But only hope.

Claudio in Measure for Measure,
3.1.2–3

He is in prison, hoping to be pardoned for getting Juliet with child.

4 True hope is swift, and flies with
   swallow's wings:

Kings it makes gods, and meaner
creatures kings.

Richmond in Richard III, 5.2.23–4

Encouraging his supporters in their drive
against Richard.

Horror

1   But that I am forbid
    To tell the secrets of my prison-
    house,
    I could a tale unfold whose lightest
    word
    Would harrow up thy soul, freeze
    thy young blood,
    Thy knotted and combinèd locks to
    part,
    And each particular hair to stand
    on end,
    Like quills upon the fretful porpen-
    tine.

Ghost in Hamlet, 1.5.14–20

Hinting at horrors he will not describe to
Hamlet; "harrow up" means lacerate; "por-
pentine" = porcupine.

Horses

1 O happy horse, to bear the weight
   of Antony!

Cleopatra in Antony and Cleopatra,
1.5.21

Thinking, with a sexual suggestiveness, of the
absent Antony.

2 I will not change my horse with any
   that treads but on four pasterns. . . .
   When I bestride him, I soar, I am a
   hawk; he trots the air.

Dauphin in *Henry V*, 3.7.11–12, 15–16

"Pasterns" = hooves.

Shepherd in *The Winter's Tale*, 4.4.62–4

Perdita is behaving as a guest rather than as the hostess.

Hospitality

Humanity

1   I have heard it said unbidden guests
Are often welcomest when they are gone.

Bedford in *Henry VI, Part 1*, 2.2.55–6

2   Ourself will mingle with society
And play the humble host.

Macbeth in *Macbeth*, 3.4.3–4

"Society" = the guests at his feast.

3   When my old wife lived, upon
This day she was both pantler, butler, cook,
Both dame and servant, welcomed all, served all,
Would sing her song and dance her turn, now here
At upper end o'the table, now i'the middle,
On his shoulder, and his, her face afire
With labor, and the thing she took to quench it
She would to each one sip.

Shepherd in *The Winter's Tale*, 4.4.55–62

Urging his (supposed) daughter Perdita to play the hostess; "pantler" = pantry server; "On his shoulder" = at his shoulder, i.e., to serve food or drink.

4   You are retired
As if you were a feasted one and not
The hostess of the meeting.

1   Yet to me what is this quintessence of dust? Man delights not me—nor woman neither, though by your smiling you seem to say so.

Hamlet in *Hamlet*, 2.2.308–10

Referring to Genesis 3:19, "For dust thou art, and to dust shalt thou return."

2   What should such fellows as I do crawling between earth and heaven?

Hamlet in *Hamlet*, 3.1.126–8

To Ophelia, accusing himself of many faults.

3   When we are born, we cry that we are come
To this great stage of fools.

King Lear in *King Lear*, 4.6.182–3

Shakespeare often compares the world to a theater in which everyone plays a part; the idea became proverbial.

4   Nature hath framed strange fellows in her time.

Antonio in *The Merchant of Venice*, 1.1.51

On the strange eccentricities of human behavior.

5   Lord, what fools these mortals be!

Puck in *A Midsummer Night's Dream*, 3.2.115

He is enjoying the confusions of the lovers, which he has brought about.

6   Throw away respect,
Tradition, form, and ceremonious
 duty,
For you have but mistook me all
 this while.
I live with bread like you, feel want,
Taste grief, need friends.

King Richard in *Richard II*, 3.2.172–6

Acknowledging his common humanity.

7   O wonder!
How many goodly creatures are
 there here!
How beauteous mankind is! O
 brave new world
That has such people in't!

Miranda in *The Tempest*, 5.1.181–4

Her first sight of a group of courtiers from
Italy, some of them in fact anything but
"goodly."

8 Who lives that's not depravèd or
 depraves?
Who dies that bears not one spurn
 to their graves
Of their friend's gift?

Apemantus in *Timon of Athens*,
1.2.140–2

A cynic's view of humanity; "spurn" = kick or
rejection.

9 The middle of humanity thou never
knewest, but the extremity of both
ends. When thou wast in thy gilt
and perfume, they mocked thee for
too much curiosity; in thy rags thou
know'st none, but art despised for
the contrary.

Apemantus in *Timon of Athens*,
4.3.300–4

Apemantus describes the once wealthy Timon,
now penniless, who has become a misan-
thropic outcast; "curiosity" = refinement.

Humility

1   Humble as the ripest mulberry
That will not hold the handling.

Volumnia in *Coriolanus*, 3.2.79–80

Advising Coriolanus how to appear to the
people.

2 I have sounded the very base string
of humility.

Prince Hal in *Henry IV, Part 1*, 2.4.5

He has been mixing with servants in an inn;
he is quibbling on "base" and "bass."

3 Then I stole all courtesy from
 heaven
And dressed my self in such humility
That I did pluck allegiance from
 men's hearts,
Loud shouts and salutations from
 their mouths,
Even in the presence of the
 crownèd king.

King Henry in *Henry IV, Part 1*,
3.2.50–4

Recalling his popularity before he became
king.

4 How like a fawning publican he
 looks!

Shylock in *The Merchant of Venice*,
1.3.41

Referring to Antonio as if he were a tax-col-
lector for the ancient Romans; an allusion to
Luke 18:10–14, where the publican looks
down humbly in contrast to the Pharisee,
showing that "everyone that exalteth himself
shall be abased; and he that humbleth himself
shall be exalted."

Hunger

1 They said they were an-hungry;
 sighed forth proverbs—

That hunger broke stone walls, that
   dogs must eat,
That meat was made for mouths,
   that the gods sent not
Corn for the rich men only.

Caius Martius, later Coriolanus, in Coriolanus, 1.1.205–8

A patrician's contempt for the starving popu-
lace of Rome.

Hunting

1   What shall he have that killed the
      deer?
His leather skin and horns to wear.
Then sing him home.
Take thou no scorn to wear the
   horn,
It was a crest ere thou wast born;
Thy father's father wore it,
And thy father bore it.
The horn, the horn, the lusty horn
Is not a thing to laugh to scorn.

Second Lord in As You Like It, 4.2.10–18

A hunting song; also an elaborate play on the
horns of a cuckold, a husband whose wife is
unfaithful.

2   As wild geese that the creeping
      fowler eye,
Or russet-pated choughs, many in
   sort,
Rising and cawing at the gun's
   report,
Sever themselves and madly sweep
   the sky—
So at his sight away his fellows fly.

Puck in A Midsummer Night's Dream, 3.2.20–4

"Russet-pated choughs, many in sort" = jackdaws with dun-colored heads in a large flock;
"sever themselves" = scatter, as Bottom's
friends scattered when they saw his ass's
head.

3   I was with Hercules and Cadmus
      once,
When in a wood of Crete they
   bayed the bear
With hounds of Sparta: never did I
   hear
Such gallant chiding; for besides the
   groves,
The skies, the fountains, every
   region near
Seemed all one mutual cry. I never
   heard
So musical a discord, such sweet
   thunder.

Hippolyta in A Midsummer Night's Dream, 4.1.112–18

Theseus is here associated with classical leg-
ends in praise of hunting with a pack of
hounds; "bayed" = brought to bay.

4   The hunt is up, the morn is bright
      and grey,
The fields are fragrant and the
   woods are green.

Titus in Titus Andronicus, 2.2.1–2

Titus and his sons, "making a noise with
hounds and horns" (stage direction), set off to
hunt.

Hypocrisy (see also Deceit, Duplicity)

1   We are oft to blame in
      this,
'Tis too much proved, that with
   devotion's visage
And pious action we do sugar o'er
The devil himself.

Polonius in Hamlet, 3.1.45–8

Using Ophelia, made to hold a prayer-book,
to spy on Hamlet; for the moment he realizes
what he is doing is wrong.

2   The lady doth protest too much,
    methinks.

Gertrude in *Hamlet*, 3.2.230

Reacting to a speech by the Player Queen,
who swears she will never remarry if left a
widow, as Gertrude herself has done.

3   Why, I can smile, and murder
    whiles I smile,
    And cry "Content!" to that which
    grieves my heart,
    And wet my cheeks with artificial
    tears,
    And frame my face to all occasions.

**Richard of Gloucester (later Richard
III) in** *Henry VI, Part 3*, 3.2.182–5

4   Would I had never trod this English
    earth!
    Or felt the flatteries that grow upon
    it;
    Ye have angels' faces, but heaven
    knows your hearts.

Queen Katherine in *Henry VIII*,
3.1.143–5

Distrusting the crafty Cardinal Wolsey, who
says he has come to counsel her.

5   When love begins to sicken and
    decay
    It useth an enforcèd ceremony.
    There are no tricks in plain and
    simple faith.

Brutus in *Julius Caesar*, 4.2.20–2

To Lucilius, who reports that Cassius appears
unfriendly.

6   Well, whiles I am a beggar, I will
    rail
    And say there is no sin but to be
    rich;
    And being rich, my virtue then shall
    be

To say there is no sin but beggary.

The Bastard Falconbridge in *King
John*, 2.1.593–6

The hypocrisy of the politicians provokes him
into cynicism.

7   I want that glib and oily art
    To speak and purpose not, since
       what I well intend,
    I'll do't before I speak.

Cordelia in *King Lear*, 1.1.224–6

Alluding to the flattering words of her sisters.

8   To show an unfelt sorrow is an
    office
    Which the false man does easy.

Malcolm in *Macbeth*, 2.3.136–7

"Easy" = easily.

9   O, what may man within him hide,
    Though angel on the outward side!

Duke in *Measure for Measure*, 3.2.271–2

Alluding to the hypocrisy of Angelo, and also
to the coin that had the figure of an angel on
its face.

10 In law, what plea so tainted and
    corrupt
    But, being seasoned with a gracious
    voice,
    Obscures the show of evil?

Bassanio in *The Merchant of Venice*,
3.2.75–7

11 Though I do hate him as I do hell
    pains,
    Yet, for necessity of present life,
    I must show out a flag and sign of
    love,
    Which is indeed but sign.

Iago in *Othello*, 1.1.154–7

Telling Roderigo his true attitude to Othello.

12   Divinity of hell!
When devils will the blackest sins
    put on,
They do suggest at first with heav-
    enly shows,
As I do now.

Iago in *Othello*, 2.3.350–3

The divinity of hell is the inverted theology
that leads people to damnation; "put on" =
encourage; "suggest" = tempt.

13   Though some of you, with Pilate,
    wash your hands,
Showing an outward pity, yet you
    Pilates
Have here delivered me to my sour
    cross.

King Richard in *Richard II*, 4.1.120–1

Referring to his nobles, who have gone over
to his rival, Bolingbroke: the biblical allusion
is to Matthew 27:24.

14   Thus I clothe my naked villainy
With odd old ends stolen forth of
    holy writ,
And seem a saint, when most I play
    the devil.

King Richard in *Richard III*, 1.3.335–7

Taking the audience into his confidence.

15   I thank my God for my humility.

King Richard in *Richard III*, 2.1.73

Speaking to all at court, after he has just
arranged the murder of his own brother,
Clarence.

16   Alas, why would you heap this care
    on me?
I am unfit for state and majesty.

I do beseech you take it not amiss,
I cannot nor I will not yield to you.

King Richard in *Richard III*, 3.7.204–7

Pretending he does not want the crown.

Identity (see also Self-Knowledge)

1   I to the world am like a drop of
    water
That in the ocean seeks another
    drop,
Who, falling there to find his fellow
    forth,
(Unseen, inquisitive) confounds
    himself.
So I, to find a mother and a
    brother,
In quest of them, unhappy, lose
    myself.

**Antipholus of Syracuse in *The Com-
edy of Errors*, 1.2.35–40**

"To the world" = in relation to the world;
"confounds himself" = mingles and loses its
identity.

2   Would you have me
False to my nature? Rather say, I
    play
The man I am.

Coriolanus in *Coriolanus*, 3.2.14–16

His mother is trying to persuade him to be
show humility.

3   Does any here know me? This is
    not Lear.
Does Lear walk thus? Speak thus?
Where are his eyes?

King Lear in *King Lear*, 1.4.226–7

The old king cannot believe his daughter
Goneril would stand up against him.

4 *Lear.* Who is it that can tell me who I am?
Fool. Lear's shadow.
King Lear, 1.4.230–1

Lear has given away his power to his daughters, hence the Fool's reply.

5 Thus play I in one person many people,
And none contented.
King Richard in *Richard II*, 5.5.31–2

Humiliated and imprisoned, Richard tries to escape from the crushing sense of his own identity.

6 I am myself alone.
Richard of Gloucester in *Henry VI, Part 3*, 5.6.83

The future Richard III prides himself on his own uniqueness.

Idleness

1 Hence! Home, you idle creatures, get you home!
Is this a holiday?
Flavius in *Julius Caesar*, 1.1.1–2

One of the tribunes orders people who have come to see Caesar to get off the streets.

Idolatry

1 'Tis mad idolatry
To make the service greater than the god.
Hector in *Troilus and Cressida*, 2.2.56–7

To offer more devotion than the "god" is worth seems mad to Hector, who is thinking of Helen.

Ignorance

1 O thou monster ignorance, how deformed dost thou look!
Holofernes in *Love's Labor's Lost*, 4.2.23

On Dull's inability to understand Latin.

2 I say there is no darkness but ignorance.
Feste in *Twelfth Night*, 4.2.42–3

Pretending to be a priest, Sir Topas, he preaches to the imprisoned Malvolio.

Imagination

1   To imagine
An Antony were nature's piece 'gainst fancy,
Condemning shadows quite.
Cleopatra in *Antony and Cleopatra*, 5.2.98–100

Claiming her dream of Antony as superman is nature's masterpiece, more valid than the "shadows" created by fancy, which have no substance.

2 Piece out our imperfections with your thoughts.
Chorus in *Henry V*, Prologue, 23

"Piece out" = make good.

3 Think, when we talk of horses, that you see them
Printing their proud hooves i' the receiving earth;
For 'tis your thoughts that now must deck our kings.
Chorus in *Henry V*, Prologue, 26–8

Calling on the spectators to use their imagination.

4 Lovers and madmen have such
   seething brains,
   Such shaping fantasies, that appre-
   hend
   More than cool reason ever com-
   prehends.
   The lunatic, the lover, and the poet
   Are of imagination all compact.
   **Theseus in *A Midsummer Night's
   Dream*, 5.1.4–8**

   In their shaping visions lovers and madmen
   conceive ("apprehend") more than cool reason understands; "compact" = composed.

5 Such tricks hath strong imagina-
   tion
   That, if it would but apprehend
   some joy,
   It comprehends some bringer of
   that joy;
   Or in the night, imagining some
   fear,
   How easy is a bush supposed a
   bear?
   **Theseus in *A Midsummer Night's
   Dream*, 5.1.18–22**

   The last line is proverbial ("bear" may = "bugbear" or hobgoblin).

6 O, who can hold a fire in his hand
   By thinking on the frosty Caucasus?
   Or cloy the hungry edge of appetite
   By bare imagination of a feast?
   Or wallow naked in December
   snow
   By thinking on fantastic summer's
   heat?
   O no, the apprehension of the good
   Gives but the greater feeling to the
   worse.
   Bolingbroke in *Richard II*, 1.3.294–301

   Rejecting his father's attempt to console him
   in his banishment; "fantastic" = imagined.

Impatience

1 Why, what a wasp-stung and impatient fool
   Art thou to break into this woman's
   mood,
   Tying thine ear to no tongue but
   thine own!
   **Northumberland in *Henry IV, Part 1*,
   1.3.236–8**

   To Hotspur, who keeps talking, too enraged to
   listen to anyone.

2 I am as poor as Job, my lord, but
   not so patient.
   Falstaff in *Henry IV, Part 2*, 1.2.126–7

   Various calamities reduce Job to poverty, but
   he does not complain (Job 1:13–22).

3 So tedious is this day
   As is the night before some festival
   To an impatient child that hath
   new robes
   And may not wear them.
   Juliet in *Romeo and Juliet*, 3.2.28–31

   Waiting impatiently for Romeo to come to her
   on her wedding night.

Improvement

1 Do thou amend thy face, and I'll
   amend my life.
   Falstaff in *Henry IV, Part 1*, 3.3.24–5

   To Bardolph, whose nose is inflamed with
   drinking.

2 Mend when thou canst, be better at
   thy leisure.
   King Lear in *King Lear*, 2.4.229

   Speaking to his daughter Goneril; "mend" =
   improve.

3   Now is the winter of our discontent
    Made glorious summer by this son
    of York.

King Richard in *Richard III*, 1.1.1–2

The "son of York" is King Edward IV, now ruling England from 1471.

Inconstancy

1   Take, O, take those lips away,
    That so sweetly were forsworn,
    And those eyes, the break of day,
    Lights that do mislead the morn;
    But my kisses bring again, bring
    again,
    Seals of love, but sealed in vain,
    sealed in vain.

Song in *Measure for Measure*, 4.1.1–6

A well-known song; the eyes are lights that "mislead the morn" by suggesting sunrise and happiness rather than being betrayed ("forsworn").

2   Not Hermia but Helena I love.
    Who will not change a raven for a
    dove?

Lysander in *A Midsummer Night's Dream*, 2.2.113–14

Puck's magic juice has made Lysander switch his affections to Helena.

3   He wears his faith but as the fashion of his hat; it ever changes with the next block.

Beatrice in *Much Ado About Nothing*, 1.1.75–7

Mocking Benedick as one who changes loyalty to friends (and perhaps religious faith) as often as he changes the fashion of his hat; "block" = mold.

4   Sigh no more, ladies, sigh no more,
    Men were deceivers ever,
    One foot in sea and one on shore,
    To one thing constant never:
    Then sigh not so, but let them go,
    And be you blithe and bonny,
    Converting all your sounds of woe
    Into Hey nonny, nonny.

Balthasar in *Much Ado About Nothing*, 2.3.62–9

One of Shakespeare's best-known songs.

5   If she be false, O then heaven
    mocks itself!
    I'll not believe't.

Othello in *Othello*, 3.3.278–9

On seeing Desdemona approaching him.

6   Ah, poor our sex! This fault in us I
    find,
    The error of our eye directs our
    mind.
    What error leads must err; O then
    conclude,
    Minds swayed by eyes are full of
    turpitude.

Cressida in *Troilus and Cressida*, 5.2.109–12

On abandoning Troilus for Diomedes.

7   Were man
    But constant, he were perfect. That
    one error
    Fills him with faults, makes him
    run through all the sins;
    Inconstancy falls off ere it begins.

Proteus in *The Two Gentlemen of Verona*, 5.4.110–13

He switched his affections from Julia to Sylvia, and now returns to Julia; "falls off ere it begins" = is unfaithful, or is a falling off from virtue, before the lover is aware of it.

Indecision

1   The swan's down feather,
That stands upon the swell at the full of tide,
And neither way inclines.

Antony in *Antony and Cleopatra*,
3.2.48–50

His image of Octavia's state of mind as she goes to Greece with him, and leaves her brother Octavius in Rome.

2   Like a man to double business bound,
I stand in pause where I shall first begin,
And both neglect.

Claudius in *Hamlet*, 3.3.41–3

He wants to pray, but cannot because of his sense of guilt.

3   'Tis with my mind
As with the tide swelled up unto his height,
That makes a still-stand, running neither way.

Northumberland in *Henry IV, Part 2*,
2.3.62–4

"Still-stand" suggests the moment at which the tide is about to turn.

4   I am a feather for each wind that blows.

Leontes in *The Winter's Tale*, 2.3.154

Inevitability (see also Fate)

1   What cannot be eschewed must be embraced.

Page in *The Merry Wives of Windsor*,
5.5.237

Accepting his daughter's marriage to Fenton.

2   *Juliet.* What must be shall be.
Friar Lawrence.   That's a certain text.

Romeo and Juliet, 4.1.21

Proverbial.

3   There is no help.
The bitter disposition of the time
Will have it so.

Paris in *Troilus and Cressida*, 4.1.48–50

On Cressida being sent to the Greek camp in exchange for Antenor.

Infancy (see also Children)

1   Peace, peace!
Dost thou not see my baby at my breast
That sucks the nurse asleep?

Cleopatra in *Antony and Cleopatra*,
5.2.308–10

Her "baby" in this beautiful image is the asp that is poisoning her.

2   At first the infant,
Mewling and puking in the nurse's arms.

Jaques in *As You Like It*, 2.7.143–4

The first of the "seven ages" of man, that of the infant crying and being sick.

3   I have given suck, and know
How tender 'tis to love the babe that milks me.

Lady Macbeth in *Macbeth*, 1.7.54–5

Infatuation (see also Adoration, Devotion, Love)

1   There is no living, none,
If Bertram be away. 'Twere all one
That I should love a bright particu-
lar star
And think to wed it, he is so above
me.

Helena in All's Well That Ends Well,
1.1.84–5

Expressing her unrequited adoration for a
social superior (" 'Twere all one That" = it is
as if).

2   But now he's gone, and my idola-
trous fancy
Must sanctify his relics.

Helena in All's Well That Ends Well,
1.1.97–8

Love ("fancy") turns into quasi-religious worship.

3   These strong Egyptian fetters I
must break,
Or lose myself in dotage.

Antony in Antony and Cleopatra,
1.2.116–17

The fetters are those of his love for Cleopatra.

4   I must from this enchanting queen
break off.

Antony in Antony and Cleopatra,
1.2.128

Recalling his responsibilities; "queen" puns on
"quean," or whore.

5   Run, run, Orlando, carve on every
tree
The fair, the chaste, the unexpressive she.

Orlando in *As You Like It*, 3.2.10

"Unexpressive" = inexpressible.

6   Loose now and then
A scattered smile, and that I'll live
upon.

Silvius in As You Like It, 3.5.103–4

Infatuated with Phebe.

7   Ever till now,
When men were fond, I smiled and
wondered how.

Angelo in Measure for Measure,
2.2.185–6

Admitting he is sexually attracted by Isabella;
"fond" = infatuated and foolish.

8   So doth the woodbine the sweet
honeysuckle
Gently entwist; the female ivy so
Enrings the barky fingers of the
elm.
O how I love thee! How I dote on
thee!

Titania in A Midsummer Night's
Dream, 4.1.42–5

Puck's magic juice has made her fall in love
with Bottom; "woodbine" is convolvulus.

9   One fairer than my love! The all-
seeing sun
Ne'er saw her match since first the
world begun.

Romeo in Romeo and Juliet, 1.2.92–3

He is infatuated with Rosaline.

10   Cesario, by the roses of the spring,
By maidhood, honor, truth, and
everything,

I love thee so, that maugre all thy pride,
Nor wit nor reason can my passion hide.

Olivia in *Twelfth Night*, 3.1.149–52

She doesn't yet know that Cesario is Viola in disguise; "maugre" = in spite of.

Infidelity

1 She was false as water.
Othello in *Othello*, 5.2.134

Proverbial; "false" = unstable, unreliable.

Inflexibility

1 I'll not be made a soft and dull-eyed fool
To shake the head, relent, and sigh, and yield
To Christian intercessors.

Shylock in *The Merchant of Venice*, 3.3.14–16

Ingratitude

1 Blow, blow thou winter wind,
Thou art not so unkind
As man's ingratitude.

Amiens in *As You Like It*, 2.7.174–7

Setting a winter scene in the forest of Arden.

2 Ingratitude is monstrous, and for the multitude to be ingrateful were to make a monster of the multitude.

Third Citizen in *Coriolanus*, 2.3.9–11

Arguing that the people should be grateful to Caius Martius for defeating the Volsces.

3 Run to your houses, fall upon your knees,
Pray to the gods to intermit the plague
That needs must light on this ingratitude.

Marullus in *Julius Caesar*, 1.1.53–5

Addressing working men who have come to see Caesar, and have forgotten Pompey (hence their "ingratitude").

4 This was the most unkindest cut of all;
For when the noble Caesar saw him stab,
Ingratitude, more strong than traitors' arms,
Quite vanquished him.

Mark Antony in *Julius Caesar*, 3.2.183–6

Pointing to the wound Brutus made.

5 The hedge-sparrow fed the cuckoo so long
That it had its head bit off by its young.

Fool in *King Lear*, 1.4.215–6

The cuckoo lays its eggs in another bird's nest, and so is an emblem of ingratitude; Lear is the sparrow and Goneril, his daughter, the cuckoo.

6 Ingratitude, thou marble-hearted fiend,
More hideous when thou show'st thee in a child
Than the sea-monster.

King Lear in *King Lear*, 1.4.259–61

Reacting to Goneril's demand that he send away half his train of followers.

7 Turn all her mother's pains and benefits
To laughter and contempt, that she may feel
How sharper than a serpent's tooth it is
To have a thankless child!
King Lear in *King Lear*, 1.4.286–9

Cursing his daughter Goneril.

8 When the mind's free,
The body's delicate; this tempest in my mind
Doth from my senses take all feeling else,
Save what beats there—filial ingratitude!
King Lear in *King Lear*, 3.4.11–14

He is wandering bareheaded in a "contentious storm" of rain and wind.

9 O, see the monstrousness of man
When he looks out in an ungrateful shape!
First Stranger in *Timon of Athens*, 3.2.72–3

Commenting on those who benefited from Timon's generosity, and refuse to help him in his need.

10 I hate ingratitude more in a man
Than lying, vainness, babbling, drunkenness,
Or any taint of vice whose strong corruption
Inhabits our frail blood.
Viola in *Twelfth Night*, 3.4.354–7

To Antonio, who mistakes her, in her disguise as Cesario, for her brother Sebastian.

Injustice

1 Some rise by sin, and some by virtue fall.
Escalus in *Measure for Measure*, 2.1.38

Thinking of the generally virtuous Claudio, sentenced to death by Angelo.

Innocence

1 Some innocents 'scape not the thunderbolt.
Cleopatra in *Antony and Cleopatra*, 2.5.77

Attacking the messenger who has brought bad news.

2 Never so much as in a thought unborn
Did I offend your Highness.
Rosalind in *As You Like It*, 1.3.51–2

Accused of treason by her uncle, Rosalind protests her innocence.

3 Our kinsman Gloucester is as innocent
From meaning treason to our royal person
As is the sucking lamb or harmless dove.
King Henry in *Henry VI, Part 2*, 3.1.69–71

The comparisons are proverbial.

4 It will help me nothing
To plead mine innocence, for that dye is on me
Which makes my whit'st part black.

Buckingham in *Henry VIII*, 1.1.207–9

On being arrested as a traitor; "nothing" = not at all.

---

5   I have done no harm. But I
     remember now
     I am in this earthly world, where to
     do harm
     Is often laudable, to do good some-
     time
     Accounted dangerous folly.

Lady Macduff in *Macbeth*, 4.2.74–7

---

6   We were as twinned lambs that did
     frisk i'the sun,
     And bleat the one at th'other.
     What we changed
     Was innocence for innocence. We
     knew not
     The doctrine of ill-doing, nor
     dreamed
     That any did.

Polixenes in *The Winter's Tale*,
1.2.67–71

On his childhood friendship with Leontes;
"changed" = exchanged.

---

7   The silence often of pure innocence
     Persuades when speaking fails.

Paulina in *The Winter's Tale*, 2.2.39–40

Proposing to present Hermione's baby to the
king, Leontes.

---

8   If powers divine
     Behold our human actions—as
     they do—
     I doubt not then but innocence
     shall make
     False accusation blush.

Hermione in *The Winter's Tale*,
3.2.28–31

Innovation

1   Things done without example in
     their issue
     Are to be feared.

King Henry in *Henry VIII*, 1.2.90–1

On learning that Cardinal Wolsey has
imposed a tax without precedent.

2   Who are the violets now
     That strew the green lap of the new-
     come spring?

Duchess of York in *Richard II*, 5.2.46–7

Asking her son Aumerle to tell her who is in
favor with the new King Henry IV.

Insects (see also Creatures)

1   When the sun shines, let foolish
     gnats make sport,
     But creep in crannies, when he
     hides his beams.

Antipholus of Syracuse in *The Comedy of Errors*, 2.2.30–1

2   I think this be the most villainous
     house in all London road for fleas.

Second Carrier in *Henry IV, Part 1*,
2.1.14–15

"House" = inn.

3   Poor harmless fly,
     That with his pretty buzzing
     melody
     Came here to make us merry. And
     thou hast killed him!

Titus in *Titus Andronicus*, 3.2.63–5

To his brother Marcus; Titus is going mad.

Instinct

1 Beware instinct—the lion will not
   touch the true prince.
   Instinct is a great matter.

   Falstaff in *Henry IV, Part 1*, 2.4.271-2

   Justifying as instinct his failure to fight the disguised Hal; "the lion will not touch the true prince" is an ancient belief.

Insults

1 I saw her hand, she has a leathern
   hand,
   A freestone-colored hand. I verily
   did think
   That her old gloves were on, but
   'twas her hands.

   Rosalind in *As You Like It*, 4.3.24-6

   Making Phebe out to be ugly; "freestone" = sandstone.

2 He is deformèd, crooked, old and
   sere,
   Ill-faced, worse bodied, shapeless
   everywhere;
   Vicious, ungentle, foolish, blunt,
   unkind,
   Stigmatical in making, worse in
   mind.

   **Adriana in *The Comedy of Errors*,
   4.2.19-22**

   On her husband, who, she thinks, has been wooing her sister Luciana; "stigmatical" = deformed.

3 Hang thyself in thine own heir-
   apparent garters!

   Falstaff in *Henry IV, Part 1*, 2.2.43-4

   A friendly insult to Prince Hal, heir to the throne.

4 Thou clay-brained guts, thou
   knotty-pated fool, thou whoreson,
   obscene, greasy tallow-catch.

   **Prince Hal in *Henry IV, Part 1*,
   2.4.226-8**

   Abusing the notoriously fat Falstaff for his lies; "knotty-pated" = blockheaded; "tallow-catch" = vessel to catch fat drippings.

5 This sanguine coward, this bed-
   presser, this horse-back-breaker,
   this huge hill of flesh.

   **Prince Hal in *Henry IV, Part 1*,
   2.4.241-3**

   Insulting Falstaff.

6 You starveling, you eel-skin, you
   dried neat's tongue, you bull's piz-
   zle, you stock-fish!

   Falstaff in *Henry IV, Part 1*, 2.4.244-5

   Getting his own back by insulting Hal; "neat's tongue" = ox tongue; "stock-fish" was dried cod.

7 O for breath to utter what is like
   thee! You tailor's yard, you sheath,
   you bowcase, you vile standing
   tuck.

   Falstaff in *Henry IV, Part 1*, 2.4.246-8

   Insulting Hal; "tuck" = rapier.

8 I scorn you, scurvy companion.
   What, you poor, base, rascally,
   cheating, lack-linen mate! Away,
   you moldy rogue, away! I am meat
   for your master.

   **Doll Tearsheet in *Henry IV, Part 2*,
   2.4.123-6**

   Dismissing Pistol; "lack-linen mate" = fellow without a shirt.

9 His wit's as thick as Tewkesbury
   mustard, there's no more conceit in
   him than is in a mallet.

Falstaff in *Henry IV, Part 2*, 2.4.240–2

Tewkesbury is a small town in Gloucestershire; "conceit" = imagination. He is speaking of Poins, who overhears his insult.

10   You blocks, you stones, you worse than senseless things!

Marullus in *Julius Caesar*, 1.1.35

To the working men who have forgotten Pompey and come out to greet Caesar.

11   Thou whoreson zed, thou unnecessary letter!

Kent in *King Lear*, 2.2.64

Expressing his contempt for Oswald, Goneril's steward.

12   A very superficial, ignorant, unweighing fellow.

Lucio in *Measure for Measure*, 3.2.139–40

Abusing the Duke to a Friar (the Duke in disguise); "unweighing" = injudicious.

13   Thou call'st me dog before thou hadst a cause,
But since I am a dog, beware my fangs.

Shylock in *The Merchant of Venice*, 3.3.6–7

Threatening Antonio.

14   Old, cold, withered, and of intolerable entrails.

Page in *The Merry Wives of Windsor*, 5.5.153–4

Page's description of Falstaff and his great belly.

15   How low am I, thou painted maypole? Speak!

Hermia in *A Midsummer Night's Dream*, 3.2.296

Angry with the taller Helena.

16   *Conrade.* Here, man, I am at thy elbow.
Borachio. Mass, and my elbow itched; I thought there would a scab follow.

Much Ado About Nothing, 3.3.98–100

"Scab" = scoundrel, as well as the literal meaning.

17   *Conrade.* Away! You are an ass, you are an ass.
Dogberry. Dost thou not suspect my place? Dost thou not suspect my years?

Much Ado About Nothing, 4.2.73–5

As usual getting the word wrong; Dogberry means "respect," not "suspect."

18   That bottled spider, that foul bunch-backed toad.

Queen Elizabeth in *Richard III*, 4.4.81

Referring to Richard; spiders and toads were thought to be venomous.

19   Thou flea, thou nit, thou winter-cricket thou.

Petruchio in *The Taming of the Shrew*, 4.3.109

An example of Petruchio's insults, here directed at a tailor; a "nit" is the egg of a louse.

Integrity (see also Honesty, Truth)

1   The good I stand on is my truth and honesty.

Archbishop Cranmer in *Henry VIII*, 5.1.122

He is about to face a hostile council.

2 When you do find him, or alive or
   dead,
   He will be found like Brutus, like
   himself.
   Lucilius in *Julius Caesar*, 5.4.24–5

To Antony, searching for Brutus now that he
and Octavius have won the battle of Philippi.

3 Truth hath a quiet breast.
   Mowbray in *Richard II*, 1.3.96

Protesting his loyalty as he is about to fight
Henry Bolingbroke.

Investment

1 *Douglas.* Now remains a sweet
   reversion—
   We may boldly spend, upon the
   hope
   Of what is to come in.
   A comfort of retirement lives in
   this.
   Hotspur. A rendezvous, a home to
   fly unto.

   Henry IV, Part 1, 4.1.53–7

Thinking of Northumberland and his army,
not with them now, as a reserve for the future;
taken in their modern sense, the lines suggest
an investment plan; "reversion" = inheritance.

Invitations

1 *Cassius.* Will you dine with me
   tomorrow?
   Casca. Ay, if I be alive, and your
   mind hold, and your dinner be
   worth the eating.
   Julius Caesar, 1.2.290–2

2 I am not bid for love, they flatter
   me.
   Shylock in *The Merchant of Venice*,
   2.5.13

On being invited to eat supper with Christians.

Isolation (see also Solitude)

1 Now I stand as one upon a rock,
   Environed with a wilderness of sea,
   Who marks the waxing tide grow
   wave by wave,
   Expecting ever when some envious
   surge
   Will in his brinish bowels swallow
   him.
   Titus in *Titus Andronicus*, 3.1.93–7

On finding his daughter Lavinia "ravished,"
and with her hands cut off and tongue cut out;
"his" = its.

Jealousy

1 How many fond fools serve mad
   jealousy?
   Luciana in *The Comedy of Errors*,
   2.1.116

2 The venom clamors of a jealous
   woman
   Poisons more deadly than a mad
   dog's tooth.
   The Abbess in *The Comedy of Errors*,
   5.1.69–70

The Abbess has drawn from Adriana the con-
fession that she constantly reproached her
husband about his unfaithfulness and supposedly drove him mad.

3 Thy jealous fits
   Have scared thy husband from the
   use of wits.
   The Abbess in *The Comedy of Errors*,
   5.1.85–6

To Adriana, whose reproaches have supposedly driven her husband Antipholus mad.

4   The Count is neither sad, nor sick,
     nor merry, nor well; but civil count,
     civil as an orange, and something of
     that jealous complexion.

Beatrice in Much Ado About Nothing,
2.1.293–5

Referring to the jealous Claudio; "civil" puns
on "Seville," where the bitter-sweet oranges
used to make marmalade are grown.

5   I do suspect the lusty Moor
     Hath leaped into my seat; the
        thought whereof
     Doth, like a poisonous mineral,
        gnaw my inwards.

Iago in Othello, 2.1.295–7

"Leaped into my seat" = made love to my
wife, Emilia.

6   O, beware, my lord, of jeal-
     ousy!
     It is the green-eyed monster which
        doth mock
     The meat it feeds on.

Iago in Othello, 3.3.165–7

Iago here plants the idea of jealousy in Othello; "mocks the meat it feeds on" = torments
the victim who suffers jealousy.

7   O, what damnèd minutes tells he
        o'er
     Who dotes, yet doubts; suspects, yet
        strongly loves!

Iago in Othello, 3.3.169–70

The clash of love and suspicion in Othello.

8   Good God, the souls of all my tribe
        defend
     From jealousy!

Iago in Othello, 3.3.175–6

9   Trifles light as air
     Are to the jealous confirmation
        strong

As proofs of holy writ.

Iago in Othello, 3.3.322–4

So he works to make Othello jealous; "holy
writ" = scripture.

10   Dangerous conceits are in their
        natures poisons,
     Which at the first are scarce found
        to distaste,
     But with a little act upon the blood
     Burn like the mines of sulphur.

Iago in Othello, 3.3.326–9

"Conceits" = fancies; mines of sulphur were
associated with the areas around Sicily and
the ever-burning volcano, Mount Etna.

11   But jealous souls will not be
        answered so;
     They are not ever jealous for the
        cause,
     But jealous for they're jealous. It is
        a monster
     Begot upon itself, born on itself.

Emilia in Othello, 3.4.159–62

Responding to Desdemona's consciousness
that she has given Othello no cause for jealousy.

12   Then must you speak
     Of one that loved not wisely but too
        well;
     Of one not easily jealous, but being
        wrought,
     Perplexed in the extreme; of one
        whose hand,
     Like the base Judean threw a pearl
        away
     Richer than all his tribe.

Othello in Othello, 5.2.343–8

"Judean" may refer to the betrayal of Christ by
Judas, who threw away the "pearl of great
price" (Matthew 13:46) which is heaven; but
the earliest text reads "Indian," suggesting an
ignorant East or West Indian who does not
know the value of a precious stone.

Jewels

1 The jewel that we find, we stoop
and take't
Because we see it; but what we do
not see
We tread upon and never think of
it.
**Angelo in *Measure for Measure*,
2.1.24–6**

2 Never so rich a gem
Was set in worse than gold.
**Prince of Morocco in *The Merchant of
Venice*, 2.7.54–5**

Convincing himself that Portia's image will be
in the golden casket.

Jokes (see also Laughter, Merriment)

1 His eye begets occasion for his wit,
For every object that the one doth
catch
The other turns to a mirth-moving
jest.
**Rosaline in *Love's Labor's Lost*,
2.1.69–71**

Describing Berowne.

2 *Maria.* Not a word with him but a
jest.
Boyet. And every jest but a word.
Love's Labor's Lost, 2.1.216

Speaking of the witty Berowne.

3 A jest's prosperity lies in the ear
Of him that hears it, never in the
tongue

Of him that makes it.
**Rosaline in *Love's Labor's Lost*,
5.2.861–3**

4 He jests at scars that never felt a
wound.
Romeo in *Romeo and Juliet*, 2.2.1

Referring to Mercutio, who has been teasing
him for being lovesick.

Joy (see also Happiness)

1 I wish you all joy of the worm.
Clown in *Antony and Cleopatra*, 5.2.260

His parting words to Cleopatra as he leaves
her the asps or snakes she uses to kill herself.

2 If he be sick with joy, he'll recover
without physic.
Prince Hal in *Henry IV, Part 2*, 4.5.15

Misunderstanding the nature of his father's illness.

3 Silence is the perfectest herald of
joy.
**Claudio in *Much Ado About Nothing*,
2.1.306**

Unable to express his happiness on being
offered Hero in marriage.

4 It gives me wonder great as my
content
To see you here before me.
Othello in *Othello*, 2.1.183–4

Greeting Desdemona on his safe arrival in
Cyprus.

5 Beseech you, sir, be merry; you
have cause,

So have we all, of joy.

Gonzalo in *The Tempest*, 2.1.1–2

Appealing to Alonso to be joyful after coming safely ashore.

6　There might you have beheld one joy crown another, so and in such manner that it seemed sorrow wept to take leave of them, for their joy waded in tears.

Third Gentleman in *The Winter's Tale*, 5.2.43–6

On the reconciliation of Leontes and Polixenes.

Judgment (see also Justice, Law)

1　Censure me in your wisdom, and awake your senses, that you may the better judge.

Brutus in *Julius Caesar*, 3.2.16–17

To the people; "censure" = judge.

2　To offend and judge are distinct offices,
And of opposèd natures.

Portia in *The Merchant of Venice*, 2.9.61–2

To the Prince of Aragon, who has judged badly in choosing the silver casket, and is offended because he feels he deserves better.

3　Seven times tried that judgment is
That did never choose amiss.
Some there be that shadows kiss,
Such have but a shadow's bliss.

Prince of Aragon in *The Merchant of Venice*, 2.9.64–7

The message in the silver casket telling him his hopes are illusory.

4　What judgment shall I dread, doing no wrong?

Shylock in *The Merchant of Venice*, 4.1.89

Going by the letter of the law.

5　A Daniel come to judgment! Yea, a Daniel!
O wise young judge, how I do honor thee!

Shylock in *The Merchant of Venice*, 4.1.223–4

On Portia, who argues the law must take its course. In the Apocrypha, Daniel rescues Susannah from her accusers, as Portia will rescue Antonio from Shylock's cruelty.

6　The urging of that word "judgment" hath bred a kind of remorse in me.

Second Murderer in *Richard III*, 1.4.107–8

Commissioned to murder Clarence, he hesitates at the thought of doomsday, or the Day of Judgment (see Matthew 10:15, etc.).

Justice (see also Judgment, Law, Punishment)

1　'Tis the sport to have the enginer Hoist with his own petard.

Hamlet in *Hamlet*, 3.4.206–7

"Enginer" = maker of military "engines" or devices; "hoist" = blown up by; "petard" = explosive device.

2　As a woodcock to mine own springe, Osric:
I am justly killed with mine own treachery.

Laertes in *Hamlet*, 5.2.306–7

He is wounded by the poisoned rapier he intended for Hamlet; "springe" = snare.

3 Sir, I desire you do me right and
justice,
And to bestow your pity on me; for
I am a most poor woman, and a
stranger,
Born out of your dominions.
Queen Katherine in *Henry VIII*,
2.4.13–16

At the divorce proceedings, she appeals to her
husband, Henry VIII.

4 Remember March, the Ides of
March remember.
Did not great Julius bleed for jus-
tice' sake?
What villain touched his body, that
did stab
And not for justice?
Brutus in *Julius Caesar*, 4.3.18–21

5 Take physic, pomp,
Expose thyself to feel what wretches
feel,
That thou mayst shake the super-
flux to them
And show the heavens more just.
King Lear in *King Lear*, 3.4.33–6

"Superflux" = superfluous possessions.

6 A man may see how this world goes
with no eyes. Look with thine ears;
see how yond justice rails upon
yond simple thief. Hark in thine
ear: change places, and handy-
dandy, which is the justice, which is
the thief?
King Lear in *King Lear*, 4.6.150–4

Addressing the blind Gloucester.

7 Through tattered clothes great vices
do appear;
Robes and furred gowns hide all.
Plate sin with gold,

And the strong lance of justice
hurtless breaks:
Arm it in rags, a pigmy's straw does
pierce it.
King Lear in *King Lear*, 4.6.164–7

Or, it is often said now, there is one justice for
the rich, and another for the poor.

8 The gods are just, and of our pleas-
ant vices
Make instruments to plague us.
Edgar in *King Lear*, 5.3.171–2

Speaking to his half-brother, the dying
Edmund, whose vices have led to his death,
just as their father Gloucester's vices have
brought about his blinding.

9 This even-handed justice
Commends the ingredients of our
poisoned chalice
To our own lips.
Macbeth in *Macbeth*, 1.7.10–12

Contemplating murdering Duncan; "even-
handed" = impartial.

10 Liberty plucks justice by the nose.
Duke in *Measure for Measure*, 1.3.29

"Liberty" = license, or excessive freedom.

11 I not deny
The jury, passing on the prisoner's
life,
May in the sworn twelve have a
thief or two
Guiltier than him they try. What's
open made to justice,
That justice seizes.
Angelo in *Measure for Measure*,
2.1.18–22

To Escalus, who has been pleading to save
Claudio from a sentence of death.

12 Under your good correction, I have
seen
When, after execution, judgment
hath
Repented o'er his doom.
Provost in *Measure for Measure,*
2.2.10–12

Cautioning Angelo against the too hasty execution of Claudio; "doom" = sentence.

13 He who the sword of heaven would
bear
Must be as holy as severe,
Pattern in himself to know,
Grace to stand and virtue go.
Duke in *Measure for Measure,* 3.2.261–4

On the need for the judge to be a model of
virtue, and have grace to be upright, as well
as virtue to lead.

14 Haste still pays haste, and leisure
answers leisure;
Like doth quit like, and measure
still for measure.
Duke in *Measure for Measure,*
5.1.410–11

Alluding to Matthew 7:2, "with what measure
ye mete, it shall be measured unto you again."

15 As thou urgest justice, be assured
Thou shalt have justice more than
thou desirest.
Portia in *The Merchant of Venice,*
4.1.315–6

The law says that Shylock must not shed the
blood of a Christian.

16 Justice is feasting while the widow
weeps.
The Rape of Lucrece, 906

Lamenting after being raped, Lucrece
becomes bitter.

Kindness

1 Kindness, nobler ever than revenge.
Oliver in *As You Like It,* 4.1.128

Speaking of Orlando's resolve to rescue his
brother from danger.

2 Yet I do fear thy nature;
It is too full o' the milk of human
kindness
To catch the nearest way.
Lady Macbeth in *Macbeth,* 1.5.16–18

Fearing Macbeth is too gentle to murder the
king ("catch the nearest way").

3 A kind heart he hath. A woman
would run through fire and water
for such a kind heart.
Mistress Quickly in *The Merry Wives
of Windsor,* 3.4.102–4

Speaking of Fenton, one of the suitors for the
hand of Anne Page.

4 Timon will to the woods, where he
shall find
Th'unkindest beast more kinder
than mankind.
Timon in *Timon of Athens,* 4.1.35–6

The beginning of his misanthropy.

Kings, see Royalty

Kinship

1 *Claudius.* But now, my cousin
Hamlet, and my son—
Hamlet. [Aside] A little more than
kin, and less than kind.

Hamlet, 1.2.64–5

"Cousin" = kinsman, here a nephew; Hamlet
is more closely related than a nephew, since
his uncle has married his mother, yet less close
than a son, and not well disposed to Claudius.

Kissing (see also Love)

1 Kingdoms are clay; our dungy earth
alike
Feeds beast as man; the nobleness
of life
Is to do thus—when such a mutual
pair
And such a twain can do't.

Antony in *Antony and Cleopatra*,
1.1.35–8

Rating an embrace with Cleopatra as worth
more than empire.

2 If she first meet the curlèd Antony,
He'll make demand of her, and
spend that kiss
Which is my heaven to have.

Cleopatra in *Antony and Cleopatra*,
5.2.301–2

Referring to her servant Iras, who has just
died; Cleopatra expects to meet Antony in
death.

3   O, a kiss
Long as my exile, sweet as my
revenge!

Coriolanus in *Coriolanus*, 5.3.44–5

Greeting his wife, Virgilia, who comes with
his son and mother to plead with him not to
make war on Rome.

4   Ere I could
Give him that parting kiss which I
had set
Betwixt two charming words,
comes in my father,
And like the tyrannous breathing of
the north
Shakes all our buds from growing.

Imogen in *Cymbeline*, 1.3.33–7

Recalling her parting from Posthumus, her
husband, who is banished; "charming words"
= words which may protect him from evil;
"north" = north wind.

5 I understand thy kisses, and thou
mine,
And that's a feeling disputation.

Mortimer in *Henry IV, Part 1*, 3.1.202–3

An Englishman speaking to his Welsh wife;
they do not speak each other's languages;
"feeling disputation" = exchange of feelings.

6 By my troth, I kiss thee with a most
constant heart.

Doll Tearsheet in *Henry IV, Part 2*,
2.4.269–70

The old whore speaking to old Falstaff.

7 I can express no kinder sign of love
Than this kind kiss.

King Henry in *Henry VI, Part 2*,
1.1.18–19

Welcoming his French queen to England.

8 *Beatrice.* Let me go with that I
came, which is, with knowing
what hath passed between you
and Claudio.

Benedick. Only foul words; and thereupon I will kiss thee.
Beatrice. Foul words is but foul wind, and foul wind is but foul breath, and foul breath is noisome; therefore I will depart unkissed.

Much Ado About Nothing, 5.2.47–54

Benedick reports he has not fought with Claudio, and Beatrice plays on the idea of the proverb, "words are but wind."

9   Kiss me, Kate; we will be married o'Sunday.

Petruchio in *The Taming of the Shrew*, 2.1.324

Speaking to the shrew, Katherine; the well-known musical, based on the play, is called "Kiss Me Kate."

Lament

1   The poor soul sat sighing by a sycamore tree,
Sing all a green willow;
Her hand on her bosom, her head on her knee,
Sing willow, willow, willow.

Desdemona in *Othello*, 4.3.40–3

Reworking an old song, Shakespeare changed the sex of the lover to suit Desdemona's sense of being forsaken.

Language (see also Solecisms, Speech, Words)

1   Thy tongue
Makes Welsh as sweet as ditties highly penned,

Sung by a fair queen in a summer's bower,
With ravishing division, to her lute.

Mortimer in *Henry IV, Part 1*, 3.1.205–8

To his wife, whose speech in Welsh he does not understand.

2   The Prince but studies his companions
Like a strange tongue, wherein, to gain the language,
'Tis needful that the most immodest word
Be looked upon and learnt, which once attained,
Your highness knows, comes to no further use
But to be known and hated.

Warwick in *Henry IV, Part 2*, 4.4.68–73

On Prince Hal as using Falstaff and others for his education.

3   I will tell thee in French—which I am sure will hang upon my tongue like a new-married wife about her husband's neck, hardly to be shook off.

King Henry in *Henry V*, 5.2.178–81

On his difficulty in finding French words in which to make love to Katherine.

4   It will be proved to thy face that thou hast men about thee that usually talk of a noun and a verb and such abominable words as no Christian ear can endure to hear.

Jack Cade in *Henry VI, Part 2*, 4.7.37–41

An illiterate peasant accusing Lord Saye of treason.

5 Those that understood him smiled
at one another and shook their
heads; but for mine own part, it was
Greek to me.
Casca in *Julius Caesar*, 1.2.282–4

Reporting Caesar's speech to the people.

6 They have been at a great feast of
languages and stolen the scraps.
Moth in *Love's Labor's Lost*, 5.1.36–7

Moth is looking at Armado, Holofernes and
Nathaniel, all lovers of wordiness.

7 The language I have learnt these
forty years,
My native English, now I must
forgo,
And now my tongue's use is to me
no more
Than an unstringèd viol or a harp.
Mowbray in *Richard II*, 1.3.159–62

On being banished to foreign parts; a "viol"
was the forerunner of the modern violin.

8 You taught me language, and my
profit on't
Is, I know how to curse. The red
plague rid you
For learning me your language!
Caliban in *The Tempest*, 1.2.363–5

To Prospero; "red" refers to red sores caused
by plague.

9 *Sir Toby Belch. Pourquoi*, my dear
knight?
Sir Andrew Aguecheek. What is
"*pourquoi*"? Do, or not do? I
would I had bestowed that time in
the tongues that I have in fencing,
dancing, and bear-baiting. O had
I but followed the arts!

Twelfth Night, 1.3.90–4

"Tongues" = languages; Sir Andrew does not
understand the simplest French, "pourquoi" =
why; setting dogs to bait bears was a popular
sport in Shakespeare's day.

Last Words

1 The rest is silence.
Hamlet in *Hamlet*, 5.2.358

2 *Et tu, Brute?*—Then fall, Caesar!
Caesar in *Julius Caesar*, 3.1.77

There is no classical source for Caesar's
famous last words, which seem to have
become well-known in Shakespeare's age,
though he did not invent them.

3 They say the tongues of dying men
Enforce attention like deep har-
mony.
Where words are scarce, they are
seldom spent in vain,
For they breathe truth that breathe
their words in pain.
John of Gaunt in *Richard II*, 2.1.5–8

Speaking on his deathbed.

4 Mount, mount, my soul! thy seat is
up on high,
Whilst my gross flesh sinks down-
ward, here to die.
King Richard in *Richard II*, 5.5. 111–2

It was proverbial that "dying men speak true."

5 A horse, a horse, my kingdom for a
horse!
King Richard in *Richard III*, 5.4.13

His last desperate cry on the field of battle
before he is killed.

6   O true apothecary!
Thy drugs are quick. Thus with a
kiss I die.

Romeo in *Romeo and Juliet*, 5.3.119–20

He kisses Juliet, supposing her to be dead.

7   This is the chase;
I am gone for ever.

**Antigonus in *The Winter's Tale*,
3.3.57–8**

He runs off "pursued by a bear" (stage direction).

Lateness

1   I am glad I was up so late, for that's
the reason I was up so early.

Cloten in *Cymbeline*, 2.3.33–4

He has been gaming all night, and so was
early enough to fee musicians to sing at sunrise to wake Imogen.

2   Better three hours too soon than a
minute too late.

**Ford in *The Merry Wives of Windsor*,
2.2.312–3**

3   Pray God we may make haste and
come too late!

King Richard in *Richard II*, 1.4.64

On his way to the dying John of Gaunt,
Richard hopes to find his uncle dead.

4   Better once than never, for never
too late.

**Petruchio in *The Taming of the Shrew*,
5.1.150**

To Katherine, on her agreeing to kiss him in
the street; proverbial: "better late than never"
and "it is never too late to mend."

5   *Sir Andrew Aguecheek.* I know, to
be up late is to be up late.

Sir Toby Belch. A false conclusion.
I hate it as an unfilled can. To be
up after midnight and to go to
bed then, is early; so that to go to
bed after midnight is to go to bed
betimes.

***Twelfth Night*, 2.3.4–9**

Sir Toby's excuse for staying up drinking.

Laughter (see also Jokes, Merriment)

1   O, you shall see him laugh till his
face be like a wet cloak ill laid up.

Falstaff in *Henry IV, Part 2*, 5.1.84–5

2   The lamentable change is from the
best,
The worst returns to laughter.

Edgar in *King Lear*, 4.1.5–6

An outcast, and disguised as a beggar Edgar
reflects on his state. The idea that at the worst
things can only get better was proverbial.

Law (see also Judgment, Justice, Punishment)

1   In the corrupted currents of this
world
Offense's gilded hand may shove by
justice,
And oft 'tis seen the wicked prize
itself
Buys out the law; but 'tis not so
above:
There is no shuffling.

Claudius in *Hamlet*, 3.3.57–61

As king, Claudius is the law in Denmark; "currents" = transactions; "gilded" = bribing;
"shove by" = push aside; "shuffling" = evasion.

2 Resolution thus fubbed as it is with the rusty curb of old father antic the law.

Falstaff in *Henry IV, Part 1*, 1.2.60–1

Falstaff's "resolution" has to do with robbery, thwarted ("fubbed") by the law.

3 Faith, I have been a truant in the law,
And never yet could frame my will to it,
And therefore frame the law unto my will.

Suffolk in *Henry VI, Part 1*, 2.4.7–9

Having neglected study of the law ("been a truant"), he makes his own, since he cannot adapt or bend ("frame") his will to it.

4 I have perhaps some shallow spirit of judgment,
But in these nice sharp quillets of the law,
Good faith, I am no wiser than a daw.

Warwick in *Henry VI, Part 1*, 2.4.16–18

"Sharp quillets" = nice distinctions; a "daw" is a jackdaw, proverbial for foolishness.

5 And what makes robbers bold but too much lenity?

Clifford in *Henry VI, Part 3*, 2.6.22

6 The law I bear no malice for my death;
'T has done upon the premises but justice;
But those that sought it I would wish more Christians.

Buckingham in *Henry VIII*, 2.1.62–4

7 We must not make a scarecrow of the law,

Setting it up to fear the birds of prey,
And let it keep one shape, till custom make it
Their perch and not their terror.

Angelo in *Measure for Measure*, 2.1.1–4

Angelo favors harsh sentencing; "fear" = frighten.

8 The law hath not been dead, though it hath slept.

Angelo in *Measure for Measure*, 2.2.90

Reminding Isabella that the laws have existed even though they have not been enforced for some time.

9 Wrest once the law to your authority:
To do a great right, do a little wrong.

Bassanio in *The Merchant of Venice*, 4.1.215–6

Asking the Duke to bend the law in order to curb Shylock.

10 I am a humble suitor to your virtues;
For pity is the virtue of the law,
And none but tyrants use it cruelly.

Alcibiades in *Timon of Athens*, 3.5.7–9

Begging the senators of Athens for the life of a friend who has killed a man in a duel.

11 There is a law in each well-ordered nation
To curb those raging appetites that are
Most disobedient and refractory.

Hector in *Troilus and Cressida*, 2.2.180–2

"Refractory" = willful, stubborn.

Lawyers

1 The first thing we do, let's kill all the lawyers.

Dick the Butcher in *Henry VI, Part 2*, 4.2.76–7

The first aim of the rebels (Shakespeare's version of the Peasants' Revolt of 1381).

2 *Kent.* This is nothing, Fool.
Fool. Then 'tis like the breath of an unfeed lawyer, you gave me nothing for't.

***King Lear*, 1.4.128–30**

Kent comments on the Fool's rhymes.

Learning (see also Books, Education, Study)

1 He was a scholar, and a ripe and good one,
Exceeding wise, fair-spoken and persuading.

Griffith in *Henry VIII*, 4.2.51–2

Speaking of Wolsey's good qualities.

23 To be a well-favored man is the gift of fortune; but to write and read comes by nature.

Dogberry in *Much Ado About Nothing*, 3.3.14–16

The comic constable, splendidly muddled as usual, has a low opinion of reading and writing; "well-favored" = good-looking.

3 For your writing and reading, let that appear when there is no need of such vanity.

Dogberry in *Much Ado About Nothing*, 3.3.20–2

Priding himself on his own illiteracy.

4 O this learning, what a thing it is!

Gremio in *The Taming of the Shrew*, 1.2.159

The foolish Gremio admires learning.

Lechery (see also Lust, Sex)

1 Sparrows must not build in his house-eaves, because they are lecherous.

Lucio in *Measure for Measure*, 3.2.175–6

Criticizing the puritanical Angelo.

2 An honest woman's son, for indeed my father did something smack, something grow to, he had a kind of taste.

Launcelot Gobbo in *The Merchant of Venice*, 2.2.16–18

Meaning that his father was known for lechery, and so was not "honest" = honorable.

3 It is impossible you should see this,
Were they as prime as goats, as hot as monkeys,
As salt as wolves in pride, and fools as gross
As ignorance made drunk.

Iago in *Othello*, 3.3.402–5

Goats were proverbially lecherous, and monkeys noted for lust, as were wolves in heat; "salt" = lustful; Iago protests that Othello cannot see Cassio and Desdemona in the act of lust.

4 There's language in her eye, her cheek, her lip,
Nay, her foot speaks; her wanton spirits look out
At every joint and motive of her body.

Ulysses in *Troilus and Cressida*,
4.5.55–7

Condemning Cressida, who has been kissed in turn by all the Greek leaders.

5 O these encounterers, so glib of tongue,
That give a coasting welcome ere it comes,
And wide unclasp the tables of their thoughts
To every ticklish reader! Set them down
For sluttish spoils of opportunity
And daughters of the game.

Ulysses in *Troilus and Cressida*,
4.5.58–63

His scornful assessment of Cressida, as she arrives in the Grecian camp; "ticklish" = lustful.

6 Lechery, lechery, still wars and lechery. Nothing else holds fashion.

Thersites in *Troilus and Cressida*,
5.2.194–5

After watching Cressida making love to Diomedes.

Leisure

1 When thou hast leisure, say thy prayers; when thou hast none, remember thy friends.

Parolles, *All's Well That Ends Well*,
1.1.212–3

His parting advice to Helena at the end of the first scene.

2 Shall I not take mine ease in mine inn?

Falstaff in *Henry IV, Part 1*, 3.3.80–1

Falstaff's way of avoiding paying what he owes.

Letters

1   Who's born that day
When I forget to send to Antony,
Shall die a beggar.

Cleopatra in *Antony and Cleopatra*,
1.5.63–5

Messages of love to the absent Antony.

2 Get posts and letters, and make friends with speed;
Never so few, and never yet more need.

Northumberland in *Henry IV, Part 2*,
1.1.214–15

"Posts" were messengers who rode by stages where they changed horses.

3 What presence must not know,
From where you do remain let paper show.

Aumerle in *Richard II*, 1.3.249–50

To the exiled Bolingbroke: "presence" = royal presence, King Richard; and also, our inability to talk face to face.

Liberality

1 Since he hath got the jewel that I loved,

And that which you did swear to
keep for me,
I will become as liberal as you,
I'll not deny him anything I have,
No, not my body nor my husband's
bed.

Portia in *The Merchant of Venice*,
5.1.224–8

Teasing Bassanio, who has given Portia's ring
to the lawyer Balthasar, not knowing that
Balthasar was his wife in disguise.

Liberty, see Freedom

Lies, see Deceit, Lying

Life

1 The web of our life is of a mingled
yarn, good and ill together.

First Lord in *All's Well That Ends
Well*, 4.3.71–2

2 I love long life better than figs.

Charmian in *Antony and Cleopatra*,
1.2.32

Figs were associated with sexual activity.

3 For some must watch while some
must sleep,
Thus runs the world away.

Hamlet in *Hamlet*, 3.2.273–4

Hamlet has been watching Claudius, who has
just hurried away from the play within the
play; "watch" = stay awake, or work.

4 O gentlemen, the time of life is
short!

To spend that shortness basely were
too long.

Hotspur in *Henry IV, Part 1*, 5.2.81–2

5 There is a history in all men's lives,
Figuring the natures of the times
deceased,
The which observed, a man may
prophesy,
With a near aim, of the main
chance of things
As yet not come to life.

Warwick in *Henry IV, Part 2*, 3.1.80–4

A chain of events ("history") in everyone's
past life may indicate pretty well ("with a near
aim") the likely shape of things to come.

6 This day I breathèd first—time is
come round,
And where I did begin, there shall I
end.
My life is run his compass.

Cassius in *Julius Caesar*, 5.3.23–5

Believing the battle is lost; "compass" = full
circle.

7   Out, out, brief candle!
Life's but a walking shadow, a poor
player
That struts and frets his hour upon
the stage
And then is heard no more. It is a
tale
Told by an idiot, full of sound and
fury,
Signifying nothing.

Macbeth in *Macbeth*, 5.5.23–8

The idea of life as fleeting and as a light or
candle is common in the Bible, as at Job 18:6,
"The light shall be dark in his dwelling, and
his candle shall be put out with him," and Job
14:1–2, "Man . . . fleeth as it were a shadow,
and never continueth in one state."

8   You take my house when you do
     take the prop
     That doth sustain my house; you
     take my life
     When you do take the means
     whereby I live.
     Shylock in _The Merchant of Venice_,
     4.1.375–7

     To the Duke, whose judgment is to pardon
     Shylock his life, but seize all his wealth.

9   This queen will live. Nature
     awakes,
     A warmth breathes out of her. She
     hath not been
     Entranced above five hours. See
     how she 'gins
     To blow into life's flower again.
     Cerimon in _Pericles_, 3.2.92–5

     Thaisa, found unconscious and coffined as if
     dead, revives; " 'gins" = begins.

10   Even through the hollow eyes of
     death
     I spy life peering.
     Northumberland in _Richard II_,
     2.1.270–1

     Even as John of Gaunt dies, word comes that
     Henry Bolingbroke is ready to make war on
     Richard.

11   _Gonzalo._ Here is everything advan-
     tageous to life.
     Antonio. True, save means to live.
     The Tempest, 2.1.50

     On Prospero's island.

12   Life's uncertain voyage.
     Timon in _Timon of Athens_, 5.1.202

Light

1   Light, seeking light, doth light of
     light beguile;
     So ere you find where light in dark-
     ness lies,
     Your light grows dark by losing of
     your eyes.
     Berowne in _Love's Labor's Lost_, 1.1.77–9

     Arguing that as too much light dazzles and
     makes the eye unable to see, so too much
     study only confuses the student.

2   Put out the light, and then put out
     the light.
     If I quench thee, thou flaming min-
     ister,
     I can again thy former light restore
     Should I repent me; but once put
     out thy light,
     Thou cunning'st pattern of
     excelling nature,
     I know not where is that
     Promethean heat
     That can thy light relume.
     Othello in _Othello_, 5.2.7–13

     The "light" is both that of the candle ("flaming
     minister") he carries, and that of Desdemona;
     Prometheus in Greek legend stole fire from
     the gods to give it to human beings; "relume"
     = light again.

Loss

1   Love that comes too late,
     Like a remorseful pardon slowly
     carried,
     To the great sender turns a sour
     offense,
     Crying, "That's good that's gone."

King of France in *All's Well That Ends Well*, 5.3.57–60

Expressing the familiar feeling of realizing that we value a thing only when it is lost.

2 I can give the loser leave to chide.

Queen Margaret in *Henry VI, Part 2*, 3.1.182

The loser is the Duke of Gloucester, arrested at her instigation.

3 O insupportable and touching loss!

Cassius in *Julius Caesar*, 4.3.151

On the news of the death of Portia, Brutus's wife.

4 "My daughter! O my ducats! O my daughter!
Fled with a Christian! O my Christian ducats!
Justice! The law! My ducats, and my daughter!"

Solanio in *The Merchant of Venice*, 2.8.15–17

Mockingly imitating Shylock's outcry on finding his daughter has stolen away with bags of ducats.

5 Thou torturest me, Tubal. It was my turquoise; I had it of Leah when I was a bachelor. I would not have given it for a wilderness of monkeys.

Shylock in *The Merchant of Venice*, 3.1.120–3

On hearing that his daughter Jessica has traded his jewel for a monkey; he refers to his dead wife, Leah.

6 But there, where I have garnered up my heart,
Where either I must live or bear no life;

The fountain from the which my current runs
Or else dries up: to be discarded thence,
Or keep it as a cistern for foul toads
To knot and gender in!

Othello in *Othello*, 4.2.57–62

"Knot and gender" = copulate and breed; the foulness is all in Othello's imagination.

7 My wife, my wife! What wife? I have no wife.
O insupportable! O heavy hour!
Methinks it should be now a huge eclipse
Of sun and moon, and that th'
affrighted globe
Should yawn at alteration.

Othello in *Othello*, 5.2.97–101

That the earth ("globe") should gape wide ("yawn") at the change brought by Desdemona's death suggests an earthquake.

8 Say, is my kingdom lost? Why, 'twas my care,
And what loss is it to be rid of care?

King Richard in *Richard II*, 3.2.95–6

Anticipating the takeover by Bolingbroke (later Henry IV).

Love (see also Adoration, Courtship, Devotion, Kissing)

1 The hind that would be mated by the lion
Must die for love.

Helena in *All's Well That Ends Well*, 1.1.91–2

On the unbridgeable gulf between herself ("hind" = deer) and Count Bertram.

2 My friends were poor, but honest,
      so's my love.
   Helena in *All's Well That Ends Well*,
   1.3.195

   On her love for Bertram, nobly born; "friends"
   here means relations.

3 Love is holy.
   Bertram in *All's Well That Ends Well*,
   4.2.32

   Said as he is trying to seduce Diana.

4   All impediments in fancy's
         course
   Are motives of more fancy.
   Bertram in *All's Well That Ends Well*,
   5.3.214–5

   "Fancy," as commonly, = love; "motives of" =
   incitements to.

5 *Cleopatra.* If it be love indeed, tell
      me how much.
   Antony. There's beggary in the love
      that can be reckoned.
   ***Antony and Cleopatra*, 1.1.14–15**

   A grand conception of love as beyond measure.

6   But you are come
   A market-maid to Rome, and have
      prevented
   The ostentation of our love.
   **Octavius Caesar in *Antony and
   Cleopatra*, 3.6.50–2**

   Octavius sees his sister returning to Rome
   with a smaller train than he thinks appropriate.

7   O thou day o' the world,
   Chain mine armed neck, leap thou,
      attire and all,

Through proof of harness to my
   heart, and there
Ride on the pants triumphing!
Antony in *Antony and Cleopatra*,
4.8.13–16

In victory he invites Cleopatra to bind
("chain") him, and leap through his strong
armor to her sexual embrace.

8 Love no man in good earnest, nor
   no further in sport neither, than
   with safety of a pure blush thou
   mayst in honor come off again.
   Celia in *As You Like It*, 1.2.27–9

   Advice to Rosalind on avoiding commitment
   in love.

9   Whose loves
   Are dearer than the natural bond of
      sisters.
   Le Beau in *As You Like It*, 1.2.275–6

   Speaking of the cousins, Rosalind and Celia.

10   As true a lover
   As ever sighed upon a midnight pil-
      low.
   Silvius in *As You Like It*, 2.4.26–7

   On the absurdity of unrequited love.

11 Alas, poor shepherd, searching of
      thy wound,
   I have by hard adventure found
      mine own.
   Rosalind in *As You Like It*, 2.4.44–5

   Examining (searching) Silvius's wound of love,
   Rosalind recognizes her own complaint.

12 We that are true lovers run into
   strange capers.
   Touchstone in *As You Like It*, 2.4.54–5

   On the folly of love.

13   Then the lover,
     Sighing like furnace, with a woeful
       ballad
     Made to his mistress' eyebrow.

Jaques in *As You Like It*, 2.7.147–9

The third of the "seven ages" of man.

14   From the east to western Inde,
     No jewel is like Rosalind.

Rosalind in *As You Like It*, 3.2.88–9

Reading one of Orlando's love poems, with its
poor rhyme ("Inde" = the Indies).

15   Your hose should be ungartered,
     your bonnet unbanded, your sleeve
     unbuttoned, your shoe untied, and
     everything about you demonstrat-
     ing a careless desolation.

Rosalind in *As You Like It*, 3.2.378–81

How the melancholy lover should look.

16   Love is merely a madness.

Rosalind in *As You Like It*, 3.2.400

17   I think he is not a pick-purse nor a
     horse-stealer, but for his verity in
     love, I do think him as concave as a
     covered goblet or a worm-eaten
     nut.

Celia in *As You Like It*, 3.4.22–5

18   The sight of lovers feedeth those in
     love.

Rosalind in *As You Like It*, 3.4.57

Going to see Silvius wooing Phebe.

19   If ever (as that ever may be near)
     You meet in some fresh cheek the
       power of fancy,

Then shall you know the wounds
  invisible
That love's keen arrows make.

Silvius in *As You Like It*, 3.5.28–31

On the power of love to hurt; the image of
Cupid shooting love's darts at random underlies these lines.

20   I pray you do not fall in love with
       me,
     For I am falser than vows made in
       wine.
     Besides, I like you not.

Rosalind in *As You Like It*, 3.5.72–4

To Phebe, while Rosalind is in disguise as a
man.

21   Dead shepherd, now I find thy saw
       of might,
     "Who ever loved that loved not at
       first sight?"

Phebe in *As You Like It*, 3.5.81–2

The quotation from Christopher Marlowe's
poem *Hero and Leander* (published 1598),
l.176, has passed into proverb lore. Marlowe
died in 1593. Phebe, a shepherdess, calls
Marlowe a shepherd.

22   O coz, coz, coz, my pretty little coz,
     that thou didst know how many
     fathom deep I am in love!

Rosalind in *As You Like It*, 4.1.205–7

Addressing Celia.

23   That same wicked bastard of Venus
     that was begot of thought, con-
     ceived of spleen, and born of mad-
     ness, that blind rascally boy that
     abuses everyone's eyes because his
     own are out, let him be judge how
     deep I am in love.

Rosalind in *As You Like It*, 4.1.211–15

"Bastard of Venus" = Cupid.

24   She could not love me
      Were man as rare as phoenix.
      Rosalind in *As You Like It*, 4.3.16–17

      Misrepresenting Phebe's letter protesting love;
      "phoenix" = a mythical bird, only one of
      which lived at a time.

25   Pacing through the forest,
      Chewing the food of sweet and bit-
      ter fancy.
      Oliver in *As You Like It*, 4.3.100–1

      Oliver's image of the love-sick Orlando.

26   Your brother and my sister no
      sooner met but they looked; no
      sooner looked but they loved; no
      sooner loved but they sighed; no
      sooner sighed but they asked one
      another the reason; no sooner knew
      the reason but they sought the rem-
      edy.
      Rosalind in *As You Like It*, 5.2.32–7

      Describing the sudden passion of Oliver and
      Celia for one another.

27   *Phebe.* Good shepherd, tell this
         youth what 'tis to love.
      Silvius. It is to be all made of sighs
         and tears.
         . . .
      It is to be all made of faith and ser-
         vice.
         . . .
      It is to be all made of fantasy,
      All made of passion, and all made
         of wishes,
      All adoration, duty, and obser-
         vance,
      All humbleness, all patience, and
         impatience,
      All purity, all trial, all observance.
      ***As You Like It*, 5.2.83–4,89,94–8**

      A definition of love by the infatuated Silvius;
      "fantasy" = imagination.

28   Hang there like fruit, my soul,
      Till the tree die!
      Posthumus in *Cymbeline*, 5.5.263–4

      Embracing Imogen, as all deceptions and mis-
      takes in the story are revealed.

29   This is the very ecstasy of love.
      Polonius in *Hamlet*, 2.1.99

      Interpreting Hamlet's strange behavior to
      Ophelia as the "ecstasy" or madness of love
      for her.

30   Doubt thou the stars are fire,
      Doubt that the sun doth move,
      Doubt truth to be a liar,
      But never doubt I love.
      Polonius in *Hamlet*, 2.2.116–19

      Quoting from Hamlet's letter to Ophelia, who
      has given it to him; "doubt" = suspect.
      (According to the Ptolemaic idea of the uni-
      verse, the sun moved round the earth).

31   *Hamlet.* Is this a prologue, or the
         posy of a ring?
      Ophelia. 'Tis brief, my lord.
      Hamlet. As woman's love.
      ***Hamlet*, 3.2.152–4**

      After the three-line prologue to the play within
      the play; "posy of a ring" = short motto
      engraved in a ring.

32   How should I your true love know
      From another one?
      By his cockle hat and staff,
      And his sandal shoon.
      Ophelia in *Hamlet*, 4.5.23–6

      Singing old songs in her madness after her
      father's death; "cockle hat" = hat bearing a
      cockle-shell, the sign, with the sandals, of a
      pilgrim; "shoon" = shoes.

33   Not that I think you did not love
         your father,
      But that I know love is begun by
         time,

And that I see, in passages of proof,
Time qualifies the spark and fire of
it.

Claudius in *Hamlet*, 4.7.110–13

To Laertes, about his love for his father, now
dead; "passages of proof" = examples that
prove what I am saying.

34 There lives within the very flame of
love
A kind of wick or snuff that will
abate it.

Claudius in *Hamlet*, 4.7.114–15

"Snuff" = charred portion of the wick.

35 Do you not love me? Do you not
indeed?
Well, do not then, for since you
love me not,
I will not love myself.

Lady Percy in *Henry IV, Part 1*, 2.3.96–8

To her husband; she is trying to get information out of him, and he says jokingly that he
does not love her.

36 *Falstaff.* I am old, I am old.
Doll Tearsheet. I love thee better
than I love e'er a scurvy young
boy of them all.

***Henry IV, Part 2*, 2.4.271–3**

"Scurvy" = contemptible; a term of abuse.

37 When love begins to sicken and
decay,
It useth an enforcèd ceremony.
There are no tricks in plain and
simple faith.

Brutus in *Julius Caesar*, 4.2.20–2

To Lucilius, who reports that Cassius is
unfriendly.

38 What shall Cordelia speak? Love,
and be silent.

Cordelia in *King Lear*, 1.1.62

On being asked to spell out how much she
loves her father.

39   I am sure my love's
More ponderous than my tongue.

Cordelia in *King Lear*, 1.1.77–8

Her love is weightier than she can put into
words.

40   Love's not love
When it is mingled with regards
that stand
Aloof from th'entire point.

King of France in *King Lear*, 1.1.238–40

"Regards" = considerations; his rival for the
hand of Cordelia has been setting conditions
for marrying her.

41 On a day—alack the day—
Love, whose month is ever May,
Spied a blossom passing fair
Playing in the wanton air.

**Dumaine in *Love's Labor's Lost*,
4.3.99–102**

Expressing his love for Katherine.

42 A lover's eyes will gaze an eagle
blind.
A lover's ear will hear the lowest
sound.

**Berowne in *Love's Labor's Lost*,
4.3.331–2**

In a speech in praise of love.

43 Love's feeling is more soft and sensible
Than are the tender horns of cockled snails.

**Berowne in *Love's Labor's Lost*,
4.3.334–5**

"Cockled" = possessing a shell.

44 When love speaks, the voice of all the gods
Make heaven drowsy with the harmony.

Berowne in *Love's Labor's Lost*,
4.3.341–2

As if the gods sing in response to human love.

45 Believe not that the dribbling dart of love
Can pierce a complete bosom.

Duke in *Measure for Measure*, 1.3.2–3

The Duke does in the end succumb to the attractions of Isabella; the "dart" suggests Cupid's arrow.

46 But love is blind, and lovers cannot see
The pretty follies that themselves commit,
For if they could, Cupid himself would blush
To see me thus transformèd to a boy.

Jessica in *The Merchant of Venice*,
2.6.36–9

She is disguised to elope with Lorenzo; "love is blind" is proverbial.

47 Beshrew me but I love her heartily,
For she is wise, if I can judge of her,
And fair she is, if that mine eyes be true,
And true she is, as she hath proved herself;
And therefore, like herself, wise, fair, and true,
Shall she be placèd in my constant soul.

Lorenzo in *The Merchant of Venice*,
2.6.52–7

On his love for Jessica.

48 One half of me is yours, the other half yours—
Mine own, I would say; but if mine, then yours,
And so all yours.

Portia in *The Merchant of Venice*,
3.2.16–18

Confessing her love to Bassanio.

49 If you do love me, you will find me out.

Portia in *The Merchant of Venice*,
3.2.41

Meaning that Bassanio will choose the right casket.

50 Tell me where is fancy bred,
Or in the heart or in the head?
How begot, how nourishèd?
Reply, reply.
It is engendered in the eyes,
With gazing fed, and fancy dies
In the cradle where it lies.
Let us all ring fancy's knell.
I'll begin it. Ding, dong, bell.

Song in *The Merchant of Venice*,
3.2.63–71

The rhymes and the idea of dying help to guide Bassanio to choose the leaden casket; love ("fancy") was supposed to enter the heart through the eyes.

51 O love, be moderate, allay thy ecstasy,
In measure rain thy joy, scant this excess!
I feel too much thy blessing; make it less,
For fear I surfeit.

Portia in *The Merchant of Venice*,
3.2.111–14

Overjoyed on seeing Bassanio choose the right casket to win her; "scant" = moderate.

52 The course of true love never did run smooth.

Lysander in *A Midsummer Night's Dream*, 1.1.134

To Hermia, whose father has forbidden her to have anything to do with Lysander.

53 Before the time I did Lysander see, Seemed Athens as a paradise to me. O then, what graces in my love do dwell, That he hath turned a heaven unto a hell?

Hermia in *A Midsummer Night's Dream*, 1.1.204–7

Her "love" is Lysander, who has provoked the anger of her father and jealousy of Demetrius, and so made Athens hell for her.

54 Things base and vile, holding no quantity, Love can transpose to form and dignity. Love looks not with the eyes, but with the mind, And therefore is winged Cupid painted blind.

Helena in *A Midsummer Night's Dream*, 1.1.232–5

Love is conventionally roused through sight, but the lover also lacks judgment in seeing beauty where others do not, hence the proverb, "Love is without reason." Cupid was often represented as blind or blindfolded, since his arrows were supposed to be fired at random.

55 Therefore is love said to be a child Because in choice he is so oft beguiled.

Helena in *A Midsummer Night's Dream*, 1.1.238–9

"Child" = both Cupid, and lovers who are so often deluded ("beguiled").

56 It is not night when I do see your face, Therefore I think I am not in the night; Nor doth this wood lack worlds of company, For you, in my respect, are all the world.

Helena in *A Midsummer Night's Dream*, 2.1.221–4

Helena's infatuation with Demetrius; "in my respect" = esteem.

57 One turf shall serve as pillow for us both; One heart, one bed, two bosoms, and one troth.

Lysander in *A Midsummer Night's Dream*, 2.2.41–2

Lysander trying to persuade Hermia to sleep by him.

58 I mean that my heart unto yours is knit, So that but one heart we can make of it: Two bosoms interchainèd with an oath, So then two bosoms and a single troth.

Lysander in *A Midsummer Night's Dream*, 2.2.47–50

A pretty idea of the union of lovers, but a bit premature for Hermia.

59 Thy fair virtue's force perforce doth move me On the first view to say, to swear, I love thee.

Titania in *A Midsummer Night's Dream*, 3.1.140–1

To Bottom, transformed by Oberon's magic into an ass; "fair virtue's force" = power of your unblemished excellence.

60 Prove that ever I lose more blood with love than I will get again with drinking, pick out mine eyes with a ballad-maker's pen and hang me up at the door of a brothel-house for the sign of blind Cupid.

Benedick in *Much Ado About Nothing*, 1.1.250–4

Sighing was thought to dry up the blood, and drinking wine to produce new blood; Benedick scorns the very idea of love by associating it with sentimental ballads and the brothel-house. Cupid was often depicted with blindfold eyes, since his arrows were shot at random.

61 How sweetly you do minister to love,
That know love's grief by his complexion!

Claudio in *Much Ado About Nothing*, 1.1.312–13

"Grief" = pangs; the lover typically had a pale appearance ("complexion").

62 All hearts in love use their own tongues.
Let every eye negotiate for itself,
And trust no agent.

Claudio in *Much Ado About Nothing*, 2.1.177–9

He thinks Don Pedro has wooed Hero for himself, and not, as he promised, for Claudio.

63 My talk to thee must be how Benedick
Is sick in love with Beatrice. Of this matter
Is little Cupid's crafty arrow made,
That only wounds by hearsay.

Hero in *Much Ado About Nothing*, 3.1.20–3

Plotting with Ursula to make Beatrice fall in love with Benedick.

64 Some Cupid kills with arrows, some with traps.

Hero in *Much Ado About Nothing*, 3.1.106

Hero's device to make Beatrice admit she loves Benedick has proved successful.

65 If he be not in love with some woman, there is no believing old signs. 'A brushes his hat o'mornings; what should that bode?

Claudio in *Much Ado About Nothing*, 3.2.40–2

On Benedick sprucing himself up.

66 I pray thee now, tell me for which of my bad parts didst thou first fall in love with me?

Benedick in *Much Ado About Nothing*, 5.2.59–61

Jokingly to Beatrice.

67 *Beatrice.* But for which of my good parts did you first suffer love for me?
Benedick. Suffer love! A good epithet. I do suffer love indeed, for I love thee against my will.

Much Ado About Nothing, 5.2.64–7

Avoiding sentiment by means of wit.

68 She loved me for the dangers I had passed,
And I loved her that she did pity them.

Othello in *Othello*, 1.3.167–8

Speaking about Desdemona.

69 If I be left behind,
A moth of peace, and he go to the war,

The rites for which I love him are
bereft me,
And I a heavy interim shall support
By his dear absence. Let me go with
him.

Desdemona in *Othello*, 1.3.255–9

Asking the Venetian senate to be allowed to
accompany her husband to Cyprus.

O anything of nothing first create,
O heavy lightness, serious vanity,
Misshapen chaos of well-seeming
forms.

Romeo in *Romeo and Juliet*, 1.1.175–9

On the miseries of unrequited love, hinting
too at the Capulet-Montague quarrel; "create"
= created.

70   The heavens forbid
But that our loves and comforts
should increase
Even as our days do grow!

Desdemona in *Othello*, 2.1.193–5

Greeting Othello on her arrival in Cyprus after
a stormy voyage.

71   Excellent wretch! Perdition catch
my soul
But I do love thee! And when I love
thee not,
Chaos is come again.

Othello in *Othello*, 3.3.90–2

Desdemona has just left the stage; "wretch"
was used as a term of endearment.

72   From forth the fatal loins of these
two foes,
A pair of star-crossed lovers take
their life.

**Chorus in *Romeo and Juliet*, Prologue,
5–6**

The foes are the clans of the Capulets and
Montagues in Verona.

73   Here's much to do with hate, but
more with love.
Why then, O brawling love, O loving hate,

74   Love is a smoke made with the
fume of sighs,
Being purged, a fire sparkling in
lovers' eyes,
Being vexed, a sea nourished with
lovers' tears.

Romeo in *Romeo and Juliet*, 1.1.190–2

A fanciful definition of love: if the "fume" or
smoke of sighs is removed, a lover's eyes
sparkle; if it is stirred up, tears are provoked.

75   Is love a tender thing? It is too
rough,
Too rude, too boisterous, and it
pricks like thorn.

Romeo in *Romeo and Juliet*, 1.4.25–6

He is still infatuated with Rosaline, who will
have nothing to do with him.

76   Did my heart love till now? Forswear it, sight,
For I ne'er saw true beauty till this
night.

Romeo in *Romeo and Juliet*, 1.5.52–3

On seeing Juliet, he dismisses his earlier passion for Rosaline.

77   It is my lady, O, it is my love.
O that she knew she were!

Romeo in *Romeo and Juliet*, 2.2.10–11

Seeing Juliet at her window.

78 With love's light wings did I o'er-
perch these walls,
For stony limits cannot hold love
out,
And what love can do, that dares
love attempt.

Romeo in *Romeo and Juliet*, 2.2.66–8

He has climbed the walls into Capulet's garden in order to watch beneath Juliet's window.

79 This bud of love by summer's
ripening breath
May prove a beauteous flower
when next we meet.

Juliet in *Romeo and Juliet*, 2.2.121–2

Reassuring herself and Romeo that their love
may flourish.

80 My bounty is as boundless as the
sea,
My love as deep. The more I give
to thee
The more I have, for both are infinite.

Juliet in *Romeo and Juliet*, 2.2.133–5

Expressing her devotion to Romeo.

81 Love's heralds should be thoughts,
Which ten times faster glides than
the sun's beams,
Driving back shadows over low'ring
hills.

Juliet in *Romeo and Juliet*, 2.5.4–6

Anxiously expecting her Nurse to return with
news of Romeo.

82 Love moderately: long love doth so.

**Friar Lawrence in *Romeo and Juliet*,
2.6.14**

Giving the hasty Romeo advice.

83 They are but beggars that can count
their worth,
But my true love is grown to such
excess
I cannot sum up sum of half my
wealth.

Juliet in *Romeo and Juliet*, 2.6.32–4

To Romeo as they go off to be married; "sum
up sum" = add up the total.

84 Is it possible
That love should of a sudden take
such hold?

**Tranio in *The Taming of the Shrew*,
1.1.146–7**

His master, Lucentio, has fallen in love at first
sight of Bianca.

85 Of all the men alive
I never yet beheld that special face
Which I could fancy more than any
other.

**Bianca in *The Taming of the Shrew*,
2.1.10–12**

Speaking to her sister Katherine.

86 Kindness in women, not their
beauteous looks,
Shall win my love.

**Hortensio in *The Taming of the
Shrew*, 4.2.41–2**

Deciding he does not want to marry Bianca.

87 Love wrought these miracles.

**Lucentio in *The Taming of the Shrew*,
5.1.124**

Speaking of the devices by which he has
deceived Bianca's father and married her.

88 Let thy song be love. This love will
undo us all.

Helen in *Troilus and Cressida*,
3.1.110–11

Calling on Pandarus to sing; "undo" = ruin.

89 Helen. In love, i'faith, to the very
tip of the nose.
Paris. He eats nothing but doves,
love, and that breeds hot blood,
and hot blood begets hot
thoughts, and hot thoughts beget
hot deeds, and hot deeds is love.

Troilus and Cressida, 3.1.127–30

They are talking about Pandarus; what Paris
describes is lechery, not love.

90 This is the monstruosity in love,
lady, that the will is infinite and the
execution confined; that the desire
is boundless, and the act a slave to
limit.

Troilus in *Troilus and Cressida*, 3.2.81–3

Speaking to Cressida.

91 They say all lovers swear more performance than they are able, and
yet reserve an ability that they never
perform; vowing more than the
perfection of ten, and discharging
less than the tenth part of one.

Cressida in *Troilus and Cressida*,
3.2.84–7

Showing her anxiety about the claims Troilus
is making for love.

92 My thoughts were like unbridled
children, grown
Too headstrong for their mother.

Cressida in *Troilus and Cressida*,
3.2.122–3

Admitting her love for Troilus.

93 Time, force, and death
Do to this body what extremes you
can,
But the strong base and building of
my love
Is as the very center of the earth,
Drawing all things to it.

Cressida in *Troilus and Cressida*,
4.2.101–5

On learning that she must leave Troilus and
go to the Greek camp; the center of the earth
was thought to act as a powerful magnet.

94 O spirit of love, how quick and
fresh art thou.

Orsino in *Twelfth Night*, 1.1.9

"Quick and fresh" = alert and vigorous.

95 O mistress mine, where are you
roaming?
O stay and hear, your true love's
coming,
That can sing both high and low.
Trip no further, pretty sweeting.
Journeys end in lovers meeting,
Every wise man's son doth know.

Feste in *Twelfth Night*, 2.3.39–44

His song of love seems to relate to the love-
tangles of the play, which do end happily.

96 What is love? 'Tis not hereafter,
Present mirth hath present laugh-
ter.
What's to come is still unsure.
In delay there lies no plenty,
Then come kiss me, sweet and
twenty.
Youth's a stuff will not endure.

Feste in *Twelfth Night*, 2.3.47–52

This stanza touches on the brevity of life and
traditional "ubi sunt" ("where are they?")
theme (as in "where have all the flowers
gone?").

97 *Sir Andrew Aguecheek.* Before me,
she's a good wench.
Sir Toby Belch. She's a beagle true
bred, and one that adores me.
What o' that?
Sir Andrew Aguecheek. I was
adored once, too.

Twelfth Night, 2.3.178–81

They speak of Maria; a "beagle" = a small,
intelligent hunting dog; Sir Andrew has his
moment of pathos.

98 There is no woman's sides
Can bide the beating of so strong a
passion
As love doth give my heart; no
woman's heart
So big, to hold so much; they lack
retention.
Alas, their love may be called
appetite.

Orsino in *Twelfth Night,* 2.4.93–7

Speaking to Cesario, really Viola in disguise;
"bide" = endure.

99 Love sought is good, but given
unsought is better.

Olivia in *Twelfth Night,* 3.1.156

100 *Julia.* His little speaking shows his
love but small.
Lucetta. Fire that's closest kept
burns most of all.
Julia. They do not love that do not
show their love.
Lucetta. O, they love least that let
men know their love.

The Two Gentlemen of Verona,
1.2.29–32

101 Sweet love, sweet lines, sweet life!
Here is her hand, the agent of her
heart;
Here is her oath for love, her
honor's pawn.

Proteus in *The Two Gentlemen of*
Verona, 1.3.45–7

He enters reading a love-letter from Julia.

102 O, how this spring of love resem-
bleth
The uncertain glory of an April day,
Which now shows all the beauty of
the sun,
And by and by a cloud takes all
away.

Proteus in *The Two Gentlemen of*
Verona, 1.3.84–7

On being sent away from Verona, and from
his love, Julia.

103 Love is blind.

Speed in *The Two Gentlemen of*
Verona, 2.1.70

Proverbial; Speed, the clown, can see better
than his master Valentine.

104 What, gone without a word?
Ay, so true love should do: it cannot speak,
For truth hath better deeds than
words to grace it.

Proteus in *The Two Gentlemen of*
Verona, 2.2.16–18

Spoken as Julia parts from him.

105 Love is like a child

That longs for everything that he
can come by.
Duke in *The Two Gentlemen of
Verona*, 3.1.124–5

For as you were when first your eye
I eyed,
Such seems your beauty still.
Sonnet 104, 1–3

106   He says he loves my daughter:
I think so too; for never gaz'd the
moon
Upon the water as he'll stand and
read
As 'twere my daughter's eyes: and,
to be plain,
I think there is not half a kiss to
choose
Who loves another best.
Shepherd in *The Winter's Tale*,
4.4.171–6

On Perdita and Florizel.

107   But if the while I think on thee,
dear friend,
All losses are restored, and sorrows
end.
Sonnet 30, 13–14

108   Take all my loves, my love, yea, take
them all.
What hast thou then more than
thou hadst before?
No love, my love, that thou mayst
true love call;
All mine was thine before thou
hadst this more.
Sonnet 40, 1–4

Does "all my loves" refer to the speaker's
male and female "friends"?

109   To me, fair friend, you never can be
old,

110   Let me not to the marriage of true
minds
Admit impediments; love is not
love
That alters where it alteration finds,
Or bends with the remover to
remove.
O no, it is an ever-fixèd mark
That looks on tempests and is never
shaken.
Sonnet 116, 1–6

A famous expression of the idea of love:
"admit" = concede that there may be; the
"alteration" may be in age or other circumstances; "Or bends with the remover to
remove" = or changes because of inconstancy
in either party. The word "impediment"
occurs in the wedding service in the Book of
Common Prayer, and the third line sums up
the promises made in that ceremony "for better for worse, for richer for poorer, in sickness
and in health."

111   Two loves I have of comfort and
despair,
Which like two spirits do suggest
me still:
The better angel is a man right
fair,
The worser spirit a woman colored
ill.
Sonnet 144, 1–4

The speaker's mistress, now involved also
with his friend, is depicted as a spirit that
tempts him (suggests) to evil; other sonnets
(130, for instance) describe her having black
hair and eyes, or "colored ill" at a time when
fair hair, a white skin and grey eyes were
prized.

Loyalty

On finding the gold left with the baby Perdita by Antigonus.

1 He'll go along o'er the wide world with me.
Celia in *As You Like It*, 1.3.132
Speaking of the clown, Touchstone.

2 I will follow thee
To the last gasp with truth and loyalty.
Adam in *As You Like It*, 2.3.69–70
Spoken by the faithful old servant Adam to Orlando as they set off for the forest of Arden.

3 A plague upon it when thieves cannot be true one to another!
Falstaff in *Henry IV, Part 1*, 2.2.27–8
His companions have taken his horse, and Falstaff is too fat to walk far.

4 My heart doth joy that yet in all my life
I found no man but he was true to me.
Brutus in *Julius Caesar*, 5.5.34–5

Luck (see also Chance, Fortune)

1 This is the third time; I hope good luck lies in odd numbers.
Falstaff in *The Merry Wives of Windsor*, 5.1.2–3

2 'Tis a lucky day, boy, and we'll do good deeds on't.
Shepherd in *The Winter's Tale*, 3.3.138–9

Lust (see also Desire, Lechery, Luxury, Sex)

1 When you have our roses,
You barely leave our thorns to prick ourselves,
And mock us with our bareness.
Diana in *All's Well That Ends Well*, 4.2.18–20
Resisting Bertram's attempt to seduce her.

2 [Antony] is become the bellows and the fan
To cool a gipsy's lust.
Philo in *Antony and Cleopatra*, 1.1.9–10
One acerbic view of the love of Antony and Cleopatra.

3 I was
A morsel for a monarch.
Cleopatra in *Antony and Cleopatra*, 1.5.30–1
Recalling her affair with Julius Caesar.

4 What hotter hours,
Unregistered in vulgar fame, you have
Luxuriously picked out.
Antony in *Antony and Cleopatra*, 3.13.118–20
Condemning Cleopatra for her past love affairs; "luxuriously" relates to lechery.

5 Thou thyself hast been a libertine,
As sensual as the brutish sting itself.

Duke Senior in *As You Like It*, 2.7.65–6

Denying Jaques the moral high ground he has claimed.

6   Rebellious hell,
If thou canst mutine in a matron's
    bones,
To flaming youth let virtue be as
    wax
And melt in her own fire.

Hamlet in *Hamlet*, 3.4.82–5

Reproaching his mother for marrying her late husband's brother, a marriage Hamlet regards as springing from lust.

7   Such is the simplicity of man to
    hearken after the flesh.

Costard in *Love's Labor' Lost*, 1.1.217

Is Costard confusing biblical echoes of such texts as "we all had our conversation in times past in the lusts of the flesh" (Ephesians 2:3)?

8   Lust is but a bloody fire
    Kindled with unchaste desire,
    Fed in heart, whose flames aspire
    As thoughts do blow them, higher
      and higher.

Song by Fairies, *The Merry Wives of Windsor*, 5.5.95–8

9   She knows the heat of a luxurious
      bed.
    Her blush is guiltiness, not mod-
      esty.

Claudio in *Much Ado About Nothing*, 4.1.41–2

Accusing Hero of being unchaste; "luxurious" could mean lecherous.

10   You seem to me as Diana in her
     orb,

As chaste as is the bud ere it be
    blown;
But you are more intemperate in
    your blood
Than Venus, or those pampered
    animals
That rage in savage sensuality.

Claudio in *Much Ado About Nothing*, 4.1.57–61

Rejecting Hero as a bride: Diana, goddess of the moon and of chastity, is contrasted with Venus, goddess of love or sexuality; "blood" = sensual appetite.

11   But we have reason to cool our rag-
    ing motions, our carnal stings, our
    unbitted lusts; whereof I take this
    that you call love to be a sect or
    scion. ... It is merely a lust of the
    blood and a permission of the will.

Iago in *Othello*, 1.3.329–32, 334–5

Iago cynically reduces all love to lust in speaking to Roderigo.

12   If ever you prove false to one
    another, since I have taken such
    pain to bring you together, let all
    pitiful goers-between be called to
    the world's end after my name; call
    them all Pandars.

Pandarus in *Troilus and Cressida*, 3.2.199–202

On providing Troilus and Cressida with a bedroom in which to make love.

13   This momentary joy breeds months
    of pain,
    This hot desire converts to cold dis-
    dain;
    Pure Chastity is ruffled of her store,
    And Lust, the thief, far poorer than
    before.

ature *The Rape of Lucrece*, 690–3

14 Th' expense of spirit in a waste of
    shame
    Is lust in action, and till action lust
    Is perjured, murderous, bloody, full
    of blame,
    Savage, extreme, rude, cruel, not to
    trust,
    Enjoyed no sooner but despisèd
    straight,
    Past reason hunted, and no sooner
    had,
    Past reason hated as a swallowed
    bait
    On purpose laid to make the taker
    mad;
    Mad in pursuit, and in possession
    so,
    Had, having, and in quest to have
    extreme,
    A bliss in proof, and proved, a very
    woe,
    Before a joy proposed, behind a
    dream.
    All this the world well knows, yet
    none knows well
    To shun the heaven that leads
    men to this hell.

Sonnet 129

The definitive account of the experience of
lust in action; "Th'expense of spirit" = the
pouring out of vital energy, involving the soul
or spirit, not just the body; "not to trust" = not
to be trusted; "in proof, and proved" = during
the experience, and afterwards.

15 Love comforteth like sunshine after
    rain,
    But lust's effect is tempest after sun;
    Love's gentle spring doth always
    fresh remain,
    Lust's winter comes ere summer
    half be done;
    Love surfeits not, lust like a glut-
    ton dies;
    Love is all truth, lust full of forgèd
    lies.

Venus and Adonis, 799–804

Adonis tries to repel the lustful advances of
Venus; the contrast between lust and love is a
recurrent topic in Shakespeare's work.

Luxury

1 The beds i'th' East are soft.

Antony in *Antony and Cleopatra*, 2.6.50

Recalling Egyptian luxury in warlike Rome.

2 The devil Luxury, with his fat rump
   and potato finger.

**Thersites in *Troilus and Cressida*,
5.2.55–6**

Luxury was not distinguished from lust; pota-
toes, first brought to England in the sixteenth
century, were thought to have aphrodisiac
qualities.

Lying

1 These lies are like their father that
   begets them, gross as a mountain,
   open, palpable.

**Prince Hal in *Henry IV, Part 1*,
2.4.225–6**

To Falstaff, who has hugely exaggerated his
account of a fight with the disguised Prince
and Poins; "gross" = huge, and hence obvi-
ous.

2 Lord, Lord, how this world is
   given to lying!

Falstaff in *Henry IV, Part 1*, 5.4.145–6

No one more than Falstaff himself.

3 For my part, if a lie may do thee
   grace,
   I'll gild it with the happiest terms I
   have.

Prince Hal in *Henry IV, Part 1,*
5.4.157–8

Falstaff claims to have killed Hotspur, and Hal does not expose the lie; "do thee grace" = bring you credit.

4 Lord, Lord, how subject we old men are to this vice of lying!

Falstaff in *Henry IV, Part 2.* 3.2.303–4

Falstaff for once speaks the truth (compare 2 above).

5 If he say so, may his pernicious soul Rot half a grain a day! He lies to the heart.

Emilia in *Othello,* 5.2.155–6

She wants Iago to rot slowly; a "grain" is the smallest measurement of weight.

6 You told a lie, an odious, damnèd lie;
Upon my soul, a lie, a wicked lie.

Emilia in *Othello,* 5.2.180–1

On learning of Iago's lies about Desdemona.

7 As many lies as will lie in thy paper, although the sheet were big enough for the bed of Ware in England.

Sir Toby Belch in *Twelfth Night,*
3.2.46–8

Advising Sir Andrew on writing a challenge; "the bed of Ware," in Hertfordshire, was famous, being ten feet square and able to accommodate twelve people.

Madness

1 Lord Hamlet, with his doublet all unbraced,
No hat upon his head, his stockings fouled,
Ungartered, and down-gyvèd to his ankle,
Pale as his shirt, his knees knocking each other,
And with a look so piteous in purport
As if he had been loosèd out of hell To speak of horrors.

Ophelia in *Hamlet,* 2.1.75–81

Describing to Polonius the distraught state of Hamlet, who appears like a ghost; "downgyved" = fallen down like fetters.

2   To define true madness, What is't but to be nothing else but mad?

Polonius in *Hamlet,* 2.2.93–4

Explaining Hamlet's madness to Claudius and Gertrude.

3   He repelled, a short tale to make, Fell into a sadness, then into a fast, Thence to a watch, thence into a weakness,
Thence to a lightness, and by this declension,
Into the madness wherein now he raves.

Polonius in *Hamlet,* 2.2.146–50

His idea of the stages of Hamlet's madness; "watch" = inability to sleep.

4 Though this be madness, yet there is method in't.

Polonius in *Hamlet,* 2.2.205–6

It dawns on him that Hamlet is not as mad as he is pretending to be; "method" = logic.

5 I am but mad north-north-west. When the wind is southerly, I know a hawk from a handsaw.

Hamlet in *Hamlet,* 2.2.378–9

Quibbling perhaps on "hernshaw" or heron.

6   This is mere madness,
And thus a while the fit will work
on him.
Anon, as patient as the female dove
When that her golden couplets are
disclosed,
His silence will sit drooping.

Gertrude in *Hamlet*, 5.1.284–8

On Hamlet's changing moods; "golden couplets" = pair of baby birds with yellow down;
"disclosed" = hatched.

7   My wits begin to turn.

King Lear in *King Lear*, 3.2.67

Realizing he is going mad.

8   O, that way madness lies; let me
shun that!

King Lear in *King Lear*, 3.4.21

"That way" = thinking about the ingratitude of
his daughters.

9   Why, he was met even now
As mad as the vexed sea, singing
aloud,
Crowned with rank fumiter and
furrow-weeds,
With hardocks, hemlock, nettles,
cuckoo-flowers,
Darnel, and all the idle weeds that
grow
In our sustaining corn.

Cordelia in *King Lear*, 4.4.1–6

The mad king has crowned himself with useless ("idle") weeds.

10 Why, this is very midsummer madness.

Olivia in *Twelfth Night*, 3.4.56

On Malvolio's strange behavior; the midsummer moon was thought to cause madness (or
"lunacy," from "luna" = moon).

Magic

1   We have the receipt of fern-seed,
we walk invisible.

Gadshill in *Henry IV, Part 1*, 2.1.86–7

"Receipt" = recipe; fern-seed was thought to
make invisible whoever carried it.

2   *Othello.* Make it a darling like your
precious eye.
To lose't or give't away were such
perdition
As nothing else could match.
Desdemona. Is't possible?
Othello. There's magic in the web
of it.

***Othello*, 3.4.69–73**

Their topic is the handkerchief that causes so
much discord between them.

3   If this be magic, let it be an art
Lawful as eating!

Leontes in *The Winter's Tale*, 5.3.110–1

Spoken as what he thinks is a statue of
Hermione comes to life.

Malice (see also Hate)

1   Ill will never said well.

Orleans in *Henry V*, 3.7.113

Proverbial.

2   If I can catch him once upon the
hip,
I will feed fat the ancient grudge I
bear him.

**Shylock in *The Merchant of Venice*,
1.3.46–7**

To "have one on the hip," or capable of being
overthrown, is a proverbial phrase, from
wrestling.

Man (see also Men, Men and Women)

Expressing the confidence of Renaissance humanism.

1 You might have been enough the man you are
With striving less to be so.

Volumnia in *Coriolanus*, 3.2.19–20

Speaking to her warrior son.

2   I'll never
Be such a gosling to obey instinct, but stand
As if a man were author of himself,
And knew no other kin.

Coriolanus in *Coriolanus*, 5.3.34–7

The gosling, or young goose, was noted for its foolishness.

3 I see a man's life is a tedious one.

Imogen in *Cymbeline*, 3.6.1

She is tired with traveling on foot disguised as a youth.

4 'A was a man, take him for all in all;
I shall not look upon his like again.

Hamlet in *Hamlet*, 1.2.186–8

Hamlet sees his father as a real man, a heroic figure, in contrast to his uncle Claudius, now King of Denmark.

5 What a piece of work is a man!
How noble in reason, how infinite in faculty, in form and moving how express and admirable, in action how like an angel, in apprehension how like a god—the beauty of the world, the paragon of animals!

Hamlet in *Hamlet*, 2.2.303–7

6   Thou art e'en as just a man
As e'er my conversation coped withal.

Hamlet in *Hamlet*, 3.2.54–5

His friend Horatio is as upright ("just") a man as any he has had dealings with ("coped withal").

7   What is a man,
If his chief good and market of his time
Be but to sleep and feed? A beast, no more.

Hamlet in *Hamlet*, 4.4.33–5

Trying to rouse himself; "market" = profit.

8 There is nothing but roguery to be found in villainous man, yet a coward is worse than a cup of sack with lime in it.

Falstaff in *Henry IV, Part 1*, 2.4.124–7

On being deserted by his friends; lime was sometimes added to poor wine to add sparkle; "sack" = dry white wine.

9 Is man no more than this? Consider him well. Thou ow'st the worm no silk, the beast no hide, the sheep no wool, the cat no perfume. Here's three on's are sophisticated. Thou art the thing itself; unaccommodated man is no more than such a poor, bare, forked animal as thou art.

King Lear in *King Lear*, 3.4.102–8

On meeting Edgar disguised as a mad beggar; Lear and his companions are clothed; Poor Tom (Edgar) is almost naked ("unaccommodated").

Manliness

1 I sprang not more in joy at first
hearing he was a man-child than
now in first seeing he had proved
himself a man.

Volumnia in *Coriolanus*, 1.3.15–17

Rejoicing that her son, Caius Martius, is a
warrior.

2 I dare do all that may become a
man;
Who dares do more is none.

Macbeth in *Macbeth*, 1.7.46–7

Lady Macbeth taunts him with cowardice, but
Macbeth replies that there is a limit to what it
is fitting for a man to do; he is resisting the
idea of murdering Duncan.

3 O that I were a man for his sake, or
that I had any friend that would be
a man for my sake! But manhood
is melted into curtsies, valor into
compliment.

**Beatrice in *Much Ado About Nothing*,
4.1.317–20**

Wishing she could challenge Claudio to a
duel.

Manners

1 Thou art too wild, too rude, and
bold of voice.

**Bassanio in *The Merchant of Venice*,
2.2.181**

On the boisterous Gratiano.

Maps

1   A plague upon it!
I have forgot the map.

Hotspur in *Henry IV, Part 1*, 3.1.5–6

The map on which the rebels were to mark
out their shares of the kingdom.

2 Give me the map there.

King Lear in *King Lear*, 1.1.37

He intends to mark on it the division of his
kingdom into three parts.

Marriage

1 A young man married is a man
that's marred.

**Parolles in *All's Well That Ends Well*,
2.3.298**

Proverbial.

2   Husband, I come!
Now to that name my courage
prove my title!

**Cleopatra in *Antony and Cleopatra*,
5.2.287–8**

Dying, she claims Antony, to whom she was
never married, as her husband.

3 As the ox hath his bow, sir, the
horse his curb, and the falcon her
bells, so man hath his desires; and
as pigeons bill, so wedlock would
be nibbling.

Touchstone in *As You Like It*, 3.3.79–82

On his desire to marry; "bow" = yoke.

4 This fellow will but join you
together as they join wainscot; then
one of you will prove a shrunk
panel, and like green timber warp,
warp.

Jaques in *As You Like It*, 3.3.86–9

To Touchstone, who has invited an illiterate
priest to marry him to Audrey.

5   Men are April when they woo,
    December when they wed; maids
    are May when they are maids, but
    the sky changes when they are
    wives.
    Rosalind in *As You Like It*, 4.1.147–9

    A woman's view of marriage.

6   Tomorrow is the joyful day,
    Audrey, tomorrow will we be
    married.
    Touchstone in *As You Like It*, 5.3.1–2

7   Wedding is great Juno's crown,
    O blessed bond of board and bed!
    'Tis Hymen peoples every town,
    High wedlock then be honorèd.
    Honor, high honor, and renown
    To Hymen, god of every town!
    Hymen in *As You Like It*, 5.4.141–6

    "Hymen" = god of marriage, and "Juno,"
    queen of the gods, also protected marriage.

8   Thy loving voyage
    Is but for two months victualled.
    Jaques in *As You Like It*, 5.4.191–2

    To Touchstone, about to marry Audrey.

9   The beasts, the fishes, and the
        wingèd fowls
    Are their males' subjects and at
        their controls:
    Man, more divine, the master of all
        these,
    Lord of the wide world and wild
        watery seas,
    Indued with intellectual sense and
        souls,
    Or more pre-eminence than fish
        and fowls,
    Are masters to their females, and
        their lords:

Then let your will attend on their
    accords.
**Luciana in *The Comedy of Errors*,
2.1.18–25**

An Elizabethan view of marriage, rejected
with spirit by her sister, Adriana, to whom the
lines are addressed.

10   My decayèd fair
    A sunny look of his would soon
    repair.
    **Adriana in *The Comedy of Errors*,
    2.1.98–9**

    Complaining about her absent husband.

11 The time was once, when thou
        unurged wouldst vow
    That never words were music to
        thine ear,
    That never object pleasing in thine
        eye,
    That never meat sweet-savored in
        thy taste,
    Unless I spake, or looked, or
        touched, or carved to thee.
    **Adriana in *The Comedy of Errors*,
    2.2.113–18**

    She is not, as she supposes, speaking to her
    straying husband, but to his twin, Antipholus
    of Syracuse.

12   As easy mayst thou fall
    A drop of water in the breaking
        gulf,
    And take unmingled thence that
        drop again,
    Without addition or diminishing,
    As take from me thyself and not me
        too.
    **Adriana in *The Comedy of Errors*,
    2.2.125–9**

    An image of unity in marriage; "fall" = let fall.

13 Thou art an elm, my husband, I a
    vine,
    Whose weakness, married to thy
    stronger state,
    Makes me with thy strength to
    communicate.
    Adriana in _The Comedy of Errors_,
    2.2.174–6

    The image of the vine embracing the elm is
    proverbial.

14 And may it be that you have quite
    forgot
    A husband's office? Shall, Antipho-
    lus,
    Even in the spring of love, thy love-
    springs rot?
    Luciana in _The Comedy of Errors_,
    3.2.1–3

    Luciana thinks she is talking to her sister's
    husband, when it is actually his twin brother.

15   I will remain
    The loyalest husband that did e'er
    plight troth.
    Posthumus in _Cymbeline_, 1.1.95–6

    To Imogen, his wife, as they are about to be
    parted.

16 If thou dost marry, I'll give thee this
    plague for thy dowry: be thou as
    chaste as ice, as pure as snow, thou
    shalt not escape calumny. Get thee
    to a nunnery, farewell! If thou wilt
    needs marry, marry a fool, for wise
    men know what monsters you
    make of them.
    Hamlet in _Hamlet_, 3.1.134–9

    Caustic advice to Ophelia.

17 Man and wife, being two, are one in
    love.
    Queen Isabel in _Henry V_, 5.2.361

18 For what is wedlock forcèd, but a
    hell,
    An age of discord and continual
    strife?
    Whereas the contrary bringeth
    bliss,
    And is a pattern of celestial peace.
    Suffolk in _Henry VI, Part 1_, 5.5.62–5

    Proposing the king should marry for love.

19 Hasty marriage seldom proveth
    well.
    **Richard of Gloucester in _Henry VI,
    Part 3_, 4.1.18**

    Varying the proverb, "Marry in haste and
    repent at leisure."

20   Am I your self
    But as it were in sort or limitation,
    To keep with you at meals, comfort
    your bed,
    And talk to you sometimes?
    Portia in _Julius Caesar_, 2.1.282–5

    To her husband, Brutus; "in sort" = up to a
    point.

21   Dwell I but in the suburbs
    Of your good pleasure? If it be no
    more,
    Portia is Brutus' harlot, not his
    wife.
    Portia in _Julius Caesar_, 2.1.285–7

    The brothels in Elizabethan London were
    located in the suburbs, beyond the jurisdiction
    of the city.

22 You are my true and honorable
    wife,
    As dear to me as are the ruddy
    drops
    That visit my sad heart.
    Brutus in _Julius Caesar_, 2.1.288–90

    To Portia.

23 What's mine is yours, and what is
   yours is mine.
   Duke in _Measure for Measure_, 5.1.537

   Offering marriage to Isabella.

24 Your wife would give you little
   thanks for that
   If she were by to hear you make the
   offer.
   Portia in _The Merchant of Venice_,
   4.1.288–9

   Disguised as a lawyer, she hears Bassanio
   value Antonio's life above everything, including herself.

25 Let me give light, but let me not be
   light,
   For a light wife doth make a heavy
   husband.
   Portia in _The Merchant of Venice_,
   5.1.129–30

   Playing on the idea of "light" as wanton or
   unchaste.

26 If there be no great love in the
   beginning, yet heaven may decrease
   it upon better acquaintance, when
   we are married and have more
   occasion to know one another.
   **Slender in _The Merry Wives of Wind-
   sor_, 1.1.246–9**

   Responding to the suggestion that he marry
   Anne Page.

27 We'll leave a proof, by that which
   we will do,
   Wives may be merry, and yet hon-
   est too.
   **Mistress Page in _The Merry Wives of
   Windsor_, 4.2.104–5**

   Plotting to expose Falstaff and remain chaste.

28 But earthlier happy is the rose distilled

Than that which, withering on the
virgin thorn,
Grows, lives, and dies in single
blessedness.
**Theseus in _A Midsummer Night's
Dream_, 1.1.76–8**

"Rose distilled" means literally distilled to perfume, but figuratively suggests marriage (and
happiness on this earth).

29 Lord, I could not endure a husband
   with a beard on his face! I had
   rather lie in the woolen.
   **Beatrice in _Much Ado About Nothing_,
   2.1.29–31**

   "Lie in the woolen" = between rough blan-
   kets, without sheets.

30 Wooing, wedding, and repenting, is
   as a Scotch jig, a measure, and a
   cinquepace; the first suit is hot and
   hasty, like a Scotch jig, and full as
   fantastical; the wedding, mannerly-
   modest, as a measure, full of state
   and ancientry; and then comes
   repentance and, with his bad legs,
   falls into the cinquepace faster and
   faster, till he sink into his grave.
   **Beatrice in _Much Ado About Nothing_,
   2.1.73–80**

   Her cynical view of marriage; "state and
   ancientry" = stateliness and old-fashioned for-
   mality; a "cinquepace" was a lively dance
   (French "cinq pas" = five paces), with a pun
   on "sink."

31 _Don Pedro._ Will you have me, lady?
   Beatrice. No, my lord, unless I
   might have another for working-
   days: your grace is too costly to
   wear every day.
   Much Ado About Nothing, 2.1.326–9

   Beatrice neatly turns aside the offer of the
   Prince of Aragon.

32 When I said I would die a bachelor,
I did not think I should live till I
were married.

Benedick in *Much Ado About Nothing,*
2.3.242–4

Explaining his sudden discovery that he loves
Beatrice.

33 He swore he would never marry,
and yet now, in despite of his heart,
he eats his meat without grudging;
and how you may be converted I
know not, but methinks you look
with your eyes as other women do.

Margaret in *Much Ado About*
Nothing, 3.4.88–92

Speaking to Beatrice about Benedick, who
now is content to be a lover ("eats his meat
without grudging").

34 *Don Pedro.* But when shall we set
the savage bull's horns on the sensible Benedick's head?
Claudio. Yes, and text underneath,
"Here dwells Benedick, the married man"?

Much Ado About Nothing, 5.1.181–4

Benedick had boasted earlier that he would
never submit to the yoke of marriage; the
"horns" as usual suggest cuckoldry.

35 Here's our own hands against our
hearts. Come, I will have thee; but,
by this light, I take thee for pity.

Benedick in *Much Ado About Nothing,*
5.4.91–3

To Beatrice; they have both expressed in writing ("hands") the love for each other they
have denied in speech.

36 I would not deny you; but, by this
good day, I yield upon great persuasion; and partly to save your life,

for I was told you were in a consumption.

Beatrice in *Much Ado About Nothing,*
5.4.94–7

Wittily accepting Benedick as a husband on
equal terms.

37 Since I do purpose to marry, I will
think nothing to any purpose that
the world can say against it; and
therefore never flout at me for what
I have said against it; for man is a
giddy thing, and this is my conclusion.

Benedick in *Much Ado About Nothing,*
5.4.105–9

Defending his change from being a confirmed
bachelor.

38 Prince, thou art sad. Get thee a
wife, get thee a wife. There is no
staff more reverend than one tipped
with horn.

Benedick in *Much Ado About Nothing,*
5.4.122–4

Jokingly hinting at the cuckold's horns.

39 A fellow almost damned in a fair
wife.

Iago in *Othello,* 1.1.22

Describing Cassio; we hear no more of this
"wife."

40 But that I love the gentle Desdemona,
I would not my unhousèd free condition
Put into circumscription and confine
For the sea's worth.

Othello in *Othello,* 1.2.25–8

As a soldier Othello has no house or domestic life; "circumscription" = restriction; Othello is fond of such big words, that here make marriage sound a little like imprisonment.

41   O curse of marriage,
That we can call these delicate creatures ours
And not their appetites!
Othello in *Othello*, 3.3.268–70

Thinking of Desdemona.

42 But I do think it is their husbands' faults
If wives do fall.
Emilia in *Othello*, 4.3.86–7

43   Let husbands know
Their wives have sense like them;
they see, and smell,
And have their palates both for sweet and sour,
As husbands have. What is it that they do
When they change us for others? Is it sport?
I think it is. And doth affection breed it?
I think it doth. Is't frailty that thus errs?
It is so, too. And have not we affections,
Desires for sport, and frailty, as men have?
Then let them use us well; else let them know,
The ills we do, their ills instruct us so.
Emilia in *Othello*, 4.3.93–103

Emilia's impassioned plea for equal moral standards for men and women.

44 The sweet silent hours of marriage joys.
King Richard in *Richard III*, 4.4.330

Trying to persuade Queen Elizabeth that he is a fit suitor for her daughter's hand.

45 Do thou but close our hands with holy words,
Then love-devouring death do what he dare,
It is enough I may but call her mine.
Romeo in *Romeo and Juliet*, 2.6.6–8

Speaking to Friar Lawrence before his marriage to Juliet, and already foreshadowing the death that will end their love.

46 We will have rings and things, and fine array,
And kiss me, Kate, we will be married o' Sunday.
Petruchio in *The Taming of the Shrew*, 2.1.323–4

"Kiss Me Kate" is the title of a musical based on the play; "we will be married o' Sunday" occurs as a refrain in ballads.

47 *Miranda.* My husband, then?
Ferdinand. Ay, with a heart as willing
As bondage e'er of freedom.
Here's my hand.
Miranda. And mine, with my heart in 't.
The Tempest, 3.1.87–90

The marriage bond for these lovers becomes paradoxically their freedom.

48 Many a good hanging prevents a bad marriage.
Feste in *Twelfth Night*, 1.5.19–20

Probably with a sexual quibble on the idea of being "well hung."

49   Let still the woman take
An elder than herself. So wears she
to him;
So sways she level in her husband's
heart.

Orsino in *Twelfth Night*, 2.4.29–31

Giving to his page Cesario (Viola in disguise)
advice that is ironically more appropriate to
Viola.

4   I speak not like a dotard nor a fool,
As under privilege of age to brag
What I have done being young, or
what would do
Were I not old.

**Leonato in *Much Ado About Nothing*,
5.1.59–62**

Old Leonato is about to challenge young
Claudio to a duel.

Maturity

1   Then the justice,
In fair round belly with good capon
lined,
With eyes severe and beard of for-
mal cut,
Full of wise saws and modern
instances;
And so he plays his part.

Jaques in *As You Like It*, 2.7.153–7

The fifth of the "seven ages" of man, when he
is full of wise sayings and trite examples. The
capon or fowl suggests he is well fed with
meat; or is it possibly a bribe?

2   O, let us have him, for his silver
hairs
Will purchase us a good opinion,
And buy men's voices to commend
our deeds.

Metellus in *Julius Caesar*, 2.1.144–6

Recommending that Cicero be invited to join
the conspirators against Caesar.

3   It shall be said his judgment ruled
our hands.
Our youths and wildness shall no
whit appear,
But all be buried in his gravity.

Metellus in *Julius Caesar*, 2.1.147–9

Arguing for the inclusion of Cicero as one of
the conspirators.

Medicine (see also Sickness)

1   I have seen a medicine
That's able to breathe life into a
stone.

**Lafew in *All's Well That Ends Well*,
2.1.72–3**

Referring to the beauty of Helena, as able to
cure the sick King of France.

2   I will through and
through
Cleanse the foul body of the
infected world
If they will patiently receive my
medicine.

Jaques in *As You Like It*, 2.7.60–1

Claiming a godlike ability to purge people of
their sins.

3   I will not cast away my physic but
on those that are sick.

Rosalind in *As You Like It*, 3.2.358–9

4   I will not let him stir
Till I have used the approvèd
means I have,
With wholesome syrups, drugs, and
holy prayers,
To make of him a formal man
again.

The Abbess in *The Comedy of Errors*,
5.1.102–5

About Antipholus of Ephesus, who is supposedly mad; "formal" = sane.

5   By medicine life may be prolonged,
    yet death
   Will seize the doctor too.

Cymbeline in *Cymbeline*, 5.5.29–30

On hearing that his Queen, who compounded
drugs herself, is dead.

6   No medicine in the world can do
    thee good;
   In thee there is not half an hour's
    life.

Laertes in *Hamlet*, 5.2.314–5

Telling Hamlet he is fatally poisoned.

7   I am bewitched with the rogue's
   company. If the rascal have not
   given me medicines to make me
   love him, I'll be hanged. It could
   not be else, I have drunk medicines.

Falstaff in *Henry IV, Part 1*, 2.2.17–20

Speaking of Prince Hal or Poins, who has hidden his horse.

8   Kill thy physician, and the fee
    bestow
   Upon the foul disease.

Kent in *King Lear*, 1.1.163–4

Kent himself is the "physician" trying to cure
Lear of madness.

9   *Macbeth.* Canst thou not minister
   to a mind diseased,
   Pluck from the memory a rooted
   sorrow,
   Raze out the written troubles of the
   brain,
   And with some sweet oblivious
   antidote

   Cleanse the stuffed bosom of that
    perilous stuff
   Which weighs upon the heart?
   Doctor. Therein the patient
   Must minister to himself.

Macbeth, 5.3.40–6

"Raze out" = erase; "oblivious" = producing
forgetfulness; the "stuff" that weighs on the
heart includes guilt for murder.

10   Throw physic to the dogs! I'll none
    of it.

Macbeth in *Macbeth*, 5.3.47

To the doctor who cannot cure his wife's disease of the mind.

11   What rhubarb, senna, or what
    purgative drug
   Would scour these English hence?

Macbeth in *Macbeth*, 5.3.55–6

Wishing he could get rid of his enemies by
purging.

12   Tenderly apply to her
   Some remedies for life.

Leontes in *The Winter's Tale*, 3.2.152–3

Anxious as Hermione faints; "for life" = to
restore her to life.

Mediocrity

1   *Touchstone.* Art rich?
   William. Faith, sir, so-so.
   Touchstone. So-so is good, very
   good, very excellent good. And
   yet it is not, it is but so-so.

As You Like It, 5.1.25–8

Touchstone is mocking the country bumpkin
William, who says he is pretty rich, by changing the meaning of so-so.

Meeting

1 Methinks King Richard and myself
should meet
With no less terror than the elements
Of fire and water, when their thun-
dering shock
At meeting tears the cloudy cheeks
of heaven.

Bolingbroke in *Richard II*, 3.3.54–7

Fire and water were two of the four elements
thought to compose all matter (the others
being earth and air).

Melancholy (see also Moods, Temperament)

1 The melancholy Jaques.

First Lord in *As You Like It*, 2.1.26

The adjective has permanently stuck to the
character.

2 I can suck melancholy out of a
song, as a weasel sucks eggs.

Jaques in *As You Like It*, 2.5.12–13

3 I have neither the scholar's melancholy, which is emulation; nor the
musician's, which is fantastical; nor
the courtier's, which is proud; nor
the soldier's, which is ambitious;
nor the lawyer's, which is politic;
nor the lady's, which is nice; nor
the lover's, which is all these.

Jaques in *As You Like It*, 4.1.10–15

Claiming his brand of melancholy is unique to
himself.

4 It is a melancholy of mine own,
compounded of many simples,
extracted from many objects.

Jaques in *As You Like It*, 4.1.15–17

"Simples" = ingredients.

5 Sweet recreation barred, what doth
ensue
But moody and dull melancholy,
Kinsman to grim and comfortless
despair.

The Abbess in *The Comedy of Errors*, 5.1.78–80

Showing Adriana the state to which she has
supposedly driven her husband.

6 He raised a sigh so piteous and pro-
found
As it did seem to shatter all his bulk
And end his being.

Ophelia in *Hamlet*, 2.1.91–3

Describing Hamlet's behavior to Polonius;
"bulk" = body.

7 *Falstaff.* 'Sblood, I am as melancholy as a gib cat, or a lugged
bear.
Prince Hal. Or an old lion, or a
lover's lute.
Falstaff. Yea, or the drone of a Lin-
colnshire bagpipe.

Henry IV, Part 1, 1.2.73–6

Falstaff swears by Christ's blood; "gib cat" =
tomcat, and a "lugged" bear is one led by a
chain for bear-baiting.

8 The sad companion, dull-eyed
melancholy.

Pericles in *Pericles*, 1.2.2

9   She never told her love,
But let concealment, like a worm i'
the bud
Feed on her damask cheek. She
pined in thought,
And with a green and yellow
melancholy
She sat like patience on a monument,
Smiling at grief. Was not this love
indeed?

Viola in *Twelfth Night*, 2.4.110–15

Disguised as Cesario, she is forced to conceal
her love for Orsino, to whom she is speaking.

Memory (see also Remembrance)

1   Though yet of Hamlet our dear
brother's death
The memory be green.

Claudius in *Hamlet*, 1.2.1–2

"Green" = fresh; he has been dead two
months.

2   Remember thee!
Ay, thou poor ghost, while memory
holds a seat
In this distracted globe.

Hamlet in *Hamlet*, 1.5.95–7

Hamlet's father's ghost has just left him with
the command, "remember me"; "globe" = his
head (or the Globe Theatre, or the world?).

3   Die two months ago, and not forgotten yet? Then there's hope a
great man's memory may outlive
his life half a year.

Hamlet in *Hamlet*, 3.2.130–2

A biting comment in response to Ophelia saying Hamlet's father died "twice two months"
ago.

4   Memory, the warder of the brain.

Lady Macbeth in *Macbeth*, 1.7.65

"Warder" = watchman.

5   I would forget it fain,
But O, it presses to my memory
Like damnèd guilty deeds to sin-
ners' minds.

Juliet in *Romeo and Juliet*, 3.2.109–11

She would forget that she heard Romeo was
banished; "fain" = gladly.

6   What seest thou else
In the dark backward and abysm of
time?

Prospero in *The Tempest*, 1.2.49–50

Asking his daughter Miranda what she
remembers of her childhood.

Men (see also Man, Men and Women)

1   In faith, he is a worthy gentleman,
Exceedingly well read, and profited
In strange concealments, valiant as
a lion,
And wondrous affable, and as
bountiful
As mines of India.

Mortimer in *Henry IV, Part 1*, 3.1.163–7

To Hotspur, about Glendower, mocked by
Hotspur; "profited" = proficient; "strange concealments" = occult arts.

2   A fellow of no mark nor livelihood.

King Henry in *Henry IV, Part 1*, 3.2.45

On what he would have been had he behaved
like Prince Hal; "livelihood" = means of
living.

3   Let the end try the man.
    Prince Hal in *Henry IV, Part 2*, 2.2.47
    "Try" = test, show the true worth of.

4   O miracle of men!
    Lady Percy in *Henry IV, Part 2*, 2.3.33
    Acclaiming Hotspur as the ideal man.

5   As young as I am, I have observed
    these three swashers. I am boy to
    them all three, but all they three,
    though they would serve me, could
    not be man to me.
    Boy in *Henry V*, 3.2.28–31
    Seeing through the swashbuckling Nym, Bar-
    dolph and Pistol, who, for all their bravado,
    are cowards; "boy" = servant.

6   For Nym, he hath heard that men
    of few words are the best men, and
    therefore he scorns to say his
    prayers, lest 'a should be thought a
    coward.
    Boy in *Henry V*, 3.2.36–8

7   You are not wood, you are not
    stones, but men;
    And being men, hearing the will of
    Caesar,
    It will inflame you, it will make you
    mad.
    Mark Antony in *Julius Caesar*, 3.2.142–4
    Addressing the people.

8   I dare do all that may become a
    man;
    Who dares do more is none.
    Macbeth in *Macbeth*, 1.7.46–7
    "Become" = be proper to, or grace, and could
    be meant in physical or moral terms.

9   When I did first impart my love to
    you,
    I freely told you all the wealth I had
    Ran in my veins: I was a gentleman;
    And then I told you true.
    Bassanio in *The Merchant of Venice*,
    3.2.253–6

10 He is the only man of Italy,
    Always excepted my dear Claudio.
    Hero in *Much Ado About Nothing*,
    3.1.92–3
    Praising Benedick in the hope of making the
    listening Beatrice fall in love with him.

11 But men are men; the best some-
    times forget.
    Iago in *Othello*, 2.3.241
    "Men are but men" is proverbial.

12 Nay, we must think men are not
    gods,
    Nor of them look for such obser-
    vancy
    As fits the bridal.
    Desdemona in *Othello*, 3.4.148–50
    Excusing Othello's anger with her by saying
    she cannot expect such attentiveness ("obser-
    vancy") as at her wedding.

Men and Women

1   That man should be at woman's
    command, and no harm done!
    Lavatch in *All's Well That Ends Well*,
    1.3.92–3
    On being ordered away by the Countess of
    Rossillion.

2   You are a thousand times a prop-
    erer man

Than she a woman. 'Tis such fools
as you
That makes the world full of ill-
favored children.

Rosalind in *As You Like It*, 3.5.51–3

Disguised as a man, she advises Silvius, who
loves Phebe, who is in love with Rosalind;
"properer" = more handsome.

3 My way is to conjure you, and I'll
begin with the women. I charge
you, O women, for the love you
bear to men, to like as much of this
play as please you. I charge you, O
men, for the love you bear to
women (as I perceive by your simpering none of you hates them),
that between you and the women,
the play may please.

**Rosalind in *As You Like It*, Epilogue,
11–17**

Appealing to her audience, which included a
lot of women.

4 Rich she shall be, that's certain;
wise, or I'll none; virtuous, or I'll
never cheapen her; fair, or I'll never
look on her; mild, or come not near
me; noble, or not I for an angel; of
good discourse, an excellent musician, and her hair shall be of what
color it please God.

**Benedick in *Much Ado About Nothing*,
2.3.30–5**

Admitting after all that he could care for a
woman—if she has all the graces.

5 They say the lady is fair; 'tis a truth,
I can bear them witness; and virtuous; so, I cannot reprove it; and
wise, but for loving me. By my
troth, it is no addition to her wit,
nor no great argument of her folly,
for I will be horribly in love with
her.

**Benedick in *Much Ado About Nothing*,
2.3.230–5**

On hearing Beatrice loves him, he is prepared
to praise her, and to love her.

6 I cannot be a man with wishing,
therefore I will die a woman with
grieving.

**Beatrice in *Much Ado About Nothing*,
4.1.322–3**

Addressing Benedick, in the hope of persuading him to challenge Claudio.

7 'Tis not a year or two shows us a
man:
They are all but stomachs, and we
all but food;
They eat us hungerly, and when
they are full
They belch us.

Emilia in *Othello*, 3.4.103–6

She may have her husband, Iago, in mind; "all
but" = nothing but; "hungerly" = hungrily.

8 Women may fall when there's no
strength in men.

**Friar Lawrence in *Romeo and Juliet*,
2.3.80**

To Romeo, alluding to St. Paul's conception of
the wife as the "weaker vessel" to be honored
and protected by her husband (I Peter 3:7).

9 Women are angels, wooing;
Things won are done; joy's soul lies
in the doing.
That she beloved knows naught
that knows not this:
Men prize the thing ungained more
than it is.

**Cressida in *Troilus and Cressida*,
1.2.286–9**

She has been holding off against her uncle
Pandarus's attempts to woo her on behalf of
Troilus.

10   Boy, however we do praise our-
     selves,
     Our fancies are more giddy and
     unfirm,
     More longing, wavering, sooner
     lost and worn,
     Than women's are.
     Orsino in *Twelfth Night,* **2.4.32–5**

     Speaking to Cesario (Viola in disguise) of
     men's loves ("fancies") as soon exhausted
     ("worn").

11   Women will love her, that she is a
     woman
     More worth than any man; men,
     that she is
     The rarest of all women.
     Servant in *The Winter's Tale,* **5.1.110–12**

     On the rare qualities of Perdita.

Mercy (see also Forgiveness)

1   Whereto serves mercy,
     But to confront the visage of
     offense?
     Claudius in *Hamlet,* **3.3.46–7**

     Hoping somehow to be forgiven for murder-
     ing old Hamlet.

2   O, let us yet be merciful.
     King Henry in *Henry V,* **2.2.47**

     On pardoning a prisoner against the advice of
     others.

3   Use mercy to them all.
     King Henry in *Henry V,* **3.3.54**

4   Mercy is not itself, that oft looks so;
     Pardon is still the nurse of second
     woe.
     Escalus in *Measure for Measure,*
     2.1.284–5

     Meaning that pardon often leads to more
     wrongdoing.

5   Yes, I do think that you might par-
     don him,
     And neither heaven nor man grieve
     at the mercy.
     Isabella in *Measure for Measure,*
     2.2.49–50

     Pleading for the life of her brother, who is
     condemned to death.

6   No ceremony that to great ones
     'longs,
     Not the king's crown, nor the
     deputed sword,
     The marshal's truncheon, nor the
     judge's robe,
     Become them with one half so good
     a grace
     As mercy does.
     Isabella in *Measure for Measure,*
     2.2.59–63

     Arguing for mercy to her condemned brother;
     " 'longs" = belongs; "deputed sword" = the
     sword of justice entrusted to the ruler or judge
     as a mark of office; "truncheon" = baton or
     staff.

7   Why, all the souls that were were
     forfeit once,
     And He that might the vantage best
     have took
     Found out the remedy. How would
     you be
     If He which is the top of judgment
     should

But judge you as you are? O, think on that,
And mercy then will breathe within your lips,
Like man new made.

Isabella in *Measure for Measure,*
2.2.73–9

In pleading for her brother's life, Isabella is recalling Christ's sermon on the mount, Matthew 7, beginning "Judge not, that ye be not judged."

8 Ignominy in ransom and free pardon
Are of two houses; lawful mercy
Is nothing kin to foul redemption.

Isabella in *Measure for Measure,*
2.4.111–13

Rejecting Angelo's offer of freedom for her brother at a price (Isabella's chastity).

9 How shalt thou hope for mercy, rendering none?

Duke in *The Merchant of Venice,* 4.1.88

To Shylock, who has refused an offer of twice what he has lent Antonio.

10 The quality of mercy is not strained,
It droppeth as the gentle rain from heaven
Upon the place beneath. It is twice blest:
It blesseth him that gives and him that takes.

Portia in *The Merchant of Venice,*
4.1.184–7

Inviting Shylock to be merciful; "strained" = forced or constrained.

11 Mercy is above this sceptered sway,

It is enthronèd in the hearts of kings,
It is an attribute to God himself;
And earthly power doth then show likest God's
When mercy seasons justice.

Portia in *The Merchant of Venice,*
4.1.193–7

Offering Shylock the chance to show mercy; "sceptered sway" = earthly rule; "attribute to" = characteristic of.

12 We do pray for mercy,
And that same prayer doth teach us all to render
The deeds of mercy.

Portia in *The Merchant of Venice,*
4.1.200–2

Inviting Shylock to be merciful.

13 *Verges.* You have always been called a merciful man, partner.
Dogberry. Truly, I would not hang a dog by my will, much more a man who hath any honesty in him.

Much Ado About Nothing, 3.3.61–4

The two comic constables discuss the law.

14 Mercy but murders, pardoning those that kill.

Prince Escalus in *Romeo and Juliet,*
3.1.197

15 Wilt thou draw near the nature of the gods?
Draw near them then in being merciful.
Sweet mercy is nobility's true badge.

Tamora in *Titus Andronicus,* 1.1.117–19

Begging Titus for mercy.

Merit (see also Deserving)

1 "Who chooseth me shall get as
   much as he deserves."
   And well said too; for who shall go
   about
   To cozen fortune, and be honorable
   Without the stamp of merit?

   Prince of Aragon in *The Merchant of*
   Venice, 2.9.36–9

   Looking at the silver casket in the hope that he
   will cheat ("cozen") fortune because he has
   the seal of approval ("stamp of merit") in
   being an aristocrat.

2 O that estates, degrees, and offices
   Were not derived corruptly, and
       that clear honor
   Were purchased by the merit of the
       wearer!

   Prince of Aragon in *The Merchant of*
   Venice, 2.9.41–3

   The aristocrat wishes status and rank were
   always the reward of merit, and could not be
   obtained by corrupt means.

Merriment (see also Jokes, Laughter)

1 *Prince Hal.* Shall we be merry?
   Poins. As merry as crickets, my lad.

   Henry IV, Part 1, 2.4.88–9

   Hal and his companions at the tavern in
   Eastcheap.

2 Berowne they call him, but a mer-
   rier man,
   Within the limit of becoming
       mirth,
   I never spent an hour's talk withal.

   Rosaline in *Love's Labor's Lost,* 2.1.66–8

   Rosaline's account of meeting with Berowne.

3   Let me play the fool,
   With mirth and laughter let old
       wrinkles come.

   Gratiano in *The Merchant of Venice,*
   1.1.79–80

   Preferring to enjoy life, and rejecting Antonio's melancholy.

4 *Don Pedro.* To be merry best
       becomes you; for, out o'question,
       you were born in a merry hour.
   Beatrice. No, sure, my lord, my
       mother cried; but then there was a
       star danced, and under that was I
       born.

   Much Ado About Nothing, 2.1.331–5

   The stars were thought to influence temperament.

5 From the crown of his head to the
   sole of his foot, he is all mirth.

   Don Pedro in *Much Ado About Noth-*
   ing, 3.2.8–10

   Describing Benedick.

6 Jog on, jog on, the footpath way,
   And merrily hent the stile-a,
   A merry heart goes all the day,
   Your sad tires in a mile-a.

   Autolycus in *The Winter's Tale,*
   4.3.123–6

   Enjoying his success as a trickster; "hent" =
   take hold of.

Middle Age

1   Think on me,
That am with Phoebus' amorous
    pinches black,
And wrinkled deep in time.

Cleopatra in *Antony and Cleopatra*,
1.5.27–8

Acknowledging her age (she was 38) and
experience in love; Phoebus was god of the
sun.

2   What, girl, though grey
Do something mingle with our
    younger brown, yet ha' we
A brain that nourishes our nerves,
    and can
Get goal for goal of youth.

Antony in *Antony and Cleopatra*,
4.8.19–22

To Cleopatra, claiming he can match the
young in fighting.

3   *Lear.* How old art thou?
   Kent. Not so young, sir, to love a
    woman for singing, nor so old to
    dote on her for anything.

***King Lear*, 1.4.36–8**

Kent goes on to say he is 48 years old.

4   I am too old to fawn upon a nurse,
Too far in years to be a pupil now.

Mowbray in *Richard II*, 1.3.170–1

Banished, he feels too old to learn a new language and way of life.

5   He has his health, and ampler
    strength indeed
Than most have of his age.

Florizel in *The Winter's Tale*, 4.4.403–4

Speaking of his father, Polixenes.

Miracles

1   They say miracles are past, and we
have our philosophical persons to
make modern and familiar things
supernatural and causeless. Hence
is it that we make trifles of terrors,
ensconcing ourselves into seeming
knowledge when we should submit
ourselves to an unknown fear.

Lafew in *All's Well That Ends Well*,
2.3.1–6

"Philosophical persons" = scientists who
make what is supernatural and unexplained in
terms of natural causes seem commonplace
("modern and familiar"); "unknown fear" =
awe in the face of what is unknowable.

2   Nothing almost sees miracles
But misery.

Kent in *King Lear*, 2.2.165–6

Those in misery are almost the only people
who see miracles (when anything happens to
bring relief).

3   Ten masts at each make not the
    altitude
Which thou hast perpendicularly
    fell.
Thy life's a miracle.

Edgar in *King Lear*, 4.6.53–5

To his father, who thinks he has jumped off a
cliff.

4   Think that the clearest gods, who
    make them honors
Of men's impossibilities, have pre-
    served thee.

Edgar in *King Lear*, 4.6.73–4

Making his father believe he has fallen off a
cliff and survived.

Misanthropy

1 What should such fellows as I do
crawling between heaven and earth?
We are arrant knaves all, believe
none of us.

Hamlet in *Hamlet*, 3.1.126–8

In Hamlet's anger against Ophelia he
denounces all men, himself included.

2 I have no brother, I am like no
brother;
And this word "love," which greybeards call divine,
Be resident in men like one
another,
And not in me: I am myself alone.

Richard of Gloucester in *Henry VI,
Part 3*, 5.6.80–3

3 I had rather hear my dog bark at a
crow than a man swear he loves me.

Beatrice in *Much Ado About Nothing*,
1.1.131–2

4 I cannot hide what I am. I must be
sad when I have cause, and smile at
no man's jests.

Don John in *Much Ado About
Nothing*, 1.3.13–14

Showing his morose nature.

5   All's obliquy;
There's nothing level in our cursèd
natures
But direct villainy. Therefore be
abhorred
All feasts, societies, and throngs of
men!

Timon in *Timon of Athens*, 4.3.18–21

Timon is expressing his misanthropy;
"obliquy" = obliquity, or deviation from moral
standards.

Misery (see also Affliction, Suffering)

1 When we our betters see bearing
our woes,
We scarcely think our miseries our
foes.
Who alone suffers, suffers most i'
the mind,
Leaving free things and happy
shows behind.
But then the mind much sufferance
doth o'erskip,
When grief hath mates, and bearing
fellowship.

Edgar in *King Lear*, 3.6.102–7

Developing the proverb, "it's good to have
company in misery"; "free" = free from misery; "happy shows" = pleasant sights; "bearing" = endurance.

2 Is wretchedness deprived that benefit
To end itself by death? 'Twas yet
some comfort
When misery could beguile the
tyrant's rage
And frustrate his proud will.

Gloucester in *King Lear*, 4.6.61–4

Stoics like Seneca defended suicide as a way
to cheat ("beguile") the enmity of tyrants like
Nero in ancient Rome.

3   Shall we rest us here,
And by relating tales of others'
griefs,
See if 'twill teach us to forget our
own?

Cleon in *Pericles*, 1.4.1–3

"Griefs" = miseries; Cleon's city is afflicted by
famine.

4 O, the fierce wretchedness that
   glory brings us!
   Who would not wish to be from
   wealth exempt,
   Since riches point to misery and
   contempt?
   Flavius in *Timon of Athens*, 4.2.30–2

   Commenting on the fall of Timon, abandoned
   by his friends.

5 When in disgrace with Fortune and
   men's eyes
   I all alone beweep my outcast
   state,
   And trouble deaf heaven with my
   bootless cries,
   And look upon myself and curse
   my fate,
   Wishing me like to one more rich
   in hope,
   Featured like him, like him with
   friends possessed,
   Desiring this man's art and that
   man's scope,
   With what I most enjoy contented
   least;
   Yet in these thoughts myself almost
   despising,
   Haply I think on thee, and then my
   state
   (Like to the lark at break of day
   arising
   From sullen earth) sings hymns at
   heaven's gate,
   For thy sweet love remembered
   such wealth brings
   That then I scorn to change my
   state with kings.
   Sonnet 29

   A poignant testimony to the power of his love
   for his friend; "in disgrace" = out of favor;
   "bootless" = unavailing, useless; "art" = skill
   (line 7 is quoted by T.S. Eliot in his poem *Ash
   Wednesday*); "haply" = perhaps.

Misogyny

1 Down from the waist they are cen-
   taurs,
   Though women all above;
   But to the girdle do the gods
   inherit,
   Beneath is all the fiends': there's
   hell, there's darkness,
   There is the sulphurous pit, burn-
   ing, scalding,
   Stench, consumption.
   King Lear in *King Lear*, 4.6.124–9

   The treatment of him by his daughters provokes this outburst of misogyny; centaurs
   were legendary creatures, half-human, half-
   horse, and notorious for lustfulness.

2 What is he for a fool that betroths
   himself to unquietness?
   Don John in *Much Ado About
   Nothing*, 1.3.47–8

   Seeing Claudio as a fool for becoming
   engaged to Hero.

3 One woman is fair, yet I am well;
   another is wise, yet I am well;
   another virtuous, yet I am well; but
   till all graces be in one woman, one
   woman shall not come in my grace.
   Benedick in *Much Ado About Nothing*,
   2.3.26–30

   Rejecting the idea of loving a woman.

4 There's no true drop of blood in
   him to be truly touched with love;
   if he be sad, he wants money.
   Don Pedro in *Much Ado About Nothing*, 3.2.18–20

   Unable to believe Benedick can fall in love;
   "wants" = is in need of, lacks.

Mistakes

1   What error drives our eyes and ears
     amiss?

Antipholus of Syracuse in *The Comedy of Errors*, 2.2.184

Amazed to find Adriana, wife of his twin
Antipholus of Ephesus, treating him as her
husband.

2   This must be patched
   With cloth of any color.

Menenius in *Coriolanus*, 3.1.251–2

Hoping to restore peace after Coriolanus has
misguidedly angered the people.

3   O hateful Error, Melancholy's
     child,
   Why dost thou show to the apt
     thoughts of men
   The things that are not?

Messala in *Julius Caesar*, 5.3.67–9

On the death of Cassius, who mistakenly
thought the battle lost, and took his own life.

4   You never spoke what did become
     you less
   Than this.

Camillo in *The Winter's Tale*, 1.2.282–3

On hearing Leontes accuse his wife of adultery.

Misunderstanding

1   Men may construe things after their
     fashion,
   Clean from the purpose of the
     things themselves.

Cicero in *Julius Caesar*, 1.3.34–5

"Construe" = interpret.

2   Your sense pursues not mine.
     Either you are ignorant,
   Or seem so, craftily; and that's not
     good.

Angelo in *Measure for Measure*, 2.4.74–5

Isabella does not understand that Angelo
wants her sexually, and he thinks she is devious, like himself.

Mockery

1   *Amiens.* What's that "ducdame"?
   Jaques. 'Tis a Greek invocation, to
     call fools into a circle.

As You Like It, 2.5.58–60

Jaques is mocking his friends with this meaningless nonsense.

2   The tongues of mocking wenches
     are as keen
   As is the razor's edge invisible.

Boyet in *Love's Labor's Lost*, 5.2.256–7

On the court ladies, who have overwhelmed
the courtiers by mocking them.

3   *Don Pedro.* She cannot endure to
     hear tell of a husband.
   Leonato. O, by no means; she
     mocks all her wooers out of suit.

***Much Ado About Nothing*, 2.1.347–50**

Referring to Beatrice.

Moderation

1   Rather rejoicing to see another
   merry, than merry at anything
   which professed to make him
   rejoice; a gentleman of all temperance.

Escalus in *Measure for Measure*,
3.2.235–7

Describing the Duke's pleasures; 'temperance'
= moderation.

2   They are as sick that surfeit with
    too much as they that starve with
    nothing. It is no mean happiness
    therefore to be seated in the mean.

    Nerissa in *The Merchant of Venice*,
    1.2.5–8

    "In the mean" = between extremes of too
    much or too little.

3   Superfluity comes sooner by white
    hairs, but competency lives longer.

    Nerissa in *The Merchant of Venice*,
    1.2.8–9

    Over-indulgence or having too much ages
    people, while those of moderate means live
    longer.

Modesty

1   It is the witness still of excellency
    To put a strange face on his own
    perfection.

    Don Pedro in *Much Ado About Noth-
    ing*, 2.3.46–7

    On the singer Balthasar; it is typical of the
    truly talented not to seem to be aware of their
    own high skill.

2   There's not a note of mine that's
    worth the noting.

    Balthasar in *Much Ado About
    Nothing*, 2.3.55

    Quibbling on "noting" and "nothing," as the
    play portrays much ado about noting (observ-
    ing or listening) and a quarrel that springs
    from nothing.

Money (see also Business, Gold, Payment)

1   Poor fellow never joyed since the
    price of oats rose, it was the death
    of him.

    First Carrier in *Henry IV, Part 1*,
    2.1.12–13

    Remembering Robin, the ostler.

2   A trifle, some eight-penny matter.

    Prince Hal in *Henry IV, Part 1*, 3.3.104

    The ring Falstaff claims has been stolen from
    him.

3   O, I do not like that paying back,
    'tis a double labor.

    Falstaff in *Henry IV, Part 1*, 3.3.179–80

    Prince Hal has returned the money they stole.

4   I can get no remedy against this
    consumption of the purse; borrow-
    ing only lingers and lingers it out,
    but the disease is incurable.

    Falstaff in *Henry IV, Part 2*, 1.2.236–8

5   Base is the slave that pays.

    Pistol in *Henry V*, 2.1.96

    Refusing to pay a gaming debt.

6   For I can raise no money by vile
    means.

    Brutus in *Julius Caesar*, 4.3.71

7   *Ford.* If money go before, all ways
    do lie open.
    Falstaff. Money is a good soldier,
    sir, and will on.

    The Merry Wives of Windsor, 2.2.168–70

    Ford, disguised, is exposing Falstaff's corrupt
    way of thinking.

8   I hate him for he is a Christian;
    But more, for that in low simplicity
    He lends out money gratis, and
        brings down
    The rate of usance here with us in
        Venice.
    Shylock in *The Merchant of Venice*,
    1.3.42–5

    On Antonio, his rival merchant; "low simplic-
    ity" can mean both modest or humble guile-
    lessness, or base folly; "usance" = usury.

9   Signior Antonio, many a time and
        oft
    In the Rialto you have rated me
    About my moneys and my usances.
    Still have I borne it with a patient
        shrug
    (For sufferance is the badge of all
        our tribe).
    Shylock in *The Merchant of Venice*,
    1.3.106–10

    "Rated" = berated; "usances" = usury.

10   Moneys is your suit.
    What should I say to you? Should I
        not say,
    "Hath a dog money? Is it possible
    A cur can lend three thousand
        ducats?" Or
    Shall I bend low and in a bond-
        man's key,
    With bated breath and whispering
        humbleness,
    Say this:
    "Fair sir, you spat on me on
        Wednesday last,
    You spurned me such a day,
        another time
    You called me dog; and for these
        courtesies
    I'll lend you thus much moneys"?
    Shylock in *The Merchant of Venice*,
    1.3.119–29

Speaking to Antonio, the "merchant" who
needs to borrow from Shylock.

11 Put money in thy purse.
    Iago in *Othello*, 1.3.339–40

    Proverbial now, implying that anything can be
    bought. He is speaking to Roderigo.

12 Why, nothing comes amiss, so
    money comes withal.
    Grumio in *The Taming of the Shrew*,
    1.2.81–2

    Arguing that any woman, however old and
    ugly, will do for a wife as long as money
    comes with her.

13 This is no time to lend money,
    especially upon bare friendship
    without security.
    Lucullus in *Timon of Athens*, 3.1.41–3

    Refusing to help Timon.

Monsters

1   Though they are of monstrous
        shape, yet note
    Their manners are more gentle,
        kind, than of
    Our human generation you shall
        find
    Many, nay, almost any.
    Gonzalo in *The Tempest*, 3.3.31–4

    On the "strange shapes" that offer Alonso and
    his courtiers a banquet.

Moods (see also Melancholy, Temperament)

1   Like to the time o'the year between
        the extremes
    Of hot and cold, he was nor sad nor
        merry.

Alexas in *Antony and Cleopatra,*
1.5.51–2

Reporting Antony's mood when he sent a
message to Cleopatra.

2 I love to cope him in these sullen
   fits,
   For then he's full of matter.
   Duke Senior in *As You Like It,*
   2.1.67–8

   Referring to the melancholy Jaques; "cope" =
   encounter.

3 *Jaques.* Why, 'tis good to be sad
   and say nothing.
   Rosalind. Why then 'tis good to be
   a post.
   As You Like It, 4.1.8–9

   In fact Jaques cannot stop talking.

4 I had rather have a fool to make me
   merry than experience to make me
   sad—and to travel for it too!
   Rosalind in *As You Like It,* 4.1.27–9

   To Jaques, who has been defining his particular melancholy.

5   So to your pleasures,
   I am for other than for dancing
   measures.
   Jaques in *As You Like It,* 5.4.92–3

   Separating himself from the general happy
   ending, Jaques returns to the cave in the forest.

6 Why should we in our peevish
   opposition
   Take it to heart?
   Claudius in *Hamlet,* 1.2.100–1

   Suggesting Hamlet is perverse in continuing to
   mourn for his father.

7 *Hamlet.* What, looked he frowningly?

Horatio.   A countenance
   more
In sorrow than in anger.
   Hamlet, 1.2.231–2

   Describing the expression of the ghost of
   Hamlet's father.

8 Why hast thou lost the fresh blood
   in thy cheeks,
   And given my treasures and my
   rights of thee
   To thick-eyed musing and cursed
   melancholy?
   Lady Percy in *Henry IV, Part 1,* 2.3.44–6

   Her husband, Hotspur, has not told her he is
   involved in plans for a rebellion against the
   king.

9 Against ill chances men are ever
   merry,
   But heaviness foreruns the good
   event.
   **Archbishop of York in *Henry IV, Part
   2,*** 4.2.81–2

   Anticipating ("against") bad luck men are
   merry, but sad or heavy before success.

10 In sooth, I know not why I am so
    sad.
    Antonio in *The Merchant of Venice,*
    1.1.1

    The opening line of this comedy; "sooth" =
    truth.

11   Let us say you are sad
    Because you are not merry; and
    'twere as easy
    For you to laugh and leap, and say
    you are merry
    Because you are not sad.
    Solanio in *The Merchant of Venice,*
    1.1.47–50

    On Antonio's unexplained melancholy.

12   Why, what's the matter,
      That you have such a February face,
      So full of frost, of storm and
      cloudiness?

Don Pedro in Much Ado About Nothing, 5.4.40–2

He is still angry with his friend Claudio.

13   I am not merry; but I do beguile
      The thing I am by seeming otherwise.

Desdemona in Othello, 2.1.122–3

She is anxiously awaiting the arrival of Othello in Cyprus.

14   I have this while with leaden
      thoughts been pressed.

Cassio in Othello, 3.4.177

He is worried about regaining his office as Othello's lieutenant; "pressed" = oppressed.

The Moon

1   How sweet the moonlight sleeps
     upon this bank!
     Here will we sit, and let the sounds
     of music
     Creep in our ears. Soft stillness and
     the night
     Become the touches of sweet harmony.

Lorenzo in The Merchant of Venice, 5.1.54–7

To Jessica, while they await the arrival of Portia.

2   The moon, like to a silver bow
     New bent in heaven, shall behold
     the night
     Of our solemnities.

Hippolyta in *A Midsummer Night's Dream,* 1.1.9–11

To Theseus, whom she is to marry.

3   Tomorrow night, when Phoebe
     doth behold
     Her silver visage in the watery glass,
     Decking with liquid pearl the
     bladed grass.

Lysander in A Midsummer Night's Dream, 1.1.209–11

"Phoebe" is another name for Diana, goddess of the moon and of chastity; "watery glass" = mirror made by water.

4   It is the very error of the moon;
     She comes more near the earth than
     she was wont
     And makes men mad.

Othello in Othello, 5.2.109–11

The term "lunacy" is derived from "luna," Latin for moon, reflecting the popular belief that underlies these lines.

Morning, see Dawn, Sunrise

Mortality (see also Death, Dying)

1   All lovers young, all lovers must
     Consign to thee and come to dust.

Guiderius and Arviragus in Cymbeline, 4.2.274–5

They address the supposedly dead body of Imogen; "Consign to thee" = share your fate.

2   Where be your gibes now, your
     gambols, your songs, your flashes

of merriment, that were wont to set the table on a roar?

Hamlet in *Hamlet*, 5.1.189–91

Holding the skull of Yorick, the king's jester.

3   *Hamlet.* To what base uses we may return, Horatio! Why may not imagination trace the noble dust of Alexander, till 'a find it stopping a bung-hole?
Horatio. 'Twere to consider too curiously to consider so.

***Hamlet*, 5.1.202–6**

Horatio pinpoints Hamlet's self-indulgence in contemplating death so minutely ("curiously").

4   Imperious Caesar, dead and turned to clay,
Might stop a hole to keep the wind away.
O that that earth which kept the world in awe
Should patch a wall t'expel the winter's flaw!

Hamlet in *Hamlet*, 5.1.213–16

A bleak view of death as mere oblivion, but recalling Genesis 3:19, where man was made of earth by God; "winter's flaw" = gust of cold wind.

5   Do not speak like a death's-head, do not bid me remember mine end.

Falstaff in *Henry IV, Part 2*, 2.4.234–5

"Death's-head" = skull, used as a *memento mori* or reminder that death awaits everyone.

6   Make less thy body hence, and more thy grace.
Leave gormandizing; know the grave doth gape

For thee thrice wider than for other men.

Prince Hal, now King Henry V, in *Henry IV, Part 2*, 5.5.52–4

Advising Falstaff to slim henceforth, abandon gluttony ("gormandizing"), and attend to his soul, to divine influence ("grace").

7   *Gloucester.* O, let me kiss that hand!
Lear. Let me wipe it first, it smells of mortality.
Gloucester. O ruined piece of nature! This great world Shall so wear out to nought.

***King Lear*, 4.6.132–5**

"Piece" = masterpiece, i.e., the old king, now mad and senile.

8   If thou art rich, thou'rt poor,
For like an ass, whose back with ingots bows,
Thou bear'st thy heavy riches but a journey,
And death unloads thee.

Duke in *Measure for Measure*, 3.1.25–8

Preparing Claudio to face death.

9   We are such stuff As dreams are made on, and our little life Is rounded with a sleep.

Prospero in *The Tempest*, 4.1.156–8

His famous comment on the insubstantiality and brevity of life; "rounded" may mean rounded off, or possibly crowned.

10   Retire me to my Milan, where Every third thought shall be my grave.

Prospero in *The Tempest*, 5.1.311–12

On returning to resume his role as Duke of Milan, and to contemplate his death.

11 Since brass, nor stone, nor earth,
    nor boundless sea,
But sad mortality o'ersways their
    power,
How with this rage shall beauty
    hold a plea,
Whose action is no stronger than a
    flower?

Sonnet 65, 1–4

A poignant sense of the fragility of mortal
beauty: "with this rage" = against this destructive power; "hold a plea" = maintain its cause
(as in a legal "action").

Mourning (see also Burials, Epitaphs, Grief, Sorrow)

1 There is nothing left remarkable
Beneath the visiting moon.

Cleopatra in *Antony and Cleopatra*,
4.15.67–8

Her view of a world without Antony.

2   With fairest flowers
Whilst summer lasts and I live here,
    Fidele,
I'll sweeten thy sad grave. Thou
    shalt not lack
The flower that's like thy face, pale
    primrose, nor
The azured harebell, like thy veins;
    no, nor
The leaf of eglantine, whom not to
    slander,
Outsweetened not thy breath.

Arviragus in *Cymbeline*, 4.2.218–24

Imogen, called Fidele in her disguise as a
youth, appears dead.

3 Fear no more the heat o'the sun,
Nor the furious winter's rages,

Thou thy worldly task hast done,
Home art gone, and ta'en thy
    wages.
Golden lads and girls all must,
As chimney-sweepers, come to
    dust.

Guiderius in *Cymbeline*, 4.2.258–63

First stanza of a song of mourning for Fidele
(the disguised Imogen), supposed dead.

4 Fear no more the frown o'the great,
Thou art past the tyrant's stroke;
Care no more to clothe and eat,
To thee the reed is as the oak.
The scepter, learning, physic, must
All follow this and come to dust.

Arviragus in *Cymbeline*, 4.2.264–9

Second stanza of a song of mourning for
Fidele (Imogen in disguise) supposed dead.

5 No exorciser harm thee.
Nor no witchcraft charm thee.
Ghost unlaid forbear thee.
Nothing ill come near thee.
Quiet consummation have,
And renownèd be thy grave.

**Guiderius and Arviragus in
Cymbeline, 4.2.276–81**

Last stanza of a song of mourning for Fidele
(really Imogen in disguise) supposed dead.

6   With a defeated joy,
With an auspicious, and a dropping
    eye,
With mirth in funeral, and with
    dirge in marriage,
In equal scale weighing delight and
    dole.

Claudius in *Hamlet*, 1.2.10–13

Describing his state of mind in marrying his
brother's widow so soon after his brother's
death; "dole" = grief.

7 Do not for ever with thy vailèd lids
   Seek for thy noble father in the
   dust.
   Thou know'st 'tis common, all that
   lives must die,
   Passing through nature to eternity.

   Gertrude in *Hamlet*, 1.2.70–3

   Offering commonplace Christian comfort to
   Hamlet, who is in mourning for his father's
   death; "vailèd lids" = downcast eyes.

8 'Tis not alone my inky cloak, good
   mother,
   Nor customary suits of solemn
   black,
   . . .
   Together with all forms, moods,
   shapes of grief,
   That can denote me truly.

   Hamlet in *Hamlet*, 1.2.77–8, 82–3

   Outward shows of mourning do not do justice
   to his inward grief for his father's death.

9 They are actions that a man might
   play,
   But I have that within which passes
   show,
   These but the trappings and the
   suits of woe.

   Hamlet in *Hamlet*, 1.2.84–6

   "Actions" = outward forms of mourning.

10 I cannot choose but weep to think
    they would lay him i'the cold
    ground.

    Ophelia in *Hamlet*, 4.5.69–70

    Mad and grieving after her father's death.

11 For this I shall have time enough to
    mourn.

    **Northumberland in *Henry IV, Part 2*,
    1.1.136**

    Bad news prompts him to action, and to put
    off mourning.

12   Thy due from me
    Is tears and heavy sorrows of the
    blood,
    Which nature, love, and filial ten-
    derness
    Shall, O dear father, pay thee plen-
    teously.

    **Prince Hal in *Henry IV, Part 2*,
    4.5.37–40**

    Thinking his father is dead.

13 O world, thou wast the forest to
    this hart,
    And this indeed, O world, the heart
    of thee!
    How like a deer, strucken by many
    princes,
    Dost thou here lie!

    **Mark Antony in *Julius Caesar*,
    3.1.207–10**

    Mourning over Caesar's dead body.

14 O, pardon me, thou bleeding piece
    of earth,
    That I am meek and gentle with
    these butchers!

    Mark Antony in *Julius Caesar*, 3.1.254–5

    Looking at the dead body of Caesar, now
    earth; compare Genesis 3:19, "dust thou art,
    and unto dust shalt thou return."

15   Bear with me;
    My heart is in the coffin there with
    Caesar,
    And I must pause till it come back
    to me.

    Mark Antony in *Julius Caesar*, 3.2.105–7

    Perhaps shedding, or faking, a tear in his effort
    to sway the people.

16   Friends, I owe more tears
To this dead man than you shall see
me pay.
I shall find time, Cassius, I shall
find time.

Brutus in *Julius Caesar*, 5.3.101–3

17   Howl, howl, howl! O, you are men
of stones!
Had I your tongues and eyes, I'd
use them so
That heaven's vault should crack.

King Lear in *King Lear*, 5.3.258–60

Carrying on stage the body of his beloved
daughter Cordelia; "men of stones" = statues,
indicating that everyone on stage stands
aghast to see the two of them.

18   Had I but died an hour before this
chance,
I had lived a blessèd time; for from
this instant
There's nothing serious in mortality.
All is but toys; renown and grace is
dead,
The wine of life is drawn, and the
mere lees
Is left this vault to brag of.

Macbeth in *Macbeth*, 2.3.91–6

Macbeth mourns in public the man he has just
murdered. "Chance" = mischance, meaning
the death of Duncan; life ("mortality") from
henceforth is trivial ("toys"); the "vault" is the
sky covering the earth.

19   If a man do not erect in this age his
own tomb ere he dies, he shall live
no longer in monument than the
bell rings and the widow weeps.

**Benedick in *Much Ado About Nothing*,
5.2.77–80**

20   No longer mourn for me when I
am dead
Than you shall hear the surly sullen
bell
Give warning to the world that I am
fled
From this vile world with vilest
worms to dwell.

Sonnet 71, 1–4

The passing bell was rung once for each year
of the dead person's life.

Murder (see also Assassination)

1   List, list, O list!
If thou didst ever thy dear father
love—
. . .
Revenge his foul and most unnatural murder.
. . .
Murder most foul, as in the best it
is,
But this most foul, strange, and
unnatural.

Ghost in *Hamlet*, 1.5.22–3, 25, 27–8

Calling on Hamlet to revenge (By killing
Claudius? And so committing another "murder most foul"?).

2   For murder, though it have no
tongue, will speak
With most miraculous organ.

Hamlet in *Hamlet*, 2.2.593–4

Another way of saying, "Murder will out."

3   So shall you hear
Of carnal, bloody, and unnatural
acts,

Of accidental judgments, casual
   slaughters,
Of deaths put on by cunning and
   forced cause,
And in this upshot, purposes mistook
Fallen on th'inventors' heads.

Horatio in *Hamlet*, 5.2.380–5

Summing up his version of the events.

4   There is no sure foundation set on
     blood;
   No certain life achieved by others'
     death.

King John in *King John*, 4.2.104–5

On hearing that the nephew he wanted out of
the way is dead.

5   Come, thick night,
   And pall thee in the dunnest smoke
     of hell,
   That my keen knife see not the
     wound it makes,
   Nor heaven peep through the blan-
     ket of the dark
   To cry, "Hold, hold!"

Lady Macbeth in *Macbeth*, 1.5.50–4

"Thee" is King Duncan, whom she thinks of
murdering in his bed; hell is proverbially
black or dark; "pall thee" = cover as with a
pall, the cloth spread over a coffin.

6   Withered murder,
   Alarumed by his sentinel, the wolf,
   Whose howl's his watch, thus with
     his stealthy pace,
   With Tarquin's ravishing strides,
     towards his design
   Moves like a ghost.

Macbeth in *Macbeth*, 2.1.52–6

The murderer is imagined as roused to action
by the howling of the wolf, and moving like

Tarquin, who raped Lucretia, the wife of Col-
latinus, in ancient Rome.

7   Though in the trade of war I have
     slain men,
   Yet do I hold it very stuff o' the
     conscience
   To do no contrived murder. I lack
     iniquity
   Sometimes to do me service.

Iago in *Othello*, 1.2.1–3

Iago's hypocritical first words to Othello.

8   When I have plucked the
     rose,
   I cannot give it vital growth again,
   It needs must wither. I'll smell it
     on the tree.

Othello in *Othello*, 5.2.13–15

Desdemona is the rose he is about to pluck, or
kill.

9   Murder's out of tune,
   And sweet revenge grows harsh.

Othello in *Othello*, 5.2.115–16

On learning that Iago has failed to kill Cassio.

10 An honorable murderer, if you will,
    For naught I did in hate, but all in
     honor.

Othello in *Othello*, 5.2.294–5

After killing Desdemona; "in honor" = from a
sense of integrity, supposing it to be the right
thing to do.

11   The great King of kings
   Hath in the table of his law com-
     manded
   That thou shalt do no murder.

Clarence in *Richard III*, 1.4.195–7

In the Ten Commandments, Exodus 20:13;
"table" = tablet or list.

12   Murder her brothers and then
       marry her—
     Uncertain way of gain, but I am in
     So far in blood that sin will pluck
     on sin.

King Richard in *Richard III*, 4.2.62–4

Richard's desperate idea of marrying the
Princess Elizabeth, whose brothers he has had
executed.

13   The tyrannous and bloody deed is
       done,
     The most arch deed of piteous mas-
       sacre
     That ever yet this land was guilty of.

Tyrell in *Richard III*, 4.3.1–3

Lamenting the murder, ordered by Richard,
of the two young princes in the Tower of
London.

Music

1   Give me some music; music,
      moody food
    Of us that trade in love.

**Cleopatra in *Antony and Cleopatra*,
2.5.1–2**

2   *Jaques.* Have you a song, forester,
      for this purpose?
    Second Lord. Yes, sir.
    Jaques. Sing it. 'Tis no matter how
      it be in tune, so it make noise
      enough.

***As You Like It*, 4.2.5–9**

The song is to celebrate the killing of a deer.

3   I am advised to give her music o'
      mornings; they say it will penetrate.

Cloten in *Cymbeline*, 2.3.11–12

The buffoon, Cloten, attempts to woo Imogen;
"penetrate" suggests his real desire.

4   It is as easy as lying. Govern these
    ventages with your fingers and
    thumbs, give it breath with your
    mouth, and it will discourse most
    eloquent music.

Hamlet in *Hamlet*, 3.2.357–9

To Guildenstern, who cannot play the
recorder; "ventages" are stops on the
instrument.

5   I framed to the harp
    Many an English ditty lovely well.

**Glendower in *Henry IV, Part 1*,
3.1.121–2**

Glendower likes to boast of his accomplish-
ments.

6   Let there be no noise made, my
      gentle friends,
    Unless some dull and favorable
      hand
    Will whisper music to my weary
      spirit.

King Henry in *Henry IV, Part 2*, 4.5.1–3

The king is sick and close to death; "dull" =
soothing, drowsy.

7   Orpheus with his lute made trees
    And the mountain tops that freeze
      Bow themselves when he did sing.
    To his music plants and flowers
    Ever sprung, as sun and showers
      There had made a lasting spring.

Song in *Henry VIII*, 3.1.3–8

Ancient Greek legend attributed these powers
to Orpheus.

8   In sweet music is such art,
    Killing care and grief of heart
    Fall asleep, or hearing die.

Song in *Henry VIII*, 3.1.12–14

9   Music oft hath such a
    charm

To make bad good, and good provoke to harm.
Duke in *Measure for Measure*, 4.1.15–16

10 Let music sound while he doth
    make his choice;
    Then if he lose he makes a swan-
    like end,
    Fading in music.
**Portia in *The Merchant of Venice*,
3.2.43–5**

The swan was proverbially supposed to sing
before dying.

11 *Jessica.* I am never merry when I
    hear sweet music.
    Lorenzo. The reason is, your spirits
    are attentive.
***The Merchant of Venice*, 5.1.69–70**

"Spirits are attentive" = faculties are engaged.

12 The man that hath no music in
    himself,
    Nor is not moved with concord of
    sweet sounds,
    Is fit for treasons, stratagems, and
    spoils;
    The motions of his spirit are dull as
    night,
    And his affections dark as Erebus:
    Let no such man be trusted.
**Lorenzo in *The Merchant of Venice*,
5.1.83–8**

"Spoils" = acts of plunder; Erebus was a place
of darkness linked with Hades in classical
mythology.

13 *Titania.* What, wilt thou hear some
    music, my sweet love?
    Bottom. I have a reasonable good
    ear in music. Let's have the tongs
    and the bones.

A Midsummer Night's Dream, 4.1.27–9

Bottom's idea of music is to play on metal
tongs and bone clappers.

14 Music, ho, music such as charmeth
    sleep!
**Titania in *A Midsummer Night's
Dream*, 4.1.83**

"Charmeth" = induces like a charm.

15 The general so likes your music,
    that he desires you for love's sake to
    make no more noise with it.
Clown in *Othello*, 3.1.11–13

Cassio arranged for musicians to play beneath
the window of Othello and Desdemona.

16 An admirable musician! O, she will
    sing the savageness out of a bear!
Othello in *Othello*, 4.1.188–9

Praising Desdemona.

17 My mother had a maid called Bar-
    bary;
    She was in love, and he she loved
    proved mad,
    And did forsake her. She had a
    song of "Willow,"
    An old thing 'twas, but it expressed
    her fortune,
    And she died singing it. That song
    tonight
    Will not go from my mind.
Desdemona in *Othello*, 4.3.26–31

The willow was the proverbial badge of a forsaken lover.

18   How sour sweet music is
    When time is broke, and no pro-
    portion kept!
    So is it in the music of men's lives.
King Richard in *Richard II*, 5.5.42–4

Reflecting on himself while in prison.

19 How silver-sweet sound lovers'
    tongues by night,
    Like softest music to attending ears!

Romeo in *Romeo and Juliet*, 2.2.165–6

Hearing Juliet call to him.

20 *Hortensio*. Madam, my instru-
    ment's in tune.
    Bianca. Let's hear. O fie, the treble
    jars.
    Lucentio. Spit in the hole, man, and
    tune again.

The Taming of the Shrew, 3.1.38–40

Hortensio's lute was a difficult instrument to
tune, and Lucentio may be advising him to
moisten the pegs.

21 Where should this music be? I'
    th'air, or th'earth?
    It sounds no more.

Ferdinand in *The Tempest*, 1.2.388–9

On hearing Ariel's spirit-music.

22 This music crept by me upon the
    waters,
    Allaying both their fury and my
    passion
    With its sweet air; thence have I fol-
    lowed it,
    Or it hath drawn me rather.

Ferdinand in *The Tempest*, 1.2.392–5

Drawn by Ariel's music; this passage was used
by T.S. Eliot in *The Waste Land*.

23 Be not afeard; the isle is full of
    noises,
    Sounds and sweet airs, that give
    delight, and hurt not.
    Sometimes a thousand twangling
    instruments
    Will hum about mine ears; and
    sometime voices,

That, if I then had waked after long
sleep,
Will make me sleep again.

Caliban in *The Tempest*, 3.2.135–40

To Stephano and Trinculo, who are scared by
Ariel's music.

24 *Alonso*. What harmony is this? My
    good friends, hark!
    Gonzalo. Marvelous sweet music!

The Tempest, 3.3.18–19

Hearing "solemn and strange" music, according to the stage direction.

25 If music be the food of love, play
    on,
    Give me excess of it; that surfeiting,
    The appetite may sicken, and so
    die.

Orsino in *Twelfth Night*, 1.1.1–3

Hoping to cure his lovesickness.

26 That strain again, it had a dying fall;
    O, it came o'er my ear like the
    sweet sound
    That breathes upon a bank of vio-
    lets,
    Stealing and giving odor. Enough,
    no more,
    'Tis not so sweet now as it was
    before.

Orsino in *Twelfth Night*, 1.1.4–8

Listening to music; "strain" = melody.

27 *Orsino*.   How dost thou like this
    tune?
    Viola. It gives a very echo to the
    seat
    Where love is throned.

Twelfth Night, 2.4.20–2

Music feeds Orsino's lovesickness.

Mutability (see also Change, Transience, Transformation)

1   This world is not for aye, nor 'tis not strange
That even our loves should with our fortunes change.

Player King in *Hamlet*, 3.2.200–1

On the theme of mutability.

2   Sweet love, I see, changing his property,
Turns to the sourest and most deadly hate.

Sir Stephen Scroop in *Richard II*, 3.2.135–6

To Richard, who has been cursing his former favorites; "property" = distinctive nature.

3   When I consider everything that grows
Holds in perfection but a little moment;
That this huge stage presenteth nought but shows
Whereon the stars in secret influence comment. . . .

***Sonnet 15*, 1–2**

On the brevity of life for all things in nature.

4   Ruin hath taught me thus to ruminate,
That Time will come and take my love away.
This thought is as a death, which cannot choose
But weep to have that which it fears to lose.

***Sonnet 64*, 11–14**

The ruins of past ages seem caught up inside the word "ruminate"; another lament for the inevitable passage of time.

Myths

1   Now I will believe
That there are unicorns; that in Arabia
There is one tree, the phoenix' throne, one phoenix
At this hour reigning there.

Sebastian in *The Tempest*, 3.3.21–4

A strange vision has made him willing to believe any traveler's tale, of mythical unicorns or the phoenix, said to renew itself periodically from the ashes of its own pyre.

Names

1   *Jaques.* Rosalind is your love's name?
Orlando. Yes, just.
Jaques. I do not like her name.
Orlando. There was no thought of pleasing you when she was christened.

***As You Like It*, 3.2.263–7**

2   *Cinna.* I am not Cinna the conspirator.
Fourth Plebeian. It is no matter, his name's Cinna! Pluck but his name out of his heart, and turn him going.

***Julius Caesar*, 3.3.32–4**

Cinna the poet has the misfortune to have the same name as a conspirator against Caesar.

3   If his name be George I'll call him Peter,
For new-made honor doth forget men's names.

The Bastard Falconbridge in *King John*, 1.1.186–7

Falconbridge has just been made a knight.

4   When tongues speak sweetly, then
      they name her name,
      And Rosaline they call her.

Berowne in Love's Labor's Lost,
3.1.166–7

Betraying his desire for Rosaline.

5   I cannot tell what the dickens his
      name is.

**Mistress Page in The Merry Wives of
Windsor,** 3.2.19–20

"Dickens" is a euphemism for the devil; she
speaks of Robin, Falstaff's page.

6   Peaseblossom, Cobweb, Moth and
      Mustardseed!

**Titania in A Midsummer Night's
Dream,** 3.1.162

The names of her fairy attendants; "Moth"
sounded like "mote" or speck.

7   O Romeo, Romeo, wherefore art
      thou Romeo?
      Deny thy father and refuse thy
      name;
      Or, if thou wilt not, be but sworn
      my love,
      And I'll no longer be a Capulet.

Juliet in Romeo and Juliet, 2.2.33–6

Realizing that she, a Capulet, has fallen in
love with a Montague, the enemy of her clan.

8   What's in a name? That which we
      call a rose
      By any other name would smell as
      sweet.

Juliet in Romeo and Juliet, 2.2.43–4

On loving Romeo, a Montague, and an
enemy.

9   *Ferdinand.* I do beseech you—
      Chiefly that I may set it in my
      prayers—

What is your name?
Miranda. Miranda.—O my father,
I have broke your hest to say so.
Ferdinand. Admired Miranda,
Indeed the top of admiration!
Worth
What's dearest to the world!

The Tempest, 3.1.34–9

Playing on the meaning of "Miranda," to be
wondered at or admired (from the Latin);
"hest" = command.

Nature

1   How hard it is to hide the sparks of
      nature!

Belarius in Cymbeline, 3.3.79

Seeing the innate nobility of the king's sons,
living with him in exile.

2   O thou goddess,
      Thou divine Nature, thou thyself
      thou blazon'st
      In these two princely boys!

Belarius in Cymbeline, 4.2.169–71

Speaking of Guiderius and Arviragus, whom
Belarius knows to be the king's sons; to "blazon" is to display, like a coat of arms.

3   Thou, Nature, art my goddess, to
      thy law
      My services are bound.

Edmund in King Lear, 1.2.1–2

Rejecting conventional morality in favor of the
law of the jungle, as he is a "natural" child, a
bastard.

4   He loves us not,
      He wants the natural touch. For
      the poor wren,
      The most diminutive of birds, will
      fight,
      Her young ones in the nest, against
      the owl.

Lady Macduff in *Macbeth*, 4.2.8–11

On Macduff, her husband, who has gone to England, and left her and her child unprotected; "wants the natural touch" = lacks natural affection.

5   The earth, that's nature's mother, is her tomb.
What is her burying grave, that is her womb.

Friar Lawrence in *Romeo and Juliet*, 2.3.9–10

"Earth is the mother of us all" was proverbial, but the Friar develops the paradox that everything nature brings to birth also dies.

6   O, mickle is the powerful grace that lies
In plants, herbs, stones, and their true qualities;
For nought so vile that on the earth doth live
But to the earth some special good doth give.

Friar Lawrence in *Romeo and Juliet*, 2.3.15–18

Celebrating the great ("mickle") goodness (as given by divine grace) in natural plants and objects.

7   I have heard it said
There is an art which in their piedness shares
With great creating nature.

Perdita in *The Winter's Tale*, 4.4.86–8

She is thinking of grafting or the cross-breeding that produces parti-colored flowers ("piedness").

8   We marry
A gentler scion to the wildest stock,
And make conceive a bark of baser kind
By bud of nobler race. This is an art

Which does mend nature—change it rather; but
The art itself is nature.

Polixenes in *The Winter's Tale*, 4.4.92–7

Instructing Perdita in the art of grafting, and, paradoxically, arguing that art is nature.

Necessity (see also Fate)

1   Be you not troubled with the time, which drives
O'er your content these strong necessities,
But let determined things to destiny
Hold unbewailed their sway.

Octavius Caesar in *Antony and Cleopatra*, 3.6.82–5

His advice to his sister now that war between him and her husband, Antony, is inevitable.

2   Are these things then necessities?
Then let us meet them like necessities.

King Henry in *Henry IV, Part 2*, 3.1.92–3

Faced with the need to fight a rebel army.

3   The deep of night is crept upon our talk,
And nature must obey necessity.

Brutus in *Julius Caesar*, 4.3.226–7

To Cassius, suggesting they take some sleep.

4   O, reason not the need! our basest beggars
Are in the poorest thing superfluous.
Allow not nature more than nature needs,
Man's life is cheap as beast's.

King Lear in *King Lear*, 2.4.264–7

On being told by Regan that he needs no servants of his own.

5   How dost, my boy? Art cold?
I am cold myself. Where is this
straw, good fellow?
The art of our necessities is strange
And can make vile things precious.

King Lear in *King Lear*, 3.2.68–71

Out in the storm, he learns there is a hovel
nearby; the "boy" is his Fool.

6   What need the bridge much
broader than the flood?

Don Pedro in *Much Ado About Nothing*, 1.1.316

Telling Claudio there is no need to do more
than is necessary to achieve his desire; "flood"
= water or river.

7   Teach thy necessity to reason thus:
There is no virtue like necessity.

John of Gaunt in *Richard II*, 1.3.277–8

Trying to comfort his banished son; proverbial
("to make a virtue of necessity").

8   I am sworn brother, sweet,
To grim Necessity, and he and I
Will keep a league till death.

King Richard in *Richard II*, 5.1.20–2

As he is being taken to prison, he meets his
queen.

9   Are you content to be our general,
To make a virtue of necessity
And live as we do in this wilderness?

Second Outlaw in *The Two Gentlemen of Verona*, 4.1.59–61

Outlaws, having captured Valentine, invite
him to be their leader; it could only happen in
romance. Compare 7 above.

Negotiation

1   In the way of bargain, mark ye me,
I'll cavil on the ninth part of a hair.

Hotspur in *Henry IV, Part 1*, 3.1.137–8

Debating the partition of the country; Hotspur
enjoys the give and take of bargaining.

2   So happy be the issue, brother England,
Of this good day and of this gracious meeting.

Queen Isabel in *Henry V*, 5.2.12–13

The French Queen hopes for a happy outcome ("issue") to the negotiations for peace.

3   Haply a woman's voice may do
some good
When articles too nicely urged be
stood on.

Queen Isabel in *Henry V*, 5.2.93–4

"Haply" = perhaps; she hopes to mediate if
too much fuss is made about details of an
agreement; "stood on" = insisted on.

News

1   The nature of bad news infects the
teller.

Messenger in *Antony and Cleopatra*, 1.2.95

2   Though it be honest, it is never
good
To bring bad news.

Cleopatra in *Antony and Cleopatra*, 2.5.85–6

3   What's the new news at the new
court?

Oliver in *As You Like It*, 1.1.96–7

"New court" because Duke Frederick has
banished his brother Duke Senior and usurped
as the new Duke.

4   Thou still hast been the father of
     good news.

Claudius in *Hamlet*, 2.2.42

To Polonius who brings news that peace is
restored between Norway and Denmark;
"still" = always.

5   This advertisement is five days old.

King Henry in *Henry IV, Part 1*, 3.2.172

"Advertisement" = information.

6   *Douglas.* That's the worst tidings
     that I hear of yet.
     Worcester. Ay, by my faith, that
     bears a frosty sound.

Henry IV, Part 1, 4.1.127–8

News that Glendower, one of the leading
rebels, cannot muster his army for fourteen
days.

7   Yea, this man's brow, like to a title-
     leaf,
     Foretells the nature of a tragic vol-
     ume.

**Northumberland in *Henry IV, Part 2*,
1.1.60–1**

The messenger's face, like the title-page of a
book, spells out bad news.

8   Yet the first bringer of unwelcome
     news
     Hath but a losing office, and his
     tongue
     Sounds ever after as a sullen bell,
     Remembered tolling a departing
     friend.

**Northumberland in *Henry IV, Part 2*,
1.1.100–3**

9   Such welcome and unwelcome
     things at once,
     'Tis hard to reconcile.

Macduff in *Macbeth*, 4.3.138–9

Hearing on the one hand that Malcolm is not
fit to rule, and on the other that he is leading
an army against Macbeth.

10   Though news be sad, yet tell them
     merrily;
     If good, thou shamest the music of
     sweet news
     By playing it to me with so sour a
     face.

Juliet in *Romeo and Juliet*, 2.5.22–4

To her Nurse, who is weary rather than sad;
Juliet is anxious for news of Romeo.

Night (see also Darkness)

1   'Tis now the very witching time of
     night,
     When churchyards yawn and hell
     itself breathes out
     Contagion to this world.

Hamlet in *Hamlet*, 3.2.388–90

He is encouraging himself to be stern with his
mother.

2   Let us be Diana's foresters, gentle-
     men of the shade, minions of the
     moon.

Falstaff in *Henry IV, Part 1*, 1.2.25–6

Falstaff prefers stealing by night to working by
day; Diana was goddess of the moon, and
associated with hunting (also, ironically here,
with chastity).

3   Now comes in the sweetest morsel
     of the night, and we must hence
     and leave it unpicked.

Falstaff in *Henry IV, Part 2*, 2.4.367–8

Summoned to the wars, he cannot go to bed
with Doll Tearsheet; "unpicked" = ungath-
ered.

4   And we shall be merry, now comes
     in the sweet o' the night.
     Shallow in *Henry IV, Part 2*, 5.3.50–1

     As they break out the wine.

5   Now entertain conjecture of a time
     When creeping murmur and the
       poring dark
     Fills the wide vessel of the universe.
     Chorus in *Henry V*, 4.Prologue, 1–3

     The dark is "poring" because people strain to
     see.

6   From camp to camp, through the
       foul womb of night,
     The hum of either army stilly
       sounds.
     Chorus in *Henry V*, 4.Prologue, 4–5

     "Stilly" = softly; the "foul womb" will give
     birth to battle at dawn.

7   The cripple tardy-gaited night,
     Who like a foul and ugly witch doth
       limp
     So tediously away.
     Chorus in *Henry V*, 4.Prologue, 20–2

     The night seems foul and tedious to the Eng-
     lish army knowing they must fight in the
     morning.

8   Hung be the heavens with black!
       Yield, day, to night!
     Bedford in *Henry VI, Part 1*, 1.1.1

     Probably referring to the canopy over the
     stage, hung with black drapes for a tragedy.

9   What a fearful night is this!
     There's two or three of us have seen
       strange sights.
     Cinna in *Julius Caesar*, 1.3.137–8

     On the stormy night before the murder of Cae-
     sar.

10   Here's a night pities neither wise
       men nor fools.
     Fool in *King Lear*, 3.2.12–13

     The stage directions call for "storm and tem-
     pest," and the text for thunder and lightning,
     wind and rain.

11   Things that love night
     Love not such nights as these.
     Kent in *King Lear*, 3.2.42–3

     Referring to the wild storm in which Lear
     wanders.

12   Now o'er the one half-world
     Nature seems dead, and wicked
       dreams abuse
     The curtained sleep.
     Macbeth in *Macbeth*, 2.1.49–51

     "Curtained" suggests both bed-curtains, and
     the unconsciousness of sleep that shuts off the
     control exerted by the conscious mind.

13   Light thickens, and the crow
     Makes wing to the rooky wood.
     Good things of day begin to droop
       and drowse,
     Whiles night's black agents to their
       prey do rouse.
     Macbeth in *Macbeth*, 3.2.50–3

     Invoking the powers of darkness preparatory
     to murdering Banquo.

14   The night is long that never finds
       the day.
     Malcolm in *Macbeth*, 4.3.240

     For him the "night" is the reign of the tyrant
     Macbeth.

15   The moon shines bright. In such a
       night as this,
     When the sweet wind did gently
       kiss the trees,

And they did make no noise, in such a night
Troilus methinks mounted the Troyan walls,
And sighed his soul toward the Grecian tents,
Where Cressida lay that night.

Lorenzo in *The Merchant of Venice*, 5.1.1–6

In Belmont, waiting for the return of Portia, Lorenzo sets the scene; Cressida turned out to be faithless to Troilus.

16 Who comes so fast in silence of the night?

Lorenzo in *The Merchant of Venice*, 5.1.25

Hearing the sound of a messenger.

17 O weary night, O long and tedious night,
Abate thy hours, shine comforts from the east.

Helena in *A Midsummer Night's Dream*, 3.2.431–2

"Abate" = cut short, abridge.

18 O grim-looked night, O night with hue so black,
O night which ever art when day is not!

Bottom in *A Midsummer Night's Dream*, 5.1.170–1

As Pyramus, addressing the night.

19 Now the hungry lion roars,
And the wolf behowls the moon,
Whilst the heavy ploughman snores,
All with weary task foredone.

Puck in *A Midsummer Night's Dream*, 5.1.371–4

"Foredone" = exhausted.

20   Come, civil night,
Thou sober-suited matron all in black.

Juliet in *Romeo and Juliet*, 3.2.10–11

"Civil" = mannerly, observing propriety; Juliet is now married, and anxiously awaiting nightfall and the coming of Romeo.

21 Come, gentle night, come, loving, black-browed night,
Give me my Romeo, and when I shall die,
Take him and cut him out in little stars
And he will make the face of heaven so fine
That all the world will be in love with night,
And pay no worship to the garish sun.

Juliet in *Romeo and Juliet*, 3.2.20–25

Expressing her adoration of Romeo.

22 The dragon wing of night o'er-spreads the earth.

Achilles in *Troilus and Cressida*, 5.8.17

Suggesting doom as well as darkness; he has just killed Hector.

23   It hath been the longest night
That e'er I watched, and the most heaviest.

Julia in *The Two Gentlemen of Verona*, 4.2.139–40

She has been watching Proteus, who has sworn his devotion to her, making love to Sylvia.

24 Sable night, mother of dread and fear.

***The Rape of Lucrece*, 117**

Nobility

1 His nature is too noble for the world;
He would not flatter Neptune for his trident,
Or Jove for 's power to thunder.

Menenius in *Coriolanus*, 3.1.254–6

Speaking about Coriolanus; "too noble" sounds like arrogance.

2 O what a noble mind is here o'erthrown!

Ophelia in *Hamlet*, 3.1.150

She thinks Hamlet to be mad after his verbal attack on her.

3 She's noble born,
And like her true nobility she has
Carried herself towards me.

King Henry in *Henry VIII*, 2.4.142–4

Praising Katherine, the wife he is about to divorce.

4 Well, Brutus, thou art noble, yet I see
Thy honorable mettle may be wrought
From that it is disposed. It is meet
That noble minds keep ever with their likes;
For who so firm that cannot be seduced.

Cassius in *Julius Caesar*, 1.2.308–12

Realizing Brutus's spirit ("mettle") may be diverted from the course he is disposed to follow; "meet" = fitting.

5 O, he sits high in all the people's hearts;
And that which would appear offense in us
His countenance, like richest alchemy,
Will change to virtue and to worthiness.

Casca in *Julius Caesar*, 1.3.157–60

Describing Brutus; "countenance" = appearance, and support; the aim of alchemy was to transmute base metals into gold.

6 This was the noblest Roman of them all.
All the conspirators save only he
Did that they did in envy of great Caesar.
He only, in a general honest thought
And common good to all, made one of them.

Mark Antony in *Julius Caesar*, 5.5.68–72

His eulogy of Brutus.

7 A brother noble,
Whose nature is so far from doing harms
That he suspects none.

Edmund in *King Lear*, 1.2.179–81

On his brother Edgar.

8 I might call him
A thing divine, for nothing natural
I ever saw so noble.

Miranda in *The Tempest*, 1.2.418–20

Miranda's first sight of a young man, Ferdinand.

9 This is the prettiest low-born lass that ever
Ran on the green-sward: nothing she does or seems
But smacks of something greater than herself,
Too noble for this place.

Polixenes in *The Winter's Tale*,
4.4.156–9

Speaking of Perdita; he doesn't yet know that she is a princess.

5   "Where is the life that late I led?"
Petruchio in *The Taming of the Shrew*,
4.1.140

The newly married Petruchio sings what seems to be the first line of a lost ballad.

Nonsense

1   This is the silliest stuff that ever I heard.
Hippolyta in *A Midsummer Night's Dream*, 5.1.210

Watching the play of "Pyramus and Thisbe."

Nostalgia

1   If ever you have looked on better days.
Orlando in *As You Like It*, 2.7.113

Asking to be pitied.

2   There lives not three good men unhanged in England, and one of them is fat and grows old.
Falstaff in *Henry IV, Part 1*, 2.4.130–2

The fat one is himself.

3   Jesu, Jesu, the mad days that I have spent! And to see how many of my old acquaintance are dead!
Shallow in *Henry IV, Part 2*, 3.2.33–4

Old justices Shallow and Silence recall their wild youth.

4   We have heard the chimes at midnight, Master Shallow.
Falstaff in *Henry IV, Part 2*, 3.2.214–15

Recalling their youth in London.

Nothing

1   *Kent.* This is nothing, Fool.
Fool. Then 'tis like the breath of an unfeed lawyer, you gave me nothing for't.
King Lear, 1.4.128–30

Kent is commenting on the Fool's rhymes.

2   Nothing can be made out of nothing.
King Lear in *King Lear*, 1.4.132–3

Proverbial (see also Proverbs)

3   Thou wast a pretty fellow when thou hadst no need to care for her frowning; now thou art an O without a figure. I am better than thou art now; I am a fool, thou art nothing.
Fool in *King Lear*, 1.4.191–4

To King Lear, who has given his lands to his daughters; an "O" is nothing without another figure in front of it.

Oaths (see also Promises, Vows)

1   Swear me, Kate, like a lady as thou art,
A good mouth-filling oath.
Hotspur in *Henry IV, Part 1*, 3.1.253–4

To his wife, who has sworn she will not sing.

2　I will die a hundred thousand
　　deaths
　　Ere break the smallest parcel of this
　　vow.
　　Prince Hal in *Henry IV, Part 1,*
　　3.2.158–9

　　Vowing his allegiance to his father and deter-
　　mination to overcome their enemy, Hotspur.

3　I have no cunning in protesta-
　　tion—only downright oaths, which
　　I never use till urged, nor never
　　break for urging.
　　King Henry in *Henry V,* 5.2.143–6

　　Plain speaking in making love to Katherine.

Obscenity

1　If bawdy talk offend you, we'll have
　　very little of it.
　　Lucio in *Measure for Measure,* 4.3.178–9

　　To the Duke, who is trying to get rid of him.

Obstinacy

1　Why should we in our peevish
　　opposition
　　Take it to heart
　　Claudius in *Hamlet,* 1.2.100–1

　　Suggesting Hamlet is pig-headed in continu-
　　ing to mourn for his father.

2　A peevish self-willed harlotry,
　　One that no persuasion can do
　　good upon.
　　Glendower in *Henry IV, Part 1,*
　　3.1.196–7

　　Speaking playfully of his daughter, who says
　　she will not be parted from her husband, who
　　is leaving for the wars; "harlotry" = hussy.

3　'Tis best to give him way, he leads
　　himself.
　　Cornwall in *King Lear,* 2.4.298

　　"Leads himself" = goes where his will leads
　　him.

4　　　O sir, to willful men
　　The injuries that they themselves
　　　procure
　　Must be their schoolmasters.
　　Regan in *King Lear,* 2.4.302–4

　　Speaking to Gloucester about her father, shut
　　out in the storm.

The Occult

1　Eye of newt and toe of frog,
　　Wool of bat and tongue of dog,
　　Adder's fork and blind-worm's
　　　sting,
　　Lizard's leg and owlet's wing,
　　For a charm of powerful trouble,
　　Like a hell-broth boil and bubble.
　　Second Witch in *Macbeth,* 4.1.14–19

　　The parts of creatures include the forked
　　tongue of the poisonous adder, and the "sting"
　　of the blind-worm, a lizard that is in fact
　　harmless.

2　Double, double, toil and trouble;
　　Fire burn, and cauldron bubble.
　　The Witches (Weird Sisters) in *Mac-
　　beth,* 4.1.20–1

　　Casting a spell.

3　*Macbeth.* How now, you secret,
　　　black, and midnight hags?
　　What is't you do?
　　Witches.　　A deed without a
　　　name.
　　Macbeth, 4.1.48–9

Old Age (see also Age)

1   "Let me not live," quoth he
"After my flame lacks oil, to be the
snuff
Of younger spirits, whose appre-
hensive senses
All but new things disdain."

**King of France in *All's Well That Ends
Well*, 1.2.58–61**

An old man's wish to die rather than oppress
the young; "snuff" = a burned wick that prevents a candle from flaming brightly.

2   They say an old man is twice a
child.

Rosencrantz in *Hamlet*, 2.2.385

To Hamlet, who has just pointed out Polonius;
proverbial.

3   There lives not three good men
unhanged in England, and one of
them is fat and grows old.

Falstaff in *Henry IV, Part 1*, 2.4.130–2

Referring to himself as "one of them."

4   Your lordship, though not clean
past your youth, have yet some
smack of age in you, some relish of
the saltness of time in you.

Falstaff in *Henry IV, Part 2*, 1.2.96–9

Addressing the Lord Chief Justice.

5   So minutes, hours, days, months,
and years,
Passed over to the end they were
created,
Would bring white hairs unto a
quiet grave.
Ah, what a life were this! How
sweet! How lovely!

**King Henry in *Henry VI, Part 3*,
2.5.38–41**

In a savage civil war the king longs for a quiet
life.

6   An old man, broken with the
storms of state,
Is come to lay his weary bones
among ye:
Give him a little earth for charity.

**Griffith, reporting Wolsey's words, in
Henry VIII, 4.2.21–3**

Wolsey's greeting to the Abbot of Leicester.

7   O sir, you are old,
Nature in you stands on the very
verge
Of her confine.

Regan in *King Lear*, 2.4.146–8

Implying that her father is not competent to
conduct his own affairs.

8   I have lived long enough: my way of
life
Is fallen into the sere, the yellow
leaf;
And that which should accompany
old age,
As honor, love, obedience, troops
of friends,
I must not look to have.

Macbeth in *Macbeth*, 5.3.22–6

Macbeth's achievement of the throne of Scotland in the end brings him no satisfaction;
"sere" = dry and withered; "as honor" = such
as honor.

9   When thou art old and rich,
Thou hast neither heat, affection,
limb, nor beauty,
To make thy riches pleasant.

Duke in *Measure for Measure*, 3.1.36–8

Preparing Claudio to face death.

10 A good old man, sir, he will be talking; as they say, "When the age is
in, the wit is out."

Dogberry in *Much Ado About
Nothing*, 3.5.33–4

On Verges, his assistant; proverbial phrases,
though the second alters the proverb, "When
the ale (or wine) is in the wit is out."

11 But old folks—many feign as they
were dead,
Unwieldy, slow, heavy, and pale as
lead.

Juliet in *Romeo and Juliet*, 2.5.16–17

Thinking of her old Nurse; "feign as" =
behave as if.

12 Give me a staff of honor for mine
age,
But not a scepter to control the
world.

Titus in *Titus Andronicus*, 1.1.198–9

Refusing to be made emperor of Rome.

13 Old Nestor—whose wit was
mouldy ere your grandsires had
nails on their toes.

Thersites in *Troilus and Cressida*,
2.1.104–6

"Wit" = intelligence; Nestor is the oldest of
the Greek generals; Thersites is speaking to
Achilles and Ajax.

14 Respect and reason wait on wrinkled age.

The Rape of Lucrece, 275

So Tarquin seeks to justify the rape by claiming it is proper for the young to pursue
desires.

Omens, see Portents

Opinion

1 Thou art a blessed fellow to think as
every man thinks. Never a man's
thought in the world keeps the
road-way better than thine.

Prince Hal in *Henry IV, Part 2*, 2.2.56–9

Mocking his friend Poins for accepting common opinion as true.

2 Come on my right hand, for this
ear is deaf,
And tell me truly what thou
think'st of him.

Caesar in *Julius Caesar*, 1.2.213–14

Inviting Antony to say what he thinks of Cassius; the all-powerful ruler has physical weak-
nesses.

3 Opinion's but a fool that makes us
scan
The outward habit for the inward
man.

Simonides in *Pericles*, 2.2.56–7

"Outward habit" = external appearance.

Opportunity

1 Who seeks and will not take when
once 'tis offered
Shall never find it more.

Menas in *Antony and Cleopatra*,
2.7.83–4

Pompey has just refused his offer to make him
emperor by assassinating Antony and
Octavius Caesar.

2 There is a tide in the affairs of men
Which, taken at the flood, leads on
to fortune;
Omitted, all the voyage of their life
Is bound in shallows and in mis-
eries.
On such a full sea are we now
afloat,
And we must take the current when
it serves,
Or lose our ventures.

Brutus in *Julius Caesar*, 4.3.218–24

The idea is that if the moment or opportunity
is neglected ("omitted"), the whole life may be
confined ("bound in") to treading water.

3 Why then, the world's mine oyster,
Which I with sword will open.

Pistol in *The Merry Wives of Windsor*,
2.2.3–4

On failing to persuade Falstaff to lend him
money; "the world's my oyster" was proverbial, meaning I'll find wealth somehow.

4 The poor, lame, blind, halt, creep,
cry out for thee,
But they ne'er meet with opportunity.

***The Rape of Lucrece*, 902–3**

Lucrece broods on the force of opportunity,
anachronistically referring to the gospels;
compare Luke 14:13, "when thou makest a
feast, call the poor, the maimed, the lame, the
blind."

Order

1 The heavens themselves, the planets, and this center
Observe degree, priority, and place.

Ulysses in *Troilus and Cressida*,
1.3.85–6

Appealing to a hierarchical concept of the
universe, with the earth at the center, as in the
Ptolemaic concept of astronomy.

2 O, when degree is shaked,
Which is the ladder to all high
designs,
The enterprise is sick.

Ulysses in *Troilus and Cressida*,
1.3.101–3

By "degree" he means hierarchy, the relative
positions of people on a social scale; "enterprise" = social or political project, here the
Trojan war.

3 Take but degree away, untune that
string,
And hark what discord follows!

Ulysses in *Troilus and Cressida*,
1.3.109–10

4 You must confine yourself within
the modest limits of order.

Maria in *Twelfth Night*, 1.3.8–9

Advising Sir Toby Belch not to stay up drinking late at night.

Overconfidence

1 The man that once did sell the
lion's skin
While the beast lived, was killed
with hunting him.

King Henry in *Henry V*, 4.3.93–4

Referring to the French, who rashly expect an
easy victory.

Painting

1 Look when a painter would surpass
   the life
   In limning out a well-proportioned
   steed,
   His art with Nature's workmanship
   at strife,
   As if the dead the living should
   exceed,
   So did this horse excel a common
   one,
   In shape, in courage, color, pace
   and bone.

   Venus and Adonis, 289–94

   "Look" = just as; "limning" = painting.

Paradoxes

1 Fair is foul and foul is fair.

   The Witches (Weird Sisters) in *Macbeth*. 1.1.11

2 Nothing is but what is not.

   Macbeth in *Macbeth*, 1.3.141–2

   Expressing the confusion in his mind as he begins to imagine murdering Duncan.

3 And I have found Demetrius, like a
   jewel,
   Mine own, and not mine own.

   Helena in *A Midsummer Night's Dream*, 4.1.191–2

   She has "found" him by chance or magic, and so, like a jewel found by accident, he may be claimed by someone else.

4 But fare thee well, most foul, most
   fair! Farewell,
   Thou pure impiety and impious
   purity!

   Claudio in *Much Ado About Nothing*, 4.1.103–4

   Dismissing Hero, whom he was to have married, and believes to have been false to him.

Parents and Children (see also Boys, Children, Girls, Youth)

1 Thou hast never in thy life
   Showed thy dear mother any cour-
   tesy,
   When she, poor hen, fond of no
   second brood,
   Has clucked thee to the wars, and
   safely home
   Loaden with honor.

   Volumnia in *Coriolanus*, 5.3.160–4

   His mother pleads with Coriolanus not to make war on Rome; a strikingly homely image for a patrician lady.

2 [*holds her by the hand, silent*] O
   mother, mother!
   What have you done? Behold, the
   heavens do ope,
   The gods look down, and this
   unnatural scene
   They laugh at. O my mother,
   mother! O!
   You have won a happy victory to
   Rome;
   But, for your son, believe it—O,
   believe it—
   Most dangerously you have with
   him prevailed,
   If not most mortal to him.

   Coriolanus in *Coriolanus*, 5.3.182–9

   The turning-point, when he agrees to spare Rome, knowing it may lead to his own ruin.

3 That thou art my son I have partly
   thy mother's word, partly my own

opinion, but chiefly a villainous trick of thine eye and a foolish hanging of thy nether lip that doth warrant me.

Falstaff in *Henry IV, Part 1*, 2.4.402–5

Falstaff is play-acting as Prince Hal's father, and invoking the common idea that one could never be sure who the father of a child was, hence the importance of resemblance to parents.

4   Why, 'tis a happy thing
To be a father unto many sons.

King Edward in *Henry VI, Part 3*, 3.2.104–5

He wants to marry Lady Grey, who has sons by a previous husband.

5   Sir, I love you more than words can
    wield the matter,
Dearer than eyesight, space, and
    liberty,
Beyond what can be valued, rich or
    rare,
No less than life, with grace, health,
    beauty, honor;
As much as child e'er loved, or
    father found,
A love that makes breath poor and
    speech unable.

Goneril in *King Lear*, 1.1.55–60

Overdoing her response to her father's demand of his daughters, "Which of you shall we say doth love us most?"

6   Now our joy,
Although our last and least.

King Lear in *King Lear*, 1.1.82–3

Addressing Cordelia, his youngest daughter (so the Folio text, 1623; the Quarto, 1608, has "not least").

7   You have begot me, bred me, loved
    me. I
Return those duties back as are
    right fit,

Obey you, love you, and most
    honor you.

Cordelia in *King Lear*, 1.1.96–8

Speaking to her father; the last line curiously echoes the marriage service.

8   Fathers that wear rags
    Do make their children blind,
    But fathers that bear bags
    Shall see their children kind.

Fool in *King Lear*, 2.4.47–50

"Bear bags" = have wealth.

9   I prithee, daughter, do not make
    me mad.
I will not trouble thee, my child;
    farewell:
We'll no more meet, no more see
    one another.
But yet thou art my flesh, my
    blood, my daughter—
Or rather a disease that's in my
    flesh,
Which I must needs call mine.

King Lear in *King Lear*, 2.4.218–23

Speaking to Goneril; he has given his power to his daughters, and now they use it against him.

10   I may neither choose who I would,
    nor refuse who I dislike; so is the
    will of a living daughter curbed by
    the will of a dead father.

Portia in *The Merchant of Venice*, 1.2.23–5

Playing on "will" as desire and as testament.

11   It is a wise father that knows his
    own child.

Launcelot Gobbo in *The Merchant of Venice*, 2.2.76–7

His blind father fails to recognize him; varying the proverb, "It is a wise child that knows his own father."

12 Farewell, and if my fortune be not
crossed,
I have a father, you a daughter, lost.

Jessica in *The Merchant of Venice*,
2.5.56–7

Said as her father, Shylock, leaves; she is aiming to elope with Lorenzo.

13 It is my cousin's duty to make
curtsy and say, "Father, as it please
you." But yet for all that, cousin,
let him be a handsome fellow, or
else make another curtsy and say,
"Father, as it please me."

Beatrice in *Much Ado About Nothing*,
2.1.52–6

Speaking of Hero; Beatrice is freer, her father
being dead.

14 Can no man tell me of my unthrifty
son?
'Tis full three months since I did
see him last.

King Henry IV in *Richard II*, 5.3.1–2

Referring to Prince Hal, as he becomes in
Henry IV; "unthrifty" = spendthrift, prodigal.

15 Earth hath swallowed all my hopes
but she;
She is the hopeful lady of my earth.

Capulet in *Romeo and Juliet*, 1.2.14–15

On his only daughter, Juliet, the heir to his
property ("earth").

16   They say we are
Almost as like as eggs. Women say
so
That will say anything.

Leontes in *The Winter's Tale*, 1.2.129–31

On the likeness of father and son.

17   Methinks a father
Is at the nuptial of his son a guest
That best becomes the table.

Polixenes in *The Winter's Tale*,
4.4.394–6

To Florizel, who has concealed his love for
Perdita from his father.

18 Thou art thy mother's glass, and
she in thee
Calls back the lovely April of her
prime.

Sonnet 3, 9–10

Addressing his "friend"; "glass" = mirror or
image.

19 A decrepit father takes delight
To see his active child do deeds of
youth.

Sonnet 37, 1–2

Was Shakespeare thinking of himself? His first
child was born when he was nineteen, in
1583.

Parting (see also Farewells)

1 Sir, you and I must part, but that's
not it;
Sir, you and I have loved, but
there's not it.

Cleopatra in *Antony and Cleopatra*,
1.3.87–8

Movingly suggesting what cannot be
expressed.

2 *Jaques.* Let's meet as little as we
can.
Orlando. I do desire we may be
better strangers.

As You Like It, 3.2.257–8

3   O the gods!
When shall we see again?

Imogen in *Cymbeline*, 1.1.123–4

To Posthumus, her husband, as they are about to be parted; "see" = see one another, meet.

4   There cannot be a pinch in death
More sharp than this is.

Imogen in *Cymbeline*, 1.1.130–1

On the banishment of her husband, Posthumus.

5   I would have broke mine eye-
strings, cracked them, but
To look upon him, till the diminution
Of space had pointed him sharp as
my needle;
Nay, followed him till he had
melted from
The smallness of a gnat to air, and
then
Have turned mine eye and wept.

Imogen in *Cymbeline*, 1.3.17–22

To Pisanio, who watched her husband, Posthumus, sail away.

6   *Polonius.* My lord, I will take my
leave of you.
Hamlet. You cannot, sir, take from
me anything that I will not more
willingly part withal—except my
life, except my life, except my life.

***Hamlet*, 2.2.213–16**

Hamlet affects madness, but his melancholy and death-wish are genuine.

7   Come, wilt thou see me ride?
And when I am a' horseback, I will
swear
I love thee infinitely.

Hotspur in *Henry IV, Part 1*, 2.3.100–2

Joking that he will love his wife only when he leaves her.

8   Art thou gone too? All comfort go
with thee,
For none abides with me.

Duchess of Gloucester in *Henry VI, Part 2*, 2.4.87–8

On being forced to part from her husband.

9   For ever and for ever farewell, Cassius!
If we do meet again, why, we shall
smile.
If not, why then this parting was
well made.

Brutus in *Julius Caesar*, 5.1.116–18

Before the battle of Philippi; they never do meet again.

10   Let us not be dainty of leave-taking,
But shift away.

Malcolm in *Macbeth*, 2.3.144–5

After the murder of their father, Duncan; "dainty of" = particular about.

11   Stand not upon the order of your
going,
But go at once.

Lady Macbeth in *Macbeth*, 3.4.118–19

The nobles at her feast would normally leave in order of precedence, but Macbeth's wild behavior on seeing the ghost of Banquo has made her eager for their departure.

12   Trouble being gone, comfort
should remain; but when you
depart from me sorrow abides, and
happiness takes his leave.

Leonato in *Much Ado About Nothing*, 1.1.100–2

An odd way to express pleasure in welcoming guests.

13   *Queen.* And must we be divided?
     Must we part?
    King Richard. Ay, hand from hand,
    my love, and heart from heart.

Richard II, 5.1.81–2

Richard is being sent north to imprisonment.

14   Love goes toward love as school-
    boys from their books,
    But love from love, toward school
    with heavy looks.

Romeo in *Romeo and Juliet,* 2.2.156–7

On leaving Juliet.

15   Good night, good night. Parting is
    such sweet sorrow
    That I shall say good night till it be
    morrow.

Juliet in *Romeo and Juliet,* 2.2.184–5

Bidding farewell from her window to Romeo
in the garden below.

16   Wilt thou be gone? It is not yet
    near day.
    It was the nightingale, and not the
    lark,
    That pierced the fearful hollow of
    thine ear;
    Nightly she sings on yond pome-
    granate tree.

Juliet in *Romeo and Juliet,* 3.5.1–4

To Romeo, who is anxious to get away at day-
break; "fearful" = anxious.

Passion

1   What to ourselves in passion we
    propose,
    The passion ending, doth the pur-
    pose lose.

Player King in *Hamlet,* 3.2.194–5

2   Is this the nature
    Whom passion could not shake?
    Whose solid virtue
    The shot of accident nor dart of
    chance
    Could neither graze nor pierce?

Lodovico in *Othello,* 4.1.265–8

Amazed at the angry passion Othello shows.

3   Is your blood
    So madly hot that no discourse of
    reason,
    Nor fear of bad success in a bad
    cause,
    Can qualify the same?

Hector in *Troilus and Cressida,*
2.2.115–18

Questioning the passion his young brother,
Troilus, has for keeping Helen.

4   An oven that is stopped, or river
    stayed,
    Burneth more hotly, swelleth with
    more rage;
    So of concealèd sorrow may be said
    Free vent of words love's fire doth
    assuage.

Venus and Adonis, 331–4

Venus, burning with love for Adonis,
approaches him.

Patience

1   I laughed him out of patience; and
    that night
    I laughed him into patience.

Cleopatra in *Antony and Cleopatra,*
2.5.19–20

Exemplifying her "infinite variety" (2.2.235).

2   Though patience be a tired mare,
    yet she will plod.

Nym in *Henry V,* 2.1.23–4

3   With meditating that she must die
    once,
    I have the patience to endure it
    now.
    Brutus in *Julius Caesar*, 4.3.191–2

    On the death of his wife, Portia.

4   I know not how,
    But I do find it cowardly and vile,
    For fear of what might fall, so to
        prevent
    The time of life—arming myself
        with patience
    To stay the providence of some
        high powers
    That govern us below.
    Brutus in *Julius Caesar*, 5.1.102–7

    Anticipating the worst, and rejecting for the
    moment the idea of suicide; "prevent" =
    anticipate.

5   No, I will be the pattern of all
        patience,
    I will say nothing.
    King Lear in *King Lear*, 3.2.37–8

    Shut out of doors in a violent storm, King Lear
    does not remain patient for long.

6   Bear free and patient thoughts.
    Edgar in *King Lear*, 4.6.80

    Advising his father; "free" = free from guilt or
    anxiety.

7   Thou must be patient; we came cry-
        ing hither.
    Thou know'st, the first time that we
        smell the air
    We wawl and cry.
    King Lear in *King Lear*, 4.6.178–80

    The old king, half-crazed, preaches to the
    blind Gloucester.

8   I do oppose
    My patience to his fury, and am
        armed
    To suffer, with a quietness of
        spirit,
    The very tyranny and rage of his.
    **Antonio in *The Merchant of Venice*,
    4.1.10–13**

    Referring to Shylock's cruelty ("tyranny").

9   If then true lovers have been ever
        crossed
    It stands as an edict in destiny.
    Then let us teach our trial
        patience,
    Because it is a customary cross,
    As due to love as thoughts, and
        dreams, and sighs,
    Wishes, and tears—poor fancy's
        followers.
    **Hermia in *A Midsummer Night's
    Dream*, 1.1.150–5**

    Speaking to Lysander; "crossed" = thwarted;
    "fancy" suggests both love and the capricious
    workings of the imagination.

10 How poor are they that have not
        patience!
    What wound did ever heal but by
        degrees?
    Iago in *Othello*, 2.3.370–1

    Recommending patience to Roderigo, who
    has been beaten by Cassio; "He that has no
    patience has nothing" is proverbial.

11   Yet thou dost look
    Like Patience gazing on kings'
        graves, and smiling
    Extremity out of act.
    Pericles in *Pericles*, 5.1.137–9

    On the sufferings of Marina; "smiling extrem-
    ity out of act" = making extreme calamities
    seem as if they never happened.

12 She sat like Patience on a monu-
    ment,
    Smiling at grief.

Viola in *Twelfth Night*, 2.4.114–5

She is describing her own concealed love for
Orsino, to whom she is speaking.

Patriotism

1 Who is here so base that would be a
   bondman? If any, speak, for him
   have I offended. Who is here so
   rude that would not be a Roman?
   If any, speak, for him have I
   offended. Who is here so vile that
   will not love his country? If any,
   speak, for him have I offended.

Brutus in *Julius Caesar*, 3.2.29–34

To the people, after the death of Caesar.

2 This England never did, nor never
   shall
   Lie at the proud foot of a conqueror,
   But when it first did help to wound
   itself.
   Now these her princes are come
   home again,
   Come the three corners of the
   world in arms,
   And we shall shock them. Nought
   shall make us rue
   If England to herself do rest but
   true!

**The Bastard Falconbridge in *King
John*, 5.7.112–18**

A rousing finish to a play much concerned
with civil discords.

Payment (see also Money)

1 Now I will look to his remuneration. Remuneration! O, that's the
   Latin word for three-farthings.

Costard in *Love's Labor's Lost*, 3.1.136–7

Armado's "reward" to him for carrying a letter
to Jaquenetta.

2 He is well paid that is well satisfied.

**Portia in *The Merchant of Venice*,
4.1.415**

Disguised as Balthasar the lawyer, she refuses
the money offered to her as a fee by her husband Bassanio.

Peace

1 The time of universal peace is near.
   Prove this a prosp'rous day, the
   three-nooked world
   Shall bear the olive freely.

**Octavius Caesar in *Antony and
Cleopatra*, 4.6.4–6**

Anticipating peace. "Prove this" = If this
prove; "three-nooked" = three-cornered.

2 *Second Servant.* As wars, in some
   sort, may be said to be a ravisher,
   so it cannot be denied but peace is
   a great maker of cuckolds.
   First Servant. Ay, and it makes men
   hate one another.
   Second Servant. Reason: because
   they then less need one another.

***Coriolanus*, 4.5.227–32**

The servants of Aufidius commenting after the
arrival of Coriolanus at his house.

3   Never was a war did cease,
Ere bloody hands were washed,
with such a peace.

Cymbeline in *Cymbeline*, 5.5.484–5

Having defeated the Romans, Cymbeline
agrees to submit to their rule.

4   All you that kiss my Lady Peace at
home.

Falstaff in *Henry IV, Part 2*, 1.2.207–8

To the Chief Justice, as Falstaff goes off to fight
rebels.

5   The dove and very blessed spirit of
peace.

**Westmorland in *Henry IV, Part 2*,
4.1.46**

On what an archbishop's vestments
symbolize.

6   Our peace shall stand as firm as
rocky mountains.

Mowbray in *Henry IV, Part 2*, 4.1.186

A rebel hopes to negotiate peace with the
king.

7   A peace is of the nature of a conquest,
For then both parties nobly are
subdued,
And neither party loser.

**Archbishop of York in *Henry IV, Part
2*, 4.2.89–91**

He does not know that Prince John is tricking
his enemies, and will promptly execute the
rebel leaders.

8   Peace puts forth her olive everywhere.

**Westmorland in *Henry IV, Part 2*,
4.4.87**

The olive branch, a traditional symbol of
peace.

9   In peace there's nothing so
becomes a man
As modest stillness and humility.

King Henry in *Henry V*, 3.1.3–4

10   Peace to this meeting, wherefore we
are met.

King Henry in *Henry V*, 5.2.1

The meeting is to settle peace between England and France.

11   Peace,
Dear nurse of arts, plenties, and
joyful births.

Burgundy in *Henry V*, 5.2.34–5

12   For blessèd are the peacemakers on
earth.

King Henry in *Henry VI, Part 2*, 2.1.34

13   In her days every man shall eat in
safety
Under his own vine what he plants,
and sing
The merry songs of peace to all his
neighbors.

**Archbishop Cranmer in *Henry VIII*,
5.4.33–5**

Anticipating the reign of Queen Elizabeth I;
the terms recall biblical passages such as
Micah 4:3–4.

14   'Tis not hard, I think,
For men so old as we to keep the
peace.

Capulet in *Romeo and Juliet*, 1.2.2–3

The prince has bound old Capulet and Montague to keep the peace.

15 I hold the olive in my hand. My
    words are as full of peace as matter.
    Viola in *Twelfth Night*, 1.5.209–11

    Bringing Orsino's message of love to Olivia.

People/Populace

1 Tonight we'll wander through the
    streets and note
    The qualities of people.
    Antony in *Antony and Cleopatra*,
    1.1.53–4

    An early instance of the popular sport of "peo-
    ple-watching."

2   This common body
    Like to a vagabond flag upon the
    stream,
    Goes to and back, lackeying the
    various tide
    To rot itself with motion.
    Octavius Caesar in *Antony and
    Cleopatra*, 1.4.44–7

    The "vagabond flag" refers to a flag iris drift-
    ing; "lackeying" = following, like a lackey or
    servant. Octavius shows his contempt for the
    people.

3 He's a very dog to the commonalty.
    First Citizen in *Coriolanus*, 1.1.28–9

    Referring to Caius Martius, later named Cori-
    olanus, one of the patricians against whom
    the citizens have begun an uprising; "com-
    monalty" = state or commonwealth.

4 What's the matter, you dissentious
    rogues,
    That rubbing the poor itch of your
    opinion
    Make yourselves scabs?
    Caius Martius, later Coriolanus, in
    Coriolanus, 1.1.164–6

    A patrician reveals his contempt for the peo-
    ple and their opinions.

5   He that trusts to you,
    Where he should find you lions,
    finds you hares;
    Where foxes, geese.
    Caius Martius, later Coriolanus, in
    Coriolanus, 1.1.170–2

    A patrician view of the people of Rome, see-
    ing them as cowardly.

6   You are no surer, no,
    Than is the coal of fire upon the ice,
    Or hailstone in the sun.
    Caius Martius, later Coriolanus, in
    Coriolanus, 1.1.172–4

    A patrician tells the people they cannot be
    trusted.

7 With every minute you do change a
    mind,
    And call him noble that was now
    your hate.
    Caius Martius, later Coriolanus, in
    Coriolanus, 1.1.177–9

    A patrician complains that the citizens of
    Rome are unstable.

8   He that depends
    Upon your favors swims with fins
    of lead,
    And hews down oaks with rushes.
    Caius Martius, later Coriolanus, in
    Coriolanus, 1.1.179–81

    A patrician view of the people as unreliable.

9 For the mutable, rank-scented
    meiny, let them
    Regard me as I do not flatter, and
    Therein behold themselves.
    Coriolanus in *Coriolanus*, 3.1.66

    A patrician claims to be telling the truth about
    the people, but shows his scorn for them at
    the same time; "meiny" = multitude.

10   You speak o'the people
As if you were a god, to punish; not
A man of their infirmity.

Brutus in *Coriolanus*, 3.1.80–2

A tribune of the people sums up the attitude of
the patrician Coriolanus.

11   You common cry of curs, whose
     breath I hate
As reek o'the rotten fens, whose
     loves I prize
As the dead carcasses of unburied
     men
That do corrupt my air—I banish
     you!

Coriolanus in *Coriolanus*, 3.3.120–3

Sicinius, a tribune of the people, has just
declared that Coriolanus should be banished.

12   Come, leave your tears. A brief
     farewell. The beast
With many heads butts me away.

Coriolanus in *Coriolanus*, 4.1.1–2

Coriolanus bids his wife farewell as he goes
from Rome, banished by the people (the
"beast with many heads").

13   The blunt monster with uncounted
     heads,
The still-discordant wav'ring multi-
     tude.

Rumor in *Henry IV, Part 2*, Induction, 18–19

14   An habitation giddy and unsure
Hath he that buildeth on the vulgar
     heart.

Archbishop of York in *Henry IV, Part 2*, 1.3.89–90

Complaining that the common people cannot
be relied on.

15   See how the giddy multitude do
     point

And nod their heads and throw
     their eyes on thee!

Duchess of Gloucester in *Henry VI, Part 2*, 2.4.21–2

To her husband, who stays with her when she
is exposed to public shame.

16   Was ever feather so lightly blown to
and fro as this multitude?

Jack Cade in *Henry VI, Part 2*, 4.8.55–6

The leader of the mob finds they readily
change allegiance.

17   I love the people,
But do not like to stage me to their
     eyes;
Though it do well, I do not relish
     well
Their loud applause and aves vehe-
     ment;
Nor do I think the man of safe dis-
     cretion
That does affect it.

Duke in *Measure for Measure*, 1.1.67–72

Deputing Angelo to rule Vienna in his place;
"aves" = cries of acclaim; "safe" = sound.

18   I will not choose what many men
     desire,
Because I will not jump with com-
     mon spirits,
And rank me with the barbarous
     multitudes.

Prince of Aragon in *The Merchant of Venice*, 2.9.31–3

"Jump" = agree, go along with.

Perception

1   Sits the wind in that corner?

Benedick in *Much Ado About Nothing*, 2.3.98

Is that how things stand?; on overhearing it
said that Beatrice loves him.

2   Grief has so wrought on him,
He takes false shadows for true substances.

Marcus in *Titus Andronicus*, 3.2.79–80

He thinks Titus is mad to identify a fly with Aaron the Moor.

3   One face, one voice, one habit, and two persons,
A natural perspective that is and is not!

Orsino in *Twelfth Night*, 5.1.216–7

On seeing the twins, Sebastian and Viola (who is dressed as a man), together for the first time; "natural perspective" = optical illusion produced by nature.

Perfection

1   You, O you,
So perfect and so peerless, are created
Of every creature's best!

Ferdinand in *The Tempest*, 3.1.46–8

Expressing his love for Miranda.

2   But no perfection is so absolute
That some impurity doth not pollute.

***The Rape of Lucrece*,** 853–4

Lucrece broods on the rape she has suffered.

3   Everything that grows
Holds in perfection but a little moment.

***Sonnet 15*,** 1–2

Perfume

1   'Tis her breathing that
Perfumes the chamber thus.

Jachimo in *Cymbeline*, 2.2.18–19

Looking at Imogen asleep.

Perplexity

1   My thoughts are whirlèd like a potter's wheel;
I know not where I am , nor what I do.

Talbot in *Henry VI, Part 1*, 1.5.19–20

He is confused by the unexpected success in battle of Joan la Pucelle (Joan of Arc).

2   My mind is troubled, like a fountain stirred,
And I myself see not the bottom of it.

Achilles in *Troilus and Cressida*, 3.3.308–9

Perseverance

1   Many strokes, though with a little axe,
Hews down and fells the hardest-timbered oak.

Messenger in *Henry VI, Part 3*, 2.1.54–5

Proverbial.

2   I am a kind of burr; I shall stick.

Lucio in *Measure for Measure*, 4.3.179

Determined to stay with the Duke, who wants to shake him off.

3   Perseverance, dear my lord,
Keeps honor bright; to have done is to hang

Quite out of fashion.

Ulysses in *Troilus and Cressida*,
3.3.150–2

He is trying to persuade the great warrior
Achilles to return to the battlefield.

5   There is no tongue that moves,
     none, none i'the world
     So soon as yours, could win me.

Polixenes in *The Winter's Tale*, 1.2.20–1

Leontes is pressing him to continue his visit to
Sicily.

Persuasion

1   But your discretions better can per-
     suade
     Than I am able to instruct or teach,
     And therefore, as we hither came in
     peace,
     So let us still continue peace and
     love.

King Henry in *Henry VI, Part 1*,
4.1.158–61

Henry is trying to preserve peace among the
quarreling factions in England.

2   What you would work me to, I have
     some aim.

Brutus in *Julius Caesar*, 1.2.163

"Aim" = idea.

3   Three parts of him
     Is ours already, and the man entire
     Upon the next encounter yields
     him ours.

Cassius in *Julius Caesar*, 1.3.154–6

Using devious means to win the support of
Brutus.

4   Let me work;
     For I can give his humor the true
     bent.

Decius in *Julius Caesar*, 2.1.209–10

Claiming he can direct Caesar's inclination
the right way.

Philosophy

1   They say miracles are past, and we
     have our philosophical persons, to
     make modern and familiar, things
     supernatural and causeless. Hence
     is it that we make trifles of terrors,
     ensconcing ourselves into seeming
     knowledge, when we should submit
     ourselves to an unknown fear.

Lafew in *All's Well That Ends Well*,
2.3.1–6

On trusting what is awesome and inexplica-
ble, rather than seeking explanations for
everything; the miracle is Helena's cure of the
king's sickness.

2   This is no flattery: these are coun-
     selors
     That feelingly persuade me what I
     am.

Duke Senior in *As You Like It*, 2.1.10–11

The Duke's philosophy in the face of wind
and cold.

3   A great cause of the night is lack of
     the sun.

Corin in *As You Like It*, 3.2.28

The shepherd's homespun philosophy.

4   I earn that I eat, get that I wear, owe
     no man hate, envy no man's happi-
     ness, glad of other men's good,
     content with my harm.

Corin in *As You Like It*, 3.2.73–6

5 *Horatio.* O day and night, but this is wondrous strange!
Hamlet. And therefore as a stranger give it welcome. There are more things in heaven and earth, Horatio, Than are dreamt of in your philosophy.

Hamlet in *Hamlet*, 1.5.164–7

After Hamlet's interview with his father's ghost; Horatio has just returned from Wittenberg to Denmark, and so is a "stranger."

6 There is nothing either good or bad, but thinking makes it so.

Hamlet in *Hamlet*, 2.2.249–50

To Rosencrantz and Guildenstern; Hamlet says Denmark is a prison and they do not think so.

7 There is something in this more than natural, if philosophy could find it out.

Hamlet in *Hamlet*, 2.2.367–8

Commenting on his uncle's popularity as king with the people who previously decried him.

8 There is some soul of goodness in things evil, Would men observingly distill it out.

King Henry in *Henry V*, 4.1.4–5

"Observingly" = observantly, with watchful care.

9 Thus may we gather honey from the weed And make a moral of the devil himself.

King Henry in *Henry V*, 4.1.11–12

Drawing encouragement from adversity.

10 'Tis good for men to love their present pains Upon example; so the spirit is eased.

King Henry in *Henry V*, 4.1.18–19

Soldiers feel better for seeing their betters like the king enduring their discomforts.

11 There is occasions and causes why and wherefore in all things.

Fluellen in *Henry V*, 5.1.3–4

The odd grammar hints at Fluellen's Welsh accent.

12 Of your philosophy you make no use If you give place to accidental evils.

Cassius in *Julius Caesar*, 4.3.145–6

To Brutus; "give place to accidental evils" = are upset by troubles caused by chance.

13 Since the affairs of men rest still incertain, Let's reason with the worst that may befall.

Cassius in *Julius Caesar*, 5.1.95–6

Contemplating battle; "reason" = reckon.

14 'Tis all men's office to speak patience To those that wring under the load of sorrow, But no man's virtue nor sufficiency To be so moral when he shall endure The like himself.

Leonato in *Much Ado About Nothing*, 5.1.27–31

He says everyone has a duty ("office") to advise patience to those who writhe ("wring") in suffering, but no one who suffers has the ability to preach patience to himself.

15   There was never yet philosopher
     That could endure the toothache
     patiently.
Leonato in *Much Ado About Nothing*,
5.1.35–6

Rejecting his brother's attempt to soothe him.

16   To mourn a mischief that is past
     and gone
     Is the next way to draw new mis-
     chief on.
Duke in *Othello*, 1.3.204–5

"Mischief" = misfortune or calamity.

17   The robbed that smiles steals some-
     thing from the thief;
     He robs himself that spends a boot-
     less grief.
Duke in *Othello*, 1.3.208–9

"Spends a bootless grief" = indulges in useless
lamenting.

18   Thoughts tending to content flatter
     themselves
     That they are not the first of for-
     tune's slaves,
     Nor shall not be the last, like silly
     beggars
     Who, sitting in the stocks, refuge
     their shame
     That many have and others must sit
     there,
     And in this thought they find a
     kind of ease.
King Richard in *Richard II*, 5.5.23–8

Meditating in prison; "silly" = simple; "refuge"
= rationalize.

19   What's gone and what's past help
     Should be past grief.
Paulina in *The Winter's Tale*, 3.2.222–3

An elegant variation on the proverb, "never
grieve for that you cannot help."

Pity

1   If ever you have looked on better
    days,
    If ever been where bells have
    knolled to church,
    If ever sat at any good man's feast,
    If ever from your eyelids wiped a
    tear,
    And know what 'tis to pity and be
    pitied,
    Let gentleness my strong enforce-
    ment be.
Orlando in *As You Like It*, 2.7.113–8

Appealing for help for his old servant, Adam.

2   Our hearts you see not; they are
    pitiful;
    And pity to the general wrong of
    Rome—
    As fire drives out fire, so pity pity—
    Hath done this deed on Caesar.
Brutus in *Julius Caesar*, 3.1.169–72

"This deed" = the assassination of Caesar.

3   O, now you weep, and I perceive
    you feel
    The dint of pity.
Mark Antony in *Julius Caesar*,
3.2.193–4

He has succeeded in making the people pity
Caesar.

4   A most poor man, made tame to
    fortune's blows,
    Who by the art of known and feel-
    ing sorrows
    Am pregnant to good pity.
Edgar in *King Lear*, 4.6.221–3

"Pregnant" = prone or predisposed.

5   Pity, like a naked, new-born babe
     Striding the blast, or heaven's
     cherubins, horsed
     Upon the sightless couriers of the
     air,
     Shall blow the horrid deed in every
     eye,
     That tears shall drown the wind.

Macbeth in *Macbeth*, 1.7.21–5

The "deed" is the murder of Duncan; in
Psalms 18:10 (Book of Common Prayer), God
"rode upon the cherubins and did fly; he
came flying upon the wings of the wind";
"sightless" = invisible.

6   *Isabella.* Yet show some pity.
     Angelo. I show it most of all when I
       show justice;
     For then I pity those I do not know,
     Which a dismissed offense would
       after gall.

Measure for Measure, 2.2.99–102

Asking mercy for her brother, sentenced to
death; "dismissed offense" = one that goes
unpunished; "after gall" = afterwards injure or
annoy.

7   My story being done,
     She gave me for my pains a world
       of sighs;
     She swore, in faith 'twas strange,
       'twas passing strange;
     'Twas pitiful, 'twas wondrous piti-
       ful.

Othello in *Othello*, 1.3.158–61

On his courtship of Desdemona by telling her
the story of his life.

8   But yet the pity of it, Iago! O Iago,
     the pity of it, Iago!

Othello in *Othello*, 4.1.195–6

Loving Desdemona even as he plans to murder her.

9   Had not God, for some strong
     purpose, steeled

The hearts of men, they must per-
     force have melted,
     And barbarism itself have pitied
     him.

York in *Richard II*, 5.2.34–6

Commenting on the harsh treatment of
Richard by the citizens of London.

10   No beast so fierce but knows some
     touch of pity.

Lady Anne in *Richard III*, 1.2.71

Plain-Speaking

1   Mark now how a plain tale shall put
     you down.

**Prince Hal in *Henry IV, Part 1*,
2.4.254–5**

Telling the true story to expose Falstaff's lies.

2   Out with it boldly; truth loves open
     dealing.

Queen Katherine in *Henry VIII*, 3.1.39

She suspects the Cardinals visiting her are not
being open.

3   What a blunt fellow is this grown to
     be!
     He was quick mettle when he went
     to school.

Brutus in *Julius Caesar*, 1.2.295–6

Describing Casca; "quick mettle" = lively in
spirit.

4   This rudeness is a sauce to his good
     wit,
     Which gives men stomach to digest
     his words
     With better appetite.

Cassius in *Julius Caesar*, 1.2.300–2

Describing Casca's forthright manner of
speaking.

5   I am no orator, as Brutus is,
    But, as you know me all, a plain
      blunt man
    That love my friend, and that they
      know full well
    That gave me public leave to speak
      of him.
    Mark Antony in *Julius Caesar*,
    3.2.217–20

    Antony is, of course, much the better orator in
    speaking of Caesar.

6   Sir, 'tis my occupation to be plain:
    I have seen better faces in my time
    Than stands on any shoulder that I
      see
    Before me at this instant.
    Kent in *King Lear*, 2.2.92–5

    Addressing his superior, the Duke of Corn-
    wall.

7   He cannot flatter, he,
    An honest mind and plain, he must
      speak truth.
    An they will take it, so; if not, he's
      plain.
    Cornwall in *King Lear*, 2.2.98–100

    Responding to the disguised Kent's blunt
    words; "an they" = if they.

8   Taffeta phrases, silken terms pre-
      cise,
    Three-piled hyperboles, spruce
      affectation,
    Figures pedantical—these summer
      flies
    Have blown me full of maggot
      ostentation.
    I do forswear them, and I here
      protest,
    By this white glove (how white the
      hand, God knows!),

Henceforth my wooing mind shall
  be expressed
In russet yeas and honest kersey
  noes.
Berowne in *Love's Labor's Lost*,
5.2.406–13

"Russet" and "kersey" were plain and rough
kinds of cloth.

9   Honest plain words best pierce the
      ear of grief.
    Berowne in *Love's Labor's Lost*, 5.2.753

    News of the death of the Princess's father
    reduces the courtiers to plain-speaking.

10 Do I entice you? Do I speak you
      fair?
    Or rather do I not in plainest truth
    Tell you I do not nor I cannot love
      you?
    **Demetrius in *A Midsummer Night's
    Dream*, 2.1.199–201**

    Rejecting Helena's love.

11 An honest tale speeds best being
      plainly told.
    Queen Elizabeth in *Richard III*, 4.4.358

    Proverbial; exposing Richard's hypocrisy.

12 I was not much afeard; for once or
      twice
    I was about to speak, and tell him
      plainly,
    The selfsame sun that shines upon
      his court
    Hides not his visage from our cot-
      tage, but
    Looks on alike.
    Perdita in *The Winter's Tale*, 4.4.442–6

    As Polixenes separates her from Florizel, his
    son and heir to the throne.

Plays (see also Acting, Theater)

He and Prince Hal are interrupted in their improvised play in which each in turn played King Henry and the Prince.

1 If it be true that good wine needs no bush, 'tis true that a good play needs no epilogue.

Rosalind in *As You Like It*, Epilogue, 3–5

It was proverbial that a good wine needed "no bush," or sign hung out to advertise sale of it.

2 My way is to conjure you, and I'll begin with the women. I charge you, O women, for the love you bear to men, to like as much of this play as please you. I charge you, O men, for the love you bear to women (as I perceive by your simpering, none of you hates them), that between you and the women the play may please.

Rosalind in *As You Like It*, Epilogue, 11–17

3 The play, I remember, pleased not the million, 'twas caviare to the general.

Hamlet in *Hamlet*, 2.2.435–7

"Caviare to the general" = too rare a delicacy for the multitude.

4   The play's the thing Wherein I'll catch the conscience of the King.

Hamlet in *Hamlet*, 2.2.604–5

"The play's the thing" is often quoted on its own; for Hamlet it is a means to expose the guilt of Claudius.

5 Play out the play!

Falstaff in *Henry IV, Part 1*, 2.4.484

6 Our wooing doth not end like an old play, Jack hath not Jill.

Berowne in *Love's Labor's Lost*, 5.2.874–5

The courtiers have to practice celibacy for a year before the ladies will have them.

Pleasure

1 There's not a minute of our lives should stretch Without some pleasure now.

Antony in *Antony and Cleopatra*, 1.1.46–7

2   The present pleasure, By revolution lowering, does become The opposite of itself.

Antony in *Antony and Cleopatra*, 1.2.123–5

"By revolution lowering" = losing its appeal as things change; "revolution" suggests the turning of Fortune's wheel.

3 I'th' East my pleasure lies.

Antony in *Antony and Cleopatra*, 2.3.41

Married, and in Rome, Antony yearns for Egypt and Cleopatra.

4   His delights Were dolphin-like, they showed his back above The element they lived in.

Cleopatra in *Antony and Cleopatra*, 5.2.88–90

Her vision of Antony, after his death.

5   Come, madam wife, sit by my
       side
And let the world slip. We shall
ne'er be younger.

Sly in *The Taming of the Shrew*,
Induction, 2.142–4

Inviting her to forget the world and watch a play.

6   *Orsino*. There's for thy pains.
Feste. No pains, sir, I take pleasure
in singing, sir.
Orsino. I'll pay thy pleasure then.
Feste. Truly, sir, and pleasure will
be paid, one time or another.

Twelfth Night, 2.4.67–71

Feste alludes to the proverbial idea that pleasure must be paid for with pain.

Plots

1   Who cannot be crushed with a
plot?

Parolles in *All's Well That Ends Well*,
4.3.325

2   O, 'tis most sweet
When in one line two crafts directly
meet.

Hamlet in *Hamlet*, 3.4.210–1

3   This falls out better than I could
devise.

Oberon in *A Midsummer Night's
Dream*, 3.2.35

Oberon has succeeded better than he expected in making Titania fall in love with an ass.

4   With as little a web as this will I
ensnare as great a fly as Cassio.

Iago in *Othello*, 2.1.168–9

Iago is observing Cassio's gallant behavior to Desdemona.

5   *Maria*. Nay, but say true, does it
work upon him?
Sir Toby Belch. Like aqua vitae with
a midwife.

Twelfth Night, 2.5.195–6

"Aqua vitae," the water of life = brandy or other spirits.

Poetry

1   Hang there, my verse, in witness of
my love.

Orlando in *As You Like It*, 3.2.1

Hanging poems in praise of Rosalind on the forest trees.

2   I'll rhyme you so eight years
together, dinners and suppers and
sleeping-hours excepted.

Touchstone in *As You Like It*, 3.2.96–7

Mocking Orlando's style of writing love poetry.

3   If a hart do lack a hind,
Let him seek out Rosalind.

Touchstone in *As You Like It*, 3.2.101–2

Parodying Orlando's verses to Rosalind.

4   The truest poetry is the most feigning.

Touchstone in *As You Like It*, 3.3.19–20

Reviving an old argument that poets who "feign," or make fictions, are liars.

5   *Orlando.* Good day and happiness,
    dear Rosalind!
    Jaques. Nay then, God buy you, an
    you talk in blank verse.
    As You Like It, 4.1.30–2

    "God buy you" spells out "goodbye"; "an" =
    if.

6   I had rather be a kitten and cry
    mew
    Than one of these same meter bal-
    lad-mongers.
    Hotspur in *Henry IV, Part 1*, 3.1.127–8

    Expressing in verse his scorn for it.

7   I had rather hear a brazen canstick
    turned,
    Or a dry wheel grate on the axle-
    tree,
    And that would set my teeth noth-
    ing on edge,
    Nothing so much as mincing
    poetry.
    'Tis like the forced gait of a shuf-
    fling nag.
    Hotspur in *Henry IV, Part 1*, 3.1.129–33

    Hotspur, speaking in verse, dismisses poetry
    as affected or effeminate ("mincing"); "can-
    stick" = candlestick; "turned" = on a lathe.

8   O for a Muse of fire, that would
    ascend
    The brightest heaven of invention!
    A kingdom for a stage, princes to
    act,
    And monarchs to behold the
    swelling scene!
    Chorus in *Henry V*, Prologue, 1–4

    "Invention" = poetic imagination.

9   Never durst poet touch a pen to
    write

Until his ink were tempered with
love's sighs.
O then his lines would ravish savage ears,
And plant in tyrants mild humility.
Berowne in *Love's Labor's Lost*,
4.3.343–6

Berowne's extravagant idea of the power of
love-poetry.

10 The poet's eye, in a fine frenzy
    rolling,
    Doth glance from heaven to earth,
    from earth to heaven;
    And as imagination bodies forth
    The forms of things unknown, the
    poet's pen
    Turns them to shapes, and gives to
    airy nothing
    A local habitation and a name.
    **Theseus in *A Midsummer Night's
    Dream*,** 5.1.12–17

    These lines might be Shakespeare's own com-
    ment on creating the fairy world of this play.

11 Marry, I cannot show it in rhyme, I
    have tried; I can find no rhyme to
    "lady" but "baby"—an innocent
    rhyme; for "scorn," "horn"—a hard
    rhyme; for "school," "fool"—a bab-
    bling rhyme; very ominous end-
    ings. No, I was not born under a
    rhyming planet, nor I cannot woo
    in festival terms.
    Benedick in *Much Ado About Nothing*,
    5.2.36–41

    Trying to express his love for Beatrice.

12 Lascivious meters, to whose venom
    sound
    The open ear of youth doth always
    listen.

York in *Richard II*, 2.1.19–20

Equivalent to the pop songs of modern times?

When those now living ("the breathers of this world") are dead, the speaker's friend will survive in remembrance through the power ("virtue") of his poetry.

13 Much is the force of heaven-bred poesy.
Duke in *The Two Gentlemen of Verona*, 3.2.71

That is, as an aid in wooing Silvia.

14 I love a ballad in print alife, for then we are sure they are true.
Mopsa in *The Winter's Tale*, 4.4.260–1

"Alife" = on my life, dearly; the peasant girl thinks anything in print must be true.

15 Not marble nor the gilded monuments
Of princes shall outlive this powerful rhyme,
But you shall shine more bright in these contents
Than unswept stone, besmeared with sluttish time.
Sonnet 55, 1–4

Shakespeare's confidence that his lines in praise of his friend would outlast monuments in stone has been validated by time.

16 Your monument shall be my gentle verse,
Which eyes not yet created shall o'er-read,
And tongues to be your being shall rehearse
When all the breathers of this world are dead;
You still shall live (such virtue hath my pen)
Where breath most breathes, even in the mouths of men.
Sonnet 81, 9–14

Poison

1 No medicine in the world can do thee good;
In thee there is not half an hour's life.
Laertes in *Hamlet*, 5.2.314–15

He has touched Hamlet with a poisoned rapier in their fencing match.

2 They love not poison that do poison need.
King Henry IV in *Richard II*, 5.6.38

Unhappy to learn that Richard II has been killed at his own suggestion.

3 There is thy gold, worse poison to men's souls,
Doing more murder in this loathsome world,
Than these poor compounds that thou mayest not sell.
I sell thee poison, thou hast sold me none.
Romeo in *Romeo and Juliet*, 5.1.80–3

Buying poison from the poor apothecary.

4 I could do this, and that with no rash potion,
But with a lingering dram, that should not work
Maliciously, like poison.
Camillo in *The Winter's Tale*, 1.2.319–21

On first hearing the king, Leontes, urge him to poison his "enemy," Polixenes.

5   There may be in the cup
A spider steeped, and one may
   drink, depart,
And yet partake no venom, for his
   knowledge
Is not infected; but if one present
Th'abhorred ingredient to his eye,
   make known
How he hath drunk, he cracks his
   gorge, his sides,
With violent hefts. I have drunk,
   and seen the spider.

Leontes in *The Winter's Tale*, 2.1.39–45

Finding the escape of Polixenes to be convincing evidence of his wife's adultery; spiders were thought to be poisonous; "hefts" =
heavings (vomiting out the poison).

Hotspur in *Henry IV, Part 1*, 1.3.239–41

Angry with the king (formerly Henry Bolingbroke), who came to power with the help of
Hotspur's family and now regards them as
rebels; "pismires" = ants; "politician" =
schemer.

4   Be it thy course to busy giddy
   minds
With foreign quarrels, that action,
   hence borne out,
May waste the memory of former
   days.

King Henry in *Henry IV, Part 2*,
4.5.213–5

The king's advice to Prince Hal, that foreign
affairs distract attention from problems at
home, has often been thought sound politics.

Politics (see also Greatness, Power)

1   The time is out of joint—O cursed
   spite,
That ever I was born to set it right!

Hamlet in *Hamlet*, 1.5.188–9

Lamenting not only the disorder of the time,
but his own nativity.

2   The great man down, you mark his
   favorite flies,
The poor advanced makes friends
   of enemies.

Player King in *Hamlet*, 3.2.204–5

"Advanced" = given promotion.

3   I am whipped and scourged with
   rods,
Nettled and stung with pismires,
   when I hear
Of this vile politician Bolingbroke.

5   Hear him debate of commonwealth
   affairs,
You would say it hath been all in all
   his study.

**Archbishop of Canterbury in *Henry
V*, 1.1.41–2**

Speaking of Prince Hal, now king.

6   Turn him to any cause of policy,
The Gordian knot of it he will
   unloose,
Familiar as his garter.

**Archbishop of Canterbury in *Henry
V*, 1.1.45–7**

It was said that whoever undid the Gordian
knot would rule Asia, and Alexander the
Great, who cut it with his sword, went on to
great conquests.

7   He was a fool,
For he would needs be virtuous.
   That good fellow,
If I command him, follows my
   appointment.

Cardinal Wolsey in *Henry VIII*,
2.2.131-3

Putting obedience above principle; the "good fellow" is Gardiner, promoted to be the king's secretary by Wolsey's scheming.

8   You ever
Have wished the sleeping of this
  business, never desired
It to be stirred, but oft have hin-
  dered, oft
The passages made toward it.

King Henry in *Henry VIII*, 2.4.163-6

Speaking to Wolsey; the "business" is the divorce proceeding against Katherine of Aragon.

9   Plague of your policy!

Surrey in *Henry VIII*, 3.2.259

To Wolsey, who contrived to have Surrey sent off to Ireland; "of" = on.

10 Let me have men about me that are
  fat,
Sleek-headed men, and such as
  sleep a-nights.
Yon Cassius has a lean and hungry
  look;
He thinks too much. Such men are
  dangerous.

Caesar in *Julius Caesar*, 1.2.192-5

Caesar's intuitive feeling about Cassius.

11 Such men as he be never at heart's
  ease
Whiles they behold a greater than
  themselves,
And therefore are they very dangerous.

Caesar in *Julius Caesar*, 1.2.208-10

Referring to Cassius.

12   Let us not break with him,
For he will never follow anything
That other men begin.

Brutus in *Julius Caesar*, 2.1.150-2

Rejecting the idea of asking Cicero to join the conspiracy against Caesar; "break with" = confide in.

13   We shall find of him
A shrewd contriver; and, you know,
  his means,
If he improve them, may well
  stretch so far
As to annoy us all.

Cassius in *Julius Caesar*, 2.1.157-60

Arguing for killing Mark Antony as well as Caesar; "shrewd contriver" = cunning and dangerous schemer.

14 What compact mean you to have
  with us?
Will you be pricked in number of
  our friends,
Or shall we on, and not depend on
  you?

Cassius in *Julius Caesar*, 3.1.215-7

Speaking to Mark Antony; "compact" = agreement; "pricked" = marked or noted down.

15 Though we lay these honors on
  this man
To ease ourselves of divers slanderous loads,
He shall but bear them as the ass
  bears gold,
To groan and sweat under the business,
Either led or driven as we point the
  way.

Mark Antony in *Julius Caesar*, 4.1.19-23

Speaking of Lepidus; Octavius and Antony plan to put on him responsibility for what they may be accused of ("slanderous loads").

16   Get thee glass eyes,
And like a scurvy politician, seem
To see the things thou dost not.

King Lear in *King Lear*, 4.6.170–2

Speaking to the blind Gloucester; "glass eyes"
may mean spectacles.

17   So we'll live,
And pray, and sing, and tell old
tales, and laugh
At gilded butterflies, and hear poor
rogues
Talk of court news; and we'll talk
with them too—
Who loses and who wins; who's in,
who's out—
And take upon 's the mystery of
things,
As if we were God's spies.

King Lear in *King Lear*, 5.3.11–17

Imagining being imprisoned with his daughter
Cordelia; "gilded butterflies" probably refers
to extravagantly dressed courtiers.

18 He cannot buckle his distempered
cause
Within the belt of rule.

Caithness in *Macbeth*, 5.2.15–16

On Macbeth as unable to put his sick or
chaotic ("distempered" may mean both) affairs
in order.

19 If I know how or which way to
order these affairs
Thus disorderly thrust into my
hands,
Never believe me.

York in *Richard II*, 2.2.108–11

He has been left to rule England in the
absence of King Richard.

20 The caterpillars of the commonwealth,

Which I have sworn to weed and
pluck away.

Bolingbroke in *Richard II*, 2.3.166–7

Describing Richard's favorites.

21 Will you enforce me to a world of
cares?
Call them again, I am not made of
stones,
But penetrable to your kind
entreaties,
Albeit against my conscience and
my soul.

King Richard in *Richard III*, 3.7.223–6

Pretending to be reluctant to accept the
crown.

22 They'll take suggestion as a cat laps
milk;
They'll tell the clock to any business
that
We say befits the hour.

Antonio in *The Tempest*, 2.1.288–90

Referring to all the courtiers except Gonzalo.

23 Men must learn now with pity to
dispense,
For policy sits above conscience.

**First Stranger in *Timon of Athens*,
3.2.86–7**

Commenting on the refusal of Timon's friends
to help him. "Policy" commonly for Shakespeare had a pejorative meaning of expedi-
ency or political cunning.

Popularity

1 And then I stole all courtesy from
heaven,

And dressed myself in such humility
That I did pluck allegiance from
men's hearts,
Loud shouts and salutations from
their mouths,
Even in the presence of the
crownèd King.

King Henry in *Henry IV, Part 1*,
3.2.50–4

Recalling his popularity before he became
king.

Portents (see also Foreboding)

1   At my nativity
The front of heaven was full of fiery
shapes
Of burning cressets, and at my
birth
The frame and huge foundation of
the earth
Shaked like a coward.

Glendower in *Henry IV, Part 1*,
3.1.13–17

Events which he says foretold that he would
be remarkable; "front" = forehead; "cressets"
= fires in metal baskets on poles.

2   The heavens were all on fire, the
earth did tremble.

Glendower in *Henry IV, Part 1*, 3.1.23

Portents, he claims, at his birth.

3   Comets, importing change of times
and states,
Brandish your crystal tresses in the
sky.

Bedford in *Henry VI, Part 1*, 1.1.2–3

Comets were thought to foretell disasters to
come.

4   It is the part of men to fear and
tremble
When the most mighty gods by
tokens send
Such dreadful heralds to astonish
us.

Casca in *Julius Caesar*, 1.3.54–6

On the ominous storms the night before Caesar is assassinated.

5   The noise of battle hurtled in the
air,
Horses did neigh, and dying men
did groan,
And ghosts did shriek and squeal
about the streets.

Calpurnia in *Julius Caesar*, 2.2.22–4

Hoping, by reporting these strange happen-
ings, to persuade her husband, Caesar, not to
go to the Capitol.

6   When beggars die there are no
comets seen;
The heavens themselves blaze forth
the death of princes.

Calpurnia in *Julius Caesar*, 2.2.30–1

7   These late eclipses in the sun and
moon portend no good to us.

Gloucester in *King Lear*, 1.2.103–4

"Late" = recent.

8   The screech-owl, screeching loud,
Puts the wretch that lies in woe
In remembrance of a shroud.

Puck in *A Midsummer Night's Dream*,
5.1.376–8

The owl was regarded as a bird of ill-omen,
often foreboding death.

9   The bay-trees in our country are all
     withered,
     And meteors fright the fixèd stars
     of heaven.
     The pale-faced moon looks bloody
     on the earth,
     And lean-looked prophets whisper
     fearful change.
     Rich men look sad, and ruffians
     dance and leap;
     The one in fear to lose what they
     enjoy,
     The other to enjoy by rage and war.
     These signs forerun the death or fall
     of kings.

Welsh Captain in *Richard II*, 2.4.8–15

Possession

1   A poor virgin, sir, an ill-favored
    thing, sir, but mine own.

Touchstone in *As You Like It*, 5.4.57–8

Introducing the sluttish Audrey to Jaques.

2   O, these naughty times
    Puts bars between the owners and
    their rights!

Portia in *The Merchant of Venice*,
3.2.18–19

"Naughty" = wicked; "bars" = barriers; she is
regretting that she cannot choose a husband
for herself.

3   Myself, and what is mine, to you
    and yours
    Is now converted.

Portia in *The Merchant of Venice*,
3.2.166–7

Giving herself to Bassanio in love.

Poverty

1   Famine is in thy cheeks,
    Need and oppression starveth in
    thy eyes,
    Contempt and beggary hangs upon
    thy back;
    The world is not thy friend, nor the
    world's law.

Romeo in *Romeo and Juliet*, 5.1.69–72

Speaking to the poor apothecary whose poison he is seeking to buy; "starveth" = are
shown by your look of starvation.

2   *Apothecary.* My poverty, but not
    my will, consents.
    Romeo. I pay thy poverty, and not
    thy will.

Romeo and Juliet, 5.1.75–6

Romeo persuades the apothecary to sell him
poison.

3   His poor self,
    A dedicated beggar to the air,
    With his disease of all-shunned
    poverty,
    Walks, like contempt, alone.

Varro's Second Servant in *Timon of*
Athens, 4.2.12–15

On the state of the once-rich Timon.

4   *Autolycus.* I am a poor fellow, sir.
    Camillo. Why, be so still; here's
    nobody will steal that from thee.

The Winter's Tale, 4.4.630–2

Power (see also Greatness, Politics, Tyranny)

1   Realms and islands were
    As plates dropped from his pocket.

Cleopatra in *Antony and Cleopatra*, 5.2.91–2

Cleopatra's dream of Antony; "plates" means coins, of silver or gold.

2   These growing feathers plucked from Caesar's wing
Will make him fly an ordinary pitch,
Who else would soar above the view of men,
And keep us all in servile fearfulness.

Flavius in *Julius Caesar*, 1.1.72–5

Caesar is imaged as a hawk that could be prevented from flying high if its feathers were plucked.

3   When Caesar says, "Do this," it is performed.

Mark Antony in *Julius Caesar*, 1.2.10

Responding to an order given by Caesar.

4   It doth amaze me
A man of such a feeble temper should
So get the start of the majestic world
And bear the palm alone.

Cassius in *Julius Caesar*, 1.2.128–31

Referring to Caesar, who in spite of physical ailments outstrips ("get the start of") all other rulers to bear the palm of victory alone.

5   Why, man, he doth bestride the narrow world
Like a colossus, and we petty men
Walk under his huge legs and peep about
To find ourselves dishonorable graves.

Cassius in *Julius Caesar*, 1.2.135–8

Referring to Caesar; the colossus was a gigantic figure of the sun-god Apollo that stood astride the entrance to the harbor at Rhodes.

6   Now could I, Casca, name to thee a man
Most like this dreadful night,
That thunders, lightens, opens graves, and roars
As doth the lion in the Capitol—
A man no mightier than thyself or me
In personal action, yet prodigious grown
And fearful, as these strange eruptions are.

Cassius in *Julius Caesar*, 1.3.72–8

Referring to Julius Caesar; the audience may have thought of the lions kept in the Tower of London.

7   Have I in conquest stretched mine arm so far
To be afeared to tell greybeards the truth?

Caesar in *Julius Caesar*, 2.2.66–7

The "greybeards" are the senators of Rome.

8   A power I have, but of what strength and nature
I am not yet instructed.

Escalus in *Measure for Measure*, 1.1.79–80

To Angelo, with whom he is to share the rule of Vienna.

9   Lord Angelo is precise,
Stands at a guard with envy, scarce confesses
That his blood flows, or that his appetite
Is more to bread than stone. Hence shall we see
If power change purpose, what our seemers be.

Duke in *Measure for Measure*, 1.3.50–4

He knows Angelo as puritanical ("precise"), and anxious about his reputation ("at a guard with envy").

10   O, it is excellent
To have a giant's strength; but it is
    tyrannous
To use it like a giant.

Isabella in *Measure for Measure*,
2.2.107–9

Pleading with Angelo for her brother's life.

11 What you will have, I'll give, and
    willing too,
For do we must what force will
    have us do.

King Richard in *Richard II*, 3.3.206–7

What Bolingbroke, later Henry IV, wants is
the kingdom.

12 The eagle suffers little birds to sing,
And is not careful what they mean
    thereby,
Knowing that with the shadow of
    his wings
He can at pleasure stint their
    melody.

Tamora in *Titus Andronicus*, 4.4.83–6

The eagle symbolizes royalty or power.

13 They that have power to hurt, and
    will do none,
That do not do the thing they most
    do show,
Who, moving others, are them-
    selves as stone,
Unmovèd, cold, and to temptation
    slow,
They rightly do inherit heaven's
    graces,
And husband nature's riches from
    expense;
They are the lords and owners of
    their faces,

Others but stewards of their excel-
    lence.

***Sonnet 94*,** 1–8

These great lines link virtue and beauty in suggesting the idea of people who in their bearing show the power they have, but possess the
mastery over themselves to exercise restraint
and preserve the gifts nature has given them
("husband nature's riches").

Praise

1   Other women cloy
The appetites they feed, but she
    makes hungry
Where most she satisfies.

Enobarbus in *Antony and Cleopatra*,
2.2.235–7

Praising Cleopatra.

2 I will praise any man that will
    praise me.

Enobarbus in *Antony and Cleopatra*,
2.6.88

3 His face was as the heavens, and
    therein stuck
A sun and moon, which kept their
    course and lighted
The little O, the earth.

Cleopatra in *Antony and Cleopatra*,
5.2.79–81

Cleopatra's image of Antony.

4 His legs bestrid the ocean, his
    reared arm
Crested the world.

Cleopatra in *Antony and Cleopatra*,
5.2.82–3

Cleopatra recalls Antony as if he were a colossal figure overawing the world; Cassius uses a similar image to describe Caesar in *Julius Caesar*; see Power 5.

5   Your praise is come too swiftly
    home before you.
    Adam in *As You Like It*, 2.2.9

    Orlando's good reputation has made his brother hate him.

6   I did not think thee lord of such a
    spirit.
    Before, I loved thee as a brother,
    John,
    But now I do respect thee as my
    soul.
    Prince Hal in *Henry IV, Part 1*,
    5.4.18–20

    Praising his brother's courage.

7   I hear as good exclamation on your
    worship as of any man in the city.
    **Dogberry in *Much Ado About
    Nothing*, 3.5.25–6**

    Mistaking the word, as usual: "exclamation" = outcry against; he perhaps means "acclamation" in speaking to Leonato, governor of Messina.

8   O slanderous world! Kate like the
    hazel twig
    Is straight and slender, and as
    brown in hue
    As hazelnuts, and sweeter than the
    kernels.
    Petruchio in *The Taming of the Shrew*,
    2.1.253–5

    Sweet-talking Katherine, who has been abusing him.

9   Thou shalt find she will outstrip
    all praise

And make it halt behind her.
Prospero in *The Tempest*, 4.1.10–11

Praising his daughter Miranda.

10 The worthiness of praise distains
    his worth
    If that the praised himself bring the
    praise forth.
    Aeneas in *Troilus and Cressida*,
    1.3.241–2

    "Distains his worth" = taints or loses its value.

11 You are as strong, as valiant, as
    wise, no less noble, much more
    gentle, and altogether more
    tractable.
    Agamemnon in *Troilus and Cressida*,
    2.3.148–50

    Comparing Ajax to Achilles.

12 Praise us as we are tasted, allow us
    as we prove.
    Troilus in *Troilus and Cressida*, 3.2.90–1

    "Allow" = commend; he is asking Cressida to let experience show how faithful he will be.

13 One good deed dying tongueless
    Slaughters a thousand waiting upon
    that;
    Our praises are our wages.
    Hermione in *The Winter's Tale*,
    1.2.92–4

    On praise as the reward of doing good.

14   Each your doing,
    So singular in each particular,
    Crowns what you are doing in the
    present deeds,
    That all your acts are queens.
    Florizel in *The Winter's Tale*, 4.4.143–6

    Praising Perdita; everything she does seems unique ("singular"), and superb; he doesn't yet know that she is in fact royal and a princess.

Prayer

1   We, ignorant of ourselves,
Beg often our own harms, which
    the wise powers
Deny us for our good; so find we
    profit
By losing of our prayers.
Menecrates in *Antony and Cleopatra*,
2.1.5–8

2   To your protection I commend me,
    gods;
From fairies and the tempters of the
    night,
Guard me, I beseech ye.
Imogen in *Cymbeline*, 2.2.8–10

As she prepares to sleep; she does not know
that Jachimo is hidden in her bedchamber.

3   Angels and ministers of grace
    defend us!
Hamlet in *Hamlet*, 1.4.39

Exclamation on first seeing his father's ghost.

4   Bow, stubborn knees, and heart,
    with strings of steel,
Be soft as sinews of the new-born
    babe!
Claudius in *Hamlet*, 3.3.70–1

Trying to pray for forgiveness for his murder of
his brother.

5   My words fly up, my thoughts
    remain below:
Words without thoughts never to
    heaven go.
Claudius in *Hamlet*, 3.3.97–8

6   O God of battles, steel my soldiers'
    hearts.

Possess them not with fear. Take
    from them now
The sense of reckoning, ere th'
    opposèd numbers
Pluck their hearts from them. Not
    today, O Lord,
O not today, think not upon the
    fault
My father made in compassing the
    crown.
King Henry in *Henry V*, 4.1.289–4

Henry IV gained ("compassed") the crown by
devious means; "sense of reckoning" = the
ability to gauge the odds against winning; the
French army is much stronger.

7   God, the best maker of all mar-
    riages,
Combine your hearts in one.
Queen Isabel in *Henry V*, 5.2.359–60

On the betrothal of Henry of England and
Katherine of France.

8   O Lord that lends me life,
Lend me a heart replete with thank-
    fulness!
King Henry in *Henry VI, Part 2*,
1.1.19–20

9   Now God be praised, that to believ-
    ing souls
Gives light in darkness, comfort in
    despair.
King Henry in *Henry VI, Part 2*,
2.1.64–5

Hearing of a miracle, that a blind man has
regained his sight.

10   O pity, God, this miserable age!
Father in *Henry VI, Part 3*, 2.5.88

On the miseries of civil war; he discovers he
has killed his own son in battle.

11 O, let me not be mad, not mad,
   sweet heaven!
   Keep me in temper, I would not be
   mad!
   King Lear in *King Lear*, 1.5.46–7

Lear's first intimation that the ingratitude of his
daughters will drive him into madness.

12   O heavens!
   If you do love old men, if your
   sweet sway
   Allow obedience, if you yourselves
   are old,
   Make it your cause; send down, and
   take my part.
   King Lear in *King Lear*, 2.4.189–92

"Allow" = approve; Lear is thinking of the dis-
obedience and ingratitude of his daughters.

13 You ever gentle gods, take my
   breath from me;
   Let not my worser spirit tempt me
   again
   To die before you please!
   Gloucester in *King Lear*, 4.6.217–9

Encountering the mad king in worse condition
than himself makes him abandon thoughts of
suicide.

14 *Hermia.* Good night, sweet friend;
   Thy love ne'er alter till thy sweet
   life end!
   Lysander. Amen, amen, to that fair
   prayer say I,
   And then end life when I end loy-
   alty!
   A Midsummer Night's Dream, 2.2.60–3

15 When holy and devout religious
   men
   Are at their beads, 'tis much to
   draw them thence,

So sweet is zealous contemplation.
Buckingham in *Richard III*, 3.7.92–4

Richard is staging an appearance between two
bishops, in order to persuade the citizens of
London that he is fit to be king.

16   Now I want
   Spirits to enforce, art to enchant,
   And my ending is despair,
   Unless I be relieved by prayer,
   Which pierces so that it assaults
   Mercy itself, and frees all faults.
   Prospero in *The Tempest*, Epilogue,
   13–18

Addressing the audience, having abandoned
his role as magician.

17 Immortal gods, I crave no pelf;
   I pray for no man but myself.
   Grant I may never prove so fond
   To trust man on his oath or bond.
   Apemantus in *Timon of Athens*,
   1.2.62–5

A cynic's prayer; "pelf" = wealth; "fond" =
foolish.

18 Lend to each man enough, that one
   need not lend to another; for were
   your godheads to borrow of men,
   men would forsake the gods.
   Timon in *Timon of Athens*, 3.6.73–5

Timon has been forsaken by his friends now
that he is poor.

19 Upon some book I love I'll pray for
   thee.
   **Proteus in *The Two Gentlemen of
   Verona*,** 1.1.20

To his friend Valentine, who is off to see the
world; he does not say what book he has in
mind.

Pregnancy

1   Your brother and his lover have
    embraced.
    As those that feed grow full, as blos-
    soming time
    That from the seedness the bare fal-
    low brings
    To teeming foison, even so her
    plenteous womb
    Expresseth his full tilth and hus-
    bandry.
    Lucio in *Measure for Measure*, 1.4.40–4

    Telling Isabella that Juliet is heavily pregnant
    by her brother; the images of plowing, sowing
    seeds, and coming to abundance ("foison")
    reflect Lucio's coarseness.

2   We have laughed to see the sails
    conceive
    And grow big-bellied with the wan-
    ton wind;
    Which she, with pretty and with
    swimming gait,
    Following (her womb then rich
    with my young squire)
    Would imitate, and sail upon the
    land.
    **Titania in *A Midsummer Night's
    Dream*, 1.2.128–32**

    On the mother of her "changeling boy."

Pride

1   Small things make base men proud.
    Suffolk in *Henry VI, Part 2*, 4.1.106

    He is angry at being taken prisoner by an
    "obscure and lousy swain."

2   Pride must have a fall.
    King Richard in *Richard II*, 5.5.88

    Proverbial.

3   The elephant hath joints, but none
    for courtesy; his legs are legs for
    necessity, not for flexure.
    **Ulysses in *Troilus and Cressida*,
    2.3.105–6**

    "Flexure" = bending; elephants were thought
    to have no joints in their knees. Ulysses refers
    to Achilles, who will not bend or show cour-
    tesy to the other Greek leaders.

4   He that is proud eats up himself.
    Pride is his own glass, his own
    trumpet, his own chronicle; and
    whatever praises itself but in the
    deed, devours the deed in the
    praise.
    **Agamemnon in *Troilus and Cressida*,
    2.3.154–7**

    Speaking to Ajax, who is as proud as any of
    the Greeks.

5   I do hate a proud man as I hate the
    engendering of toads.
    Ajax in *Troilus and Cressida*, 2.3.158–9

    Nestor wisely comments, "And yet he loves
    himself."

6   I see you what you are, you are too
    proud;
    But if you were the devil, you are
    fair.
    Viola in *Twelfth Night*, 1.5.250–1

    On Olivia; "if" = even if.

Promises (see also Oaths, Vows)

1   The oath of a lover is no stronger
    than the word of a tapster; they are
    both the confirmer of false reckon-
    ings.

Celia in *As You Like It*, 3.4.30–2

A lover's promises are no more to be trusted than an innkeeper's reckonings; on Orlando, who has failed to keep his appointment with Rosalind.

2 O, that's a brave man! He writes brave verses, speaks brave words, swears brave oaths, and breaks them bravely.

Celia in *As You Like It*, 3.4.40–2

Mocking Orlando; "brave" = fine, used ironically.

3 Breaking his oath and resolution like
A twist of rotten silk.

Aufidius in *Coriolanus*, 5.6.94–5

Accusing Coriolanus of disloyalty to the Volscians.

4   Every drop of blood
That every Roman bears, and nobly bears,
Is guilty of a several bastardy
If he do break the smallest particle
Of any promise that hath passed from him.

Brutus in *Julius Caesar*, 2.1.136–40

Expressing his confidence in the idea of being a Roman.

5 I will not hold thee long. If I do live,
I will be good to thee.

Brutus in *Julius Caesar*, 4.3.265–6

Asking his servant Lucius to play music.

6 He promised to meet me two hours since, and he was ever precise in promise-keeping.

Lucio in *Measure for Measure*, 1.2.74–6

To a gentleman, remarking on Claudio's failure to keep an appointment.

7 I'll take thy word for faith, not ask thine oath;
Who shuns not to break one will crack them both.

Pericles in *Pericles*, 1.2.120–2

8 Promising is the very air o'the time;
It opens the eyes of expectation.
Performance is ever the duller for his act.

Painter in *Timon of Athens*, 5.1.22–4

"For his act" = when the performance is carried out.

Promptness

1 You come most carefully upon your hour.

Francisco in *Hamlet*, 1.1.6

Greeting Barnardo, succeeding him as a guard on the king's castle in Elsinore.

Proof

1 Be sure of it. Give me the ocular proof.

Othello in *Othello*, 3.3.360

To Iago, demanding to see Desdemona and Cassio making love.

2 Make me to see't, or at the least so prove it
That the probation bear no hinge nor loop
To hang a doubt on.

Othello in *Othello*, 3.3.364–6

He seeks proof that Desdemona has committed adultery; "probation" = proof.

Prophecy

1 In nature's infinite book of secrecy
A little I can read.
Soothsayer in *Antony and Cleopatra*,
1.2.10–11

His prophecies turn out to be accurate.

2 *Ghost.* The serpent that did sting
thy father's life
Now wears his crown.
Hamlet.   O my prophetic
soul!
My uncle?
Ghost. Ay, that incestuous, that
adulterate beast.
Hamlet, 1.5.39–42

Hamlet has half-guessed what the ghost
reveals, that old Hamlet was murdered by his
brother, who then married his widow, a marriage regarded as incestuous in Shakespeare's
time.

3 The hope and expectation of thy
time
Is ruined, and the soul of every man
Prophetically do forethink thy fall.
King Henry in *Henry IV, Part 1*,
3.2.36–8

To Prince Hal, heir to the crown, who finds
Falstaff and tavern life more interesting than
the court.

4 The blood weeps from my heart
when I do shape,
In forms imaginary, th' unguided
days
And rotten times that you shall
look upon
When I am sleeping with my ancestors.
King Henry in *Henry IV, Part 2*,
4.4.58–61

Anticipating disorder after his death.

5 Over thy wounds now do I proph-
esy
. . .
A curse shall light upon the limbs
of men,
Domestic fury and fierce civil strife
Shall cumber all the parts of Italy.
**Mark Antony in *Julius Caesar*, 3.1.259,
262–4**

The wounds are those of the assassinated
Julius Caesar.

6 If you can look into the seeds of
time,
And say which grain will grow and
which will not,
Speak then to me.
Banquo in *Macbeth*, 1.3.58–60

Speaking to the three witches.

7 The night has been unruly. Where
we lay,
Our chimneys were blown down,
and, as they say,
Lamentings heard i' th' air, strange
screams of death,
And prophesying with accents terri-
ble
Of dire combustion and confused
events,
New-hatched to the woeful time.
Lennox in *Macbeth*, 2.3.54–9

Describing the night of Duncan's murder;
"combustion" = tumult.

8 Be bloody, bold, and resolute; laugh
to scorn
The power of man; for none of
woman born
Shall harm Macbeth.
Second Apparition in *Macbeth*,
4.1.79–81

A prophecy that makes Macbeth overconfi-
dent.

9 Macbeth shall never vanquished be
   until
   Great Birnam Wood to high Dunsi-
   nane Hill
   Shall come against him.
   Third Apparition in Macbeth, 4.1.92–4

The "wood" does move, in the form of soldiers carrying a screen of branches.

Prostitution

1 *Escalus.* What do you think of the
   trade, Pompey? Is it a lawful
   trade?
   Pompey. If the law would allow it,
   sir.
   Escalus. But the law will not allow
   it, Pompey; nor it shall not be
   allowed in Vienna.
   Pompey. Does your worship mean
   to geld and spay all the youth of
   the city?
   Escalus. No, Pompey.
   Pompey. Truly, sir, in my poor
   opinion they will to't then.
   Measure for Measure, 2.1.225–35

Pompey is defending his trade as a bawd.

Proverbs

1 Neither rhyme nor reason can
   express how much.
   Orlando in As You Like It, 3.2.398–9

Proverbial; he has been trying to express in
rhymes how much he is in love.

2 He will give the devil his due.
   Prince Hal in Henry IV, Part 1, 1.2.119

Proverbial; the phrase occurs too in *Henry V*;
see The Devil 4.

3 But since all is well, keep it so, wake
   not a sleeping wolf.
   Chief Justice in Henry IV, Part 2,
   1.2.153–4

Advising Falstaff not to get into trouble with
the law.

4 One for superfluity, and another
   for use.
   Prince Hal in Henry IV, Part 2,
   2.2.17–18

Mockingly suggesting a spare clean shirt is
superfluous, more than his friend Poins needs.

5 *Falstaff.* What wind blew you
   hither, Pistol?
   Pistol. Not the ill wind which blows
   no man to good.
   Henry IV, Part 2, 5.3.85–6

Pistol brings news that Hal is now king, bending the proverb, "it's an ill wind that blows no
man good."

6 I did never know so full a voice
   issue from so empty a heart. But
   the saying is true: "The empty vessel makes the greatest sound."
   Boy in Henry V, 4.4.67–9

Proverbial; referring to the empty boasting of
Pistol.

7 I shall not want false witness to
   condemn me,
   Nor store of treasons to augment
   my guilt.
   The ancient proverb will be well
   effected:
   "A staff is quickly found to beat a
   dog."
   Gloucester in Henry VI, Part 2,
   3.1.168–71

On being accused of treason.

8 As dead as a doornail.

Jack Cade in *Henry VI, Part 2*, 4.10.40–1

Shakespeare may have established this phrase
as proverbial.

9 Ill blows the wind that profits
nobody.

Soldier in *Henry VI, Part 3*, 2.5.55

10 Courage mounteth with occasion.

Duke of Austria in *King John*, 2.1.82

"Occasion" = emergency, or occasion calling
for action; from a proverb.

11 The better act of purposes mistook
Is to mistake again; though indirect,
Yet indirection thereby grows
direct,
And falsehood falsehood cures, as
fire cools fire
Within the scorchèd veins of one
who burns.

Cardinal Pandulph in *King John*,
3.1.274–8

The crafty Cardinal casuistically uses
proverbs, that one deceit ("indirection") drives
out another, just as one fire drives out another
(it was thought burns could be cured by
warmth), to excuse wrongdoing.

12 Nothing will come of nothing.

King Lear in *King Lear*, 1.1.90

13 Striving to better, oft we mar what's
well.

Albany in *King Lear*, 1.4.346

Varying the proverb, "let well alone."

14 We'll set thee to school to an ant, to
teach thee there's no laboring i' the
winter.

Fool in *King Lear*, 2.4.67–8

Proverbs 6:6; Proverbs 30:25.

15 The younger rises when the old
doth fall.

Edmund in *King Lear*, 3.3.25

Varying the proverb, "the rising of one man is
the falling of another."

16 Jesters do oft prove prophets.

Regan in *King Lear*, 5.3.71

Varying the proverb, "there's many a true
word spoken in jest."

17 It will have blood, they say; blood
will have blood.

Macbeth in *Macbeth*, 3.4.121

Proverbial, and echoing Genesis 9:6, "Whoso
sheddeth man's blood, by man shall his blood
be shed."

18 Give me your blessing; truth will
come to light; murder cannot be
hid long; a man's son may, but in
the end truth will out.

Launcelot Gobbo in *The Merchant of
Venice*, 2.2.78–80

Comically acknowledging that he is old
Gobbo's son.

19 The old proverb is very well parted
between my master Shylock and
you, sir: you have the grace of God,
sir, and he hath enough.

Launcelot Gobbo in *The Merchant of
Venice*, 2.2.149–51

The proverb is "the grace of God is great
enough"; Launcelot means that his father has
grace, and Shylock enough in the sense of
wealth.

20 The ancient saying is no heresy,
Hanging and wiving goes by destiny.

Nerissa in *The Merchant of Venice*,
2.9.82–3

Proverbial, implying that men may easily be
misled in their choice of a wife.

21 And the country proverb known,
That every man should take his
own,
In your waking shall be shown.
Jack shall have Jill,
Nought shall go ill:
The man shall have his mare again,
and all shall be well.

Puck in *A Midsummer Night's Dream*,
3.2.458–63

These phrases are proverbial; Puck is squeez-
ing magic juice on the eyelids of the sleeping
lovers to restore peace and reconciliation.

22 An two men ride of a horse, one
must ride behind.

**Dogberry in *Much Ado About
Nothing*,** 3.5.36–7

Thinking of himself as at the front, of course.

23   Ha? No more moving?
Still as the grave.

Othello in *Othello*, 5.2.93–4

"Still (or silent) as the grave (or death)" was
proverbial.

24 Things past redress are now with
me past care.

York in *Richard II*, 2.3.171

Rephrasing the proverb, "past cure, past care."

25 Small herbs have grace; great weeds
do grow apace.

York in *Richard III*, 2.4.13

Citing Richard's comment, a criticism of the
fast-growing boy; proverbial; "grace" = good
qualities.

26 *Duchess of York.* Good madam, be
not angry with the child.
Queen Elizabeth. Pitchers have
ears.

Richard III, 2.4.36–7

Referring to the precocious Duke of York; the
proverb ran usually "small pitchers have large
ears."

27 He that dies pays all debts.

Stephano in *The Tempest*, 3.2.131

Rephrasing a common proverb.

28 Blunt wedges rive hard knots.

Ulysses in *Troilus and Cressida*, 1.3.316

He has in mind getting the proud Achilles to
return to the battlefield.

29 The raven chides blackness.

Ulysses in *Troilus and Cressida*, 2.3.211

On Ajax criticizing Achilles for his pride.

30 The old saying is "The third pays
for all."

Feste in *Twelfth Night*, 5.1.37

The phrase has to do with the mystique
attaching to the number three.

31   It is yours,
And might we lay th'old proverb to
your charge,
So like you, 'tis the worse.

Paulina in *The Winter's Tale*, 2.3.96–8

Showing Leontes his baby daughter; implying
that it would be better for the child if she were
not like her father.

32   Were beauty under twenty locks
     kept fast,
     Yet love breaks through and picks
     them all at last.
     Venus and Adonis, 575–6

Varying the proverb, "love conquers all."

33   Make use of time, let not advantage
     slip;
     Beauty within itself should not be
     wasted.
     Fair flowers that are not gathered
     in their prime
     Rot and consume themselves in
     little time.
     Venus and Adonis, 129–32

Venus seeks to seduce Adonis by the common
plea of lovers; "advantage" = opportunity.
The idea relates to the proverb, "Take occasion (opportunity) by the forelock, for she is
bald behind."

Providence

1   Be not with mortal cares oppressed,
    No care of yours it is; you know 'tis
    ours.
    Whom best I love, I cross, to make
    my gift
    The more delayed, delighted.
    Jupiter in *Cymbeline*, 5.4.99–102

Jupiter advises Posthumus to trust in providence; "delighted" = delighted in.

2   Our indiscretion sometime serves
    us well
    When our deep plots do pall, and
    that should learn us
    There's a divinity that shapes our
    ends,
    Rough-hew them how we will.
    Hamlet in *Hamlet*, 5.2.8–11

Acting rashly has saved his life, by revealing
Claudius's plot to have Hamlet executed in
England; "learn" = teach.

3   There is special providence in the
    fall of a sparrow. If it be now, 'tis
    not to come; if it be not to come, it
    will be now; if it be not now, yet it
    will come—the readiness is all.
    Hamlet in *Hamlet*, 5.2.219–22

Punishment (see also Justice, Law)

1   Here feel we not the penalty of
    Adam,
    The seasons' difference.
    Duke Senior in *As You Like It*, 2.1.6

There were no seasons until Adam was
expelled from the Garden of Eden.

2   Where the offense is, let the great
    axe fall.
    Claudius in *Hamlet*, 4.5.219

Promising to punish the killer of Polonius, but
ironic in relation to Claudius's greater
"offense" in murdering old Hamlet.

3   That high All-seer which I dallied
    with
    Hath turned my feignèd prayer on
    my head,
    And given in earnest what I begged
    in jest.
    Buckingham in *Richard III*, 5.1.20–2

Buckingham had called on God to punish him
if he was ever false to King Edward, and now
goes to his death, executed by Richard.

4   Friend or brother,
    He forfeits his own blood that kills
    another.

First Senator in *Timon of Athens*, 3.5.86–7

The context suggests that Shakespeare did not approve of this strict devotion to capital punishment.

Purgatory

1 *Ghost.*   My hour is almost come
When I to sulph'rous and torment-
ing flames
Must render up myself.
Hamlet.   Alas, poor ghost!

Hamlet, 1.5.2–4

"Sulph'rous and tormenting flames" = purgatorial fire.

2   But that I am forbid
To tell the secrets of my prison-
house,
I could a tale unfold whose lightest
word
Would harrow up thy soul, freeze
thy young blood.

Ghost in *Hamlet*, 1.5.13–16

Effectively suggesting the horrors of purgatory to Hamlet; "harrow up" = lacerate.

Quarrels

1 I know when seven justices could
not take up a quarrel, but when the
parties met themselves, one of them
thought but of an If, as, "If you said
so, then I said so"; and they shook
hands and swore brothers. Your If
is your only peacemaker; much
virtue in If.

Touchstone in *As You Like It*, 5.4.98–103

"Take up" = settle

2 'Tis dangerous when the baser
nature comes
Between the pass and fell incensèd
points
Of mighty opposites.

Hamlet in *Hamlet*, 5.2.60

Hamlet is thinking of himself as opposed to Claudius; "pass" = thrust, as with a sword (hence "points"); "fell" = fierce. The "baser nature" refers to Rosencrantz and Guildenstern, whom he has sent to their deaths.

3 By my troth, this is the old fashion.
You two never meet but you fall to
some discord.

Hostess in *Henry IV, Part 2*, 2.4.55–6

On Falstaff and Doll Tearsheet.

4 How irksome is this music to my
heart!
When such strings jar, what hope of
harmony?

King Henry in *Henry VI, Part 2*, 2.1.54–5

Referring to his lords who quarrel at court.

5 Thrice is he armed that hath his
quarrel just,
And he but naked, though locked
up in steel,
Whose conscience with injustice is
corrupted.

King Henry in *Henry VI, Part 2*, 3.2.233–5

Henry's wishful thinking has little effect on his contentious nobles and citizens.

6 Urge me no more, I shall forget
myself.

Cassius in *Julius Caesar*, 4.3.35

To Brutus; "urge" = provoke.

7 *Cassius.* Must I endure all this?
   Brutus. All this? Ay, more! Fret till
   your proud heart break.
   Julius Caesar, 4.3.41–2

Brutus has accused Cassius of being corrupt.

8 Do not presume too much upon
   my love,
   I may do that I shall be sorry for.
   Cassius in *Julius Caesar,* 4.3.63–4

Quarreling with Brutus.

9 I am the unhappy subject of these
   quarrels.
   Antonio in *The Merchant of Venice,*
   5.1.238

Fearing he has provoked discord in Belmont.

10 Never since the middle summer's
   spring
   Met we on hill, in dale, forest, or
   mead,
   By pavèd fountain or by rushy
   brook,
   Or in the beachèd margent of the
   sea
   To dance our ringlets to the
   whistling wind,
   But with thy brawls thou hast dis-
   turbed our sport.
   Titania in *A Midsummer Night's
   Dream,* 2.1.82–7

The quarrel between Oberon and Titania has
gone on since the beginning of summer; a
"paved" fountain flows over stones; "margent"
= margin, and "ringlets" are circular dances
that mark the grass with fairy rings.

11 This same progeny of evils comes
   From our debate, from our dissension.

Titania in *A Midsummer Night's
Dream,* 2.1.115–16

On the disorder resulting from her quarrel
("debate") with Oberon.

12 Who set this ancient quarrel new
   abroach?
   Montague in *Romeo and Juliet,* 1.1.104

The quarrel between the clans of the Montagues and Capulets; "abroach" = flowing, as
in opening or broaching a cask.

13 Thou wilt quarrel with a man for
   cracking nuts, having no other reason but because thou hast hazel
   eyes.
   Mercutio in *Romeo and Juliet,* 3.1.18–20

Mocking his friend Benvolio.

14 Thy head is as full of quarrels as an
   egg is full of meat.
   Mercutio in *Romeo and Juliet,* 3.1.22–3

The "meat" of the egg is what can be eaten.

15 Be thou armed for some unhappy
   words.
   Baptista in *The Taming of the Shrew,*
   2.1.139

Advising Petruchio what to expect from
Katherine.

16 *Katherine.* Asses are made to bear,
   and so are you.
   Petruchio. Women are made to
   bear, and so are you.
   Katherine. No such jade as you, if
   me you mean.
   The Taming of the Shrew, 2.1.199–201

Playing on various senses of "bear," including
bearing children; a "jade" is a worn-out horse,
a hack.

17 No man hath any quarrel to me.
My remembrance is very free and
clear from any image of offense
done to any man.
Viola in *Twelfth Night,* 3.4.226–8

Responding to Sir Toby's demand that she
meet the challenge of Sir Andrew Aguecheek.

Queens, see Royalty

Readiness

1 All things are ready if our minds be
so.
King Henry in *Henry V,* 4.3.71

On being prepared to fight the French.

2 Let's lack no discipline, make no
delay:
For, lords, tomorrow is a busy day.
King Richard in *Richard III,* 5.3.17–18

Preparing to fight the forces of Richmond.

3 I would have been much more a
fresher man
Had I expected thee.
Hector in *Troilus and Cressida,* 5.6.20–1

Hector did not anticipate fighting with
Achilles, who had been sulking in his tent.

Reading (see also Books, Study)

1 *Polonius.* What do you read, my
lord?
Hamlet. Words, words, words.
Hamlet, 2.2.191–2

Hamlet affecting madness answers Polonius's
question literally.

2 He reads much,
He is a great observer, and he looks
Quite through the deeds of men.
Caesar in *Julius Caesar,* 1.2.201–3

Describing Cassius.

3 How well he's read, to reason
against reading!
King of Navarre in *Love's Labor's Lost,*
1.1.94

Responding to Berowne's arguments against
poring over a book.

Reason/Reasons (see also Argument)

1 They say every why hath a where-
fore.
Dromio of Syracuse in *The Comedy of
Errors,* 2.2.43

Meaning another reason can always be found
to support a case.

2 Sure He that made us with such
large discourse,
Looking before and after, gave us
not
That capability and godlike reason
To fust in us unused.
Hamlet in *Hamlet,* 4.4.36–9

Reason is "godlike" as shared with the creator,
and marking the difference between human
beings and beasts.

3 Give you a reason on compulsion?
If reasons were as plentiful as black-
berries, I would give no man a reason upon compulsion, I.
Falstaff in *Henry IV, Part 1,* 2.4.238–40

Evading a direct answer to Poins and Hal;
"reasons" would have sounded like "raisins."

4   O judgment, thou art fled to
     brutish beasts,
     And men have lost their reason!

Mark Antony in *Julius Caesar*, 3.2.104–5

Otherwise, he implies, they would all mourn
for Caesar.

5   Gratiano speaks an infinite deal of
     nothing, more than any man in all
     Venice. His reasons are as two
     grains of wheat hid in two bushels
     of chaff; you shall seek all day ere
     you find them, and when you have
     them, they are not worth the
     search.

**Bassanio in *The Merchant of Venice*,
1.1.114–18**

6   To say the truth, reason and love
     keep little company together nowa-
     days.

**Bottom in *A Midsummer Night's
Dream*, 3.1.143–4**

Amazed that Titania makes love to him.

7   Reason and respect
     Make livers pale, and lustihood
     deject.

**Troilus in *Troilus and Cressida*,
2.2.49–50**

Reason here is matched with "respect" or caution as breeding cowardice (pale livers) and
inertia; Troilus is eager to fight to keep Helen
in Troy.

Rebellion

1   Rebellion lay in his way, and he
     found it.

Falstaff in *Henry IV, Part 1*, 5.1.28

On the Earl of Worcester, who says he did not
seek rebellion.

2   To face the garment of rebellion
     With some fine color that may
     please the eye
     Of fickle changelings and poor dis-
     contents,
     Which gape and rub the elbow at
     the news
     Of hurly-burly innovation.

**King Henry in *Henry IV, Part 1*,
5.1.74–8**

Rebels can always attract support; "face" =
trim; "changelings" are turncoats who greet
with pleasure ("rub the elbow") news of
revolution.

Recklessness

1   If I be foiled, there is but one
     shamed that was never gracious; if
     killed, but one dead that is willing
     to be so.

Orlando in *As You Like It*, 1.2.187–9

Not caring whether he is overthrown
("foiled"), as he volunteers to wrestle with a
deadly professional.

2   I do not set my life at a pin's fee,
     And for my soul, what can it do to
     that,
     Being a thing immortal as itself?

Hamlet in *Hamlet*, 1.4.65–7

He is determined to follow the ghost, not
knowing whether it is a good or evil spirit;
"fee" = worth.

3   I am one, my liege,
     Whom the vile blows and buffets of
     the world
     Hath so incensed that I am reckless
     what
     I do to spite the world.

**Second Murderer in *Macbeth*,
3.1.107–10**

So he is ready to murder Banquo.

Reconciliation

1 Love and be friends, as two such men should be.

Poet in *Julius Caesar*, 4.3.131

To the quarreling Brutus and Cassius.

2 This was an ill beginning of the night. Never come such division 'tween our souls!

Cassius in *Julius Caesar*, 4.3.234–5

To Brutus, after their quarrel.

3 You must bear with me. Pray you now, forget and forgive; I am old and foolish.

King Lear in *King Lear*, 4.7.82–3

Asking forgiveness of his daughter, Cordelia.

4 Come, let's away to prison: We two alone will sit like birds i' the cage; When thou dost ask me blessing, I'll kneel down And ask of thee forgiveness.

King Lear in *King Lear*, 5.3.8–11

To his daughter Cordelia when they are taken prisoner.

5 Now thou and I are new in amity.

Oberon in *A Midsummer Night's Dream*, 4.1.87

Reconciled to his Queen, Titania.

Reformation

1 Like bright metal on a sullen ground, My reformation, glitt'ring o'er my fault,

Shall show more goodly and attract more eyes Than that which hath no foil to set it off.

Prince Hal in *Henry IV, Part 1*, 1.2.212–15

Hal plans to humor his companions for a while, joining in their dissolute life, in order to cast them off later; "sullen ground" = dark background.

2 If I do grow great, I'll grow less, for I'll purge and leave sack, and live cleanly as a nobleman should do.

Falstaff in *Henry IV, Part 1*, 5.4.163–5

Imagining he may be rewarded for his claim to have killed Hotspur, he thinks of slimming and giving up drinking ("sack" = sherry).

3 When wilt thou leave fighting o' days and foining o' nights, and begin to patch up thine old body for heaven?

Doll Tearsheet in *Henry IV, Part 2*, 2.4.231–3

To Falstaff, who has just driven ancient Pistol out of doors; "foining" = fornicating.

4 Presume not that I am the thing I was.

Prince Hal, now King Henry V, in *Henry IV, Part 2*, 5.5.56

Marking the change in him now that he is king.

5 Consideration like an angel came And whipped th' offending Adam out of him.

Archbishop of Canterbury in *Henry V*, 1.1.28–9

On Prince Hal's reformation now that he is king; Adam was guilty of the first, original sin in disobeying God (see Romans 5:12–14).

Regret

1 What our contempts doth often
    hurl from us,
    We wish it ours again.
Antony in *Antony and Cleopatra*,
1.2.123–4

Regret for what is scorned and thrown away.

2   Things without all rem-
    edy
    Should be without regard. What's
    done is done.
Lady Macbeth in *Macbeth*, 3.2.11–12

"Be without regard" = not brooded on.

Rejection

1 O that a lady, of one man refused,
    Should of another therefore be
    abused!
**Helena in *A Midsummer Night's
    Dream*, 2.2.133–4**

Helena finds herself scorned by both Lysander
and Demetrius.

2 I have told you enough of this. For
    my part I'll not meddle nor make
    no farther.
Pandarus in *Troilus and Cressida*,
1.1.13–14

"Meddle nor make" was a proverbial phrase,
"make" meaning "have anything to do with
it"; he is refusing to help Troilus.

3 I will acquaintance strangle, and
    look strange.
***Sonnet 89*, 8**

Rejecting his friend; "acquaintance strangle" =
cease to be familiar.

Religion

1 The gross band of the unfaithful.
Rosalind in *As You Like It*, 4.1.194–5

To Orlando, merging love and religion.

2 It is religion that doth make vows
    kept.
Cardinal Pandulph in *King John*,
1.1.172

3 Hath not a Jew eyes? Hath not a
    Jew hands, organs, dimensions,
    senses, affections, passions; fed with
    the same food, hurt with the same
    weapons, subject to the same dis-
    eases, healed by the same means,
    warmed and cooled by the same
    winter and summer, as a Christian
    is?
Shylock in *The Merchant of Venice*,
3.1.59–64

His famous defense of the shared humanity of
Jews.

4   In religion,
    What damnèd error but some sober
    brow
    Will bless it, and approve it with a
    text,
    Hiding the grossness with fair orna-
    ment?
Bassanio in *The Merchant of Venice*,
3.2.77–80

"Approve" = confirm.

5 Whether, if you yield not to your
    father's choice,
    You can endure the livery of a nun,
    For aye to be in shady cloister
    mewed,

To live a barren sister all your life,
Chanting faint hymns to the cold
fruitless moon.
Thrice blessèd they that master so
their blood
To undergo such maiden pilgrimage.

Theseus in *A Midsummer Night's
Dream*, 1.1.69–75

To Hermia, who has refused to marry
Demetrius, the suitor favored by her father.

6   God save the foundation!
Dogberry in *Much Ado About
Nothing*, 5.1.318

On being given money by Leonato, Dogberry
responds as if he had been given alms at some
religious house or foundation.

Remembrance (see also Memory)

1   Praising what is lost
Makes the remembrance dear.
King of France in *All's Well That Ends
Well*, 5.3.19–20

2   *Hamlet.* Methinks I see my father.
Horatio. Where, my lord?
Hamlet. In my mind's eye, Hora-
tio.

Hamlet, 1.2.184–5

Recalling the appearance of the ghost of old
Hamlet in the previous scene.

3   Old men forget; yet all shall be forgot,
But he'll remember, with advantages,

What feats he did that day.
King Henry in *Henry V*, 4.3.49–51

4   Men's evil manners live in brass,
their virtues
We write in water.
Griffith in *Henry VIII*, 4.2.45–6

Speaking of the dead Cardinal Wolsey; "live
in brass" = are long remembered; the idea
was proverbial.

5   After my death I wish no other her-
ald,
No other speaker of my living
actions
To keep mine honor from corrup-
tion,
But such an honest chronicler as
Griffith.
Queen Katherine in *Henry VIII*,
4.2.69–72

Griffith has just spoken of the good qualities
of Wolsey.

6   Remember that you call on me
today.
Be near me, that I may remember
you.
Caesar in *Julius Caesar*, 2.2.122–3

To Trebonius, who is one of the conspirators
plotting to murder Caesar.

7   My love to Hermia,
Melted as the snow, seems to me
now
As the remembrance of an idle
gaud
Which in my childhood I did dote
upon.
Demetrius in *A Midsummer Night's
Dream*, 4.1.165–8

"Idle gaud" = worthless plaything.

8   Let us not burden our remem-
     brances
     With a heaviness that's gone.

Prospero in *The Tempest*, 5.1.198–9

"Heaviness" = grief.

9   When to the sessions of sweet silent
     thought
     I summon up remembrance of
     things past,
     I sigh the lack of many a thing I
     sought,
     And with old woes new wail my
     dear time's waste.

***Sonnet* 30, 1–4**

These famous lines seem to be recalled in the
general title of Marcel Proust's sequence of
novels, *A la recherche du temps perdu*; "dear"
= precious.

Renunciation

1   What must the King do now? Must
     he submit?
     The King shall do it. Must he be
     deposed?
     The King shall be contented. Must
     he lose
     The name of King? A' God's name
     let it go.

King Richard in *Richard II*, 3.3.143–6

Anticipating the loss of his throne.

2   I'll give my jewels for a set of beads,
     My gorgeous palace for a hermitage,
     . . .
     And my large kingdom for a little
     grave,
     A little, little grave, an obscure
     grave.

**King Richard in *Richard II*, 3.3.147–8,
153–4**

Already yielding in mind to his inevitable
deposition from the throne.

3   Now mark me how I will undo
     myself.
     I give this heavy weight from off my
     head,
     And this unwieldy scepter from my
     hand,
     The pride of kingly sway from out
     my heart.
     With mine own tears I wash away
     my balm,
     With mine own hands I give away
     my crown.

King Richard in *Richard II*, 4.1.203–8

Deposing himself.

4   Graves at my command
     Have waked their sleepers, oped,
     and let 'em forth
     By my so potent art. But this rough
     magic
     I here abjure.

Prospero in *The Tempest*, 5.1.48–51

Renouncing his magical powers; "oped" =
opened.

5   I'll break my staff,
     Bury it certain fathoms in the earth,
     And deeper than did ever plummet
     sound
     I'll drown my book.

Prospero in *The Tempest*, 5.1.54–7

Abandoning his magic powers by discarding
his staff and book; "plummet" = plumb-line, a
line weighted with lead to measure depth.

Repentance

1   Try what repentance can. What
     can it not?
     Yet what can it, when one cannot
     repent?

Claudius in *Hamlet*, 3.3.65–6

Wishing he could find forgiveness for the murder of old Hamlet.

2 Well, I'll repent, and that suddenly, while I am in some liking. I shall be out of heart shortly, and then I shall have no strength to repent.

Falstaff in *Henry IV, Part 1*, 3.3.4–7

"Suddenly" = at once; "in some liking" = inclined to do it.

3   More will I do,
Though all that I can do is nothing worth,
Since that my penitence comes after all,
Imploring pardon.

King Henry in *Henry V*, 4.1.302–5

Nothing he can do in penitence for his past sins is any use, because ("since that") he still has to seek pardon.

4 Woe, that too late repents!

King Lear in *King Lear*, 1.4.257

"Woe" = woe to the person; Lear finds Goneril ungrateful and regrets giving her half his kingdom.

5 Well, if my wind were but long enough to say my prayers, I would repent.

Falstaff in *The Merry Wives of Windsor*, 4.5.102–3

On being cheated and beaten; "wind" = breath.

Repetition

1 *Richard.* Harp not on that string, madam, that is past.
Queen Elizabeth. Harp on it still shall I till heart-strings break.

Richard III, 4.4.364–5

He wants to talk of marriage, but she reminds him of the murders he has perpetrated.

Reputation (see also Fame, Slander)

1   I have offended reputation,
A most unnoble swerving.

Antony in *Antony and Cleopatra*, 3.11.49–50

After turning tail at the battle of Actium.

2 I would to God thou and I knew where a commodity of good names were to be bought.

Falstaff in *Henry IV, Part 1*, 1.2.82–3

To Prince Hal, implying they both have a bad reputation; "commodity" = goods for sale, supply.

3 My credit now stands on such slippery ground
That one of two bad ways you must conceit me,
Either a coward or a flatterer.

Mark Antony in *Julius Caesar*, 3.1.191–3

Speaking to the conspirators who have killed Caesar; "conceit" = think of.

4 He hath honored me of late, and I have bought
Golden opinions from all sorts of people,
Which would be worn now in their newest gloss,
Not cast aside so soon.

Macbeth in *Macbeth*, 1.7.32–5

Resisting the idea of murdering King Duncan to get the throne.

5   I do know of these
That therefore only are reputed
  wise
For saying nothing; when I am very
  sure
If they should speak, would almost
  damn those ears
Which hearing them would call
  their brothers fools.

Gratiano in *The Merchant of Venice*,
1.1.95–9

Alluding to Matthew 5:22, "And whosoever
saith unto his brother . . . Fool, shall be worthy to be punished with hell fire." (Geneva
version.)

6   Reputation, reputation, reputation!
O, I have lost my reputation! I
have lost the immortal part of
myself, and what remains is bestial.

Cassio in *Othello*, 2.3.262–4

On being cashiered for drinking and
quarreling.

7   Reputation is an idle and most false
imposition; oft got without merit,
and lost without deserving.

Iago in *Othello*, 2.3.268–70

"Imposition" = what is attributed to someone
by other people; this is said for the benefit of
Cassio; see next entries.

8   Good name in man and woman,
  dear my lord,
Is the immediate jewel of their
  souls.

Iago in *Othello*, 3.3.155–6

Iago praises reputation to Othello, having earlier made little of it to Cassio at 2.3.268–70.

9   He that filches from me my good
  name
Robs me of that which not enriches
  him,

And makes me poor indeed.

Iago in *Othello*, 3.3.159–61

Provoking Othello to be suspicious of Desdemona.

10   But, alas, to make me
A fixèd figure for the time of scorn
To point his slow unmoving finger
  at!

Othello in *Othello*, 4.2.53–5

Imagining everyone will always point him out
as a cuckold.

11   The purest treasure mortal times
  afford
Is spotless reputation.

Mowbray in *Richard II*, 1.1.177–8

On being accused of treason.

12   The King's name is a tower of
  strength.

King Richard in *Richard III*, 5.3.12

Relying on his reputation in fighting against
Richmond.

13   Perseverance, dear my lord,
Keeps honor bright; to have done is
  to hang
Quite out of fashion, like a rusty
  mail,
In monumental mockery.

Ulysses in *Troilus and Cressida*,
3.3.150–3

"Rusty mail" = rusty suit of armor; addressing
Achilles, who has refused to fight for the
Greeks.

14   Take the instant way,
For honor travels in a strait so narrow,

Where one but goes abreast. Keep then the path,
For emulation hath a thousand sons
That one by one pursue. If you give way,
Or hedge aside from the direct forthright,
Like to an entered tide, they all rush by
And leave you hindmost.

Ulysses in *Troilus and Cressida*, 3.3.153–60

Depicting life as a rat-race to Achilles in an effort to get him to fight again.

15 I see my reputation is at stake,
My fame is shrewdly gored.

Achilles in *Troilus and Cressida*, 3.3.227–8

"Shrewdly gored" = badly wounded; responding to Ulysses.

16 Thence comes it that my name receives a brand,
And almost thence my nature is subdued
To what it works in, like the dyer's hand.

Sonnet 111, 5–7

As the dyer's hand is stained by his work, so the speaker (Shakespeare himself presumably) is tainted (as with a brand) and conditioned by his work as an actor and writer for the stage.

17 'Tis better to be vile than vile esteemed,
When not to be receives reproach of being.

Sonnet 121, 1–2

It is better to be vile when, not being vicious, one is thought to be so, and reproached for it.

Resignation

1 All strange and terrible events are welcome,
But comforts we despise.

Cleopatra in *Antony and Cleopatra*, 4.15.3–4

Preparing for the worst.

2 Night hangs upon mine eyes; my bones would rest,
That have but labored to attain this hour.

Brutus in *Julius Caesar*, 5.5.41–2

Anticipating his death.

3 Cold indeed, and labor lost:
Then farewell heat, and welcome frost!

Prince of Morocco in *The Merchant of Venice*, 2.7.74–5

Before choosing the wrong casket, he had sworn never to marry.

4 I am a tainted wether of the flock,
Meetest for death; the weakest kind of fruit
Drops earliest to the ground, and so let me.

Antonio in *The Merchant of Venice*, 4.1.114–16

"Tainted wether" literally = sickly castrated ram; Antonio offers himself, as it were, for sacrifice.

5 But why should honor outlive honesty?
Let it go all.

Othello in *Othello*, 5.2.245–6

Having lost his integrity ("honesty") he no longer sees a need to maintain his reputation as a warrior.

6   Here is my journey's end, here is
     my butt
     And very sea-mark of my utmost
     sail.
     Othello in *Othello*, 5.2.267–8

Meaning the journey of life; "butt" = goal; a
sea-mark was a beacon or landmark to guide
ships to harbor.

Resistance

1   Fight to the last gasp; I'll be your
     guard.
     Joan la Pucelle in *Henry VI, Part 1*,
     1.2.127

Urging the French to resist the attack by the
English on Orleans.

2   What fates impose, that men must
     needs abide;
     It boots not to resist both wind and
     tide.
     King Edward in *Henry VI, Part 3*,
     4.4.58–9

He has been taken prisoner; "It boots not" = it
is pointless.

3   I'll not budge an inch.
     **Sly in *The Taming of the Shrew*,
     Induction, I.14**

Threatened with the Constable, he refuses to
leave the inn where he has broken some
glasses.

Resolution (see also Determination)

1   I have nothing
     Of woman in me; now from head
     to foot

I am marble-constant.
Cleopatra in *Antony and Cleopatra*,
5.2.237–40

Cleopatra prepares for death.

2   Thy commandment all alone shall
     live
     Within the book and volume of my
     brain
     Unmixed with baser matter.
     Hamlet in *Hamlet*, 1.5.102–4

Taking the Ghost's demand for revenge as a
military order (command), and a biblical
injunction (commandment).

3   I am fresh of spirit and resolved
     To meet all perils very constantly.
     Cassius in *Julius Caesar*, 5.1.90–1

Rejecting the bad omens seen before the battle of Philippi.

4   Put on
     The dauntless spirit of resolution.
     **The Bastard Falconbridge in *King
     John*, 5.1.52–3**

Urging King John to stand firm.

5   I am settled, and bend up
     Each corporal agent to this terrible
     feat.
     Macbeth in *Macbeth*, 1.7.79–80

"Bend up" = brace every nerve in my body
(from bringing a bow into tension); he is ready
to murder Duncan (the "terrible feat").

6   It makes us, or it mars us, think on
     that,
     And fix most firm thy resolution.
     Iago in *Othello*, 5.1.4–5

"Makes or mars" was proverbial = succeed or
be destroyed; to Roderigo, as they ambush
Cassio.

Respect

1   That title of respect
Which the proud soul ne'er pays
but to the proud.

King Henry in *Henry IV, Part 1*, 1.3.8–9

He thinks he can only earn respect by being tough.

Retirement

1   I could be well content
To entertain the lag end of my life
With quiet hours.

Worcester in *Henry IV, Part 1*, 5.1.23–5

2   'Tis our fast intent
To shake all cares and business
   from our age,
Conferring them on younger
   strengths, while we
Unburdened crawl toward death.

King Lear in *King Lear*, 1.1.38–41

Kings are not expected to retire, and Lear brings disaster when he gives his power to his daughters.

Revels

1   See, Antony, that revels long a-
   nights,
Is notwithstanding up.

Caesar in *Julius Caesar*, 2.2.116–17

Greeting Antony.

2   Revels, dances, masques, and
   merry hours
Forerun fair love, strewing her way
with flowers.

Berowne in *Love's Labor's Lost*,
4.3.376–7

Berowne's plan to win over the ladies of the court.

3   Come now, what masques, what
   dances shall we have
To wear away this long age of three
   hours
Between our after-supper and bed-
   time?

**Theseus in *A Midsummer Night's
Dream*, 5.1.32–4**

"Masques" were courtly entertainments based on the idea of masked dancers.

4   Say, what abridgement have you for
   this evening?
What masque, what music? How
   shall we beguile
The lazy time if not with some
   delight?

**Theseus in *A Midsummer Night's
Dream*, 5.1.39–41**

"Abridgement" = amusement to make the time pass quickly.

5   I am a fellow o'the strangest mind
i'the world; I delight in masques
and revels sometimes altogether.

**Sir Andrew Aguecheek in *Twelfth
Night*, 1.3.112–14**

He has just changed his mind about staying in Illyria.

Revenge

1   Haste me to know it, that I with
   wings as swift
As meditation, or the thoughts of
   love,
May sweep to my revenge.

Hamlet in *Hamlet*, 1.5.29–31

Impulsively eager to rush to the revenge his father's ghost has demanded; "swift as thought" is proverbial.

2 How all occasions do inform
    against me,
And spur my dull revenge!

Hamlet in *Hamlet*, 4.4.32–3

"Inform against me" = accuse me of inaction.

3 *Salerio.* Why, I am sure if he forfeit
    thou wilt not take his flesh.
    What's that good for?
    Shylock. To bait fish withal—if it
    will feed nothing else, it will feed
    my revenge.

The Merchant of Venice, 3.1.51–4

On the news that ships bearing Antonio's
goods have been lost.

4 If you prick us, do we not bleed? If
you tickle us, do we not laugh? If
you poison us, do we not die? And
if you wrong us, shall we not
revenge? If we are like you in the
rest, we will resemble you in that.
If a Jew wrong a Christian, what is
his humility? Revenge. If a Christian wrong a Jew, what should his
sufferance be by Christian example?
Why, revenge. The villainy you
teach me, I will execute, and it
shall go hard but I will better the
instruction.

Shylock in *The Merchant of Venice*,
3.1.64–73

Intending to demand his pound of flesh from
Antonio.

5   Nothing can or shall content
    my soul
Till I am evened with him, wife for
    wife,
Or failing so, yet that I put the
    Moor
At least into a jealousy so strong
That judgment cannot cure.

Iago in *Othello*, 2.1.298–302

Imagining Othello has slept with his wife,
Emilia.

6 All my fond love thus do I blow to
    heaven.
'Tis gone.
Arise, black vengeance, from the
    hollow hell!

Othello in *Othello*, 3.3.445–7

The turning point, as his love for Desdemona
turns to hate.

7   Like to the Pontic Sea,
Whose icy current and compulsive
    course
Ne'er knows retiring ebb, but keeps
    due on
To the Propontic and the Helle-
    spont,
Even so my bloody thoughts with
    violent pace
Shall ne'er look back, ne'er ebb to
    humble love,
Till that a capable and wide revenge
Swallow them up.

Othello in *Othello*, 3.3.453–60

The "Pontic Sea" is the Black Sea; the "Propontic" or Sea of Marmora, and the "Helle-
spont," the straits of the Dardanelles, both
connect the Black Sea with the Aegean Sea in
the Mediterranean.

8 To revenge is no valor, but to bear.

First Senator in *Timon of Athens*, 3.5.39

Claiming that true valor lies in being able to
endure rather than seek revenge.

9 I'll be revenged on the whole pack
of you.

Malvolio in *Twelfth Night*, 5.1.378

His famous exit-line, after being duped and
treated as mad.

Revolution

1 Pluck down my officers, break my
   decrees,
   For now a time is come to mock at
   form.

King Henry in *Henry IV, Part 2,*
4.5.117–8

Imagining what will happen when Prince
Hal becomes king; "form" = ceremony or
tradition.

Risk

1   Were it good
   To set the exact wealth of all our
      states
   All at one cast? To set so rich a
      main
   On the nice hazard of one doubtful
      hour?
   It were not good, for therein should
   we read
   The very bottom and the soul of
      hope,
   The very list, the very utmost
      bound
   Of all our fortunes.

Hotspur in *Henry IV, Part 1,* 4.1.45–52

Convincing himself it is as well to keep the
forces of his father, who pleads sickness, in
reserve; "exact wealth of all our states" =
whole of our resources; "main" = stake; "nice
hazard" = tricky gamble; "list" = boundary.

2 "Who chooseth me must give and
   hazard all he hath."
   Must give—for what? For lead,
   hazard for lead?
   This casket threatens. Men that
   hazard all
   Do it in hope of fair advantages;

A golden mind stoops not to shows
of dross.

Prince of Morocco in *The Merchant of
Venice,* 2.7.16–20

Reading the message he finds on the leaden
casket.

Rivalry

1   Think not, Percy,
   To share with me in glory any
      more.
   Two stars keep not their motion in
   one sphere.

Prince Hal in *Henry IV, Part 1,* 5.4.63–5

To Hotspur; the last line means two stars cannot share the same orbit.

Rivers

1 There is a river in Macedon, and
   there is moreover a river in Mon-
   mouth. It is called Wye at Mon-
   mouth, but it is out of my prains
   what is the name of the other river;
   but 'tis all one, 'tis alike as my fingers is to my fingers, and there is
   salmons in both.

Fluellen in *Henry V,* 4.7.26–31

Fluellen's logic is as quaint as his language as
he "proves" that Henry V is as great a soldier
as Alexander the Great.

2 Smooth runs the water where the
   brook is deep.

Suffolk in *Henry VI, Part 2,* 3.1.53

Accusing Humphrey, Duke of Gloucester, of
hypocrisy; proverbial.

3 The current that with gentle mur-
mur glides,
Thou know'st, being stopped,
impatiently doth rage;
But when his fair course is not hin-
derèd,
He makes sweet music with th'
enameled stones,
Giving a gentle kiss to every sedge
He overtaketh in his pilgrimage.

**Julia in _The Two Gentlemen of
Verona_, 2.7.25–30**

She is really thinking of the course of her love
for Valentine.

Royalty

1   There is gold, and here
My bluest veins to kiss—a hand
that kings
Have lipped, and trembled kissing.

**Cleopatra in _Antony and Cleopatra_,
2.5.28–30**

Allowing a messenger to kiss the royal hand.

2 Show me, my women, like a queen;
go fetch
My best attires. I am again for Cydnus
To meet Mark Antony.

**Cleopatra in _Antony and Cleopatra_,
5.2.227–9**

Dressing up to recapture her first glamorous
meeting with Antony.

3 Give me my robe, put on my
crown, I have
Immortal longings in me.

**Cleopatra in _Antony and Cleopatra_,
5.2.280–1**

Preparing for death as a queen.

4 _First Guard._ Is this well done?
Charmian. It is well done, and fit-
ting for a princess
Descended of so many royal kings.

Antony and Cleopatra, 5.2.325–7

Caesar's guards find Cleopatra dead.

5   Never alone
Did the King sigh, but with a general groan.

Rosencrantz in _Hamlet_, 3.3.22–3

The obsequious courtier speaking to Claudius.

6 There's such divinity doth hedge a
king
That treason can but peep to what
it would,
Acts little of his will.

Claudius in _Hamlet_, 4.5.124–6

James I liked to claim that kings were gods on
earth. It is ironic that Claudius, who murdered King Hamlet, should claim divine protection; "his" = its.

7   Let four captains
Bear Hamlet like a soldier to the
stage,
For he was likely, had he been put
on,
To have proved most royally.

Fortinbras in _Hamlet_, 5.2.395–8

Hamlet receives a soldier's funeral.

8 The skipping King, he ambled up
and down,
With shallow jesters and rash bavin
wits,
Soon kindled and soon burnt,
carded his state,
Mingled his royalty with cap'ring
fools.

King Henry in *Henry IV, Part 1*,
3.2.60–3

Speaking to his son of Richard II; "bavin" =
brushwood; "carded his state" = weakened his
power.

9   No extraordinary gaze,
Such as is bent on sunlike majesty
When it shines seldom in admiring
eyes.
King Henry in *Henry IV, Part 1*,
3.2.78–80

Advising Prince Hal that kings should rarely
display themselves.

10 The King himself is to be feared as
the lion.
Falstaff in *Henry IV, Part 1*, 3.3.149

As the lion is king of the beasts.

11 Uneasy lies the head that wears a
crown.
King Henry in *Henry IV, Part 2*, 3.1.31

The king's best-known line.

12 O polished perturbation! Golden
care!
That keep'st the ports of slumber
open wide
To many a watchful night.
Prince Hal in *Henry IV, Part 2*,
4.5.23–5

Commenting on the crown that lies on his sick
father's pillow; "ports" = gates.

13 This new and gorgeous garment,
majesty,
Sits not so easy on me as you think.
Prince Hal in *Henry IV, Part 2*, 5.2.44–5

On taking the throne as Henry V.

14 The mirror of all Christian kings.
Chorus in *Henry V*, 2.Prologue, 6

Praising Henry V as the model for all kings.

15 Never was monarch better feared
and loved
Than is your Majesty.
Cambridge in *Henry V*, 2.2.25–6

He is about to be exposed as a traitor.

16   Mean and gentle all
Behold, as may unworthiness
define,
A little touch of Harry in the night.
Chorus in *Henry V*, 4.Prologue, 45–7

High and low ("mean and gentle") alike are
influenced by the king's personality (the familiar "Harry," not Henry); the Chorus apologizes
for his "unworthiness" in attempting to
describe it.

17 I think the King is but a man, as I
am. The violet smells to him as it
doth to me.
King Henry in *Henry V*, 4.1.101–2

Henry is in disguise, speaking with common
soldiers.

18 Upon the King! Let us our lives,
our souls,
Our debts, our careful wives,
Our children, and our sins lay on
the King!
We must bear all. O hard condi-
tion,
Twin-born with greatness, subject
to the breath
Of every fool.
King Henry in *Henry V*, 4.1.230–5

Lamenting the hardship of bearing responsibility.

19 'Tis not the balm, the scepter, and
   the ball,
The sword, the mace, the crown
   imperial,
The intertissued robe of gold and
   pearl,
   . . .
Not all these, laid in bed majestical,
Can sleep so soundly as the
   wretched slave
Who with a body filled and vacant
   mind
Gets him to rest, crammed with
   distressful bread.
King Henry in *Henry V*, 4.1.260–2,
267–70

The poor laborer whose food is earned by
hard toil (hence "distressful") sleeps easier
than a king, for all his luxury.

20 I am glad thou canst speak no better English, for if thou couldst, thou
   wouldst find me such a plain king
   that thou wouldst think I had sold
   my farm to buy my crown.
King Henry in *Henry V*, 5.2.123–6

Apologizing to Katherine for his roughness.

21 How sweet a thing it is to wear a
   crown,
Within whose circuit is Elysium
And all that poets feign of bliss and
   joy.
**Richard of Gloucester in *Henry VI*,
Part 3,** 1.2.29–31

Elysium was the heaven of Greek mythology,
where the spirits of the blessed dwelled.

22 *Second Keeper.* But if thou be a
   king, where is thy crown?
King Henry. My crown is in my
   heart, not on my head;
Not decked with diamonds and
   Indian stones,

Nor to be seen: my crown is called
   content;
A crown it is that seldom kings
   enjoy.
Henry VI, Part 3, 3.1.61–5

The king, in disguise, encounters two game-
keepers; "Indian stones" = precious gems from
India.

23 I swear again, I would not be a
   queen
For all the world.
Anne Boleyn in *Henry VIII*, 2.3.45–6

Ironic both in relation to the quibble on
"quean" or whore, and in view of what happened to her; she became queen, and was
later beheaded.

24   Thou art alone
(If thy rare qualities, sweet gentle-
   ness,
Thy meekness saintlike, wife-like
   government,
Obeying in commanding, and thy
   parts
Sovereign and pious else, could
   speak thee out)
The queen of earthly queens.
King Henry in *Henry VIII*, 2.4.137–42

Praising Katherine, the wife he is divorcing;
"government" = conduct; her "sovereign
parts" are her excellent qualities.

25 *Gloucester.* Is't not the King?
Lear. Ay, every inch a king!
When I do stare, see how the sub-
   ject quakes!
King Lear, 4.6.107–8

26 We were not born to sue, but to
   command.
King Richard in *Richard II*, 1.1.196

27 Four lagging winters and four wanton springs
    End in a word: such is the breath of kings.

Bolingbroke in *Richard II*, 1.3.214–5

King Richard has reduced his term of banishment by four years.

28 Not all the water in the rough rude sea
    Can wash the balm off from an anointed king;
    The breath of worldly men cannot depose
    The deputy elected by the Lord.

King Richard in *Richard II*, 3.2.54–7

Alluding to the "divine right" of a king, consecrated with holy oil ("balm"), and God's deputy on earth.

29 Is not the king's name twenty thousand names?
    Arm, arm, my name! A puny subject strikes
    At thy great glory.

King Richard in *Richard II*, 3.2.85–7

Having no soldiers, he tries to cheer himself up.

30 See, see, King Richard doth himself appear,
    As doth the blushing discontented sun
    From out the fiery portal of the east.

Bolingbroke in *Richard II*, 3.3.62–4

Richard appears on the battlements of a castle (or balcony on the stage).

31 Yet looks he like a king. Behold, his eye,
    As bright as is the eagle's, lightens forth
    Controlling majesty.

York in *Richard II*, 3.3.68–70

In defeat Richard still has a good appearance; "lightens forth" = flashes like lightning.

32   She is
    The queen of curds and cream.

Camillo in *The Winter's Tale*, 4.4.160–1

Seeing Perdita, really a princess, among the country shepherds and shepherdesses.

33 For princes are the glass, the school, the book
    Where subjects' eyes do learn, do read, do look.

The Rape of Lucrece, 615–6

Ruin

1 Leave not the mansion so long tenantless
   Lest, growing ruinous, the building fall
   And leave no memory of what it was.

Valentine in *The Two Gentlemen of Verona*, 5.4.7–10

Appealing to Sylvia; the "mansion" is his heart.

Rumor

1 Let every feeble rumor shake your hearts.

Coriolanus in *Coriolanus*, 3.3.125

To the people as he goes into exile.

2 *Enter Rumor, painted full of tongues.*
Open your ears; for which of you
    will stop
The vent of hearing when loud
    Rumor speaks?

**Rumor in *Henry IV, Part 2*, Induction,
1–2, and stage direction**

The Chorus to the play.

3   Rumor is a pipe
Blown by surmises, jealousies, con-
    jectures.

**Rumor in *Henry IV, Part 2*, Induction,
15–16**

How rumor spreads, like music.

4   From Rumor's tongues
They bring smooth comforts false,
    worse than true wrongs.

**Rumor in *Henry IV, Part 2*, Induction,
39–40**

"They" are people spreading reports.

5 Rumor doth double, like the voice
    and echo,
The numbers of the feared.

Warwick in *Henry IV, Part 2*, 3.1.97–8

Referring to the size of a rebel army.

6 I heard a bustling rumor like a fray,
And the wind blows it from the
    Capitol.

Portia in *Julius Caesar*, 2.4.18–19

"Bustling rumor like a fray" = confused noise
like a brawl.

Ruthlessness (see also Cruelty)

1 There is no more mercy in him
than there is milk in a male tiger.

Menenius in *Coriolanus*, 5.4.27–8

Referring to Coriolanus, who is threatening to
conquer Rome.

2 Down, down to hell, and say I sent
    thee thither—
I that have neither pity, love, nor
    fear.

**Richard of Gloucester in *Henry VI,
Part 3*, 5.6.67–8**

Stabbing the already dead King Henry VI.

3   Make thick my blood,
Stop up th' access and passage to
    remorse,
That no compunctious visitings of
    nature
Shake my fell purpose.

Lady Macbeth in *Macbeth*, 1.5.43–6

If the blood is "thick" no pity or remorse
("compunctious visitings") can flow from the
heart; the "purpose" is murder.

4   I have given suck, and know
How tender 'tis to love the babe
    that milks me;
I would, while it was smiling in my
    face,
Have plucked my nipple from his
    boneless gums
And dashed the brains out, had I so
    sworn
As you have done to this.

Lady Macbeth in *Macbeth*, 1.7.54–9

To Macbeth, who is hesitating about murdering Duncan.

5 Tear-falling pity dwells not in this
    eye.

King Richard in *Richard III*, 4.2.65

Sacrifice

1 Let us be sacrificers, but not butchers, Caius.

Brutus in *Julius Caesar*, 2.1.166

On the idea of killing Caesar.

2 Upon such sacrifices, my Cordelia,
The gods themselves throw incense.

King Lear in *King Lear*, 5.3.20–1

Lear here seems to anticipate the death of Cordelia, who is soon to be hanged in prison.

Safety

1 Would I were in an alehouse in London. I would give all my fame for a pot of ale, and safety.

Boy in *Henry V*, 3.2.12–13

He is with the English forces attacking Harfleur in France; a wry comment on the militarism of Henry V.

2   I am sure 'tis safer to
Avoid what's grown than question how 'tis born.

Camillo in *The Winter's Tale*, 1.2.432–3

To Polixenes, who cannot conceive how his old friend, Leontes, should wish to murder him.

Sanity

1 My pulse as yours doth temperately keep time,
And makes as healthful music. It is not madness
That I have uttered.

Hamlet in *Hamlet*, 3.4.140–2

To Gertrude, who thinks Hamlet is mad.

Scorn (see also Contempt)

1 Disdain and scorn ride sparkling in her eyes,
Misprising what they look on, and her wit
Values itself so highly that to her
All matter else seems weak.

Hero in *Much Ado About Nothing*, 3.1.51–4

Characterizing Beatrice as self-centered in her cleverness ("wit") and despising ("misprising") what anyone else says as trivial.

2 Teach not thy lip such scorn, for it was made
For kissing, lady, not for such contempt.

King Richard in *Richard III*, 1.2.171–2

Wooing the Lady Anne, whose father-in-law he killed.

Sea

1 The wild and wasteful ocean.

King Henry in *Henry V*, 3.1.14

2   The murmuring surge,
That on th' unnumbered idle pebble chafes,
Cannot be heard so high.

Edgar in *King Lear*, 4.6.20–2

Imagining being on the cliffs at Dover.

3 I never did like molestation view
On the enchafèd flood.

Second Gentleman in *Othello*, 2.1.16–17

"Like molestation" = disturbance like this; he is looking out to sea ("flood") for the ship bringing Othello.

4   *Gonzalo.* Nay, good, be patient.
     Boatswain. When the sea is.
     Hence! What cares these roarers
     for the name of king?
     The Tempest, 1.1.15–17

     The storm has no respect for social rank.

5   Now would I give a thousand fur-
     longs of sea for an acre of barren
     ground, long heath, brown furze,
     anything.
     Gonzalo in The Tempest, 1.1.65–7

     Facing shipwreck.

6   Come unto these yellow sands,
     And then take hands.
     Curtsied when you have and kissed
     The wild waves whist,
     Foot it featly here and there;
     And, sweet sprites, the burden bear.
     Ariel in The Tempest, 1.2.375–80

     Summoning spirits to calm the waves into
     silence ("kissed/The wild waves whist"),
     dance, and sing the refrain ("the burden
     bear").

Seasons

1   Here feel we not the penalty of
     Adam,
     The seasons' difference.
     Duke Senior in As You Like It, 2.1.6

     There were no seasons until Adam was
     expelled from the Garden of Eden.

2   Freeze, freeze, thou bitter sky,
     That dost not bite so nigh
     As benefits forgot.
     Amiens in As You Like It, 2.7.184–6

     Establishing the idea of winter in the forest of
     Arden.

3   It was a lover and his lass,
     With a hey, and a ho, and a hey
     nonino,
     That o'er the green corn-field did
     pass,
     In spring time, the only pretty ring
     time,
     When birds do sing, hey ding a
     ding, ding,
     Sweet lovers love the spring.
     Between the acres of the rye,
     With a hey, and a ho, and a hey
     nonino,
     These pretty country folks would
     lie,
     In spring time.
     Song in As You Like It, 5.3.16–25

     One of Shakespeare's best known lyrics.

4   As full of spirit as the month of
     May,
     And gorgeous as the sun at mid-
     summer.
     Vernon in Henry IV, Part 1, 4.1.101–2

     Describing Prince Hal and his comrades, in
     armor to fight against the rebel noblemen.

5   In an early spring
     We see th'appearing buds, which to
     prove fruit
     Hope gives not so much warrant, as
     despair
     That frosts will bite them.
     Lord Bardolph in Henry IV, Part 2,
     1.3.38–41

     Fear of a killing frost tends to outweigh hope
     for a plentiful crop.

6   The seasons change their manners,
     as the year
     Had found some months asleep
     and leapt them over.
     Gloucester in Henry IV, Part 2, 4.4.123–4

     "As" = as if; on unseasonable and strange
     weather.

7 As clear as is the summer's sun.

Archbishop of Canterbury in *Henry V*, 1.2.86

He is "proving" Henry's claim to rule France.

8 Thus sometimes hath the brightest
day a cloud,
And after summer evermore succeeds
Barren winter, with his wrathful
nipping cold;
So cares and joys abound, as seasons fleet.

Gloucester in *Henry VI, Part 2*,
2.4.1–4

He has lost his office of Protector of the King,
and his wife has been banished.

9 At Christmas I no more desire a
rose
Than wish a snow in May's new-
fangled shows,
But like of each thing that in season
grows.

Berowne in *Love's Labor's Lost*,
1.1.105–7

Berowne rejects the idea of mature men
devoting themselves to study.

10 When daisies pied and violets blue,
And lady-smocks, all silver-white,
And cuckoo-buds of yellow hue
Do paint the meadows with delight,
The cuckoo then on every tree
Mocks married men, for thus sings
he:
Cuckoo!
Cuckoo, cuckoo—O word of fear,
Unpleasing to a married ear.

Spring in *Love's Labor's Lost*,
5.2.894–902

The first stanza of the song of Spring at the
end of the play; the cuckoo's habit of using

the nests of other birds suggests cuckoldry,
and the refrain conflicts with the delights of
spring.

11 When icicles hang by the wall,
And Dick the shepherd blows his
nail,
And Tom bears logs into the hall,
And milk comes frozen home in
pail;
When blood is nipped, and ways be
foul,
Then nightly sings the staring owl:
Tu-whit, tu-whoo!—
A merry note,
While greasy Joan doth keel the
pot.

Winter in *Love's Labor's Lost*, 5.2.912–20

The first stanza of the song of Winter at the
end of the play; the refrain ends in merriment
in spite of winter.

12 How many things by season seasoned are
To their right praise and true perfection!

Portia in *The Merchant of Venice*,
5.1.107–8

"By season" = by fit occasion, playing on the
notion of seasoning.

13 The seasons alter; hoary-headed
frosts
Fall in the fresh lap of the crimson
rose,
And on old Hiems' thin and icy
crown
An odorous chaplet of sweet summer buds
Is, as in mockery, set.

Titania in *A Midsummer Night's Dream*, 2.1.107–11

"Hiems" is the personification of winter, hoary
and old.

14   The spring, the summer,
The childing autumn, angry winter
change
Their wonted liveries, and the
mazèd world
By their increase now knows not
which is which.

**Titania in *A Midsummer Night's
Dream*, 2.1.111–14**

On the confusion brought about by her quarrel with Oberon; "childing" = fruitful;
"mazed" = bewildered.

15   Such comfort as do lusty young
men feel
When well-appareled April on the
heel
Of limping winter treads.

Capulet in *Romeo and Juliet*, 1.2.26–8

Referring to the feast and dance Capulet is
planning.

16   Winter tames man, woman, and
beast.

**Grumio in *The Taming of the Shrew*,
4.1.23–4**

17   When daffodils begin to peer,
With heigh, the doxy over the dale,
Why then comes in the sweet o'the
year,
For the red blood reigns in the winter's pale.

Autolycus in *The Winter's Tale*, 4.3.1–4

The rogue Autolycus bursts in to change the
mood from winter to spring, singing of
renewed vitality ("red blood") doing away
with the paleness of winter; a "doxy" is slang
for a wench or, in modern slang, a floozy.

18   That time of year thou may'st in me
behold
When yellow leaves, or none, or
few, do hang

Upon those boughs which shake
against the cold,
Bare ruined choirs where late the
sweet birds sang.

***Sonnet* 73, 1–4**

The speaker represents himself to his younger
lover as aged and close to death (Shakespeare
was 45 when the Sonnets were first published
in 1609, and they are thought to have been
written much earlier).

19   The teeming autumn, big with rich
increase.

***Sonnet* 97, 6**

Secrets

1   Two may keep counsel when the
third's away.

Aaron in *Titus Andronicus*, 4.2.144

He kills the nurse he is speaking to so that she
cannot betray him; she is the "third" who
knows about the birth of his son; proverbial.

2   I have unclasped
To thee the book even of my secret
soul.

Orsino in *Twelfth Night*, 1.4.13–14

To Cesario (Viola in disguise), whom he is
sending to Olivia as his go-between.

Security

1   And you all know security
Is mortals' chiefest enemy.

Hecate in *Macbeth*, 3.5.32–3

Hecate, the goddess of witchcraft, speaks to
the Witches.

2   The wound of peace is
surety,

Surety secure, but modest doubt is
called
The beacon of the wise.

Hector in *Troilus and Cressida*,
2.2.15–16

Arguing that a sense of safety endangers
peace, and that it is best to maintain a moderate degree of wariness ("modest doubt").

Self-Harm

1   Those wounds heal ill that men do
give themselves.

Patroclus in *Troilus and Cressida*,
3.3.229

Referring to Achilles, whose reputation has
been damaged by his idleness.

Self-Importance

1   There are a sort of men whose visages
Do cream and mantle like a standing pond,
And do a willful stillness entertain,
With purpose to be dressed in an
opinion
Of wisdom, gravity, profound conceit,
As who should say, "I am Sir Oracle,
And when I ope my lips let no dog
bark!"

Gratiano in *The Merchant of Venice*,
1.1.88–94

The idea is that their faces take on a set
expression, like the puckered or wrinkled
scum on a stagnant pond; "opinion" = reputation; "conceit" = imagination.

2   Masters, do not forget to specify,
when time and place shall serve,
that I am an ass.

**Dogberry in *Much Ado About
Nothing*, 5.1.255–6**

Dogberry exposes the comic aspects of self-
importance.

3   The best persuaded of himself, so
crammed, as he thinks, with excel-
lencies, that it is his grounds of
faith that all that look on him love
him.

Maria in *Twelfth Night*, 2.3.150–2

On Malvolio; "The best persuaded of himself"
= having the best opinion of himself.

Self-Interest

1   That same purpose-changer, that
sly devil,
That broker that still breaks the
pate of faith,
That daily break-vow, he that wins
of all,
Of kings, of beggars, old men,
young men, maids . . .
That smooth-faced gentleman, tickling commodity,
Commodity, the bias of the world.

**The Bastard Falconbridge in *King
John*, 2.1.567–9, 573–4**

"Commodity" = selfish interest, or concern
with profit; it is imaged as a middleman or
bawd ("broker"), a plausible rogue ("smooth-
faced gentleman"), and as the weight (from
the game of bowls) that influences dealings in
the world.

2   Let me, if not by birth, have lands
by wit;
All with me's meet that I can fashion fit.

Edmund in *King Lear*, 1.2.183–4

Everything that serves his purpose ("can fashion fit") is permissible or justifiable ("meet").

3   That sir which serves and seeks for
    gain,
    And follows but for form,
    Will pack when it begins to rain,
    And leave thee in the storm.

Fool in *King Lear*, 2.4.78–81

"Sir" = man; "pack" = pack up and go.

4   In following him, I follow but
    myself.

Iago in *Othello*, 1.1.58

Referring to Othello.

Self-Knowledge (see also Identity)

1   I will chide no breather in the
    world but myself, against whom I
    know most faults.

Orlando in *As You Like It*, 3.2.280–1

Refusing to join Jaques in abusing the world.

2   Mistress, know yourself, down on
    your knees,
    And thank heaven, fasting, for a
    good man's love.

Rosalind in *As You Like It*, 3.5.57–8

To Phebe, who rejects Silvius's love.

3   Lord, we know what we are, but
    know not what we may be.

Ophelia in *Hamlet*, 4.5.43–4

Wise in her madness.

4   I know myself now, and I feel
    within me
    A peace above all earthly dignities,
    A still and quiet conscience.

Cardinal Wolsey in *Henry VIII*,
3.2.378–80

In his downfall he finds peace, and knows his
faults and limitations.

5   Since you know you cannot see
    yourself
    So well as by reflection, I, your
    glass,
    Will modestly discover to yourself
    That of yourself which yet you
    know not of.

Cassius in *Julius Caesar*, 1.2.67–70

Telling Brutus he can, like a mirror ("glass")
reveal discreetly ("modestly discover") what
Brutus fails to understand about himself.

6   'Tis the infirmity of his age, yet he
    hath ever but slenderly known him-
    self.

Regan in *King Lear*, 1.1.293–4

On Lear casting off his daughter Cordelia.

7   To know my deed, 'twere best not
    know myself.

Macbeth in *Macbeth*, 2.2.70

The "deed" is the murder of Duncan.

8   *Duke (in disguise).* I pray you, sir, of
    what disposition was the Duke?
    Escalus. One that, above all other
    strifes, contended especially to
    know himself.

Measure for Measure, 3.2.230–3

To know oneself was to know how to balance
understanding against the will and the senses;
"strifes" = efforts, endeavors.

9   I have much ado to know myself.

Antonio in *The Merchant of Venice*,
1.1.7

He cannot understand why he is melancholy.

10 I do begin to perceive that I am
   made an ass.
   Falstaff in *The Merry Wives of Wind-*
   sor, 5.5.119

   Realizing how much he has been fooled.

11   I'll read enough
   When I do see the very book indeed
   Where all my sins are writ, and
      that's myself.
   King Richard in *Richard II,* 4.1.273–5

   On being pressed to read a list of his crimes.

12 *Feste.* The better for my foes and
      the worse for my friends.
   Orsino. Just the contrary: the better
      for thy friends.
   Feste. No, sir, the worse.
   Orsino. How can that be?
   Feste. . . . They praise me, and
      make an ass of me. Now my foes
      tell me plainly I am an ass; so that
      by my foes, sir, I profit in the
      knowledge of myself, and by my
      friends I am abused.
   Twelfth Night, 5.1.12–20

   Feste's friends flatter him, so that he is
   deceived and badly treated ("abused").

Self-Love

1 Self-love, my liege, is not so vile a
   sin
   As self-neglecting.
   Dauphin in *Henry V,* 2.4.74–5

   Advising his father, the King of France, to confront the English invaders.

2   She cannot love,
   Nor take no shape nor project of
      affection,

She is so self-endeared.
Hero in *Much Ado About Nothing,*
3.1.54–6

Commenting on Beatrice in the knowledge
that she is listening.

3 O, you are sick of self-love, Malvolio, and taste with a distempered
   appetite.
   Olivia in *Twelfth Night,* 1.5.90–1

   Malvolio has been criticizing Feste; "distempered" = diseased.

4 Sin of self-love possesseth all mine
      eye,
   And all my soul, and all my every
      part;
   And for this sin there is no remedy,
   It is so grounded inward in my
      heart.
   Sonnet 62, 1–4

   The aging poet, "chopped with tanned antiquity," paradoxically sees himself reflected in
   the beauty of his lover, even as he acknowl-
   edges the "sin" of indulging that love.

Self-Pity

1   Here I stand your slave,
   A poor, infirm, weak, and despised
      old man.
   King Lear in *King Lear,* 3.2.19–20

   He is at the mercy of the elements, cast out in
   a storm.

2   I am a man
   More sinned against than sinning.
   King Lear in *King Lear,* 3.2.59–60

   The cry of someone who is as yet unwilling
   fully to acknowledge his own faults?

3   Give me that glass, and therein will
     I read.
     No deeper wrinkles yet? Hath sor-
     row struck
     So many blows upon this face of
     mine
     And made no deeper wounds?

King Richard in *Richard II*, 4.1.276–9

Looking at himself in a mirror.

Self-Reliance

1   Our remedies oft in ourselves do lie
     Which we ascribe to heaven.

Helena in *All's Well That Ends Well*,
1.1.216–7

2   Simply the thing I am
     Shall make me live.

Parolles in *All's Well That Ends Well*,
4.3.333–4

Bouncing back from humiliation.

Senses

1   Dark night, that from the eye his
     function takes,
     The ear more quick of apprehen-
     sion makes;
     Wherein it doth impair the seeing
     sense
     It pays the hearing double recom-
     pense.

**Hermia in *A Midsummer Night's
Dream*,** 3.2.177–80

2   The eye of man hath not heard, the
     ear of man hath not seen, man's
     hand is not able to taste, his tongue

to conceive, nor his heart to report
what my dream was!

**Bottom in *A Midsummer Night's
Dream*,** 4.1.211–4

Bottom mixes up senses in misquoting a passage from I Corinthians 2:9–10, but perhaps
his dream was one of the "things which God
hath prepared for them that love him."

Service

1   I have lost my teeth in your service.

Adam in *As You Like It*, 1.1.82–3

The faithful old servant is cast out.

2   O good old man, how well in thee
     appears
     The constant service of the antique
     world,
     When service sweat for duty, not
     for meed!

Orlando in *As You Like It*, 2.3.56–8

Imagining a golden age when doing the job
was its own reward.

3   I had rather be their servant in my
     way
     Than sway with them in theirs.

Coriolanus in *Coriolanus*, 2.1.203–4

Responding to his mother's wish that he
accept the public office of Consul in Rome.

4   My endeavors
     Have ever come too short of my
     desires,
     Yet filed with my abilities.

Cardinal Wolsey in *Henry VIII*,
3.2.169–71

"Filed" = kept pace with; he claims he has
done the best he could.

5   Had I but served my God with half
       the zeal
     I served my king, he would not in
       mine age
     Have left me naked to mine ene-
       mies.
     Cardinal Wolsey in *Henry VIII*,
     3.2.455–7

6   Remember I have done thee worthy
       service,
     Told thee no lies, made no mistak-
       ings, served
     Without or grudge or grumblings.
     Ariel in *The Tempest*, 1.2.247–9

     Prospero's "airy spirit" reminds Prospero of
     the service he has given.

7   Hear my soul speak:
     The very instant that I saw you, did
     My heart fly to your service, there
       resides
     To make me slave to it.
     Ferdinand in *The Tempest*, 3.1.63–6

     His love makes him a willing "servant" to
     Miranda.

Servitude

1   Our fathers' minds are dead,
     And we are governed with our
       mothers' spirits.
     Our yoke and sufferance show us
       womanish.
     Cassius in *Julius Caesar*, 1.3.82–4

     "Yoke and sufferance" = servitude and patient
     submission to it.

2   Every bondman in his own hand
       bears

The power to cancel his captivity.
Casca in *Julius Caesar*, 1.3.101–2

The ultimate way out of slavery, by suicide.

3   I am all the subjects that you have,
     Which first was mine own king.
     Caliban in *The Tempest*, 1.2.341–2

To Prospero, who has made him a slave.

Sex (see also Lechery, Lust)

1   *Gertrude.* Come hither, my dear
       Hamlet, sit by me.
     Hamlet. No, good mother, here's
       metal more attractive.
     ***Hamlet*, 3.2.108–9**

Hamlet implies he is drawn like a magnet to
Ophelia; he wants to be where he can watch
Claudius at the play, but it is as if he cannot
leave Ophelia alone. Does he touch or
embrace her here? Whatever, the phrase
"here's metal more attractive" has passed into
common use to indicate any kind of preference. See next entry.

2   *Hamlet.* Lady, shall I lie in your
       lap?
     Ophelia. No, my lord.
     Hamlet. I mean, my head upon
       your lap?
     Ophelia. Ay, my lord.
     Hamlet. Do you think I meant
       country matters?
     Ophelia. I think nothing, my lord.
     Hamlet. That's a fair thought to lie
       between maids' legs.
     ***Hamlet*, 3.2.112–8**

This is Hamlet at his least attractive, vexing
Ophelia with the obscene pun in "country"
and sexual innuendo in "fair thought."

3   Come, Kate, thou art perfect in
    lying down.
    Come, quick, quick, that I may lay
    my head in thy lap.

Hotspur in *Henry IV, Part 1*, 3.1.226–7

Teasing his wife, as Mortimer's wife prepares
to sing.

4   Well, while I live I'll fear no other
    thing
    So sore, as keeping safe Nerissa's
    ring.

Gratiano in *The Merchant of Venice*,
5.1.306–7

Pleased to find Nerissa has the ring he thought
he had given away, Gratiano exploits a sexual
play on the word.

5   *Don Pedro.* You have put him
    down, lady, you have put him
    down.
    Beatrice. So I would not he should
    do me, my lord, lest I should
    prove the mother of fools.

***Much Ado About Nothing*,** 2.1.283–6

Beatrice has outsmarted Benedick, but she
jokingly takes "put him down" literally.

6   *Beatrice.* I am stuffed, cousin, I
    cannot smell.
    Margaret. A maid, and stuffed!
    There's goodly catching of cold.

***Much Ado About Nothing*,** 3.4.64–6

Beatrice is "stuffed" with a cold in the head,
but Margaret takes the word in a bawdy sense.

7   *Beatrice.* Will you go hear this
    news, signor?
    Benedick. I will live in thy heart, die
    in thy lap and be buried in thy
    eyes; and moreover, I will go with
    thee to thy uncle's.

***Much Ado About Nothing*,** 5.2.101–4

Benedick's witty response to her question
plays on "die" as referring to sexual orgasm, a
common image in poetry of Shakespeare's age.

8   Do not give dal-
    liance
    Too much the rein. The strongest
    oaths are straw
    To the fire in the blood.

Prospero in *The Tempest*, 4.1.51–3

Cautioning Ferdinand and Miranda in their
lovemaking.

9   These lovers cry, O ho they die!
    Yet that which seems the wound to
    kill
    Doth turn O ho! to ha, ha, he!
    So dying love lives still.

Pandarus in *Troilus and Cressida*,
3.1.121–4

Pandarus's song about sexual consummation.

Shame

1   Alack, when once our grace we
    have forgot,
    Nothing goes right; we would, and
    we would not.

Angelo in *Measure for Measure*,
4.4.33–4

Ashamed, he thinks he has forced Isabella to
have sex with him, and executed her brother
Claudio; "grace" = sense of right, and the
divine grace given to man.

Shiftiness

1   You have been a boggler ever.

Antony in *Antony and Cleopatra*,
3.13.110

Accusing Cleopatra of having been always
shifty and unreliable.

Ships

1   The barge she sat in, like a burnished throne,
Burnt on the water. The poop was beaten gold;
Purple the sails, and so perfumèd that
The winds were love-sick with them.

Enobarbus in *Antony and Cleopatra*, 2.2.191–4

Describing Cleopatra as she first appeared to Antony, on the River Cydnus; quoted by T.S. Eliot in *The Waste Land*.

2   Play with your fancies: and in them behold
Upon the hempen tackle ship-boys climbing;
Hear the shrill whistle which doth order give
To sound confused; behold the threaden sails
Borne with th' invisible and creeping wind.

Chorus in *Henry V*, 3.Prologue, 7–11

Urging the audience to imagine ships sailing to France; "threaden" = woven with thread.

3   A city on th' inconstant billows dancing;
For so appears this fleet majestical.

Chorus in *Henry V*, 3.Prologue, 15–16

Imagining the English fleet sailing to France.

4   Ships are but boards, sailors but men; there be land-rats and water-rats, water-thieves and land-thieves, I mean pirates, and then there is the peril of waters, winds, and rocks.

Shylock in *The Merchant of Venice*, 1.3.22–5

On Antonio's business ventures, his goods sent off on various ships; the heavy-handed joke on "pi-rats" marks Shylock's odd sense of humor.

5   A rotten carcass of a butt, not rigged,
Nor tackle, sail, nor mast—the very rats
Instinctively have quit it.

Prospero in *The Tempest*, 1.2.146–8

Describing to Miranda the miserable boat ("butt" = cask) in which they were exiled from his dukedom.

6   Light boats sail swift, though greater hulks draw deep.

Agamemnon in *Troilus and Cressida*, 2.3.266

"Hulks" = larger and clumsier vessels, like Ajax and Achilles, the great but not very bright warriors of the Greeks.

Shopping

1   Haply your eye shall light upon some toy
You have desire to purchase.

Antonio in *Twelfth Night*, 3.3.44–5

Giving his friend Sebastian his purse; "Haply" = perhaps; "toy" = trifle.

Sickness (see also Medicine)

1   I know the more one sickens the worse at ease he is.

Corin in *As You Like It*, 3.2.23–4

On the basic facts of life.

2   I am ill, but your being by me
    Cannot amend me; society is no
    comfort
    To one not sociable. I am not very
    sick,
    Since I can reason of it.
    Imogen in *Cymbeline*, 4.2.11–14

    She is begging to be left alone.

3   Lay not that flattering unction to
    your soul,
    That not your trespass but my
    madness speaks;
    It will but skin and film the ulcer-
    ous place,
    Whilst rank corruption, mining all
    within,
    Infects unseen.
    Hamlet in *Hamlet*, 3.4.145–9

    To Gertrude, who thinks he is mad; "flattering
    unction" = soothing ointment of flattery.

4   Diseases desperate grown
    By desperate appliance are relieved,
    Or not at all.
    Claudius in *Hamlet*, 4.3.9–11

    Proverbial.

5   How has he the leisure to be
    sick
    In such a jostling time?
    Hotspur in *Henry IV, Part 1*, 4.1.17–18

    Referring to his father, who was to have
    brought an army to support Hotspur's rebellion
    against the king; "jostling time" = time of strife.

6   This sickness doth infect
    The very life-blood of our enter-
    prise.
    Hotspur in *Henry IV, Part 1*, 4.1.28–9

    The enterprise is the rebellion against King
    Henry; the sickness of Northumberland pre-
    vents him from taking part.

7   Worse than the sun in March,
    This praise doth nourish agues.
    Hotspur in *Henry IV, Part 1*, 4.1.111–12

    On hearing praise of Prince Hal; "agues" =
    fevers, thought to come from mists raised by
    the sun.

8   It is the disease of not listening, the
    malady of not marking, that I am
    troubled withal.
    Falstaff in *Henry IV, Part 2*, 1.2.121–2

    Refusing to heed the advice of the Chief Jus-
    tice.

9   In poison there is physic, and these
    news,
    Having been well, that would have
    made me sick,
    Being sick, have in some measure
    made me well.
    Northumberland in *Henry IV, Part 2*,
    1.1.137–9

    Bad news stimulates him to act.

10 A pox of this gout! Or a gout of
    this pox! For the one or the other
    plays the rogue with my great toe.
    Falstaff in *Henry IV, Part 2*, 1.2.243–5

    Diseases brought on by lechery ("pox" =
    syphilis) and drinking.

11 Before the curing of a strong dis-
    ease,
    Even in the instant of repair and
    health,
    The fit is strongest.
    Lewis the Dauphin in *King John*,
    3.4.112–14

    "Repair" = restoration, cure.

12 This fever that hath troubled me so
    long

Lies heavy on me. O, my heart is
sick!

King John in _King John_, 5.3.3–4

Spoken shortly before his death.

13 Infirmity doth still neglect all office
Whereto our health is bound; we
are not ourselves
When nature, being oppressed,
commands the mind
To suffer with the body.

King Lear in _King Lear_, 2.4.106–9

Ill health makes us neglect the duties ("all
office") we are obliged to do when well.

14   Where the greater malady is
fixed,
The lesser is scarce felt.

King Lear in _King Lear_, 3.4.8–9

His inner torment prevents Lear from being
troubled by the storm raging around him.

15 How now, which of your hips has
the most profound sciatica?

First Gentleman in _Measure for Measure_, 1.2.58–9

Greeting the bawd, Mistress Overdone.

16 For let our finger ache, and it
endues
Our other healthful members even
to a sense
Of pain.

Desdemona in _Othello_, 3.4.146–8

"Endues" = brings.

17   Be cured
Of this diseased opinion, and
betimes,
For 'tis most dangerous.

Camillo in _The Winter's Tale_, 1.2.296–8

Realizing Leontes is mentally unbalanced.

Silence

1 Thou art a soldier only, speak no
more.

Antony in _Antony and Cleopatra_, 2.2.107

Rebuking his lieutenant Enobarbus.

2 My gracious silence, hail!

Coriolanus in _Coriolanus_, 2.1.175

Returning victorious from battle, he at last
notices his wife, Virgilia.

3 Holds her by the hand, silent.

Stage Direction, _Coriolanus_, 5.3.182

This striking gesture to his mother marks the
yielding by Coriolanus to her plea that he
spare Rome, and leads to his death at the
hands of Aufidius.

4 The rest is silence.

Hamlet in _Hamlet_, 5.2.358

Hamlet's last words.

5 Madam, you have bereft me of all
words.

Bassanio in _The Merchant of Venice_, 3.2.175

6 Demand me nothing; what you
know, you know.
From this time forth I never will
speak word.

Iago in _Othello_, 5.2.303–4

7 _Troilus._ You have bereft me of all
words, lady.
Pandarus. Words pay no debts,
give her deeds.

Troilus and Cressida, 3.2.54–5

Echoing Bassanio, Troilus is overwhelmed by
his first encounter with Cressida; see 5 above.

8   I like your silence, it the more
      shows off
      Your wonder.
      Paulina in *The Winter's Tale,* 5.3.21–2

      Leontes is struck dumb on seeing, as he
      thinks, so lifelike a statue of Hermione.

Simplicity

1   How green you are, and fresh in
      this old world!
      Cardinal Pandulph in *King John,*
      3.4.145

      The Cardinal finds the young Dauphin of
      France to be politically naive.

2   Never anything can be amiss
      When simpleness and duty tender
      it.
      Theseus in *A Midsummer Night's*
      Dream, 5.1.82–3

3   Home-keeping youth have ever
      homely wits.
      Valentine in *The Two Gentlemen of*
      Verona, 1.1.2

Sin

1   I will weep for thee,
      For this revolt of thine methinks is
      like
      Another fall of man.
      King Henry in *Henry V,* 2.2.140–2

      Speaking to the traitor, Lord Scroop, and refer-
      ring to Adam's original transgression (Genesis
      3).

2   Forbear to judge, for we are sinners
      all.
      King Henry in *Henry VI, Part 2,* 3.3.31

      On the tormented dying of Cardinal Beaufort.

3   Some sins do bear their privilege on
      earth,
      And so doth yours; your fault was
      not your folly.
      The Bastard Falconbridge in *King*
      John, 1.1.261–2

      The Bastard Falconbridge tells his mother she
      is not to blame for her adultery; "do bear their
      privilege" = may be excused.

4   I am a man
      More sinned against than sinning.
      King Lear in *King Lear,* 3.2.59–60

      A dubious claim, as he has not yet come to
      terms with his own tyrannical behavior in
      casting out his daughter Cordelia.

5   Impose me to what penance your
      invention
      Can lay upon my sin; yet sinned I
      not
      But in mistaking.
      Claudio in *Much Ado About Nothing,*
      5.1.273–5

      Contrite after his public denunciation of Hero,
      he invites Leonato to subject him to any
      penance.

6   Few love to hear the sins they love
      to act.
      Pericles in *Pericles,* 1.1.92

      On discovering the incestuous relationship
      between King Antiochus and his daughter;
      "hear" = hear described.

7   One sin, I know, another doth pro-
      voke.

Murder's as near to lust as flame to smoke.

Pericles in *Pericles*, 1.1.137–8

Fearing for his life now he has revealed the incest of the King and his daughter.

8 Anything that's mended is but patched; virtue that transgresses is but patched with sin, and sin that amends is patched with virtue.

Feste in *Twelfth Night*, 1.5.47–9

The fool's understanding of human nature as imperfect.

Sincerity

1 I hold you as a thing enskied, and sainted,
By your renouncement an immortal spirit,
And to be talked with in sincerity,
As with a saint.

Lucio in *Measure for Measure*, 1.4.34–7

Addressing the novice Isabella at the gate of the nunnery; "enskied" = in heaven.

2 Pleads he in earnest? Look upon his face.
His eyes do drop no tears, his prayers are in jest.
His words come from his mouth; ours from our breast.
He prays but faintly, and would be denied;
We pray with heart and soul, and all beside.

Duchess of York in *Richard II*, 5.3.100–4

Pleading against her husband with Henry IV to save her traitorous son, Aumerle.

3 His words are bonds, his oaths are oracles,
His love sincere, his thoughts immaculate,
His tears pure messengers sent from his heart,
His heart as far from fraud as heaven from earth.

Julia in *The Two Gentlemen of Verona*, 2.7.75–8

Mistakenly trusting the unfaithful Proteus.

Singing

1 *Amiens.* My voice is ragged, I know I cannot please you.
Jaques. I do not desire you to please me, I do desire you to sing.

As You Like It, 2.5.15–18

2 Warble, child, make passionate my sense of hearing.

Armado in *Love's Labor's Lost*, 3.1.1–2

Armado's absurd way of asking his page, Moth, to sing.

3 I love a ballad but even too well, if it be doleful matter merrily set down, or a very pleasant thing indeed, and sung lamentably.

Clown in *The Winter's Tale*, 4.4.188–90

He likes a mixture of emotions in his ballads; "pleasant" = merry.

4 He has the prettiest love-songs for maids, so without bawdry, which is strange.

Servant in *The Winter's Tale*, 4.4.193–4

On Autolycus, who is peddling ballads.

Slander (see also Reputation)

1 For slander lives upon succession,
   For ever housèd where it gets possession.

   Balthazar in *The Comedy of Errors*,
   3.1.105–6

   "Lives upon succession" = is handed down
   from one generation to the next.

2   'Tis slander,
   Whose edge is sharper than the
   sword, whose tongue
   Outvenoms all the worms of Nile,
   whose breath
   Rides on the posting winds, and
   doth belie
   All corners of the world.

   Pisanio in *Cymbeline*, 3.4.33–7

   In early maps the winds were often shown as
   faces puffing from the four corners; "worms" =
   snakes, like the asp with which Cleopatra kills
   herself.

3 Be thou as chaste as ice, as pure as
   snow, thou shalt not escape
   calumny.

   Hamlet in *Hamlet*, 3.1.135–6

   Addressing Ophelia.

4 Upon my tongues continual slanders ride,
   The which in every language I pro-
   nounce,
   Stuffing the ears of men with false
   reports.

   **Rumor in *Henry IV, Part 2*, Induction,
   6–8**

5 No might nor greatness in mortality

Can censure scape; back-wounding
calumny
The whitest virtue strikes. What
king so strong
Can tie the gall up in the slanderous
tongue?

Duke in *Measure for Measure*, 3.2.185–8

Not even the most virtuous can escape
("scape") slander; the Duke, in disguise, has
listened to Lucio slandering him.

6 If thou dost slander her and torture
   me,
   Never pray more; abandon all
   remorse;
   On horror's head horrors accumu-
   late;
   Do deeds to make heaven weep, all
   earth amazed;
   For nothing canst thou to damnation add
   Greater than that.

   Othello in *Othello*, 3.3.368–73

   An ironic threat against Iago, since he does
   indeed slander Desdemona.

7 I am disgraced, impeached, and
   baffled here,
   Pierced to the soul with slander's
   venomed spear.

   Mowbray in *Richard II*, 1.1.170–1

   He has been accused of being a traitor; "baffled" = publicly denounced.

8   Calumny will sear
   Virtue itself.

   Leontes in *The Winter's Tale*, 2.1.73–4

   Varying the proverb, "envy shoots at the
   fairest mark."

9   Slander,
   Whose sting is sharper than the
   sword's.

Paulina in *The Winter's Tale*, 2.3.86–7

Convinced that Hermione is wrongly accused and slandered.

Sleep (see also Dreams)

1   Weariness
Can snore upon the flint, when resty sloth
Finds the down pillow hard.

Belarius in *Cymbeline*, 3.6.33–5

"Resty" = lazy, indolent.

2 Thy spirit within thee hath been so at war,
And thus hath so bestirred thee in thy sleep,
That beads of sweat have stood upon thy brow,
Like bubbles in a late-disturbèd stream.

Lady Percy in *Henry IV, Part 1*, 2.3.56–9

Describing Hotspur's troubled state of mind as he plots a rebellion against the king.

3 She will sing the song that pleaseth you,
And on your eyelids crown the god of sleep,
Charming your blood with pleasing heaviness.

Glendower in *Henry IV, Part 1*, 3.1.213–15

Translating his daughter's words to her husband, Mortimer.

4 Making such difference 'twixt wake and sleep
As is the difference betwixt day and night

The hour before the heavenly-harnessed team
Begins his golden progress in the east.

Glendower in *Henry IV, Part 1*, 3.1.216–19

Describing the effect his daughter's singing will have on her sleepy husband.

5 Why rather, sleep, liest thou in smoky cribs

. . .

Than in the perfumed chambers of the great,
Under the canopies of costly state,
And lulled with sound of sweetest melody?

King Henry in *Henry IV, Part 2*, 3.1.9, 12–14

Sleep comes easier in a smoky hovel ("crib") than in a palace.

6 Enjoy the honey-heavy dew of slumber.
Thou hast no figures, nor no fantasies,
Which busy care draws in the brains of men;
Therefore thou sleep'st so sound.

Brutus in *Julius Caesar*, 2.1.230–3

To his boy, Lucius, who has no anxieties.

7 I will not do thee so much wrong to wake thee.

Brutus in *Julius Caesar*, 4.3.270

His servant, Lucius, has fallen asleep.

8 Our foster-nurse of nature is repose.

Doctor in *King Lear*, 4.4.12

"Foster-nurse" = what naturally restores us.

9 A heavy summons lies like lead
     upon me,
   And yet I would not sleep.

Banquo in *Macbeth*, 2.1.6–7

Weariness summons him to sleep, but he is
troubled in mind.

10 Methought I heard a voice cry
      "Sleep no more!
    Macbeth does murder sleep," the
      innocent sleep,
    Sleep that knits up the ravelled
      sleave of care,
    The death of each day's life, sore
      labor's bath,
    Balm of hurt minds, great nature's
      second course,
    Chief nourisher in life's feast.

Macbeth in *Macbeth*, 2.2.32–7

"Ravelled sleave" = tangled thread; "second
course" = main and most nourishing course
(feasts had two courses as a rule).

11 You lack the season of all natures,
      sleep.

Lady Macbeth in *Macbeth*, 3.4.140

"Season" may mean necessary period of rest,
or the seasoning that preserves.

12   Thy best of rest is sleep,
    And that thou oft provok'st, yet
      grossly fear'st
    Thy death, which is no more.

Duke in *Measure for Measure*, 3.1.17–19

Disguised as a Friar, he is preparing Claudio
to face death.

13   Sleep, that sometimes shuts up
      sorrow's eye,
    Steal me awhile from mine own
      company.

*Helena in *A Midsummer Night's*
Dream,* 3.2.435–6

Thinking she is abandoned in the woods by
night.

14   Not poppy, nor mandragora,
     Nor all the drowsy syrups of the
       world
     Shall ever medicine thee to that
       sweet sleep
     Which thou owed'st yesterday.

Iago in *Othello*, 3.3.330–3

Opiates were derived from poppy (opium) and
mandragora (mandrake, of the deadly night-
shade family).

15 *Emilia.* How do you, madam? How
      do you, good lady?
    Desdemona. Faith, half asleep.

Othello, 4.2.96–7

Desdemona's reaction to being treated by
Othello as a whore seems wonderfully apt.

16 Thou art inclined to sleep; 'tis a
      good dullness,
    And give it way.

Prospero in *The Tempest*, 1.2.185–6

Putting Miranda to sleep by his magic; "dull-
ness" = drowsiness.

17 *Alonso.* What, all so soon asleep! I
      wish mine eyes
    Would, with themselves, shut up
      my thoughts. I find
    They are inclined to do so.
    Sebastian.   Please you, sir,
    Do not omit the heavy offer of it.
    It seldom visits sorrow; when it
      doth,
    It is a comforter.

The Tempest, 2.1.191–6

Ariel's music has made them drowsy.

18 When will this fearful slumber have
    an end?

Titus in *Titus Andronicus*, 3.1.252

Thinking all the horrors that have happened
may be a dream.

19 Weary with toil, I haste me to my
    bed,
    The dear repose for limbs with
    travel tired,
    But then begins a journey in my
    head
    To work my mind when body's
    work's expired.

Sonnet 27, 1–4

"Travel" was not distinguished from "travail"
or labor, the spelling in the first edition of
1609.

Sleeplessness

1   O sleep! O gentle sleep!
    Nature's soft nurse, how have I
    frighted thee,
    That thou no more wilt weigh my
    eyelids down,
    And steep my senses in forgetful-
    ness?

King Henry in *Henry IV, Part 2*, 3.1.5–8

The king, burdened with cares, cannot sleep.

2 I have been up this hour, awake all
    night.

Brutus in *Julius Caesar*, 2.1.88

Greeting Cassius and the conspirators against
Caesar.

3 What watchful cares do interpose
    themselves
    Betwixt your eyes and night?

Brutus in *Julius Caesar*, 2.1.98–9

"Watchful cares" = anxieties preventing sleep.

4 Sleep shall neither night nor day
    Hang upon his penthouse lid;
    He shall live a man forbid;
    Weary sev'n-nights, nine times
    nine,
    Shall he dwindle, peak and pine;
    Though his bark cannot be lost,
    Yet it shall be tempest-tossed.

First Witch in *Macbeth*, 1.3.19–25

Putting a curse on a ship's captain; "pent-
house lid" = eyelid, that slopes like a pent-
house roof; "forbid" = accursed; "peak and
pine" = waste away.

5 Still it cried, "Sleep no more!" to all
    the house:
    "Glamis hath murdered sleep, and
    therefore Cawdor
    Shall sleep no more, Macbeth shall
    sleep no more!"

Macbeth in *Macbeth*, 2.2.38–40

Imagining he hears a voice; Macbeth by now
is Thane (Lord) of Glamis and Cawdor.

6 For never yet one hour in his bed
    Did I enjoy the golden dew of sleep,
    But with his timorous dreams was
    still awaked.

Lady Anne in *Richard III*, 4.1.82–4

On the misery of being married to Richard III.

7 Care keeps his watch in every old
    man's eye,
    And where care lodges, sleep will
    never lie;
    But where unbruisèd youth with
    unstuffed brain
    Doth couch his limbs, there golden
    sleep doth reign.

**Friar Lawrence in *Romeo and Juliet*,
2.3.35–8**

The old friar is interrupted early in the morning by Romeo.

8   Nor night, nor day, no rest.
     Leontes in *The Winter's Tale*, 2.3.1
     Obsessed with the idea of his wife's adultery.

Snakes

1   He's speaking now,
     Or murmuring, "Where's my ser-
     pent of old Nile?"
     (For so he calls me).
     **Cleopatra in *Antony and Cleopatra*,
     1.5.24–6**

     Antony's affectionate phrase also suggests evil
     (Satan as serpent), and the "worm" that gives
     Cleopatra her death-wound.

2   *Cleopatra.* Hast thou the pretty
     worm of Nilus there,
     That kills and pains not?
     Clown. Truly, I have him; but I
     would not be the party that
     should desire you to touch him,
     for his biting is immortal; those
     that do die of it do seldom or
     never recover.
     ***Antony and Cleopatra*, 5.2.243–8**

     The Clown is delivering the asps with which
     Cleopatra kills herself.

3   Wouldst thou have a serpent sting
     thee twice?
     **Shylock in *The Merchant of Venice*,
     4.1.69**

     The "serpent" is Antonio, whose death he
     seeks.

Sobriety

1   This same young sober-blooded
     boy doth not love me, nor a man

cannot make him laugh, but that's
no marvel, he drinks no wine.
Falstaff in *Henry IV, Part 2*, 4.3.87–9

Referring to Prince John.

2   Let not the sound of shallow fop-
     pery enter
     My sober house.
     **Shylock in *The Merchant of Venice*,
     2.5.35–6**

     Telling his daughter Jessica to close up his
     house while he is away, and not listen to the
     Christians reveling outside.

Society (see also Fellowship, Hospitality)

1   Company, villainous company,
     hath been the spoil of me.
     Falstaff in *Henry IV, Part 1*, 3.3.9–10

     As usual putting the blame on others; "spoil"
     = ruin.

2   It is certain that either wise bearing
     or ignorant carriage is caught, as
     men take diseases, one of another;
     therefore let men take heed of their
     company.
     Falstaff in *Henry IV, Part 2*, 5.1.75–7

     "Carriage" = behavior.

3   He is given
     To sports, to wildness, and much
     company.
     Brutus in *Julius Caesar*, 2.1.188–9

     Describing Mark Antony.

4   Society, saith the text, is the happi-
     ness of life.
     Nathaniel in *Love's Labor's Lost*, 4.2.161

The "text" should be biblical, and possibly the reference is to Ecclesiastes 4:8–12, "Two are better than one," etc.

5   To make society
The sweeter welcome, we will keep
     ourself
Till supper-time alone.
Macbeth in *Macbeth*, 3.1.41–3

6   Nay, I'll go with thee, cheek by
jowl.
Demetrius in *A Midsummer Night's Dream*, 3.2.338

Going off to fight with Lysander.

7   I promise you, but for your company,
I would have been a-bed an hour
ago.
Capulet in *Romeo and Juliet*, 3.4.6–7

To Paris, who has been hoping to see Juliet.

8   I would not wish
Any companion in the world but
you.
Miranda in *The Tempest*, 3.1.54–5

Admitting her love for Ferdinand.

Soldiers (see also Fighting, War)

1   Then a soldier,
Full of strange oaths, and bearded
like the pard,
Jealous in honor, sudden, and
quick in quarrel,
Seeking the bubble reputation
Even in the cannon's mouth.
Jaques in *As You Like It*, 2.7.149–53

The fourth of the "seven ages" of man; he has moustaches (any facial hair was a beard) like a leopard.

2   If you have writ your annals true,
'tis there
That, like an eagle in a dove-cote, I
Fluttered your Volscians in Cori-
oles.
Alone I did it.
Coriolanus in *Coriolanus*, 5.3.113–16

Boasting of his achievements in battle.

3   Sharked up a list of lawless res-
olutes.
For food and diet to some enter-
prise
That hath a stomach in't.
Horatio in *Hamlet*, 1.1.98–100

Speaking of young Fortinbras of Norway and his way of getting an army together; "sharked up" = collected up indiscriminately.

4   Let four captains
Bear Hamlet like a soldier to the
stage,
For he was likely, had he been put
on,
To have proved most royal.
Fortinbras in *Hamlet*, 5.2.395–8

Hamlet's body is treated with respect; "stage" = platform (it is not clear how this was staged); "put on" = tested by becoming king.

5   I will redeem all this on Percy's
head,
And in the closing of some glorious
day,
Be bold to tell you that I am your
son.
Prince Hal in *Henry IV, Part 1*, 3.2.132–4

To his father, boasting that he will defeat the renowned Hotspur.

6   I saw young Harry with his beaver
    on,
    His cuishes on his thighs, gallantly
    armed,
    Rise from the ground like feathered
    Mercury,
    And vaulted with such ease into his
    seat
    As if an angel dropped down from
    the clouds
    To turn and wind a fiery Pegasus,
    And witch the world with noble
    horsemanship.

Vernon in *Henry IV, Part 1*, 4.1.104–10

Prince Hal, ready to fight against the rebels;
"beaver" = helmet; "cuishes" = cuisses, thigh
armor; "Mercury" was the messenger of the
gods, who had winged heels; "wind" = wheel
round; "Pegasus" = mythical flying horse.

7   Tut, tut, good enough to toss, food
    for powder, food for powder; they'll
    fill a pit as well as better. Tush,
    man, mortal men, mortal men.

Falstaff in *Henry IV, Part 1*, 4.2.65–7

Describing his conscripts; "powder" = gun-
powder (compare the modern "cannon fod-
der").

8   I do not think a braver gentleman,
    More active-valiant or more
    valiant-young,
    More daring, or more bold, is now
    alive
    To grace this latter age with noble
    deeds.

**Prince Hal in *Henry IV, Part 1*,
5.1.89–92**

Praising Hotspur.

9   Be he as he will, yet once ere night
    I will embrace him with a soldier's
    arm
    That he shall shrink under my
    courtesy.

Hotspur in *Henry IV, Part 1*, 5.2.72–4

Promising to fight with Prince Hal.

10 A soldier is better accommodated
    than with a wife.

Bardolph in *Henry IV, Part 2*, 3.2.66–7

Referring to Falstaff who is provided ("accommodated") with Doll Tearsheet as a companion.

11 He hath a killing tongue and a quiet
    sword.

Boy in *Henry V*, 3.2.34

On ancient Pistol.

12   As I am a soldier,
    A name that in my thoughts
    becomes me best.

King Henry in *Henry V*, 3.3.5–6

13 A soldier firm and sound of heart.

Pistol in *Henry V*, 3.6.25

Praising Bardolph, who is to be hanged for
stealing from a church.

14   Art thou officer,
    Or art thou base, common, and
    popular?

Pistol in *Henry V*, 4.1.37–8

Addressing the king, who is disguised.

15 A good old commander and a most
    kind gentleman.

Williams in *Henry V*, 4.1.95–6

On Sir Thomas Erpingham.

16 We are but warriors for the work-
    ing day.
    Our gayness and our gilt are all
    besmirched

With rainy marching in the painful field.

King Henry in *Henry V*, 4.3.109–11

On the bedraggled English army.

17 I speak to thee plain soldier. If thou canst love me for this, take me.

King Henry in *Henry V*, 5.2.149–50

His method of making love to the French Princess Katherine.

18 Your son, my lord, has paid a soldier's debt.

Ross in *Macbeth*, 5.9.5

On young Siward, killed in battle.

19   Mere prattle without practice
Is all his soldiership.

Iago in *Othello*, 1.1.26–7

Abusing Cassio to Roderigo.

20 I have served him, and the man commands
Like a full soldier.

Montano in *Othello*, 2.1.35–6

Referring to Othello.

21 You may relish him more in the soldier than in the scholar.

Cassio in *Othello*, 2.1.165–6

Cassio's account of Iago.

22   A soldier's a man,
O, man's life's but a span,
Why then, let a soldier drink.

Iago in *Othello*, 2.3.71–3

A "span" is literally a hand's breadth from thumb to little finger; here a short time, as in Psalms 38:5 (Book of Common Prayer); the phrase "life's but a span" became proverbial.

23 He's a soldier fit to stand by Caesar
And give direction.

Iago in *Othello*, 2.3.122–3

Praising Cassio to Montano (but see 19 above).

24   'Tis the soldier's life
To have their balmy slumbers
waked with strife.

Othello in *Othello*, 2.3.257–8

25   But we are soldiers,
And may that soldier a mere recreant prove,
That means not, hath not, or is not in love.

Agamemnon in *Troilus and Cressida*, 1.3.286–8

Responding to Hector's challenge; "recreant" = traitor.

Solecisms

1 Dost thou infamonize me among potentates?

Armado in *Love's Labor's Lost*, 5.2.678

Getting wrong "infamonize" = defame, and overdoing it with "potentates" in reference to the company with him.

2 I pray, let none of your people stir me; I have an exposition of sleep come upon me.

Bottom in *A Midsummer Night's Dream*, 4.1.38–9

Presumably meaning "a disposition to."

3   *Quince.* He is a very paramour for
a sweet voice.
Flute. You must say "paragon." A
paramour is, God bless us, a thing
of naught.

A Midsummer Night's Dream,
4.2.11–14

Comically alluding to Bottom, who has been
temporarily Titania's paramour.

4   *Dogberry.* Are you good men and
true?
Verges. Yea, or else it were pity but
they should suffer salvation, body
and soul.

Much Ado About Nothing, 3.3.1–3

Possibly the earliest comic policemen
addressing the watchmen; Verges means to
say "damnation."

5   Comparisons are odorous.
**Dogberry in *Much Ado About
Nothing,*** 3.5.16

Meaning "odious," and getting the proverb
amusingly wrong.

6   O villain! Thou wilt be condemned
into everlasting redemption for
this.
**Dogberry in *Much Ado About
Nothing,*** 4.2.56–7

Interrogating his prisoner, Borachio; he means
to say "damnation," not "redemption."

Solitude (see also Isolation)

1   I had as lief have been myself alone.
Jaques in *As You Like It,* 3.2.254

Preferring to be left alone.

2   I and my bosom must debate
awhile,
And then I would no other company.
King Henry in *Henry V,* 4.1.31–2

Preparing himself for battle.

3   Then how can it be said I am alone
When all the world is here to look
on me?
**Helena in *A Midsummer Night's
Dream,*** 2.11

Her world is Demetrius, with whom she is
alone.

4   I myself am best
When least in company.
Orsino in *Twelfth Night,* 1.4.37–8

The lovesick Orsino prefers to be alone.

5   Here can I sit alone, unseen of any,
And to the nightingale's complain-
ing notes
Tune my distresses and record my
woes.
**Valentine in *The Two Gentlemen of
Verona,*** 5.4.4–6

Sorrow (see also Affliction, Grief, Mourning)

1   When sorrows come, they come
not single spies,
But in battalions.
Claudius in *Hamlet,* 4.5.78–9

Proverbial; "spies" = soldiers sent ahead to
reconnoiter.

2   One woe doth tread upon another's
heel,

So fast they follow.

Gertrude in *Hamlet*, 4.7.163–4

Ophelia's death by drowning follows on the killing of Polonius.

3   Down, thou climbing sorrow,
    Thy element's below.

King Lear in *King Lear*, 2.4.57–8

Afraid his heart will burst; "element" = proper place.

4   Let us seek out some desolate
    shade, and there
    Weep our sad bosoms empty.

Malcolm in *Macbeth*, 4.3.1–2

5   Each new morn
  New widows howl, new orphans
    cry, new sorrows
  Strike heaven on the face.

Macduff in *Macbeth*, 4.3.4–6

On the affliction Macbeth has brought to Scotland.

6   My particular grief
  Is of so flood-gate and o'erbearing
    nature
  That it engluts and swallows other
    sorrows,
  And it is still itself.

Brabantio in *Othello*, 1.3.55–8

Overwhelmed (as if a "flood-gate" were open) by the loss of his daughter, his grief engulfs ("engluts") other feelings.

7   One sorrow never comes but brings
    an heir
  That may succeed as his inheritor.

Cleon in *Pericles*, 1.4.63–4

Proverbial.

8   Sorrow ends not when it seemeth
    done.

Duchess of Gloucester in *Richard II*, 1.2.61

Lamenting her murdered husband.

9   For gnarling sorrow hath less power
    to bite
  The man that mocks at it and sets it
    light.

John of Gaunt in *Richard II*, 1.3.292–3

"Gnarling" = biting or snarling; "sets it light" = makes light of it.

10   Sorrow and grief of heart
  Makes him speak fondly like a fran-
    tic man.

Northumberland in *Richard II*, 3.3.184–5

Reporting the behavior of Richard to Henry Bolingbroke; "fondly" = foolishly.

11 Sorrow breaks seasons and reposing
    hours,
  Makes the night morning and the
    noontide night.

Brakenbury in *Richard III*, 1.4.76–7

Commenting on Clarence, whose terrible dream kept him awake all night.

12 Griefs of mine own lie heavy in my
    breast.

Romeo in *Romeo and Juliet*, 1.1.186

Meaning his unrequited love for Rosaline.

13   All these woes shall serve
  For sweet discourses in our times to
    come.

Romeo in *Romeo and Juliet*, 3.5.52–3

Leaving Juliet and Verona as a banished man.

14 Is there no pity sitting in the clouds,
That sees into the bottom of my
grief?
Juliet in *Romeo and Juliet*, 3.5.196–7

To her mother, making grief for her cousin
Tybalt's death a reason for delaying the pro-
posed marriage with Paris.

15 For never was a story of more woe
Than this of Juliet and her Romeo.
**Prince of Escalus in *Romeo and Juliet*,
5.3.309–10**

The Prince of Verona pronouncing an epitaph
on the dead lovers.

16 I have, as when the sun doth light a
storm,
Buried this sigh in wrinkle of a
smile;
But sorrow that is couched in seeming gladness
Is like that mirth fate turns to sudden sadness.
**Troilus in *Troilus and Cressida*,
1.1.37–40**

He has been pretending to be happy in order
to conceal his lovesickness from his brother
and father.

17 If all the world could have seen 't,
the woe had been universal.
**Third Gentleman in *The Winter's
Tale*, 5.2.91–2**

On the reporting of the (supposed) death of
Hermione.

18 Though woe be heavy, yet it seldom
sleeps,
And they that watch see time how
slow it creeps.
***The Rape of Lucrece*, 1574–5**

The Soul

1 I do not set my life at a pin's fee,
And for my soul, what can it do to
that,
Being a thing immortal as itself?
Hamlet in *Hamlet*, 1.4.65–7

Determined to follow the ghost, not knowing
whether it is a good or evil spirit; "fee" =
worth.

2 Well, God's above all; and there be
souls must be saved, and there be
souls must not be saved.
Cassio in *Othello*, 2.3.102–4

Cassio, tipsy, may be recalling such biblical
phrases as "whosoever shall call on the name
of the Lord shall be saved" (Acts 2:21).

3 I think nobly of the soul.
Malvolio in *Twelfth Night*, 4.2.55

Protesting his sanity.

4 Poor soul, the center of my sinful
earth.
***Sonnet* 146, 1**

"Earth" is both the speaker's body ("The first
man is of the earth, earthy," I Corinthians
15:47), and his world.

Speculation

1 In my school-days, when I had lost
one shaft,
I shot his fellow of the self-same
flight
The self-same way with more
advisèd watch
To find the other forth, and by
adventuring both
I oft found both.

Bassanio in *The Merchant of Venice*,
1.1.140–4

The image is from archery; "advised watch" = careful estimation; "forth" = out.

Speech (see also Eloquence, Talking, Words)

1 What I think I utter, and spend my malice in my breath.

Menenius in *Coriolanus*, 2.1.53–4

2   His heart's his mouth;
What his breast forges, that his tongue must vent.

Volumnia in *Coriolanus*, 3.1.256–7

3 Speaking thick, which nature made his blemish,
Became the accents of the valiant;
For those that could speak low and tardily
Would turn their own perfection to abuse
To seem like him.

Lady Percy in *Henry IV, Part 2*, 2.3.24–8

Everyone tried to adopt Hotspur's impetuous ("thick") way of speaking.

4 Good phrases are surely, and ever were, very commendable.

Shallow in *Henry IV, Part 2*, 3.2.70–1

He is impressed by Bardolph's rather absurd use of the word "accommodated" in relation to Falstaff and Doll Tearsheet.

5 Wherefore do you so ill translate yourself
Out of the speech of peace that bears such grace,

Into the harsh and boisterous tongue of war?

Westmorland in *Henry IV, Part 2*,
4.1.47–9

On an archbishop transforming (translating) himself into a soldier, and changing his speech.

6 Speak on, but be not over-tedious.

Burgundy in *Henry VI, Part 1*, 3.3.43

Allowing Joan la Pucelle (Joan of Arc) to have her say.

7 For things are often spoke and seldom meant.

Suffolk in *Henry VI, Part 2*, 3.1.268

Claiming that he always means what he says.

8 I have neither wit, nor words, nor worth,
Action, nor utterance, nor the power of speech
To stir men's blood; I only speak right on.

Mark Antony in *Julius Caesar*, 3.2.221–3

He has already stirred the people in speaking about the killing of Caesar.

9   I cannot heave
My heart into my mouth. I love your Majesty
According to my bond, no more nor less.

Cordelia in *King Lear*, 1.1.91–3

"Bond" disturbingly suggests the natural tie between father and child, but also a formal agreement or limitation, and a fetter.

10   Mend your speech a little,
Lest you may mar your fortunes.

King Lear in *King Lear*, 1.1.94–5

On Cordelia refusing to say she loves him.

11 Thy youngest daughter does not
   love thee least,
   Nor are those empty-hearted whose
   low sounds
   Reverb no hollowness.
   Kent in *King Lear*, 1.1.152–4

Proverbial ("the emptiest vessel makes the
greatest sound").

12   Her voice was ever soft,
   Gentle, and low, an excellent thing
   in woman.
   King Lear in *King Lear*, 5.3.273–4

Referring to his daughter Cordelia.

13 It is not enough to speak, but to
   speak true.
   **Lysander in *A Midsummer Night's
   Dream*,** 5.1.120

Quince's misreading of the prologue to "Pyramus and Thisbe" prompts Lysander to think of
this "good moral."

14 She speaks poniards, and every
   word stabs.
   Benedick in *Much Ado About Nothing*,
   2.1.247–8

On Beatrice's sharp tongue.

15 If her breath were as terrible as her
   terminations, there were no living
   near her; she would infect to the
   north star.
   Benedick in *Much Ado About Nothing*,
   2.1.248–50

On Beatrice's sharp tongue; "terminations" =
the barbed endings of her sentences.

16 He was wont to speak plain and to
   the purpose, like an honest man

and a soldier, and now is he turned
orthography; his words are a very
fantastical banquet, just so many
strange dishes.
Benedick in *Much Ado About Nothing*,
2.3.18–21

On Claudio's rhetorical flourishes now he has
become a lover; "turned orthography" =
become pedantic.

17 He hath a heart as sound as a bell
   and his tongue is the clapper, for
   what his heart thinks, his tongue
   speaks.
   **Don Pedro in *Much Ado About Noth-
   ing*,** 3.2.12–14

Praising Benedick.

18   Rude am I in my speech,
   And little blessed with the soft
   phrase of peace.
   Othello in *Othello*, 1.3.81–2

Eloquently addressing the Venetian senate.

19   Little of this great world can I
   speak
   More than pertains to feats of broils
   and battle,
   And therefore little shall I grace my
   cause
   In speaking for myself.
   Othello in *Othello*, 1.3.86–9

Othello in fact speaks magnificently; "broils"
= quarrels or fights.

20 Soft you, a word or two before you
   go.
   Othello in *Othello*, 5.2.338

Prefacing his final speech; "soft you" = hold
on, wait a moment.

21 Speak of me as I am; nothing exten-
uate,
Nor set down aught in malice.
Othello in *Othello*, 5.2.342–3

22 Your fair discourse hath been as
sugar,
Making the hard way sweet and
delectable.
Northumberland in *Richard II*, 2.3.6–7

Flattering Henry Bolingbroke.

23 You never spoke what did become
you less
Than this.
Camillo in *The Winter's Tale*, 1.2.282–3

On hearing Leontes accuse his wife of adultery.

Speechmaking (see also Eloquence)

1 I'll mountebank their
loves,
Cog their hearts from them, and
come home beloved
Of all the trades in Rome.
Coriolanus in *Coriolanus*, 3.2.132–4

Promising his mother he will dissemble like a
quack medicine-man ("mountebank"), and
beguile ("Cog") the citizens into voting for
him.

2 Hear me for my cause, and be
silent, that you may hear.
Brutus in *Julius Caesar*, 3.2.13–14

Opening his speech to the people after the
death of Caesar.

3 In the modesty of fearful duty
I read as much as from the rattling
tongue
Of saucy and audacious eloquence.
Love, therefore, and tongue-tied
simplicity
In least speak most, to my capacity.
**Theseus in *A Midsummer Night's
Dream*, 5.1.101–5**

"To my capacity" = in my judgment.

4 Runs not this speech like iron
through your blood?
**Don Pedro in *Much Ado About Noth-
ing*, 5.1.245**

To Claudio, on learning they were misled into
thinking Hero false.

5 *Katherine.* Where did you study all
this goodly speech?
Petruchio. It is extempore, from my
mother-wit.
The Taming of the Shrew, 2.1.262–3

Petruchio has been praising Katherine for
sweetness of temper.

6 I would be loath to cast away my
speech, for besides that it is excellently well penned, I have taken
great pains to con it.
Viola in *Twelfth Night*, 1.5.172–4

Addressing Olivia with a speech on behalf of
Orsino; "con" = learn by heart.

Speed

1 Celerity is never more admired
Than by the negligent.
**Cleopatra in *Antony and Cleopatra*,
3.7.24–5**

"A good rebuke," as Antony remarks.

2 I have speeded hither with the very
   extremest inch of possibility.
   Falstaff in *Henry IV, Part 2*, 4.3.34–5

   Excusing himself for being late.

3   We may outrun
   By violent swiftness that which we
     run at,
   And lose by over-running.
   Norfolk in *Henry VIII*, 1.1.141–3

   Varying the proverb, "make haste slowly"
   (Latin "festina lente").

4 I will be here again, even with a
   thought.
   Titinius in *Julius Caesar*, 5.3.19

   Reporting to Cassius on the state of the battle
   of Philippi.

5 I drink the air before me, and
     return
   Or ere your pulse twice beat.
   Ariel in *The Tempest*, 5.1.102–3

   To Prospero, as he is sent off to fetch the captain and boatswain of Alonso's ship.

Sport

1 What sport shall we devise here in
     this garden
   To drive away the heavy thought of
     care?
   Queen in *Richard II*, 3.4.1–2

   Speaking to the women who attend on her.

2 There be some sports are painful,
     and their labor
   Delight in them sets off.
   Ferdinand in *The Tempest*, 3.1.1–2

   Forced by Prospero to heave logs, Ferdinand
   finds consolation in his love for Miranda.

3 Hark what good sport is out of
   town today.
   Aeneas in *Troilus and Cressida*, 1.1.113

   By "sport" he means fighting with the Greeks.

Spring, see Seasons

Stoicism

1 A man that Fortune's buffets and
     rewards
   Hath ta'en with equal thanks.
   Hamlet in *Hamlet*, 3.2.67–8

   Describing his friend Horatio.

2 *Brutus.* Now, as you are a Roman,
     tell me true.
   Messala. Then like a Roman bear
     the truth I tell,
   For certain she is dead, and by
     strange manner.
   Brutus. Why, farewell, Portia. We
     must die, Messala.
   ***Julius Caesar*,** 4.3.187–90

   Brutus's stoic response to the news of the
   death of his wife.

Stories

1 If thou didst ever hold me in thy
     heart,
   Absent thee from felicity awhile,
   And in this harsh world draw thy
     breath in pain
   To tell my story.
   Hamlet in *Hamlet*, 5.2.346–9

   As he lies dying, he prevents Horatio from
   committing suicide; Hamlet pleads with him
   to live on to tell the world the truth.

2 So shall you hear
Of carnal, bloody, and unnatural
acts,
Of accidental judgments, casual
slaughters,
Of deaths put on by cunning and
forced cause,
And in this upshot, purposes mis-
took,
Fallen on the inventors' heads.

Horatio in *Hamlet*, 5.2.380–5

Horatio's version of events makes *Hamlet*
sound like a detective fiction.

3 Yet by your gracious
patience
I will a round unvarnished tale
deliver
Of my whole course of love.

Othello in *Othello*, 1.3.89–91

Explaining to the Venetian senate his
courtship of Desdemona.

4 If I should tell my history, 'twould
seem
Like lies, disdained in the reporting.

Marina in *Pericles*, 5.1.118–19

In response to Pericles's questions about her;
"in the reporting" = in the act of telling.

5 For God's sake let us sit upon the
ground
And tell sad stories of the death of
kings.

King Richard in *Richard II*, 3.2.155–6

Yielding to despair, and foreshadowing his
own death.

6 *First Lady.* Madam, we'll tell tales.
Queen. Of sorrow or of joy?
First Lady. Of either, madam.
Queen. Of neither, girl.
For if of joy, being altogether want-
ing,

It doth remember me the more of
sorrow.
Or if of grief, being altogether had,
It adds more sorrow to my want of
joy.

Richard II, 3.4.10–16

"Remember" = remind.

7 In winter's tedious nights, sit by the
fire
With good old folks, and let them
tell thee tales
Of woeful ages long ago betid.

King Richard in *Richard II*, 5.1.40–2

Speaking to his queen as if he were a character in an old tale.

8 An honest tale speeds best being
plainly told.

**Queen Elizabeth in *Richard III*,
4.4.357–8**

Responding to Richard's flattery; "speeds" =
succeeds.

9 I'll to thy closet and go read with
thee
Sad stories chancèd in the times of
old.

Titus in *Titus Andronicus*, 3.2.82–3

To his mutilated daughter, Lavinia; "closet" =
private room.

10 *Hermione.* Pray you sit by us,
And tell's a tale.
Mamillius. Merry or sad shall't be?
Hermione. As merry as you will.
Mamillius. A sad tale's best for
winter. I have one
Of sprites and goblins.

The Winter's Tale, 2.1.22–6

Mother and child are talking; a "winter's tale"
was the sort of fable or old wives' tale that
would pass the time on a dark winter evening.

Storms

1   The southern wind
Doth play the trumpet to his purposes,
And by his hollow whistling in the
leaves,
Foretells a tempest and a blustering
day.

Prince Hal in *Henry IV, Part 1*, 5.1.3–6

The day he fights the rebels at the battle of
Shrewsbury.

2   When from thy shore the tempest
beat us back,
I stood upon the hatches in the
storm.

Queen Margaret in *Henry VI, Part 2*,
3.2.102–3

Her account of sailing to England.

3   Who ever knew the heavens menace so?

Casca in *Julius Caesar*, 1.3.44

On the night before the assassination of Caesar.

4   Why now, blow wind, swell billow,
and swim bark!
The storm is up, and all is on the
hazard.

Cassius in *Julius Caesar*, 5.1.67–8

Anticipating the battle to come.

5   So foul a sky clears not without a
storm.

King John in *King John*, 4.2.108

He refers to the consequences of the death of
his nephew, young Arthur.

6   Alack, the night comes on, and the
bleak winds

Do sorely ruffle; for many miles
about
There's scarce a bush.

Gloucester in *King Lear*, 2.4.300–2

As Lear rushes off into the storm; "ruffle" =
rage.

7   Blow, winds, and crack your
cheeks! Rage, blow!
You cataracts and hurricanoes,
spout
Till you have drenched our steeples,
drowned the cocks!

King Lear in *King Lear*, 3.2.1–3

Cast out in the storm, he welcomes it with a
storm of words; "cocks" = weathercocks.

8   And thou, all-shaking thunder,
Strike flat the thick rotundity o' the
world!
Crack nature's molds, all germens
spill at once
That makes ingrateful man!

King Lear in *King Lear*, 3.2.6–9

Jupiter spoke in thunder, which is the voice of
God in the book of Job too; "molds" are the
forms with which nature creates living beings;
"germens" = seeds.

9   Rumble thy bellyful! Spit, fire!
Spout, rain!
Nor rain, wind, thunder, fire are
my daughters.
I tax you not, you elements, with
unkindness;
I never gave you kingdom, called
you children.

King Lear in *King Lear*, 3.2.14–17

Welcoming thunder, lightning and rain in his
anger.

10   Since I was man,
Such sheets of fire, such bursts of
horrid thunder,

Such groans of roaring wind and
rain, I never
Remember to have heard. Man's
nature cannot carry
Th'affliction nor the fear.

Kent in *King Lear*, 3.2.45–9

Describing the storm as more than human
nature can bear ("carry").

11   O my soul's joy,
If after every tempest come such
calms,
May the winds blow till they have
wakened death!
And let the laboring bark climb
hills of seas
Olympus-high, and duck again as
low
As hell's from heaven!

Othello in *Othello*, 2.1.184–9

On finding Desdemona safe in Cyprus; Mount
Olympus was the seat of the ancient Greek
gods.

12 Yet cease your ire, you angry stars
of heaven!
Wind, rain, and thunder, remember earthly man
Is but a substance that must yield to
you.

Pericles in *Pericles*, 2.1.1–3

Seeing the storm that has shipwrecked him as
marking the anger of the heavens.

13 The god of this great vast, rebuke
these surges,
Which wash both heaven and hell;
and thou that hast
Upon the winds command, bind
them in brass,
Having called them from the deep!
O, still
Thy deaf'ning dreadful thunders,
gently quench

Thy nimble sulphurous flashes!

Pericles in *Pericles*, 3.1.1–6

Pericles is imagined as on shipboard in a
storm; "vast" = huge desolate sea (suggesting
also "waste").

14 The sky it seems would pour down
stinking pitch,
But that the sea, mounting to the
welkin's cheek,
Dashes the fire out.

Miranda in *The Tempest*, 1.2.3–5

Describing the storm she has seen; "welkin's
cheek" = the clouds in the sky.

15 Here's neither bush nor shrub to
bear off any weather at all. And
another storm brewing, I hear it
sing i' the wind. Yond same black
cloud, yond huge one, looks like a
foul bombard that would shed his
liquor. If it should thunder as it did
before, I know not where to hide
my head. Yond same cloud cannot
choose but fall by pailfuls.

Trinculo in *The Tempest*, 2.2.18–24

A "bombard" was a large leather container for
liquor.

16 I will here shroud till the dregs of
the storm be past.

Trinculo in *The Tempest*, 2.2.40–1

Taking cover under Caliban's cloak.

17 When heaven doth weep, doth not
the earth o'erflow?
If the winds rage, doth not the sea
wax mad,
Threatening the welkin with his
big-swollen face?

Titus in *Titus Andronicus*, 3.1.221–3

Titus is raging at the barbarous mutilation of
his daughter.

18   I never saw
The heavens so dim by day. A savage clamor!

Antigonus in *The Winter's Tale*,
3.3.55–6

The ominous storm bodes the death of
Antigonus.

Strength

1   Then join you with them like a rib
of steel,
To make strength stronger.

Lady Percy in *Henry IV, Part 2*, 2.3.54–5

Advising Northumberland not to join rebels in
fighting the king until he is sure of their
power.

2   O, it is excellent
To have a giant's strength, but it is
tyrannous
To use it like a giant.

Isabella in *Measure for Measure*,
2.2.107–9

3   Love give me strength, and strength
shall help afford!

Juliet in *Romeo and Juliet*, 4.1.125

She needs strength to take the drug Friar
Lawrence has given her.

Study (see also Books, Education, Learning)

1   *Berowne.* What is the end of study,
let me know?
King of Navarre. Why, that to
know which else we should not
know.

Love's Labor's Lost, 1.1.55–6

Speaking of the little academy they propose to
set up.

2   Study is like the heaven's glorious
sun,
That will not be deep searched with
saucy looks;
Small have continual plodders ever
won,
Save base authority from others'
books.

Berowne in *Love's Labor's Lost*, 1.1.84–7

"Small" = little; "base" = second-hand, hack-
neyed.

3   So study evermore is overshot;
While it doth study to have what it
would.
It doth forget to do the thing it
should.

Berowne in *Love's Labor's Lost*,
1.1.142–4

Proposing to keep away from women, his
companions have forgotten a planned visit by
the Princess of France; "is overshot" = misses
the target.

4   No profit grows where is no pleasure ta'en.
In brief, sir, study what you most
affect.

Tranio in *The Taming of the Shrew*,
1.1.39–40

Advising his master Lucentio; "affect" = find
pleasing.

5   My books and instruments shall be
my company,
On them to look and practice by
myself.

Bianca in *The Taming of the Shrew*,
1.1.82–3

To her father Baptista, submitting (for the
moment) to his wishes.

Stupidity

1 O that he were here to write me
down an ass! But, masters, remember that I am an ass; though it be
not written down, yet forget not
that I am an ass.
**Dogberry in *Much Ado About
Nothing*, 4.2.75–8**

Keen to have his own stupidity recorded for
posterity.

2 The plague of Greece upon thee,
thou mongrel beef-witted lord!
**Thersites in *Troilus and Cressida*,
2.1.12–13**

Bandying insults with Ajax; a diet of beef was
thought to make people stupid.

3 Thou hast no more brain than I
have in mine elbows.
**Thersites in *Troilus and Cressida*,
2.1.43–4**

Insulting the slow-witted Ajax.

4 An honest fellow enough, and one
that loves quails, but he has not so
much brain as ear-wax.
**Thersites in *Troilus and Cressida*,
5.1.51–3**

His description of Agamemnon, the leader of
the Greeks.

Suffering (see also Affliction, Grief)

1 You do me wrong to take me out o'
the grave:
Thou art a soul in bliss, but I am
bound
Upon a wheel of fire, that mine
own tears
Do scald like molten lead.
King Lear in *King Lear*, 4.7.44–7

Lear thinks he is in hell; in classical and Christian mythology a wheel of fire was a traditional form of torture for the damned.

2 Vex not his ghost. O, let him pass;
he hates him
That would upon the rack of this
tough world
Stretch him out longer.
Kent in *King Lear*, 5.3.314–6

On the dying King Lear; "ghost" = departing
spirit.

3 He jests at scars that never felt a
wound.
Romeo in *Romeo and Juliet*, 2.2.1

The lover responds to the mockery of Mercutio and Benvolio.

4   O, I have suffered
With those that I saw suffer!
Miranda in *The Tempest*, 1.2.5–6

She thinks she has seen a ship wrecked, and
all the crew drowned.

Suicide (see also Death-Wish)

1   There is left us
Ourselves to end ourselves.
**Antony in *Antony and Cleopatra*,
4.14.21–2**

His despairing last resort.

2 The long day's task is done,
And we must sleep.
**Antony in *Antony and Cleopatra*,
4.14.35–6**

Deciding to die, on hearing of Cleopatra's
supposed death.

3   Since the torch is out,
Lie down and stray no further.

Antony in *Antony and Cleopatra*,
4.14.46–7

The "torch" is the light of his life, Cleopatra.

4   I will be
A bridegroom in my death, and run
    into't
As to a lover's bed.

Antony in *Antony and Cleopatra*,
4.14.99–101

Turning suicide into a fantasy of marriage.

5   None but Antony
Should conquer Antony.

Cleopatra in *Antony and Cleopatra*,
4.15.16–17

For her suicide shows the courage to remain in control of oneself.

6   Is it sin
To rush into the secret house of
    death
Ere death dare come to us?

Cleopatra in *Antony and Cleopatra*,
4.15.80–2

Contemplating suicide, and perhaps recalling oddly the biblical injunction against killing, as at Matthew 5:21.

7   What's brave, what's noble,
Let's do't after the high Roman
    fashion,
And make death proud to take us.

Cleopatra in *Antony and Cleopatra*,
4.15.86–8

Determined to control her destiny.

8   It is great
To do that thing that ends all other
    deeds,

Which shackles accidents and bolts
up change.

Cleopatra in *Antony and Cleopatra*,
5.2.4–6

Contemplating suicide after Antony's death, in the Stoic fashion defended by Seneca as a positive act.

9   Bravest at the last,
She leveled at our purposes, and
    being royal
Took her own way.

Octavius Caesar in *Antony and Cleopatra*, 5.2.335–7

Finding Cleopatra dead by her own hand.

10   Against self-slaughter
There is a prohibition so divine
That cravens my weak hand.

Imogen in *Cymbeline*, 3.4.76–8

Alluding to the Christian injunction against suicide.

11 O that this too too solid flesh would
    melt,
Thaw, and resolve itself into a dew!
Or that the Everlasting had not
    fixed
His canon 'gainst self-slaughter!

Hamlet in *Hamlet*, 1.2.129–32

"Canon" = the Sixth Commandment, "Thou shalt not kill"; "solid" puns on "sullied," contaminated.

12 To be or not to be, that is the ques-
    tion.

Hamlet in *Hamlet*, 3.1.55

Taken by itself, this most famous of Hamlet's lines suggests a death-wish, though he goes on to define the "question" as a choice between endurance and action (see also Choice 1).

13 For who would bear the whips and
    scorns of time,

Th'oppressor's wrong, the proud
man's contumely,
The pangs of despised love, the
law's delay,
The insolence of office, and the
spurns
That patient merit of the unworthy
takes,
When he himself might his quietus
make
With a bare bodkin.

Hamlet in *Hamlet*, 3.1.69–75

A bodkin could mean a dagger, or even a pin
for the hair; "contumely" = contemptuous
abuse.

14 I am more an antique Roman than
a Dane.

Horatio in *Hamlet*, 5.2.341

Meaning he chooses the Stoic path of suicide,
recommended by Seneca, rather than the
modern Christian one of survival.

15 Life, being weary of these worldly
bars,
Never lacks power to dismiss itself.

Cassius in *Julius Caesar*, 1.3.96–7

A Stoic attitude that sees suicide positively as
having power over oneself.

16 Why should I play the Roman fool
and die
On my own sword?

Macbeth in *Macbeth*, 5.8.1–2

Suicide was advocated by the Roman Stoics,
notably Seneca.

Summer, see Seasons

Sunrise (see also Dawn)

1 Hark, hark, the lark at heaven's gate
sings,

And Phoebus 'gins arise,
His steeds to water at those springs
On chaliced flowers that lies;
And winking Mary-buds begin to
ope their golden eyes;
With everything that pretty is, my
lady sweet, arise;
Arise, arise!

Song in *Cymbeline*, 2.3.20–26

Sung to wake Imogen.

2 But we are spirits of another sort.
I with the morning's love have oft
made sport,
And like a forester the groves may
tread
Even till the eastern gate, all fiery-
red,
Opening on Neptune with fair
blessèd beams,
Turns into yellow gold his salt
green streams.

**Oberon in *A Midsummer Night's
Dream*, 3.2.388–93**

The fairies, being benign spirits, do not have
to disappear with the dawn, but can greet the
rising sun that changes the color of the sea
(Neptune).

3 All the world is cheered by the
sun.

King Richard in *Richard III*, 1.2.129

So, he claims, he is cheered by the beauty of
Anne.

4 All so soon as the all-cheering sun
Should in the farthest east begin to
draw
The shady curtains from Aurora's
bed.

**Montague in *Romeo and Juliet*,
1.1.134–6**

5 But soft, what light through yonder
window breaks?
It is the east, and Juliet is the sun.

Romeo in *Romeo and Juliet*, 2.2.2–3

Looking up as a light appears in Juliet's
window.

6 Full many a glorious morning have
I seen
Flatter the mountain tops with sov-
ereign eye.

***Sonnet 33*, 1–2**

The "sovereign eye" is the sun, soon to be
covered by clouds.

7 Lo here the gentle lark, weary of
rest,
From his moist cabinet mounts up
on high,
And wakes the morning, from
whose silver breast
The sun ariseth in his majesty,
Who doth the world so gloriously
behold
That cedar tops and hills seem
burnished gold.

***Venus and Adonis*, 853–8**

In these beautiful lines, the lark is imaged as
soaring from its damp or dewy nest ("moist
cabinet") as the sun (Apollo) rises from the
breast of his lover, the dawn (Aurora).

Sunset

1 The west yet glimmers with some
streaks of day.
Now spurs the lated traveler apace
To gain the timely inn.

First Murderer in *Macbeth*, 3.3.5–7

2 The weary sun hath made a golden
set,
And by the bright track of his fiery
car

Gives token of a goodly day tomorrow.

Richmond in *Richard III*, 5.3.19–21

Cheerfully anticipating victory in the battle
with Richard the next morning.

3 The sun begins to gild the western
sky.

**Eglamour in *The Two Gentlemen of
Verona*, 5.1.1**

The Supernatural

1 *Glendower.* I can call spirits from
the vasty deep.
Hotspur. Why, so can I, or so can
any man.
But will they come when you do
call for them?

***Henry IV, Part 1*, 3.1.52–4**

Glendower's claims undermined; "vasty
deep" = great abyss, the underworld.

2 *First Witch.* When shall we three
meet again?
In thunder, lightning, or in rain?
Second Witch. When the hurly-
burly's done,
When the battle's lost and won.
Third Witch. That will be ere set of
sun.
First Witch. Where the place?
Second Witch.   Upon the
heath.
Third Witch. There to meet with
Macbeth.

***Macbeth*, 1.1.1–7**

"Hurly-burly" = tumult of war.

3   What are these
So withered and so wild in their
attire,
That look not like th' inhabitants o'
th' earth,

And yet are on't?

Banquo in *Macbeth*, 1.3.39–42

On first seeing the three Witches.

4   This supernatural soliciting
Cannot be ill; cannot be good.

Macbeth in *Macbeth*, 1.3.130–1

Reflecting on what the Weird Sisters have told him.

Superstition

1   He is superstitious grown of late,
Quite from the main opinion he
held once
Of fantasy, of dreams, and cere-
monies.

Cassius in *Julius Caesar*, 2.1.195–7

Claiming that Caesar has changed his basic opinion about things imagined ("fantasy"), dreams, and divination based on ceremonial rites.

Suspicion

1   The bird that hath been limèd in a
bush
With trembling wings misdoubteth
every bush.

**King Henry in *Henry VI, Part 3*,
5.6.13–14**

"Limèd" = caught with birdlime; "misdoubteth" = suspects; the idea is proverbial.

2   Is whispering nothing?
Is leaning cheek to cheek? Is meeting noses?
Kissing with inside lip? Stopping
the career
Of laughter with a sigh?—A note
infallible

Of breaking honesty.

Leontes in *The Winter's Tale*, 1.2.284–8

Evidence to him that his wife's chastity ("honesty") is suspect; "career" = full gallop.

Swimming

1   I saw him beat the surges under
him,
And ride upon their backs. He trod
the water,
Whose enmity he flung aside, and
breasted
The surge most swoll'n that met
him.

Francisco in *The Tempest*, 2.1.115–18

Telling Alonso that his son may be safe.

2   His bold head
'Bove the contentious waves he
kept, and oared
Himself with his good arms in lusty
stroke
To the shore.

Francisco in *The Tempest*, 2.1.118–21

Describing Ferdinand swimming from the
shipwreck.

Sympathy

1   Hast thou, which art but air, a
touch, a feeling
Of their afflictions, and shall not
myself,
One of their kind, that relish all as
sharply
Passion as they, be kindlier moved
than thou art?

Prospero in *The Tempest*, 5.1.21–4

To Ariel, who has encouraged Prospero to
have pity on his enemies.

Talking (see also Speech, Words)

1 I love not many words.

Parolles in *All's Well That Ends Well*,
3.6.84

The braggart whose very name means
"words" protests that he is not a talker.

2   He talks well—
But what care I for words?

Phebe in *As You Like It*, 3.5.110–1

She is attracted to Rosalind, disguised as a
man.

3 These are but wild and whirling
words, my lord.

Horatio in *Hamlet*, 1.5.133

Commenting on Hamlet's overexcited
response to seeing the ghost of his father.

4 If I chance to talk a little wild, forgive me;
I had it from my father.

Lord Sands in *Henry VIII*, 1.4.26–7

He is being bold with the court ladies.

5   Agèd ears play truant at his tales,
And younger hearings are quite
ravishèd,
So sweet and voluble is his discourse.

Rosaline in *Love's Labor's Lost*, 2.1.74–6

Praising Berowne; "play truant" = cease to
attend to serious business; "voluble" = lively,
quick.

6 A gentleman, Nurse, that loves to
hear himself talk, and will speak
more in a minute than he will stand
to in a month.

Romeo in *Romeo and Juliet*, 2.4.147–9

Describing his friend Mercutio to the Nurse;
"stand to" = defend.

7 What, this gentleman will out-talk
us all.

Gremio in *The Taming of the Shrew*,
1.2.246

On hearing Tranio, disguised as Lucentio,
offering to woo Bianca.

Tears

1 The April's in her eyes, it is love's
spring,
And these the showers to bring it
on.

Antony in *Antony and Cleopatra*,
3.2.43–4

On Octavia weeping as she parts from her
brother, Octavius Caesar.

2 Fall not a tear, I say, one of them
rates
All that is won and lost.

Antony in *Antony and Cleopatra*,
3.11.69–70

Spoken to the penitent Cleopatra after the Battle of Actium; "Fall" = let fall.

3   The big round tears
Coursed one another down his
innocent nose
In piteous chase.

First Lord in *As You Like It*, 2.1.38–40

Describing the weeping of a wounded stag.

4 At a few drops of women's rheum,
which are
As cheap as lies, he sold the blood
and labor
Of our great action.

Aufidius in *Coriolanus*, 5.6.45–7

Speaking of Coriolanus, who yielded to the
entreaties of his wife and mother to spare
Rome; "rheum" = tears.

5   There will be a world of water shed
    Upon the parting of your wives and
    you.
    Glendower in *Henry IV, Part 1*, 3.1.93–4

    He is to bring the rebels' wives to take leave
    before the wars.

6   All my mother came into mine eyes
    And gave me up to tears.
    Exeter in *Henry V*, 4.6.31–2

    On the death in battle of Suffolk and York.

7   I did not think to shed a tear
    In all my miseries; but thou hast
        forced me,
    Out of thy honest truth, to play the
        woman.
    Cardinal Wolsey in *Henry VIII*,
    3.2.428–30

    To his devoted supporter Cromwell.

8   If you have tears, prepare to shed
    them now.
    Mark Antony in *Julius Caesar*, 3.2.169

    Displaying the body of Caesar to the people.

9   I am ashamed
    That thou hast power to shake my
        manhood thus,
    That these hot tears, which break
        from me perforce,
    Should make thee worth them.
    King Lear in *King Lear*, 1.4.296–9

    In distress at the way his daughter Goneril has
    been treating him.

10   Touch me with noble anger,
    And let not women's weapons,
        water-drops,
    Stain my man's cheeks!
    King Lear in *King Lear*, 2.4.276–8

Reacting to the rejection of him by his daughters, Goneril and Regan.

11   You think I'll weep:
    No, I'll not weep.
    I have full cause of weeping, but
        this heart
    Shall break into a hundred thou-
        sand flaws
    Or ere I'll weep.
    King Lear in *King Lear*, 2.4.282–6

    The old king in fact is impotent to do more
    than weep and curse; "flaws" = fragments; "or
    ere" = before.

12   You have seen
    Sunshine and rain at once; her
        smiles and tears
    Were like a better way: those happy
        smilets
    That played on her ripe lip seemed
        not to know
    What guests were in her eyes, which
        parted thence
    As pearls from diamonds dropped.
    Gentleman in *King Lear*, 4.3.17–22

    Cordelia here becomes an emblem of pity;
    "like" = alike.

13 How much better is it to weep at
    joy than to joy at weeping!
    Leonato in *Much Ado About Nothing*,
    1.1.27–9

    On Claudio's uncle, who weeps for joy that
    his nephew is safe.

14 If that the earth could teem with
        woman's tears,
    Each drop she falls would prove a
        crocodile.
    Othello in *Othello*, 4.1.245–6

    Accusing Desdemona of deception; croco-
    diles proverbially shed hypocritical tears over
    their victims.

15 His tears runs down his beard like
   winter's drops
   From eaves of reeds.

Ariel in *The Tempest*, 5.1.16–17

Referring to old Gonzalo, whose tears show
his pity for the madness afflicting Alonso.

16 Tears harden lust, though marble
   wear with raining.

The Rape of Lucrece, 560

The effect on Tarquin of Lucrece's tears.

Tediousness

1   O, he is as tedious
   As a tired horse, a railing wife,
   Worse than a smoky house.

Hotspur in *Henry IV, Part 1*, 3.1.157–9

Meaning Glendower.

2 Life is as tedious as a twice-told tale,
   Vexing the dull ear of a drowsy
   man.

Lewis the Dauphin in *King John*,
3.4.108–9

3 This will last out a night in Russia
   When nights are longest there.

Angelo in *Measure for Measure*,
2.1.134–5

Bored with the interrogation of the bawd,
Pompey.

4 *Dogberry.* If I were as tedious as a
   king, I could find in my heart to
   bestow it all on your worship.
   Leonato. All thy tediousness on me,
   ha?

Much Ado About Nothing, 3.5.21–3

Dogberry seems to think "tedious" means
"wealthy"; Leonato is indeed finding him very
tedious.

Temperament (see also Melancholy, Moods)

1 My master is of churlish disposition,
   And little recks to find the way to
   heaven
   By doing deeds of hospitality.

Corin in *As You Like It*, 2.4.80–82

"Recks" means cares.

2   Blest are those
   Whose blood and judgment are so
   well commingled
   That they are not a pipe for For-
   tune's finger
   To sound what stop she please.

Hamlet in *Hamlet*, 3.2.68–71

Referring to Horatio; "blood" = passions;
"commingled" = mixed.

3   Give me that man
   That is not passion's slave, and I
   will wear him
   In my heart's core, ay, in my heart
   of heart,
   As I do thee.

Hamlet in *Hamlet*, 3.2.71–4

Praising Horatio.

4 I am now of all humors that have
   showed themselves humors since
   the old days of goodman Adam to
   the pupil age of this present twelve
   o'clock at midnight.

Prince Hal in *Henry IV, Part 1*,
2.4.92–5

Feeling ready for anything; "goodman" =
farmer or gardener.

Temperance

1
        I am sure,
Though you can guess what tem-
   perance should be,
You know not what it is.

Antony in *Antony and Cleopatra*,
3.13.120–2

Criticizing Cleopatra.

Temptation

1   Why do I yield to that suggestion
Whose horrid image doth unfix my
   hair
And make my seated heart knock at
   my ribs
Against the use of nature?

Macbeth in *Macbeth*, 1.3.134–7

The "horrid image" is the idea of murdering
King Duncan.

2   'Tis one thing to be tempted,
   Escalus,
Another thing to fall.

Angelo in *Measure for Measure*,
2.1.17–18

To Escalus, who has been pleading for Claudio, sentenced to death by Angelo for getting
Juliet with child.

3   What's this, what's this? Is it her
   fault or mine?
The tempter, or the tempted, who
   sins most, ha?

Angelo in *Measure for Measure*,
2.2.162–3

Finding he is sexually attracted by the novice,
Isabella.

4   O cunning enemy, that to catch a
   saint,
With saints doth bait thy hook!
   Most dangerous
Is that temptation that doth goad
   us on
To sin in loving virtue.

Angelo in *Measure for Measure*,
2.2.179–82

Angelo imagines Satan (the "enemy") as causing him to be attracted sexually by Isabella.

5   But something may be done that we
   will not,
And sometimes we are devils to
   ourselves,
When we will tempt the frailty of
   our powers,
Presuming on their changeful
   potency.

Troilus in *Troilus and Cressida*, 4.4.94–7

Anxious about Cressida's promise to be faithful to him; "changeful potency" = unstable
strength.

Thanks

1   I thank you. I am not of many
words, but I thank you.

**Don John in *Much Ado About
Nothing*,** 1.1.157–8

On being welcomed by Leonato, Don John
establishes his taciturn nature.

2
        I greet thy love,
Not with vain thanks, but with
   acceptance bounteous.

Othello in *Othello*, 3.3.469–70

Accepting Iago's offer to do anything, even
murder, for him.

3   My recompense is thanks, that's all,
     Yet my good will is great, though
       the gift small.

Thaisa in *Pericles*, 3.4.17–18

To Cerimon, who has brought her back to life.

4   Evermore thanks, the exchequer of
       the poor.

Bolingbroke in *Richard II*, 2.3.65

Having no other reward to give; "exchequer"
= treasury, purse.

5   The poorest service is repaid with
       thanks.

Petruchio in *The Taming of the Shrew*,
4.3.45

Demanding that Katherine thank him before
she gets anything to eat.

6   I can no other answer make but
       thanks,
     And thanks.

Sebastian in *Twelfth Night*, 3.3.14–15

Thanking his friend Antonio.

Theater (see also Acting, Plays)

1   The quick comedians
     Extemporally will stage us, and pre-
       sent
     Our Alexandrian revels: Antony
     Shall be brought drunken forth,
       and I shall see
     Some squeaking Cleopatra boy my
       greatness
     I' the posture of a whore.

Cleopatra in *Antony and Cleopatra*,
5.2.216–21

A direct allusion to Shakespeare's own theater, in which female characters were played
by boy actors.

2   This wide and universal theatre
     Presents more woeful pageants than
       the scene
     Wherein we play in.

Duke Senior in *As You Like It*, 2.7.136–9

He has just heard from Orlando of Adam's
sufferings from age and hunger; Shakespeare
exploits the traditional idea of the world as a
theater.

3   All the world's a stage,
     And all the men and women merely
       players;
     They have their exits and their
       entrances,
     And one man in his time plays
       many parts,
     His acts being seven ages.

Jaques in *As You Like It*, 2.7.139–43

A most brilliant formulation of a proverbial
idea.

4   I have heard
     That guilty creatures sitting at a
       play
     Have by the very cunning of the
       scene
     Been struck so to the soul, that
       presently
     They have proclaimed their male-
       factions.

Hamlet in *Hamlet*, 2.2.588–92

Thinking of ways to expose Claudius's guilt;
"malefactions" = crimes, evil-doing.

5   O for a Muse of fire, that would
       ascend
     The brightest heaven of invention!

A kingdom for a stage, princes to act,
And monarchs to behold the swelling scene!

Chorus in *Henry V*, 1.1–4

"Invention" = poetic imagination.

6   Can this cockpit hold
The vasty fields of France? Or may we cram
Within this wooden O the very casques
That did affright the air at Agincourt?

Chorus in *Henry V*, 1.11–14

The "wooden O" refers to multi-sided theaters like the Globe, where Shakespeare's plays were staged; "casques" = helmets.

7   Thus with imagined wing our swift scene flies
In motion of no less celerity
Than that of thought.

Chorus in *Henry V*, 3.1–3

"As swift as thought" was proverbial.

8   Sit and see,
Minding true things by what their mockeries be.

Chorus in *Henry V*, 4.52–3

Asking the audience to imagine the battle of Agincourt as it really happened.

9   Thus far with rough and all-unable pen
Our bending author hath pursued the story,
In little room confining mighty men.

Chorus in *Henry V*, 5.Epilogue, 1–3

The "little room" refers to the theater.

10   *Brutus.* How many times shall Caesar bleed in sport,
That now on Pompey's basis lies along,
No worthier than the dust!
Cassius.   So oft as that shall be,
So often shall the knot of us be called
The men that gave their country liberty.

Julius Caesar, 3.1.114–18

Caesar's body is supposed to have fallen at the base of the statue of his old enemy, Pompey.

11   *Quince.* Marry, our play is "The most lamentable comedy and most cruel death of Pyramus and Thisbe."
Bottom. A very good piece of work, I assure you, and a merry.

A Midsummer Night's Dream, 1.2.11–14

Shakespeare was mocking a fashion for elaborate titles that confounded genres, such as the "Tragical Comedy of Apius and Virginia" (1575).

12   Here's a marvelous convenient place for our rehearsal.

Quince in *A Midsummer Night's Dream*, 3.1.2–3

13   "A tedious brief scene of young Pyramus
And his love Thisbe, very tragical mirth"—
Merry and tragical? Tedious and brief?
That is hot ice and wondrous strange snow!

Theseus in *A Midsummer Night's Dream*, 5.1.56–9

The absurd title of the play put on by Bottom, Quince and their crew parodies the titles of some earlier Elizabethan plays.

14 A play there is, my lord, some ten words long,
Which is as brief as I have known a play,
But by ten words, my lord, it is too long,
Which makes it tedious.

Philostrate in *A Midsummer Night's Dream*, 5.1.61–4

Advising Theseus not to watch "Pyramus and Thisbe."

15 No epilogue, I pray you; for your play needs no excuse. Never excuse; for when the players are all dead, there need none to be blamed.

Theseus in *A Midsummer Night's Dream*, 5.1.355–7

Speaking to the players after watching "Pyramus and Thisbe"; the players are "dead" at the end of the tragedy.

16 If we shadows have offended,
Think but this, and all is mended,
That you have but slumbered here
While these visions did appear.

Puck in *A Midsummer Night's Dream*, 5.1.423–6

The word shadow was often opposed to substance; so spirits were shadows, and so were actors playing roles; the word also suggests the illusions of the theater.

17 As in a theater the eyes of men,
After a well-graced actor leaves the stage,
Are idly bent on him that enters next,
Thinking his prattle to be tedious,
Even so, or with much more contempt, men's eyes
Did scowl on gentle Richard.

York in *Richard II*, 5.2.23–8

Commenting on the disrespect shown to Richard by the people of London.

18 The two hours' traffic of our stage.

Chorus in *Romeo and Juliet*, Prologue, 12

Suggesting how swift the action of a play was on Shakespeare's stage.

19 If this were played upon a stage now, I could condemn it as an improbable fiction.

Fabian in *Twelfth Night*, 3.4.127–8

Referring to Malvolio's absurd confidence that Olivia is in love with him.

20 A great while ago the world begun,
With hey, ho, the wind and the rain,
But that's all one, our play is done,
And we'll strive to please you every day.

Feste in *Twelfth Night*, 5.1.405–8

Bringing the play to an end on a slight note of melancholy.

Theft

1 *Prince Hal.* I see a good amendment of life in thee, from praying to purse-taking.
Falstaff. Why, Hal, 'tis my vocation, Hal; 'tis no sin for a man to labor in his vocation.

***Henry IV, Part 1*, 1.2.102–5**

Falstaff wittily invokes a biblical echo of Ephesians 4:1, "beseech you that ye walk worthy of the vocation wherewith ye are called."

2 Rob me the exchequer the first thing thou dost, and do it with unwashed hands too.

Falstaff in *Henry IV, Part 1*, 3.3.183–4

To Prince Hal now that he is reconciled with the king.

3   They will steal anything, and call it purchase.

Boy in *Henry V*, 3.2.41–2

Referring to Nym, Bardolph and Pistol; "purchase" = plunder.

4   They would have me as familiar with men's pockets as their gloves or their handkerchiefs; which makes much against my manhood, if I should take from another's pocket to put into mine; for it is plain pocketing up of wrongs.

Boy in *Henry V*, 3.2.47–51

His employers, Nym, Bardolph and Pistol, would turn the boy into a pickpocket.

5   To England will I steal, and there I'll steal.

Pistol in *Henry V*, 5.1.87

Humiliated in France, he plans to steal off to England.

6   Thieves for their robbery have authority
When judges steal themselves.

Angelo in *Measure for Measure*, 2.2.175–6

The hitherto upright judge finds he cannot control his lust for Isabella.

7   If you meet a thief, you may suspect him, by virtue of your office, to be no true man.

Dogberry in *Much Ado About Nothing*, 3.3.50–1

Comically laying down the law.

8   The most peaceable way for you, if you do take a thief, is to let him

show himself what he is and steal out of your company.

Dogberry in *Much Ado About Nothing*, 3.3.57–60

The incompetent constable instructs the watchmen who patrol the town at night.

9   The robbed that smiles steals something from the thief.

Duke in *Othello*, 1.3.208

Advising Brabantio to accept the loss of his daughter, Desdemona.

10   He that is robbed, not wanting what is stolen,
Let him not know't, and he's not robbed at all.

Othello in *Othello*, 3.3.342–3

"Wanting" = missing; the idea became proverbial.

11   I'll example you with thievery:
The sun's a thief, and with his great attraction
Robs the vast sea; the moon's an arrant thief,
And her pale fire she snatches from the sun.

Timon in *Timon of Athens*, 4.3.435–8

Timon seeks to prove everything in nature is a thief. Nabokov used the phrase "pale fire" as the title of a novel.

12   My father named me Autolycus, who being, as I am, littered under Mercury, was likewise a snapper-up of unconsidered trifles.

Autolycus in *The Winter's Tale*, 4.3.24–6

Mercury was the god of thieves; in the *Odyssey*, Autolycus, the grandfather of Ulysses, was supposed to be a son of Mercury.

Thinness

1 When I was about thy years, Hal, I was not an eagle's talon in the waist, I could have crept into any alderman's thumb-ring. A plague of sighing and grief, it blows a man up like a bladder.

Falstaff in *Henry IV, Part 1*, 2.4.329–33

2 Do I not bate? Do I not dwindle? Why, my skin hangs about me like an old lady's loose gown; I am withered like an old apple-john.

Falstaff in *Henry IV, Part 1*, 3.3.2–4

"Bate" = abate, grow thin; "apple-john" = kind of apple which was kept until the skin shriveled.

3 I am famished in his service; you may tell every finger I have with my ribs.

Launcelot Gobbo in *The Merchant of Venice*, 2.2.106–7

Launcelot is servant to Shylock; "tell" = count.

4 I am not tall enough to become the function well, nor lean enough to be thought a good student.

Feste in *Twelfth Night*, 4.2.6–8

About to put on a gown and pretend to be the curate, Sir Topas; the typical student was assumed to be poor and thin.

5 You'd be so lean that blasts of January Would blow you through and through.

Perdita in *The Winter's Tale*, 4.4.111–12

To Camillo, who is so taken by her beauty that he says he could feed by staring at her.

Thought

1 *Rosalind.* There's a girl goes before the priest, and certainly a woman's thought runs before her actions.
Orlando. So do all thoughts, they are winged.

As You Like It, 4.1.139–42

Disguised as a man, Rosalind gets Celia to "marry" her to Orlando; does he penetrate her disguise?

2 Pacing through the forest, Chewing the food of sweet and bitter fancy.

Oliver in *As You Like It*, 4.3.100–1

On Orlando mulling over his thoughts of love ("fancy").

3 Our thoughts are ours, their ends none of our own.

Player King in *Hamlet*, 3.2.213

On the gap between thoughts and deeds.

4 *Prince Hal.* I never thought to hear you speak again.
King Henry. Thy wish was father, Harry, to that thought.

Henry IV, Part 2, 4.5.91–2

The king thinks his son wished him dead.

5 Thus with imagined wing our swift scene flies
In motion of no less celerity
Than that of thought.

Chorus in *Henry V*, 3.Prologue, 1–3

"As swift as thought" was proverbial.

6 In the quick forge and working-house of thought.

Chorus in *Henry V*, 5.Prologue, 23

A fine image of the working of the imagination.

7 My thoughts are whirlèd like a potter's wheel,
I know not where I am, nor what I do.

Talbot in *Henry VI, Part 1*, 1.5.19–20

He is amazed at the power shown by Joan la Pucelle (Joan of Arc) in fighting him.

8 Faster than springtime showers comes thought on thought.

York in *Henry VI, Part 2*, 3.1.337

Brooding on his ambition for the throne.

9 I hear, yet say not much, but think the more.

Richard of Gloucester in *Henry VI, Part 3*, 4.1.83

Richard stirs up quarrels at court while watching for his chance to seize power.

10 My noble friend, chew upon this.

Brutus in *Julius Caesar*, 1.2.171

To Cassius; "chew" = ruminate, reflect.

11   Merciful powers,
Restrain in me the cursèd thoughts that nature
Gives way to in repose!

Banquo in *Macbeth*, 2.1.7–9

"Powers" may refer to the order of angels deputed to resist demons; the orders are listed in John Milton's *Paradise Lost*, V.601, as "Thrones, Dominations, Princedoms, Virtues, Powers."

12   By heaven, he echoes me,
As if there were some monster in his thought

Too hideous to be shown.

Othello in *Othello*, 3.3.106–8

Iago echoes the suspicion already forming in Othello's thought.

13 Thought is free.

Maria in *Twelfth Night*, 1.3.69

To Sir Andrew Aguecheek, meaning "you may think what you like"; proverbial.

14 Thoughts are but dreams till their effects be tried.

The Rape of Lucrece, 353

Thrift

1 Thrift, thrift, Horatio; the funeral baked meats
Did coldly furnish forth the marriage tables.

Hamlet in *Hamlet*, 1.2.180–1

Horatio has remarked that Hamlet's mother married again soon after her first husband's death; "coldly" = when cold.

2 This was a way to thrive, and he was blest;
And thrift is blessing, if men steal it not.

Shylock in *The Merchant of Venice*, 1.3.89–90

Defending usury by reference to Jacob's skill in increasing his flocks of sheep and goats (Genesis 30:32–43).

3   Fast bind, fast find,
A proverb never stale in thrifty mind.

Shylock in *The Merchant of Venice*, 2.5.54–5

Meaning keep things secure and they are readily found.

Time

Time is measured by clocks in the world of business and the court, not in the forest of Arden.

1 Let's take the instant by the forward top;
For we are old, and on our quick'st decrees
Th'inaudible and noiseless foot of time
Steals ere we can effect them.

King of France in All's Well That Ends Well, 5.3.40–2

Being old, he must move quickly if he is to see the results of his actions; compare the proverb, "seize Occasion by the forelock, for she is bald behind."

2 'Tis but an hour ago since it was nine,
And after one hour more 'twill be eleven,
And so from hour to hour, we ripe and ripe,
And then from hour to hour, we rot and rot;
And thereby hangs a tale.

Jaques in As You Like It, 2.7.24–8

Quoting Touchstone's basic view of life.

3 Whate'er you are
That in this desert inaccessible,
Under the shade of melancholy boughs,
Lose and neglect the creeping hours of time.

Orlando in As You Like It, 2.7.109–12

Meeting Duke Senior's company in the forest of Arden, he sees them as wasting time.

4 *Rosalind.* I pray you, what is't o'clock?
Orlando. You should ask me what time o' day; there's no clock in the forest.

As You Like It, 3.2.299–305

5 Time travels in divers paces with divers persons.

Rosalind in As You Like It, 3.2.308–9

Time passes at different speeds according to the person.

6 *Orlando.* Who stays it still withal?
Rosalind. With lawyers in the vacation; for they sleep between term and term, and then they perceive not how Time moves.

As You Like It, 3.2.330–3

On the perception of time, mocking lawyers.

7 There's a time for all things.

Antipholus of Syracuse in The Comedy of Errors, 2.2.65

Proverbial; from Ecclesiastes 3:1, "To every thing there is a season."

8 Time is a very bankrupt and owes more than he's worth to season.
Nay, he's a thief too: have you not heard men say,
That Time comes stealing on by night and day?

Dromio of Syracuse in The Comedy of Errors, 4.2.58–60

Time proverbially steals away; "season" = opportunity, with a quibble on "seizing," linking with "thief."

9 But thoughts, the slaves of life, and life, time's fool,
And time, that takes survey of all the world,
Must have a stop.

Hotspur in Henry IV, Part 1, 5.4.80–3

He is dying as he speaks these words.

10 Past and to come seems best; things present, worst.

Archbishop of York in *Henry IV, Part 2*, 1.3.108

Everything seems to be at its worst for the rebels.

11 We are time's subjects, and time bids be gone.

Hastings in *Henry IV, Part 2*, 1.3.110

Time calls on the rebels to act, not to go on talking.

12 Well, thus we play the fools with the time, and the spirits of the wise sit in the clouds and mock us.

Prince Hal in *Henry IV, Part 2*, 2.2.142–3

Recognizing that in fooling with his tavern companions he is wasting time.

13   I feel me much to blame So idly to profane the precious time.

Prince Hal in *Henry IV, Part 2*, 2.4.361–2

News of war makes Hal realize he is wasting time; "profane" = violate, treat with contempt.

14 We see which way the stream of time doth run.

Archbishop of York in *Henry IV, Part 2*, 4.2.70

Accepting what is inevitable.

15   Now he weighs time Even to the utmost grain.

Exeter in *Henry V*, 2.4.137–8

Recalling how as Prince Hal, Henry wasted time; a grain is the smallest unit of weight.

16 Old Time the clock-setter, that bald sexton Time!

The Bastard Falconbridge in *King John*, 3.1.324

Referring both to the proverb, "Take occasion/time by the forelock for she/he is bald behind," and also to time as bringing death, since the sexton often doubled as grave-digger.

17 Time shall unfold what plighted cunning hides, Who covert faults at last with shame derides.

Cordelia in *King Lear*, 1.1.280–1

Compare the proverb, "Time brings truth to light"; "plighted" = pleated.

18   Come what come may, Time and the hour runs through the roughest day.

Macbeth in *Macbeth*, 1.3.146–7

Recalling the proverb, "time and tide stay for no man."

19 *Seyton.* The Queen, my lord, is dead. *Macbeth.* She should have died hereafter; There would have been a time for such a word.— Tomorrow, and tomorrow, and tomorrow, Creeps in this petty pace from day to day, To the last syllable of recorded time; And all our yesterdays have lighted fools The way to dusty death.

Macbeth, 5.5.16–23

Macbeth has lost the ability to feel grief, or any emotion. The lines gain power from the common biblical associations of light with life, and of the body with dust; see, for example, Ecclesiastes 3:20, "All go unto one place; all are of the dust, and all turn to dust again."

20 There are many events in the womb of time which will be delivered.

Iago in *Othello*, 1.3.369–70

21 What, keep a week away? Seven days and nights,
Eightscore-eight hours, and lovers' absent hours
More tedious than the dial eightscore times!
A weary reckoning!

Bianca in *Othello*, 3.4.173–6

On Cassio's neglect of her.

22 I see that Time's the king of men;
He's both their parent, and he is their grave,
And gives them what he will, not what they crave.

Pericles in *Pericles*, 2.3.45–7

After suffering misfortunes, Pericles, against expectations, wins a tournament and a bride.

23 O call back yesterday, bid time return!

Salisbury in *Richard II*, 3.2.69

Reporting that the Welsh have deserted Richard.

24 I wasted time, and now doth time waste me.

King Richard in *Richard II*, 5.5.49

Playing on "waste" as meaning 1. squander; 2. wear away and destroy.

25 Sad hours seem long.

Romeo in *Romeo and Juliet*, 1.1.161

The lovelorn Romeo finds time hangs on his hands.

26 The bawdy hand of the dial is now upon the prick of noon.

Mercutio in *Romeo and Juliet*, 2.4.112–13

Teasing Juliet's nurse, who is something of a bawd.

27 Now is the sun upon the highmost hill
Of this day's journey.

Juliet in *Romeo and Juliet*, 2.5.9–10

It is noon, and she has been waiting three hours for her nurse to return.

28 Time hath, my lord, a wallet at his back,
Wherein he puts alms for oblivion,
A great-sized monster of ingratitudes:
Those scraps are good deeds past, which are devoured
As fast as they are made, forgot as soon
As done.

Ulysses in *Troilus and Cressida*, 3.3.145–50

Trying to persuade the idle Achilles to fight again for the Greeks; Time was often personified as an old man.

29 Time is like a fashionable host,
That slightly shakes his parting guest by the hand,
And with his arms outstretched, as he would fly,
Grasps in the comer: the welcome ever smiles,
And farewell goes out sighing.

Ulysses in *Troilus and Cressida*, 3.3.165–9

Telling Achilles that his past achievements are soon forgotten.

30 For beauty, wit,
High birth, vigor of bone, desert in service,

Love, friendship, charity, are subjects all
To envious and calumniating time.
Ulysses in *Troilus and Cressida*, 3.3.171–4

Inviting Achilles to contemplate the brevity of life and all human attributes in an effort to get him to fight.

31 Injurious Time now, with a robber's haste,
Crams his rich thievery up, he knows not how;
As many farewells as be stars in heaven,
With distinct breath and consigned kisses to them,
He fumbles up into a loose adieu,
And scants us with a single famished kiss,
Distasted with the salt of broken tears.
Troilus in *Troilus and Cressida*, 4.4.42–8

On parting from Cressida; "he knows not how" = indiscriminately; numberless farewells, each with its kisses, are crammed into a casual ("loose") parting.

32 *Aeneas.* 'Tis the old Nestor.
Hector. Let me embrace thee, good old chronicle,
That hast so long walked hand in hand with time.
***Troilus and Cressida*,** 4.5.201–3

Aeneas is introducing Hector to the Greek warriors during a truce.

33   The end crowns all;
And that old common arbitrator, Time,
Will one day end it.
Hector in *Troilus and Cressida*, 4.5.224–6

Refusing to accept Ulysses's prophecy that Troy will fall.

34 What else may hap, to time I will commit.
Viola in *Twelfth Night*, 1.2.60

"Hap" = chance to happen.

35 O time, thou must untangle this, not I.
It is too hard a knot for me t'untie.
Viola in *Twelfth Night*, 2.2.40–1

On realizing that Olivia has fallen in love with her, supposing her to be a man (Cesario).

36 The clock upbraids me with a waste of time.
Olivia in *Twelfth Night*, 3.1.130

Conscious of spending too much time with Cesario (the disguised Viola).

37 Thus the whirligig of time brings in his revenges.
Feste in *Twelfth Night*, 5.1.376–7

Marking the comeuppance afflicted on Malvolio; a "whirligig" is a spinning top.

38 Time is the nurse and breeder of all good.
Proteus in *The Two Gentlemen of Verona*, 3.1.245

A truism perhaps, but he is in the act of deceiving his friend Valentine.

39 I that please some, try all, both joy and terror
Of good and bad, that makes and unfolds error.
Time in *The Winter's Tale*, 4.1.1–2

Time, the Chorus, proclaims his proverbial impartiality or indifference in relation to humanity ("time tries all things").

40   Time's glory is to calm contending
kings,
To unmask falsehood and bring
truth to light,
To stamp the seal of time in agèd
things,
To wake the morn and sentinel the
night.

The Rape of Lucrece, 939–42

"Sentinel" = keep guard during.

41   Nothing 'gainst Time's scythe can
make defense.

Sonnet 12, 13

A traditional image of time as a reaper.

42   Devouring Time, blunt thou the
lion's paws,
And make the earth devour her
own sweet brood.

Sonnet 19, 1–2

On Time personified as destructive (Latin
"edax rerum," or consuming all things).

43   Like as the waves make towards the
pebbled shore,
So do our minutes hasten to their
end;
Each changing place with that
which goes before,
In sequent toil all forwards do con-
tend.

Sonnet 60, 1–4

The inexorable passage of time is a recurrent
theme of Shakespeare's sonnets; here it is as if
each minute struggles onward painfully ("in
sequent toil").

44   No, Time, thou shalt not boast that
I do change;

Thy pyramids built up with newer
might
To me are nothing novel, nothing
strange;
They are but dressings of a former
sight.
Our dates are brief, and therefore
we admire
What thou dost foist upon us that
is old,
And rather make them born to our
desire
Than think that we before have
heard them told.

Sonnet 123, 1–8

The pyramids recall ancient Egypt, and may
refer also to obelisks or other buildings set up
in London; new constructions seem recre-
ations ("dressings") of old ones, and we
admire old forms by reinventing them to our
taste rather than remembering how we have
heard them described ("told").

45   Make use of time, let not advantage
slip;
Beauty within itself should not be
wasted.
Fair flowers that are gathered in
their prime
Rot and consume themselves in
little time.

Venus and Adonis, 129–32

Venus is seeking to seduce Adonis by a
common plea of lovers; "advantage" =
opportunity.

Time of Day

1   In the dead waste and middle of the
night.

Horatio in *Hamlet*, 1.2.198

He describes the time when he saw the ghost
of Hamlet's father; "waste" suggests barren-
ness, and could be heard also as "waist" or
middle. The earliest text has "vast."

2   But soft, methinks I scent the
morning air,
Brief let me be.
Ghost in *Hamlet*, 1.5.58–9

The ghost has to return to his "prison-house"
by day.

3   The glow-worm shows the matin to
be near,
And 'gins to pale his uneffectual
fire.
Ghost in *Hamlet*, 1.5.89–90

Signaling the end of the interview between
Hamlet and the ghost of his father as day
approaches.

4   What time of day is it, lad?
Falstaff in *Henry IV, Part 1*, 1.2.1

Addressing Prince Hal as "lad" shows the
close relationship between them.

5   What a devil hast thou to do with
the time of the day? Unless hours
were cups of sack, and minutes
capons, and clocks the tongues of
bawds, and dials the signs of leaping-houses, and the blessed sun
himself a fair hot wench in flame-
colored taffeta, I see no reason why
thou shouldst be so superfluous to
demand the time of the day.
Prince Hal in *Henry IV, Part 1*, 1.2.6–12

On Falstaff's feckless way of life, consisting of
drinking ("sack"), eating ("capons" or fowl)
and lechery; "leaping-houses" = brothels.

6   From the rising of the lark to the
lodging of the lamb.
Dauphin in *Henry V*, 3.7.31–2

That is, from dawn to dusk, when the lamb
lies down to sleep.

7   *Macbeth*. What is the night?
Lady Macbeth. Almost at odds with
morning, which is which.
Macbeth, 3.4.125–6

8   The iron tongue of midnight hath
told twelve.
Lovers, to bed; 'tis almost fairy
time.
**Theseus in *A Midsummer Night's
Dream*, 5.1.363–4**

"Iron tongue" = clapper of a bell.

9   'Tis fresh morning with me
When you are by at night.
Ferdinand in *The Tempest*, 3.1.33–4

To Miranda, whom he loves; "by" = nearby.

Timeserving

1   A hovering temporizer, that
Canst with thine eyes at once see
good and evil,
Inclining to them both.
Leontes in *The Winter's Tale*, 1.2.302–4

His misguided perception of his good coun-
selor, Camillo.

Torture

1   I fear you speak upon the rack,
Where men enforcèd do speak anything.
**Portia in *The Merchant of Venice*,
3.2.32–3**

She fears Bassanio may not be honest in his
protestations of love.

2 What studied torments, tyrant, hast
   for me?
   What wheels, racks, fires? What
   flaying, boiling
   In leads or oils? What old or newer
   torture
   Must I receive, whose every word
   deserves
   To taste of thy most worst?
   Paulina in *The Winter's Tale*, 3.2.175–9

Emphasizing what a tyrant Leontes has been,
but knowing that he is not really going to punish her now he has come to his senses.

Transformation (see also Change, Mutability)

1   I do not shame
   To tell you what I was, since my
   conversion
   So sweetly tastes, being the thing I
   am.
   Oliver in *As You Like It*, 4.3.135–7

Saved from death by his brother, Orlando, the
malicious Oliver suddenly becomes gentle
and loving.

2   Something have you heard
   Of Hamlet's transformation; so I
   call it,
   Since not th' exterior nor the
   inward man
   Resembles that it was.
   Claudius in *Hamlet*, 2.2.4–7

To Rosencrantz and Guildenstern, summoned
to try to find out what is troubling Hamlet.

3 Full fathom five thy father lies,
   Of his bones are coral made;
   Those are pearls that were his eyes;
   Nothing of him that doth fade,
   But doth suffer a sea-change

Into something rich and strange.
Sea-nymphs hourly ring his knell:
Ding-dong.
Hark! Now I hear them—ding-
dong bell.
Ariel in *The Tempest*, 1.2.397–405

Ariel's best-known song, for Ferdinand's benefit, misleading him about his father, who is not
dead; the idea of change or transformation is
important in the play.

Transience (see also Change, Mutability)

1 The sun of Rome is set. Our day is
   gone;
   Clouds, dews, and dangers come;
   our deeds are done.
   Titinius in *Julius Caesar*, 5.3.63–4

On finding Cassius dead at the battle of
Philippi.

2 Swift as a shadow, short as any
   dream,
   Brief as the lightning in the collied
   night,
   That in a spleen unfolds both
   heaven and earth,
   And, ere a man hath power to say
   "Behold!,"
   The jaws of darkness do devour it
   up.
   So quick bright things come to con-
   fusion.
   **Lysander in *A Midsummer Night's
   Dream*, 1.1.144–9**

On the nature of human love, and life; "collied" = blackened (as with coal dust); "in a
spleen" = fit of temper.

3 His rash fierce blaze of riot cannot
   last,
   For violent fires soon burn out
   themselves;

Small showers last long, but sudden
storms are short.

John of Gaunt in *Richard II*, 2.1.33–5

Referring to Richard.

4   O momentary grace of mortal men,
Which we more hunt for than the
grace of God!

Hastings in *Richard III*, 3.4.96–7

Playing on the meanings of "grace" = 1. the
condition of being in favor; 2. divine grace.
Hastings has just been sentenced to death.

5   These violent delights have violent
ends,
And in their triumph die, like fire
and powder,
Which as they kiss consume.

**Friar Lawrence in *Romeo and Juliet*,
2.6.9–11**

On Romeo and Juliet as they rush into marriage; the Friar's words seem to anticipate
their death.

6   The cloud-capped towers, the gorgeous palaces,
The solemn temples, the great globe
itself,
Yea, all which it inherit, shall dis-
solve,
And, like this insubstantial pageant
faded,
Leave not a rack behind.

Prospero in *The Tempest*, 4.1.152–6

The "globe" may have made Shakespeare's
audience think of the Globe Theatre as well as
the world.

7   When forty winters shall besiege
thy brow
And dig deep trenches in thy
beauty's field,
Thy youth's proud livery, so gazed
on now,

Will be a tattered weed of small
worth held.

Sonnet 2, 1–4

On the speed with which the good looks of
his friend will fade.

Travel

1   *Rosalind.* Well, this is the forest of
Arden.
Touchstone. Ay, now am I in
Arden, the more fool I. When I
was at home, I was in a better
place, but travelers must be content.

As You Like It, 2.4.15–18

2   I fear you have sold your own lands
to see other men's; then to have
seen much, and to have nothing, is
to have rich eyes and poor hands.

Rosalind in *As You Like It*, 4.1.22–5

To Jaques, defining the true traveler.

3   I'll view the manners of the town,
Peruse the traders, gaze upon the
buildings,
And then return and sleep within
mine inn,
For with long travel I am stiff and
weary.

**Antipholus of Syracuse in *The Com-
edy of Errors*, 1.2.12–15**

On arriving in Ephesus.

4   I will go lose myself,
And wander up and down to view
the city.

**Antipholus of Syracuse in *The Com-
edy of Errors*, 1.2.30–1**

The city is Ephesus.

5 They say this town is full of cozenage:
As nimble jugglers that deceive the
eye,
Dark-working sorcerers that change
the mind,
Soul-killing witches that deform the
body,
Disguisèd cheaters, prating mountebanks,
And many such-like liberties of sin.

**Antipholus of Syracuse in *The Com-
edy of Errors*, 1.2.97–102**

The reputation of Ephesus, where Antipholus
has just arrived; "mountebanks" were quack
doctors or charlatans.

6 O for a horse with wings!

Imogen in *Cymbeline*, 3.2.48

Imogen learns that her husband, Posthumus, is
at Milford-Haven.

7 Whither I go, thither shall you go
too;
Today will I set forth, tomorrow
you.

Hotspur in *Henry IV, Part 1*, 2.3.115–16

Leaving his wife, without telling her that he is
going to lead a rebellion against the king.

8 Thou and I
Have thirty miles to ride yet ere
dinner-time.

**Prince Hal in *Henry IV, Part 1*,
3.3.197–8**

To Peto, on their way to fight with rebels.

9 I hope to see London once ere I die.

Davy in *Henry IV, Part 2*, 5.3.60

Davy, a servant, has lived all his life in the
country.

10 'Tis ever common
That men are merriest when they
are from home.

King Henry in *Henry V*, 1.2.271–2

11 Now sits the wind fair, and we will
aboard.

King Henry in *Henry V*, 2.2.12

Preparing to sail for France.

12 A man of travel, that hath seen the
world.

Armado in *Love's Labor's Lost*, 5.1.107–8

Making the claim for himself.

13 Come away!
For you shall hence upon your
wedding day.

**Portia in *The Merchant of Venice*,
3.2.310–11**

Sending Bassanio off with money to pay his
friend Antonio's debts.

14 I'll put a girdle round about the
earth
In forty minutes!

**Puck in *A Midsummer Night's Dream*,
2.1.175–6**

Puck travels at fairy speed to serve Oberon.

15 We the globe can compass soon,
Swifter than the wandering moon.

**Puck and Oberon in *A Midsummer
Night's Dream*, 4.1.97–8**

On the power of fairies to circle the earth in
no time.

16 My travel's history,
Wherein of antres vast and deserts
idle,

Rough quarries, rocks, and hills
whose heads touch heaven,
It was my hint to speak—such was
my process—
And of the cannibals that each
other eat,
The anthropophagi, and men
whose heads
Do grow beneath their shoulders.
Othello in *Othello*, 1.3.139–45

On his exotic past; "antres" = caves; "rough
quarries" = rugged precipices; "anthropophagi," or cannibals, and headless men
were reported by Pliny, and figured in travel-
books still in the 16th century.

17 All places that the eye of heaven vis-
its
Are to a wise man ports and happy
havens.
John of Gaunt in *Richard II*, 1.3.275–6
Advising his banished son, Bolingbroke.

18 These high wild hills and rough
uneven ways
Draws out our miles and makes
them wearisome.
Northumberland in *Richard II*, 2.3.4–5
He is a stranger in Gloucestershire.

19 *Hortensio.* What happy gale
Blows you to Padua here from old
Verona?
Petruchio. Such wind as scatters
young men through the world
To seek their fortunes farther than
at home,
Where small experience grows.
The Taming of the Shrew, 1.2.48–52

20 Crowns in my purse I have, and
goods at home,
And so am come abroad to see the
world.

Petruchio in *The Taming of the Shrew*,
1.2.57–8
He has just arrived in Padua from Verona.

21 All torment, trouble, wonder, and
amazement
Inhabits here. Some heavenly
power guide us
Out of this fearful country!
Gonzalo in *The Tempest*, 5.1.104–6
Concerned at the distraction suffered by
Alonso; the "country" is Prospero's island.

22 *Olivia.* There lies your way, due
west.
Viola. Then westward ho!
Twelfth Night, 3.1.134
Viola picks up on the cry of watermen who
ferried people across the Thames to Westmin-
ster.

23   What's to do?
Shall we go see the relics of this
town?
Sebastian in *Twelfth Night*, 3.3.18–19
To Antonio, on arriving in Illyria; "relics" =
antiquities.

24 I pray you let us satisfy our eyes
With the memorials and the things
of fame
That do renown this city.
Sebastian in *Twelfth Night*, 3.3.22–4
Anxious to see the sights of Illyria.

25 Beguile the time, and feed your
knowledge
With viewing of the town.
Antonio in *Twelfth Night*, 3.3.41–2
Urging Sebastian to look around Illyria.

26 Alas, the way is wearisome and long.

Lucetta in *The Two Gentlemen of Verona*, 2.7.8

Trying to persuade Julia not to follow her "loving Proteus" from Verona to Milan.

27 The climate's delicate, the air most sweet,
Fertile the isle, the temple much surpassing
The common praise it bears.

Cleomenes in *The Winter's Tale*, 3.1.1–3

Describing their visit to the oracle at Delphos.

Treachery

1 I fear me you but warm the starvèd snake,
Who, cherished in your breasts, will sting your hearts.

York in *Henry VI, Part 2*, 3.1.343–4

Plotting rebellion.

Treason

1 Treason is not inherited, my lord.

Rosalind in *As You Like It*, 1.3.61

Protesting her innocence after her father has been banished.

2 Suspicion all our lives shall be stuck full of eyes;
For treason is but trusted like the fox,
Who never so tame, so cherished and locked up,
Will have a wild trick of his ancestors.

Worcester in *Henry IV, Part 1*, 5.2.8–11

The rebels should not make terms with the king since they will always be watched and never trusted.

3 Treason and murder ever kept together,
As two yoke-devils sworn to either's purpose.

King Henry in *Henry V*, 2.2.105–6

"Yoke-devils" = devils in partnership, yoked together.

4 O, what a fall was there, my countrymen!
Then I, and you, and all of us fell down,
Whilst bloody treason flourished over us.

Mark Antony in *Julius Caesar*, 3.2.190–2

On the death of Caesar.

Trees

1 Under an oak, whose antique root peeps out
Upon the brook that brawls along this wood.

First Lord in *As You Like It*, 2.1.31–2

2 Under an old oak, whose boughs were mossed with age
And high top bald with dry antiquity.

Oliver in *As You Like It*, 4.3.104–5

3 There is a willow grows aslant a brook
That shows his hoar leaves in the glassy stream.

Gertrude in *Hamlet*, 4.7.166–7

"His" = its; "hoar" = frost; the undersides of willow leaves are greyish white, like frost.

Trials

1   Let your fair eyes and gentle wishes
    go with me to my trial.
    Orlando in *As You Like It*, 1.2.185–7

Addressing Rosalind and Celia before he wrestles with Charles.

Truisms

1   The property of rain is to wet and
    fire to burn.
    Corin in *As You Like It*, 3.2.26–7

The shepherd's common sense.

2   *Hamlet*. There's never a villain
       dwelling in all Denmark
    But he's an arrant knave.
    Horatio. There needs no ghost, my
       lord, come from the grave
    To tell us this.
    Hamlet, 1.5.123–6

Hamlet fends off questions about his interview with his father's ghost.

3   Every cloud engenders not a storm.
    Clarence in *Henry VI, Part 3*, 5.3.13

Trust

1   Constant you are,
    But yet a woman, and for secrecy
    No lady closer, for I well believe
    Thou wilt not utter what thou dost
    not know,

And so far will I trust thee, gentle
Kate.
Hotspur in *Henry IV, Part 1*, 2.3 108–12

Refusing to tell his wife about his involvement in rebellion against the king.

2   There's no more faith in thee than
    in a stewed prune.
    Falstaff in *Henry IV, Part 1*, 3.3.112–13

Insulting the Hostess, who denies he has been robbed in her tavern; stewed prunes were associated with brothels, where regular food could not be served.

3   I took him for the plainest harmless
       creature
    That breathed upon the earth a
       Christian;
    Made him my book, wherein my
       soul recorded
    The history of all her secret
       thoughts.
    King Richard in *Richard III*, 3.5.25–8

Protesting his love for Hastings, whose execution he has just plotted.

4   My trust,
    Like a good parent, did beget of
       him
    A falsehood in its contrary, as great
    As my trust was; which had indeed
       no limit,
    A confidence sans bound.
    Prospero in *The Tempest*, 1.2.93–7

On being betrayed by his brother Antonio; recalling the proverb, "trust is the mother of deceit."

5   I wonder men dare trust themselves
    with men.
    Apemantus in *Timon of Athens*, 1.2.43

Seeing that Timon's guests are destroying him.

Truth (see also Honesty, Integrity)

1 If circumstances lead me, I will find
   Where truth is hid, though it were
      hid indeed
   Within the center.

   Polonius in *Hamlet*, 2.2.157–9

   Boasting of his political skills.

2 I can teach thee, coz, to shame the
      devil
   By telling truth: tell truth and
      shame the devil.

   Hotspur in *Henry IV, Part 1*, 3.1.57–8

   To Glendower ("coz" = cousin), who has
   been claiming supernatural powers; "tell truth
   and shame the devil" was proverbial (as the
   devil was the father of lies).

3 Whom I most hated living, thou
      hast made me
   With thy religious truth and mod-
      esty,
   Now in his ashes honor.

   Queen Katherine in *Henry VIII*, 4.2.73–5

   Changing her opinion of Cardinal Wolsey;
   "modesty" = moderation.

4 What in the world should make me
      now deceive,
   Since I must lose the use of all
      deceit?
   Why should I then be false, since it
      is true
   That I must die here and live hence
      by truth?

   Melune in *King John*, 5.3.26–9

   Melune, wounded and at the point of death,
   develops the proverb "Dying men speak true"
   to include the idea of an afterlife in which he
   will have to "live . . . by truth."

5   Truth is truth
   To the very end of reckoning.

   Isabella in *Measure for Measure*, 5.1.45–6

6 Promise me life, and I'll confess the
      truth.

   Bassanio in *The Merchant of Venice*, 3.2.34

   To Portia, who is anxious to be assured of his
   love.

7 Methinks the truth should live
      from age to age,
   As 'twere retailed to all posterity,
   Even to the general all-ending day.

   Prince Edward in *Richard III*, 3.1.76–8

   "Retailed" = handed down; by the "all-ending
   day" he means doomsday.

Twins

1 Methinks you are my glass, and not
      my brother:
   I see by you I am a sweet-faced
      youth.

   Dromio of Ephesus in *The Comedy of Errors*, 5.1.418–19

   The twins meet at last.

2 We came into the world like
      brother and brother;
   And now let's go hand in hand, not
      one before another.

   Dromio of Ephesus in *The Comedy of Errors*, 5.1.425–6

   To his twin, Dromio of Syracuse, at the end of
   the play.

3   So we grew together
   Like to a double cherry, seeming
      parted,

But yet an union in partition,
Two lovely berries molded on one
stem.

**Helena in *A Midsummer Night's
Dream*, 3.2.208–11**

4   An apple cleft in two is not more
     twin
     Than these two creatures.

Antonio in *Twelfth Night*, 5.1.223–4

The twins, Viola and Sebastian, are at last
revealed, and meet one another.

Tyranny (see also Power)

1   For how can tyrants safely govern
     home,
     Unless abroad they purchase great
     alliance?

**Queen Margaret in *Henry VI, Part 3*,
3.3.69–70**

2   Brutus had rather be a villager
     Than to repute himself a son of
     Rome
     Under these hard conditions as this
     time
     Is like to lay upon us.

Brutus in *Julius Caesar*, 1.2.172–5

Expecting that Caesar may turn out to be a
tyrant; "is like" = may well.

3   That part of tyranny that I do bear
     I can shake off at pleasure.

Cassius in *Julius Caesar*, 1.3.99–100

He means by taking his own life.

4   Thy brother by decree is banishèd.
     If thou dost bend, and pray, and
     fawn for him,
     I spurn thee like a cur out of my
     way.

Caesar in *Julius Caesar*, 3.1.44–6

To Metellus, who pleads for his exiled
brother; "spurn" = kick.

5   I begin to find an idle and fond
     bondage in the oppression of aged
     tyranny, who sways, not as it hath
     power, but as it is suffered.

Gloucester in *King Lear*, 1.2.49–51

"Suffered" = allowed, by the young who
could seize power.

6   'Tis time to fear when tyrants seem
     to kiss.

Pericles in *Pericles*, 1.2.79

After discovering the guilty secret of Antiochus's incest with his own daughter, Pericles
distrusts the tyrant's honeyed words.

7   The orphan pines while the oppres-
     sor sleeps.

The Rape of Lucrece, 905

After being raped, Lucrece thinks of the injustice in the world.

Unkindness

1   Hath homely age th' alluring beauty
     took
     From my poor cheek? Then he
     hath wasted it.
     Are my discourses dull? Barren my
     wit?
     If voluble and sharp discourse be
     marred,
     Unkindness blunts it more than
     marble hard.

**Adriana in *The Comedy of Errors*,
2.1.89–93**

On her absent husband; "wasted" = squan-
dered and laid waste to.

2   My decayèd fair
    A sunny look of his would soon
      repair.

Adriana in *The Comedy of Errors*,
2.1.98–9

Complaining about her absent husband.

3   Unkindness may do much,
    And his unkindness may defeat my
      life,
    But never taint my love.

Desdemona in *Othello*, 4.2.159–61

On Othello's harsh treatment of her; "defeat"
= destroy.

4   In nature there's no blemish but the
      mind;
    None can be called deformed but
      the unkind.

Antonio in *Twelfth Night*, 3.4.367–8

Mistaking Cesario (the disguised Viola) for
Sebastian, he accuses him/her of being unnatural and ungrateful ("unkind").

Utopias

1   I'the commonwealth I would by
     contraries
  Execute all things; for no kind of
     traffic
  Would I admit; no name of magis-
     trate;
  Letters should not be known;
     riches, poverty,
  And use of service, none; contract,
     succession,
  Bourn, bound of land, tilth, vine-
     yard, none;
  No use of metal, corn, or wine, or
     oil;

  No occupation; all men idle, all,
  And women too, but innocent and
     pure.

Gonzalo in *The Tempest*, 2.1.148–56

His utopian vision of himself as king in a
golden age with no rules or private property
("Bourn, bound of land"); "traffic" = trade;
"use of service" = employment of servants.

Valor (see also Courage)

1   I will reward thee
  Once for thy sprightly comfort, and
     tenfold
  For thy good valor.

Antony in *Antony and Cleopatra*,
4.7.14–16

The "comfort" is news of victory.

2   O infinite virtue, com'st thou smil-
     ing from
  The world's great snare uncaught?

Cleopatra in *Antony and Cleopatra*,
4.8.17–18

On Antony returning from his one defeat of
Octavius's army; "virtue" here = valor.

3   He is a lion
  That I am proud to hunt.

**Caius Martius, later Coriolanus, in
Coriolanus,** 1.1.235–6

A warrior's admiration for his rival, Tullus
Aufidius, leader of the Volsces.

4   He is himself alone,
  To answer all the city.

First Soldier in *Coriolanus*, 1.4.51–2

On Caius Martius, who has fought his way
alone into the city of Corioli.

5   It is held
That valor is the chiefest virtue, and
Most dignifies the haver.
Cominius in *Coriolanus*, 2.2.83–5

Praising Coriolanus for his courage in battle
("haver" = possessor).

6   O, the blood more stirs
To rouse a lion than to start a hare!
Hotspur in *Henry IV, Part 1*, 1.3.197–8

Imagining himself as the lion; the hare was
proverbially fearful.

7   There's no more valor in that Poins
than in a wild duck.
Falstaff in *Henry IV, Part 1*, 2.2.101

After a robbery, from which Poins was absent
by design.

8   The better part of valor is discretion, in the which better part I have
saved my life.
Falstaff in *Henry IV, Part 1*, 5.4.119–20

Falstaff's "discretion" means avoiding danger
on the battlefield by pretending to be dead.

9   His valors shown upon our crests
today
Have taught us how to cherish such
high deeds
Even in the bosom of our adversaries.
Prince Hal in *Henry IV, Part 1*,
5.5.29–31

Freeing the prisoner, Douglas, who has fought
heroically.

10   Thou wilt be as valiant as the
wrathful dove or most magnanimous mouse.

Falstaff in *Henry IV, Part 2*, 3.2.159–60

On recruiting little Feeble, a tailor, as a
soldier.

11   That's a valiant flea that dare eat his
breakfast on the lip of a lion.
Orleans in *Henry V*, 3.7.145–6

Seeing the English as foolish to engage the
French army.

12   'Tis much he dares,
And to that dauntless temper of his
mind,
He hath a wisdom that doth guide
his valor
To act in safety.
Macbeth in *Macbeth*, 3.1.50–3

Describing Banquo.

13   In a false quarrel there is no true
valor.
Benedick in *Much Ado About Nothing*,
5.1.120

To Don Pedro and Claudio, and their mockery
of old Leonato's quarrel with them.

14   He is as valiant as the lion, churlish
as the bear, slow as the elephant.
Alexander in *Troilus and Cressida*,
1.2.20–1

Describing the huge but dim-witted Ajax.

15   To awake your dormouse valor, to
put fire in your heart, and brimstone in your liver.
Fabian in *Twelfth Night*, 3.2.19–21

Trying to provoke Sir Andrew to challenge
Cesario (Viola); "brimstone" = sulphur.

Value

1   The jewel that we find, we stoop
    and take it
    Because we see it; but what we do
    not see
    We tread upon and never think of
    it.

    Angelo in *Measure for Measure*, 2.1.24–6

2   What we have we prize not to the
    worth
    Whiles we enjoy it, but being lacked
    and lost,
    Why, then we rack the value, then
    we find
    The virtue that possession would
    not show us
    Whiles it was ours.

    **Friar Francis in *Much Ado About
    Nothing*,** 4.1.218–22

    He says we do not value at its true worth what
    we possess, but when we lose a possession,
    we exaggerate ("rack") its value; he is thinking
    of Claudio's harsh treatment of Hero.

3   What, is the jay more precious than
    the lark
    Because his feathers are more beau-
    tiful?
    Or is the adder better than the eel
    Because his painted skin contents
    the eye?

    Petruchio in *The Taming of the Shrew*,
    4.3.175–8

    "Painted" = brightly colored.

4   What's aught but as 'tis valued?

    Troilus in *Troilus and Cressida*, 2.2.52

    The Trojans are debating whether to keep
    Helen or return her to the Greeks.

5   Value dwells not in particular
    will;

It holds his estimate and dignity
As well wherein 'tis precious of
    itself
As in the prizer.

Hector in *Troilus and Cressida*, 2.2.53–6

Arguing that value depends on intrinsic worth,
not on the particular preference of any individual; the debate is about keeping Helen or
returning her to the Greeks.

6   Is she worth keeping? Why, she is a
    pearl
    Whose price hath launched above a
    thousand ships.

    Troilus in *Troilus and Cressida*, 2.2.81–2

    Referring to Helen, whose rape by Paris
    caused the Trojan war, and echoing a famous
    passage in Christopher Marlowe's play, *Doc-
    tor Faustus*.

7   Nature, what things
    there are
    Most abject in regard, and dear in
    use!
    What things again most dear in the
    esteem
    And poor in worth!

    Ulysses in *Troilus and Cressida*,
    3.3.127–30

    Pointing out that things of low esteem may
    have great practical value, while what is
    highly esteemed may be of little use.

Vanity

1   There was never yet fair woman but
    she made mouths in a glass.

    Fool in *King Lear*, 3.2.35–6

2   Light vanity, insatiate cormorant,
    Consuming means, soon preys on
    itself.

John of Gaunt in *Richard II*, 2.1.38–9

Prophesying that the extravagance of King Richard, by devouring the means of sustaining life, will lead to disaster; the cormorant is noted for its gluttony.

3   A lover may bestride the gossamers
That idles in the wanton summer
air,
And yet not fall; so light is vanity.
Friar Lawrence in *Romeo and Juliet*,
2.6.18–20

On Juliet's arrival, "light of foot"; "wanton" = playful.

4   What a sweep of vanity comes this
way!
Apemantus in *Timon of Athens*, 1.2.132

A cynic's comment on the arrival at Timon's feast of a group of dancers dressed as Amazons.

Vegetables

1   I am qualmish at the smell of leek.
Pistol in *Henry V*, 5.1.21

He is insulting Fluellen, who wears a leek to identify himself as Welsh (usually worn on St. David's Day, the patron saint of Wales).

2   Midnight mushrooms.
Prospero in *The Tempest*, 5.1.39

"Mushrumps" in the original text, imagined as brought into being by Prospero's spirits.

Vertigo

1   How fearful
And dizzy 'tis, to cast one's eyes so
low!

The crows and choughs that wing
the midway air
Show scarce so gross as beetles.
Half way down
Hangs one that gathers samphire,
dreadful trade!
Edgar in *King Lear*, 4.6.11–15

Imagining the prospect from the cliffs at Dover; "choughs" = crows or jackdaws; "gross" = large; "samphire" is an herb used in pickling.

Vice

1   When we in our viciousness grow
hard
(O, misery on't!), the wise gods seel
our eyes,
In our own filth drop our clear
judgments, make us
Adore our errors, laugh at us while
we strut
To our confusion.
Antony in *Antony and Cleopatra*,
3.13.111–5

"Seel" = blind (a term from hawking; the eyes of the hawk are covered in order to train it).

2   That reverend Vice, that grey Iniquity, that father Ruffian, that Vanity in years.
Prince Hal in *Henry IV, Part 1*,
2.4.453–4

Meaning Falstaff; "Vice," "Iniquity," "Ruffian," and "Vanity" are type names suggesting a morality play.

3   Virtue itself turns vice, being misapplied,
And vice sometime by action dignified.
Friar Lawrence in *Romeo and Juliet*,
2.3.21–2

4   There is no man hath a virtue that he hath not a glimpse of, nor any man an attaint but he carries some stain of it.

Alexander in *Troilus and Cressida*, 1.2.24–6

Referring to Ajax; "attaint" = vice.

5   O what a mansion have those vices got
Which for their habitation chose out thee,
Where beauty's veil doth cover every blot,
And all things turns to fair that eyes can see!

***Sonnet* 95,** 9–12

"All things turns to fair" = makes all appear beautiful.

Victory

1   The harder matched, the greater victory.

King Edward in *Henry VI, Part 3*, 5.1.70

The king is about to engage in battle; the idea is based on the proverb, "The more danger the more honor."

2   A victory is twice itself when the achiever brings home full numbers.

Leonato in *Much Ado About Nothing*, 1.1.8–9

On a battle won with almost no loss of life.

3   Now are our brows bound with victorious wreaths.

King Richard in *Richard III*, 1.1.5

At the end of the civil wars that plagued the reign of Henry VI.

Vigilance

1   I am as vigilant as a cat to steal cream.

Falstaff in *Henry IV, Part 1*, 4.2.58–9

Villainy

1   O villain, villain, smiling, damned villain!
My tables—meet it is I set it down
That one may smile, and smile, and be a villain!

Hamlet in *Hamlet*, 1.5.106–8

Brooding on his uncle Claudius, the "villain" who murdered his father; "tables" = writing tables.

2   I like not fair terms and a villain's mind.

Bassanio in *The Merchant of Venice*, 1.3.179

On Shylock's offer to lend Antonio 3,000 ducats.

3   Though I cannot be said to be a flattering honest man, it must not be denied but I am a plain-dealing villain.

Don John in *Much Ado About Nothing*, 1.3.30–2

Showing his true nature to his companion, Conrade.

4   If I had my mouth, I would bite; if I had my liberty, I would do my liking. In the meantime, let me be that I am, and seek not to alter me.

Don John in *Much Ado About Nothing*, 1.3.34–7

If he cannot do any harm, he can be morose and surly.

5 We have here recovered the most dangerous piece of lechery that ever was known in the commonwealth.

Second Watchman in *Much Ado About Nothing*, 3.3.167–8

The comic watchman means to say "discovered" and "treachery."

6 He is composed and framed of treachery,
And fled he is upon this villainy.

Don Pedro in *Much Ado About Nothing*, 5.1.249–50

On Don John, who set up the plot to ruin the marriage of Claudio and Hero.

7 Since I cannot prove a lover
To entertain these fair well-spoken days,
I am determinèd to prove a villain
And hate the idle pleasures of these days.

King Richard in *Richard III*, 1.1.28–31

Announcing his intentions in his opening soliloquy.

Virginity (see also Chastity)

1 Man is an enemy to virginity. How may we barricado it against him?

Helena in *All's Well That Ends Well*, 1.1.112–3

She is somewhat oddly seeking advice of the corrupt Parolles.

2 It is not politic in the commonwealth of nature to preserve virginity. Loss of virginity is rational increase, and there was never virgin got till virginity was first lost.

Parolles in *All's Well That Ends Well*, 1.1.126–8

The sardonic response of Parolles to Helena.

3 The imperial votaress passed on,
In maiden meditation, fancy-free.

Oberon in *A Midsummer Night's Dream*, 2.1.163–4

On Cupid's arrow missing the vestal virgin or "imperial votaress," perhaps Queen Elizabeth.

Virtue (see also Goodness)

1 Where an unclean mind carries virtuous qualities, there commendations go with pity; they are virtues and traitors too.

Countess of Rossillion, *All's Well That Ends Well*, 1.1.41–3

Virtuous qualities become "traitors" if they are used for wicked purposes.

2 Honesty coupled to beauty is to have honey a sauce to sugar.

Touchstone in *As You Like It*, 3.3.30–1

Trying to persuade her not to be virtuous ("honest").

3 Our virtues
Lie in the interpretation of the time.

Aufidius in *Coriolanus*, 4.7.49–50

The leader of the Volscians finds his abilities no longer appreciated now that he shares authority with Coriolanus.

4   Thou wrong'st a gentleman, who is
     as far
     From thy report as thou from
     honor, and
     Solicits here a lady that disdains
     Thee and the devil alike.

Imogen in _Cymbeline_, 1.6.145–8

Rejecting Jachimo's account of Posthumus's
unfaithfulness.

5   Virtue itself scapes not calumnious
     strokes.

Laertes in _Hamlet_, 1.3.39–40

Warning Ophelia against Hamlet.

6   But virtue, as it never will be
     moved,
     Though lewdness court it in a shape
     of heaven,
     So lust, though to a radiant angel
     linked,
     Will sate itself in a celestial bed
     And prey on garbage.

Ghost in _Hamlet_, 1.5.53–7

Accusing his widow Gertrude of lust in marrying a brother he despises, a marriage he
regards as incestuous; "shape of heaven" =
angelic form; "sate itself" = gratify its appetite
to the point of disgust.

7   _Polonius._ What do you think of
     me?
     Claudius. As of a man faithful and
     honorable.

Hamlet, 2.2.129–30

Appealing to Claudius for confirmation of his
integrity.

8   My heart laments that virtue can-
     not live
     Out of the teeth of emulation.

**Artemidorus in _Julius Caesar_,
2.3.13–14**

Thinking of Caesar; "Out of the teeth of emulation" = beyond the bite of envious rivalry.

9   Fairest Cordelia, that art most rich
     being poor,
     Most choice forsaken, and most
     loved despised,
     Thee and thy virtues here I seize
     upon.

King of France in _King Lear_, 1.1.250–2

Taking her in marriage with no dowry and
hated by her father.

10   This Duncan
     Hath borne his faculties so meek,
     hath been
     So clear in his great office, that his
     virtues
     Will plead like angels, trumpet-
     tongued, against
     The deep damnation of his taking-
     off.

Macbeth in _Macbeth_, 1.7.16–20

Duncan has wielded power so mildly
("meek"), and been blameless ("clear") as
king, hence the "deep damnation" of killing
him.

11   The king-becoming graces,
     As justice, verity, temperance, sta-
     bleness,
     Bounty, perseverance, mercy, lowli-
     ness,
     Devotion, patience, courage, forti-
     tude,
     I have no relish of them.

Malcolm in _Macbeth_, 4.3.91–5

Malcolm denigrates himself, afraid that Macduff may be a spy.

12 Heaven doth with us as we with torches do,
Not light them for themselves; for if our virtues
Did not go forth of us, 'twere all alike
As if we had them not.

Duke in *Measure for Measure*, 1.1.32–5

Echoing various injunctions of Jesus in the gospels, as at Matthew 5:14–16 and Luke 8:16, e.g., "Let your light so shine before men, that they may see your good works"; "all alike" = just the same.

13 The hand that hath made you fair hath made you good.

Duke in *Measure for Measure*, 3.1.180–1

Greeting the novice Isabella; the hand is God's.

14 Virtue is bold, and goodness never fearful.

Duke in *Measure for Measure*, 3.1.208

Varying the proverb, "innocence is bold."

15 He who the sword of heaven will bear
Must be as holy as severe;
Pattern in himself to know,
Grace to stand, and virtue go.

Duke in *Measure for Measure*, 3.2.261–4

The last two lines may be understood as meaning he must know himself as a model for judging others, stand firm with grace, and act with virtue.

16 Your father was ever virtuous, and holy men at their death have good inspirations.

Nerissa in *The Merchant of Venice*, 1.2.27–8

Defending the will made by Portia's father that restricts her choice in marriage.

17 Virtue? A fig! 'Tis in ourselves that we are thus or thus. Our bodies are our gardens, to the which our wills are gardeners.

Iago in *Othello*, 1.3.319–21

"A fig!" implies the scornful gesture of thrusting the thumb between the first and second fingers.

18 She is of so free, so kind, so apt, so blessed a disposition, she holds it a vice in her goodness not to do more than she is requested.

Iago in *Othello*, 2.3.319–22

A perceptive description of Desdemona.

19   If Cassio do remain,
He hath a daily beauty in his life
That makes me ugly.

Iago in *Othello*, 5.1.18–20

Meaning "if Cassio remains alive."

20 Virtue itself turns vice, being misapplied,
And vice sometime's by action dignified.

Friar Lawrence in *Romeo and Juliet*, 2.3.21–2

21 Is it a world to hide virtues in?

Sir Toby Belch in *Twelfth Night*, 1.3.131–2

Encouraging the foolish Sir Andrew to show how well he can dance.

22 Anything that's mended is but patched; virtue that transgresses is but patched with sin, and sin that amends is patched with virtue.

Feste in *Twelfth Night*, 1.5.47–9

23 *Sir Toby Belch.* Dost thou think because thou art virtuous there shall be no more cakes and ale? *Feste.* Yes, by Saint Anne, and ginger shall be hot i'the mouth, too.

Twelfth Night, 2.3.114–18

Referring to Malvolio's puritanical streak; "cakes and ale" were associated with church feasts, the ale often spiced with ginger.

24 Virtue is beauty, but the beauteous evil
Are empty trunks o'erflourished by the devil.

Antonio in *Twelfth Night*, 3.4.369–70

That is, those who are beautiful on the outside but evil within are like vacant bodies or chests covered over with ornament.

Vows (see also Oaths, Promises)

1 'Tis not the many oaths that makes the truth,
But the plain single vow that is vowed true.
What is not holy, that we swear not by,
But take the Highest to witness.

Diana in *All's Well That Ends Well*, 4.2.21–2

Rejecting Bertram's protestations of love as unholy.

2 I swear to thee by Cupid's strongest bow,
By his best arrow with the golden head,
By the simplicity of Venus' doves,
By that which knitteth souls and prospers loves,
. . .

By all the vows that ever men have broke
(In number more than ever women spoke).

Hermia in *A Midsummer Night's Dream*, 1.1.169–72, 175–6

Cupid used arrows of gold to cause love, and lead to repel it; doves were sacred to Venus, as symbolizing fidelity and freedom from deceit ("simplicity").

3 For, ere Demetrius looked on Hermia's eyne,
He hailed down oaths that he was only mine,
And when this hail some heat from Hermia felt,
So he dissolved, and showers of oaths did melt.

Helena in *A Midsummer Night's Dream*, 1.1.242–5

"Eyne" = eyes.

4 *Romeo.* Lady, by yonder blessèd moon I vow,
That tips with silver all these fruit tree tops—
Juliet. O, swear not by the moon, th' inconstant moon,
That monthly changes in her circled orb,
Lest that thy love prove likewise variable.

Romeo and Juliet, 2.2.107–11

5 It is the purpose that makes strong the vow,
But vows to every purpose must not hold.

Cassandra in *Troilus and Cressida*, 5.3.23–4

She is trying to persuade Hector to break for one day an engagement he has made to fight the Greeks.

War (see also Fighting, Soldiers)

1 Wars is no strife
To the dark house and the detested wife.
Bertram in *All's Well That Ends Well,* 2.3.291–2

Preferring the risks of war to being at home.

2 They come like sacrifices in their trim,
And to the fire-eyed maid of smoky war
All hot and bleeding will we offer them.
Hotspur in *Henry IV, Part 1,* 4.1.113–15

Expecting to defeat Prince Hal and his army; "fire-eyed maid" = Bellona, goddess of war.

3 I would 'twere bed-time, Hal, and all well.
Falstaff in *Henry IV, Part 1,* 5.1.125

Showing his fear of dying in battle.

4 Sound all the lofty instruments of war,
And by that music let us all embrace,
For, heaven to earth, some of us never shall
A second time do such a courtesy.
Hotspur in *Henry IV, Part 1,* 5.2.97–100

5 God keep lead out of me!
Falstaff in *Henry IV, Part 1,* 5.3.34

Referring to bullets.

6 O yet for God's sake, go not to these wars!

Lady Percy in *Henry IV, Part 2,* 2.3.9

Hotspur's widow begs her father-in-law not to fight.

7 The hideous god of war.
Lady Percy in *Henry IV, Part 2,* 2.3.35

Mars seems hideous to her now that her husband has been killed in battle.

8 In cases of defense 'tis best to weigh
The enemy more mighty than he seems.
Dauphin in *Henry V,* 2.4.43–4

Advising the King of France not to underestimate the strength of English forces.

9 He bids you . . . to take mercy
On the poor souls for whom this hungry war
Opens his vasty jaws.
Exeter in *Henry V,* 2.4.93, 103–5

Henry's message to the King of France.

10 Once more unto the breach, dear friends, once more.
King Henry in *Henry V,* 3.1.1

Henry's famous battle-cry at the gap or breach in the walls of Harfleur.

11 When the blast of war blows in our ears,
Then imitate the action of the tiger;
Stiffen the sinews, conjure up the blood,
Disguise fair nature with hard-favored rage;
Then lend the eye a terrible aspect.
King Henry in *Henry V,* 3.1.5–9

Encouraging his soldiers to fight.

12 I see you stand like greyhounds in
      the slips,
    Straining upon the start. The
      game's afoot!
    Follow your spirit, and upon this
      charge
    Cry, "God for Harry, England and
      Saint George!"

King Henry in *Henry V*, 3.1.31–4

Seeing his troops as like greyhounds leashed
("in the slips") and waiting to be loosed to
hunt game. St. George is the patron saint of
England.

13 What is it then to me, if impious
      War,
    Arrayed in flames like to the prince
      of fiends,
    Do with his smirched complexion
      all fell feats
    Enlinked to waste and desolation?

King Henry in *Henry V*, 3.3.15–18

Blaming war rather than individuals for the
cruelty ("fell feats") and devastation it brings.

14 Advantage is a better soldier than
    rashness.

Montjoy in *Henry V*, 3.6.120

Better to wait for a favorable opportunity than
act rashly in war; so the French King makes
the best of losing Harfleur to the English.

15 Gentlemen in England now abed
    Shall think themselves accursed
      they were not here,
    And hold their manhoods cheap
      whiles any speaks
    That fought with us upon Saint
      Crispin's Day.

King Henry in *Henry V*, 4.3.64–7

Encouraging his army to fight the French;
Saint Crispin was martyred on 25th October,
the date of the Battle of Agincourt.

16 Caesar's spirit, ranging for
      revenge,
    With Ate by his side, come hot
      from hell,
    Shall in these confines, with a
      monarch's voice,
    Cry "Havoc!" and let slip the dogs
      of war.

Mark Antony in *Julius Caesar*, 3.1.270–3

Ate was the Greek goddess of discord and
destruction; the cry "Havoc!" was the signal
to kill and pillage without mercy.

17 I pray you, how many hath he
    killed and eaten in these wars? But
    how many hath he killed? For
    indeed, I promised to eat all of his
    killing.

Beatrice in *Much Ado About Nothing*,
1.1.42–5

Mocking Benedick's achievement as a soldier.

18 The tyrant custom, most grave sen-
      ators,
    Hath made the flinty and steel
      couch of war
    My thrice-driven bed of down.

Othello in *Othello*, 1.3.229–31

As a soldier, he is used to living rough.

19 Farewell the neighing steed and the
      shrill trump,
    The spirit-stirring drum, th' ear-
      piercing fife,
    The royal banner and all quality,
    Pride, pomp, and circumstance of
      glorious war!

Othello in *Othello*, 3.3.351–4

Bidding farewell to the glamour and ceremony ("circumstance") of his profession as a
general; "trump" = trumpet. Edward Elgar
chose to name his famous marches with the
phrase "pomp and circumstance."

20   He is come to open
The purple testament of bleeding
war.

King Richard in *Richard II*, 3.3.93–4

On Henry Bolingbroke; blood was often
described as purple.

21 Contumelious, beastly, mad-
brained, war.

Timon in *Timon of Athens*, 5.1.174

His response to the senators of Athens when
they want him to defend them against Alcibiades; "contumelious" = insolent.

22 She is a theme of honor and
renown,
A spur to valiant and magnanimous
deeds,
Whose present courage may beat
down our foes,
And fame in time to come canonize
us.

**Hector in *Troilus and Cressida*,
2.2.199–202**

Hector's reasons for keeping Helen in Troy.

23 All the argument is a whore and a
cuckold, a good quarrel to draw
emulous factions and bleed to
death upon!

**Thersites in *Troilus and Cressida*,
2.3.72–4**

A cynic's view of the Trojan war; Helen is the
"whore," and Menelaus the "cuckold";
"draw" = attract.

Weakness

1 Frailty, thy name is woman!

Hamlet in *Hamlet*, 1.2.146

Generalizing from Gertrude, his mother, and
her hasty marriage to her dead husband's
brother.

2   We are all men,
In our own natures frail and capa-
ble
Of our flesh.

**Lord Chamberlain in *Henry VIII*,
5.2.45–7**

"Capable" = susceptible to temptation. Compare Matthew 26:41, "the spirit indeed is willing, but the flesh is weak."

3 We are all frail.

Angelo in *Measure for Measure*, 2.4.121

Proverbial, from the apocryphal Ecclesiasticus
8:5; frail means liable to sin, rather than phys-
ically weak. See also Psalms 39:4.

4 Bear with my weakness. My old
brain is troubled.
Be not disturbed with my infirmity.

Prospero in *The Tempest*, 4.1.159–60

5 Now my charms are all o'erthrown,
And what strength I have's mine
own,
Which is most faint.

**Prospero in *The Tempest*, Epilogue,
1–3**

Appealing to the audience in his epilogue.

6 I am weaker than a woman's tear,
Tamer than sleep, fonder than
ignorance,
Less valiant than the virgin in the
night,
And skilless as unpracticed infancy.

Troilus in *Troilus and Cressida*, 1.1.9–12

"Fonder" = more foolish; his love for Cressida
prevents him from fighting against the Greeks.

Weariness

1   Weariness
Can snore upon the flint, when resty sloth
Finds the down pillow hard.

Belarius in *Cymbeline*, 3.6.33–5

"Resty" = sluggish.

2   By my troth, Nerissa, my little body is aweary of this great world.

Portia in *The Merchant of Venice*, 1.2.1–2

Portia's first words in the play.

3   I can go no further, sir.
My old bones aches.

Gonzalo in *The Tempest*, 3.3.1–2

The third person plural ending in "s," as in "aches," was very common in Shakespeare's day. Gonzalo has been helping to search the island for Ferdinand.

Weather

1   *Hamlet.* The air bites shrewdly, it is very cold.
Horatio. It is a nipping and an eager air.

***Hamlet*, 1.4.1–2**

On the battlements of the castle, waiting for the ghost to appear; "shrewdly" = keenly; "eager" = sharp, bitter.

2   Is not their climate foggy, raw and dull,
On whom, as in despite, the sun looks pale,
Killing their fruit with frowns?

Constable in *Henry V*, 3.5.16–18

On the English climate.

3   Many can brook the weather that love not the wind.

Nathaniel in *Love's Labor's Lost*, 4.2.33

Proverbial, meaning we must endure ("brook") much we may not like.

4   So foul and fair a day I have not seen.

Macbeth in *Macbeth*, 1.3.38

5   Men judge by the complexion of the sky
The state and inclination of the day.

Sir Stephen Scroop in *Richard II*, 3.2.194–5

His gloomy looks match the bad news he brings.

6   The skies look grimly
And threaten present blusters.

Mariner in *The Winter's Tale*, 3.3.3–4

7   The day frowns more and more.

Antigonus in *The Winter's Tale*, 3.3.54

8   Like a red morn that ever yet betokened
Wrack to the seaman, tempest to the field,
    Sorrow to shepherds, woe unto the birds,
    Gusts and foul flaws to herdsmen and to herds.

***Venus and Adonis*, 453–6**

It was proverbial that a red sky in the morning heralded bad weather; "wrack" = shipwreck; "flaws" = blasts of wind.

Weeping, see Tears

Welcome (see also Greetings)

1   At first
And last, the hearty welcome.

Macbeth in *Macbeth*, 3.4.1–2

"At first/And last" = once and for all.

2   What's past and what's to come is
strewed with husks
And formless ruin of oblivion;
But in this extant moment, faith
and truth,
Strained purely from all hollow
bias-drawing,
Bids thee, with most divine
integrity,
From heart of very heart, great
Hector, welcome!

Agamemnon in *Troilus and Cressida*, 4.5.166–71

Greeting Hector with pleasure in a moment of truce, free from all insincerity or deviation from truth ("hollow bias-drawing").

3   Pray you bid
These unknown friends to 's welcome, for it is
A way to make us better friends,
more known.

Shepherd in *The Winter's Tale*, 4.4.64–6

On the arrival of the disguised Polixenes and Camillo; "to's" = each to his.

4   Welcome hither,
As is the spring to th' earth.

Leontes in *The Winter's Tale*, 5.1.151–2

Welcoming Florizel at his court.

Wilderness

1   Thou wilt be a wilderness again,
Peopled with wolves, thy old inhabitants!

King Henry in *Henry IV, Part 2*, 4.5.136–7

Referring to his kingdom.

2   The commonwealth of Athens is
become a forest of beasts.

Apemantus in *Timon of Athens*, 4.3.347–8

His cynical view of the state of Athens.

3   Dost thou not perceive
That Rome is but a wilderness of
tigers?

Titus in *Titus Andronicus*, 3.1.53–4

Speaking to his son, Lucius, who has just been banished from Rome.

Winter, see Seasons

Wisdom

1   Thus men may grow wiser every
day.

Touchstone in *As You Like It*, 1.2.137

On hearing the destruction of three young men by a wrestler described as sport for ladies; Touchstone is being ironic.

2   The fool doth think he is wise, but
the wise man knows himself to be a
fool.

Touchstone in *As You Like It*, 5.1.30–2

3   Wisdom cries out in the streets, and no man regards it.

Prince Hal in Henry IV, Part 1, 1.2.88–9

Echoing the Bible, Proverbs 1:23–4.

4   I never knew so young a body with so old a head.

Duke in The Merchant of Venice, 4.1.163–4

Citing the letter commending the legal ability of the disguised Portia.

5   There's not one wise man among twenty that will praise himself.

Beatrice in Much Ado About Nothing, 5.2.73–5

To Benedick, varying the proverb, "he must praise himself since no-one else will."

6   You are wise,
Or else you love not, for to be wise and love
Exceeds man's might.

Cressida in Troilus and Cressida, 3.2.155–7

Speaking to Troilus.

Wit

1   Make the door upon a woman's wit, and it will out at the casement; shut that, and 'twill out at the keyhole; stop that, 'twill fly with the smoke out at the chimney.

Rosalind in As You Like It, 4.1.161–4

2   Brevity is the soul of wit.

Polonius in Hamlet, 2.2.90

Ironically, he is tediously long-winded himself; "wit" could mean wisdom, but shades into its modern meaning.

3   I am not only witty in myself, but the cause that wit is in other men.

Falstaff in Henry IV, Part 2, 1.2.9–10

In this play Falstaff becomes the butt of other men's wit.

4   Thy wit is as quick as the greyhound's mouth; it catches.

Benedick in Much Ado About Nothing, 5.2.11–12

To Margaret, who seizes on unintended meanings as quick as a hound catches its prey.

5   A college of wit-crackers cannot flout me out of my humor. Dost thou think I care for a satire or an epigram?

Benedick in Much Ado About Nothing, 5.4.100–2

Having sworn he would never marry, he is teased by Don Pedro for agreeing to marry Beatrice; "college" = assembly.

6   Look, he's winding up the watch of his wit; by and by it will strike.

Sebastian in The Tempest, 2.1.12–13

Scornfully referring to Gonzalo, who is trying to comfort Alonso; "wit" = intelligence or thought.

7   A sentence is but a cheveril glove to a good wit. How quickly the wrong side may be turned outward!

Feste in Twelfth Night, 3.1.11–13

A "sentence" could be any utterance or opinion; "cheveril" = kidskin, noted for being pliable.

Women (see also Men and Women)

1   No more but e'en a woman, and commanded

By such poor passion as the maid
that milks
And does the meanest chares.

Cleopatra in *Antony and Cleopatra*,
4.15.73–5

In grief the queen discovers her common
humanity.

2 Those that she makes fair she scarce
makes honest, and those that she
makes honest she makes very ill-
favoredly.

Celia in *As You Like It*, 1.2.37–9

Discussing with Rosalind Fortune's contrary
gifts to women.

3 Alas, what danger will it be to us,
Maids as we are, to travel forth so
far!
Beauty provoketh thieves sooner
than gold.

Rosalind in *As You Like It*, 1.3.108–10

Celia has suggested that they go to the forest
of Arden.

4 I must comfort the weaker vessel, as
doublet and hose ought to show
itself courageous to petticoat.

Rosalind in *As You Like It*, 2.4.5–7

Rosalind is dressed as a man, and refers to
Celia in the biblical phrase as a woman or
"weaker vessel" (Paul's first epistle to Peter
3:7).

5 Dost thou think, though I am
caparisoned like a man, I have a
doublet and hose in my disposition?

Rosalind in *As You Like It*, 3.2.194–7

Dressed as a man, but with a woman's heart,
she is eager for Celia to tell her who has been
posting verses about her.

6 Do you not know I am a woman?
When I think, I must speak.

Rosalind in *As You Like It*, 3.2.249–50

7 I thank God I am not a woman, to
be touched with so many giddy
offenses as he hath generally taxed
their whole sex withal.

Rosalind in *As You Like It*, 3.2.347–50

She is disguised as a boy, and mocks her own
sex in speaking to Orlando.

8 I know a wench of excellent discourse,
Pretty and witty; wild, and yet, too,
gentle.

Antipholus of Ephesus in *The Comedy
of Errors*, 3.1.109–10

9 Alas, poor women, make us but
believe
(Being compact of credit) that you
love us;
Though others have the arm, show
us the sleeve;
We in your motion turn, and you
may move us.

Luciana in *The Comedy of Errors*,
3.2.21–4

Speaking to Antipholus of Syracuse; "compact
of credit" = quick to believe; "motion" refers
to the orbit of a heavenly sphere.

10 My gracious silence, hail!
Wouldst thou have laughed had I
come coffined home,
That weep'st to see me triumph?

Coriolanus in *Coriolanus*, 2.1.175

To his wife, Virgilia, who weeps with relief
that he has returned alive from battle.

11 Is there no way for men to be, but women
    Must be half-workers?

Posthumus in *Cymbeline*, 2.5.1–2

Beginning Posthumus's outburst of misogyny when he falsely believes Imogen to be unfaithful; "half-workers" = accessories, part responsible.

12   There's no motion
    That tends to vice in man, but I affirm
    It is the woman's part.

Posthumus in *Cymbeline*, 2.5.20–22

Posthumus turns against all women, falsely believing Imogen to be unfaithful; "motion" = impulse.

13 I have heard of your paintings, too, well enough. God hath given you one face, and you make yourselves another.

Hamlet in *Hamlet*, 3.1.142–4

To Ophelia, in his misogyny denouncing her and women in general.

14 Now get you to my lady's chamber, and tell her, let her paint an inch thick, to this favor she must come; make her laugh at that.

Hamlet in *Hamlet*, 5.1.192–5

Addressing the skull of Yorick, the king's jester.

15   Constant you are,
    But yet a woman, and for secrecy,
    No lady closer, for I well believe
    Thou wilt not utter what thou dost not know,
    And so far will I trust thee, gentle Kate.

Hotspur in *Henry IV, Part 1*, 2.3.108–12

Refusing to tell her his purpose of armed rebellion against the king.

16 She's beautiful, and therefore to be wooed;
    She is a woman, therefore to be won.

Suffolk in *Henry VI, Part 1*, 5.3.78–9

Seeing Margaret of France as a match for King Henry.

17 You, that have so fair parts of woman on you,
    Have too a woman's heart, which ever yet
    Affected eminence, wealth, sovereignty;
    Which, to say sooth, are blessings.

Old Lady in *Henry VIII*, 2.3.27–30

To Anne Boleyn, who has said she does not want to be queen; "affected" = desired.

18 Alas, I am a woman friendless, hopeless!

Queen Katherine in *Henry VIII*, 3.1.80

Divorced by Henry and bullied by Cardinal Wolsey.

19 I grant I am a woman; but withal
    A woman that Lord Brutus took to wife.
    I grant I am a woman; but withal
    A woman well-reputed, Cato's daughter.
    Think you I am no stronger than my sex,
    Being so fathered and so husbanded?

Portia in *Julius Caesar*, 2.1.292–7

Cato was noted for his integrity; he supported Pompey against Caesar, and committed suicide rather than submit to Caesar.

20   How hard it is for women to keep counsel.

Portia in *Julius Caesar*, 2.4.9

21   Ay me, how weak a thing
      The heart of woman is!

Portia in *Julius Caesar*, 2.4.39–40

22   *Cassio.* The divine Desdemona.
      Montano.   What is
      she?
      Cassio. She that I spake of, our
      great captain's captain.

***Othello*, 2.1.73–4**

Implying that Desdemona now commands Othello.

23   She that was ever fair, and never proud,
      Had tongue at will, and yet was never loud,
      . . .
      She that could think, and ne'er disclose her mind,
      See suitors following, and not look behind.
      She was a wight, if ever such wight were—
      . . .
      To suckle fools and chronicle small beer.

Iago in *Othello*, 2.1.148–9, 156–8, 160

Any woman ("wight") so perfect would be fit only to have fools for children and be concerned with trivialities ("small beer"); Iago's litany ends characteristically in contempt.

24   O, the world hath not a sweeter creature! She might lie by an emperor's side and command him tasks.

Othello in *Othello*, 4.1.183–5

Praising Desdemona.

25   A woman moved is like a fountain troubled,
      Muddy, ill-seeming, thick, bereft of beauty,
      And while it is so, none so dry or thirsty
      Will deign to sip or touch one drop of it.

Katherine in *The Taming of the Shrew*, 5.2.142–5

Katherine lectures the angry ("moved") Widow; "ill-seeming" = ugly.

26   Now I see our lances are but straws,
      Our strength as weak, our weakness past compare,
      That seeming to be most which we indeed least are.

Katherine in *The Taming of the Shrew*, 5.2.173–5

Saying, for the benefit of the headstrong Widow and Bianca, that women's weapons (words, temper, anger) are weak, offering a mere appearance of strength.

27   *Orsino.* For women are as roses, whose fair flower
      Being once displayed, doth fall that very hour.
      Viola. And so they are. Alas, that they are so:
      To die even when they to perfection grow.

***Twelfth Night*, 2.4.38–41**

Transience, the swift passage of life, is a recurrent topic in the play; the image of a woman as a rose, fading as soon as it is full-blown ("displayed") is common.

28 *Lucetta.* Of many good, I think him best.
Julia. Your reason?
Lucetta. I have no other but a woman's reason:
I think him so because I think him so.

The Two Gentlemen of Verona, 1.2.21–4

Wonder

1 I was seven of the nine days out of the wonder before you came.

Rosalind in *As You Like It*, 3.2.174–5

The wonder was caused by Rosalind finding the love-rhymes Orlando hung on trees in the forest of Arden; alluding to the proverb "a wonder lasts but nine days."

2   You are made
Rather to wonder at the things you hear
Than to work any.

Posthumus in *Cymbeline*, 5.3.53–5

To a British Lord, astonished that two boys and an old man could win a battle against the Romans.

3 That would be ten days' wonder at the least.

Richard of Gloucester in *Henry VI, Part 3*, 3.2.113

On King Edward IV's idea of marrying Lady Grey; a ten days' wonder would be one more than the proverbial nine.

4   Be collected.
No more amazement. Tell your piteous heart
There's no harm done.

Prospero in *The Tempest*, 1.2.13–15

The storm his daughter Miranda witnessed was created by his magic.

Words (see also Speech, Talking, Words and Deeds)

1   Oft
When blows have made me stay, I fled from words.

Coriolanus in *Coriolanus*, 2.2.71–2

The warrior would rather fight than deal in words.

2 That ever this fellow should have fewer words than a parrot, and yet the son of a woman!

Prince Hal in *Henry IV, Part 1*, 2.4.98–9

Meaning Francis, the apprentice tapster; Prince Hal has given him little chance to talk.

3 Zounds, I was never so bethumped with words
Since I first called my brother's father 'dad'!

The Bastard Falconbridge in *King John*, 2.1.466–7

On hearing the long speech of Hubert in an effort to make peace between France and England; he prefers war.

4 I marvel thy master hath not eaten thee for a word, for thou art not so long by the head as honorificabilitudinitatibus.

Costard in *Love's Labor's Lost*, 5.1.39–41

The last word is said to be the longest known; the dative plural of a medieval term meaning the condition of being loaded with honors.

5 *Holofernes.* Goodman Dull, thou hast spoken no word all this while.

Dull. Nor understood none, neither.

Love's Labor's Lost, 5.1.149–51

An apt response to the absurdly learned dia-
logue of Holofernes, Nathaniel and Armado.

6   How every fool can play upon the
word!

Lorenzo in *The Merchant of Venice,*
3.5.43

On Launcelot Gobbo.

7   Thou wilt be like a lover presently
And tire the hearer with a book of
words.

**Don Pedro in *Much Ado About Noth-
ing,*** 1.1.306–7

To Claudio, who waxes lyrical in praise of
Hero, the woman he wants to marry.

8   Thou hast frighted the word out of
his right sense, so forcible is thy wit.

Benedick in *Much Ado About Nothing,*
5.2.55–6

To Beatrice, who has deliberately twisted
Benedick's attempt to persuade her to accept
a kiss.

9   You cram these words into mine
ears against
The stomach of my sense.

Alonso in *The Tempest,* 2.1.107–8

To Gonzalo, who has been trying to comfort
him; he fears his son is drowned.

10   Words, words, mere words, no
matter from the heart.

Troilus in *Troilus and Cressida,* 5.3.108

On receiving a letter from Cressida, whose
love for Diomedes he has witnessed.

Words and Deeds

1   'Tis a kind of good deed to say
well,
And yet words are no deeds.

King Henry in *Henry VIII,* 3.2.153–4

2   Your words and performances are
no kin together.

Roderigo in *Othello,* 4.2.182–3

On the gap between what Iago promises and
what he does.

3   Talkers are no good doers. Be
assured,
We go to use our hands and not
our tongues.

First Murderer in *Richard III,*
1.3.350–1

Assuring Richard they will not listen to
Clarence before murdering him.

4   A true knight,
Not yet mature, yet matchless, firm
of word,
Speaking in deeds, and deedless in
his tongue.

Ulysses in *Troilus and Cressida,*
4.5.96–8

Describing Troilus as one who keeps his
promises ("firm of word"), and who lets his
actions speak for themselves.

5   His insolence draws folly from my
lips,
But I'll endeavor deeds to match
these words.

Hector in *Troilus and Cressida,*
4.5.258–9

Realizing it is stupid to boast as Achilles has
done about what he will do in battle.

Work

1 I am indeed, sir, a surgeon to old shoes; when they are in great danger I recover them.

Cobbler in *Julius Caesar*, 1.1.23–4

Playing on "recover" as cure and resole.

2 When workmen strive to do better than well,
They do confound their skill in covetousness,
And oftentimes excusing of a fault,
Doth make the fault worse by the excuse.

Pembroke in *King John*, 4.2.28–31

"Confound their skill in covetousness" = spoil what they are skilled at by emulation, or trying to be too clever.

3 I cannot draw a cart, nor eat dried oats;
If it be man's work, I'll do't.

Captain in *King Lear*, 5.3.38–9

Accepting a commission to kill Lear and Cordelia.

4 The labor we delight in physics pain.

Macbeth in *Macbeth*, 2.3.50

"Physics pain" = relieves pain, or the trouble we have taken.

5 Now have I done a good day's work.

King Edward in *Richard III*, 2.1.1

Thinking he has reconciled his quarreling nobles.

6 These sweet thoughts do even refresh my labors.

Ferdinand in *The Tempest*, 3.1.14

Thoughts, i.e., of Miranda, with whom he is in love.

The World

1 His face was as the heav'ns, and therein stuck
A sun and moon, which kept their course, and lighted
The little O, th' earth.

Cleopatra in *Antony and Cleopatra*, 5.2.79–81

The dead Antony becomes godlike in her imaginative recall.

2 His legs bestrid the ocean, his reared arm
Crested the world.

Cleopatra in *Antony and Cleopatra*, 5.2.82–3

Her magnificent, inflated vision of the dead Antony as superman, a colossus.

3 This goodly frame, the earth, seems to me a sterile promontory.

Hamlet in *Hamlet*, 2.2.298–9

4 This most excellent canopy, the air, look you, this brave o'erhanging firmament, this majestical roof fretted with golden fire, why, it appeareth nothing to me but a foul and pestilent congregation of vapors.

Hamlet in *Hamlet*, 2.2.299–303

Hamlet may be telling his old school fellows, whom he now knows were sent for to spy on him, what he wants them to think.

5 World, world, O world!
But that thy strange mutations make us hate thee,
Life would not yield to age.

Edgar in *King Lear*, 4.1.9–11

"Life would not yield to age" = we would not be reconciled to growing old.

6   This world's a city full of straying streets,
And death the market-place where each one meets.
Third Queen in *The Two Noble Kinsmen*, 1.5.15–16

Writing

1   Devise, wit; write, pen; for I am for whole volumes in folio.
Armado in *Love's Labor's Lost*, 1.2.184–5

To express his love for the country wench, Jaquenetta.

Wrongdoing (see also Crime, Evil)

1   I'll so offend to make offense a skill,
Redeeming time when men least think I will.
Prince Hal in *Henry IV, Part 1*, 1.2.216–17

Planning to make up for wasted time.

2   Didst thou never hear
That things ill got had ever bad success?
King Henry in *Henry VI, Part 3*, 2.2.45–6

Varying the proverb, "evil-gotten goods never prove well."

3   How oft the sight of means to do ill deeds

Make ill deeds done!
King John in *King John*, 4.2.219

Claiming that it was seeing Hubert as his agent that made him think of killing his nephew, Arthur.

4   I cannot wish the fault undone, the issue of it being so proper.
Kent in *King Lear*, 1.1.17–18

On learning that the handsome ("proper") Edmund is the "issue" of Gloucester's adultery.

5   *Don Pedro.* Officers, what offense have these men done?
Dogberry. Marry, sir, they have committed false report; moreover they have spoken untruths; secondarily, they are slanders; sixth and lastly, they have belied a lady; thirdly, they have verified unjust things; and, to conclude, they are lying knaves.
Much Ado About Nothing, 5.1.213–19

Dogberry's list is wonderfully muddled; by "slanders" he means slanderers.

6   Thus to persist
In doing wrong extenuates not wrong,
But makes it much more heavy.
Hector in *Troilus and Cressida*, 2.2.186–8

Seeing that the Trojans are wrong to want to keep Helen.

7   I see this is the time that the unjust man doth thrive.
Autolycus in *The Winter's Tale*, 4.4.673–4

He has benefited by an exchange of clothes with Prince Florizel.

8 Think but how vile a spectacle it
were
To view thy present trespass in
another,
Men's faults do seldom to themselves appear;
Their own transgressions partially
they smother.

The Rape of Lucrece, 631–4

Lucrece pleads with Tarquin, who intends to
rape her.

9 No more be grieved at that which
thou hast done:
Roses have thorns, and silver fountains mud;
Clouds and eclipses stain both sun
and moon,
And loathsome canker lives in
sweetest bud.

Sonnet 35, 1–4

On some wrong the loved friend has done
him; the "canker" is a worm that blights the
rose, symbol of beauty.

Youth (see also Boys, Girls, Parents and Children)

1 This thorn
Doth to our rose of youth rightly
belong.

Countess of Rossillion in *All's Well
That Ends Well,* 1.3.129–30

The "thorn" is Helena's unrequited love.

2 If the quick fire of youth light not
your mind,
You are no maiden, but a monument.

When you are dead, you should be
such a one
As you are now; for you are cold
and stern.

Bertram in *All's Well That Ends Well,*
4.2.5–9

Bertram, married to Helena, attempts to
seduce the chaste Diana.

3 My salad days,
When I was green in judgment,
cold in blood,
To say as I said then!

Cleopatra in *Antony and Cleopatra,*
1.5.73–5

Dismissing her earlier love for Julius Caesar.

4 He wears the rose
Of youth upon him.

Antony in *Antony and Cleopatra,*
3.13.20–1

Referring to the young Octavius.

5 Briefly die their joys
That place them on the truth of
girls and boys.

Lucius in *Cymbeline,* 5.5.106

Imogen, disguised as his page, abandons him
for the man she loves, Posthumus.

6 In the morn and liquid dew of
youth
Contagious blastments are most
imminent.
Be wary then; best safety lies in fear.
Youth to itself rebels, though none
else near.

Laertes in *Hamlet,* 1.3.41–4

Warning his sister Ophelia against Hamlet's
advances; "contagious blastments" = disease-
bringing blights.

7 In the very May-morn of his youth,
Ripe for exploits and mighty enter-
prises.
Bishop of Ely in *Henry V*, 1.2.120–1

On the newly-crowned Henry V.

8 Now all the youth of England are
on fire,
And silken dalliance in the
wardrobe lies.
Chorus in *Henry V*, 2.Prologue, 1–2

9 For who is he, whose chin is but
enriched
With one appearing hair, that will
not follow
These culled and choice-drawn cav-
aliers to France?
Chorus in *Henry V*, 3.Prologue, 22–4

On the English army sailing to France;
"choice-drawn" = carefully chosen.

10 So wise so young, they say, do never
live long.
King Richard in *Richard III*, 3.1.79

Commenting on the clever talk of the young
Prince Edward; reformulating a proverb, "too
soon wise to live long."

11 Not yet old enough for a man, nor
young enough for a boy; as a
squash is before 'tis a peascod, or a
codling when 'tis almost an apple.
'Tis with him in standing water
between boy and man.
Malvolio in *Twelfth Night*, 1.5.156–9

Describing Cesario, Orsino's page (the disguised Viola); a "squash" was an unripe pea-
pod; and a "codling" an unripe apple.

12 I would there were no age between
ten and three-and-twenty, or that
youth would sleep out the rest; for
there is nothing in the between but
getting wenches with child, wrong-
ing the ancientry, stealing, fighting.
**Shepherd in *The Winter's Tale*,
3.3.59–63**

"Ancientry" = old people.

13 Would any but these boiled-brains
of nineteen and two-and-twenty
hunt this weather?
**Shepherd in *The Winter's Tale*,
3.3.63–5**

That is, in the gloom of a great storm.

Character Index

fulness 1, 2; Generosity 1; Horses 1; Imagination 1; Infancy 1; Innocence 1; Kissing 2; Letters 1; Love 5; Lust 3; Marriage 2; Middle Age 1; Mourning 1; Music 1; News 2; Parting 1; Patience 1; Pleasure 4; Power 1; Praise 3, 4; Resignation 1; Resolution 1; Royalty 1, 2, 3; Snakes 1, 2; Speed 1; Suicide 5, 6, 7, 8; Theater 1; Valor 2; Women 1; World 1, 2; Youth 3

Clifford (Henry VI, Part 3):
Courage 3; Law 5

Cloten (Cymbeline):
Gold 2; Lateness 1; Music 3

Clown (Antony and Cleopatra):
Death 4; Joy 1; Snakes 2

Clown (Othello):
Music 15

Clown (The Winter's Tale):
Authority 11; Cowardice 8; Feasts 4; Singing 3

Cobbler (Julius Caesar):
Work 1

Cominius (Coriolanus):
Authority 3; Valor 5

Conrade (Much Ado About Nothing):
Fashion 8; Insults 16, 17

Constable (Henry V):
Action 6; Flattery 3; Weather 2

Constance (King John):
Death-Wish 7; Grief 8, 9

Cordelia (King Lear):
Hypocrisy 7; Love 38, 39; Madness 9; Parents and Children 7; Speech 9; Time 17

Corin (As You Like It):
Aphorisms 1; Contentment 1; Philosophy 3, 4; Sickness 1; Temperament 1; Truisms 1

Coriolanus (Caius Martius) (Coriolanus):
Absence 2; Acting 2, 3; Authority 2; Chastity 1; Confusion 1; Custom 1; Exile 2; Friendship 2; Hunger 1; Identity 2; Kissing 3; Man 2; Parents and Children 2; People 4, 5, 6, 7, 8, 9, 11, 12; Rumor 1; Service 3; Silence 2; Soldiers 2; Speechmaking 1; Valor 3; Women 10; Words 1

Cornwall (King Lear):
Obstinacy 3; Plain-Speaking 7

Costard (Love's Labor's Lost):
Lust 7; Payment 1; Words 4

Countess of Rossillion (All's Well That Ends Well):
Advice 1, 2; Evil 1; Virtue 1; Youth 1

Cressida (Troilus and Cressida):
Constancy 8; Courtship 22; Desire 15; Fear 16; Inconstancy 6; Love 91, 92, 93; Men and Women 9; Wisdom 6

Cromwell (Henry VIII):
Downfall 3

Cymbeline (Cymbeline):
Medicine 5; Peace 3

Dauphin (Henry V):
Horses 2; Self-Love 1; Time of Day 6; War 8

Davy (Henry IV, Part 2):
Travel 9

Decius (Julius Caesar):
Flattery 4; Persuasion 4

Demetrius (A Midsummer Night's Dream):
Devotion 2, 3; Plain-Speaking 10; Remembrance 7; Society 6

Demetrius (Titus Andronicus):
Courtship 21

Desdemona (Othello):
Devotion 5; Duty 5; Education 4; Endings 3; Friendship 24; Lament 1; Love 69, 70; Magic 2; Men 12; Moods 13; Music 17; Sickness 16; Sleep 15; Unkindness 3

Diana (All's Well That Ends Well):
Lust 1; Vows 1

Dick the Butcher (Henry VI, Part 2):
Lawyers 1

Diomedes (Troilus and Cressida):
Familiarity 1

Doctor (Gentleman) (King Lear):
Sleep 8

Doctor (Macbeth):
Guilt 9; Medicine 9

Doctor Pinch (The Comedy of Errors):
Exorcism 1

Dogberry (Much Ado About Nothing):
Blessings 4; Condescension 1, 2; Dignity 1; Honesty 4; Insults 17; Learning 2, 3; Mercy 13; Old Age 10; Praise 7; Proverbs 22; Religion 6; Self-Importance 2; Solecisms 4, 5, 6; Stupidity 1; Tediousness 4; Theft 7, 8; Wrongdoing 5

Dolabella (Antony and Cleopatra):
Dreams 2

Doll Tearsheet (Henry IV, Part 2):
Friendship 8; Insults 8; Kissing 6; Love 36; Reformation 3

Don John (Much Ado About Nothing):
Constraint 2; Hate 2; Hindrance 1; Misanthropy 4; Misogyny 2; Thanks 1; Villainy 3, 4

Don Pedro (Much Ado About Nothing):
Friendship 22; Generosity 4; Marriage 31, 34; Merriment 4, 5; Misogyny 4; Mockery 3; Modesty 1; Moods 12; Necessity 6; Sex 5; Speech 17; Speechmaking 4; Villainy 6; Words 7; Wrongdoing 5

Donalbain (Macbeth):
Danger 12

Douglas (Henry IV, Part 1):
Honor 4; Investment 1; News 6

Dromio of Ephesus (The Comedy of Errors):
Twins 1, 2

Dromio of Syracuse (The Comedy of Errors):
Reason 1; Time 8

Duchess of Gloucester (Henry VI, Part 2):
Parting 8; People 15

Duchess of Gloucester (Richard II):
Cowardice 5; Sorrow 8

Duchess of York (Richard II):
Flowers 7; Innovation 2; Sincerity 2

Duchess of York (Richard III):
Deceit 16; Proverbs 26

Recklessness 2; Remembrance 2; Resolution 2; Revenge 1, 2; Sanity 1; Sex 1, 2; Sickness 3; Silence 4; Slander 3; Soul 1; Stoicism 1; Stories 1; Suicide 11, 12, 13; Temperament 2, 3; Theater 4; Thrift 1; Truisms 2; Villainy 1; Weakness 1; Weather 1; Women 13, 14; World 3, 4

Hastings (Henry IV, Part 2):
Home 1; Hope 1; Time 11

Hastings (Richard III):
Appearances 10; Grace 2; Transience 4

Hecate (Macbeth):
Security 1

Hector (Troilus and Cressida):
Argument 5, 6; Honor 22; Idolatry 1; Law 11; Passion 3; Readiness 3; Security 2; Time 32, 33; Value 5; War 22; Words and Deeds 5; Wrongdoing 6

Helen (Troilus and Cressida):
Love 88, 89

Helena (All's Well That Ends Well):
Achievement 1; Arrogance 1; Endings 1; Expectation 1; Freedom 1; God 1; Infatuation 1, 2; Love 1, 2; Self-Reliance 1; Virginity 1

Helena (A Midsummer Night's Dream):
Anger 5; Beauty 15; Courtship 14; Friendship 21; Love 54, 55, 56; Night 17; Paradoxes 1; Rejection 1; Sleep 13; Solitude 3; Twins 3; Vows 3

Hermia (A Midsummer Night's Dream):
Comparisons 1; Constancy 4; Insults 15; Love 53; Patience 9; Prayer 14; Senses 1; Vows 2

Hermione (The Winter's Tale):
Action 16; Conspiracy 9; Death-Wish 11; Grief 15; Innocence 8; Praise 13; Stories 10

Hero (Much Ado About Nothing):
Criticism 3; Egotism; Love 63, 64; Men 10; Scorn 1; Self-Love 2

Hippolyta (A Midsummer Night's Dream):
Acting 25; Hunting 3; Moon 2; Nonsense 1

Holofernes (Love's Labor's Lost):
Affectation 1; Argument 4; Ignorance 1; Words 5

Horatio (Hamlet):
Apparitions 1, 2, 3; Belief 1; Dawn 1; Epitaphs 5; Faces 2; Foreboding 3, 4; Ghosts 1, 3, 5, 6, 8; Moods 7; Mortality 3; Murder 3; Philosophy 5; Remembrance 2; Soldiers 3; Stories 2; Suicide 14; Talking 3; Time of Day 1; Truisms 2; Weather 1

Hortensio (The Taming of the Shrew):
Choice 8; Love 86; Music 20; Travel 19

Host (The Merry Wives of Windsor):
Courtship 13

Hostess (Henry IV, Part 1):
Acting 12

Hostess (Henry IV, Part 2):
Quarrels 3

Hotspur (Henry IV, Part 1):
Business 2; Cowardice 2; Danger 1; Death 11; Devil 3; Doomsday 1; Earthquakes 1; Effeminacy 1; Flattery 2; Friendship 6; Greatness 5; Honor 3; Investment 1; Life 4; Maps 1; Negotiation 1; Oaths 1; Parting 7; Poetry 6, 7; Politics 3; Risk 1; Sex 3; Sickness 5, 6, 7;

Soldiers 9; Supernatural 1; Tediousness 1; Time 9; Travel 7; Trust 1; Truth 2; Valor 6; War 2, 4; Women 15

Hymen (As You Like It):
Marriage 7

Iago (Othello):
Action 14; Advice 14; Aphorisms 10, 11; Appearance 8; Chance 1; Character 4; Criticism 4; Deceit 12, 13, 14; Drinking 23; Evil 10; Honesty 7; Hypocrisy 11, 12; Jealousy 5, 6, 7, 8, 9, 10; Lechery 3; Lust 11; Marriage 39; Men 11; Money 11; Murder 7; Patience 10; Plots 4; Reputation 7, 8, 9; Resolution 6; Revenge 5; Self-Interest 4; Silence 6; Sleep 14; Soldiers 19, 22, 23; Time 20; Virtue 17, 18, 19; Women 23

Imogen (Cymbeline):
Countries 1, 2; Death-Wish 4; Deceit 2; Doubt 1; Eyes 4, 5; Hate 1; Kissing 4; Man 3; Parting 3, 4, 5; Prayer 2; Sickness 2; Suicide 10; Travel 6; Virtue 4

Iras (Antony and Cleopatra):
Death-Wish 2

Isabella (Measure for Measure):
Authority 9, 10; Death 27; Desire 11; Mercy 5, 6, 7, 8; Pity 6; Power 10; Strength 2; Truth 5

Jachimo (Cymbeline):
Action 2; Beauty 5, 6; Eyes 3; Perfume 1

Jack Cade (Henry VI, Part 2):
Books 1; Education 1; Gardens 4; Language 4; People 16; Proverbs 8

Jaques (As You Like It):
Age 4, 5; Argument 2; Body 1; Boys 1; Country Life 5; Faults 4; Fools 1, 2, 3, 4, 6; Freedom 2; Height 1; Infancy 2; Love 13; Marriage 4, 8; Maturity 1; Medicine 2; Melancholy 2, 3, 4; Mockery 1; Moods 3, 5; Music 2; Names 1; Parting 2; Poetry 5; Singing 1; Soldiers 1; Solitude 1; Theater 3; Time 2

Jessica (The Merchant of Venice):
Love 46; Music 11; Parents and Children 12

Joan la Pucelle (Henry VI, Part 1):
Anxiety 3; Chastity 7; Fear 4; Glory 1; Resistance 1

John of Gaunt (Richard II):
Countries 5, 6, 7; Eating 11; Endings 4; Grief 13; Last Words 3; Necessity 7; Sorrow 9; Transience 3; Travel 17; Vanity 2

Julia (The Two Gentlemen of Verona):
Love 100; Night 23; Rivers 3; Sincerity 3; Women 28

Juliet (Romeo and Juliet):
Anticipation 3; Anxiety 9; Deceit 22, 23; Despair 8; Devotion 6; Fear 15; Impatience 3; Inevitability 2; Love 79, 80, 81, 83; Memory 5; Names 7, 8; News 10; Night 20, 21; Old Age 11; Parting 15, 16; Sorrow 14; Strength 3; Time 27; Vows 4

Juno (The Tempest):
Blessings 5

Jupiter (Cymbeline):
Providence 1

Katherine (Love's Labor's Lost):
Cheerfulness 1

Katherine (The Taming of the Shrew):
Quarrels 16; Speechmaking 5; Women 25

Kent (King Lear):
Astrology 3; Authority 6; Doomsday 2; Duty 4; Farewells 12; Fortune 13, 14; Insults 11; Lawyers 2; Medicine 8; Middle Age 3; Miracles 2; Night 11; Nothing 1; Plain-Speaking 6; Speech 11; Storms 10; Suffering 2; Wrongdoing 4

King Edward (Henry VI, Part 3):
Action 8; Body 4; Fate 4; Parents and Children 4; Resistance 2; Victory 1

King Edward (Richard III):
Work 5

King Henry (Henry IV, Part 1):
Anxiety 2; Authority 5; Birds 1; Business 3; Eating 3; Enemies 1; Fame 1; Greatness 4; Humility 3; Men 2; News 5; Popularity 1; Prophecy 3; Rebellion 2; Respect 1; Royalty 8, 9

King Henry (Henry IV, Part 2):
Avarice 1; Birds 3; Charity 1; Despair 2; Deviousness 3; Fate 3; Fortune 8; Friendship 9; Gardens 1; Gold 3; Music 6; Necessity 2; Politics 4; Prophecy 4; Revolution 1; Royalty 11; Sleep 5; Sleeplessness 1; Thought 4; Wilderness 1

King Henry (Henry V):
Age 18, 19; Business 5; Ceremony 1, 2; Courtship 7, 8, 9, 10, 11; Custom 4; Crime 1; Danger 3, 4; Death 16; Deceit 3; Duty 2; Eloquence 4; Evil 2; Fellowship 2; Festivals 3, 4; God 2, 3; Greetings 1; Honor 8, 9, 10; Language 3; Mercy 2, 3; Oaths 3; Overconfidence 1; Peace 9, 10; Philosophy 8, 9, 10; Prayer 6; Readiness 1; Remembrance 3; Repentance 3; Royalty 17, 18, 19, 20; Sea 1; Sin 1; Soldiers 12, 16, 17; Solitude 2; Travel 10, 11; Treason 3; War 10, 11, 12, 13, 15

King Henry (Henry VI, Part 1):
Civil War 1; Persuasion 1

King Henry (Henry VI, Part 2):
God 5, 6, 7; Heaven 2; Honor 11; Innocence 3; Kissing 7; Peace 12; Prayer 8, 9; Quarrels 4, 5; Sin 2

King Henry (Henry VI, Part 3):
Animals 7; Happiness 3; Old Age 5; Royalty 22; Suspicion 1; Wrongdoing 2

King Henry (Henry VIII):
Action 11; Beauty 9; Conscience 3; Eating 6; Eloquence 4; Enemies 3; Innovation 1; Nobility 3; Politics 8; Royalty 24; Words and Deeds 1

King Henry IV (Richard II):
Conspiracy 8; Honor 20; Parents and Children 14; Poison 2

King John (King John):
Comfort 4; Dying 11; Murder 4; Sickness 12; Storms 5; Wrongdoing 3

King Lear (King Lear):
Adultery 1; Affliction 4; Age 26, 27; Anger 4; Authority 6, 7; Cause 4; Country Life 11; Danger 11; Death 20, 21; Dogs 3; Evil 4; Fashion 6; Flattery 5; Fools 8; Gold 4; Homelessness 1, 2; Humanity 3; Identity 3, 4; Improvement 2; Ingratitude 6, 7, 8; Justice 5, 6, 7; Madness 7, 8; Man 9; Maps 2; Middle Age 3; Misogyny 1; Mortality 7; Mourning 17; Necessity 4, 5; Nothing 2; Parents and Children 6, 9; Patience 5, 7;

Politics 16, 17; Prayer 11, 12; Proverbs 12; Reconciliation 3, 4; Repentance 4; Retirement 2; Royalty 25; Sacrifice 2; Self-Pity 1, 2; Sickness 13, 14; Sin 4; Sorrow 3; Speech 10, 12; Storms 7, 8, 9; Suffering 1; Tears 9, 10, 11

King of France (All's Well That Ends Well):
Girls 1; Honor 1; Loss 1; Old Age 1; Remembrance 1; Time 1

King of France (King Lear):
Love 40; Virtue 9

King of Navarre (Love's Labor's Lost):
Fame 2; Fashion 7; Reading 3; Study 1

King Richard (Richard II):
Angels 2; Animals 9; Betrayal 2; Death 33, 34, 35; Death-Wish 9; Deserving 3; Despair 5, 6; Discontent 1; Eloquence 6; Epitaphs 13; Farewells 15; Flattery 6; Greetings 11; Grief 14; Humanity 6; Hypocrisy 13; Identity 5; Lateness 3; Last Words 4; Loss 8; Music 18; Necessity 8; Parting 13; Philosophy 18; Power 11; Pride 2; Renunciation 1, 2, 3; Royalty 26, 28, 29; Self-Knowledge 11; Self-Pity 3; Stories 5, 6; Time 24; War 20

King Richard (Richard III):
Apologies 4; Boys 3; Conscience 6, 7, 8; Courtship 17, 18; Cowardice 6; Dancing 2; Deceit 20; Dejection 4; Deserving 4; Despair 7; Desperation 1; Duplicity 6, 7; Excuses 4; Execution 1; Foreboding 13; Gifts 4; Hypocrisy 14, 15, 16; Improvement 3; Last Words 5; Marriage 44; Murder 12; Politics 21; Readiness 2; Repetition 1; Reputation 12; Ruthlessness 5; Scorn 2; Sunrise 3; Trust 3; Victory 3; Villainy 7; Youth 10

Knight (King Lear):
Ceremony 3

Lady Anne (Richard III):
Animals 11; Pity 10; Sleeplessness 6

Lady Macbeth (Macbeth):
Ambition 11; Aphorisms 4, 7; Birds 8; Ceremony 4; Courage 6; Cowardice 4; Cruelty 3; Death 22; Deceit 4; Desire 10; Drinking 13; Evil 6; Eyes 9; Faces 6; Foreboding 9; Guilt 6, 7, 8; Hell 4; Infancy 3; Kindness 2; Memory 4; Murder 5; Parting 11; Regret 2; Ruthlessness 3, 4; Sleep 11; Time of Day 7

Lady Macduff (Macbeth):
Fear 13; Innocence 5; Nature 4

Lady Percy (Henry IV, Part 1):
Love 35; Moods 8; Sleep 2

Lady Percy (Henry IV, Part 2):
Fashion 3, 4; Speech 3; Strength 1; War 6, 7

Laertes (Hamlet):
Burial 3; Chastity 4, 5, 6; Flowers 1; Justice 2; Medicine 6; Poison 1; Virtue 5; Youth 6

Lafew (All's Well That Ends Well):
Clothing 1; Grief 1; Medicine 1; Miracles 1; Philosophy 1

Launce (The Two Gentlemen of Verona):
Dogs 7

Launcelot Gobbo (The Merchant of Venice):
Food 8; Fortune 19; Lechery 2; Parents and Children 11; Proverbs 18, 19; Thinness 3

els 3, 4; Simplicity 2; Speechmaking 3; Theater 13, 15; Time of Day 8
Theseus (Two Noble Kinsmen):
Epitaphs 17; Gods and Goddesses 4
Third Apparition (Macbeth):
Prophecy 9
Third Citizen (Coriolanus):
Ingratitude 2
Third Citizen (Richard III):
Change 1; Government 4
Third Fisherman (Pericles):
Fish 1
Third Gentleman (The Winter's Tale):
Joy 6; Sorrow 17
Third Queen (Two Noble Kinsmen):
Cities 3; World 6
Time (The Winter's Tale):
Time 39
Timon (Timon of Athens):
Ceremony 5; Dying 16; Epitaphs 15; Flattery 9; Friendship 28, 29, 30; Generosity 5, 6; Gold 6; Helping 2; Kindness 4; Life 12; Misanthropy 5; Prayer 18; Theft 11; War 21
Titania (A Midsummer Night's Dream):
Dancing 1; Fairies 5, 7; Food 11; Infatuation 8; Love 59; Music 13, 14; Names 6; Pregnancy 2; Quarrels 10, 11; Seasons 13, 14
Titinius (Julius Caesar):
Speed 4; Transience 1
Titus (Titus Andronicus):
Books 5; Epitaphs 16; Hunting 4; Insects 3; Isolation 1; Old Age 12; Sleep 18; Stories 9; Storms 17; Wilderness 3
Touchstone (As You Like It):
Body 2; Court 1; Country Life 6, 7; Food 4, 5; Fools 5; Honesty 1; Love 12; Marriage 3; Mediocrity 1; Poetry 2, 3, 4; Possession 1; Quarrels 1; Travel 1; Virtue 2; Wisdom 1, 2
Tranio (The Taming of the Shrew):
Friendship 27; Love 84; Study 4
Trebonius (Julius Caesar):
Chaos 1
Trinculo (The Tempest):
Clothing 11; Fellowship 3; Fish 2; Storms 15, 16
Troilus (Troilus and Cressida):
Anticipation 4; Conscience 9; Dawn 8; Constancy 7; Love 90; Praise 12; Reason 7; Silence 7; Sorrow 16; Temptation 5; Time 31; Value 4, 6; Weakness 6; Words 10
Tyrell (Richard III):
Murder 13
Ulysses (Troilus and Cressida):
Anarchy 2; Arrogance 2; Business 9; Fashion 11; Friendship 31; Government 6; Lechery 4, 5; Order 1, 2, 3; Perseverance 3; Pride 3; Proverbs 28, 29; Reputation 13, 14; Time 28, 29, 30; Value 7; Words and Deeds 4
Ursula (Much Ado About Nothing):
Fishing 2

Valentine (The Two Gentlemen of Verona):
Courtship 24; Custom 5; Experience 5; Friendship 32; Gifts 5; Happiness 7; Ruin 1; Simplicity 3; Solitude 5
Varro's Second Servant (Timon of Athens):
Homelessness 3; Poverty 3
Ventidius (Antony and Cleopatra):
Ambition 1
Verges (Much Ado About Nothing):
Solecisms 1
Vernon (Henry IV, Part 1):
Animals 4; Seasons 4; Soldiers 6
Vernon (Henry VI, Part 1):
Flowers 4
Vincentio (The Taming of the Shrew):
Education 5
Viola (Twelfth Night):
Acting 29; Appearance 11; Beauty 24, 25; Countries 8; Courtship 23; Fools 15; Ingratitude 10; Melancholy 9; Music 27; Patience 12; Peace 15; Pride 6; Quarrels 17; Speechmaking 6; Time 34, 35; Travel 22; Women 27
Volumnia (Coriolanus):
Action 1; Anger 1; Humility 1; Man 1; Manliness 1; Parents and Children 1; Speech 2
Warwick (Henry IV, Part 2):
Language 2; Life 5; Rumor 5
Warwick (Henry VI, Part 1):
Law 4
Warwick (Henry VI, Part 3):
Dying 9
Welsh Captain (Richard II):
Portents 9
Westmorland (Henry IV, Part 2):
Peace 5, 8; Speech 5
Widow (The Taming of the Shrew):
Giddiness 1
William (As You Like It):
Mediocrity 1
Williams (Henry V):
Danger 4; Soldiers 15
Winter (Love's Labor's Lost):
Seasons 11
Witches (Weird Sisters) (Macbeth):
Air 1; Confusion 2; Eyes 10; Occult 2, 3; Paradoxes 4; Supernatural 2
Worcester (Henry IV, Part 1):
Birds 2; Conspiracy 1; Friendship 7; News 6; Retirement 1; Treason 2
York (Henry VI, Part 2):
Thought 8; Treachery 1
York (Henry VI, Part 3):
Beauty 8; Cruelty 1; Dying 8
York (Richard II):
Affliction 11; Confusion 7; Fashion 9; Grace 1; Pity 9; Poetry 12; Politics 19; Proverbs 24; Royalty 31; Theater 17
York (Richard III):
Proverbs 25

Play Index

Poem Index

Keyword Index

alliance:
  Good lord, for a. (Celibacy 3)
all-seer:
  that high a. which I dallied with (Punishment 3)
alone:
  here can I sit a. (Solitude 5)
  how can it be said I am a. (Solitude 3)
Alps:
  on the A. ... thou didst eat strange flesh (Eating 1)
altitude:
  the a. which thou hast ... fell (Miracles 3)
amaze:
  it doth a. me that such a man (Power 4)
amazed:
  I am a. ... and lose my way (Danger 10)
amazement:
  be collected. No more a. (Wonder 4)
ambition:
  a.'s debt is paid (Ambition 8)
  a., the soldier's virtue (Ambition 1)
  art not without a. (Ambition 11)
  become a churchman better than a. (Ambition 6)
  death for his a.(Caesar 3)
  fling away a. (Ambition 5)
  ill-weaved a. (Ambition 2)
  lowliness is young a.'s ladder (Ambition 7)
  the big wars that makes a. virtue (Farewells 14)
  thriftless a. (Ambition 13)
  vaulting a. (Ambition 12)
  virtue is choked with foul a. (Ambition 3)
ambitious:
  the very substance of the a. (Dreams 4)
Amen:
  a., a. to that fair prayer (Prayer 14)
amend:
  do thou a. thy face, and I'll a. my life (Faces 3)
amendment:
  I see a good a. of life (Theft 1)
amiable:
  O a., lovely Death! (Death-Wish 5)
amity:
  now thou and I are new in a. (Reconciliation 4)
  the a. that wisdom knits not (Friendship 31)
anatomy:
  a mere a. (Character 1)
angel:
  art thou... some angel (Apparitions 5)
  a. is like you, Kate (Courtship 8)
  better a. is a man (Love 111)
  how like an a. (Man 5)
  she is an a. (Beauty 11)
  speak again, bright a. (Adoration 1)
  though a. on the outward side (Hypocrisy 9)
angels:
  a. and ministers of grace (Prayer 3)
  a. are bright still (Angels 1)
  flights of a. sing thee to thy rest (Epitaphs 5)
  if a. fight weak men must fall (Angels 2)
anger:
  a.'s my meat (Anger 1)

contempt and a. of his lip (Contempt 4)
  more in sorrow than in a. (Moods 7)
  to be in a. is impiety (Anger 9)
  touch me with noble a. (Tears 10)
angle:
  give me mine a. (Fishing 1)
angling:
  pleasant'st a. is to see the fish (Fishing 2)
angry:
  be a. when you will (Forbearance 1)
  when she is a. she is keen (Anger 5)
animal:
  a poor., bare, forked a. (Man 9)
animals:
  the paragon of a. (Man 5)
annals:
  if you have writ your a. true (Soldiers 2)
answer:
  still a. nay and take it (Deceit 19)
  your a., sir, is enigmatical (Answers 1)
ant:
  set thee to school to an a. (Proverbs 14)
anthropophagi:
  the a., and men whose heads (Travel 16)
antic:
  there the a. sits (Death 35)
antiquity:
  every part ... blasted with a. (Age 12)
Antony:
  A. that revels long a-nights (Revels 1)
  as she would catch another A. (Death 6)
  bear the weight of A. (Horses 1)
  none but A. should conquer A. (Suicide 5)
  to imagine an A. (Imagination 1)
  when I forget to send to A. (Letters 1)
anything:
  a. that's mended is but patched (Virtue 22, Sin 8)
ape:
  like an angry a. (Authority 9)
Apollo:
  A. a poor humble swain (Gods 5)
apothecary:
  O true a. (Last Words 6)
apparel:
  a. oft proclaims the man (Clothing 3)
  a. vice like virtue's harbinger (Deceit 1)
  fashion wears out more a. (Fashion 8)
appetite:
  a. an universal wolf (Anarchy 1)
  cloy the hungry edge of a. (Imagination 6)
  good digestion wait on a. (Eating 7)
  sharpen with cloyless sauce his a. (Food 2)
  taste with a distempered a. (Self-Love 3)
  their l. may be called a. (Love 98)
  who riseth from a feast with that keen a. (Eating 8)
appetites:
  curb those a. (Law 11)
  other women cloy the a. (Praise 1)
applause:
  their loud a. and aves vehement (People 17)

apple:
a goodly a. rotten at the heart (Duplicity 4)
an a. cleft in twain (Twins 4)

apple-john:
I am withered like an old a. (Thinness 2)

apples:
small choice in rotten a. (Choice 8)

apricots:
feed him with apricots (Food 11)
go bind ... yon dangling a. (Gardens 5)

April:
a day in A. never came so sweet (Anticipation 2)
he smells A. and May (Courtship 13)
men are A. when they woo (Marriage 5)
the A.'s in her eyes (Tears 1)
uncertain glory of an A. day (Love 102)

aqua-vitae:
like a. with a midwife (Plots 5)

arch:
the wide a. of the ranged empire fall (Empire 1)

Arden:
in the forest of A. (Country Life 1)
now I am in A., the more fool I (Travel 1)

argument:
all the a. is a whore (War 23)
finer than the staple of his a. (Argument 4)

are:
a. you good men and true? (Solecisms 4)

Aristotle:
A. thought unfit to hear ... philosophy (Argument 3)

armed:
be thou a. for some unhappy words (Quarrels 15)

armor:
the very a. he had on (Ghosts 1)

arms:
a., take your last embrace (Farewells 19)
my father's spirit in a.! (Foreboding 5)
take a. against a sea of troubles (Choice 1)

arrest:
Death is strict in his a. (Death 9)

art:
a. made tongue-tied (Censorship 1)
a. of our necessities (Necessity 5)
a. which does change nature (Nature 8)
a. which in their piedness shares (Nature 7)
a. with nature's workmanship at strife (Painting 1)
desiring this man's a. (Misery 5)
in sweet music is such a. (Music 8)
I want that glib and oily a. (Hypocrisy 7)
let it be an a. lawful as eating (Magic 3)
more matter with less a. (Eloquence 2)
no a. to find the mind's construction (Appearance 2)

artery:
makes each petty a. in this body (Fate 1)

Arthur's bosom:
(Afterlife 4)

arts:
had I but followed the a. (Language 9)
peace, dear nurse of a. (Peace 11)

asleep:
faith, half a. (Sleep 15)
what, all so soon a. (Sleep 17)

ass:
forget not that I am an a. (Stupidity 1)
I ... perceive that I am made an a. (Self-Knowledge 10)
my foes tell me plainly I am an a. (Self-Knowledge 12)
specify ... that I am an a. (Self-Importance 2)
that any man turn a. (Country Life 5)
you are an a. (Insults 17)

assays:
with a. of bias (Deviousness 1)

assassination:
if th' a. could trammel up (Action 12)

asses:
a. are made to bear (Quarrels 16)
tenderly led by the nose as a. are (Deceit 12)

Athens:
seemed A. as a paradise (Love 53)

atomies:
eyes ... shut their coward gates on a. (Eyes 1)

attention:
tongues of dying men enforce a. (Last Words 3)

attribute:
much a. he hath (Fame 5)

aught:
what's a. but as 'tis valued? (Value 4)

augmentation:
new map with the a. of the Indies (Faces 6)

Aurora:
yonder shines A's harbinger (Dawn 4)

authorities:
manage those a. (Age 21)
when two a. are up (Confusion 1)

authority:
art made tongue-tied by a. (Censorship 1)
a., though it err like others (Authority 10)
man ... dressed in a little brief a. (Authority 9)
the demigod, a. (Authority 8)
the great image of a. (Authority 5)
there is no fettering of a. (Authority 1)
though a. be a stubborn bear (Authority 11)
what a. and show of truth (Deceit 9)
wrest once the law to your a. (Law 7)
you have that in your countenance ... a. (Authority 6)

autumn:
the childing a. (Seasons 14)
the teeming a. (Seasons 19)
an a. ... that grew the more by reaping (Generosity 1)

avoided:
what can be a., whose end is purposed? (Fate 4)

away:
a. and mock the time (Deceit 5)

awe:
live to be in a. of such a thing (Freedom 2)

aweary:
Cassius is a. of the world (Criticism 2)

axe:
    let the great a. fall (Punishment 2)
babbled:
    'a b. of green fields (Dying 6)
babe:
    how tender 'tis to love the b. (Infancy 1, Ruthlessness 4)
    pity like a naked new-born b. (Pity 5)
babes:
    old fools are b. again (Age 25)
baby:
    dost thou not see my b.? (Infancy 1)
bachelor:
    b. of threescore (Celibacy 1)
    when I said I would die a b. (Marriage 32)
backward:
    dark b. and abysm of time (Memory 6)
bait:
    your b. of falsehood takes this carp (Deviousness 1)
ballad:
    I love a b. in print (Poetry 14, Singing 3)
ballad-mongers:
    these same meter b. (Poetry 6)
balm:
    I wash away my b. (Renunciation 3)
    'tis not the b., the scepter and the ball (Royalty 19)
band:
    the gross b. of the unfaithful (Religion 1)
banishment:
    Ha, b.? Be merciful, say death (Exile 8)
bankrupt:
    time is a very b. (Time 8)
Banquo:
    B, thy soul's flight (Death 24)
bar:
    any b., any cross (Hindrance 1)
barbarism:
    b. itself have pitied him (Pity 9)
Barbary:
    a maid called B. (Music 16)
barber's:
    I must to the b. (Hair 3)
barefoot:
    walked b. to Palestine (Desire 14)
bargain:
    in the way of b. (Business 2, Negotiation 1)
barge:
    the b. she sat in (Ships 1)
barnes:
    b. are blessings (Children 1)
bars:
    life being weary of these worldly b. (Suicide 15)
base:
    art thou b., common, and popular? (Soldiers 14)
    b. is the slave that pays (Money 5)
    who is here so b.? (Patriotism 1)
bastard:
    that same wicked b. of Venus (Love 23)
    I am a bastard too (Bastardy 2)

bastardizing:
    star...twinkled on my b. (Astrology 2)
bastards:
    gods, stand up for b. (Bastardy 1)
bat:
    ere the b. hath flown (Evil 7)
bate:
    do I not b.? (Thinness 2)
battle:
    the noise of b. hurtled (Portents 5)
    when the b.'s lost and won (Supernatural 2)
battlements:
    entrance of Duncan under my b. (Foreboding 9)
bawdy:
    if b. talk offend you (Obscenity 1)
bay-trees:
    the b. ... are all withered (Portents 9)
be:
    be it thy course to busy giddy minds (Politics 4)
    be not afeared (Music 22)
    be not easily won (Deceit 19)
    be you not troubled with the time (Necessity 1)
    to be or not to be (Choice 1, Suicide 12)
beacon:
    modest doubt ... the b. of the wise (Security 2)
beagle:
    a b., true-bred (Love 97)
bear:
    exit pursued by a b. (Animals 12)
    b. free and patient thoughts (Patience 6)
    b. with me good boy (Forbearance 3)
    b. with my weakness (Weakness 4)
    sing the savageness out of a b. (Music 15)
    though authority be a stubborn b. (Authority 11)
beard:
    a husband with a b. on his face (Marriage 29)
    black b. will turn white (Courtship 11)
    he that hath a b. (Celibacy 2)
    what a b. hast thou got (Appearance 4)
    younger ... by the loss of a b. (Appearance 6)
bearing:
    either wise b. or ignorant carriage (Society 2)
bears:
    wolves and b. (Creatures 5)
beast:
    a b., no more (Man 7)
    Caesar should be a b. without a heart (Fear 8)
    he is little better than a b. (Drinking 15)
    no b. so fierce (Animals 11, Pity 10)
    the b. with many heads (People 12)
    unkindest b. more kinder than mankind (Kindness 4)
beasts:
    gods ... have taken the shapes of b. (Gods 5)
    here comes a pair of very strange b. (Fools 6)
    the b., the fishes and the wingèd fowls (Marriage 9)
beating:
    b. and hanging are terrors to me (Afterlife 6)
beautiful:
    she's b., and therefore to be wooed (Women 16)

beauty:
b. and honor in her (Beauty 10)
b. doth varnish age (Beauty 13)
b. itself doth of itself persuade (Beauty 29)
b. my prize (Desire 19)
b. provoketh thieves (Women 3)
b.'s ensign yet is crimson (Death 38)
b.'s rose might never die (Beauty 30)
b. too rich for use (Beauty 22)
b. within itself should not be wasted (Time 45)
for b. lives with kindness (Beauty 27)
for b., wit, high birth (Time 30)
grief, that's b.'s canker (Beauty 23)
he hath a daily b. in his life (Virtue 19)
how much more doth b. beauteous seem (Beauty 32)
I ne'er saw true b. (Love 70)
look on b., and you shall see (Beauty 14)
most radiant, exquisite ... b. (Beauty 24)
my b., though but mean (Beauty 12)
O b., till now I never knew thee (Beauty 9)
orators are dumb when b. pleadeth (Eloquence 8)
'tis b. that doth oft make women proud (Beauty 8)
unmask her b. to the moon (Chastity 5)
virtue is b. (Virtue 24)
were b. under twenty locks (Proverbs 32)
bed:
heat of a luxurious b. (Lust 9)
how bravely thou becom'st thy b. (Beauty 5)
I haste me to my b. (Sleep 19)
made his pendant b.(Birds 7)
never yet one hour in his b. (Sleeplessness 6)
run into't as to a lover's b. (Death 1)
bedfellows:
misery acquaints a man with strange b. (Fellowship 3)
beds:
the b. i'th' east are soft (Luxury 1)
bed-time:
I would 'twere b.-time (War 3)
bee:
where the b. sucks there suck I (Fairies 9)
beef:
I am a great eater of b. (Eating 13)
what say you to a piece of b.? (Food 14)
beer:
show vilely in me to desire small b. (Drinking 8)
beetle:
poor b. that we tread upon (Death 27)
shard-borne b. with his drowsy hums (Evil 7)
beetles:
b. black approach not near (Creatures 4)
beggar:
a dedicated b. to the air (Poverty 3)
farmer's dog bark at a b. (Authority 7)
whiles I am a b. I will rail (Hypocrisy 6)
beggars:
our basest b. (Necessity 4)
they are but b. (Love 83)
when b. die there are no comets (Portents 6)

beggary:
there's b. in the love (Love 5)
begging:
here's them ... gets more with b. (Begging 2)
begot:
you have b. me (Parents and Children 7)
beguile:
to b. the time (Deceit 4)
believe:
b. me for mine honor (Honor 14)
b. not that the ... dart of love (Love 45)
I might not this b. (Belief 1)
make thee b. I love (Courtship 1)
bell:
she strike upon the b. (Bells 1)
the b. invites me (Bells 2)
the sullen, surly b. (Mourning 20)
bellman:
the fatal b. (Birds 8)
bellows:
the b. and the fan (Lust 2)
bells:
like sweet b. jangled (Dejection 4)
bellyful:
rumble thy b. (Storms 9)
benefits:
we are born to do b. (Friendship 29)
benison:
God's b. go with you (Blessings 1)
beseech:
b. you sir, be merry (Joy 5)
best:
the b. persuaded of himself (Self-Importance 3)
the b. in this kind (Acting 25)
'tis b. to give him way (Obstinacy 3)
when he is b. (Drinking 15)
betray:
to b. us in deepest consequence (Evil 5)
betrothed:
to her ... was I b. (Devotion 3)
better:
b. a little chiding (Chiding 1)
b. a witty fool than a foolish wit (Fools 11)
b. once than never (Lateness 4)
b. three hours too soon (Lateness 2)
I could have b. spared a b. man (Farewells 7)
betters:
when we see our b. (Misery 1)
bid:
b. that welcome which comes to punish (Endurance 2)
big:
looked b. and spit at him (Cowardice 8)
big-bellied:
see the sails conceive and grow b. (Pregnancy 2)
bird:
b. of dawning singeth (Festivals 1)
sweet b.'s throat (Country Life 3)
the b. that hath been limèd (Suspicion 1)

this b. hath made his procreant bed (Birds 7)
thou art a summer b. (Birds 3)
birds:
the eagle suffers little b. to sing (Birds 14, Power 12)
birth:
bring this monstrous b. to the world's light (Evil 10)
birthday:
it is my b. (Birthdays 1)
biting:
his b. is immortal (Death 4, Snakes 1)
blanket:
heaven peep through the b. (Murder 5)
blastments:
contagious b. are most imminent (Chastity 6)
blasts:
b. of January would blow you (Thinness 5)
many b. to shake them (Greatness 10)
blaze:
rash fierce b. of riot (Transience 3)
blazon:
eternal b. must not be (Afterlife 1, Eternity 2)
blessedness:
lives and dies in single b. (Marriage 28)
blessings:
barnes are b. (Children 1)
blest:
b. are those whose blood (Temperament 2)
blind:
b. fear that seeing reason leads (Fear 16)
he that is strucken b. (Eyes 13)
now you strike like the b. man (Anger 6)
blindworms:
newts and b. do no wrong (Creatures 4)
blocks:
you b., you stones (Insults 10)
blood:
every drop of blood (Promises 4)
here's the smell of the b. still (Guilt 8)
his b. is very snow-broth (Asceticism 1)
I am in b. stepped in so far (Crime 2)
I am in so far in b. (Murder 12)
I'll not shed her b. (Beauty 18)
is your b. so madly hot (Passion 3)
it will have b. ... b. will have b. (Proverbs 17)
lost the fresh b. in thy cheeks (Moods 8)
make thick my b. (Ruthlessness 3)
Neptune's ocean wash this b. (Guilt 5)
no sure foundation set on b. (Murder 4)
no true drop of b. in him (Misogyny 4)
the b. more stirs to rouse a lion (Valor 6)
the b. weeps from my heart (Prophecy 4)
the warming of the b. (Drinking 10)
those whose b. and judgment (Temperament 2)
bloody:
be b. , bold and resolute (Prophecy 8)
blossom:
I pluck this pale and maiden b. here (Flowers 4)
O that this b. could be kept from cankers (Flowers 3)

blow:
that but this b. might be the be-all (Action 12)
blows:
oft when b. have made me stay (Words 1)
words before b. (Councils 3)
boast:
now b. thee, death (Death 5)
boats:
fortune brings in some b. (Fortune 6)
light b. sail swift (Ships 6)
bodies:
our b. are our gardens (Virtue 17)
bodkin:
his quietus make with a bare b. (Suicide 13)
body:
bear your b. more seeming (Body 2)
done with the dead b. (Burial 1)
make less thy b. hence (Mortality 6)
my little b. is aweary (Weariness 2)
so young a b. with so old a head (Wisdom 4)
the foul b. of the infected world (Body 1)
this common b. (People 2)
what is the b.? (Body 4)
boggler:
you have been a b. ever (Shiftiness 1)
boiled-brains:
would any but these b. (Youth 13)
bold:
that which hath made them drunk hath made me b.
(Drinking 13)
bolt:
a fool's b. is soon shot (Fools 7)
marked I where the b. of Cupid fell (Flowers 5)
bolting-hutch:
that b. of beastliness (Fatness 4)
bombard:
that huge b. of sack (Fatness 4)
bombast:
my sweet creature of b. (Fatness 2)
bond:
b. cracked 'twixt son and father (Disorder 1)
I'll have my b. (Determination 2)
natural b. of sisters (Love 7)
tear to pieces that great b. (Evil 8)
bondage:
as b. e'er of freedom (Marriage 47)
I begin to find an idle ... b. (Tyranny 5)
bondman:
checked like a b. (Criticism 2)
every b. in his own hand bears (Servitude 2)
who ... would be a b.? (Patriotism 1)
bonds:
my b. in thee are all determinate (Farewells 21)
bones:
my old b. aches (Weariness 3)
book:
painfully to pore upon a b. (Books 2)
shut the b. and sit him down and die (Despair 2)

canopy:
   this most excellent c. (World 4)
cantle:
   the greater c. of the world is lost (Empire 2)
cantons:
   loyal c. of contemnèd love (Courtship 23)
capability:
   that c. and godlike reason (Reason 1)
capers:
   he c., he dances (Courtship 13)
   he c. nimbly in a lady's chamber (Dancing 2)
   true lovers run into strange c. (Love 12)
captain:
   our great c.'s c. (Women 22)
captains:
   let four c. bear Hamlet (Royalty 7, Soldiers 4)
caraways:
   we will eat ... a dish of c. (Eating 5)
carcass:
   a rotten c. of a butt (Ships 5)
care:
   buy it with much c. (Anxiety 8)
   c. is no cure (Anxiety 3)
   c. keeps his watch (Sleeplessness 7)
   c.'s an enemy to life (Hedonism 1)
   no c., no stop; so senseless of expense (Extravagance 3)
   wan with c. (Anxiety 2)
   what though c. killed a cat (Encouragement 3)
   why would you heap this c. on me (Hypocrisy 16)
career:
   down the hill he holds his fierce c. (Evil 2)
cares:
   be not with mortal c. oppressed (Providence 1)
   enforce me to a world of c. (Politics 21)
   forfeited to c. for ever (Anxiety 1)
   intent to shake all c. ... from our age (Retirement 2)
   what watchful c. do interpose (Sleeplessness 3)
carnations:
   the fairest flowers ... are our c. (Flowers 10)
carp:
   bait of falsehood takes this c. of truth (Deviousness 1)
cart:
   I cannot draw a c. (Work 3)
Cassius:
   C. is aweary of the world (Criticism 2)
cast:
   set the exact wealth ... all at one c. (Risk 1)
castle:
   this c. hath a pleasant seat (Castles 1)
   there stands the c. (Castles 2)
castles:
   though c. topple (Chaos 2)
cat:
   harmless necessary c. (Animals 8)
   I am as melancholy as a gib c. (Melancholy 7)
   poor c. i' th' adage (Cowardice 4)
   the c. will mew (Animals 3)
   vigilant as a c. (Vigilance 1)

what though care killed a c. (Encouragement 3)
catalogue:
   in the c. ye go for men (Dogs 4)
cataracts:
   you c. and hurricanoes, spout (Storms 7)
caterpillars:
   the c. of the commonwealth (Politics 20)
cattle:
   get your living by the copulation of c. (Country Life 6)
Caucasus:
   thinking on the frosty C. (Imagination 6)
cause:
   a great c. of the night (Philosophy 1)
   hear me for my c. (Speechmaking 2)
   he cannot buckle his distempered c. (Politics 18)
   I know no personal c. (Cause 1)
   is there any c. in nature? (Cause 4)
   it is the c. (Cause 5)
   love him, not without c. (Cause 3)
   on the cause ... have glozed (Argument 5)
   the c. is in my will (Cause 2)
   wrenching the true c. the false way (Deviousness 2)
caviare:
   'twas c. to the general (Plays 3)
cavil:
   c. on the ninth part of a hair (Business 2)
celerity:
   c. is never more admired (Speed 1)
cell:
   death ... thine eternal cell (Death 10)
cellarage:
   you hear this fellow in the c. (Ghosts 10)
censure:
   c. me in your wisdom (Judgment 1)
   no might nor greatness ... can c. scape (Slander 5)
censurers:
   to cope malicious c. (Action 9)
ceremony:
   c. was but devised at first (Ceremony 5)
   love...useth an enforcèd c. (Hypocrisy 5, Love 37)
   no c. that to great ones 'longs (Mercy 6)
   the sauce to meat is c. (Ceremony 4)
   thou idol, c. (Ceremony 2)
   what have kings ... save c. (Ceremony 1)
Cesario:
   C., by the roses of the spring (Infatuation 10)
chalice:
   th'ingredients of our poisoned c. (Justice 9)
challenge:
   here's the c. (Challenges 2)
chamber:
   get you to my lady's c. (Women 14)
chameleon:
   add colors to the c. (Duplicity 2)
   the c. love can feed on the air (Food 15)
chance:
   c. as fair (Choice 7)
   in the reproof of c. (Chance 2)

the slaves of c. (Chance 3)

chances:
against ill c. (Moods 9)

change:
the lamentable c. is from the best (Hope 2, Laughter 2)

changes:
full of c. (Age 20)

chaos:
misshapen c. (Love 73)
c. is come again (Love 71)

chapmen:
you do as c. do (Business 10)

character:
thy fair and outward c. (Appearance 11)

charity:
am so near the lack of c. (Hate 1)
bound in c. against it (Contempt 1)
c. itself fulfills the law (Charity 2)
melting c. (Charity 1)
'twere good you do so much for c. (Charity 3)

charm:
for a c. of powerful trouble (Occult 1)
music oft hath such a c. (Music 9)

charmers:
O you heavenly c. (Gods and Goddesses 4)

charms:
now my c. are all o'erthrown (Weakness 5)

charter:
I must have ... as large a c. (Freedom 1)
the c. of thy worth gives thee releasing (Farewells 21)

chase:
this is the c. (Last Words 7)

chaste:
be thou as c. as ice (Slander 1)
c. and immaculate (Chastity 7)
c. as the icicle (Chastity 1)

chastity:
cold, my girl, even like thy c. (Affliction 10)
pure c. is ruffled (Lust 13)

cheer:
receive what c. you may (Aphorisms 6)
small c. and great welcome (Feasts 3)

cheese:
my c., my digestion, (Fools 10)

cherry:
we grew together, like to a double c. (Twins 3)

cherubins:
still quiring to the young-eyed c. (Heaven 3)

chestnut:
c. the only color (Hair 1)

chew:
my noble friend, c. upon this (Thought 10)

chickens:
all my pretty c. (Cruelty 4)

chiding:
better a little c. than ... heartbreak (Chiding 1)

child:
an impatient c. (Impatience 3)

as much as c. e'er loved (Parents and Children 5)
grief fills the room up of my absent c. (Grief 9)
love is like a c. (Love 105)
old man is twice a c. (Old Age 2)
to have a thankless c. (Ingratitude 7)
to see his active c. do deeds (Parents and Children 19)
wise father that knows his own c. (Parents and Children 11)
woe to that land that's governed by a c. (Government 4)

childbed:
a terrible c. (Birth and Death 1)

childhood:
eye of c. fears a painted devil (Death 22)

childishness:
second c. and mere oblivion (Age 5)

childness:
his varying c. (Children 2)

children:
fathers ... make their c. blind (Parents and Children 7)
thoughts like unbridled c. (Love 92)
when scepters are in c's hands (Cities 2)

chimes:
we have heard the c. at midnight (Nostalgia 4)

chin:
who is he whose c. (Youth 9)

choice:
there's small c. in rotten apples (Choice 8)

choirs:
bare ruined c. where late (Seasons 18)

choler:
your rash c. (Anger 2)

choose:
fools, when they do c. (Choice 4)
here c. I (Choice 6)
here do I c. (Choice 3)
I may neither c. who I would (Parents and Children 7)
let me c. (Choice 5)
you that c. not by the view (Choice 7)

choughs:
russet-pated c. (Hunting 2)

Christ:
so Judas did to C. (Betrayal 2)

Christian:
as I am a C. faithful man (Dreams 8)
I hate him for he is a C. (Money 8)

Christians:
making of C. will raise the price of hogs (Food 8)

chronicle:
let me embrace thee, good old c. (Time 32)

chronicles:
abstracts and brief c. (Acting 5)
time's doting c. (Age 16)

chrysolite:
world of one entire and perfect c. (Constancy 5)

church:
I can see a c. by daylight (Eyes 12)

when beggars die there are no c. (Portents 6)
comfort:
    all c. go with thee (Parting 8)
    be c. to my age (Age 2)
    c. should remain (Parting 12)
    c.'s in heaven (Affliction 11)
    he receives c. like cold porridge (Comfort 6)
    I beg cold c. (Comfort 4)
    I must c. the weaker vessel (Comfort 3)
    my c. is that old age ... no more spoil (Age 19)
    of c. no man speak (Despair 5)
    reward thee ... for thy sprightly c. (Comfort 1, Valor 1)
    society is no c. (Sickness 2)
    such c. as do lusty young men feel (Seasons 15)
    that spring whence c. seemed to come (Confusion 3)
    this must my c. be (Exile 3)
    two loves I have of c. and despair (Love 111)
    what c. have we now? (Despair 6)
comforts:
    we make us c. of our losses (Comfort 2)
command:
    achievement is c. (Desire 15)
    exactly do at all points my c. (Freedom 5)
commander:
    a good old c. (Soldiers 15)
commandment:
    thy c. all alone shall live (Resolution 2)
commodity:
    c. the bias of the world (Self-Interest 1)
    turn diseases to c. (Business 4)
common:
    thou know'st 'tis c. (Mourning 7)
commonwealth:
    caterpillars of the c. (Politics 20)
    i'the c. I would by contraries (Utopias 1)
    the c. of Athens is become a forest (Wilderness 2)
    worm that gnaws the bowels of the c. (Civil War 1)
compact:
    what c. mean you to have with us? (Friendship 14)
companion:
    I scorn you, scurvy c. (Insults 8)
    I would not wish any c. (Society 8)
    sad c., dull-eyed melancholy (Melancholy 8)
companions:
    in c. that do converse (Friendship 19)
    the prince but studies his c. (Language 2)
company:
    best when least in c. (Solitude 4)
    but for your c. I would have been in bed (Society 7)
    c., villainous c. hath been the spoil (Society 1)
    he is given to sports ... and much c. (Society 3)
    he is too disputable for my c. (Argument 2)
    I cannot live out of her c. (Friendship 1)
    I would no other c. (Solitude 2)
    let men take heed of their c. (Society 2)
    my books and instruments shall be my c. (Study 5)
comparisons:
    c. are odorous (Solecisms 5)

compass:
    my life is run his c. (Life 5)
competency:
    c. lives longer (Moderation 3)
complexion:
    c. of the element (Conspiracy 3)
    mislike me not for my c. (Appearance 3)
    the best thing about him is his c. (Faces 1)
compliment:
    demonstrate ... my heart in c. externe (Deceit 10)
comrade:
    to be a c. with the wolf (Homelessness 1)
concealment:
    let c. like a worm i'the bud (Melancholy 9)
conceits:
    dangerous c. are ... poisons (Jealousy 10)
conclusion:
    lame and impotent c.! (Endings 3)
concord:
    sweet milk of c.(Chaos 3)
condition:
    unhousèd, free c. (Marriage 40)
confine:
    spirit hies to his c. (Ghosts 6)
confusion:
    c. now hath made his masterpiece (Confusion 5)
    how soon c. may enter (Confusion 1)
conquest:
    a peace is of the nature of a c. (Peace 7)
    death makes no c. of this conqueror (Fame 4)
    have I in c. stretched mine arm? (Power 7)
    made a shameful c. of itself (Countries 7)
conquests:
    are all thy c. ... shrunk (Epitaphs 8)
conscience:
    c. is born of love (Conscience 10)
    c. is but a word (Conscience 8)
    for policy sits above c. (Politics 23)
    haunt thee like a wicked c. (Conscience 9)
    hulling in the wild sea of my c. (Conscience 3)
    my c. hath a thousand several tongues (Conscience 7)
    O coward c. (Conscience 6)
    their best c. is not to leave't undone (Deceit 14)
    the worm of c. (Conscience 4)
    thus c. does make cowards (Conscience 2)
    where's thy c. now? (Conscience 5)
consecrate:
    did I my soul and fortunes c. (Devotion 4)
consent:
    government ... doth keep in one c. (Government 2)
consider:
    'twere to c. too curiously (Mortality 3)
consideration:
    c. like an angel came (Reformation 5)
conspiracy:
    for c., I know not how it tastes (Conspiracy 9)
    heinous, strong and bold c. (Conspiracy 8)
    security gives way to c. (Conspiracy 6)

cowardice:
patience is pale cold c. (Cowardice 5)
cowards:
a plague of all c. (Cowardice 3)
as many other mannish c. do (Cowardice 1)
conscience doth make c. (Conscience 2)
c. die many times before their deaths (Death 17)
word that c. use (Conscience 8)
cowslip:
crimson drops i'the bottom of a c. (Beauty 6)
hang a pearl in every c.'s ear (Fairies 2)
in a c.'s bell I lie (Fairies 9)
the freckled c., burnet and green clover (Farming 2)
cozenage:
this town is full of c. (Corruption 1)
Crab:
I think C., my dog, be the sourest-natured (Dogs 7)
crabs:
bring thee where c. grow (Education 6)
cracks:
now c. a noble heart (Epitaphs 5)
cradle:
procreant c. (Birds 7)
crafts:
in one line two c. directly meet (Plots 2)
crannies:
creep in c. (Insects 1)
creature:
I took him for the plainest ... c. (Trust 3)
there is no c. loves me (Despair 7)
the world hath not a sweeter c. (Women 24)
wine is a good familiar creature (Drinking 23)
creatures:
call these delicate c. ours (Marriage 41)
from fairest c. we desire increase (Beauty 30)
guilty c. sitting at a play (Theater 4)
home, you idle c. (Idleness 1)
how many goodly c. are there here (Humanity 7)
those wicked c. yet do look (Evil 4)
credit:
my c. now stands (Reputation 3)
crickets:
as merry as c. (Merriment 1)
crimes:
the foul c. done in my days of nature (Ghosts 9)
cripple:
c. tardy-gaited night (Night 7)
Crispian:
this day is called the feast of C. (Festivals 3)
tomorrow is Saint C. (Festivals 4)
critical:
I am nothing if not c. (Criticism 4)
crocodile:
what manner o'thing is your c.? (Creatures 1)
cross:
delivered me to my sour c. (Hypocrisy 13)
crow:
c. doth sing as sweetly as the lark (Birds 10)

c. makes wing to the rooky wood (Night 13)
waked the ribald c. (Dawn 8)
crown:
by what ... crooked ways I met this c. (Deviousness 3)
from the c. of his head (Merriment 5)
how sweet ... it is to wear a c. (Royalty 21)
my c. is in my heart (Royalty 22)
put on my c. (Death-Wish 3, Royalty 3)
the sword, the mace, the c. imperial (Royalty 19)
uneasy lies the head that wears a c. (Royalty 11)
within the hollow c. (Death 35)
with mine own hands I give away my c. (Renunciation 3)
crowns:
c. in my purse I have (Travel 20)
cruel:
c. are the times (Confusion 6)
cruelty:
fill me ... top-full of direst c. (Cruelty 3)
'tis a c. to load a falling man (Downfall 3)
cry:
c. woe, destruction, ruin (Death 33)
you common c. of curs (People 11)
crying:
we came c. hither (Patience 7)
cuckolds:
have been c. ... ere now (Adultery 2)
cuckoo:
as the c. is in June (Birds 1)
c., c. - O word of fear (Seasons 10)
hedge-sparrow fed the c. (Ingratitude 5)
plainsong c. grey (Birds 13)
the c.'s bird useth the sparrow (Birds 2)
cue:
were it my c. to fight (Fighting 4)
cup:
there may be in the c. a spider (Poison 5)
Cupid:
C. himself would blush (Love 46)
C. is a knavish lad (Gods 3)
I saw ... C. all armed (Gods 2)
little C.'s crafty arrow (Love 63)
marked I where the bolt of C. fell (Flowers 5)
sign of blind C. (Love 60)
some C. kills with arrows (Love 64)
winged C. painted blind (Love 54)
cur:
this cruel-hearted c. (Dogs 7)
cure:
care is no c. (Anxiety 3)
current:
the c. that with gentle murmur (Rivers 3)
curs:
like to village c., bark (Enemies 3)
you common cry of c. (People 11)
curse:
a c. shall light upon the limbs (Prophecy 5)
I know how to c. (Language 8)
shall we c. the planets (Curses 1)

curse (cont'd.)
the common c. of mankind (Curses 9)
wish for me to help thee c. (Curses 7)
curses:
c. not loud but deep (Curses 5)
curtains:
the fringèd c. of thine eyes (Eyes 14)
custom:
a c. more honored in the breach (Custom 2)
c. calls me to't (Custom 1)
c. stale her infinite variety (Charm 3)
hath not old c. made this life more sweet (Exile 1)
some other c. of entertainment (Drinking 20)
the tyrant c. (War 18)
customs:
new c. though they be never so ridiculous (Fashion 5)
nice c. curtsy to great kings (Custom 4)
cut:
the most unkindest c. (Ingratitude 4)
cypress:
in sad c. let me be laid (Death 40)
daffodils:
d. that come before the swallow dares (Flowers 12)
when d. begin to peer (Seasons 17)
dagger:
a d. of the mind (Apparitions 7)
hath no man's d. here a point for me (Death-Wish 8)
is this a d.? (Apparitions 6)
daggers:
there's d. in men's smiles (Danger 12)
dainty:
let us not be d. of leave-taking (Parting 10)
daisies:
when d. pied and violets blue (Seasons 10)
dalliance:
do not give d. too much the rein (Sex 6)
dame:
both d. and servant (Hospitality 3)
damned:
d. be he that first cries "Hold, enough!" (Fighting 2)
dance:
if you will patiently d. (Dancing 1)
when you do d. (Dancing 4)
dancing:
say I am d. (Capriciousness 1)
you are I are past our d. days (Dancing 3)
danger:
d. knows full well (Danger 8)
I must go and meet with d. (Danger 2)
out of this nettle, d. (Danger 1)
we are in great d. (Danger 3)
what d. will it be to us (Beauty 2, Women 3)
dangerous:
'tis d. when the baser nature comes (Quarrels 2)
dangers:
d. are to me indifferent (Confidence 1)
loved me for the d. I had passed (Love 68)
Daniel:
a D. come to judgment (Judgment 5)

dare:
how you d., with what you d. (Challenges 1)
letting I d. not wait upon I would (Cowardice 4)
darkling:
d. stand the varying shore (Darkness 1)
darkness:
I will encounter d. as a bride (Death 28)
no d. but i. (Ignorance 2)
prince of d. is a gentleman (Devil 5)
the instruments of d. tell us truths (Evil 5)
this thing of d. I acknowledge (Darkness 3)
dates:
our d. are brief (Time 44)
daughter:
d., do not make me mad (Parents and Children 9)
he says he loves my d. (Love 106)
my d.! O my ducats! (Loss 4)
thou art my flesh, my blood, my d. (Parents and Children 9)
thy youngest d. does not love thee least (Speech 11)
will of a living d. curbed (Parents and Children 10)
daws:
wear my heart ... for d. to peck at (Deceit 10)
day:
bright d. brings forth the adder (Danger 6)
busy d. waked by the lark (Dawn 8)
d. will come when thou shalt wish for me (Curses 7)
let never d. nor night (God 6)
O thou d. o'the world (Love 7)
so foul and fair a d. (Weather 4)
sometimes hath the brightest d. a cloud (Seasons 8)
the bright d. is done (Death-Wish 2)
the d. frowns more and more (Weather 7)
this d. is called the feast of Crispian (Festivals 3)
who dares not stir by d. (Fear 9)
days:
looked on better d. (Nostalgia 1)
my salad d., when I was green (Youth 2)
past our dancing d. (Dancing 3)
seen better d. (Adversity 6)
shorten my d. thou canst (Grief 13)
the mad d. that I have spent (Nostalgia 3)
dead:
as d. as a doornail (Proverbs 8)
better be with the d. (Anxiety 6)
he is d. and gone, lady (Death 8)
I know when one is d. (Death 20)
sheeted d. did squeak (Apparitions 3)
spirits o'the d. may walk again (Ghosts 15)
the sleeping and the dead (Death 22)
death:
a dateless bargain to engrossing d. (Farewells 19)
after my d. I wish no other herald (Remembrance 5)
a man that apprehends d. (Death 31)
a royal fellowship of d. (Death 16)
be absolute for d. (Death 26)
be merciful, say "death" (Exile 8)
come away, come away d. (Death 40)
d., a necessary end, will come (Death 18)
d., as the psalmist saith (Death 13)

d., d.! O amiable, lovely d.! (Death-Wish 7)
d. is a fearful thing (Death 29)
d. lies on her like an untimely frost (Death 37)
d. makes no conquest of this conqueror (Fame 4)
d. may usurp on nature (Death 32)
d. once dead there's no more dying then (Eternity 4)
d., that hath sucked the honey (Death 38)
d. the market-place (World 6)
downy sleep. d.'s counterfeit (Death 23)
drop into the rotten mouth of d. (Decline 2)
for restful d. I cry (Death-Wish 12)
grim d., how foul (Death 39)
I will be a bridegroom in my d. (Death 2)
keeps d. his court (Death 35)
love-devouring d. (Marriage 45)
nothing we can call our own but d. (Death 34)
now boast thee, d. (Death 5, Epitaphs 2)
O proud d., what feast is toward (Death 10)
set honor in one eye and d. i'th' other (Honor 12)
the sense of d. (Death 27)
the stroke of d. is as a lover's pinch (Dying 3)
the worst is d. (Death 33)
this fell sergeant, d. (Death 9)
thou owest God a d. (Death 12)
through the hollow eyes of d. (Life 10)
we owe God a d. (Death 14)
what sights of ugly d. within mine eyes (Dreams 9)
where art thou, d.? (Death 3)
death's head:
do not speak like a d. (Mortality 5)
deaths:
d. put on by cunning (Murder 3)
debt:
ambition's d. is paid (Ambition 8)
debts:
he that dies pays all d. (Proverbs 27)
decay:
this muddy vesture of d. (Heaven 3)
deceit:
that d. should steal such gentle shape (Deceit 16)
the fairest show means most d. (Deceit 15)
deceits:
the tongues of men are full of d. (Deceit 3)
deceived:
she has d. her father (Deceit 11)
December:
D.'s bareness (Absence 3)
D. when they are wed (Marriage 5)
makes a July's day short as D. (Children 2)
rain and wind beat dark D. (Country Life 10)
decrees:
break my d. (Revolution 1)
deed:
a little water clears us of this d. (Guilt 6)
one good d. dying (Praise 13)
so shines a good d. (Goodness 3)
this d. is chronicled in hell (Devil 10)
'tis a kind of good d. to say well (Action 11)
to know my d. (Self-Knowledge 7)
tyrannous and bloody d. (Murder 13)

deeds:
a spur to valiant ... d. (War 22)
foul d. will rise (Foreboding 5)
give her d. (Silence 7)
hot d. is love (Love 89)
I'll endeavor d. (Words and Deeds 5)
pity choked with custom of fell d. (Cruelty 2)
speaking in deeds (Words and Deeds 4)
the sight of means to do ill d. (Wrongdoing 3)
unnatural d. (Guilt 9)
words are no d. (Action 11, Words and Deeds 1)
deer:
what shall he have that killed the d. (Hunting 1)
defeatures:
written strange d. on my face (Grief 3)
defect:
make d. perfection (Charm 2)
defense:
in cases of d. 'tis best to weigh (War 8)
deformed:
he is d., crooked (Insults 2)
defy:
what man, d. the devil (Devil 11)
degree:
take but d. away (Order 3)
the heavens ... observe d. (Order 1)
when d. is shaked (Order 2)
degrees:
d. were not derived corruptly (Merit 2)
deject:
I of ladies most d. (Dejection 3)
delays:
d. have dangerous ends (Delay 3)
delight:
all for your d. (Acting 24)
delights:
all d. are vain (Books 2)
his d. were dolphin-like (Pleasure 4)
these violent d. have violent ends (Transience 5)
demand:
d. me nothing (Silence 6)
demigod:
d. authority (Authority 8)
denial:
he's fortified against any d. (Determination 4)
deny:
I would not d. you (Marriage 36)
Denmark:
rotten in the state of D. (Corruption 2)
depraved:
who lives that's not d. ? (Corruption 6, Humanity 8)
Desdemona:
the divine D. (Women 22)
desert:
in this d. inaccessible (Time 3)
use every man after your own d. (Deserving 2, Generosity 2)
deserts:
not my d., but what I will deserve (Deserving 4)

deserve:
 well you d. (Deserving 3)
deserves:
 get as much as he d. (Choice 2)
deservings:
 make foul the clearness of our d. (Deserving 1)
desire:
 a great d. for a bottle of hay (Eating 9)
 can one d. to much of a good thing (Desire 5)
 d. is boundless (Love 90)
 d. my pilot is (Desire 19)
 d. should ... outlive performance (Desire 7)
 gain what many men d. (Desire 12, 13)
 how far I am from the d. of this (Deceit 20)
 I hope it is no dishonest d. (Desire 6)
 in night ... d. sees best of all (Desire 21)
 provokes the d. (Drinking 14)
 so sweet as when d. did sue (Desire 15)
 tend upon the ... times of your d. (Devotion 7)
 the trustless wings of false d. (Desire 17)
desires:
 my black and deep d. (Desire 9)
 my d., like fell and cruel hounds (Desire 16)
 thy d. are wolvish (Cruelty 7)
 your heart's d. be with you (Desire 3)
desolation:
 a careless d. (Love 15)
despair:
 grim and comfortless d. (Melancholy 5)
 I shall d. (Despair 7)
 I will d. and be at enmity (Despair 4)
 two loves ... of comfort and d. (Love 111)
despise:
 how much I could d. this man (Contempt 1)
despising:
 d. for you the city (Exile 2)
destruction:
 cry woe, d., ruin (Death 33)
device:
 who ... cannot see this palpable d. (Deceit 18)
devil:
 a d., a born d. (Education 7)
 a d. more damned to top Macbeth (Hell 3)
 art thou ... some d. (Apparitions 5)
 d., he's an enemy to mankind (Devil 11)
 eye of childhood fears a painted d. (Death 22)
 give the d. his due (Devil 4, Proverbs 2)
 he must needs go that the d. drives (Devil 1)
 hypocrisy against the d. (Devil 9)
 I perceive the d. understands Welsh (Devil 3)
 sugar o'er the d. himself (Hypocrisy 1)
 the d. can cite scripture (Devil 8)
 the d. damn thee black (Curses 4)
 the d. take one party (Curses 6)
 the d. that told me I did well (Devil 10)
 the spirit ... may be the d. (Devil 2)
 what a d. hast thou to do (Time of Day 5)
 what, can the d. speak true (Devil 7)

 what man, defy the d. (Devil 11)
devil-porter:
 I'll d. it no further (Hell 2)
devils:
 d. soonest tempt (Devil 6)
 when d. ... the blackest sins put on (Hypocrisy 12)
 whip me, ye d. (Hell 6)
devouring:
 d. time, blunt thou the lion's paws (Time 42)
devout:
 a most d. coward (Cowardice 7)
dewdrops:
 I must go seek some d. (Fairies 2)
devices:
 our d. all are overthrown (Fate 1)
devil:
 seem a saint when most I play the d. (Hypocrisy 14)
devotion:
 with d.'s visage (Hypocrisy 1)
dial:
 the bawdy hand of the d. (Time 26)
Dian:
 as D. in her orb (Lust 10)
 icicle ... hangs on D.'s temple (Chastity 1)
Diana:
 D's lip is not more rubious (Androgyny 1)
 let us be D.'s foresters (Night 2)
die:
 all shall d. (Death 13)
 a man can d. but once (Death 14)
 d. all, d. merrily (Death 11, Doomsday 1)
 d. two months ago (Memory 3)
 find myself so apt to d. (Death-Wish 6)
 if it were now to die (Happiness 6)
 lovers cry, O ho they d. (Sex 9)
 that we shall d. we know (Death 19)
 'tis a vile thing to d. (Death 36)
 to d. and go we know not where (Graves 1)
 to d., to sleep, perchance to dream (Death 7)
died:
 he d. as one ... studied in his death (Dying 13)
dies:
 he that d. pays all debts (Proverbs 27)
difference:
 O the d. of man and man! (Desire 8)
digestion:
 good d. wait on appetite (Eating 7)
 things sweet to taste prove in d. sour (Eating 11)
digestions:
 unquiet meals make ill d. (Eating 2)
diminution:
 a d. in our captain's brain (Folly 2)
dine:
 will you d. with me? (Invitations 1)
dinner:
 I will make an end of my d. (Food 9)
disasters:
 make guilty of our d. the sun (Astrology 1)

the e. suffers little birds to sing (Birds 14, Power 12)
ear:
a jest's prosperity lies in the e. (Jokes 3)
give every man thy e. (Advice 5)
this e. is deaf (Opinion 2)
early:
the reason I was up so e. (Lateness 1)
earn:
I e. that I eat (Contentment 1)
earnest:
I love no man in good e. (Love 8)
pleads he in e.? (Sincerity 2)
ears:
aged e. play truant at his tales (Talking 5)
lend me your e. (Epitaphs 10)
O that men's e. should be to counsel deaf (Flattery 8)
shake your Rome about your e. (Authority 3)
to e. of flesh and blood (Afterlife 1)
earth:
beauty for … e. too dear (Beauty 22)
canst work i'th' e. so fast? (Ghosts 11)
e. hath swallowed all my hopes (Parents and Children 15)
e.'s increase, foison plenty (Blessings 6)
from the four corners of the e. (Fame 3)
greet I thee, my e. (Greetings 11)
lards the lean e. as he walks along (Fatness 1)
lay her i'th'e. (Burial 3)
teeming e. is with a kind of colic pinched (Earthquakes 1)
the e. that's nature's mother (Nature 5)
this goodly frame, the e. (World 3)
thou bleeding piece of e. (Mourning 14)
earthlier:
e. happy is the rose distilled (Marriage 28)
ease:
take mine e. in mine inn (Leisure 2)
east:
e., west, north, south (Home 1)
from the e. to western Inde (Love 14)
i'th' e. my pleasure lies (Pleasure 3)
easy:
as e. mayst thou fall (Marriage 12)
eat:
e. no onions nor garlic (Eating 10)
nothing but sit and sit, and e. and e. (Eating 12)
we will e. a last year's pippin (Eating 5)
eaten:
he hath e. me out of house and home (Eating 4)
eater:
I am a great e. of beef (Eating 13)
eating:
e. the bitter bread of banishment (Exile 7)
eclipse:
should be now a huge e. (Loss 7)
eclipses:
these late e. in the sun (Portents 7)
ecstasy:
allay thy e. (Love 51)

restless e. (Anxiety 6)
the very e. of love (Love 29)
Eden:
this other E., demi-paradise (Countries 5)
edict:
it stands as an e. in destiny (Patience 9)
egg:
full of quarrels as an e. is full of meat (Quarrels 14)
thou art damned, like an ill-roasted e. (Food 4)
eglantine:
with sweet musk-roses and with e. (Flowers 6)
Egypt:
I am dying, E., dying (Dying 1)
Egyptian:
he will to his E. dish again (Desire 2)
eight:
eyes were set at e. i' the morning (Drinking 28)
elbow:
my e. itched (Insults 16)
elements:
I tax you not, you e. (Storms 9)
life consist of the four e. (Hedonism 2)
the e. so mixed in him (Epitaphs 12)
to the e. be free (Freedom 9)
unfriendly e. forgot thee (Birth and Death 1)
with no less terror than the e. (Meeting 1)
elephant:
the e. hath joints (Pride 3)
elm:
thou art an e., my husband (Marriage 13)
eloquence:
action is e. (Action 1)
more e. in a sugar touch (Eloquence 4)
saucy and audacious e. (Speechmaking 3)
she uttereth piercing e. (Courtship 20)
Elsinore:
what make you at E.? (Friendship 4)
elves:
ye e. of hills, brooks, standing lakes (Fairies 8)
Elysium:
my brother he is in E. (Countries 8)
emulation:
e. hath a thousand sons (Reputation 14)
encounterers:
these e., so glib of tongue (Lechery 5)
end:
bid me remember mine e. (Mortality 5)
here is my journey's e. (Resignation 6)
is this the promised e.? (Doomsday 2)
let the e. try the man (Men 3)
the e. crowns all (Time 33)
whose e. is purposed by the mighty gods (Fate 6)
endeavors:
my e. have ever come too short (Service 4)
ends:
delays have dangerous e. (Delay 3)
more are men's e. marked (Endings 3)
endure:
men must e. their going hence (Endurance 2)
must I e. all this? (Quarrels 7)

enemies:
bayed about with many e. (Danger 9)
our e. have beat us to the pit (Defeat 1)
such men my friends than e. (Enemies 4)
you have many e. (Enemies 3)
enemy:
common e. of man (Damnation 1)
easier ... than fight with mine e. (Fighting 3)
if the e. is an ass and a fool (Enemies 2)
my nearest and dearest e. (Enemies 1)
O cunning e. (Temptation 4)
put an e. into their mouths (Drinking 22)
security is mortals' chiefest e. (Security 2)
though mine e. (Honor 20)
engendered:
I have 't. It is e. (Evil 10)
enginer:
have the e. hoist with his own petard (Justice 1)
England:
E. breeds very valiant creatures (Dogs 2)
if E. to herself do rest but true (Patriotism 2)
old Robin Hood of E. (Country Life 1)
save back to E. all the world's my way (Exile 5)
that E. that was wont to conquer (Countries 7)
then E.'s ground farewell (Exile 6)
this blessed plot, this E. (Countries 6)
this E. never did (Patriotism 2)
to E. will I steal (Theft 5)
why was he sent into E.? (Countries 3)
English:
my native E. I must now forgo (Language 7)
trick of our E. nation (Countries 4)
Englishman:
though banished, yet a true-born E. (Exile 6)
enigmatical:
your answer, sir, is e. (Meaning 1, Answers 1)
enjoy:
e. the honey-heavy dew of slumber (Sleep 6)
enmity:
be at e. with any cozening hope (Despair 4)
enough:
lend to each man enough (Prayer 18)
entice:
do I e. you? (Plain-Speaking 10)
entrails:
of intolerable e. (Insults 14)
turns our swords in our own proper e. (Caesar 5)
entrance:
the fatal e. of Duncan (Foreboding 9)
envy:
e. breeds unkind division (Civil War 2)
men that make ... nourishment (Envy 1)
Epicurean:
E. cooks sharpen ... his appetite (Food 2)
epilogue:
no e., I pray you (Theater 15)
epithet:
singular and choice e. (Affectation 1)
suffer love! a good e. (Love 67)

Eros:
unarm E. (Death-Wish 1)
error:
e. of our eye (Inconstancy 6)
mountainous e. be ... heaped (Custom 1)
O hateful e. (Mistakes 3)
the very e. of the moon (Moon 4)
what e. drives our eyes and ears amiss? (Mistakes 1)
eruption:
this bodes some strange e. (Foreboding 3)
eruptions:
earth breaks out in strange e. (Earthquakes 1)
eschewed:
what cannot be e. (Inevitability 1)
esperance:
stands still in e. (Hope 2)
essence:
his glassy e. (Authority 9)
estate:
what thinks he of our e.? (Danger 4)
wish th'e. o'the world were now undone (Despair 3)
estates:
O that e. ... were not derived corruptly (Merit 2)
et:
et tu Brute (Last Words 2)
eternal:
this e. blazon must not be (Afterlife 1, Eternity 2)
thy e. summer shall; not fade (Eternity 3)
eternity:
e. was in our lips and eyes (Eternity 1)
make us heirs of all e. (Fame 2)
who ... sells e. to gain a toy? (Desire 18)
evening:
how still the e. is (Evening 1)
events:
many e. in the womb of time (Time 20)
ever:
e. till now when men were fond (Infatuation 7)
for e. and for e. farewell (Parting 9)
everyone:
e. can master a grief (Aphorisms 9)
everything:
e. that grows holds in perfection (Perfection 3)
evil:
e. soul producing holy witness (Duplicity 1)
obscures the show of e. (Hypocrisy 10)
the beauteous e. (Virtue 24)
the e. that men do (Epitaphs 10)
evils:
pitch our e. there (Building 3)
this same progeny of e. (Quarrels 11)
example:
things done without e. (Innovation 1)
excellent:
e. wretch! (Love 71)
so e. a king (Excellence 1)
excess:
is wasteful and ridiculous e. (Extravagance 2)

what f. impose (Fate 4, Resistance 2)

father:
a decrepit f. takes delight (Parents and Children 19)
a f.'s at the nuptial of his son (Parents and Children 17)
as a f. to my youth (Advice 8)
I am glad thy f.'s dead (Grief 12)
I am thy f.'s spirit (Ghosts 9)
I have a f., you a daughter lost (Parents and Children 12)
my f. did something smack (Lechery 2)
my f. named me Autolycus (Theft 12)
my f. will grant precious things (Generosity 7)
she has deceived her f. (Deceit 11)
to be a f. unto many sons (Parents and Children 4)
wise f. that knows his own child (Parents and Children 11)
your f. was ever virtuous (Virtue 16)

fathers:
f. that wear rags (Parents and Children 7)

fathom:
full f. five thy father lies (Transformation 3)
how many f. deep I am in love (Love 22)

fatter:
would he were f. (Fear 7)

fault:
Fie, 'tis a f. to heaven (Faults 5)
I cannot wish the f. undone (Wrongdoing 4)
if sack and sugar be a f. (Age 9)
is it her f. or mine? (Temptation 3)
pardon this f. (Apologies 3)
the f., dear Brutus, is not in our stars (Faults 6)
the worst f. you have (Faults 4)
think not upon the f. (Prayer 6)
this f. I find (Inconstancy 6)

faults:
all his f. observed (Criticism 2)
a man who is the abstract of all f. (Faults 1)
best men are molded out of f. (Faults 8)
f. that are rich are fair (Generosity 5)
I do not like your f. (Faults 7)
if little f. ... shall not be winked at (Crime 1)
myself, against whom I know most f. (Self-Knowledge 1)
one error fills him with f. (Inconstancy 7)
who covert f. ... with shame derides (Time 17)
you gods will give us some f. (Faults 3)

favors:
he that depends upon your f. (People 8)
remember the f. of these men (Betrayal 2)

fear:
blind f. that seeing reason (Fear 16)
f. is most accursed (Fear 4)
f. no more the frown (Mourning 4)
f. no more the heat (Mourning 3)
I f. him not (Fear 7)
if he should stay at home ... for f. (Fear 8)
I have a faint cold f. (Fear 15)
know not what we f. (Confusion 5)
'tis time to fear (Tyranny 6)

to be feared than what I f. (Caesar 1)
true nobility is exempt from f. (Fear 5)
you may f. too far (Fear 11)

fearful:
how f. and dizzy 'tis (Vertigo 1)

fears:
he that but f. the thing (Fear 3)
I have almost forgot the taste of f. (Fear 14)
not mine own f. (Anxiety 11)
our f. do make us traitors (Fear 13)
present f. are less (Fear 12)

feast:
buy for our sheep-shearing f. (Feasts 4)
not yet an Alexandrian f. (Feasts 1)
one f., one house (Happiness 7)
proud death, what f. is toward (Death 10)
small cheer ... makes a merry f. (Feasts 3)
the beginning of a f. (Fighting 1)
the f. of Crispian (Festivals 2)
who riseth from a f. with that keen appetite (Eating 8)

feasts:
be abhorred all f. (Misanthropy 5)

feather:
I am a f. for each wind (Indecision 4)
the swan's down f. (Indecision 1)
was ever f. so lightly blown (People 16)

feathers:
these growing f. plucked (Power 2)

February:
such a F. face (Moods 12)

fee:
the golden f. for which I plead (Eloquence 7)

feeble:
not enough to help the f. up (Helping 2)

feed:
f. him with apricots and dewberries (Food 11)

felicity:
absent thee from f. (Stories 1)

fellow:
a barren-spirited f. (Contempt 3)
a f. almost damned (Marriage 39)
a f. of a good respect (Honor 17)
a f. of infinite jest (Epitaphs 3)
a f. of no mark (Men 2)
an honest f. enough (Stupidity 4)
a very tainted fellow (Evil 1)
ignorant, unweighing f. (Insults 12)
love a f. of this temper (Courtship 10)
poor f. never joyed (Money 1)
that ever this f. should have fewer words (Words 2)
this f. is wise enough to play the fool (Fools 15)
this f.'s of exceeding honesty (Honesty 6)
this f. will but join you (Marriage 4)
thou art a blessed f. (Opinion 1)
thou art a f. of a good respect (Honor 17)
what a blunt f. is this grown (Plain-Speaking 3)

fellows:
nature hath framed strange f. (Humanity 4)
what should such f. as I do? (Humanity 2, Misanthropy 1)

fellowship:
   a royal f. of death (Death 16)
   f. in woe doth woe assuage (Fellowship 4)
fen:
   perfumed by a f. (Air 2)
fertility:
   corrupting in its own f. (Farming 1)
festival:
   the night before some f. (Impatience 3)
fetters:
   these strong Egyptian f. (Infatuation 3)
fever:
   after life's fitful f. (Death 25)
   this f. that has troubled me (Sickness 12)
few:
   f. love to hear the sins (Sin 6)
fiend:
   beneath is all the f.'s (Misogyny 1)
   it was some f. (Demons 1)
   thou marble-hearted f. (Ingratitude 6)
fiends:
   methought a legion of foul f. (Dreams 11)
fight:
   f. to the last gasp (Resistance 1)
   we cannot f. for love (Courtship 14)
   were it my cue to f. (Fighting 5)
fighting:
   when wilt thou leave f. (Reformation 3)
figs:
   love long life better than f. (Life 2)
figure:
   to make me a fixèd f. (Reputation 10)
finch:
   the f., the sparrow (Birds 13)
find:
   when you do f. him (Integrity 2)
finger:
   for let our f. ache (Sickness 16)
fingers:
   contaminate our f. with base bribes (Corruption 6)
   ill cook that cannot lick his own f. (Cooking 2)
finish:
   f., good lady (Death-Wish 2)
fire:
   a little f. is quickly trodden out (Fire 1)
   as f. cools f. (Proverbs 11)
   f. that's closest (Love 100)
   frighted with false f. (Fear 2)
   one f. burns out another's (Fire 3)
   pale his ineffectual f. (Dawn 3)
   shunned the f. for fear of burning (Danger 15)
   such sheets of f. (Storms 10)
   the f. in the flint shows not (Fire 5)
   those that ... will make a mighty f. (Fire 2)
   who can hold a f. in his hand (Imagination 6)
fires:
   confined to fast in f. (Ghosts 9)
   when two raging f. meet (Fire 4)
first:
   at f. and last, the hearty welcome (Welcome 1)

fish:
   a f., he smells like a f. (Fish 2)
   here's a f. hangs in the net (Fishing 3)
   we'll have ... f. for fasting-days (Food 13)
fishes:
   I marvel how the f. live (Fish 1)
fit:
   then comes my f. (Anxiety 7)
fits:
   cope him in these sullen f. (Moods 2)
   thy jealous f. (Jealousy 2)
flame:
   the f. o'the taper bows toward her (Eyes 3)
   within the very f. of love (Love 34)
flames:
   to sulphurous and tormenting f. (Purgatory 1)
flapjacks:
   puddings and f. (Food 13)
flatter:
   he cannot f., he (Plain-Speaking 7)
flattered:
   he that loves to be f. (Flattery 7)
   why should the poor be f. (Flattery 1)
flatterers:
   when I tell him he hates f. (Flattery 4)
flatteries:
   felt the f. that grow upon it (Hypocrisy 4)
   wounds me with the f. of his tongue (Flattery 6)
flattery:
   there is f. in friendship (Flattery 3)
   this is no f. (Philosophy 2)
   to counsel deaf, but not to f. (Flattery 8)
   when power to f. bows (Duty 3)
flea:
   that's a valiant f. that dare (Valor 11)
   thou f., thou nit (Insults 19)
fleas:
   villainous house ... for f. (Insects 2)
fleet:
   this f. majestical (Ships 3)
flesh:
   as pretty a piece of f. as any in Messina (Dignity 1)
   fair and unpolluted f. (Burial 3)
   foul tainted f. (Guilt 10)
   huge hill of f. (Insults 5)
   I have more f. than another man (Excuses 3)
   O that this too too solid f. (Suicide 11)
   pound of f. which I demand (Cruelty 6)
   this f. keep in a little life (Farewells 7)
   thou didst eat strange f. (Eating 1)
   we'll have f. for holidays (Food 13)
flies:
   as f. to wanton boys (Gods 1)
flood:
   an age since the great f. (History 2)
   the enchafèd f. (Sea 3)
   what if it tempt you toward the f. (Ghosts 8)
flower:
   a little western f. (Flowers 5)
   look like the innocent f. (Deceit 4)

not a f., not a f. sweet (Graves 2)
sweetest f. of all the field (Death 37)
the summer's f. (Flowers 14)
we pluck this f., safety (Danger 1)
flowers:
    fair f. that are gathered (Time 45)
    here's f. for you (Flowers 11)
    lulled in these f. (Flowers 6)
    suck ... fertility from wholesome f. (Gardens 6)
    to sweet beds of f. (Flowers 8)
    with fairest f. I'll sweeten (Mourning 2)
fly:
    poor harmless f. (Insects 3)
foes:
    two such friends should be long f. (Friendship 32)
    why, Harry, do I tell thee of my f. (Enemies 1)
fog:
    hover through the f. (Air 1)
foiled:
    if I be f. (Recklessness 1)
following:
    in f. him, I follow but myself (Self-Interest 4)
folly:
    amity ... f. may easily untie (Friendship 31)
    common curse of mankind, f. (Curses 9)
    the purpose must weigh with the f. (Folly 3)
    to do good ... accounted dangerous f. (Innocence 4)
fond:
    when men were f. (Infatuation 7)
food:
    chewing the f. of ... fancy (Thought 2)
    f. for powder, f. for powder (Soldiers 7)
    if music be the f. of love (Music 25)
    like a sickness did I loathe this f. (Devotion 3)
    music, moody f. of us (Music 1)
    the f. of sweet and bitter fancy (Love 25)
foolish:
    f. fond old man (Age 27)
    she never yet was f. that was fair (Aphorisms 10)
fool:
    a f., a f., I met a f. (Fools 1)
    a f.'s bolt is soon shot (Fools 7)
    a f. that betrothes himself (Misogyny 2)
    and my poor f. is hanged (Death 21)
    better a witty f. (Fools 11)
    dost thou call me f.? (Fools 8)
    he was a f. (Politics 7)
    how every f. can play upon the word (Words 6)
    I am indeed not her f. (Fools 14)
    I was seeking for a f. (Fools 4)
    knotty-pated f. (Insults 4)
    lead her in a f.'s paradise (Deceit 21)
    let me play the f. (Merriment 3)
    love's not Time's f. (Constancy 12)
    made a soft and dull-eyed f. (Inflexibility 1)
    opinion's but a f. (Appearance 9)
    O that I were a f. (Fools 2)
    O wretched f. (Honesty 7)
    she will keep no f. (Fools 13)
    the f. doth think he is wise (Fools 5)

transformed into a strumpet's f. (Folly 1)
what a wasp-stung and impatient f. (Impatience 1)
why should I play the Roman f. (Suicide 16)
wise enough to play the f. (Fools 15)
foolery:
    by f. thrive (Foolery 1)
    f., sir, does walk about the orb (Foolery 3)
    there was more f. yet (Foolery 2)
fooling:
    the knight's in admirable f. (Fools 12)
fools:
    beasts ... called f. (Fools 6)
    f. by heavenly compulsion (Astrology 1)
    f. of Time (Constancy 13)
    how many fond f. serve mad jealousy? (Jealousy 1)
    life ... that none but f. would keep (Death 26)
    old f. are babes again (Age 22)
    these deliberate f. (Choice 4)
    this great stage of f. (Humanity 3)
    we play the f. with the time (Time 12)
    what f. these mortals be (Fools 9, Humanity 9)
foppery:
    let not the sound of shallow f. (Sobriety 2)
force:
    do we must what f. will have us do (Power 11)
    f. should be right (Anarchy 2)
forefathers:
    our f. had no other books (Books 1)
forest:
    already in the f. of Arden (Country Life 1)
    I met a fool in the f. (Fools 1)
    pacing through the f. (Love 25)
    there's no clock in the f. (Time 4)
    well, this is the f. of Arden (Travel 1)
foresters:
    Let us be Diana's f. (Night 2)
forests:
    with shadowy f. ... riched (Country Life 11)
forge:
    in the quick f. and working-house (Thought 6)
forget:
    f. and forgive (Reconciliation 3)
forgive:
    I as free f. you (Forgiveness 4)
    with them, f. yourself (Forgiveness 6)
forgot:
    great thing of us f. (Forgetfulness 3)
fortified:
    he's f. against any denial (Determination 4)
fortress:
    God is our f. (God 4)
fortune:
    a good man's f. (Fortune 13)
    a man whom f. hath cruelly scratched (Fortune 1)
    blind f. leading me (Fortune 17)
    doth f. play the huswife (Fortune 10)
    fools of f. (Flattery 9)
    f. brings in some boats (Fortune 6)
    f., good night (Fortune 14)
    f. is merry (Fortune 11)

fortune (cont'd.)

f. is painted blind (Fortune 9)

f. knows we scorn her most (Fortune 2)

f. now to my heart's hope (Fortune 20)

f. reigns in the gifts of the world (Fortune 4)

f.'s bastard be unfathered (Constancy 13)

f.'s buffets and rewards (Fortune 7, Stoicism 1)

good f. then (Fortune 18)

greatness once fallen out with f. (Decline 3)

herein f. shows herself more kind (Fortune 21)

if f. be a woman (Fortune 19)

if my f. be not crossed (Parents and Children 12)

I see f. would not suffer me (Fortune 24)

I thank my f. for it (Business 6)

joy for his f. (Caesar 3)

mock the good huswife of f. (Fortune 3)

most dejected thing of f. (Hope 2)

O lady f., stand you (Fortune 23)

one out of suits with f. (Fortune 5)

poor man made tame to f.'s blows (Pity 4)

since this f. falls to you (Choice 7)

slings and arrows of outrageous f. (Choice 1)

some unborn sorrow ripe in f.'s womb (Foreboding 12)

tide leads on to f. (Opportunity 2)

to cozen f. (Merit 1)

when f. means to men most good (Fortune 12)

when in disgrace with f. (Misery 5)

will f. never come (Fortune 8)

fortunes:

all my f. at thy foot I'll lay (Devotion 6)

f. will ever after droop (Astrology 4)

least rub in your f. (Betrayal 1)

loves should with our f. change (Mutability 1)

make content with his f. fit (Fortune 15)

fortune-teller:

one Pinch ... a f. (Character 1)

foster-nurse:

our f. of nature is repose (Sleep 8)

foul:

f. is fair (Confusion 2)

most f., most fair (Paradoxes 2)

so f. and fair a day I have not seen (Weather 4)

foundation:

God save the f.! (Religion 6)

no sure f. set on blood (Murder 4)

fountain:

f. from the which my current runs (Loss 6)

troubled like a f. stirred (Perplexity 2)

four:

f. lagging winters (Royalty 27)

fowler:

geese that the creeping f. eye (Hunting 2)

fox:

the f. barks not when he would steal (Animals 5)

when the f. hath once got in his nose (Animals 6)

frail:

we are all f. (Weakness 3)

frailty:

f., thy name is woman (Weakness 1)

I have more flesh ... and therefore more f. (Excuses 3)

frame:

this goodly f., the earth (World 3)

France:

churlish turf of F. (Age 18)

fray:

latter end of a f. (Fighting 1)

free:

be as f. as mountain winds (Freedom 7)

to the elements be f. (Freedom 9)

freedom:

f., high-day! high-day f.! (Freedom 8)

liberty! f.! (Freedom 4)

freeze:

f., f. thou bitter sky (Seasons 2)

French:

I will tell thee in F. (Language 3)

fret:

f. till your proud heart break (Quarrels 4)

friend:

a f. i'the court (Friendship 11)

a f. should bear his f.'s infirmities (Friendship 17)

f. or brother, he forfeits (Punishment 4)

he was my f., faithful and just to me (Friendship 16)

if I had a f. that loved her (Courtship 16)

I weigh my f.'s affection (Friendship 30)

my noble f., chew upon this (Thought 10)

think on thee, dear f. (Love 107)

to me, fair f., you never can be old (Love 109)

friends:

come, I'll be f. with thee (Friendship 8)

eat and drink as f. (Friendship 27)

f. am I with you all, and love you all (Friendship 15)

f., I owe more tears (Mourning 16)

f., Romans, countrymen (Epitaphs 10)

good f., go in (Friendship 13)

good morrow, f. (Greetings 6)

happy ... in remembering my good f. (Friendship 25)

I had rather have such men my f. than enemies (Enemies 4)

joy, gentle f. (Greetings 7)

love and be f. (Reconciliation 1)

make f. and give your heart to (Betrayal 1)

make f. of foes (Blessings 1)

make f. with speed (Diplomacy 1, Letters 2)

my f. were poor, but honest (Love 2)

pity two such f. should be long foes (Friendship 32)

pricked in number of our f. (Friendship 14)

those f. thou hast (Friendship 3)

'twixt such f. as we few words suffice (Friendship 26)

what need we have any f.? (Friendship 28)

you dare easier be f. with me (Fighting 3)

friendship:

f. is constant in all other things (Friendship 23)

if I do vow a f. (Friendship 24)

in the beaten way of f. (Friendship 4)

love cools, f. falls off (Disorder 1)

most f. is feigning (Disillusion 1)

there is flattery in f. (Flattery 3)

where there is true f. (Ceremony 5)

frost:
death lies on her like an untimely f. (Death 37)
the third day comes a f., a killing f. (Farewells 10)

frown:
fear no more the f. (Mourning 4)

frowningly:
what, looked he f.? (Faces 2)

fruit:
the ripest f. first falls (Epitaphs 13)

full:
f. fathom five (Transformation 2)
f. many a glorious morning (Sunrise 6)

full-gorged:
my falcon ... must not be f. (Falconry 1)

function:
f. is smothered in surmise (Confusion 4)

funeral:
come I to speak in Caesar's f. (Honor 15)
with mirth in f. (Mourning 6)

furnace:
heat not a f. for your foe (Advice 9)

fury:
fires ... consume the thing that feeds their f. (Fire 4)

gaberdine:
my Jewish g. (Anti-Semitism 1)

gain:
sir which serves and seeks for g. (Self-Interest 3)

gale:
what happy g. blows you to Padua? (Travel 19)

gallop:
g. apace, you fiery-footed steeds (Anticipation 3)

gap:
sleep out this great g. of time (Forgetfulness 2)

garden:
old Adam's likeness, set to dress this g. (Gardens 8)
our sea-walled g. the whole land (Disorder 3)
this world ... 'tis an unweeded g. (Dejection 1)

gardener:
Adam was a g. (Gardens 4)

garland:
withered is the g. of the war (Epitaphs 1)

garlic:
eat no onions nor g. (Eating 10)

garment:
this new and gorgeous g. (Royalty 13)

garments:
our g. poor (Clothing 10)

garter:
knights of the g. (Chivalry 1)

garters:
hang thyself in thine own ... g. (Insults 3)

gasp:
fight to the last g. (Resistance 1)

gauds:
all, with one consent, praise new-born g. (Fashion 11)

gaudy:
let's have one other g. night (Feasts 2)

gaze:
no extraordinary g. (Royalty 9)

geese:
wild g. that the creeping fowler eye (Hunting 2)

geld:
g. and spay all the youth (Prostitution 1)

gem:
never so rich a g. (Jewels 2)

general:
are you content to be our g.? (Necessity 9)
the g. so likes your music (Music 15)

gentleman:
a g. ... that loves to hear himself talk (Talking 6)
a most kind g. (Soldiers 15)
he is a worthy g. (Men 1)
I do not think a braver g. (Soldiers 8)
I was a g. (Men 9)
prince of darkness is a g. (Devil 5)
smooth-faced g., tickling commodity (Self-Interest 1)
the g. is learned (Eloquence 5)
this g. will out-talk us all (Talking 7)
thou wrong'st a g. (Virtue 4)

gentlemen:
g. in England now abed (War 15)

gentleness:
I have not from your eyes that g. (Friendship 12)
the g. of all the gods go with thee (Farewells 20)

germens:
all g. spill at once (Storms 6)

get:
g. you hence, sirrah! (Dismissal 1)

ghost:
I'll make a g. of him that lets me (Determination 1)
there needs no g., my lord (Truisms 2)

giant:
excellent to have a g.'s strength (Strength 2)
pang as great as when a g. dies (Death 27)
sleeping g. (Action 15)

gibes:
where be your g. now? (Mortality 2)

giddy:
he that is g. (Giddiness 1)

gift:
action did outsell her g. (Action 2)
make my g. the more delayed (Providence 1)
this rich and precious g. (Gifts 1)
though the g. small (Gifts 3)

gifts:
the g. she looks from me (Gifts 6)
why do you make us love your goodly g.? (Gifts 2)
win her with g. (Gifts 5)

gild:
to g. refinèd gold (Extravagance 2)

gillyvors:
our carnations and streaked g. (Flowers 10)

ginger:
and g. shall be hot (Virtue 23)

girdle:
but to the g. do the gods inherit (Misogyny 1)
I'll put a g. round about the earth (Travel 14)

girl:
an unlessoned g., unschooled (Girls 3)

girl (cont'd.)
there's a g. goes before the priest (Thought 1)
girls:
the truth of g.'s and boys (Girls 2)
those g. of Italy (Girls 1)
give:
g. me my robe (Death-Wish 3)
g. me that glass (Self-Pity 3)
g. me that man that is not passion's slave (Freedom 5)
g. me the map there (Maps 2)
g. the Devil his due (Devil 4)
glass:
fair woman but she made mouths in a g. (Vanity 1)
give me that g. (Self-Pity 3)
he was the mark and g., copy and book (Fashion 4)
methinks you are my g. (Twins 1)
the g. of fashion and the mold of form (Fashion 2)
the g. wherein the noble youth (Fashion 3)
globe:
th'affrighted g. (Loss 7)
this distracted g. (Memory 2)
we the g. can compass soon (Travel 15)
glory:
fierce wretchedness that g. brings (Misery 4)
g. is like a circle in the water (Glory 1)
greater g. dim the less (Comparisons 2)
think not ... to share with me in g. (Rivalry 1)
times's g. is to calm (Time 40)
uncertain g. of an April day (Love 102)
glove:
a cheveril g. to a good wit (Wit 7)
gloves:
g. as sweet as damask roses (Clothing 15)
glow-worm:
g. shows the matin to be near (Dawn 3, Time of Day 3)
gnats:
let foolish g. make sport (Insects 1)
go:
he must needs go that the devil drives (Devil 1)
goats:
as prime as g. (Lechery 3)
wanton as youthful g. (Animals 4)
goblin:
be thou ... a g. damned (Ghosts 7)
God:
an attribute to G. himself (Mercy 9)
art thou some g. (Apparitions 5)
for G.'s sake go not to these wars (War 6)
for G.'s sake let us sit (Stories 5)
G. doth know and you may partly see (Deceit 20)
G. is our fortress (God 4)
G. keep lead out of me (War 5)
G. keep your worship (Blessings 4)
G.'s above all (Soul 2)
G. save the foundation! (Religion 6)
G.'s benison go with you (Blessings 1)
G. shall be my hope (God 7)

G. the best maker of all marriages (Prayer 7)
had I but served my G. (Service 4)
had not G. for some strong purpose (Pity 9)
in apprehension how like a g. (Man 5)
I thank G. I am not a woman (Women 7)
make the service greater than the g. (Idolatry 1)
now G. be praised (God 5, Prayer 9)
O G. of battles (Prayer 6)
O G., that men should put an enemy (Drinking 22)
O G., that one might read the book of fate (Fate 3)
O G., thy arm was here (God 3)
O pity, G., this miserable age! (Prayer 10)
the g. of this great vast (Storms 13)
the hideous g. of w. (War 7)
thou owest G. a death (Death 12)
we are in G.'s hands (God 2)
we owe G. a death (Death 14)
what kind of g. art thou (Ceremony 2)
godheads:
were your g. to borrow of men (Prayer 18)
gods:
as flies ... are we to the g. (Gods 1)
draw near the nature of the g. (Mercy 15)
g. are just (Justice 8)
g. stand up for bastards (Bastardy 1)
g. themselves humbling their deities (Gods 5)
g., why do you make us love your ... gifts (Gifts 2)
immortal g., I crave no pelf (Prayer 17)
nature of the g. (Mercy 12)
the clearest g. ... have preserved thee (Miracles 4)
the voice of all the g. (Love 44)
to your protection I commend me, g. (Prayer 2)
you ever gentle g. (Prayer 13)
goers-between:
let all pitiful g. (Lust 12)
gold:
all that glisters is not g. (Gold 5)
g., worse poison to men's souls (Poison 3)
g., yellow, glistering, precious g. (Gold 6)
I am not covetous for g. (Honor 9)
plate sin with g. (Gold 4)
poop was beaten g. (Ships 2)
saint-seducing g. (Courtship 19)
the g. bides still (Gold 1)
there is g. (Royalty 1)
'tis g. which makes the true man killed (Gold 2)
when g. becomes her object (Avarice 1, Gold 3)
golden age:
t'excel the g. (Government 5)
golden world:
carelessly as they did in the g. (Golden Age 1)
gone:
art thou g. too ? (Parting 8)
wilt thou be g.? (Parting 16)
good:
g. fortune then! To make me blest (Fortune 18)
g. friends, go in and taste some wine (Friendship 13)
g. Hamlet, cast thy nighted color (Clothing 2)
I never did repent for doing g. (Goodness 2)

it is not, nor it cannot come to g. (Grief 6)
make g. of bad (Blessings 1)
so shines a g. deed (Goodness 3)
the g. is oft interrèd with their bones (Epitaphs 10)
the g. I stand on (Integrity 1)
they should be g. men (Goodness 1)
'tis g. for men to love their ... pains (Philosophy 10)
to do g. accounted dangerous folly (Innocence 4)
goodly:
a g. portly man, i'faith (Fatness 3)
good will:
my g. w. is great (Gifts 3)
when g. w. is showed (Acting 1)
goodness:
g. to the vile seem vile (Aphorisms 3)
some soul of g. in things evil (Philosophy 8)
goose:
when every g. is cackling (Birds 11)
gorgeous:
nature needs not what thou g. wear'st (Fashion 5)
gosling:
I'll never be such a g. (Man 2)
gossamers:
lover may bestride the g. (Vanity 3)
gout:
a pox of this g. (Sickness 10)
govern:
I would with such perfection g. (Government 5)
government:
g., though high and low (Government 2)
we be men of good g. (Government 1)
gowns:
one that hath two g. (Dignity 1)
grace:
g. and remembrance be to you (Flowers 9)
g. me no g. (Grace 1)
g. of heaven ... enwheel thee round (Greetings 10)
heaven such g. did lend her (Beauty 26)
he does it with a better g. (Fools 12)
her strong toil of g. (Death 6)
if a lie may do thee g. (Lying 3)
in all external g. (Constancy 11)
mickle is the powerful g. (Nature 6)
O momentary g. of mortal men (Grace 2, Transience 4)
things foul would wear the brows of g. (Angels 1)
this action ... is for my better g. (Action 16)
what a g. was seated on this brow (Beauty 7)
when once our g. we have forgot (Shame 1)
you have the g. of God (Proverbs 19)
graces:
g. her subjects (Beauty 19)
the king-becoming g. (Virtue 11)
grain:
'tis in g. ... 'twill endure wind (Beauty 25)
grass:
how lush and lusty the g. looks (Gardens 10)
grave:
a little g., an obscure g. (Renunciation 2)

do me wrong to take me out o' the g. (Suffering 1)
Duncan is in his g. (Death 25)
every third thought shall be my g. (Mortality 10)
no g. upon the earth shall clip (Epitaphs 3)
renownèd be thy g. (Mourning 5)
still as the g. (Proverbs 23)
sweeten thy sad g. (Mourning 2)
the g. doth gape for thee (Mortality 6)
thy ignominy sleep with thee in the g. (Epitaphs 7)
tomorrow you shall find me a g. man (Dying 15)
true lover never find my g. (Graces 2)
graves:
bears not one spurn to their g. (Corruption 7)
g. at my command (Renunciation 4)
g. stood tenantless (Apparitions 3)
let's talk of g. (Despair 5)
the g. all gaping wide (Ghosts 14)
grave-stone:
let my g. be your oracle (Epitaphs 15)
gravity:
g. out of his bed at midnight (Age 7)
great:
g. thing of us forgot! (Forgetfulness 3)
he was g. of heart (Greatness 9)
if I do grow g., I'll grow less (Reformation 2)
it is g. to do that thing (Suicide 8)
rightly to be g. (Greatness 2)
some are born g. (Greatness 11)
thou wouldst be g. (Ambition 11)
what g. ones do the less will prattle of (Gossip 1)
greatest:
g. scandal waits on g. state (Greatness 12)
greatness:
a long farewell to all my g. (Farewells 10)
g. going off (Greatness 1)
g. knows itself (Greatness 5)
g. once fallen out with fortune (Decline 3)
possessed he is with g. (Arrogance 2)
some achieve g. (Greatness 11)
th'abuse of g. (Greatness 6)
touched the highest point of all my g. (Downfall 1)
Greece:
in our country of G. (Begging 2)
Greek:
it was G. to me (Language 5)
green:
how g. you are, and fresh (Simplicity 1)
greenwood:
under the g. tree (Country Life 3)
greeting:
bear my g. to the senators (Greetings 3)
grey:
though g. do something mingle (Middle Age 2)
greyhound:
fawning g. then did proffer (Flattery 1)
greyhounds:
I see you stand like g. (War 12)
grief:
crosses, cares and g. (Affliction 11)

grief (cont'd.)
everyone can master a g. (Aphorisms 9)
full of g. as age (Affliction 4)
g. fills the room up (Grief 9)
g. has so wrought on him (Perception 2)
g. hath changed me (Grief 3)
he robs himself that spends a bootless g. (Philosophy 17, Theft 9)
I have that honorable g. (Grief 15)
it were a g. ... to part with thee (Farewells 17)
my g. lies all within (Grief 14)
my g.'s so great (Grief 8)
my heart of g. (Grief 7)
my particular g. (Sorrow 6)
pure g. shore his old thread (Grief 12)
something stained with g. (Beauty 23)
speak comfort to that g. (Experience 3)
the g. that does not speak (Grief 10)
griefs:
factious for redress of all these g. (Conspiracy 2)
g. of mine own lie heavy (Sorrow 12)
great g., I see, medicine the less (Grief 4)
relating tales of others' g. (Misery 3)
sick of many g. (Affliction 2)
suffer'st ... mortal g. (Ceremony 2)
to speak my g. unspeakable (Grief 2)
grieved:
no more be g. (Wrongdoing 8)
grim:
g. death, how foul (Death 39)
gross:
in the g. and scope of mine opinion (Foreboding 3)
ground:
having waste g. enough (Building 3)
the hopes we have in him touch g. (Disappointment 1)
lay him in the cold g. (Burial 2)
grudge:
the ancient g. I bear him (Malevolence 2)
guest:
beginning of a feast ... fits ... a keen g. (Fighting 1)
guests:
unbidden g. (Hospitality 1)
guilt:
they whose g. within their bosoms lie (Guilt 11)
full of artless jealousy is g. (Guilt 4)
gulfs:
wash me in steep-down g. (Hell 6)
gull:
that ungentle g. (Birds 2)
guts:
thou clay-brained g. (Insults 4)
habit:
costly thy h. as thy purse can buy (Clothing 3)
honor peereth in the meanest h. (Clothing 10)
how use doth breed a h. (Custom 5)
habitation:
an h. giddy and unsure (People 14)

hags:
secret, black and midnight h. (Occult 3)
hail:
h. to thee, lady (Greetings 10)
hair:
h. shall be of what color it please God (Men and Women 4)
his very h. is of the dissembling color (Hair 1)
many a man has more h. than wit (Hair 2)
hairs:
his silver h. (Maturity 2)
if h. be wires (Beauty 33)
spread ... thy golden h. (Courtship 4)
white h. (Age 8, 17)
half:
one h. of me is yours (Love 48)
half-world:
now o'er the one h. (Night 12)
hand:
each man render me his bloody h. (Greetings 4)
h. in h. with fairy grace (Fairies 7)
I saw her h. ... a leathern h. (Insults 1)
let me kiss that h. (Mortality 7)
the bawdy h. of the dial (Time 26)
the eye wink at the h. (Desire 9)
the fairest h. I ... touched (Beauty 9)
the h. that hath made you fair (Virtue 13)
what if this cursèd h. were thicker (Forgiveness 3)
hands:
close our h. with holy words (Marriage 45)
give me your h. all over (Greetings 2)
our own h. against our hearts (Marriage 35)
these h. do lack nobility (Assault 1)
handy-dandy:
h., which is the justice (Justice 6)
hang:
h. me up at the door of a brothel-house (Love 60)
h. there like fruit (Love 28)
h. there, my verse (Poetry 1)
h. thyself (Insults 3)
hanging:
beating and h. are terrors to me (Afterlife 6)
h. and wiving goes by destiny (Proverbs 20)
many a good h. prevents a bad marriage (Marriage 48)
happiness:
envy no man's h. (Contentment 1)
look into h. through another man's eyes (Happiness 1)
one mutual h. (Happiness 7)
society ... is the h. of life (Society 4)
happy:
h. thou art not (Happiness 5)
methinks it were a h. life (Happiness 3)
so h. be the issue (Negotiation 2)
'twere now to be most h. (Happiness 6)
harbinger:
apparel vice like virtue's h. (Deceit 1)

shines Aurora's h. (Dawn 4)
harder:
  the h. matched, the greater victory (Victory 1)
hark:
  h., h., the lark at heaven's gate (Sunrise 1)
  h. what good sport is out of town (Sport 3)
harlot:
  Portia is Brutus's h. (Marriage 21)
harlotry:
  peevish, self-willed h. (Obstinacy 2)
harm:
  I have done no h. (Innocence 5)
  know'st thou any h.'s intended (Foreboding 7)
harmony:
  hushed on purpose to grace h. (Evening 1)
  make heaven drowsy with the h. (Love 44)
  such h. is in immortal souls (Heaven 3)
  what h. is this? (Music 24)
harp:
  h. not on that string (Repetition 1)
  I framed to the h. (Music 5)
hart:
  if a h. do lack a hind (Poetry 3)
  that instant was I turned into a h. (Desire 16)
hast:
  h. thou, which art but air (Sympathy 1)
haste:
  h. still pays h. (Justice 14)
  pray God we may make h. (Lateness 3)
hat:
  'a brushes his h. o'mornings (Love 65)
  as the fashion of his h. (Inconstancy 3)
hate:
  lesser hide his love or h. (Appearance 10)
  much to do with h. (Love 73)
  naught I did in h. (Murder 10)
haunt:
  h. thee like a wicked conscience (Conscience 9)
have:
  they well deserve to h. (Deserving 2)
  to h. what we would h. (Desire 11)
hawk:
  I soar, I am a h. (Horses 2)
hay:
  a bottle of h. Good h., sweet h. (Eating 9)
hazard:
  give and h. all he hath (Risk 2)
  the nice h. of one doubtful hour (Risk 1)
he:
  he bids you ... to take mercy (War 9)
  he does me double wrong (Flattery 6)
  he does smile his face (Faces 7)
  he hath a heart as sound as a bell (Speech 17)
  he hath borne himself (Courage 7)
  he hath disgraced me (Anti-Semitism 2)
  he hath honored me (Reputation 4)
  he hath ribbons of all the colors (Clothing 14)
  he is as valiant as the lion (Valor 14)

he is come to open the purple testament (War 20)
he is composed and framed of treachery (Villainy 6)
he is himself alone (Valor 4)
he is too disputable (Argument 2)
he repelled ... fell into a sadness (Madness 3)
he's as tall a man (Appearance 12)
he seemed to find his way without his eyes (Eyes 6)
he's truly valiant (Endurance 4)
he talks well (Talking 2)
he that but fears the thing (Fear 3)
he that depends upon your favors (People 8)
he that filches from me (Reputation 9)
he that is strucken blind (Eyes 13)
he that loves to be flattered (Flattery 7)
he that of greatest works is finisher (God 1)
he that plays the king (Acting 5)
he that shall see this day (Festivals 4)
he that trusts to you (the People 5)
he was wont to speak plain (Speech 16)
he who the sword of heaven will bear (Justice 13, Virtue 15)
he will to his Egyptian dish (Desire 2)
head:
  his bold h. 'bove the ... waves (Swimming 2)
  no house to put his h. in (Homelessness 3)
  off with his h. (Execution 1)
  thy h. is as full of quarrels (Quarrels 14)
  uneasy lies the h. (Royalty 11)
  what is the body when the h. is off? (Body 4)
health:
  as in h. come to my natural taste (Devotion 3)
  h. and fair time of day (Greetings 1)
  he has his h. (Middle Age)
healths:
  with drinking h. to my niece (Drinking 27)
hear:
  h. him debate of commonwealth affairs (Politics 5)
  h. me for my cause (Speechmaking 2)
heart:
  a good h. is the sun and the moon (Courtship 11)
  a kind h. he hath (Kindness 3)
  a light h. lives long (Cheerfulness 1)
  a merry h. goes all the way (Endurance 5)
  break, my h. (Grief 6)
  did my h. love till now? (Love 76)
  fare thee well, great h.! (Farewells 6)
  he has my h. yet (Devotion 1)
  he hath a h. as sound as a bell (Speech 17)
  he was great of h. (Greatness 9)
  his flawed h., alack too weak (Dying 12)
  his h.'s his mouth (Speech 2)
  how ill all's here about my h. (Foreboding 6)
  how weak a thing the h. of woman is (Women 20)
  I cannot heave my h. (Speech 9)
  infinite h.'s ease (Ceremony 1)
  I saw his h. in his face (Faces 8)
  I will live in thy h. (Sex 7)
  I would eat his h. (Anger 7)

heart (cont'd.)
just as high as my h. (Height 1)
like none for constant h. (Constancy 11)
my h. doth joy (Loyalty 4)
my h. hath one poor string (Dying 11)
my h. is in the coffin (Mourning 15)
my h. is turned to stone (Affliction 8)
my h. laments that virtue (Virtue 8)
my h. prays for him (Forgiveness 1)
my h.'s subdued (Devotion 4)
my h. unto yours is knit (Love 58)
my old h. is cracked (Affliction 3)
no matter from the h. (Words 10)
now cracks a noble h. (Epitaphs 5)
one h., one bed (Love 57)
O serpent h. (Deceit 22)
show his eyes and grieve his h. (Eyes 10)
the poor h. would fain deny (Curses 5)
thy breast encloseth my poor h. (Courtship 17)
wear him in my h.'s core, ay, in my h. of h. (Friendship 5)
wear my h. upon my sleeve (Deceit 10)
what the false h. doth know (Deceit 5)
where I have garnered up my h. (Loss 6)
whispers the o'er-fraught h. (Grief 10)
with a h. as willing (Marriage 47)
your h's desires be with you (Desire 3)
heart-break:
better a little chiding than ... h. (Chiding 1)
hearts:
all h. in love (Love 62)
for our h., he knows no more of mine (Deceit 17)
he sits high in all the people's h. (Nobility 5)
let our h. stir up their servants (Assassination 2)
makes these hard h. (Cause 4)
our h. you see not (Pity 2)
our own hands against our h. (Marriage 35)
heat:
the h. of a luxurious bed (Lust 9)
heaven:
comfort's in h. (Affliction 11)
either in h. or hell (Afterlife 3)
h. doth with us as we with torches (Virtue 12)
h. give thee joy (Blessings 2)
h. give you ... merry days (Blessings 3)
he hath turned a h. unto a hell (Love 53)
he who the sword of h. will bear (Justice 13)
h. is above all yet (God 8)
h. mocks itself (Inconstancy 5)
h. still guards the right (Angels 2)
hurl my soul from h. (Affliction 10)
leave her to h. (Conscience 1)
lightning seemed to open the breast of h. (Courage 5)
make h. drowsy (Love 44)
make my h. in a lady's lap (Courtship 12)
my sole earth's h. (Courtship 5)
plays tricks before high h. (Authority 9)
steep and thorny way to h. (Advice 4)
summons thee to h. (Bells 2)
that kiss which is my h. to have (Kissing 2)

the front of h. was full of fiery shapes (Portents 1)
the help of h. we count the act of men (Arrogance 1)
there's husbandry in h. (Darkness 2)
thy soul's flight, if it find h. (Death 24)
when h. doth weep (Storms 17)
heavens:
do as the h. have done (Forgiveness 6)
his face was as the h. (Praise 3)
hung be the h. with black (Night 8)
if that the h. do not their visible spirits (Anarchy 1)
I never saw the h. so dim (Storms 18)
the h. forbid but that our loves (Love 70)
the h. hold firm the walls (Chastity 2, Wishes 2)
the h. themselves blaze forth (Portents 6)
the h. themselves ... observe degree (Order 1)
the h. were all on fire (Portents 2)
who ever knew the h. menace so? (Storms 3)
Hecate:
the triple H.'s team (Fairies 6)
Hecuba:
What's H. to him, or he to H.? (Acting 8)
hedgehogs:
thorny h. (Creatures 3)
hedge-sparrow:
the h. fed the cuckoo so long (Ingratitude 5)
heigh-ho:
sing h. unto the green holly (Disillusion 1)
height:
with her h. ... she hath prevailed (Comparisons 1)
heir:
folly helped her to an h. (Aphorisms 10)
hell:
all h. shall stir for this (Hell 1)
could not believe but that I was in h. (Dreams 11)
down, down to h. (Ruthlessness 2)
either in heaven or h. (Afterlife 3)
h. is murky (Hell 4)
he's not in h. (Afterlife 4)
keeps the gate of h. (Hell 5)
loosèd out of h. (Madness 1)
not in the legions of horrid h. (Hell 3)
rebellious h. (Lust 6)
summons thee to ... h. (Bells 2)
there's h., there's darkness (Misogyny 1)
this place is too cold for h. (Hell 2)
wedlock forcèd but a h. (Marriage 18)
hell-fire:
I never see thy face but I think upon h. (Faces 4)
help:
it appears you need my h. (Help 1)
there is no h. (Inevitability 3)
'tis not enough to h. the feeble (Help 2)
hen:
she, poor h., has clucked thee (Parents and Children
1)
herald:
I wish no other h. (Remembrance 5)
the lark, the h. of the morn (Dawn 6)
heralds:
love's h. should be thoughts (Love 81)

immortal:
his biting is i. (Death 4)
impatience:
i. hath his privilege (Anger 3)
impatient:
wasp-stung and i. fool (Impatience 1)
impediment:
any cross, any i. (Hindrance 1)
impediments:
all i. in fancy's course (Love 4)
imperfections:
piece out our i. (Imagination 2)
imperious:
i. Caesar, dead (Mortality 4)
impiety:
to be in anger is i. (Anger 9)
thou pure i. and impious purity (Paradoxes 4)
importunity:
his unmastered i. (Chastity 4)
impose:
i. me to what penance (Sin 5)
impossibilities:
make them honors of men's i. (Miracles 4)
inch:
I will not budge an i. (Resistance 3)
inconstancy:
i. falls off before it begins (Inconstancy 7)
India:
bountiful as mines of I. (Men 1)
Indian:
scarf veiling an I. beauty (Deceit 8)
Indies:
new map with the augmentation of the I. (Faces 7)
indirections:
by i. find directions out (Deviousness 1)
indiscretions:
our i. sometimes serve us well (Providence 2)
industry:
experience is by i. achieved (Experience 4)
inestimable:
i. stones, unvalued jewels (Dreams 10)
infamonize:
dost thou i. me? (Solecisms 1)
infancy:
her tender i. (Chastity 7)
infant:
at first the i. (Infancy 2)
infected:
i. be the air on which they ride (Curses 3)
infirmities:
a friend should bear his friend's i. (Friendship 17)
infirmity:
i. doth still neglect all office (Sickness 13)
'tis the i. of his age (Self-Knowledge 6)
ingratitude:
filial i. (Ingratitude 8)
I hate i. more in a man (Ingratitude 10)
i. is monstrous (Ingratitude 2)
i., more strong than traitors' arms (Ingratitude 4)
i., thou marble-hearted fiend (Ingratitude 6)

not so unkind as man's i. (Ingratitude 1)
plague ... must light on this i. (Ingratitude 3)
iniquity:
I lack i. (Murder 7)
that grey i. (Vice 2)
injuries:
i. that they themselves procure (Obstinacy 4)
ink
fallen into a pit of i. (Guilt 10)
inn:
take mine ease in mine i. (Leisure 2)
innocence:
childhood i. (Friendship 21)
i. shall make false accusation blush (Innocence 8)
the silence often of pure i. (Innocence 7)
to plead mine i. (Innocence 4)
what we changed was i. for i. (Innocence 6)
innocency:
thou knowest in the state of i. Adam fell (Excuses 2)
innocent:
our kinsman Gloucester is as i. (Innocence 3)
innocents:
some i. scape not the thunderbolt (Innocence 1)
insolence:
his i. draws folly from my lips (Words and Deeds 5)
instant:
let's take the i. (Time 1)
instinct:
beware i. (Instinct 1)
instrument:
my i.'s in tune (Music 20)
instruments:
a thousand twangling i. (Music 23)
insupportable:
O i. and touching loss (Loss 3)
O i.! O heavy hour! (Loss 7)
intent:
'tis our fast i. (Retirement 2)
intercessors:
yield to Christian i. (Inflexibility 1)
interpretation:
our virtues lie in the i. (Virtue 3)
invisible:
we walk i. (Magic 1)
invocation:
'tis a Greek i. (Mockery 1)
ire:
yet cease your i., you angry stars (Storms 12)
irksome:
how i. is this music (Quarrels 4)
iron:
else the i. cools (Action 7)
isle:
the i. is full of noises (Music 23)
issue:
for Banquo's i. (Damnation 1)
so happy be the i. (Negotiation 2)
issues:
spirits are not finely touched but to great i. (Greatness 8)

knights:
k. of the garter (Chivalry 1)
knot:
it is too hard a k. for me (Time 35)
know:
contended especially to k. himself (Self-Knowledge 8)
does any here k. me? (Identity 3)
I have much ado to k. myself (Self-Knowledge 9)
I k. myself now (Self-Knowledge 4)
none that I k. will be (Foreboding 7)
to k. my deed (Self-Knowledge 7)
we k. each other well (Familiarity 1)
you k. you cannot see yourself (Self-Knowledge 5)
knowledge:
feed your k. with viewing of the town (Travel 25)
I profit in the k. of myself (Self-Knowledge 12)
k. the wing wherewith we fly to heaven (Education 2)
known:
ever but slenderly k. himself (Self-Knowledge 6)
labor:
cold indeed and l. lost (Resignation 3)
the l. we delight in (Work 4)
laboring:
there's no l. in the winter (Proverbs 14)
labors:
sweet thoughts do even refresh my l. (Work 6)
ladies:
good night, sweet l. (Farewells 4)
lads:
golden l. and girls (Mourning 3)
two l. that thought (Boys 5)
lady:
get you to my l.'s chamber (Women 14)
I have flattered a l. (Court 1)
it is my l. (Love 77)
l., by yonder blessèd moon (Vows 4)
l. doth protest too much (Hypocrisy 2)
l., shall I lie in your lap (Sex 2)
make my heaven in a l.'s lap (Courtship 12)
the sweetest l. that ever I looked on (Eyes 11)
they say the l. is fair (Men and Women 5)
thou art a l.; if only to go warm (Fashion 6)
why, that's the l. (Desire 13)
will you have me, l.? (Marriage 31)
you have put him down, l. (Sex 2)
lamb:
innocent ... as is the sucking l. (Innocence 3)
in the figure of a l. the feats of a lion (Courage 7)
the fox ... would steal the l. (Animals 5)
when the lion fawns upon the l. (Animals 7)
lambs:
we were as twinned l. (Innocence 6)
lame:
most l. and impotent conclusion (Endings 3)
the poor, l., blind ... cry out for thee (Opportunity 4)
lances:
now I see our l. are but straws (Women 26)
land:
the whole l. is full of weeds (Disorder 2)

woe to that l. that's governed by a child (Government 4)
land-rats:
there be l. and water-rats (Ships 4)
lands:
let me...have l. by wit (Self-Interest 2)
you have sold your own l. (Travel 2)
language:
there's l. in her eye (Lechery 4)
to gain the l. (Language 2)
you taught me l. (Language 8)
languages:
a great feast of l. (Language 6)
l. I have learnt (Language 7)
speaks three or four l. (Character 5)
lap:
I will...die in thy l. (Sex 7)
ope her l. to saint-seducing gold (Courtship 19)
shall I lie in your lap? (Sex 2)
lapwing:
far from her nest the l. cries away (Forgiveness 1)
lards:
l. the lean earth as he walks (Fatness 1)
largess:
a l. universal, like the sun (Generosity 3)
lark:
busy day, waked by the l. (Dawn 8)
crow doth sing as sweetly as the l. (Birds 10)
from the rising of the l. (Time of Day 6)
is the jay more precious than the l.? (Value 3)
lo, here the gentle l. (Sunrise 7)
more tunable than l. to shepherd's ear (Beauty 15)
the finch, the sparrow and the l. (Birds 13)
the l. at heaven's gate sings (Sunrise 1)
the l., the herald of the morn (Dawn 6)
lascivious:
l. meters, to whose venom sound (Poetry 12)
lass:
a l. unparalleled (Death 5, Epitaphs 2)
the prettiest low-born l. (Nobility 9)
last:
the l. of all the Romans, fare thee well (Epitaphs 11)
late:
better ... too soon than a minute too l. (Lateness 2)
I am glad I was up so l. (Lateness 1)
it is so very l. that we may call it early (Farewells 18)
never too l. (Lateness 4)
to be up l. is to be up l. (Lateness 5)
lated:
I am so l. in the world (Despair 1)
laugh:
you shall see him l. (Laughter 1)
laughter:
the worst returns to l. (Hope 1, Laughter 2)
lavender:
hot l. (Flowers 11)
law:
a l. in each well-ordered nation (Law 11)
I have been a truant in the l. (Law 3)
in l. what plea so tainted (Hypocrisy 10)

law (cont'd.)
  like a poor man's right in the l. (Fishing 3)
  make a scarecrow of the l. (Law 7)
  old father antic the l. (Law 2)
  pity is the virtue of the l. (Law 10)
  sharp quillets of the l. (Law 4)
  the l. hath not been dead (Law 8)
  the l. I bear no malice (Law 6)
  thou know'st no l. (Animals 11)
  wicked prize ... buys out the l. (Law 1)
  wrest once the l. (Law 9)
lawn:
  l. as white as driven snow (Clothing 15)
lawyer:
  the breath of an unfeed l. (Lawyers 2)
lawyers:
  let's kill all the l. (Lawyers 1)
  with l. in the vacation (Time 6)
lay:
  l. on, Macduff (Fighting 2)
lead:
  God keep l. out of me! (War 5)
lean:
  l. enough to be thought a good student (Thinness 4)
  you'd be so l. (Thinness 5)
leap:
  methinks it were an easy l. (Honor 1)
Lear:
  this is not L. (Identity 3)
learning:
  O this l., what a thing it is! (Learning 4)
leave:
  I will take my l. of you (Parting 6)
  l. not the mansion ... tenantless (Ruin 1)
leave-taking:
  let us not be dainty of l. (Parting 10)
lechery:
  l., l. still wars and l. (Lechery 6)
  l., sir, it provokes and unprovokes (Drinking 14)
  the most dangerous piece of l. (Villainy 5)
leek:
  I am qualmish at the smell of l. (Vegetables 1)
leg:
  a good l. will fall (Courtship 11)
legacy:
  no l. is so rich as honesty (Honor 2)
legion:
  methought a l. of foul fiends (Dreams 11)
legs:
  his l. are l. for courtesy (Pride 3)
  his l. bestrid the ocean (Praise 4, World 2)
leisure:
  how has he the l. to be sick? (Sickness 5)
  when thou hast l. (Leisure 1)
lend:
  l. to each man enough (Prayer 18)
lender:
  neither a borrower nor a l. be (Advice 6)
Lent:
  what's a joint of mutton or two in a whole L. (Food 7)

leopards:
  lions make l. tame (Animals 9)
leprosy:
  make the hoar l. adored (Gold 6)
lesson:
  any hard l. that may do thee good (Friendship 22)
let:
  l. every feeble rumor shake (Rumor 1)
  l. me, if not by birth (Self-Interest 2)
  l. us ... mock the good huswife fortune (Fortune 3)
  l. us not break with him (Politics 12)
  l. us not burden our remembrances (Remembrance 8)
  l. us seek out some desolate shade (Sorrow 4)
Lethe:
  weed that roots itself ... on L. wharf (Action 3)
letter:
  thou unnecessary l. (Insults 11)
letters:
  get posts and l. (Letters 2)
liberal:
  I will become as l. as you (Liberality 1)
  where you are l. of your loves (Betrayal 1)
  you are l. in offers (Begging 1)
libertine:
  reckless l. (Advice 4)
  the air, a chartered l. is still (Eloquence 3)
  thou thyself hast been a l. (Lust 5)
liberty:
  I must have l. (Freedom 2)
  l.! freedom! tyranny is dead (Freedom 4)
  l. plucks justice by the nose (Freedom 6, Justice 10)
library:
  furnished me from mine own l. (Books 4)
  make choice of all my l. (Books 5)
  my l. was dukedom large enough (Books 3)
lids:
  with thy vailèd l. (Mourning 7)
lie:
  if a l. may do thee grace (Lying 3)
  you told a l. ... a wicked l. (Lying 6)
lies:
  as many l. as will lie in thy paper (Lying 7)
  he l. to the heart (Lying 5)
  these l. are like their father (Lying 1)
life:
  after l.'s fitful fever (Death 25)
  aim of all is but to nurse the l. (Ambition 14)
  all the courses of my l. do show (Greatness 3)
  a man's l.'s but a span (Soldiers 22)
  care's an enemy to l. (Hedonism 1)
  entertain the lag-end of my l. (Retirement 1)
  everything advantageous to l. (Life 10)
  farewell l. (Farewells 9)
  fie upon this quiet l. (Action 4)
  for the l. to come (Afterlife 6)
  grunt and sweat under a weary l. (Afterlife 2)
  his l. was gentle (Epitaphs 12)
  I do not set my l. at a pin's fee (Recklessness 2)
  I love long l. (Life 2)

I spy l. peering (Life 10)
l. being weary of these worldly bars (Suicide 15)
l. consists of the four elements (Hedonism 2)
l. every man holds dear (Honor 22)
l. is as tedious (Tediousness 2)
l. itself, my wife and all the world (Friendship 20)
l.'s but a walking shadow (Life 7)
l.'s uncertain voyage (Life 12)
l., time's fool (Time 9)
merriment ... lengthens l. (Acting 27)
methinks it were a happy l. (Happiness 3)
mine honor is my l. (Honor 17)
my l. is run his compass (Life 6)
our little l. (Mortality 9)
promise me l., and I'll confess (Truth 6)
reason thus with l. (Death 25)
sands are numbered that makes up my l. (Dying 8)
the time of l. is short (Life 4)
the web of our l. (Life 1)
this l. is nobler (Country Life 9)
this our l., exempt from public haunt (Country Life 2)
to me can l. be no commodity (Death-Wish 11)
very vile l. (Country Life 7)
weariest ... worldly l. (Death 30)
we'd jump the l. to come (Action 12)
when a painter would surpass the l. (Painting 1)
where is the l. (Nostalgia 5)
you take my l. (Life 8)
light:
God ... give l. in darkness (God 5)
let me give l. (Marriage 25)
let not l. see my black and deep desires (Desire 9)
l., seeking l. (Light 1)
l. thickens, and the crow (Night 13)
put out the l. (Light 2)
what l. through yonder window breaks (Sunrise 5)
lightning:
brief as the l. (Transience 2)
the cross blue l. (Courage 5)
too like the l. (Anxiety 9)
like:
so l. you 'tis the worse (Proverbs 31)
likelihood:
l. and forms of hope (Hope 1)
lilies:
l. that fester smell far worse (Flowers 14)
lily:
fresh l. (Beauty 5)
to paint the l. (Extravagance 2)
limitation:
your self but ... in sort or l. (Marriage 20)
limits:
stony l. cannot hold love out (Love 78)
line:
will the l. stretch out? (Doomsday 3)
lion:
doing ... the feats of a l. (Courage 7)
hardy as the Nemean l.'s nerve (Fate 2)
he is a l. I am proud to hunt (Valor 3)

he is as valiant as the l. (Valor 14)
hind that would be mated by the l. (Love 1)
l. dying ... wounds the earth (Animals 10)
l. will not touch the true prince (Instinct 1)
now the hungry l. roars (Night 19)
the blood more stirs to rouse a l. (Valor 6)
the king ... is to be feared as the l. (Royalty 10)
when the l. fawns upon the lamb (Animals 7)
lioness:
a l. with udders all drawn dry (Animals 1)
lions:
l. make leopards tame (Animals 9)
two l. littered in one day (Danger 8)
lip:
for a touch of his nether l. (Desire 14)
lips:
eternity was in our l. and eyes (Eternity 1)
take those l. away (Inconstancy 1)
liquor:
this grand l. that hath gilded 'em (Drinking 25)
liquors:
I never did apply hot ... l. (Drinking 2)
list:
l., l., O list (Murder 1)
little:
a l. fire is quickly trodden out (Fire 1)
a l. more than a l. is by much too much (Eating 3)
a very l. (Action 6)
l. of this great world can I speak (Speech 19)
live:
let me not l. (Old Age 1)
l., and deal with others better (Forgiveness 2)
l. a thousand years (Death-Wish 6)
l. we how we can, yet die we must (Dying 9)
so we'll l., and pray (Politics 17)
this queen will l. (Life 8)
livery:
light and careless l. (Clothing 4)
lives:
a history in all men's l. (Life 5)
living:
there is no l., none (Infatuation 1)
lo:
lo, here the gentle lark (Sunrise 7)
locks:
never shake thy gory l. at me (Ghosts 13)
loins:
from forth the fatal l. (Love 72)
London:
I hope to see L. (Travel 9)
longings:
I have immortal l. in me (Death-Wish 3)
look:
l., I draw the sword myself (Death-Wish 4)
l. so piteous in purport (Madness 1)
l. to her, Moor (Deceit 11)
l. what a wardrobe here is for thee (Clothing 11)
l. what is done cannot now be amended (Excuses 4)
looks:
elder than thy l. (Appearance 5)

loon:
thou cream-faced l. (Curses 4)

Lord:
L. Angelo is precise (Power 9)
L. Hamlet with his doublet (Madness 1)
L., L., how this world is given (Lying 2)
l. of the wide world (Marriage 9)
L., what fools these mortals be (Fools 9, Humanity 5)
O L. that lends me life (Prayer 8)
remember what the L. hath done (God 6)

loser:
give the l. leave to chide (Loss 2)

loss:
O insupportable and touching l. (Loss 3)
what l. is it to be rid of care? (Loss 8)
wise men ne'er sit and wail their l. (Encouragement 1)

losses:
all l. are restored (Love 107)

love:
a braver place in my heart's l. (Friendship 6)
all hearts in l. (Love 62)
Benedick is sick in l. (Love 63)
but that I l. the gentle Desdemona (Marriage 40)
can lesser hide his l. (Appearance 10)
canst l. a fellow of this temper (Courtship 10)
chameleon l. can feed on air (Food 15)
course of true l. (Love 52)
did my heart l. till now? (Love 76)
do not fall in l. with me (Love 20)
do not presume too much upon my l. (Quarrels 8)
do you not l. me? (Love 35)
even in the spring of l. (Marriage 14)
ever I lose more blood with l. (Love 60)
first fall in l. (Love 66)
first suffer l. for me (Love 67)
for his verity in l. (Love 17)
have you not l. enough to bear with me? (Forbearance 2)
hind ... must die for l. (Love 1)
honest, so's my l. (Love 2)
how deep I am in l. (Love 23)
how many fathom deep I am in l. (Love 22)
how should I your true l. know (Love 32)
how this spring of l. (Love 102)
if ever thou shalt l. (Constancy 9)
if he be not in l. (Love 65)
if it be l. indeed (Love 5)
if music be the food of l. (Music 25)
if my dear l. were but the child of state (Constancy 13)
if there be no great l. (Marriage 26)
if you do l. me (Love 49)
I l. her heartily (Love 47)
I l. thee better (Love 36)
I l. you more than words (Parents and Children 5)
in l., i'faith (Love 89)
innocent mansion of my l., my heart (Death-Wish 4)
I owe him a little duty and less l. (Duty 2)
is l. a tender thing? (Love 75)
it is my l. (Love 77)

I will be horribly in l. with her (Men and Women 5)
let thy song be l. (Love 88)
l. all (Advice 1)
l. and be friends (Reconciliation 1)
l. and be silent (Love 38)
l. and meekness (Ambition 6)
l. breaks through (Proverbs 32)
l. comforteth like sunshine (Lust 15)
l. cools, friendship falls off (Disorder 1)
l. friendship, charity are subjects all (Time 30)
l. give me strength (Strength 3)
l. goes toward l. as schoolboys (Parting 14)
l. is a smoke (Love 74)
l. is begun by time (Love 33)
l. is blind (Love 46, 103)
l. is holy (Love 3)
l. is like a child (Love 105)
l. is merely a madness (Love 16)
l. is not l. (Love 110)
l. is too young (Conscience 10)
l. looks not with the eyes (Love 54)
l. me ... Fridays and Saturdays and all (Courtship 3)
l. moderately (Love 82)
l. no man in good earnest (Love 8)
l.'s feeling is more soft (Love 43)
l. said to be a child (Love 55)
l.'s heralds should be thoughts (Love 81)
l.'s keen arrows (Love 19)
l.'s not l. when it is mingled (Love 40)
l.'s not Time's fool (Constancy 12)
l. sought is good (Love 99)
l. that comes too late (Loss 1)
l. thyself last (Corruption 4)
l. whose month is ever May (Love 41)
l. wrought these miracles (Love 87)
loyal cantons of contemnèd l. (Courtship 23)
men have died ... but not for l. (Dying 5)
minister to l. (Love 61)
monstruosity in l. (Love 90)
my l. as deep (Love 80)
my l. doth so approve him (Devotion 5)
my l. is thine to teach (Friendship 22)
my l. shall hear the music of my hounds (Dogs 5)
my l.'s more ponderous (Love 39)
my l. to Hermia melted (Remembrance 7)
my true l. is grown (Love 83)
never doubt I l. (Love 30)
no kinder sign of l. (Kissing 7)
O brawling l. (Love 73)
O l., be moderate (Love 51)
O spirit of l. (Love 94)
ostentation of our l. (Love 6)
prosperity the very bond of l. (Affliction 13)
reason and l. keep little company (Reason 6)
rites for which I l. him (Love 69)
seat where l. is throned (Music 27)
she cannot l. (Self-Love 2)
she could not l. me (Love 24)
she never told her l. (Melancholy 7)

O, see the monstrousness of m. (Ingratitude 9)
O that I were a m. (Manliness 3)
O, that's a brave m. (Promises 5)
O, the difference of m. and m. (Desire 8)
ruins of the noblest m. (Epitaphs 9)
slight, unmeritable m. (Contempt 2)
stand as if a m. were author of himself (Man 2)
state of m. like to a little kingdom (Anxiety 4)
suffer the worst that m. can breathe (Endurance 4)
that a m. might know the end (Foreboding 8)
that I might see but such another m. (Dreams 1)
that m. should be at woman's command (Men and
Women 1)
that m. that hath a tongue (Courtship 24)
that's a brave m. (Promises 2)
the great m. down (Politics 2)
the m. nearest my soul (Friendship 9)
the m. shall have his mare again (Proverbs 21)
the m. that hath no music (Music 12)
there is no m. hath a virtue (Vice 4)
there's not one wise m. among twenty (Wisdom 5)
there's place and means for every m. (Foolery 1)
the simplicity of m. (Lust 7)
the time that the unjust m. doth thrive (Wrongdoing
7)
think you there ... might be such a m.? (Dreams 2)
this is the state of m. (Farewells 10)
thou art e'en as just a m. (Man 6)
though I am caparisoned like a m. (Women 5)
'tis not a year or two shows us a m. (Men and
Women 7)
to be a well-favored m. (Learning 2)
turns she every m. the wrong side out (Criticism 3)
unaccommodated m. (Man 9)
villainous m. (Man 8)
were m. but constant (Inconstancy 7)
what a piece of work is a m. (Man 5)
what is a m. (Man 7)
what m. may within him hide (Hypocrisy 9)
what wouldst thou do, old m.? (Duty 4)
who is m. that is not angry (Anger 9)
winter tames m. (Seasons 16)
you might have been enough the m. (Man 1)
young m. married (Marriage 1)
mandragora:
give me to drink m. (Forgetfulness 2)
manhood:
m. is melted into curtsies (Manliness 3)
mankind:
he's an enemy to m. (Devil 11)
how beauteous m. is! (Humanity 7)
the common curse of m. (Curses 9)
manners:
I'll view the m. of the town (Travel 3)
men's evil m. live in brass (Remembrance 4)
their m. are more gentle (Monsters 1)
we are the makers of m. (Custom 4)
mansion:
innocent m. of my love (Death-Wish 2)

leave not the m. so long tenantless (Ruin 1)
Timon hath made his everlasting m. (Epitaphs 15)
what a m. have those vices got (Vice 5)
mantle:
morn in russet m. clad (Dawn 1)
map:
give me the m. there (Maps 2)
I have forgot the m. (Maps 1)
new m. with the augmentation (Faces 7)
marble:
not m. nor the gilded monuments (Poetry 15)
marigold:
the m. that goes to bed with the sun (Flowers 11)
mark:
a fellow of no m. (Men 2)
he was the m. and glass (Fashion 3)
love ... is an ever-fixèd m. (Love 110)
m. how a plain tale (Plain-Speaking 1)
market-maid:
you are come a m. to Rome (Love 6)
markets:
not for all m. (Advice 3)
marmoset:
snare the nimble m. (Education 6)
marriage:
a good hanging prevents a bad m. (Marriage 48)
hasty m. seldom proveth well (Marriage 19)
let me not to the m. (Love 110)
O curse of m. (Marriage 41)
sweet silent hours of m. joys (Marriage 44)
with dirge in m. (Mourning 6)
marriage-blessing:
honor, riches, m. (Blessings 5)
marriages:
God, the best maker of all (Prayer 7)
married:
a young man m. (Marriage 1)
Benedick, the m. man (Marriage 34)
we will be m. o' Sunday (Marriage 46)
marry:
he swore he would never m. (Marriage 33)
if thou dost m. (Marriage 16)
if thou wilt needs m., m. a fool (Marriage 16)
since I do purpose to m. (Marriage 37)
Mars:
an eye like M. (Beauty 7)
think what Venus did with M. (Desire 1)
this seat of M. (Countries 5)
martlet:
the temple-haunting m. (Birds 6)
masks:
m. for faces (Clothing 15)
masons:
the singing m. (Building 2)
masque:
what m., what music? (Revels 4)
masques:
I delight in m. (Revels 5)
what m., what dances shall we have (Revels 3)

m. are flesh and blood (Constancy 2)
m. are m. (Men 11)
m. are merriest when they are from home (Travel 10)
m. are not gods (Men 12)
m. at some time are masters of their fates (Fate 5)
m. have died from time to time (Dying 5)
m. judge by the complexion of the sky (Weather 5)
m. may construe things (Misunderstanding 1)
m. must endure their going hence (Endurance 3)
m. must learn now with pity to dispense (Politics 23)
m. must needs abide (Fate 4)
m. of few words are the best (Men 6)
m. prize the thing ungained (Men and Women 9)
m.'s evil manners live in brass (Remembrance 3)
m. shall deal unadvisedly sometimes (Excuses 4)
m. should be what they seem (Appearance 8)
m. shut their doors against a setting sun (Downfall 4)
m. that make envy ... nourishment (Envy 1)
m. that she is the rarest (Men and Women 11)
m. that talk of a noun and a verb (Language 4)
m. were deceivers ever (Inconstancy 4)
m., wives, and children stare (Chaos 1)
m. would forsake the gods (Prayer 18)
most strange that m. should fear (Death 18)
of all the m. alive (Love 85)
O miracle of m. (Men 4)
such m. as he be never at heart's ease (Politics 11)
that we women had m.'s privilege (Courtship 22)
there are a sort of m. (Self-Importance 1)
there lives not three good m. unhanged (Nostalgia 2, Old Age 3)
the true proof of m. (Chance 2)
they should be good m. (Goodness 1)
thus m. may grow wiser (Wisdom 1)
tongues of m. are full of deceits (Deceit 3)
to willful m. the injuries (Obstinacy 4)
we are all m. (Weakness 2)
what m. dare do (Action 13)
when holy and devout religious m. (Prayer 15)
when there's no strength in m. (Men and Women 8)
wise m. ne'er sit and wail (Encouragement 1)
you are m. of stones (Mourning 17)
you are not stones, but m. (Men 7)
mend:
m. when thou canst (Improvement 2)
merchants:
like m. show our foulest wares (Business 9)
merciful:
O let us yet be m. (Mercy 2)
Mercury:
rise from the ground like feathered M. (Soldiers 6)
mercy:
half so good a grace as m. (Mercy 6)
how shalt thou hope for m.? (Mercy 9)
lawful m. (Mercy 6)
m. but murders, pardoning (Mercy 14)
m. is above this sceptered sway (Mercy 11)

m. is not itself that oft looks so (Mercy 4)
m. then will breathe (Mercy 7)
nor man grieve at the m. (Mercy 5)
quality of m. (Mercy 10)
sweet m. is nobility's true badge (Mercy 15)
there is no more m. in him (Ruthlessness 1)
use m. to them all (Mercy 3)
we do pray for m. (Mercy 12)
void ... from any dram of m. (Cruelty 5)
whereto serves m.? (Mercy 1)
meridian:
from that full m. of my glory (Downfall 1)
merit:
honorable without the stamp of m. (Merit 1)
purchased by the m. (Merit 2)
merrier:
a m. man (Merriment 2)
merriment:
mirth and m. (Acting 27)
your flashes of m. (Mortality 2)
merry:
a m. heart goes all the day (Merriment 6)
I am never m. when I hear (Music 11)
I am not m. (Moods 13)
men are ever m. (Moods 9)
neither sad nor m. (Moods 1)
rejoicing to see another m. (Moderation 1)
shall we be m.? (Merriment 1)
to be m. best becomes you (Merriment 4)
we shall be m. (Night 4)
you are m. because you are not sad (Moods 11)
message:
horrid m. for a challenge (Challenges 3)
metal:
here's metal more attractive (Sex 1)
meteors:
m. fright the fixèd stars (Portents 9)
meters:
lascivious m. to whose venom sound (Poetry 12)
methinks:
m. I see my father (Remembrance 2)
m. it were an easy leap (Honor 3)
m. King Richard and myself (Meeting 1)
m. the truth should live (Truth 7)
mettle:
thy honorable m. may be wrought (Nobility 4)
method:
there's m. in't (Madness 4)
mickle:
O, m,. is the powerful grace (Nature 6)
middle:
the m. of humanity thou never knewest (Humanity 9)
midnight:
out of his bed at m.(Age 7)
the iron tongue of m. (Time of Day 8)
to be up after m. (Lateness 5)
midsummer:
as gorgeous as the sun at m. (Seasons 4)
this is very m. madness (Madness 10)

moneys:
    m. is your suit (Money 10)
money-bags:
    I did dream of money-bags tonight (Foreboding 10)
monkeys:
    as hot as m. (Lechery 3)
    a wilderness of m. (Loss 5)
monks:
    all hoods make not m. (Goodness 1)
monster:
    a m. begot upon itself (Jealousy 11)
    as if there were some m. in his thought (Thought 12)
    the blunt m. with uncounted heads (People 13)
    the green-eyed m. (Jealousy 6)
monstruosity:
    this is the m. in love (Love 90)
monstrousness:
    O, see the m. of man (Ingratitude 9)
monument:
    your m. shall be my gentle verse (Poetry 16)
moon:
    beneath the visiting m. (Mourning 1)
    by yonder blessèd m. I swear (Vows 4)
    if she unmask her beauty to the m. (Chastity 5)
    m. like to a silver bow (Moon 2)
    never gazed the m. (Love 106)
    swifter than the m.'s sphere (Fairies 1)
    the cold fruitless m. (Religion 5)
    the m.'s an arrant thief (Theft 11)
    the m. shines bright (Night 15)
    the pale-faced m. (Honor 3)
    the very error of the m. (Moon 4)
moonlight:
    how sweet the m. sleeps (Moon 1)
    ill met by m. (Greetings 5)
Moor:
    the M. is of a free and open nature (Deceit 12)
    look to her, M. (Deceit 11)
    suspect the lusty M. (Jealousy 5)
    the M. ... is of a ... noble nature (Character 4, Constancy 5)
more:
    m. are men's ends marked than their lives (Endings 4)
more-having:
    my m. would be as a sauce (Greed 1)
morn:
    grey-eyed m. smiles on the ... night (Dawn 5)
    in the m. ... of youth (Chastity 6, Youth 6)
    like a red m. that ever yet betokened (Weather 8)
    m. in russet mantle clad (Dawn 1)
    the lark, the herald of the m. (Dawn 6)
morning:
    full many a glorious m. (Sunrise 6)
    'tis fresh m. with me (Time of Day 9)
morsel:
    I found you as a m., cold (Food 3)
    I was a m. for a monarch (Lust 3)
    sweetest m. of the night (Night 3)

mortality:
    insensible of m. (Death 31)
    it smells of m. (Mortality 7)
    nothing serious in m. (Mourning 18)
    sad m. o'ersways their power (Mortality 11)
mortals:
    what fools these m. be (Fools 9)
mote:
    a m. it is to trouble the mind's eye (Foreboding 4)
moth:
    left behind, a m. of peace (Love 69)
    Peaseblossom, Cobweb, M., and Mustardseed (Fairies 6)
    thus hath the candle singed the m. (Disappointment 2)
mother:
    all my m. came into mine eyes (Tears 6)
    a long-parted m. with her child (Greetings 11)
    my m. had a maid (Music 17)
    O m., m.! What have you done? (Parents and Children 2)
    showed thy dear m. any courtesy (Parents and Children 1)
    thou art thy m.'s glass (Parents and Children 18)
motion:
    in fear our m. will be mocked (Action 10)
    no m. that tends to vice in man (Women 12)
motley:
    I am ambitious for a m. coat (Fools 3)
    made myself a m. to the view (Folly 5)
    m.'s the only wear (Fools 2)
mount:
    m., m. my soul (Last Words 4)
mountebank:
    a mere anatomy, a m. (Character 1)
    I'll m. their loves (Speechmaking 1)
mountebanks:
    prating m. (Corruption 1)
mourn:
    I shall have time enough to m. (Mourning 11)
    no longer m. for me (Mourning 20)
    to m. a mischief (Philosophy 16)
mouse:
    not a m. shall disturb this hallowed house (Fairies 6)
mouth:
    drop into the rotten m. of death (Decline 2)
    his heart's his m. (Speech 2)
    if I had my m. I would bite (Villainy 4)
mouth-honor:
    curses not loud but deep, m. (Curses 5)
much:
    m. is the force (Poetry 13)
mulberry:
    humble as the ripest m. (Humility 2)
multitude:
    still-discordant, wavering m. (People 13)
    the fool m. that choose by show (Desire 13)
    the giddy m. (People 15)
multitudes:
    the barbarous m. (People 18)

murder:

   a brother's m. (Guilt 1)

   conscience to do no contrived m. (Murder 7)

   most sacrilegious m. (Confusion 5)

   m. cannot be hid (Proverbs 18)

   m. her brothers (Murder 12)

   m. most foul (Murder 1)

   m.'s as near to lust (Sin 7)

   m.'s out of tune (Murder 9)

   m., though it have no tongue (Murder 2)

   m. yet is but fantastical (Confusion 3)

   thou shalt do no m. (Murder 11)

   withered m. (Murder 6)

murderer:

   an honorable m. (Murder 10)

murderers:

   purgers, not m. (Assassination 2)

muse:

   O for a m. of fire (Poetry 8, Theater 5)

mushrooms:

   midnight m. (Vegetables 2)

music:

   discourse most eloquent m. (Music 4)

   give me some m. (Music 1)

   how irksome is this m. (Quarrels 4)

   how sour sweet m. is (Music 18)

   I am advised to give her m. (Music 3)

   if m. be the food of love (Music 25)

   in sweet m. is such art (Music 8)

   I will play the swan and die in m. (Dying 14)

   let m. sound (Music 10)

   let the sounds of m. creep (Moon 1)

   like softest m. (Music 19)

   marvelous sweet m. (Music 24)

   much m. ... in this little organ (Character 2)

   m. at the close ... is sweetest last (Endings 3)

   m., ho! m. such as charmeth (Music 14)

   m. oft hath such a charm (Music 9)

   my love shall hear the m. of my hounds (Dogs 5)

   never merry when I hear sweet m. (Music 11)

   the general so likes your m. (Music 15)

   the man that hath no m. (Music 12)

   this m. crept by me (Music 22)

   to his m. plants and flowers (Music 7)

   where should this m. be (Music 21)

   whisper m. to my weary spirit (Music 6)

   wilt thou hear some m.? (Music 13)

musician:

   an admirable m. (Music 16)

musk-roses:

   with sweet m. and with eglantine (Flowers 6)

mustachioed:

   these mad, m. maltworms (Drinking 6)

mustard:

   his wit's as thick as Tewkesbury m. (Insults 9)

Mustardseed:

   Peaseblossom, Cobweb, Moth, and M. (Fairies 6)

mutable:

   m. rank-scented meiny (People 9)

mutations:

   world! but that thy strange m. (World 5)

mutinies:

   in cities m. (Disorder 1)

mutton:

   what's a joint of m. or two in a whole Lent (Food 7)

muzzle:

   I am trusted with a m. (Constraint 2)

myself:

   m. and what is mine (Possession 3)

mystery:

   m. in the soul of state (Government 6)

   pluck out the heart of my m. (Character 2)

   take upon's the m. of things (Politics 17)

naked:

   n. in bed, Iago, and not mean harm? (Devil 9)

   when he was n. (Body 3)

name:

   good n. in man and woman (Reputation 8)

   he that filches from my good n. (Reputation 9)

   his n.'s Cinna (Names 2)

   I do not like her n. (Names 1)

   if his n. be George (Names 3)

   if my n. were liable to fear (Fear 7)

   is not the king's n. (Royalty 29)

   my n. receives a brand (Reputation 16)

   refuse thy n. (Names 7)

   the king's n. is a tower of strength (Reputation 12)

   they n. her n. and Rosaline they call her (Names 4)

   to that n. my courage prove my title (Courage 1)

   what is your n.? (Names 9)

   what's in a n.? (Names 8)

   what the dickens his n. is (Names 5)

names:

   where a commodity of good n. (Reputation 2)

nation:

   a law in each well-ordered n. (Law 11)

   trick of our English n. (Countries 4)

native:

   though I am n. here (Custom 2)

nativity:

   at my n. the front of heaven (Portents 1)

   n. was under Ursa Major (Astrology 2)

natural:

   I do it more n. (Fools 12)

natural:

   he wants the n. touch (Nature 4)

   something in this more than n. (Philosophy 7)

nature:

   allow not n. more (Necessity 4)

   all the good gifts of n. (Character 5)

   any cause in n. (Cause 4)

   crack n.'s molds (Storms 8)

   cunning'st pattern of excelling n. (Light 2)

   death may usurp on n. (Death 32)

   diseasèd n. oft breaks out (Earthquakes 1)

   face with n.'s own hand painted (Androgyny 2)

   fancy outwork n. (Beauty 1)

   great creating n. (Nature 7)

hard to hide the sparks of n. (Nature 1)
his n. is too noble (Nobility 1)
how that might change his n. (Cause 1)
I do fear thy n. (Kindness 2)
in n.'s infinite book of secrecy (Prophecy 1)
is this the n.? (Passion 2)
life that age ... can lay on n. (Death 30)
Moor is of a free and open n. (Deceit 12)
Moor is of a ... noble n. (Character 3)
n. awakes (Life 9)
n. framed strange fellows (Humanity 4)
n. in you stands on the very verge (Old Age 7)
n. might stand up and say (Epitaphs 12)
n. must obey necessity (Necessity 2)
n. needs not what thou gorgeous wear'st (Fashion 6)
n. quickly falls into revolt (Avarice 1)
n. seems dead (Night 12)
n.'s germens tumble (Chaos 2)
n.'s own sweet and cunning hand (Beauty 25)
n. stands on the very verge of his confine (Age 25)
n., what things there are (Value 7)
n. whom passion could not shake (Passion 1)
one touch of n. makes the whole world kin (Fashion 11)
O ruined piece of n. (Mortality 7)
the art itself is n. (Nature 8)
the earth, that's n.'s mother (Nature 5)
things rank and gross in n. (Dejection 1)
thou goddess, thou divine n.! (Nature 2)
thou, N. art my goddess (Nature 3)
use amost can change the stamp of n. (Custom 3)
violet in the youth of primy n. (Flowers 1)
when the baser n. comes (Quarrels 2)
would you have me false to my n. (Identity 2)
natures:
men, in our own n. frail (Weakness 2)
necessities:
are these things then n.? (Necessity 2)
art of our n. is strange (Necessity 5)
call in question our n.(Councils 2)
these strong n. (Necessity 1)
necessity:
brother, sweet, to grim n. (Necessity 8)
for n. of present life (Hypocrisy 11)
make a virtue of n. (Necessity 9)
nature must obey n. (Necessity 3)
n.'s sharp pinch (Homelessness 1)
teach thy n. to reason thus (Necessity 7)
need:
reason not the n. (Necessity 4)
never so few and never yet more n. (Diplomacy 1)
neighbor:
our bad n. makes us early stirrers (Business 5)
pond fished by his n. (Adultery 2)
neighborly:
is not that n. (Desire 4)
Nemean:
hardy as the N. lion's nerve (Fate 2)

Neptune:
the green N. a ram (Gods 5)
ye that ... do chase the ebbing N. (Fairies 8)
nettle:
out of this n., danger (Danger 1)
the strawberry grows underneath the n. (Gardens 2)
never:
n. anything can be amiss (Simplicity 2)
n. come such division (Reconciliation 2)
n. durst poet touch a pen (Poetry 9)
n., never, never, never (Death 21)
n. since the middle summer's spring (Quarrels 10)
n. so much as in a thought unborn (Innocence 2)
n. was a story of more woe (Sorrow 15)
n. was a war did cease (Peace 3)
new-born:
met'st ... with things n. (Birth and Death 2)
news:
first bringer of unwelcome n. (News 8)
never good to bring bad n. (News 2)
the father of good n. (News 4)
the nature of bad n. (News 1)
though n. be sad (News 10)
what's the new n.? (News 3)
newts:
n. and blindworms (Creatures 4)
night:
come, civil n. (Night 20)
come, gentle n. (Night 21)
come, seeling n. (Evil 6)
comes in the sweet o' the n. (Night 4)
comes so fast in silence of the n. (Night 16)
come, thick n. (Murder 5)
converses with the buttock of the n. (Drinking 4)
cripple tardy-gaited n. (Night 7)
dark n. that from the eye (Senses 1)
dragon wing of n. (Night 22)
foul womb of n. (Night 6)
here's a n. pities neither wise men (Night 10)
in n. ... desire sees best of all (Desire 21)
in such a n. as this (Night 15)
it hath been the longest n. (Night 23)
it is not n. when I do see (Love 56)
let's have one other gaudy n. (Feasts 2)
n. is long that never finds the day (Aphorisms 6, Night 14)
nor n. nor day no rest (Sleeplessness 8)
now it is the time of n. (Ghosts 14)
n.'s black agents to their preys do rouse (Night 13)
n.'s candles are burnt out (Dawn 7)
O grim-looked n. (Night 18)
O weary n. (Night 17)
sable n., mother of dread (Night 24)
smiles on the frowning n. (Dawn 5)
sweetest morsel of the n. (Night 3)
the n. comes on, and the bleak winds (Storms 6)
the n. has been unruly (Prophecy 7)
things that love n. (Night 11)
this is the n. (Chance 1)

night (cont'd.)
 this will last out a n. in Russia (Tediousness 3)
 to dwell in solemn shades of endless n. (Exile 4)
 usurp'st this time of n. (Apparitions 2)
 very witching time of n. (Night 1)
 what a fearful n. is this! (Night 9)
 what is the n.? (Time of Day 7)
 yield day to n. (Night 8)

nightingale:
 it was the lark … no n. (Dawn 6)
 it was the n. and not the lark (Parting 16)
 she sings as sweetly as a n. (Courtship 20)
 the n., if she should sing by day (Birds 11)

night-shriek:
 senses would have cooled to hear a n. (Fear 14)

nit:
 thou flea, thou n. (Insults 19)

nobility:
 hands do lack n. (Assault 1)
 mercy is n.'s true badge (Mercy 15)
 true n. is exempt from fear (Fear 4)

noble:
 a brother n. (Nobility 7)
 his nature is too n. (Nobility 1)
 nothing natural I ever saw so n. (Nobility 8)
 she's n. born (Nobility 3)
 too n. for this place (Nobility 9)
 well, Brutus, thou n. art (Nobility 4)
 what a n. mind is here o'erthrown (Nobility 2)

nobleness:
 the n. of life is to do thus (Kissing 1)

noblest:
 this was the n. Roman (Nobility 6)

noise:
 let there be no n. (Music 6)
 the n. of b. hurtled in the air (Portents 5)

noises:
 the isle is full of n. (Music 23)

none:
 n. can truly say he gives (Generosity 5)

north:
 tyrannous breathing of the n. (Kissing 4)

Norway:
 when he the ambitious N. combated (Ghosts 1)

nose:
 his n. was a sharp as a pen (Dying 6)

nose-painting:
 drink especially provoke? … n. (Drinking 14)

note:
 not a n. of mine that's worth noting (Modesty 2)

nothing:
 before I knew thee, I knew n. (Character 3)
 demand me n. (Silence 6)
 Gratiano speaks an infinite deal of n. (Reason 5)
 I am a fool; thou art n. (Nothing 3)
 n. almost sees miracles (Miracles 2)
 n. but sit and sit, and eat and eat (Eating 12)
 n. brings me all things (Dying 16)
 n. can be made out of n. (Nothing 2)

 n. can come between me and … my hopes (Confidence 2)
 n. can … content my soul (Revenge 5)
 n. can we call our own but death (Death 34)
 n. comes amiss so money comes (Money 12)
 n. either good or bad (Philosophy 6)
 n. extenuate (Speech 21)
 n. 'gainst time's scythe (Time 41)
 n. ill can dwell in such a temple (Goodness 4)
 n. in his life became him (Dying 13)
 n. is but what is not (Confusion 4, Paradoxes 2)
 n. left remarkable (Mourning 1)
 nor any man … with n. shall be pleased (Discontent 1)
 n. will come of n. (Proverbs 12)
 reputed wise for saying n. (Reputation 5)
 this is n., Fool (Lawyers 2, Nothing 1)
 thou talk'st of n. (Dreams 13)

nought:
 n.'s had, all's spent (Desire 10)
 n. shall go ill (Proverbs 21)

now:
 n. could I, Casca, name to thee (Power 6)
 n. he weighs time (Time 15)
 n. is the sun upon the highmost hill (Time 27)
 n. is the winter of our discontent (Improvement 3)
 n. let it work (Evil 3)
 n. mark me how I will undo myself (Renunciation 3)
 n. the hungry lion roars (Night 19)
 n. thou and I are new in amity (Reconciliation 5)
 n. would I give a thousand furlongs (Sea 5)

nun:
 endure the livery of a n. (Religion 5)

nunnery:
 get thee to a n. (Marriage 16)

nurse:
 dear n. of arts (Peace 11)
 mewling and puking in the n.'s arms (Infancy 2)
 time is the n. and breeder of all good (Time 38)

nurture:
 on whose nature n. can never stick (Education 7)

nut:
 sweetest n. hath sourest rind (Food 5)

nuts:
 quarrel with a man for cracking n. (Quarrels 13)

nutshell:
 I could be bounded in a n. (Dreams 3)

O:
 cram within this wooden O (Theater 6)
 O beware, my lord, of jealousy (Jealousy 6)
 O God of battles (Prayer 6)
 O God, that men should put an enemy (Drinking 22)
 O good old man, how well (Service 2)
 O heavens! If you do love old men (Prayer 12)
 O how I love thee (Infatuation 8)
 O how much more doth beauty (Beauty 32)
 O lady fortune, stand you auspicious (Fortune 23)
 O let me clip ye in arms as sound (Friendship 2)
 O let me not be mad (Prayer 11)
 O let us have him (Maturity 2)

O let us yet be merciful (Mercy 1)
O Lord, methought what pain it was to drown (Dreams 9)
O Lord that lends me life (Prayer 8)
O mighty Caesar! Dost thou lie so low (Epitaphs 8)
O mischief, thou art swift (Evil 9)
O pity, God (Prayer 10)
O, sir, your presence is too bold (Authority 5)
O that a lady of one man refused (Rejection 1)
O that I were a fool (Fools 3)
O that I were a man (Manliness 3)
O that I were a mockery king (Death-Wish 9)
O that's a brave man (Promises 2)
O that this too too solid flesh (Suicide 11)
O, 'tis most sweet (Plots 2)
O, what a goodly outside (Duplicity 5)
O, what damnèd minutes tells he o'er (Jealousy 7)
O, what men dare do (Action 13)
the little O, the earth (Praise 3)
thou art an O without a figure (Nothing 3)
oak:
under an o., whose antique root (Trees 1)
under an old o. (Trees 2)
oars:
fish cut with her golden o. the silver stream (Fishing 2)
oath:
breaking his o. and resolution (Promises 3)
never more break an o. (Apologies 3)
swear me ... a good mouth-filling o. (Oaths 1)
the o. of a lover is no stronger (Promises 1)
oaths:
downright o. (Oaths 3)
he hailed down o. that he was only mine (Vows 3)
his o. are oracles (Sincerity 3)
soldier, full of strange o. (Soldiers 1)
the strongest o. are straw (Sex 6)
'tis not the many o. that makes the truth (Vows 1)
oats:
I could munch your good dry o. (Eating 9)
since the price of o. rose (Money 1)
object:
o. and pleasure of mine eye (Devotion 2)
objects:
one that feeds on o. (Contempt 3)
oblivion:
blind o. swallowed cities up (Constancy 8)
formless ruin of o. (Welcome 2)
my o. is a very Antony (Forgetfulness 1)
second childishness and mere o. (Age 5)
the dust of old o. (History 1)
obloquy:
all's o. (Misanthropy 5)
observer:
he is a great o. (Reading 2)
observers:
the observed of all o. (Fashion 2)
obstruction:
to lie in cold o. (Graves 1)
occasions:

how all o. do inform (Revenge 2)
there is o. and causes (Philosophy 11)
occupation:
'tis my o. to be plain (Plain-Speaking 6)
ocean:
his legs bestrid the o. (Praise 4)
the wild and wasteful o. (Sea 1)
water that in the o. seeks another drop (Identity 1)
will all great Neptune's o. wash (Guilt 5)
oceans:
drinking o. dry (Futility 1)
offend:
to o. and judge are distinct offices (Judgment 2)
offense:
confront the visage of o. (Mercy 1)
every nice o. bear his comment (Criticism 1)
my o. is rank (Guilt 1)
o.'s gilded hand (Law 1)
some sick o. within your mind (Anxiety 5)
so offend to make o. a skill (Wrongdoing 1)
what o. have these men done (Wrongdoing 5)
where the o. is (Punishment 2)
offenses:
I would I could quit all o. (Excuses 1)
made old o. of affections new (Folly 5)
make us pay down for our o. (Authority 6)
office:
infirmity doth still neglect all o. (Sickness 13)
save in the o. and affairs of love (Friendship 23)
the o. opposite Saint Peter (Hell 5)
'tis all men's o. to speak patience (Philosophy 14)
officer:
art thou o.? (Soldiers 14)
offices:
o. were not derived corruptly (Merit 2)
sell and mart your o. for gold (Corruption 5)
oftentimes:
o. to win us to our harm (Evil 5)
old:
a good o. man, sir (Old Age 10)
an o. man broken (Old Age 6)
an o. man, sir, and his wits are not so blunt (Honesty 4)
foolish fond o. man (Age 27)
how o. art thou? (Middle Age 3)
I am o., I am o. (Love 36)
I am too o. to fawn (Middle Age 4)
I confess that I am o. (Age 26)
o. and reverend (Age 23)
o., cold, withered (Insults 14)
o. fashions please me best (Fashion 9)
o. folks ... unwieldy, slow (Old Age 11)
o. man is twice a child (Old Age 2)
o. men forget (Remembrance 3)
o. Nestor (Old Age 13)
o. till thou hadst been wise (Age 24)
one of them is fat and grows o. (Old Age 3)
she cannot choose but be o. (Age 14)
sir, you are old (Age 25, Old Age 7)

palm:
bear the p. alone (Power 4)
palpable:
who cannot see this p. device? (Deceit 18)
Pandars:
call them all p. (Lust 12)
pansies:
there is p., that's for thoughts (Flowers 2)
pantaloon:
lean and slippered p. (Age 4)
pantler:
she was both p., butler, cook (Hospitality 3)
pants:
ride on the p. triumphing (Love 7)
paper:
as many lies as will lie in thy p. (Lying 7)
let p. show (Letters 3)
paradise:
lead her in a fool's p. (Deceit 21)
paramour:
he's a very p. for a sweet voice (Solecisms 3)
parasites:
most smiling, smooth, detested p. (Flattery 9)
pardon:
free p. (Mercy 8)
p. is still the nurse (Mercy 4)
p. me, thou bleeding piece of earth (Mourning 14)
you might p. him (Mercy 5)
part:
answer to his p. (Acting 31)
his p. is played (Epitaphs 17)
I have forgot my p. (Acting 3)
I must bear a p. (Acting 30)
it is the p. of men to fear (Portents 4)
lion's p. (Acting 20)
more willingly p. withal (Parting 6)
must we p.? (Parting 13)
p. to tear a cat in (Acting 19)
question's out of my p. (Acting 29)
sir, you and I must p. (Parting 1)
speak all your p. at once (Acting 23)
stage where every man must play a p. (Acting 17)
you have put me to such a p. (Acting 2)
parted:
'A p. even just between twelve and one (Dying 6)
particular:
why seems it so p. (Appearance 1)
parting:
p. is such sweet sorrow (Parting 15)
this p. was well made (Parting 9)
parts:
for which of my bad p. (Love 66)
for which of my good p. (Love 67)
three p. of him is ours (Persuasion 3)
passages:
in p. of proof (Love 33)
passion:
hot p. of distempered blood (Argument 6)
man that is not p.'s slave (Friendship 5)
nature whom p. could not shake (Passion 2)

nor wit nor reason can my p. hide (Infatuation 10)
the beating of so strong a p. (Love 98)
'twixt two extremes of p., joy and grief (Dying 12)
what to ourselves in p. we propose (Passion 1)
passions:
of all base p., fear (Fear 4)
past:
p. and to come seems best (Time 10)
what's p. and what's to come (Welcome 2)
patched:
p. with cloth of any color (Mistakes 2)
patience:
all men's office to speak p. (Philosophy 14)
arming myself with p. (Patience 4)
found ... a drop of p. (Affliction 9)
how poor are they that have not p. (Patience 10)
I have the p. to endure it (Patience 3)
I laughed him out of p. (Patience 1)
I will be the pattern of all p. (Patience 5)
I will with p. hear (Consideration 1)
let us teach our trial p. (Patience 9)
like p. gazing on kings' graves (Patience 11)
oppose my p. to his fury (Patience 8)
p. is pale cold cowardice (Cowardice 5)
sat like p. on a monument (Melancholy 9, Patience 12)
though p. be a tired mare (Patience 2)
patient:
bear free and p. thoughts (Patience 6)
p. must minister to himself (Medicine 9)
thou must be p. (Patience 7)
patiently:
if you will p. dance in our round (Dancing 1)
pattern:
I will be the p. of all patience (Patience 5)
pause:
stand in p. where I shall first begin (Indecision 2)
peace:
a moth of p. (Love 69)
a p. is of the nature of a conquest (Peace 7)
blessed spirit of p. (Peace 5)
for men as old as we to keep the p. (Peace 14)
frighted p. to pant (Anxiety 1)
I feel within me a p. (Self-Knowledge 4)
in p. there's nothing (Peace 9)
kiss my lady p. at home (Peace 4)
my words are as full of p. (Peace 15)
our p. shall stand as firm (Peace 6)
p., dear nurse of arts (Peace 11)
p. is a great maker of cuckolds (Peace 2)
p., p! dost thou not see? (Infancy 1)
p. puts forth her olive (Peace 8)
p. to this meeting (Peace 10)
the merry songs of p. (Peace 13)
the wound of p. is surety (Security 2)
time of universal p. (Peace 2)
uproar the universal p. (Chaos 3)
we, to gain our p., have sent to p. (Anxiety 6)
peacemakers:
blessèd are the p. on earth (Peace 12)

Pilate:
some of you, with P. wash (Hypocrisy 13)
pilchards:
fools are like husbands as p. are to herrings (Fools 12)
pilgrimage:
his time is spent; our p. must be (Epitaphs 13)
pillar:
the triple p. of the world transformed (Folly 1)
pillow:
sighed upon a midnight p. (Love 8)
pilot:
desire my p. is (Desire 19)
pinch:
as a lover's p., which hurts and is desired (Dying 3)
there cannot be a p. in death (Parting 4)
they brought one P. (Character 1)
pinches:
Phoebus' amorous p. (Middle Age 1)
pink:
I am the very p. of courtesy (Courtesy 2)
pipe:
rumor is a p. blown by surmises (Rumor 3)
pippin:
a last year's p. of my own grafting (Eating 5)
pippins:
there's p. and cheese to come (Food 9)
pirates:
water-thieves ... I mean p. (Ships 4)
pit:
enemies have beat us to the p. (Defeat 1)
she is fallen into a p. of ink (Guilt 10)
pitchers:
p. have ears (Proverbs 26)
pitiful:
'twas p., 'twas wondrous p. (Pity 7)
pity:
am pregnant to good p. (Pity 4)
a tear for p. (Charity 1)
but yet the p. of it, Iago! (Pity 8)
I perceive you feel the dint of p. (Pity 3)
is there no p. sitting in the clouds (Sorrow 14)
know what 'tis to p. and be pitied (Pity 1)
men must learn now with p. to dispense (Politics 23)
p. choked with custom of fell deeds (Cruelty 2)
p. is the virtue of the law (Law 10)
p. like a naked new-born babe (Pity 5)
p. to the general wrong of Rome (Pity 2)
p. two such friends ... be long foes (Friendship 32)
showing an outward p. (Hypocrisy 13)
tear-falling p. dwells not (Ruthlessness 5)
wretch uncapable of p. (Cruelty 5)
yet show some p. (Pity 6)
place:
dost thou not suspect my p. (Insults 17)
here's a marvelous convenient p. (Theater 12)
this p. is too cold for hell (Hell 2)
places:
all p. that the eye of heaven visits (Travel 17)
plague:
a p. on these pickle herring (Eating 14)

a p. of sighing and grief (Thinness 1)
a p. upon it! (Maps 1)
a p. upon it when thieves (Loyalty 3)
p. of all cowards (Cowardice 3)
p. of your policy (Politics 9)
p. on both your houses (Curses 8)
the p. of Greece upon thee (Stupidity 2)
the p. that needs must (Ingratitude 3)
plain:
an honest mind and p. (Plain-Speaking 7)
a p. tale shall put you down (Plain-Speaking 1)
honest p. words best pierce (Plain-Speaking 9)
'tis my occupation to be p. (Plain-Speaking 6)
planets:
curse the p. of mishap (Curses 1)
play:
a good p. needs no epilogue (Plays 1)
a p. there is ... some ten words long (Theater 14)
guilty creatures sitting at a p. (Theater 4)
I see the p. so lies (Acting 30)
like as much of this p. as please you (Men and Women 3, Plays 2)
our p. is done (Theater 20)
our wooing doth not end like an old p. (Plays 6, Endings 6)
p. out the p. (Plays 5)
p. with your fancies (Ships 2)
the p. ... pleased not the million (Plays 3)
the p.'s the thing (Plays 4)
thought it good you hear a p. (Acting 27)
thus play I in one person (Identity 5)
your p. needs no excuse (Theater 15)
you would p. upon me (Character 2)
player:
a poor p. that struts (Life 7)
players:
harlotry p. (Acting 12)
p. well bestowed (Acting 7)
playing:
the purpose of p. (Acting 11)
plead:
p. what I will be (Deserving 4)
pleads:
p. he in earnest? (Sincerity 2)
pleasure:
I take p. in singing (Pleasure 6)
i' th'east my p. lies (Pleasure 3)
lives should stretch without some p. (Pleasure 1)
my lawful p. she restrained (Chastity 3)
p. and action (Action 14)
p. and revenge have ears (Argument 6)
the present p. by revolution lowering (Pleasure 2)
what other p. can the world afford? (Courtship 12)
pleasures:
so to your p. (Moods 5)
plodders:
small have continual p. ever won (Study 2)
plot:
first survey the p. (Building 1)
who cannot be crushed with a p. (Plots 1)

unless I be relieved by p. (Prayer 16)

prayers:

fall to thy p. (Age 17)

find we profit by losing of our p. (Prayer 1)

he has my heart yet and shall have my p. (Devotion 1)

my wind were but long enough to say my p. (Repentance 6)

when thou hast leisure, say thy p. (Leisure 1)

presence:

what p. must not know (Letters 3)

your p. is too bold (Authority 5)

presume:

do not p. too much (Quarrels 8)

p. not that I am the thing I was (Reformation 4)

presumption:

most it is p. in us (Arrogance 1)

prick:

if you p. us (Revenge 4)

pricked:

will you be p. in number? (Friendship 14)

pricking:

by the p. of my thumbs (Evil 9)

price:

make what p. they will (Business 8)

pride:

p. is his own glass (Pride 4)

p. must have a fall (Pride 2)

p. that quarrels at self-breath (Arrogance 2)

primrose:

p. path of dalliance (Advice 4)

p. way to the everlasting bonfire (Hell 2)

primroses:

pale p., that die unmarried (Flowers 13)

prince:

p., thou art sad (Marriage 38)

the p. of darkness (Devil 5)

princes:

for p. are the glass, the school (Royalty 33)

princess:

p. descended from ... royal kings (Royalty 4)

principle:

the first humane p. I should teach (Drinking 12)

printing:

caused p. to be used (Books 1)

prison:

come, let's away to p. (Reconciliation 4)

prison-house:

tell the secrets of my p. (Horror 1, Purgatory 1)

privilege:

impatience hath his p. (Anger 3)

profit:

find we p. by losing of our prayers (Prayer 1)

no p. grows where is no pleasure (Study 4)

progeny:

this same p. of evils (Quarrels 11)

prologue:

is this a p. (Love 31)

promise:

p. me life and I'll confess (Truth 6)

smallest particle of any p. (Promises 4)

promised:

he p. to meet me (Promises 6)

promising:

p. is the very air o' the time (Promises 8)

promontory:

like one that stands upon a p. (Aspiration)

promotion:

none will sweat but for p. (Fashion 1)

prompter:

I should have known it without a p. (Fighting 4)

proof:

give me the ocular p. (Proof 1)

the true p. of men (Chance 2)

we'll leave a p. (Marriage 27)

property:

sweet love, changing his p. (Mutability 2)

prophesy:

over thy wounds now do I p. (Prophecy 5)

prophesying:

p. with accents terrible (Prophecy 7)

prophetic:

O my p. soul! (Prophecy 2)

proportion:

a like p. of lineaments (Friendship 19)

prosperity:

Death ... thou hate and terror to p. (Death-Wish 5)

p. begins to mellow (Decline 2)

p.'s the very bond of love (Affliction 13)

protestation:

I have no cunning in p. (Oaths 3)

proud:

he that is p. eats up himself (Pride 4)

I do hate a p. man (Pride 5)

small things make base men p. (Pride 1)

you are too p. (Pride 6)

prove:

p. that ever I lose more blood (Love 60)

so p. it that the probation bear (Proof 2)

provender:

a peck of p. (Eating 9)

proverb:

fast find, fast bind, a p. never stale (Thrift 3)

lay the old p. to your charge (Proverbs 31)

the country p. known (Proverbs 21)

the old p. ... you have the grace (Proverbs 19)

proverbs:

they ... sighed forth p. (Hunger 1)

providence:

special p. in the fall (Providence 3)

prune:

no more faith in thee than in a stewed p. (Trust 2)

psalmist:

death, as the p. saith (Death 13)

publican:

how like a fawning p. he looks (Humility 4)

Puck:

those that hobgoblin call you and sweet P. (Fairies 4)

pudding:

ox with the p. in his belly (Fatness 4)

puddings:
p. and flapjacks (Food 13)

puddle:
thou didst drink ... the gilded p. (Endurance 1)

pudency:
with a p. so rosy (Chastity 3)

pullet-sperm:
I'll no p. in my brewage (Drinking 19)

pulse:
my p. as yours doth temperately (Sanity 1)

purchase:
steal anything and call it p. (Theft 3)

purgatory:
no world without Verona walls but p. (Exile 9)

purgers:
we shall be called p. (Assassination 2)

purity:
pure impiety and impious p. (Paradoxes 4)

purpose:
p. of playing (Acting 11)
the p. must weigh with the folly (Folly 3)
'tis the p. that makes strong the vow (Vows 5)

purpose-changer:
that same p., that sly devil (Self-Interest 1)

purse:
consumption of the p. (Money 4)
put money in thy p. (Money 11)
show the inside of your p. (Authority 11)

purses:
our p. shall be proud (Clothing 10)

pursuit:
mad in p. (Lust 14)

pyramids:
p. slope their heads (Chaos 2)

Pyramus:
what is P.? (Acting 18)

quality:
the q. of mercy (Mercy 10)

quarrel:
in a false q. (Valor 13)
no man hath any q. to me (Quarrels 17)
seven justices could not take up a q. (Quarrels 1)
that hath his q. just (Quarrels 5)
the q. will bear no color (Conspiracy 4)
thou wilt q. with a man (Quarrels 13)

quarrels:
busy giddy minds with foreign q. (Politics 4)
the unhappy subject of these q. (Quarrels 9)
thy head is as full of q. (Quarrels 14)

queen:
death ... come and take a q. (Death 3)
fie, wrangling q. (Charm 1)
from this enchanting q. break off (Infatuation 4)
in the remembrance of a weeping q. (Gardens 9)
I would not be a q. (Royalty 23)
she is the q. of curds and cream (Royalty 32)
show me, My women, like a q. (Royalty 2)
the q., my lord, is dead (Time 19)
this q. will live (Life 9)

thou art ... the q. of earthly queens (Royalty 24)

quenched:
what hath q. them hath given me fire (Drinking 13)

quietus:
he himself might his q. make (Suicide 13)

quillets:
sharp q. of the law (Law 4)

quips:
shall quips ... awe a man (Aphorisms 8)

quit:
I would I could q. all offenses (Excuses 1)

rack:
I fear you speak upon the r. (Torture 1)
I live upon the r. (Choice 5)

radish:
like a forked r. (Body 3)

rage:
how with this r. shall beauty (Mortality 11)
lion ... with r. to be o'erpowered (Animals 8)
stir ... to an act of rage (Assassination 2)
swells the r. of Bolingbroke (Anger 8)

raggedness:
looped and windowed r. (Homelessness 2)

rail:
say that she r. (Courtship 20)

raiment:
ask me what r. I'll wear (Clothing 9)

rain:
is there not r. enough? (Forgiveness 3)
it droppeth as the gentle r. (Mercy 10)
the property of r. is to wet (Truisms 1)
the r. it raineth every day (Boys 4, Fortune 12)

rancors:
put r. in the vessel of my peace (Damnation 1)

raven:
as doth the r. o'er the infected house (Foreboding 11)
change a r. for a dove (Inconstancy 2)
the r. chides blackness (Proverbs 29)
the r. himself is hoarse (Foreboding 9)

ravens:
instruct the kites and r. (Creatures 5)

read:
how well he's r. to reason against reading (Reading 3)
r. o'er this, ... and then to breakfast (Eating 6)
r. you matter deep and dangerous (Conspiracy 1)
what do you r., my lord? (Reading 1)

reads:
he r. much (Reading 2)

ready:
all things are r. (Readiness 1)

realms:
r. and islands were as plates (Power 1)

reason:
capability and godlike r. (Reason 2)
deprive your sovereignty of r. (Ghosts 8)
give you a r. on compulsion (Reason 3)
men have lost their r. (Reason 4)
more than cool r. (Imagination 4)
past r. hunted (Lust 14)

r. and love keep little company (Reason 6)
r. and respect make livers pale (Reason 7)
r. not the need (Necessity 4)
respect and r. wait on wrinkled age (Old Age 14)
r. ... whose common theme is death (Faults 5)
that noble and most sovereign r. (Dejection 4)
we have r. to cool our raging motions (Lust 11)
with my nobler r. 'gainst my fury (Forgiveness 5)
your r.? I have no other but a woman's r. (Women 28)
reasons:
his r. are as two grains of wheat (Reason 5)
r. you allege (Argument 6)
your r. at dinner (Argument 3)
rebellion:
r. lay in his way (Rebellion 1)
to face the garment of r. (Rebellion 2)
receipt:
we have the r. of fern-seed (Magic 1)
reckoning:
a trim r. (Honor 4)
I am ill at r. (Arithmetic 1)
recompense:
my r. is thanks (Thanks 3)
recreation:
sweet r. barred (Melancholy 5)
redemption:
condemned into everlasting r. (Solecisms 6)
nothing kin to foul r. (Mercy 6)
reeling:
Trinculo is r. ripe (Drinking 25)
reflection:
the eye sees not itself but by r. (Eyes 7)
you cannot see yourself but by r. (Self-Knowledge 5)
reformation:
my r. glittering o'er my fault (Reformation 1)
rehearsal:
convenient place for our r. (Theater 12)
rehearse:
r. most obscenely (Acting 22)
rein:
what r. can hold licentious wickedness? (Evil 2)
relics:
sanctify his r. (Infatuation 2)
shall we go see the r. of this town ? (Travel 23)
relief:
for this r., much thanks (Foreboding 2)
religion:
in r. what damnèd error (Religion 4)
it is r. that doth make vows kept (Religion 2)
religions:
knit and break r. (Gold 6)
relish:
imaginary r. is so sweet (Anticipation 4)
remedies:
apply to her some r. (Medicine 12)
our r. oft in ourselves do lie (Self-Reliance 1)
remedy:
no r. against this consumption (Money 4)
things without all r. (Aphorisms 4, Regret 2)

remember:
I well r. the favors (Betrayal 2)
r. I have done thee worthy service (Service 6)
r. March, the Ides of March r. (Justice 4)
r. that you call on me today (Remembrance 6)
r. thee! Ay, thou poor ghost (Memory 2)
remembrance:
as the r. of an idle gaud (Remembrance 7)
I summon up r. of things past (Remembrance 9)
praising makes the r. dear (Remembrance 1)
rosemary, that's for r. (Flowers 2)
rue ... in the r. of a weeping queen (Gardens 9)
writ in r. more than things long past (Endings 4)
remembrances:
let us nor burden our r. (Remembrance 8)
remorse:
greatness ... disjoins r. from power (Greatness 4)
stop up th' access ... to r. (Ruthlessness 3)
remuneration:
now I will look to his r. (Payment 1)
rendezvous:
a r., a home to fly unto (Investment 1)
renown:
r. and grace is dead (Mourning 18)
rents:
what are thy r.? (Ceremony 2)
repent:
I'll r., and that suddenly (Repentance 2)
repentance:
try what r. can (Repentance 1)
repents:
woe, that too late r. (Repentance 4)
report:
r. of fashions in proud Italy (Fashion 9)
repose:
our foster-nurse of nature is r. (Sleep 8)
r. you here in rest (Epitaphs 16)
reproof:
in the r. of chance (Chance 2)
reputation:
I have offended r. (Reputation 1)
I see my r. is at stake (Reputation 15)
r., r., r.! O I have lost my r. (Reputation 6)
r. is an idle ... imposition (Reputation 7)
seeking the bubble r. (Soldiers 1)
spotless r. (Reputation 11)
resist:
it boots not to r. both wind and tide (Resistance 2)
resolutes:
a list of lawless r. (Soldiers 3)
resolution:
breaking his oath and r. (Promises 3)
fix most firm thy r. (Resolution 6)
native hue of r. (Conscience 2)
r. thus fubbed with ... the law (Law 2)
the dauntless spirit of r. (Resolution 4)
respect:
is there no r. of place ... in you ? (Disorder 5)
men so noble ... should find r. (Downfall 3)

respect (cont'd.)

reason and r. make livers pale (Reason 7)

r. and reason wait on wrinkled age (Old Age 14)

that title of r. (Respect 1)

throw away r. (Humanity 6)

too much r. upon the world (Anxiety 7)

use him with all r. (Burial 4)

rest:

the r. is silence (Last Words 1)

nor night, nor day, no r. (Sleeplessness 8)

set up my everlasting r. (Death-Wish 10)

thy best of r. is sleep (Sleep 12)

retire:

r. me to my Milan (Mortality 10)

retirement:

a comfort of r. (Investment 1)

return:

at your r. visit our house (Friendship 10)

r. to her? (Homelessness 1)

returning:

r. were as tedious as go o'er (Crime 2)

revels:

Antony that r. long a-nights (Revels 1)

I delight in masques and r. (Revels 5)

our r. now are ended (Acting 28)

r., dances, masques (Revels 2)

see our moonlight r. (Dancing 1)

revenge:

a capable and wide r. (Revenge 7)

Caesar's spirit, ranging for r. (War 16)

I ... may sweep to my r. (Revenge 1)

it will feed my r. (Revenge 3)

kindness, nobler than r. (Kindness 1)

pleasure and r. (Argument 6)

r. his foul and most unnatural murder (Murder 1)

spur my dull r. (Revenge 2)

sweet as my r. (Kissing 3)

sweet r. grows harsh (Murder 9)

to r. is no valor (Revenge 8)

what should his sufferance be? ... Why, r. (Revenge 4)

revenged:

I'll be r. on the whole pack (Revenge 9)

reverend:

as you are old and r. (Age 23)

reversion:

remains a sweet r. (Investment 1)

revolution:

pleasure by r. lowering (Pleasure 2)

see the r. of the times (Fate 3)

rhubarb:

what r., senna (Medicine 11)

rhyme:

I cannot show it in r. (Poetry 11)

I'll r. you so eight years (Poetry 2)

neither r. nor reason (Proverbs 1)

outlive this powerful r. (Poetry 15)

Rialto:

in the R. you have rated me (Money 9)

ribbons:

r. of all the colors (Clothing 14)

rich:

art r.? (Mediocrity 1)

if thou art r. thou art poor (Mortality 8)

poorly rich ... pineth still for more (Avarice 2)

r. she shall be (Men and Women 4)

riches:

honor, r., marriage-blessing (Blessings 5)

show r. ready to drop upon me (Dreams 15)

since r. point to misery (Misery 4)

r. strewed herself in the streets (Cities 2)

ride:

come, wilt thou see me r.? (Parting 7)

rigol:

from this golden r. hath divorced (Death 15)

ring:

keeping safe Nerissa's r. (Sex 4)

look how my r. encompasseth thy finger (Courtship 17)

r. parts from this finger (Constancy 3)

rings:

we will have r. and things (Marriage 46)

riot:

his rash fierce blaze of r. (Transience 3)

ripeness:

r. is all (Endurance 3)

rising:

from the r. of the lark (Time of Day 6)

rite:

observe the r. of May (Festivals 5)

river:

there is a r. in Macedon (Rivers 1)

roarers:

what cares these r. for the name (Sea 4)

rob:

r. me the exchequer (Theft 2)

robbed:

he that is r. (Theft 10)

the r. that smiles (Philosophy 17, Theft 9)

robbers:

what makes r. bold? (Law 5)

robbery:

thieves for their r. have authority (Theft 6)

robe:

giant's r. upon a ... thief (Clothing 7)

give me my r. (Death-Wish 3, Royalty 3)

like a r. pontifical (Greatness 4)

this r. of mine does change my disposition (Clothing 13)

robes:

r. and furred gowns hide all (Justice 7)

Robin:

sprite called R. Goodfellow (Fairies 3)

Robin Hood:

old R.H. of England (Country Life 1)

rock:

I stand as one upon a r. (Isolation 1)

rods:
whipped and scourged with r. (Politics 3)
rogue:
satirical r. (Age 6)
roguery:
nothing but r. (Man 8)
rogues:
you dissentious r. (People 4)
Roman:
a R. thought hath struck him (Duty 1)
like a R. bear the truth (Stoicism 2)
more an antique R. than a Dane (Suicide 14)
R. actors (Acting 15)
the noblest R. of them all (Nobility 6)
Romans:
the last of all the R., fare thee well (Epitaphs 11)
Rome:
be to R. as is the osprey to the fish (Authority 4)
high and palmy state of R. (Apparitions 3)
let R. in Tiber melt (Empire 1)
shake your R. about your ears (Authority 2)
that ever Brutus will go bound to R. (Greatness 7)
Romeo:
wherefore art thou R.? (Names 7)
roofs:
singing masons building r. of gold (Building 2)
Rosalind:
R. is your love's name (Names 1)
rose:
a r. by any other name (Names 8)
beauty's r. might never die (Beauty 30)
earthlier happy is the r. distilled (Marriage 28)
he wears the r. of youth (Youth 4)
this thorn doth to our r. of youth (Youth 1)
when I have plucked the r. (Murder 8)
when you have our r. (Lust 1)
rosemary:
there's r. and rue (Flowers 9)
there's r., that's for remembrance (Flowers 2)
roses:
as clear as morning r. (Courtship 20)
r. have thorns (Wrongdoing 8)
women are as r. (Women 27)
rot:
a man may r. even here (Endurance 3)
rotten:
something is r. in the state of Denmark (Corruption 2)
round:
dance in our r. (Dancing 1)
royal:
this r. throne of kings (Countries 5)
royally:
likely ... to have proved most r. (Royalty 7)
royalty:
mingled his r. with cap'ring fools (Royalty 8)
rub:
there's the r. (Death 7)

rude:
r. am I in my speech (Speech 18)
rudeness:
this r. is a sauce (Plain-Speaking 4)
rue:
I'll set a bank of r. (Gardens 9)
there's rosemary and r. (Flowers 9)
ruin:
r. hath taught me (Mutability 4)
ruins:
thou art the r. of the noblest man (Epitaphs 9)
rumble:
r. thy bellyful (Storms 9)
rumor:
Enter R., painted full of tongues (Rumor 2)
from r's tongues they bring (Rumor 4)
hold r. from what we fear (Confusion 6)
I heard a bustling r. (Rumor 6)
let every feeble r. shake (Rumor 1)
r. doth double, like the voice (Rumor 5)
r. is a pipe, blown by surmises (Rumor 3)
run:
now bid me r. (Fitness 1)
r., r., Orlando (Infatuation 5)
r. to your houses (Ingratitude 3)
runs:
r. not this speech like iron (Speechmaking 4)
russet:
morn in r. mantle clad (Dawn 1)
r. yeas and honest kersey nos (Plain-Speaking 8)
Russia:
last out a night in R. (Tediousness 3)
sack:
addict themselves to s. (Drinking 12)
brew me a pottle of s. (Drinking 19)
this intolerable deal of s. (Drinking 7)
you love s. and so do I (Drinking 18)
sacrificers:
let us be s., but not butchers (Sacrifice 1)
sacrifices:
they come like s. (War 2)
upon such s., my Cordelia (Sacrifice 2)
sad:
experience to make me s. (Moods 4)
he was nor s. nor merry (Moods 1)
if you find him s. (Capriciousness 1)
I know not why I am so s. (Moods 10)
I must be s. when I have cause (Misanthropy 4)
let us say you are s. (Moods 11)
'tis good to be s. (Moods 3)
safer:
'tis s. to avoid what's grown (Safety 2)
safety:
give all ... for a pot of ale and s. (Safety 1)
we pluck this flower, s. (Danger 1)
sails:
behold the threaden s. (Ships 2)
laughed to see the s. conceive (Pregnancy 2)

saint:
seem a s. when … I play the devil (Hypocrisy 14)
this mortal-breathing s. (Fame 3)
to catch a s. with saints doth bait (Temptation 4)
tomorrow is S. Valentine's day (Festivals 2)
salad:
my s. days, when I was green (Youth 3)
salvation:
pity but they should suffer s. (Solecisms 4)
samphire:
hangs one that gathers s. (Vertigo 1)
sanctuary:
shall we desire to raze the s.? (Building 3)
sand:
as men wrecked upon a s. (Danger 4)
sands:
numbering s. and drinking oceans (Futility 1)
the s. are numbered (Dying 8)
Satan:
I charge thee, S. (Exorcism 1)
Saturn:
warmed old S. (Chastity 3)
satyr:
Hyperion to a s. (Excellence 1)
saucy:
s. fellow, hence! (Dismissal 1)
savior:
our s.'s birth is celebrated (Festivals 1)
saws:
full of wise s. (Maturity 1)
say:
s., is my kingdom lost? (Loss 8)
saying:
the ancient s. is no heresy (Proverbs 20)
the old s. is "the third pays for all" (Proverbs 30)
scab:
I thought there would a s. follow (Insults 16)
scaffold:
this unworthy s. (Acting 13)
scandal:
greatest s. waits on greatest state (Greatness 12)
scarecrow:
make a s. of the law (Law 7)
scarf:
beauteous s. veiling an Indian beauty (Deceit 8)
s. up the tender eye of pitiful day (Evil 8)
scars:
he jests at s. that never felt a wound (Jokes 4)
scene:
allowing him … a little s. (Death 35)
a tedious brief s. (Theater 13)
last s. of all (Age 5)
our swift s. flies (Thought 5, Theater 7)
this our lofty s. (Acting 16)
scepters:
when s. are in children's hands (Civil War 2)
scholar:
he was a s. (Learning 1)
I have neither the s.'s melancholy (Melancholy 3)

more in the soldier than in the s. (Soldiers 21)
thou'rt a s. (Hedonism 2)
school:
in erecting a grammar s. (Education 1)
like a s. broke up (Home 1)
schoolboy:
the whining s. (Boys 1)
school-days:
in my s. when I had lost a shaft (Speculation 1)
sciatica:
has the most profound s. (Sickness 15)
scion:
we marry a gentler s. (Nature 8)
scope:
the fated sky gives us free s. (Freedom 1)
scorched:
we have s. the snake (Danger 13)
score:
no other books but the s. (Books 1)
scorn:
disdain and s. ride sparkling (Scorn 1)
teach not thy lip such s. (Scorn 2)
what a deal of s. looks beautiful (Contempt 4)
scorpions:
full of s. … is my mind (Affliction 7)
screech-owl:
the s., screeching loud (Portents 8)
scripture:
the devil can cite s. (Devil 8)
sea:
all scattered in the bottom of the s. (Dreams 10)
a wilderness of s. (Isolation 1)
be patient. When the s. is (Sea 4)
boundless as the s. (Love 80)
drenched me in the s. (Danger 15)
float upon a wild and violent s. (Confusion 6)
give a thousand furlongs of s. (Sea 5)
horns whelked … like the enridgèd s. (Demons 1)
wild s. of my conscience (Conscience 3)
wish you a wave o' the s. (Dancing 4)
sea-change:
suffer a s. (Transformation 3)
sea-monster:
more hideous … than the s. (Ingratitude 6)
seas:
the multitudinous s. incarnadine (Guilt 5)
season:
ever 'gainst that s. comes (Festivals 1)
how many things by s. seasoned are (Seasons 12)
like of each thing that in s. grows (Seasons 9)
you lack the s. of all natures (Sleep 11)
seasons:
feel we not … the s.'s difference (Seasons 1)
sorrow breaks s. (Sorrow 11)
the s. alter (Seasons 13)
the s. change their manners (Seasons 6)
seat:
castle hath a pleasant s. (Castles 1)
secrecy:
nature's infinite book of s. (Prophecy 1)

s. lives upon succession (Slander 1)
s.'s venomed spear (Slander 7)
s., whose sting is sharper (Slander 9)
'tis s., whose edge is sharper (Slander 2)
slanders:
upon my tongues continual s. ride (Slander 4)
slaughters:
casual s. (Murder 2)
slave:
being your s. what should I do (Devotion 7)
here I stand your s. (Self-Pity 1)
this yellow s. will knit and break religions (Gold 6)
slaves:
s. of chance (Chance 3)
sleep:
apprehends death ... as a drunken s. (Death 31)
I have an exposition of s. (Solecisms 2)
in s. a king, but waking no such matter (Dreams 17)
Macbeth does murder s. (Sleep 10)
making such difference 'twixt wake and s. (Sleep 4)
medicine thee to that sweet s. (Sleep 14)
music such as charmeth s. (Music 14)
on your eyelids crown the god of s. (Sleep 3)
O s.! O gentle s.! (Sleeplessness 1)
O, such another s. (Dreams 1)
she looks like s. (Death 6)
s. dwell upon thine eyes (Farewells 16)
s. shall neither night nor day (Sleeplessness 4)
s. that knits up the ravelled sleeve (Sleep 10)
s. that ... shuts up sorrow's eye (Sleep 13)
so bestirred thee in thy s. (Sleep 2)
still it cried "s. no more" (Sleeplessness 5)
that I might s. out this great gap (Forgetfulness 2)
the flattering truth of s. (Dreams 14)
the golden dew of s. (Sleeplessness 6)
this downy s., death's counterfeit (Death 23)
this s. is sound indeed (Death 15)
thou art inclined to s. (Sleep 16)
thy best of rest is s. (Sleep 12)
to die, to s., perchance to dream (Death 7)
where care lodges, s. will never lie (Sleeplessness 7)
why rather, s., liest thou in smoky cribs (Sleep 5)
you lack the season of all natures, s. (Sleep 11)
sleeper:
long a s. (Apologies 4)
sleeping:
the s. and the dead (Death 22)
sloth:
s. finds the down pillow hard (Sleep 1, Weariness 1)
slumber:
enjoy the honey-heavy dew of s. (Sleep 6)
when will this fearful s. have an end (Sleep 18)
smell:
compound of villainous s. (Clothing 8)
here's the s. of the blood still (Guilt 8)
smile:
I can s., and murder while I s. (Duplicity 1, Hypocrisy 3)
lose now and then a scattered s. (Infatuation 6)

smiles:
there's daggers in men's s. (Danger 12)
smoke:
love is a s. (Love 74)
snail:
creeping like s. (Boys 1)
worm nor s. do no offense (Creatures 3)
snails:
tender horns of cockled s. (Love 43)
snake:
scorched the s. not killed it (Danger 13)
you but warm the starvèd s. (Snakes 3)
snakes:
you spotted s. (Creatures 3)
snapper-up:
a s. of unconsidered trifles (Theft 12)
snow:
a mockery king of s. (Death-Wish 9)
chaste as unsunned s. (Chastity 3)
wallow naked in December s. (Imagination 6)
so:
so long as men can breathe (Eternity 3)
so may I, blind fortune leading me (Fortune 17)
so may the outward shows (Deceit 6)
so shall I live, supposing thou art true (Deceit 24)
society:
s. is no comfort to one not sociable (Sickness 2)
s. ... is the happiness of life (Society 4)
to make s. the sweeter welcome (Society 5)
soft:
but s., methinks I scent (Dawn 2, Time of Day 2)
s., behold! lo, where it comes again (Ghosts 3)
s. you, a word or two (Speech 20)
soil:
most subject is the fattest s. to weeds (Gardens 1)
soldier:
as I am a s. (Soldiers 12)
a s. firm and sound of heart (Soldiers 13)
a s. fit to stand by Caesar (Soldiers 23)
a s. is better accommodated (Soldiers 10)
a s.'s a man (Soldiers 22)
bear Hamlet like a s. (Soldiers 4, Royalty 7)
embrace him with a s.'s arm (Soldiers 9)
I speak to thee plain s. (Soldiers 17)
teach a s. terms (Courtship 7)
the man commands like a full s. (Soldiers 20)
then a s. full of strange oaths (Soldiers 1)
the s.'s pole is fallen (Epitaphs 1)
thou art a s. only, speak no more (Silence 1)
'tis the s.'s life (Soldiers 24)
you may relish him more in the s. (Soldiers 21)
your son ... hath paid a s.'s debt (Soldiers 18)
soldiers:
but we are s. (Soldiers 25)
soldiership:
prattle ... is all his s. (Soldiers 19)
soliciting:
this supernatural s. (Supernatural 4)
solitary:
in respect it is s. (Country Life 7)

state (cont'd.)
  greatest scandal waits on greatest s. (Greatness 12)
  I am unfit for s. (Hypocrisy 16)
  my s. ... showed like a feast (Greatness 4)
  mystery in the soul of s. (Government 6)
state-statues:
  sit s. only (Action 10)
stature:
  what s. is she of? (Height 1)
staying:
  when you sued s. (Eternity 1)
steal:
  they will s. anything (Theft 3)
  to England will I s., and there I'll s. (Theft 5)
steeds:
  you fiery-footed s. (Anticipation 3)
stench:
  death ... thou odoriferous s. (Death-Wish 7)
sticking-place:
  screw your courage to the s. (Courage 6)
still:
  s. as the grave (Proverbs 23)
  s. it cried "sleep no more" (Sleeplessness 5)
sting:
  sensual as the brutish s. (Lust 5)
  slander, whose s. is sharper (Slander 9)
stirrers:
  bad neighbor makes us early s. (Business 5)
stomach:
  my s. is not constant (Drinking 24)
stone:
  heart is turned to s. (Affliction 8)
stones:
  you are men of s. (Mourning 17)
stories:
  sad s. chancèd in the times of old (Stories 9)
  tell sad s. of the death of kings (Stories 5)
storm:
  another s. brewing (Storms 15)
  every cloud engenders not a s. (Truisms 3)
  shroud till the dregs of the s. be past (Storms 16)
  so foul a sky clears not without a s. (Storms 5)
  the pelting of this pitiless s. (Homelessness 2)
  the s. is up, and all is on the hazard (Storms 4)
story:
  draw thy breath in pain to tell my s. (Stories 1)
  my s. being done (Pity 7)
  never was a s. of more woe (Sorrow 15)
  our bending author hath pursued the s. (Theater 9)
  tell my s. and that would woo her (Courtship 16)
  the subject of my s. (Honor 13)
strain:
  that s. again (Music 26)
strange:
  this is wondrous s. (Philosophy 5)
strangers:
  desire we may be better s. (Parting 2)
straw:
  to find quarrel in a s. (Greatness 1)

strawberry:
  the s. grows underneath the nettle (Gardens 2)
straws:
  a mighty fire begin it with weak s. (Fire 2)
stray:
  now no way can I s. (Exile 5)
stream:
  which way the s. of time doth run (Time 14)
strength:
  excellent to have a giant's s. (Strength 2)
  love give me s. (Strength 3)
  rib of steel to make s. stronger (Strength 1)
strike:
  s. a meaner than myself (Assault 1)
  s. now (Action 7)
string:
  harp not on that s. (Repetition 1)
striving:
  s. to better oft we mar (Proverbs 13)
stroke:
  the s. of death is as a lover's pinch (Dying 3)
strokes:
  many s. ... fells the...oak (Perseverance 1)
strong:
  you are as s. (Praise 11)
stubbornness:
  his s., his checks, ... have grace (Devotion 5)
student:
  lean enough to be thought a good s. (Thinness 4)
studied:
  one that had been s. in his death (Dying 13)
study:
  s. evermore is overshot (Study 3)
  s. is like the heaven's glorious sun (Study 2)
  s. what you most affect (Study 4)
  what is the end of s.? (Study 1)
stuff:
  this is the silliest s. (Nonsense 1)
  we are such s. as dreams are made on (Mortality 9)
stuffed:
  I am s., cousin (Sex 6)
stumble:
  they s. that run fast (Haste 2)
subjects:
  I am all the s. that you have (Servitude 3)
substance:
  the very s. of the ambitious (Dreams 4)
substitute:
  s. shines brightly as a king (Comparisons 2)
suburbs:
  dwell I but in the s. (Marriage 21)
succession:
  slander lives upon s. (Slander 1)
sudden:
  he's s. (Action 8)
sufferance:
  in corporal s. finds a pang (Death 27)
  s. is the badge of all our tribe (Money 9)
suffered:
  I have s. with those that I saw s. (Suffering 4)

suffers:
who alone s. (Misery 1)
sugar:
why strew'st thou s. on that...spider (Danger 14)
suggestion:
they'll take s. as a cat laps milk (Politics 22)
why do I yield to that s. (Temptation 1)
suitor:
I am a humble s. (Law 10)
suits:
customary s. of solemn black (Mourning 8)
sulphur:
burn like the mines of s. (Jealousy 10)
roast me in s. (Hell 6)
summer:
after s. evermore succeeds (Seasons 8)
as a fair day in s. (Beauty 20)
as clear as is the s.'s sun (Seasons 7)
a s. bird (Birds 3)
costly s. (Anticipation 2)
fantastic s.'s heat (Imagination 6)
shall I compare thee to a s.'s day? (Beauty 31)
s.'s lease hath too short a date (Beauty 31)
s.'s ripening breath (Love 79)
the spring, the s., the childing autumn (Seasons 14)
this guest of s. (Birds 6)
thy eternal s. shall not fade (Eternity 3)
summons:
a guilty thing upon a fearful s. (Ghosts 5)
a heavy s. lies like lead (Sleep 9)
ere to black Hecate's s. (Evil 7)
sun:
all so soon as the all-cheering s. (Sunrise 4)
all the world is cheered by the s. (Sunrise 3)
hath Britain all the s.? (Countries 1)
I am too much i'the s. (Grief 5)
I 'gin to be aweary of the s. (Despair 3)
Juliet is the s. (Sunrise 5)
men shut their doors against a setting s. (Downfall 4)
now is the s. upon the highmost hill (Time 27)
O s., burn the great sphere (Darkness 1)
O, 'tis the s. that maketh all things shine (Beauty 13)
the all-seeing s. (Infatuation 9)
the blushing, discontented s. (Royalty 30)
the setting s. and music at the close (Endings 4)
the s. ariseth in his majesty (Sunrise 7)
the s. begins to gild the western sky (Sunset 3)
the s. of Rome is set (Transience 1)
the s. that warms you here (Exile 3)
the s. was not more true (Constancy 4)
the weary s. hath made a golden set (Sunset 2)
when the s. shines (Insects 1)
who ... loves to live i' the s. (Country Life 4)
who saw the s. today? (Foreboding 13)
sunburning:
face is not worth s. (Courtship 10)
sunburnt:
I am s. (Celibacy 3)
sunshine:
you have seen s. and rain (Tears 12)

superfluity:
one for s. and another for use (Proverbs 4)
s. comes sooner by white hairs (Moderation 3)
superflux:
shake the s. to them, (Justice 5)
superstitious:
he is s. grown of late (Superstition 1)
superstitiously:
s. I will be squared by this (Dreams 16)
sure:
s. He that made us (Reason 2)
surer:
you are no s. (People 6)
surety:
the wound of peace is s. (Security 2)
surfeit:
a s. of the sweetest things (Food 10)
surge:
the murmuring s. (Sea 2)
surgeon:
I am ... a s. to old shoes (Work 1)
surges:
I saw him beat the s. (Swimming 1)
suspicion:
s. all our lives shall be (Treason 2)
s. always haunts the guilty mind (Fear 6)
swain:
happy life to be ... a homely s. (Happiness 3)
swallow:
daffodils that come before the s. dares (Flowers 12)
hope ... flies with s.'s wings (Hope 4)
swan:
in a great pool a s.'s nest (Countries 2)
play the s. and die in music (Dying 14)
the s. her downy cygnets save (Birds 5)
swashers:
I have observed these three s. (Men 5)
swashing:
a s. and a martial outside (Cowardice 1)
swear:
s. me, Kate, like a lady (Oaths 1)
sweep:
what a s. of vanity comes this way (Vanity 4)
sweet:
how s. the moonlight sleeps (Moon 1)
s. peace conduct his soul (Epitaphs 14)
sweetest:
s. nut hath sourest rind (Food 5)
sweetness:
began to loathe the taste of s. (Eating 3)
sweets:
s. to the sweet, farewell (Farewells 5)
the s. we wish for (Desire 20)
swift:
s. as a shadow (Transience 2)
swoop:
at one fell s. (Cruelty 4)
sword:
a killing tongue and quiet s. (Soldiers 11)
he who the s. of heaven (Justice 13, Virtue 15)

sword (cont'd.)
   I draw the s. myself (Death-Wish 4)
   slander, whose edge is sharper than the s. (Slander 2)
swords:
   keep up your bright s. (Fighting 4)
sympathy:
   would you desire better s.? (Drinking 18)
taffeta:
   t. phrases, silken terms (Plain-Speaking 8)
taint:
   t. not thy mind (Conscience 1)
taints:
   his t. and honors waged equal (Faults 2)
take:
   t., o, t. those lips away (Inconstancy 1)
   t. the instant way (Reputation 14)
tale:
   an honest t. speeds best (Plain-Speaking 11, Stories 8)
   a plain t. shall put you down (Plain-Speaking 1)
   a round unvarnished t. (Stories 3)
   a sad t.'s best for winter (Stories 10)
   a t. told by an idiot (Life 7)
   I could a t. unfold (Purgatory 2)
tales:
   aged ears play truant at his t. (Talking 5)
   Madam, we'll tell t. (Stories 7)
   relating t. of others' griefs (Misery 3)
   tell thee t. of woeful ages (Stories 6)
talk:
   if I chance to t. a little wild (Talking 4)
   loves to hear himself t. (Talking 6)
   my t. to thee must be (Love 63)
talkers:
   t. are no good doers (Words and Deeds 3)
talks:
   he t. well (Talking 2)
tall:
   he is not very t. (Height 2)
tallow-catch:
   obscene, greasy t. (Insults 4)
talon:
   not an eagle's t. in the waist (Thinness 1)
tame:
   be not too t. neither (Acting 8)
tangle:
   she means to t. my eyes (Eyes 2)
taper:
   how ill this t. burns (Apparitions 4)
   sit we close about this t. (Councils 2)
   the flame o'the t. bows toward her (Eyes 3)
tapster:
   the spirit of a t. (Arithmetic 1)
task:
   a heavier t. could not have been imposed (Grief 2)
   the long day's t. is done (Death-Wish 1, Suicide 2)
   the t. he undertakes is numbering sands (Futility 1)
taste:
   things sweet to t. prove in digestion sour (Eating 11)
taught:
   he must be t. and trained (Contempt 3, Education 3)

teach:
   t. not thy lip such scorn (Scorn 2)
   those that do t. young babes (Education 4)
   we'll t. you to drink deep (Drinking 5)
teaching:
   follow mine own t. (Advice 11)
tear:
   a t. for pity (Charity 1)
   fall not a t. (Tears 2)
   here did she fall a t. (Gardens 9)
   I did not think to shed a t. (Tears 7)
tears:
   ask some t. (Acting 18)
   come, leave your t. (People 12)
   earth could teem with women's t. (Tears 14)
   gave me up to t. (Tears 6)
   her smiles and t. were like (Tears 12)
   his t. run down his beard (Tears 15)
   if you have t. (Tears 8)
   t. harden lust (Tears 16)
   the big round t. (Tears 3)
   there is t. for his love (Caesar 3)
   these hot t. that break from me (Tears 9)
   thy due from me is t. (Mourning 12)
tedious:
   he is as t. as a tired horse (Tediousness 1)
   if I were as t. as a king (Tediousness 4)
   life is as t. (Tediousness 2)
   so t. is this day (Impatience 3)
   'tis better, sir, than to be t. (Brevity 2)
tell:
   t. me where is fancy bred (Love 50)
temper:
   that dauntless t. of his mind (Valor 12)
temperance:
   a gentleman of all t. (Moderation 1)
   you cannot guess what t. should be (Temperance 1)
tempest:
   if after every t. come such calms (Storms 11)
   the southern wind ... foretells a t. (Storms 1)
   this t. in my mind (Ingratitude 8)
   when from thy shore the t. beat us (Storms 2)
temple:
   nothing ill can dwell in such a t. (Goodness 4)
temporizer:
   a hovering t. (Timeserving 1)
tempt:
   devils soonest t. (Devil 6)
   t. the frailty of our powers (Temptation 5)
temptation:
   is that t. that doth goad us on? (Temptation 4)
tempted:
   'tis one thing to be t. (Temptation 2)
tempter:
   the t. or the tempted, who sins most (Temptation 3)
tenderly:
   t. apply some remedies (Medicine 12)
terms:
   buy t. divine (Eternity 4)

thou (cont'd.)
t. canst not say I did it (Ghosts 13)
t. hast my love (Desire 4)
t.'lt come no more (Death 21)
t. shalt be as free (Freedom 7)
t. shalt find she will outstrip (Praise 9)
t. still hast been the father (News 4)
t. wilt be like a lover (Words 7)
t. wouldst be great (Ambition 11)
though:
t. some of you, with Pilate (Hypocrisy 13)
thought:
a Roman t. hath struck him (Duty 1)
as if there were some monster in his t. (Thought 12)
a woman's t. runs before her actions (Thought 1)
comes t. on t. (Thought 8)
every third t. shall be my grave (Mortality 10)
honor's t. reigns solely (Honor 7)
in a t. unborn (Innocence 2)
of no less celerity than that of t. (Thought 5)
pale cast of t. (Conscience 2)
quick forge and working-house of t. (Thought 6)
t. is free (Thought 13)
t. whose murder yet is but fantastical (Confusion 4)
thy wish was father ... to that t. (Thought 4)
thoughts:
fair t. and happy hours (Farewells 13)
hot blood begets hot t. (Love 89)
I have ... with leaden t. been pressed (Moods 13)
my bloody t. with violent pace (Revenge 7)
my t. are whirled (Perplexity 1, Thought 7)
my t. remain below (Prayer 5)
my t. were like unbridled children (Love 92)
our t. are ours, their ends (Thought 3)
pansies, that's for t. (Flowers 2)
swift to enter in the t. of men (Evil 9)
the cursèd t. that nature gives way to (Thought 11)
these sweet t. do even refresh my labors (Work 6)
t. are but dreams (Thought 14)
t. tending to content (Philosophy 18)
t. that would thick my blood (Children 2)
t. the slaves of life (Time 9)
what, in ill t. again? (Endurance 3)
words without t. never to heaven go (Prayer 5)
your t. must deck our kings (Imagination 3)
thread:
he draweth out the t. (Argument 4)
threats:
sir, spare your t. (Death-Wish 11)
three:
t. parts of him is ours (Persuasion 3)
thrice:
t. is he armed (Quarrels 5)
thrift:
t. is blessing (Thrift 2)
t., t., Horatio (Food 6, Thrift 1)
thrive:
t. I as I may (Choice 3)
throne:
like a burnished t. (Ships 1)

throstle:
t. with his note so true (Birds 12)
thunder:
such bursts of horrid t. (Storms 10)
thou all-shaking t. (Storms 8)
thunderbolt:
some innocents scape not the t. (Innocence 1)
thus:
t. play I in one person (Identity 5)
thyme:
a bank whereon the wild t. grows (Flowers 6)
thyself:
t. mine own self's better part (Courtship 5)
Tiber:
wine with not a drop of allaying T. (Drinking 3)
tide:
a t. in the affairs of men (Opportunity 2)
on the swell at full of t. (Indecision 1)
'tis with my mind as with the t. (Indecision 3)
washed off at the next t. (Danger 4)
tidings:
the worst t. that I hear of (News 6)
tiger:
milk in a male t. (Ruthlessness 1)
t's heart wrapped in a woman's hide (Cruelty 1)
time:
bank and shoal of t. (Action 11)
beguile the t. (Travel 25)
be you not troubled with the t. (Necessity 1)
bid t. return (Time 23)
bitter disposition of the t. (Inevitability 3)
clock upbraids me with a waste of t. (Time 36)
companions that ... waste the t. (Friendship 19)
creeping hours of t. (Time 3)
dark backward and abysm of t. (Memory 6)
devouring t., blunt thou (Time 42)
envious and calumniating t. (Time 30)
fleet the t. carelessly (Golden Age 1)
had I but t. (Death 9)
help t. to furrow me with age (Grief 13)
his t. is spent (Epitaphs 13)
I have no precious t. to spend (Devotion 7)
inaudible and noiseless foot of t. (Time 1)
injurious t. (Time 31)
in such a t. as this (Criticism 1)
I shall find t., Cassius (Mourning 16)
I shall have t. enough (Mourning 11)
I wasted t. (Time 24)
look into the seeds of t. (Prophecy 6)
love's not T.'s fool (Constancy 12)
make use of t. (Proverbs 33, Time 45)
many events in the womb of t. (Time 20)
mock the t. with fairest show (Deceit 5)
nothing 'gainst t.'s scythe can make defense (Time 41)
no, t., thou shalt not boast (Time 44)
now he weighs t. (Time 15)
old folk, t.'s doting chronicles (Age 16)
old t. the clock-setter (Time 16)
O t., thou must untangle this (Time 35)

perceive not how t. moves (Time 6)
relish of the saltness of t. (Age 10)
so idly to profane the precious t. (Time 13)
so long walked hand in hand with t. (Time 32)
spite of cormorant devouring t. (Fame 2)
subject to t.'s love (Constancy 13)
that old common arbitrator, t. (Time 33)
that t. of year thou may'st in me behold (Seasons 18)
there's a t. for all things (Time 7)
there would have been a t. (Time 19)
the t. is out of joint (Politics 1)
the t. of life is short (Life 3)
the t. was once (Marriage 11)
the whirligig of t. (Time 37)
this great gap of time (Forgetfulness 3)
this is no t. to lend money (Money 13)
though t. seem so adverse (Endings 1)
t. and the hour runs through (Time 18)
t. comes stealing on (Time 8)
t., force and death (Love 93)
t. hath, my lord, a wallet (Time 28)
t. is a very bankrupt (Time 8)
t. is like a fashionable host (Time 29)
t. is the nurse and breeder (Time 38)
t. ... must have a stop (Time 9)
t. of universal peace (Peace 2)
t. qualifies the spark (Love 33)
t.'s deformèd hand (Grief 3)
t.'s glory is to calm (Time 40)
t. shall unfold (Time 17)
t.'s the king of men (Time 22)
t. travels in divers paces (Time 5)
t. will come and take my love (Mutability 4)
'tis but the t. ... that men stand upon (Death 19)
to beguile the t., look like the t. (Deceit 4)
trencher-friends, t.'s flies (Flattery 7)
we are t.'s subjects (Time 11)
we have seen the best of our t. (Disorder 2)
we play the fools with the t. (Time 12)
what else may hap, to t. I will commit (Time 34)
what hast thou to do with the t. (Time of Day 5)
what t. of day is it, lad? (Time of Day 4)
when t. is old (Constancy 8)
which way the stream of t. doth run (Time 14)
who would bear the whips and scorns of t. (Suicide 13)
wide gap of t. (Acting 31)
witching t. of night (Night 1)
you shall have t. to wrangle in (Argument 1)
times:
but cruel are the t. (Confusion 6)
how many t. shall Caesar (Theater 10)
O these naughty t. (Possession 2)
Timon:
T. hath made his everlasting mansion (Epitaphs 15)
T. will to the woods (Kindness 4)
tinkers:
to gabble like t. (Disorder 4)
tiptoe:
jocund day stand t. (Dawn 7)

tired:
t. with all these (Death-Wish 12)
Titania:
proud T. (Greetings 5)
title:
his t. hang loose about him (Clothing 7)
that t. of respect (Respect 1)
titles:
all thy other t. thou hast given away (Fools 8)
toad:
foul bunch-backed t. (Insults 18)
like the t., ugly and venomous (Adversity 2)
poisonous bunch-backed t. (Curses 7)
toads:
foul t. to knot and gender in (Loss 6)
I hate the engendering of t. (Pride 5)
together:
they have seemed to be t. (Friendship 33)
toil:
in her strong t. of grace (Death 6)
tombs:
gilded t. do worms infold (Gold 5)
tomorrow:
such a day t. as is today (Boys 5)
t., and t., and t. (Time 19)
t. is Saint Valentine's day (Festivals 2)
t. is the joyful day (Marriage 6)
t. night, when Phoebe (Moon 3)
tongs:
the t. and the bones (Music 13)
tongue:
deedless in his t. (Words and Deeds 3)
he hath a killing t. (Soldiers 11)
I must hold my t. (Grief 6)
like a strange t. (Language 2)
love's more ponderous than my t. (Love 39)
murder, though it have no t. (Murder 2)
no power in the t. of man to alter me (Determination 3)
that man that hath a t. (Courtship 24)
the iron t. of midnight (Time of Day 8)
there is no t. that moves (Persuasion 5)
t.'s sweet air (Beauty 15)
trippingly on the t. (Acting 7)
thy t. makes Welsh as sweet (Language 1)
wounds me with the flatteries of his t. (Flattery 4)
tongues:
bestowed that time in the t. (Language 9)
conscience hath a thousand t. (Conscience 7)
finds t. in trees (Country Life 2)
how silver-sweet sound lovers' t. (Music 19)
t. of dying men (Last Words 3)
t. of men are full of deceits (Deceit 3)
t. of mocking wenches (Mockery 2)
upon my t. continual slanders ride (Slander 4)
tonight:
t. we'll wander through the streets (People 1)
tooth:
a mad dog's t. (Jealousy 2)
sharper than a serpent's t. (Ingratitude 7)

trusts:
    he that t. to you (People 5)
truth:
    bear the t. I tell (Stoicism 2)
    good I stand on is my t. (Integrity 1)
    he found t. in one (Betrayal 2)
    his simple t. must be abused (Duplicity 3)
    I'll confess the t. (Truth 6)
    I must ... live hence by t. (Truth 4)
    I will find where t. is hid (Truth 1)
    methinks the t. should live (Truth 7)
    seeming t. that cunning times put on (Deceit 8)
    show of t. can cunning sin cover itself (Deceit 9)
    swerve a hair from t. (Constancy 8)
    tell t. and shame the devil (Truth 2)
    that sweet ornament which t. (Beauty 32)
    the map of honor, t. and loyalty (Honor 11)
    the naked t. of it is (Clothing 6)
    they breathe t. that breathe ... in pain (Last Words 3)
    to seek the light of t. (Books 2)
    trust the flattering t. of sleep (Dreams 14)
    t. hath a quiet breast (Integrity 3)
    t. hath better deeds (Love 104)
    t. is truth (Truth 5)
    t. loves open dealing (Plain-Speaking 2)
    t. will come to light (Proverbs 18)
    with thy religious t. (Truth 3)
tuck:
    vile standing t. (Insults 7)
tune:
    how dost thou like this t.? (Music 27)
turf:
    at his head a grass-green t. (Death 8)
    one t. shall serve as pillow (Love 57)
turn:
    a t. or two I'll walk (Exercise 1)
    do not t. me about (Drinking 24)
    t. him to any cause (Politics 4)
turquoise:
    it was my t. (Loss 5)
turtle-doves:
    a pair of loving t. (Birds 4)
tut:
    t. man, one fire burns out another's (Fire 3)
    t., t., good enough to toss (Soldiers 7)
twig:
    Kate, like the hazel t., is straight (Praise 8)
two:
    an t. men ride of a horse (Proverbs 22)
    t. may keep counsel (Secrets 1)
tyrannous:
    the t. and bloody deed (Murder 13)
tyranny:
    liberty! freedom! t. is dead (Freedom 3)
    that part of t. that I do bear (Tyranny 3)
    the oppression of aged t. (Tyranny 5)
tyrant:
    how fine this t. can tickle (Deceit 2)
tyrants:
    fear when t. seem to kiss (Tyranny 6)

how can t. safely govern home (Tyranny 1)
ulcerous:
    skin and film the u. place (Sickness 2)
unarm:
    u. Eros, the long day's task is done (Dying 1)
unction:
    lay not that flattering u. (Corruption 3, Sickness 2)
underlings:
    the fault ... that we are u. (Faults 6)
undeserver:
    u. may sleep (Action 5)
undeservers:
    sell ... offices for gold to u. (Corruption 5)
undone:
    u. and forfeited to cares (Anxiety 1)
uneasy:
    u. lies the head (Royalty 11)
uneven:
    all is uneven (Confusion 7)
unfaithful:
    the gross band of the u. (Religion 1)
unhand:
    u. me gentlemen (Determination 1)
unicorns:
    I will believe that there are u. (Myths 1)
university:
    spend all at the u. (Education 5)
unkindness:
    drink down all u. (Drinking 17)
    u. blunts it (Unkindness 1)
    u. may do much (Unkindness 3)
unnecessary:
    age is u. (Age 26)
unpin:
    prithee u. me (Devotion 5)
unquietness:
    betroths himself to u. (Misogyny 2)
unsex:
    u. me here (Cruelty 3)
unstaid:
    u. and skittish in all motions else (Constancy 9)
urge:
    u. me no more (Quarrels 6)
Ursa Major:
    nativity was under U. (Astrology 2)
use:
    abject in regard and dear in u. (Value 7)
    how u. doth breed a habit (Custom 5)
    make u. of time (Proverbs 33)
    u. almost can change (Custom 3)
uses:
    to what base u. (Mortality 3)
utterance:
    with all the gracious u. thou hast (Eloquence 6)
Valentine:
    Saint V. is past (Greetings 6)
    to be your V. (Festivals 2)
valiant:
    he is as v. as the lion (Valor 14)
    he's truly v. (Endurance 4)

viol:
he plays o' the v.-de-gamboys (Character 5)
violet:
a v. in the youth of primy nature (Flowers 1)
to throw a perfume on the v. (Extravagance 2)
where oxlips and the nodding v. grows (Flowers 6)
violets:
breathes upon a bank of v. (Music 26)
may v. spring (Burial 3)
who are the v. now (Flowers 7, Innovation 2)
virgin:
a poor v., sir ... but mine own (Possession 1)
a v. from her very infancy (Chastity 7)
virginity:
loss of v. is rational increase (Virginity 2)
man is an enemy to v. (Virginity 1)
virtue:
according to his v. (Burial 4)
but v., as it never will be moved (Virtue 6)
calumny will sear v. itself (Slander 8)
grace to stand and v. go (Virtue 15)
I will not change for your best v. (Faults 4)
king of every v. (Beauty 19)
let v. be as wax (Lust 6)
my heart laments that v. cannot live (Virtue 8)
no v. like necessity (Necessity 6)
O infinite v. (Valor 2)
some by v. fall (Injustice 1)
the devil their v. tempts (Devil 9)
the rarer action is in v. than in vengeance (Forgiveness 5)
there is no man hath a v. (Vice 3)
thy fair v.'s force (Love 59)
valor is the chiefest v. (Valor 5)
vice ... assumes some mark of v. (Deceit 7)
v.? a fig! 'tis in ourselves (Virtue 17)
v. cannot live out of the teeth (Virtue 8)
v. is beauty (Virtue 24)
v. is bold (Virtue 14)
v. itself scapes not calumnious strokes (Virtue 5)
v. itself turns vice (Virtue 20)
v. that transgresses (Virtue 22)
virtues:
his v. will plead like angels (Virtue 10)
if our v. did not go forth of us (Virtue 12)
is it a world to hide v. in? (Virtue 21)
our v. lie in the interpretation (Virtue 3)
thee and thy v. here I seize upon (Virtue 9)
they are v. and traitors (Virtue 1)
virtuous:
a fool for he would needs be v. (Politics 7)
dost think, because thou art v. (Virtue 23)
your father was ever v. (Virtue 16)
visage:
I saw Othello's v. in his mind (Devotion 4)
mask thy monstrous v. (Conspiracy 5)
visages:
men whose v. do cream (Self-Importance 1)
vision:
fatal v. (Apparitions 7)

I have had a most rare v. (Dreams 6)
visor:
with a virtuous v. hide deep vice (Deceit 16)
vixen:
she was a v. (Anger 5)
vocation:
why, Hal, 'tis my v. (Theft 1)
voice:
a woman's v. may do some good (Negotiation 3)
give ... few thy v. (Advice 5)
her v. was ever soft (Speech 12)
I will aggravate my v. (Acting 21)
my v. is ragged (Singing 1)
so full a v. from so empty a heart (Proverbs 6)
volubility:
I'll commend her v. (Courtship 20)
votaress:
the imperial v. passed on (Virginity 3)
vouchsafe:
v. to teach a soldier terms (Courtship 7)
vow:
break the smallest parcel of this v. (Oaths 2)
by yonder blessèd moon I vow (Vows 4)
the purpose that makes strong the vow (Vows 5)
the plain single v. (Vows 1)
vows:
by all the v. that ever men have broke (Vows 2)
sucked the honey of his music v. (Dejection 3)
voyage:
thy loving v. (Marriage 8)
life's uncertain v. (Life 12)
wages:
our praises are our wages (Praise 13)
wainscot:
join you as they join w. (Marriage 4)
waist:
from the w. they are centaurs (Misogyny 1)
wake:
do thee so much wrong to w. thee (Sleep 7)
wallet:
time hath ... a w. at his back (Time 28)
wanderer:
I am that merry w. of the night (Fairies 4)
war:
impious w. (War 13)
in the trade of w. I have slain men (Murder 7)
let slip the dogs of w. (War 16)
never was a w. did cease (Peace 3)
pomp, and circumstance of glorious w. (War 19)
the fire-eyed maid of smoky w. (War 2)
the flinty and steel couch of w. (War 18)
the hideous god of w. (War 7)
the lofty instruments of w. (War 4)
the purple testament of bleeding w. (War 20)
this hungry w. opens his vasty jaws (War 9)
when the blast of w. blows (War 11)
warble:
w. , child, make passionate (Singing 2)
warder:
memory, the w. of the brain (Memory 4)

wardrobe:
look what a w. here is for thee (Clothing 11)
wares:
show our foulest w. (Business 9)
warrior:
the painful w. famousèd for fight (Honor 23)
warriors:
we are but w. for the working day (Soldiers 16)
wars:
as w. ... may be said to be a ravisher (Peace 2)
go not to these w. (Wars 6)
how many hath he killed ... in these w.? (War 17)
still w. and lechery (Lechery 6)
the big w. that makes ambition virtue (Farewells 14)
thou art going to the wars (Friendship 8)
w. is no strife to the dark house (War 1)
waste:
in the dead w. (Time of Day 1)
your w. is great (Extravagance 1)
watch:
he's winding up the w. of his wit (Wit 6)
some must w. while some must sleep (Life 3)
w. tonight, pray tomorrow (Fellowship 1)
water:
a little w. clears us of this deed (Guilt 6)
as false as w. (Infidelity 1)
a world of w. shed (Tears 5)
fall a drop of w. in the breaking gulf (Marriage 12)
honest w. (Drinking 26)
I to the world am like a drop of w. (Identity 1)
like a circle in the w. (Glory 1)
not all the w. in the rough rude sea (Royalty 28)
smooth runs the w. (Rivers 2)
w. in a sieve (Advice 13)
w. that ne'er left man i' the mire (Drinking 26)
what dreadful noise of w. in my ears (Dreams 9)
wave:
I wish you a w. o'the sea (Dancing 4)
waves:
as the w. make towards the pebbled shore (Time 43)
head 'bove the contentious w. (Swimming 2)
way:
in the beaten w. of friendship (Friendship 4)
my w. is to conjure you (Men and Women 3, Plays 2)
my w. of life is fallen into the sere (Old Age 8)
take the instant w. (Reputation 14)
there lies your w. (Travel 22)
the w. is wearisome (Travel 26)
this w. a w. to thrive (Thrift 2)
ways:
by what ... crooked w. (Deviousness 3)
waywardness:
unruly w. (Capriciousness 2)
we:
so we grew together (Twins 3)
we are all frail (Weakness 3)
we are all men (Weakness 2)
we are oft to blame in this (Hypocrisy 1)
we do not come (Acting 24)

we few, we happy few (Fellowship 2)
we have here recovered (Villainy 5)
we have laughed to see the sails (Pregnancy 2)
we have seen the best of our time (Disorder 2)
we, ignorant of ourselves (Prayer 1)
we know each other's faces (Deceit 17)
we know what we are (Self-Knowledge 3)
we'll set thee to school to an ant (Proverbs 14)
we two alone will sing (Reconciliation 4)
we were not born to sue (Royalty 26)
we were the first ... of your friends (Friendship 7)
we wound our modesty (Deserving 1)
weak:
how w. a thing the heart of woman is (Women 21)
weaker:
I am w. than a woman's tear (Weakness 6)
weakness:
bear with my w. (Weakness 4)
our w. past compare (Women 26)
'twere childish w. to lament (Courage 4)
wealth:
all the w. I had (Men 9)
sum up sum of half my w. (Love 83)
weapon:
thought he had no w. (Greatness 9)
weariness:
w. can snore upon the flint (Sleep 1)
weary:
how w., flat, stale and unprofitable (Dejection 1)
weapons:
women's w., water-drops (Tears 9)
wear:
w. this for me (Fortune 5)
weariness:
w. can snore upon the flint (Weariness 1)
weary:
w. with toil, I hast me (Sleep 19)
weather:
many can brook the w. (Weather 3)
web:
with as little a w. as this (Plots 4)
wedding:
the w. mannerly-modest (Marriage 30)
w. is great Juno's crown (Marriage 7)
wedges:
blunt w. rive hard knots (Proverbs 28)
w. of gold, great anchors (Dreams 10)
wedlock:
high w. then be honorèd (Marriage 7)
w. would be nibbling (Marriage 3)
what is w. forcèd (Marriage 18)
weed:
fat w. that roots itself (Action 3)
thou w. who art so lovely fair (Beauty 17)
weeds:
all the idle w. that grow (Madness 9)
great w. do grow apace (Proverbs 25)
I will go root away the noisome w. (Gardens 6)
lilies that fester smell far worse than w. (Flowers 14)

most subject is the fattest soil to w. (Gardens 1)
w. are shallow-rooted (Gardens 3)
week:
what, keep a w. away (Time 21)
weep:
come w. with me (Despair 8)
how much better is it to w. at joy (Tears 13)
I cannot choose but w. (Mourning 10, Burial 2)
you think I'll w. (Tears 11)
weeping:
I am not prone to w. (Grief 15)
welcome:
at first and last, the hearty w. (Welcome 1)
bid that w. which comes to punish (Endurance 2)
bid these unknown friends to's w. (Welcome 3)
great Hector, w.! (Welcome 2)
great w. makes a merry feast (Feasts 3)
such w. and unwelcome things (News 9)
the w. ever smiles (Time 29)
w. hither as is the spring (Welcome 4)
well:
the hurt ... is not so deep as a w. (Dying 15)
since all is w., keep it so (Proverbs 3)
Welsh:
the devil understands W. (Devil 3)
thy tongue makes W. as sweet (Language 1)
wench:
I know a w. of excellent discourse (Women 8)
ill-starred w. (Affliction 10)
she's a good w. (Love 97)
wenches:
tongues of mocking w. (Mockery 2)
west:
the w. yet glimmers (Sunset 1)
w. of this place (Country Life 8)
westward:
then w. ho! (Travel 22)
wether:
I am a tainted w. of the flock (Resignation 4)
what:
w., all so soon asleep? (Sleep 17)
w. a pair of spectacles (Eyes 16)
w. a piece of work is a man (Man 5)
w. are these, so withered? (Supernatural 3)
w. can be avoided? (Fate 6)
w. cannot be eschewed (Inevitability 1)
w. else may hap (Time 34)
w., frighted with false fire? (Fear 2)
w., girl, though grey (Middle Age 2)
w., gone without a word? (Love 104)
w. is a man (Man 7)
w. is it then to me (War 13)
w. I think I utter (Speech 1)
w., keep a week away? (Time 21)
w. must be shall be (Inevitability 2)
w. says she, fair one? (Deceit 3)
w. say you to a piece of beef (Food 14)
w. seest thou else (Memory 6)
w.'s gone and w.'s past help (Philosophy 19)

w. shall Cordelia speak? (Love 38)
w.'s mine is yours (Marriage 23)
w. to ourselves in passion we propose (Passion 1)
w. we have we prize not (Value 2)
w. win I if I gain the thing I seek? (Desire 17)
w. you will have, I'll give (Power 11)
wheel:
fortune ..., turn thy wheel (Fortune 14)
I am bound upon a w. of fire (Suffering 1)
the w. is come full circle (Fortune 16)
thoughts are whirlèd like a potter's w. (Perplexity 1)
w. runs down a hill (Advice 10)
when:
w. holy and devout religious men (Prayer 15)
w. icicles hang by the wall (Seasons 11)
w. I consider everything (Mutability 3)
w. I have plucked the rose (Murder 8)
w. I tell him he hates flatterers (Flattery 4)
w. shall we three meet again? (Supernatural 12)
w. thou hast leisure (Leisure 1)
w. to the sessions of sweet silent thought (Remembrance 9)
w. we in our viciousness grow hard (Vice 1)
w. will this fearful slumber (Sleep 18)
w. you depart from me (Parting 12)
where:
w. did you study? (Speechmaking 5)
w. should this music be? (Music 21)
while:
w. I live I'll fear (Sex 4)
whipping:
who should 'scape w.? (Generosity 2)
whips:
who would bear the w. and scorns of time (Suicide 13)
whirligig:
the w. of time brings ... revenges (Time 37)
whispering:
is w. nothing? (Suspicion 2)
whisperings:
foul w. are abroad (Guilt 9)
whither:
w. I go, thither shall you (Travel 7)
who:
w. are the violets now? (Innovation 2, Flowers 7)
w. can control his fate? (Fate 7)
w. can converse with a dumb show? (Conversation 2)
w. cannot be crushed? (Plots 1)
w. chooseth me must give (Risk 2)
w. chooseth me shall gain (Desire 12, 13)
w. chooseth me shall get (Merit 1)
w. comes so fast? (Night 16)
w. dares not stir by day (Fear 9)
w. is it that can tell me who I am? (Identity 4)
w. is Silvia? (Beauty 26)
w. lives that's not depravèd (Corruption 7, Humanity 8)
w. makes the fairest show (Deceit 15)
w.'s born that day when I forget (Letters 1)

w. cries out in the streets (Wisdom 3)
wise:
   not one w. man among twenty (Wisdom 5)
   so w., so young, they say (Youth 10)
   the fool doth think he is w. (Fools 5)
   the w. man knows himself to be a fool (Wisdom 2)
   to be w. and love exceeds man's might (Wisdom 6)
   too w. to woo peaceably (Courtship 15)
   w. men put on their cloaks (Change 1)
   you are w. or else you love not (Wisdom 6)
wisely:
   w. and slow (Haste 2)
wiser:
   men may grow w. (Wisdom 1)
wishes:
   let your fair eyes and gentle w. go (Trials 1)
wit:
   a cheveril glove to a good w. (Wit 7)
   better a witty fool than a foolish w. (Fools 10)
   brevity is the soul of w. (Wit 1)
   devise, w. (Writing 1)
   good w. ... make use of anything (Business 4)
   have you no w., manners, nor modesty (Disorder 4)
   he's winding up the watch of his w. (Wit 6)
   he that has and a little tiny w. (Fortune 15)
   his w.'s as thick as Tewkesbury mustard (Insults 9)
   I believe that does harm to my w. (Eating 13)
   I have neither w., nor words (Speech 4)
   I will keep where there is w. stirring (Folly 4)
   make the door upon a woman's w. (Wit 1)
   many a man has more hair than w. (Hair 2)
   the cause that w. is in other men (Wit 3)
   thy w. is as quick as the greyhound's mouth (Wit 4)
   when the age is in the w. is out (Old Age 10)
witch:
   no w. hath power to charm (Festivals 1)
witchcraft:
   you have w. in your lips, Kate (Eloquence 4)
witches:
   soul-killing w. that deform (Corruption 1)
witching:
   w. time of night (Night 1)
wit-crackers:
   a college of w. cannot flout (Wit 5)
withered:
   so w. and so wild (Supernatural 3)
   w. is the garland of the war (Epitaphs 1)
witness:
   I shall not want false w. (Proverbs 7)
   the w. still of excellency (Modesty 1)
wits:
   if our w. run the wild-goose chase (Futility 2)
   my w. begin to turn (Madness 7)
witty:
   I am not only w. in myself (Wit 3)
wives:
   if w. do fall (Marriage 42)
   revolted w. (Adultery 3)

wives and children stare (Chaos 1)
   w. may be merry (Marriage 27)
woe:
   cry w., destruction, ruin (Death 33)
   fellowship in w. doth w. assuage (Fellowship 4)
   never was a story of more w. (Sorrow 15)
   one w. doth tread upon another's heel (Sorrow 2)
   the w. had been universal (Sorrow 17)
   though w. be heavy (Sorrow 18)
   w., that too late repents (Repentance 4)
woes:
   all these w. shall serve (Sorrow 13)
   ne'er wail their w. (Advice 15)
wolf:
   be a comrade with the w. (Homelessness 1)
   the w. behowls the moon (Night 19)
   trusts in the tameness of a w. (Aphorisms 2)
   wake not a sleeping w. (Proverbs 3)
wolves:
   as salt as w. in pride (Lechery 3)
   howling of Irish w. (Animals 2)
   w. and bears ... done offices of pity (Creatures 5)
woman:
   alas, I am a w. friendless (Women 18)
   a properer man than she a w. (Beauty 4, Men and Women 2)
   a w. and therefore may be wooed (Courtship 21)
   a w. impudent and mannish grown (Effeminacy 3)
   a w. moved is like a fountain troubled (Women 25)
   a w.'s thought runs before her actions (Thought 1)
   constant you are, but yet a w. (Women 15)
   desire to be a w. of the world (Desire 6)
   do you not know I am a w. (Women 6)
   fair w. but she made mouths in a glass (Vanity 1)
   how weak a thing the heart of w. is (Women 21)
   if fortune be a w. (Fortune 19)
   I grant I am a w. (Women 19)
   I have no other but a w.'s reason (Women 28)
   I have nothing of w. in me (Resolution 1)
   I thank God I am not a w. (Women 7)
   I will die a w. with grieving (Men and Women 6)
   jewels ... move a w.'s mind (Gifts 3)
   let still the w. take (Marriage 49)
   no more but e'en a w. (Women 1)
   one w. is fair (Misogyny 3)
   semblative a w.'s part (Androgyny 1)
   she is a w., therefore may be won (Women 21)
   that man should be at w.'s command (Men and Women 1)
   there is no w.'s sides (Love 98)
   tiger's heart wrapped in a w's hide (Cruelty 1)
   venom clamors of a jealous w. (Jealousy 2)
   vice ... it is the w.'s part (Women 12)
   was ever w. in this humor wooed (Courtship 18)
   w.'s face ... gentle heart (Androgyny 2)
   w.'s voice may do some good (Negotiation 3)
   you that have so fair parts of w. (Women 17)
women:
   alas, poor w., make us but believe (Women 9)

women (cont'd.)

all men idle, all, and w. too (Utopias 1)

how hard it is for w. to keep counsel (Women 20)

I'll begin with the w. (Men and Women 3, Plays 2)

kindness in w. (Love 86)

no way ... but w. must be half-workers (Women 11)

O that we w. had men's privilege (Courtship 22)

other w. cloy the appetite (Praise 1)

sooner lost and worn that w.'s are (Men and Women 10)

'tis beauty that doth oft make w. proud (Beauty 8)

w. are angels wooing (Men and Women 9)

w. are as roses (Women 27)

w. are made to bear (Quarrels 16)

w. may fall (Men and Women 8)

w. say so that will say anything (Parents and Children 16)

w. will love her (Men and Women 11)

wonder:

it gives me w. great as my content (Joy 4)

it the more shows off your w. (Silence 8)

seven of the nine days out of the w. (Wonder 1)

that would be ten days' w. (Wonder 3)

you are made rather to w. (Wonder 2)

woo:

come w. me, w. me (Courtship 2)

too wise to w. peaceably (Courtship 15)

we ... were not made to w. (Courtship 14)

wood:

rooky w. (Night 13)

woodbine:

overcanopied with luscious w. (Flowers 6)

so doth the w. the sweet honeysuckle (Infatuation 8)

woodbirds:

begin these w. but to couple now? (Greetings 6)

woodcock:

as a w. to mine own springe (Justice 2)

wooers:

mocks her w. out of suit (Mockery 3)

wooing:

our w. doth not end like an old play (Endings 2)

w., wedding, and repenting (Marriage 30)

woolward:

I go w. for penance (Clothing 5)

word:

a true knight ... firm of w. (Words and Deeds 4)

but a w. that cowards use (Conscience 8)

how every fool can play upon the w. (Words 6)

I'll take your w. for faith (Promises 7)

not a w. but a jest, and every jest a w. (Jokes 2)

suit the action to the w. (Acting 10)

thou hast frighted the w. (Words 8)

thou hast spoken no w. (Words 5)

what is honor? a w. (Honor 6)

words:

w. are no deeds (Action 11)

armed for some unhappy w. (Quarrels 15)

endeavor deeds to match these w. (Words and Deeds 5)

foul w. is but foul wind (Kissing 8)

his w. are bonds (Sincerity 3)

honest plain w. (Plain-Speaking 9)

I am ... her corrupter of w. (Fools 14)

I am not of many w. (Thanks 1)

I fled from w. (Words 1)

I have neither wit, nor w. (Speech 4)

I love not many w. (Talking 1)

I was never so bethumped with w. (Words 3)

my w. fly up (Prayer 5)

never w. were music to thine ear (Marriage 11)

such abominable w. (Language 4)

that ever this fellow should have fewer w. (Words 2)

tire the hearer with a book of w. (Words 7)

what care I for w.? (Talking 2)

wild and whirling w. (Talking 3)

w. before blows (Councils 3)

w. pay no debts (Silence 7)

w. that in an honest suit might move (Courtship 6)

w., w., mere w. (Words 10)

write her fair w. in the foulest terms (Fortune 8)

you cram these w. into mine ears (Words 9)

you have bereft me of all w., lady (Silence 7)

your w. and performances (Words and Deeds 2)

work:

w. that will make sick men whole (Health 1)

does it w. upon him? (Plots 5)

if it be man's w. (Work 3)

I want w. (Action 4)

let me w. (Persuasion 4)

now have I done a good day's w. (Work 5)

to sport would be as tedious as to w. (Holidays 1)

what a piece of w. is a man (Man 5)

what you would w. me to (Persuasion 2)

w. we have in hand, most bloody-fiery (Conspiracy 3)

working-days:

have another for w. (Marriage 31)

workmen:

when w. strive to do better (Work 2)

world:

a good deed in a naughty w. (Goodness 3)

a great while ago the w. began (Theater 20)

all the uses of this w. (Dejection 1)

all the w.'s a stage (Theater 3)

all the w. is cheered by the sun (Sunrise 3)

all this the w. well knows (Lust 14)

best actors in the w. (Acting 6)

come the three corners of the w. (Patriotism 2)

enforce me t a w. of cares (Politics 21)

fleet the time ... in the golden w. (Golden Age 1)

foul body of th' infected w. (Body 1)

go along o'er the wide w. (Loyalty 1)

he doth bestride the narrow w. (Power 5)

here's a good w. the while (Deceit 18)

his reared arm crested the w. (World 2)

how this w. is given to lying (Lying 2)

I am in this earthly w. (Innocence 5)

I hold the w. but as the w. (Acting 17)

in a better w. than this (Farewells 2)

is it a w. to hide virtues in? (Virtue 21)

i'the w.'s volume (Countries 2)
I think he only loves the w. for him (Friendship 18)
let the w. slip (Pleasure 5)
O brave new w. (Humanity 7)
O slanderous w.! (Praise 8)
O w., thou wast the forest (Mourning 13)
the corrupted currents of this w. (Law 1)
the poor w. is ... six thousand years old (Dying 4)
there is no w. without Verona walls (Exile 9)
there is a w. elsewhere (Exile 2)
the w. hath not a sweeter creature (Women 24)
the w.'s mine oyster (Opportunity 3)
the w.; 'tis furnished well with men (Constancy 2)
thinks the w. turns round (Giddiness 1)
this dull w. (Absence 1)
this great w. shall so wear out (Mortality 7)
this little w. ... this England (Countries 6)
this troublous w. (Afterlife 5)
this working-day w. (Adversity 1)
this w. is not for aye (Mutability 1)
this w.'s a city full of straying streets (World 6)
thorns and dangers of this w. (Danger 10)
thus runs the w. away (Life 3)
too much respect upon the w. (Anxiety 8)
varying shore o' the w. (Darkness 1)
what in the w. should make me (Truth 4)
w. of one entire ... chrysolite (Constancy 5)
w., w., O w., but that thy ... mutations (World 5)
you ... are all the w. (Love 56)
worm:
  I wish you joy of the w. (Joy 1)
  smallest w. will turn (Courage 3)
  the pretty w. of Nilus (Snakes 2)
  viperous w. that gnaws (Cities 1)
  w. nor snail do no offense (Creatures 4)
  w. of conscience (Conscience 4)
wormholes:
  the w. of long-vanished days (History 1)
worms:
  shall w., inheritors of this excess (Eternity 4)
worse:
  w. than the sun in March (Sickness 7)
worst:
  the w. returns to laughter (Laughter 2)
  things at the w. will cease (Comfort 5)
  to fear the w. oft cures the w. (Fear 16)
  we can say "This is the w." (Affliction 5)
worth:
  beggars that can count their w. (Love 83)
  what we have we prize not to the w. (Value 2)
worthiness:
  the w. of praise distains his worth (Praise 10)
would:
  this "w." ... hath abatements and delays (Delay 2)
wound:
  what w. did ever heal (Patience 10)
wounds:
  those w. heal ill (Self-Harm 1)
wreaths:
  brows bound with victorious w. (Victory 3)

wrecks:
  I saw a thousand fearful w. (Dreams 10)
wren:
  no better a musician than the w. (Birds 11)
  w. with little quill (Birds 12)
wrenching:
  w. the true cause the false way (Deviousness 2)
wrest:
  w. once the law (Law 9)
wrestled:
  you have w. well (Conquest 1)
wretch:
  an inhuman w. (Cruelty 5)
  excellent w. (Love 71)
wretched:
  how w. is that poor man (Downfall 2)
wretchedness:
  is w. deprived that benefit? (Misery 2)
  the fierce w. that glory brings (Misery 4)
wretches:
  feel what w. feel (Justice 5)
  poor naked w. (Homelessness 2)
wrinkled:
  w. deep in time (Middle Age 1)
writ:
  old ends stolen forth of holy w. (Hypocrisy 14)
write:
  to w. and read comes by nature (Learning 2)
writing:
  for your w. and reading (Learning 3)
wrong:
  Caesar doth not w. (Caesar 2)
  do w. ... to none (Advice 1)
  he does me double w. (Flattery 6)
  I do the w. and first being to brawl (Duplicity 7)
  to persist in doing w. (Wrongdoing 6)
  we do it w., being so majestical (Ghosts 4)
  you do me w. (Suffering 1)
wrongs:
  with their high w. I am struck (Forgiveness 4)
wounds:
  the w. invisible (Love 19)
yard:
  you tailor's y. (Insults 7)
yarn:
  web of our life is of a mingled y. (Life 1)
year:
  the y. growing ancient (Flowers 10)
years:
  his y. but young (Experience 5)
  when I was about thy y., Hal (Thinness 1)
yesterday:
  O call back y. (Time 23)
yet:
  y. cease your ire, you angry stars (Storms 10)
  y. I'll not shed her blood (Beauty 18)
yield:
  y. day to night (Night 8)
yielded:
  he saw me and y. (Conquest 2)